Internetworking Technologies Handbook,

Second Edition

Kevin Downes
Merilee Ford
H. Kim Lew
Steve Spanier
Tim Stevenson

CISCO SYSTEMS

CISCO PRESS

M
T|P
MACMILLAN
TECHNICAL
PUBLISHING
U·S·A

Macmillan Technical Publishing
201 West 103rd Street
Indianapolis, IN 46290 USA

Internetworking Technologies Handbook, Second Edition

Published by:
Macmillan Technical Publishing
201 West 103rd Street
Indianapolis, IN 46290 USA

Printed in the United States of America 1 2 3 4 5 6 7 8 9 0

Library of Congress Cataloging-in-Publication Number 98-86495

ISBN: 1-57870-102-3

Warning and Disclaimer

This book is designed to provide information about Internetworking technologies. Every effort has been made to make this book as complete and accurate as possible, but no warranty or fitness is implied.

The information is provided on an "as is" basis. The author, Macmillan Technical Publishing, and Cisco Systems, Inc. shall have neither liability nor responsibility to any person or entity with respect to any loss or damages arising from the information contained in this book or from the use of the discs or programs that may accompany it.

The opinions expressed in this book belong to the author and are not necessarily those of Cisco Systems, Inc.

Feedback Information

At Cisco Press, our goal is to create in-depth technical books of the highest quality and value. Each book is crafted with care and precision, undergoing rigorous development that involves the unique expertise of members from the professional technical community.

Readers' feedback is a natural continuation of this process. If you have any comments regarding how we could improve the quality of this book, or otherwise alter it to better suit your needs, you can contact us at ciscopress@mcp.com. Please make sure to include the book title and ISBN in your message.

We greatly appreciate your assistance.

Associate Publisher	Jim LeValley
Executive Editor	Alicia Buckley
Cisco Systems Program Manager	H. Kim Lew
Managing Editor	Caroline Roop
Acquisitions Editor	Lynette Quinn
Development Editor	Kitty Jarrett
Project Editors	Sherri Fugit
	Jen Nuckles
Technical Editors	Jacqueline Kim
	Tim Boyles
Team Coordinator	Amy Lewis
Production Team	Argosy
Indexer	Kevin Fulcher

Trademark Acknowledgments

All terms mentioned in this book that are known to be trademarks or service marks have been appropriately capitalized. Macmillan Technical Publishing or Cisco Systems, Inc. cannot attest to the accuracy of this information. Use of a term in this book should not be regarded as affecting the validity of any trademark or service mark.

Table of Contents

Preface and Acknowledgments

Data communications technologies are evolving and expanding at an unparalleled rate. The growth in demand for Internet access and intranet services continues to fuel rapid technical adaptation by both implementers and developers. Unfortunately, creating an information resource such as the Internetworking Technologies Handbook requires a certain recognition by its authors that some information is likely to be obsolete the day it appears in print.

The authors of Internetworking Technologies Handbook approached its development with a commitment to helping readers make informed technology decisions and develop a keen awareness of this dilemma. We hope that this first release is a step in the correct direction, and that, together with other books planned for the Cisco Press program, you will be able to identify technologies that will accommodate working network solutions as your requirements change.

This chapter discusses the objectives, intended audiences, and overall organization of the *Internetworking Technologies Handbook, Second Edition.*

OBJECTIVES

This publication provides technical information addressing Cisco-supported internetworking technologies. It is designed for use in conjunction with other Cisco manuals or as a stand-alone reference.

Internetworking Technologies Handbook, Second Edition is not intended to provide all possible information on the included technologies. Because a primary goal of this publication is to help network administrators configure Cisco products, the publication emphasizes Cisco-supported technologies; however, inclusion of a technology in this publication does not necessarily imply Cisco support for that technology.

AUDIENCE

Internetworking Technologies Handbook, Second Edition was written for anyone who wants to understand internetworking. We anticipate that most readers will use the information in this publication to assess the applicability of specific technologies for their environments.

ORGANIZATION

This publication is divided into eight parts. Each part is concerned with introductory material or a major area of internetworking technology and comprises chapters describing related tasks or functions.

- Part 1, "Introduction to Internetworking," presents concepts basic to the understanding of internetworking and network management.

- Part 2, "LAN Protocols," describes standard protocols used for accessing network physical media.

- Part 3, "WAN Technologies," describes standard protocols used to implement wide-area networking.

- Part 4, "Bridging and Switching," describes protocols and technologies used to provide Layer 2 connectivity between subnetworks.

- Part 5, "Network Protocols," describes standard networking protocol stacks that can be routed through an internetwork.

- Part 6, "Routing Protocols," describes protocols used to route information through an internetwork.

- Part 7, "Internet Access Technologies," describes security, network caching technologies and directory services.

- Part 8, "Network Management," describes the architecture and operation of common network management implementations.

ACKNOWLEDGMENTS

This book was written as a collaborative effort. It represents several years of information compilation and the integration of information products developed by Cisco Knowledge Products developers. Principal authors for this publication were Merilee Ford, H. Kim Lew, Steve Spanier, and Tim Stevenson. During the last process of consolidation, Kevin Downes contributed to integrating the material into this product.

The authors want to acknowledge the many contributions of Cisco subject-matter experts for their participation in reviewing material and providing insights into the technologies presented here. Folks who added to this compilation include Priscilla Oppenheimer, Aviva Garrett, Steve Lin, Manoj Leelanivas, Kent Leung, Dave Stine, Ronnie Kon, Dino Farinacci, Fred Baker, Kris Thompson, Jeffrey Johnson, George Abe, Yakov Rekhter, Abbas Masnavi, Alan Marcus, Laura Fay, Anthony Alles, David Benham, Debra Gotelli, Ed Chapman, Bill Erdman, Tom Keenan, Soni Jiandani, and Derek Yeung, among a number of other Cisco contributors. The authors appreciate the time and critical reviews each of these participants provided in helping to develop the source material for the Internetworking Technologies Handbook, Second Edition.

This publication borrows liberally from publications and training products previously developed by Cisco. In particular, the Internetworking Technology Overview publication and the Cisco Connection Training multimedia CD-ROM provided the foundation from which this compilation was derived.

PART 1

Introduction to Internetworking

Part 1, "Introduction to Internetworking," provides a bird's eye view of internetworking technologies and terminology. Individual chapters discuss the following topics:

Internetworking Basics—Covers the basics of internetworking, including the OSI model, addressing, network services, and more.

Introduction to LAN Protocols—Presents an overview of the popular LAN data-link and physical-layer protocols.

Introduction to WAN Technologies—Presents an overview of WAN protocols, devices, and implementations.

Bridging and Switching Basics—Presents an overview of bridging and switching technologies.

Routing Basics—Provides an introduction to the routing protocols.

Network Management Basics—Provides a brief overview of network management and the OSI network management model.

CHAPTER 1

Internetworking Basics

This chapter works with the next six chapters to act as a foundation for the technology discussions that follow. In this chapter, some fundamental concepts and terms used in the evolving language of internetworking are addressed. In the same way that this book provides a foundation for understanding modern networking, this chapter summarizes some common themes presented throughout the remainder of this book. Topics include flow control, error checking, and multiplexing, but this chapter focuses mainly on mapping the *Open Systems Interconnect (OSI)* model to networking/internetworking functions and summarizing the general nature of addressing schemes within the context of the OSI model.

WHAT IS AN INTERNETWORK?

An internetwork is a collection of individual networks, connected by intermediate networking devices, that functions as a single large network. Internetworking refers to the industry, products, and procedures that meet the challenge of creating and administering internetworks. Figure 1–1 illustrates some different kinds of network technologies that can be interconnected by routers and other networking devices to create an internetwork:

3

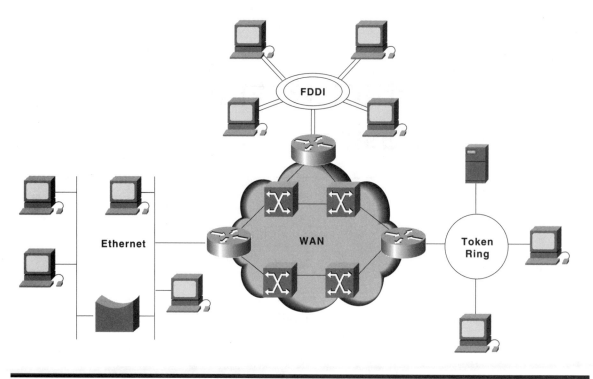

Figure 1–1
Different network technologies can be connected to create an internetwork.

History of Internetworking

The first networks were time-sharing networks that used mainframes and attached terminals. Such environments were implemented by both IBM's System Network Architecture (SNA) and Digital's network architecture.

Local area networks (LANs) evolved around the PC revolution. LANs enabled multiple users in a relatively small geographical area to exchange files and messages, as well as access shared resources such as file servers.

Wide-area networks (WANs) interconnect LANs across normal telephone lines (and other media), thereby interconnecting geographically dispersed users.

Today, high-speed LANs and switched internetworks are becoming widely used, largely because they operate at very high speeds and support such high-bandwidth applications as voice and videoconferencing.

Internetworking evolved as a solution to three key problems: isolated LANs, duplication of resources, and a lack of network management. Isolated LANS made electronic communication between different offices or departments impossible. Duplication of resources meant that the same hardware and software had to be supplied to each office or department, as did a separate support staff. This lack of network management meant that no centralized method of managing and troubleshooting networks existed.

Internetworking Challenges

Implementing a functional internetwork is no simple task. Many challenges must be faced, especially in the areas of connectivity, reliability, network management, and flexibility. Each area is key in establishing an efficient and effective internetwork.

The challenge when connecting various systems is to support communication between disparate technologies. Different sites, for example, may use different types of media, or they might operate at varying speeds.

Another essential consideration, reliable service, must be maintained in any internetwork. Individual users and entire organizations depend on consistent, reliable access to network resources.

Furthermore, network management must provide centralized support and troubleshooting capabilities in an internetwork. Configuration, security, performance, and other issues must be adequately addressed for the internetwork to function smoothly.

Flexibility, the final concern, is necessary for network expansion and new applications and services, among other factors.

OPEN SYSTEMS INTERCONNECTION (OSI) REFERENCE MODEL

The Open Systems Interconnection (OSI) reference model describes how information from a software application in one computer moves through a network medium to a software application in another computer. The OSI reference model is a conceptual model composed of seven layers, each specifying particular network functions. The model was developed by the International Organization for Standardization (ISO) in 1984, and it is now considered the primary architectural model for intercomputer communications. The OSI model divides the tasks involved with moving information between networked computers into seven smaller, more manageable task groups. A task or group of tasks is then assigned to each of the seven OSI layers. Each layer is reasonably self-contained, so that the tasks assigned to each layer can be implemented independently. This enables the solutions offered by one layer to be updated without adversely affecting the other layers. The following list details the seven layers of the Open System Interconnection (OSI) reference model:

- Layer 7—Application layer
- Layer 6—Presentation layer
- Layer 5—Session layer
- Layer 4—Transport layer
- Layer 3—Network layer
- Layer 2—Data Link layer
- Layer 1—Physical layer

Figure 1–2 illustrates the seven-layer OSI reference model.

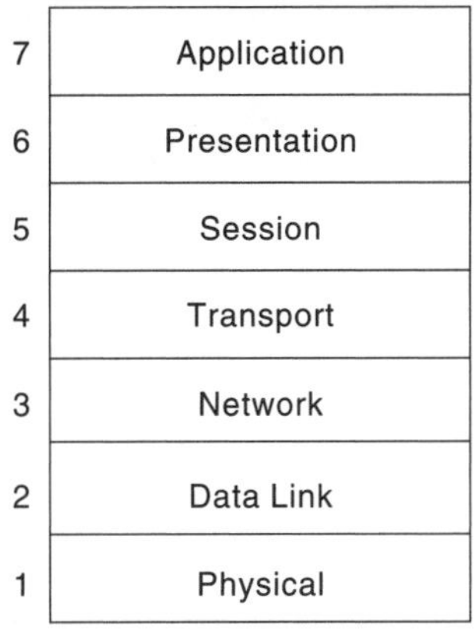

7	Application
6	Presentation
5	Session
4	Transport
3	Network
2	Data Link
1	Physical

Figure 1–2
The OSI reference model contains seven independent layers.

Characteristics of the OSI Layers

The seven layers of the OSI reference model can be divided into two categories: *upper layers* and *lower layers*.

The *upper layers* of the OSI model deal with application issues and generally are implemented only in software. The highest layer, application, is closest to the end user. Both users and application-layer processes interact with software applications that contain a communications component. The term upper layer is sometimes used to refer to any layer above another layer in the OSI model.

The *lower layers* of the OSI model handle data transport issues. The physical layer and data link layer are implemented in hardware and software. The other lower layers generally are implemented only in software. The lowest layer, the physical layer, is closest to the physical network medium (the network cabling, for example) and is responsible for actually placing information on the medium.

Figure 1–3 illustrates the division between the upper and lower OSI layers.

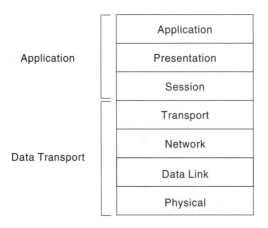

Figure 1–3
Two sets of layers make up the OSI layers.

Protocols

The OSI model provides a conceptual framework for communication between computers, but the model itself is not a method of communication. Actual communication is made possible by using communication protocols. In the context of data networking, a *protocol* is a formal set of rules and conventions that governs how computers exchange information over a network medium. A protocol implements the functions of one or more of the OSI layers. A wide variety of communication protocols exist, but all tend to fall into one of the following groups: *LAN protocols*, *WAN protocols*, *network protocols*, and *routing protocols*. *LAN protocols* operate at the physical and data link layers of the OSI model and define communication over the various LAN media. *WAN protocols* operate at the lowest three layers of the OSI model and define communication over the various wide-area media. *Routing protocols* are network-layer protocols that are responsible for path determination and traffic switching. Finally, *network protocols* are the various upper-layer protocols that exist in a given protocol suite.

OSI Model and Communication Between Systems

Information being transferred from a software application in one computer system to a software application in another must pass through each of the OSI layers. If, for example, a software application in System A has information to transmit to a software application in System B, the application program in System A will pass its information to the application layer (Layer 7) of System A. The application layer then passes the information to the presentation layer (Layer 6), which relays the data to the session layer (Layer 5), and so on down to the physical layer (Layer 1). At the physical layer, the information is placed on the physical network medium and is sent across the medium to System B.The physical layer of System B removes the information from the physical medium, and then its physical layer passes the information up to the data link layer (Layer 2), which passes it to the network layer (Layer 3), and so on until it reaches the application layer (Layer 7) of System B. Finally, the application layer of System B passes the information to the recipient application program to complete the communication process.

Interaction Between OSI Model Layers

A given layer in the OSI layers generally communicates with three other OSI layers: the layer directly above it, the layer directly below it, and its peer layer in other networked computer systems. The data link layer in System A, for example, communicates with the network layer of System A, the physical layer of System A, and the data link layer in System B. Figure 1–4 illustrates this example.

OSI-Layer Services

One OSI layer communicates with another layer to make use of the services provided by the second layer. The services provided by adjacent layers help a given OSI layer communicate with its peer layer in other computer systems. Three basic elements are involved in layer services: the service user, the service provider, and the service access point (SAP).

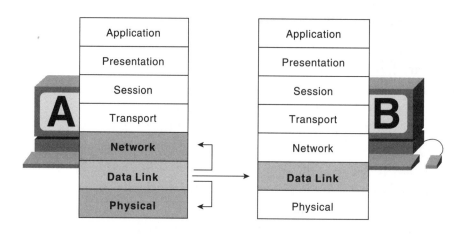

Figure 1–4
OSI model layers communicate with other layers.

In this context, the service *user* is the OSI layer that requests services from an adjacent OSI layer. The service *provider* is the OSI layer that provides services to service users. OSI layers can provide services to multiple service users. The *SAP* is a conceptual location at which one OSI layer can request the services of another OSI layer.

Figure 1–5 illustrates how these three elements interact at the network and data link layers.

OSI Model Layers and Information Exchange

The seven OSI layers use various forms of control information to communicate with their peer layers in other computer systems. This *control information* consists of specific requests and instructions that are exchanged between peer OSI layers.

Control information typically takes one of two forms: headers and trailers. Headers are prepended to data that has been passed down from upper layers. Trailers are appended to data that has been passed down from upper layers. An OSI layer is not required to attach a header or trailer to data from upper layers.

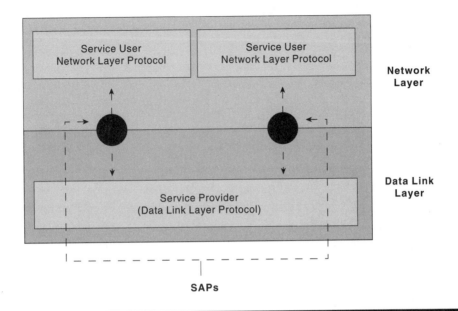

Figure 1–5
Service users, providers, and SAPs interact at the network and data link layers.

Headers, trailers, and data are relative concepts, depending on the layer that analyzes the information unit. At the network layer, an information unit, for example, consists of a Layer 3 header and data. At the data link layer, however, all the information passed down by the network layer (the Layer 3 header and the data) is treated as data.

In other words, the data portion of an information unit at a given OSI layer potentially can contain headers, trailers, and data from all the higher layers. This is known as *encapsulation*. Figure 1–6 shows how the header and data from one layer are encapsulated into the header of the next lowest layer.

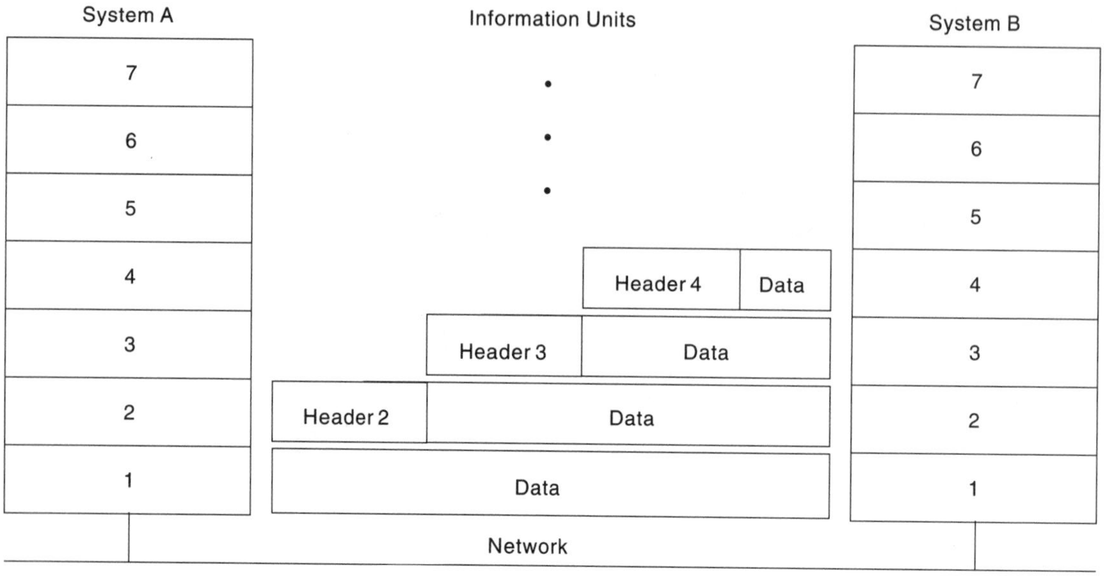

Figure 1–6
Headers and data can be encapsulated during information exchange.

Information Exchange Process

The information exchange process occurs between peer OSI layers. Each layer in the source system adds control information to data and each layer in the destination system analyzes and removes the control information from that data.

If System A has data from a software application to send to System B, the data is passed to the application layer. The application layer in System A then communicates any control information required by the application layer in System B by prepending a header to the data. The resulting information unit (a header and the data) is passed to the presentation layer, which prepends its own header containing control information intended for the presentation layer in System B. The information unit grows in size as each layer prepends its own header (and in some cases a trailer) that contains control information to be used by its peer layer in System B. At the physical layer, the entire information unit is placed onto the network medium.

The physical layer in System B receives the information unit and passes it to the data link layer. The data link layer in System B then reads the control information contained in the header prepended by the data link layer in System A. The header is then removed, and the remainder of the information unit is passed to the network layer. Each layer performs the same actions: The layer reads the header from its peer layer, strips it off, and passes the remaining information unit to the next highest layer. After the application layer performs these actions, the data is passed to the recipient software application in System B, in exactly the form in which it was transmitted by the application in System A.

OSI Model Physical Layer

The physical layer defines the electrical, mechanical, procedural, and functional specifications for activating, maintaining, and deactivating the physical link between communicating network systems. Physical layer specifications define characteristics such as voltage levels, timing of voltage changes, physical data rates, maximum transmission distances, and physical connectors. Physical-layer implementations can be categorized as either LAN or WAN specifications. Figure 1–7 illustrates some common LAN and WAN physical-layer implementations.

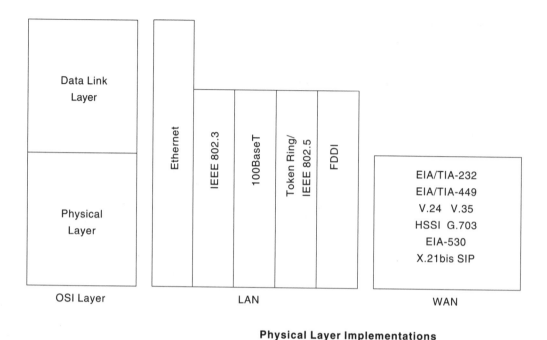

Physical Layer Implementations

Figure 1–7
Physical-layer implementations can be LAN or WAN specifications.

OSI Model Data Link Layer

The data link layer provides reliable transit of data across a physical network link. Different data link layer specifications define different network and protocol characteristics, including physical addressing, network topology, error notification, sequencing of frames, and flow control. Physical addressing (as opposed to network addressing) defines how devices are addressed at the data link layer. Network topology consists of the data link layer specifications that often define how devices are to be physically connected, such as in a bus or a ring topology. Error notification alerts upper-layer protocols that a transmission error has occurred, and the sequencing of data frames reorders frames that are transmitted out of sequence. Finally, flow control moderates the transmission of data so that the receiving device is not overwhelmed with more traffic than it can handle at one time.

The Institute of Electrical and Electronics Engineers (IEEE) has subdivided the data link layer into two sublayers: Logical Link Control (LLC) and Media Access Control (MAC). Figure 1–8 illustrates the IEEE sublayers of the data link layer.

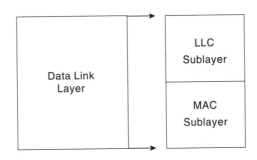

Figure 1–8
The data link layer contains two sublayers.

The Logical Link Control (LLC) sublayer of the data link layer manages communications between devices over a single link of a network. LLC is defined in the IEEE 802.2 specification and supports both connectionless and connection-oriented services used by higher-layer protocols. IEEE 802.2 defines a number of fields in data link layer frames that enable multiple higher-layer protocols to share a single physical data link. The Media Access Control (MAC) sublayer of the data link layer manages protocol access to the physical network medium. The IEEE MAC specification defines MAC addresses, which enable multiple devices to uniquely identify one another at the data link layer.

OSI Model Network Layer

The network layer provides routing and related functions that enable multiple data links to be combined into an internetwork. This is accomplished by the logical addressing (as opposed to the physical addressing) of devices. The network layer supports both connection-oriented and connectionless service from higher-layer protocols. Network-layer protocols typically are routing protocols, but other types of protocols are implemented at the network layer as well. Some common routing protocols include Border Gateway Protocol (BGP), an Internet interdomain routing protocol; Open Shortest Path First (OSPF), a link-state, interior gateway protocol developed for use in TCP/IP networks; and Routing Information Protocol (RIP), an Internet routing protocol that uses hop count as its metric.

OSI Model Transport Layer

The transport layer implements reliable internetwork data transport services that are transparent to upper layers. Transport-layer functions typically include flow control, multiplexing, virtual circuit management, and error checking and recovery.

Flow control manages data transmission between devices so that the transmitting device does not send more data than the receiving device can process. Multiplexing enables data from several applications to be transmitted onto a single physical link. Virtual circuits are established, maintained, and terminated by the transport layer. Error checking involves creating various mechanisms for detecting transmission errors, while error recovery involves taking an action, such as requesting that data be retransmitted, to resolve any errors that occur.

Some transport-layer implementations include Transmission Control Protocol, Name Binding Protocol, and OSI transport protocols. Transmission Control Protocol (TCP) is the protocol in the TCP/IP suite that provides reliable transmission of data. Name Binding Protocol (NBP) is the protocol that associates AppleTalk names with addresses. OSI transport protocols are a series of transport protocols in the OSI protocol suite.

OSI Model Session Layer

The session layer establishes, manages, and terminates communication sessions between presentation layer entities. Communication sessions consist of service requests and service responses that occur between applications located in different network devices. These requests and responses are coordinated by protocols implemented at the session layer. Some examples of session-layer implementations include Zone Information Protocol (ZIP), the AppleTalk protocol that coordinates the name binding process; and Session Control Protocol (SCP), the DECnet Phase IV session-layer protocol.

OSI Model Presentation Layer

The presentation layer provides a variety of coding and conversion functions that are applied to application layer data. These functions ensure that information sent from the application layer of one system will be readable by the application layer of another system. Some examples of presentation-layer coding and conversion schemes include common data representation formats, conversion of character representation formats, common data compression schemes, and common data encryption schemes.

Common data representation formats, or the use of standard image, sound, and video formats, enable the interchange of application data between different types of computer systems. Conversion schemes are used to exchange information with systems by using different text and data representations, such as EBCDIC and ASCII. Standard data compression schemes enable data that is compressed at the source device to be properly decompressed at the destination. Standard data encryption schemes enable data encrypted at the source device to be properly deciphered at the destination.

Presentation-layer implementations are not typically associated with a particular protocol stack. Some well-known standards for video include QuickTime and Motion Picture Experts Group (MPEG). QuickTime is an Apple Computer specification for video and audio, and MPEG is a standard for video compression and coding.

Among the well-known graphic image formats are Graphics Interchange Format (GIF), Joint Photographic Experts Group (JPEG), and Tagged Image File Format (TIFF). GIF is a standard for compressing and coding graphic images. JPEG is another compression and coding standard for graphic images, and TIFF is a standard coding format for graphic images.

OSI Model Application Layer

The application layer is the OSI layer closest to the end user, which means that both the OSI application layer and the user interact directly with the software application.

This layer interacts with software applications that implement a communicating component. Such application programs fall outside the scope of the OSI model. Application-layer functions typically include identifying communication partners, determining resource availability, and synchronizing communication.

When identifying communication partners, the application layer determines the identity and availability of communication partners for an application with data to transmit. When determining resource availability, the application layer must decide whether sufficient network resources for the requested communication exist. In synchronizing communication, all communication between applications requires cooperation that is managed by the application layer.

Two key types of application-layer implementations are TCP/IP applications and OSI applications. TCP/IP applications are protocols, such as Telnet, File Transfer Protocol (FTP), and Simple Mail Transfer Protocol (SMTP), that exist in the Internet Protocol suite. OSI applications are protocols, such as File Transfer, Access, and Management (FTAM), Virtual Terminal Protocol (VTP), and Common Management Information Protocol (CMIP), that exist in the OSI suite.

INFORMATION FORMATS

The data and control information that is transmitted through internetworks takes a wide variety of forms. The terms used to refer to these information formats are not used consistently in the internetworking industry but sometimes are used interchangeably. Common information formats include frame, packet, datagram, segment, message, cell, and data unit.

A frame is an information unit whose source and destination are data link layer entities. A frame is composed of the data-link layer header (and possibly a trailer) and upper-layer data. The header and trailer contain control information intended for the data-link layer entity in the destination system. Data from upper-layer entities is encapsulated in the data-link layer header and trailer. Figure 1–9 illustrates the basic components of a data-link layer frame.

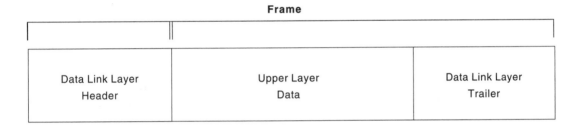

Figure 1–9
Data from upper-layer entities makes up the data link layer frame.

A packet is an information unit whose source and destination are network-layer entities. A packet is composed of the network-layer header (and possibly a trailer) and upper-layer data. The header and trailer contain control information intended for the network-layer entity in the destination system. Data from upper-layer entities is encapsulated in the network-layer header and trailer. Figure 1–10 illustrates the basic components of a network-layer packet.

Packet

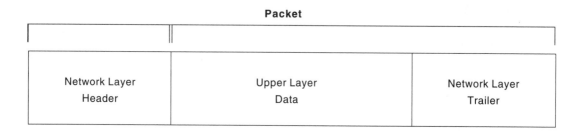

| Network Layer
Header | Upper Layer
Data | Network Layer
Trailer |

Figure 1–10
Three basic components make up a network-layer packet.

The term *datagram* usually refers to an information unit whose source and destination are network-layer entities that use connectionless network service.

The term *segment* usually refers to an information unit whose source and destination are transport-layer entities.

A *message* is an information unit whose source and destination entities exist above the network layer (often the application layer).

A *cell* is an information unit of a fixed size whose source and destination are data-link layer entities. Cells are used in switched environments, such as Asynchronous Transfer Mode (ATM) and Switched Multimegabit Data Service (SMDS) networks. A cell is composed of the header and payload. The header contains control information intended for the destination data-link layer entity and is typically 5 bytes long. The payload contains upper-layer data that is encapsulated in the cell header and is typically 48 bytes long.

The length of the header and the payload fields always are exactly the same for each cell. Figure 1–11 depicts the components of a typical cell.

Data unit is a generic term that refers to a variety of information units. Some common data units are service data units (SDUs), protocol data units, and bridge protocol data units (BPDUs). SDUs are information units from upper-layer protocols that define a service request to a lower-layer protocol. PDU is OSI terminology for a packet. BPDUs are used by the spanning-tree algorithm as hello messages.

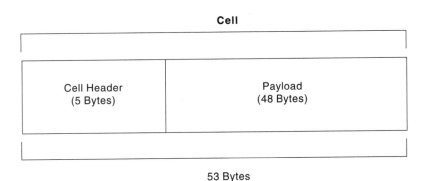

Figure 1–11
Two components make up a typical cell.

ISO HIERARCHY OF NETWORKS

Large networks typically are organized as hierarchies. A hierarchical organization provides such advantages as ease of management, flexibility, and a reduction in unnecessary traffic. Thus, the International Organization for Standardization (ISO) has adopted a number of terminology conventions for addressing network entities. Key terms, defined in this section, include *end system* (ES), *intermediate system* (IS), *area*, and *autonomous system* (AS).

An *ES* is a network device that does not perform routing or other traffic-forwarding functions. Typical ESs include such devices as terminals, personal computers, and printers. An *IS* is a network device that performs routing or other traffic-forwarding functions. Typical ISs include such devices as routers, switches, and bridges. Two types of IS networks exist: intradomain IS and interdomain IS. An intradomain IS communicates within a single autonomous system, while an interdomain IS communicates within and between autonomous systems. An *area* is a logical group of network segments and their attached devices. Areas are subdivisions of autonomous systems (ASs). An AS is a collection of networks under a common administration that share a common routing strategy. Autonomous systems are subdivided into areas, and an AS is sometimes called a *domain*. Figure 1–12 illustrates a hierarchical network and its components.

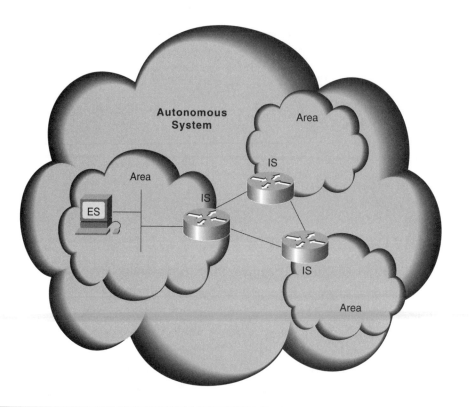

Figure 1–12
A hierarchical network contains numerous components.

CONNECTION-ORIENTED AND CONNECTIONLESS NETWORK SERVICES

In general, networking protocols and the data traffic that they support can be characterized as being either connection-oriented or connectionless. In brief, connection-oriented data handling involves using a specific path that is established for the duration of a connection. Connectionless data handling involves passing data through a permanently established connection.

Connection-oriented service involves three phases: connection establishment, data transfer, and connection termination.

During the connection-establishment phase, a single path between the source and destination systems is determined. Network resources typically are reserved at this time to ensure a consistent grade of service, such as a guaranteed throughput rate.

In the data-transfer phase, data is transmitted sequentially over the path that has been established. Data always arrives at the destination system in the order in which it was sent.

During the connection-termination phase, an established connection that is no longer needed is terminated. Further communication between the source and destination systems requires that a new connection be established.

Connection-oriented network service carries two significant disadvantages over connectionless, static-path selection and the static reservation of network resources. Static-path selection can create difficulty because all traffic must travel along the same static path. A failure anywhere along that path causes the connection to fail. Static reservation of network resources causes difficulty because it requires a guaranteed rate of throughput and, thus, a commitment of resources that other network users cannot share. Unless the connection uses full, uninterrupted throughput, bandwidth is not used efficiently.

Connection-oriented services, however, are useful for transmitting data from applications that don't tolerate delays and packet resequencing. Voice and video applications are typically based on connection-oriented services.

As another disadvantage, connectionless network service does not predetermine the path from the source to the destination system, nor are packet sequencing, data throughput, and other network resources guaranteed. Each packet must be completely addressed because different paths through the network may be selected for different packets, based on a variety of influences. Each packet is transmitted independently by the source system and is handled independently by intermediate network devices.

Connectionless service, however, offers two important advantages over connection-oriented service: dynamic-path selection and dynamic-bandwidth allocation. Dynamic-path selection enables traffic to be routed around network failures because paths are selected on a packet-by-packet basis. With dynamic-bandwidth allocation, bandwidth is used more efficiently because network resources are not allocated a bandwidth that they will not use.

Connectionless services are useful for transmitting data from applications that can tolerate some delay and resequencing. Data-based applications typically are based on connectionless service.

INTERNETWORK ADDRESSING

Internetwork addresses identify devices separately or as members of a group. Addressing schemes vary depending on the protocol family and the OSI layer. Three types of internetwork addresses are commonly used: data link-layer addresses, Media Access Control (MAC) addresses, and network-layer addresses.

Data Link Layer

A data link-layer address uniquely identifies each physical network connection of a network device. Data-link addresses sometimes are referred to as *physical* or *hardware* addresses. Data-link addresses usually exist within a flat address space and have a pre-established and typically fixed relationship to a specific device.

End systems generally have only one physical network connection, and thus have only one data-link address. Routers and other internetworking devices typically have multiple physical network connections and therefore also have multiple data-link addresses. Figure 1–13 illustrates how each interface on a device is uniquely identified by a data-link address.

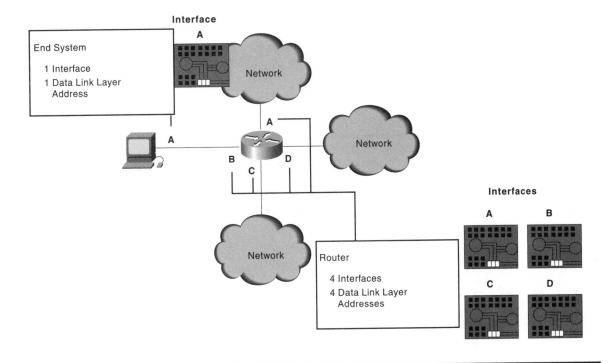

Figure 1–13
Each interface on a device is uniquely identified by a data-link address.

MAC Addresses

Media Access Control (MAC) addresses consist of a subset of data link-layer addresses. MAC addresses identify network entities in LANs that implement the IEEE MAC addresses of the data link layer. As with most data-link addresses, MAC addresses are unique for each LAN interface. Figure 1–14 illustrates the relationship between MAC addresses, data-link addresses, and the IEEE sublayers of the data link layer.

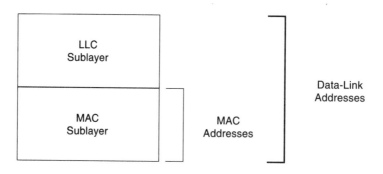

Figure 1–14
MAC addresses, data-link addresses, and the IEEE sublayers of the data-link layer are all related.

MAC addresses are 48 bits in length and are expressed as 12 hexadecimal digits. The first 6 hexadecimal digits, which are administered by the IEEE, identify the manufacturer or vendor and thus comprise the Organizational Unique Identifier (OUI). The last 6 hexadecimal digits comprise the interface serial number, or another value administered by the specific vendor. MAC addresses sometimes are called *burned-in addresses* (BIAs) because they are burned into read-only memory (ROM) and are copied into random-access memory (RAM) when the interface card initializes. Figure 1–15 illustrates the MAC address format.

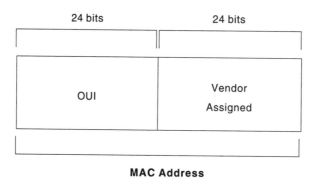

Figure 1–15
The MAC address contains a unique format of hexadecimal digits.

Different protocol suites use different methods for determining the MAC address of a device. The following three methods are used most often. Address Resolution Protocol (ARP) maps network addresses to MAC addresses. Hello protocol enables network devices to learn the MAC addresses of other network devices. MAC addresses are either embedded in the network-layer address or are generated by an algorithm.

Address resolution is the process of mapping network addresses to Media Access Control (MAC) addresses. This process is accomplished by using the Address Resolution Protocol (ARP), which is implemented by many protocol suites.When a network address is successfully associated with a MAC address, the network device stores the information in the ARP cache. The ARP cache enables devices to send traffic to a destination without creating ARP traffic because the MAC address of the destination is already known.

The process of address resolution differs slightly, depending on the network environment. Address resolution on a single LAN begins when End System A broadcasts an ARP request onto the LAN in an attempt to learn the MAC address of End System B. The broadcast is received and processed by all devices on the LAN, although only End System B replies to the ARP request by sending an ARP reply containing its MAC address to End System A. End System A receives the reply and saves the MAC address of End System B in its ARP cache. (The ARP cache is where network addresses are associated with MAC addresses.)Whenever End System A must communicate with End System B, it checks the ARP cache, finds the MAC address of System B, and sends the frame directly without first having to use an ARP request.

Address resolution works differently, however, when source and destination devices are attached to different LANs that are interconnected by a router. End System Y broadcasts an ARP request onto the LAN in an attempt to learn the MAC address of End System Z. The broadcast is received and processed by all devices on the LAN, including Router X, which acts as a proxy for End System Z by checking its routing table to determine that End System Z is located on a different LAN. Router X then replies to the ARP request from

End System Y, sending an ARP reply containing its *own* MAC address as if it belonged to End System Z. End System Y receives the ARP reply and saves the MAC address of Router X in its ARP cache in the entry for End System Z. When End System Y must communicate with End System Z, it checks the ARP cache, finds the MAC address of Router X, and sends the frame directly without using ARP requests. Router X receives the traffic from End System Y and forwards it to End System Z on the other LAN.

The Hello protocol is a network-layer protocol that enables network devices to identify one another and indicate that they are still functional. When a new end system powers up, for example, it broadcasts Hello messages onto the network. Devices on the network then return Hello replies, and Hello messages are also sent at specific intervals to indicate that they are still functional. Network devices can learn the MAC addresses of other devices by examining Hello-protocol packets.

Three protocols use predictable MAC addresses. In these protocol suites, MAC addresses are predictable because the network layer either embeds the MAC address in the network-layer address or uses an algorithm to determine the MAC address. The three protocols are Xerox Network Systems (XNS), Novell Internetwork Packet Exchange (IPX), and DECnet Phase IV.

Network-Layer Addresses

A network-layer address identifies an entity at the network layer of the OSI layers. Network addresses usually exist within a hierarchical address space and sometimes are called *virtual* or *logical* addresses.

The relationship between a network address and a device is logical and unfixed; it typically is based either on physical network characteristics (the device is on a particular network segment) or on groupings that have no physical basis (the device is part of an AppleTalk zone). End systems require one network-layer address for each network-layer protocol they support. (This assumes that the device has only one physical network connection.) Routers and other internetworking devices require one network-layer address per physical network connection for each network-layer protocol supported. A router, for example, with three interfaces each running AppleTalk, TCP/IP, and OSI must have three network-layer addresses for each interface. The router therefore has nine network-layer addresses. Figure 1–16 illustrates how each network interface must be assigned a network address for each protocol supported.

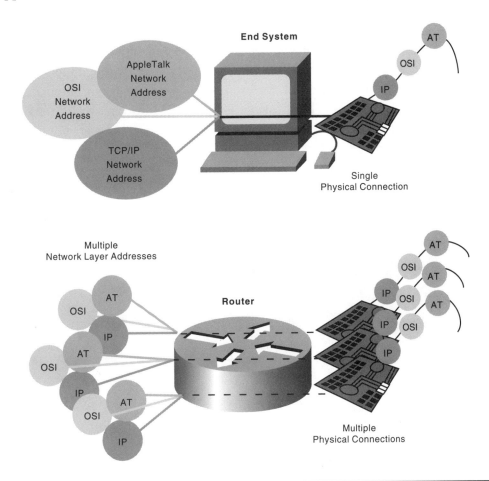

Figure 1–16
Each network interface must be assigned a network address for each protocol supported.

Hierarchical Versus Flat Address Space

Internetwork address space typically takes one of two forms: hierarchical address space or flat address space. A hierarchical address space is organized into numerous subgroups, each successively narrowing an address until it points to a single device (in a manner similar to street addresses). A flat address space is organized into a single group (in a manner similar to U.S. Social Security numbers).

Hierarchical addressing offers certain advantages over flat-addressing schemes. Address sorting and recall is simplified through the use of comparison operations. Ireland, for example, in a street address eliminates any other country as a possible location. Figure 1–17 illustrates the difference between hierarchical and flat-address spaces.

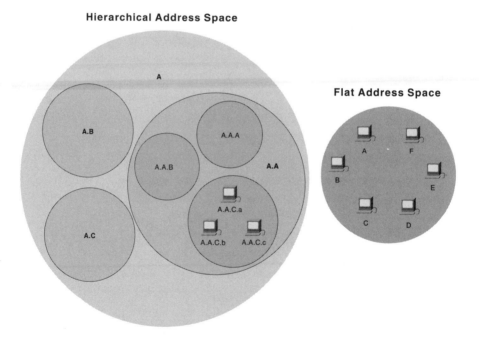

Figure 1–17

Hierarchical and flat address spaces differ in comparison operations.

Address Assignments

Addresses are assigned to devices as one of three types: *static*, *dynamic*, or *server* addresses. *Static addresses* are assigned by a network administrator according to a preconceived internetwork addressing plan. A static address does not change until the network administrator manually changes it. *Dynamic addresses* are obtained by devices when they attach to a network, by means of some protocol-specific process. A device using a dynamic address often has a different address each time it connects to the network. Addresses assigned by a server are given to devices as they connect to the network. Server-assigned addresses are recycled for reuse as devices disconnect. A device is therefore likely to have a different address each time it connects to the network.

Addresses Versus Names

Internetwork devices usually have both a name and an address associated with them. Internetwork names typically are location-independent and remain associated with a device wherever that device moves (for example, from one building to another). Internetwork addresses usually are location-dependent and change when a device is moved (although MAC addresses are an exception to this rule). Names and addresses represent a logical identifier, which may be a local system administrator or an organization, such as the Internet Assigned Numbers Authority (IANA).

FLOW-CONTROL BASICS

Flow control is a function that prevents network congestion by ensuring that transmitting devices do not overwhelm receiving devices with data. Countless possible causes of network congestion exist. A high-speed computer, for example, may generate traffic faster than the network can transfer it, or faster than the destination device can receive and process it. The three commonly used methods for handling network congestion are buffering, transmitting source-quench messages, and windowing.

Buffering is used by network devices to temporarily store bursts of excess data in memory until they can be processed. Occasional data bursts are easily handled by buffering. Excess data bursts can exhaust memory, however, forcing the device to discard any additional datagrams that arrive.

Source-quench messages are used by receiving devices to help prevent their buffers from overflowing. The receiving device sends source-quench messages to request that the source reduce its current rate of data transmission. First, the receiving device begins discarding received data due to overflowing buffers. Second, the receiving device begins sending source-quench messages to the transmitting device at the rate of one message for each packet dropped. The source device receives the source-quench messages and lowers the data rate until it stops receiving the messages. Finally, the source device then gradually increases the data rate as long as no further source-quench requests are received.

Windowing is a flow-control scheme in which the source device requires an acknowledgment from the destination after a certain number of packets have been transmitted. With a window size of three, the source requires an acknowledgment after sending three packets, as follows. First, the source device sends three packets to the destination device. Then, after receiving the three packets, the destination device sends an acknowledgment to the source. The source receives the acknowledgment and sends three more packets. If the destination does not receive one or more of the packets for some reason, such as overflowing buffers, it does not receive enough packets to send an acknowledgment. The source then retransmits the packets at a reduced transmission rate.

ERROR-CHECKING BASICS

Error-checking schemes determine whether transmitted data has become corrupt or otherwise damaged while traveling from the source to the destination. Error-checking is implemented at a number of the OSI layers.

One common error-checking scheme is the cyclic redundancy check (CRC), which detects and discards corrupted data. Error-correction functions (such as data retransmission) are left to higher-layer protocols. A CRC value is generated by a calculation that is performed at the source device. The destination device compares this value to its own calculation to determine whether errors occurred during transmission. First, the source device performs a predetermined set of calculations over the contents of the packet to be sent. Then, the source places the calculated value in the packet and sends the packet to the destination. The destination performs the same predetermined set of calculations over the contents of the packet and then compares its computed value with that contained in the packet. If the values are equal, the packet is considered valid. If the values are unequal, the packet contains errors and is discarded.

MULTIPLEXING BASICS

Multiplexing is a process in which multiple data channels are combined into a single data or physical channel at the source. Multiplexing can be implemented at any of the OSI layers. Conversely, demultiplexing is the process of separating multiplexed data channels at the destination. One example of multiplexing is when data from multiple applications is multiplexed into a single lower-layer data packet. Figure 1–18 illustrates this example.

Another example of multiplexing is when data from multiple devices is combined into a single physical channel (using a device called a multiplexer). Figure 1–19 illustrates this example.

A multiplexer is a physical-layer device that combines multiple data streams into one or more output channels at the source. Multiplexers demultiplex the channels into multiple data streams at the remote end and thus maximize the use of the bandwidth of the physical medium by enabling it to be shared by multiple traffic sources.

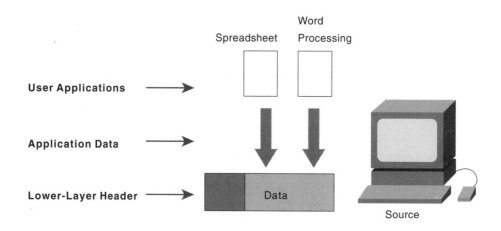

Figure 1–18

Multiple applications can be multiplexed into a single lower-layer data packet.

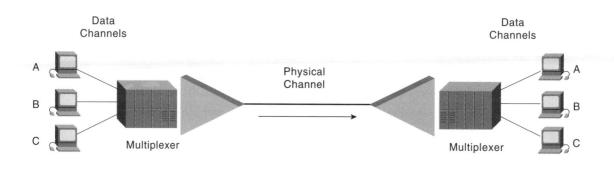

Figure 1–19

Multiple devices can be multiplexed into a single physical channel.

Some methods used for multiplexing data are time-division multiplexing (TDM), asynchronous time-division multiplexing (ATDM), frequency-division multiplexing (FDM), and statistical multiplexing.

In TDM, information from each data channel is allocated bandwidth based on preassigned time slots, regardless of whether there is data to transmit. In

ATDM, information from data channels is allocated bandwidth as needed, by using dynamically assigned time slots. In FDM, information from each data channel is allocated bandwidth based on the signal frequency of the traffic. In statistical multiplexing, bandwidth is dynamically allocated to any data channels that have information to transmit.

STANDARDS ORGANIZATIONS

A wide variety of organizations contribute to internetworking standards by providing forums for discussion, turning informal discussion into formal specifications, and proliferating specifications after they are standardized.

Most standards organizations create formal standards by using specific processes: organizing ideas, discussing the approach, developing draft standards, voting on all or certain aspects of the standards, and then formally releasing the completed standard to the public.

Some of the best-known standards organizations that contribute to internetworking standards include:

- *International Organization for Standardization (ISO)*—ISO is an international standards organization responsible for a wide range of standards, including many that are relevant to networking. Their best-known contribution is the development of the OSI reference model and the OSI protocol suite.

- *American National Standards Institute (ANSI)*—ANSI, which is also a member of the ISO, is the coordinating body for voluntary standards groups within the United States. ANSI developed the Fiber Distributed Data Interface (FDDI) and other communications standards.

- *Electronic Industries Association (EIA)*—EIA specifies electrical transmission standards, including those used in networking. The EIA developed the widely used EIA/TIA-232 standard (formerly known as RS-232).

- *Institute of Electrical and Electronic Engineers (IEEE)*—IEEE is a professional organization that defines networking and other standards. The IEEE developed the widely used LAN standards IEEE 802.3 and IEEE 802.5.

- *International Telecommunication Union Telecommunication Standardization Sector (ITU-T)*—Formerly called the Committee for International Telegraph and Telephone (CCITT), ITU-T is now an international organization that develops communication standards. The ITU-T developed X.25 and other communications standards.

- *Internet Activities Board (IAB)*—IAB is a group of internetwork researchers who discuss issues pertinent to the Internet and set Internet policies through decisions and task forces. The IAB designates some Request For Comments (RFC) documents as Internet standards, including Transmission Control Protocol/Internet Protocol (TCP/IP) and the Simple Network Management Protocol (SNMP).

CHAPTER 2

Introduction
to LAN Protocols

This chapter introduces the various media-access methods, transmission methods, topologies, and devices used in a local area network (LAN). Topics addressed focus on the methods and devices used in Ethernet/IEEE 802.3, Token Ring/IEEE 802.5, and Fiber Distributed Data Interface (FDDI). Subsequent chapters in Part 2, "LAN Protocols," of this book address specific protocols in more detail. Figure 2–1 illustrates the basic layout of these three implementations.

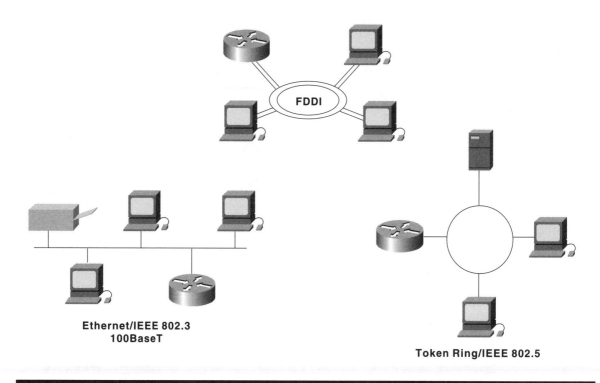

Figure 2–1
Three LAN implementations are used most commonly.

WHAT IS A LAN?

A LAN is a high-speed, fault-tolerant data network that covers a relatively small geographic area. It typically connects workstations, personal computers, printers, and other devices. LANs offer computer users many advantages, including shared access to devices and applications, file exchange between connected users, and communication between users via electronic mail and other applications.

LAN PROTOCOLS AND THE OSI REFERENCE MODEL

LAN protocols function at the lowest two layers of the OSI reference model, as discussed in Chapter 1, "Internetworking Basics," between the physical layer and the data link layer. Figure 2–2 illustrates how several popular LAN protocols map to the OSI reference model.

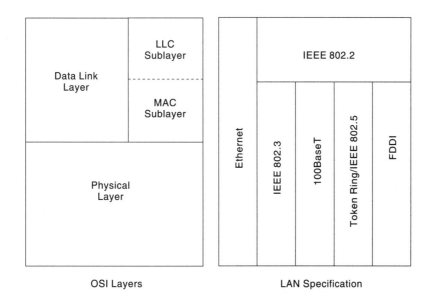

Figure 2–2
Popular LAN protocols mapped to the OSI reference model.

LAN MEDIA-ACCESS METHODS

LAN protocols typically use one of two methods to access the physical network medium: *carrier sense multiple access collision detect* (CSMA/CD) and *token passing.*

In the CSMA/CD media-access scheme, network devices contend for use of the physical network medium. CSMA/CD is therefore sometimes called *contention access*. Examples of LANs that use the CSMA/CD media-access scheme are Ethernet/IEEE 802.3 networks, including 100BaseT.

In the token-passing media-access scheme, network devices access the physical medium based on possession of a token. Examples of LANs that use the token-passing media-access scheme are Token Ring/IEEE 802.5 and FDDI.

LAN TRANSMISSION METHODS

LAN data transmissions fall into three classifications: *unicast*, *multicast*, and *broadcast*. In each type of transmission, a single packet is sent to one or more nodes.

In a unicast transmission, a single packet is sent from the source to a destination on a network. First, the source node addresses the packet by using the address of the destination node. The package is then sent onto the network, and finally, the network passes the packet to its destination.

A multicast transmission consists of a single data packet that is copied and sent to a specific subset of nodes on the network. First, the source node addresses the packet by using a multicast address. The packet is then sent into the network, which makes copies of the packet and sends a copy to each node that is part of the multicast address.

A broadcast transmission consists of a single data packet that is copied and sent to all nodes on the network. In these types of transmissions, the source node addresses the packet by using the broadcast address. The packet is then sent into the network, which makes copies of the packet and sends a copy to every node on the network.

LAN TOPOLOGIES

LAN topologies define the manner in which network devices are organized. Four common LAN topologies exist: bus, ring, star, and tree. These topologies are logical architectures, but the actual devices need not be physically organized in these configurations. Logical bus and ring topologies, for example, are commonly organized physically as a star. A bus topology is a linear LAN architecture in which transmissions from network stations propagate the length of the medium and are received by all other stations. Of the three most widely used LAN implementations, Ethernet/IEEE 802.3 networks—including 100BaseT—implement a bus topology, which is illustrated in Figure 2–3.

Figure 2–3
Some networks implement a local bus topology.

A ring topology is a LAN architecture that consists of a series of devices connected to one another by unidirectional transmission links to form a single closed loop. Both Token Ring/IEEE 802.5 and FDDI networks implement a ring topology. Figure 2–4 depicts a logical ring topology.

A star topology is a LAN architecture in which the endpoints on a network are connected to a common central hub, or switch, by dedicated links. Logical bus and ring topologies are often implemented physically in a star topology, which is illustrated in Figure 2–5.

A tree topology is a LAN architecture that is identical to the bus topology, except that branches with multiple nodes are possible in this case. Figure 2–5 illustrates a logical tree topology.

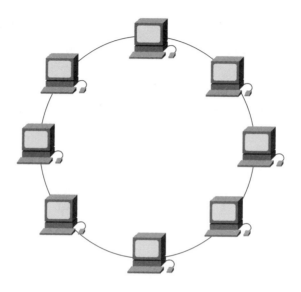

Figure 2–4

Some networks implement a logical ring topology.

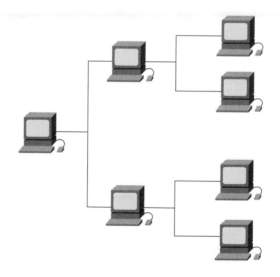

Figure 2–5

A logical tree topology can contain multiple nodes.

LAN DEVICES

Devices commonly used in LANs include *repeaters*, *hubs*, *LAN extenders*, *bridges*, *LAN switches*, and *routers*.

NOTES

Repeaters, hubs, and LAN extenders are discussed briefly in this section. The function and operation of bridges, switches, and routers are discussed generally in Chapter 4, "Bridging and Switching Basics," and Chapter 5, "Routing Basics."

A *repeater* is a physical layer device used to interconnect the media segments of an extended network. A repeater essentially enables a series of cable segments to be treated as a single cable. Repeaters receive signals from one network segment and amplify, retime, and retransmit those signals to another network segment. These actions prevent signal deterioration caused by long cable lengths and large numbers of connected devices. Repeaters are incapable of performing complex filtering and other traffic processing. In addition, all electrical signals, including electrical disturbances and other errors, are repeated and amplified. The total number of repeaters and network segments that can be connected is limited due to timing and other issues. Figure 2–6 illustrates a repeater connecting two network segments.

A *hub* is a physical-layer device that connects multiple user stations, each via a dedicated cable. Electrical interconnections are established inside the hub. Hubs are used to create a physical star network while maintaining the logical bus or ring configuration of the LAN. In some respects, a hub functions as a multiport repeater.

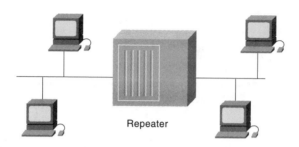

Figure 2-6

A repeater connects two network segments.

A LAN *extender* is a remote-access multilayer switch that connects to a host router. LAN extenders forward traffic from all the standard network-layer protocols (such as IP, IPX, and AppleTalk), and filter traffic based on the MAC address or network-layer protocol type. LAN extenders scale well because the host router filters out unwanted broadcasts and multicasts. LAN extenders, however, are not capable of segmenting traffic or creating security firewalls. Figure 2-7 illustrates multiple LAN extenders connected to the host router through a WAN.

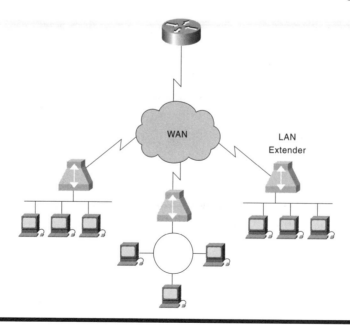

Figure 2-7

Multiple LAN extenders can connect to the host router through a WAN.

CHAPTER 3

Introduction to WAN Technologies

This chapter introduces the various protocols and technologies used in wide-area network (WAN) environments. Topics summarized here include point-to-point links, circuit switching, packet switching, virtual circuits, dialup services, and WAN devices. Chapters in Part 3, "WAN Technologies," of this book address specific technologies in more detail.

WHAT IS A WAN?

A WAN is a data communications network that covers a relatively broad geographic area and often uses transmission facilities provided by common carriers, such as telephone companies. WAN technologies function at the lower three layers of the OSI reference model: the physical layer, the data link layer, and the network layer. Figure 3–1 illustrates the relationship between the common WAN technologies and the OSI model.

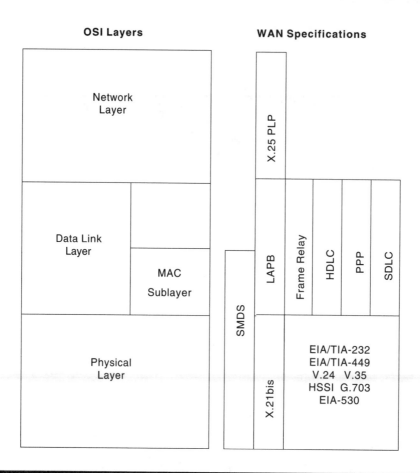

Figure 3–1
WAN technologies operate at the lowest levels of the OSI model.

POINT-TO-POINT LINKS

A *point-to-point link* provides a single, preestablished WAN communications path from the customer premises through a carrier network, such as a telephone company, to a remote network. A point-to-point link is also known as a leased line because its established path is permanent and fixed for each remote network reached through the carrier facilities. The carrier company reserves point-to-point links for the private use of the customer. These links accommodate two types of transmissions: datagram transmissions, which are composed of individually addressed frames, and data-stream transmissions, which are composed of a stream of data for which address checking occurs only once. Figure 3–2 illustrates a typical point-to-point link through a WAN.

Figure 3–2
A typical point-to-point link operates through a WAN to a remote network.

CIRCUIT SWITCHING

Circuit switching is a WAN switching method in which a dedicated physical circuit is established, maintained, and terminated through a carrier network for each communication session. Circuit switching accommodates two types of transmissions: datagram transmissions and data-stream transmissions. Used extensively in telephone company networks, circuit switching operates much like a normal telephone call. Integrated Services Digital Network (ISDN) is an example of a circuit-switched WAN technology, and is illustrated in Figure 3–3.

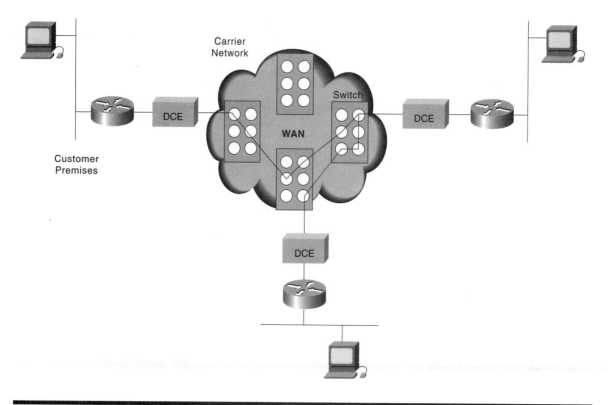

Figure 3–3

A circuit-switched WAN undergoes a process similar to that used for a telephone call.

PACKET SWITCHING

Packet switching is a WAN switching method in which network devices share a single point-to-point link to transport packets from a source to a destination across a carrier network. Statistical mutliplexing is used to enable devices to share these circuits. Asynchronous Transfer Mode (ATM), Frame Relay, Switched Multimegabit Data Service (SMDS), and X.25 are examples of packet-switched WAN technologies (see Figure 3–4).

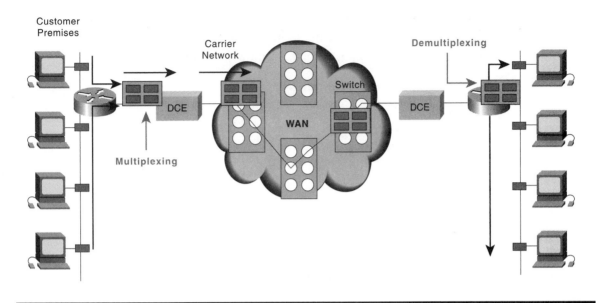

Figure 3–4
Packet switching transfers packets across a carrier network.

WAN VIRTUAL CIRCUITS

A virtual circuit is a logical circuit created to ensure reliable communication between two network devices. Two types of virtual circuits exist: switched virtual circuits (SVCs) and permanent virtual circuits (PVCs).

SVCs are virtual circuits that are dynamically established on demand and terminated when transmission is complete. Communication over an SVC consists of three phases: circuit establishment, data transfer, and circuit termination. The establishment phase involves creating the virtual circuit between the source and destination devices. Data transfer involves transmitting data between the devices over the virtual circuit, and the circuit-termination phase involves tearing down the virtual circuit between the source and destination devices. SVCs are used in situations in which data transmission between devices is sporadic, largely because SVCs increase bandwidth used due to the circuit establishment and termination phases, but decrease the cost associated with constant virtual circuit availability.

A *PVC* is a permanently established virtual circuit that consists of one mode: data transfer. PVCs are used in situations in which data transfer between devices is constant. PVCs decrease the bandwidth use associated with the establishment and termination of virtual circuits, but increase costs due to constant virtual circuit availability.

WAN DIALUP SERVICES

Dialup services offer cost-effective methods for connectivity across WANs. Two popular dialup implementations are dial-on-demand routing (DDR) and dial backup.

DDR is a technique whereby a router can dynamically initiate and close a circuit-switched session as transmitting end station demand. A router is configured to consider certain traffic interesting (such as traffic from a particular protocol) and other traffic uninteresting. When the router receives interesting traffic destined for a remote network, a circuit is established and the traffic is transmitted normally. If the router receives uninteresting traffic and a circuit is already established, that traffic also is transmitted normally. The router maintains an idle timer that is reset only when interesting traffic is received. If the router receives no interesting traffic before the idle timer expires, however, the circuit is terminated. Likewise, if uninteresting traffic is received and no circuit exists, the router drops the traffic. Upon receiving interesting traffic, the router initiates a new circuit. DDR can be used to replace point-to-point links and switched multiaccess WAN services.

Dial backup is a service that activates a backup serial line under certain conditions. The secondary serial line can act as a backup link that is used when the primary link fails or as a source of additional bandwidth when the load on the primary link reaches a certain threshold. Dial backup provides protection against WAN performance degradation and downtime.

WAN Devices

WANs use numerous types of devices that are specific to WAN environments. WAN switches, access servers, modems, CSU/DSUs, and ISDN terminal adapters are discussed in the following sections. Other devices found in WAN environments that are exclusive to WAN implementations include routers, ATM switches, and multiplexers.

WAN Switch

A WAN switch is a multiport internetworking device used in carrier networks. These devices typically switch such traffic as Frame Relay, X.25, and SMDS and operate at the data link layer of the OSI reference model. Figure 3–5 illustrates two routers at remote ends of a WAN that are connected by WAN switches.

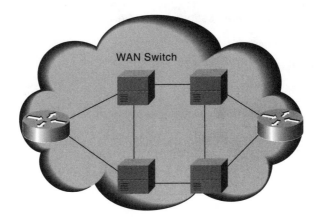

Figure 3–5
Two routers at remote ends of a WAN can be connected by WAN switches.

Access Server

An access server acts as a concentration point for dial-in and dial-out connections. Figure 3–6 illustrates an access server concentrating dial-out connections into a WAN.

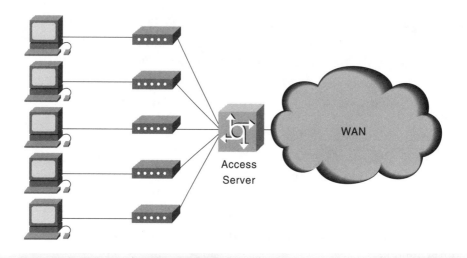

Figure 3–6
An access server concentrates dial-out connections into a WAN.

Modem

A modem is a device that interprets digital and analog signals, enabling data to be transmitted over voice-grade telephone lines. At the source, digital signals are converted to a form suitable for transmission over analog communication facilities. At the destination, these analog signals are returned to their digital form. Figure 3–7 illustrates a simple modem-to-modem connection through a WAN.

Figure 3-7
A modem connection through a WAN handles analog and digital signals.

CSU/DSU

A channel service unit/digital service unit (CSU/DSU) is a digital-interface device (or sometimes two separate digital devices) that adapts the physical interface on a data terminal equipment (DTE) device (such as a terminal) to the interface of a data circuit-terminating (DCE) device (such as a switch) in a switched-carrier network. The CSU/DSU also provides signal timing for communication between these devices. Figure 3-8 illustrates the placement of the CSU/DSU in a WAN implementation.

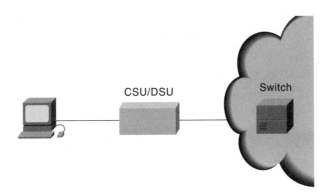

Figure 3-8
The CSU/DSU stands between the switch and the terminal.

ISDN Terminal Adapter

An ISDN terminal adapter is a device used to connect ISDN Basic Rate Interface (BRI) connections to other interfaces, such as EIA/TIA-232. A terminal adapter is essentially an ISDN modem. Figure 3–9 illustrates the placement of the terminal adapter in an ISDN environment.

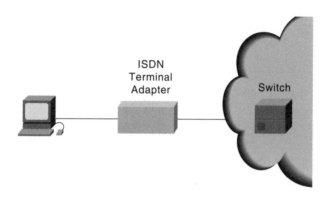

Figure 3–9

The terminal adapter connects the ISDN terminal adapter to other interfaces.

CHAPTER 4

Bridging and Switching Basics

This chapter introduces the technologies employed in devices loosely referred to as *bridges* and *switches*. Topics summarized here include general link-layer device operations, local and remote bridging, ATM switching, and LAN switching. Chapters in Part 4, "Bridging and Switching," of this book address specific technologies in more detail.

WHAT ARE BRIDGES AND SWITCHES?

Bridges and switches are data communications devices that operate principally at Layer 2 of the OSI reference model. As such, they are widely referred to as data link-layer devices.

Bridges became commercially available in the early 1980s. At the time of their introduction, bridges connected and enabled packet forwarding between homogeneous networks. More recently, bridging between different networks has also been defined and standardized.

Several kinds of bridging have proven important as internetworking devices. *Transparent bridging* is found primarily in Ethernet environments, while *source-route bridging* occurs primarily in Token Ring environments.

Translational bridging provides translation between the formats and transit principles of different media types (usually Ethernet and Token Ring). Finally, *source-route transparent bridging* combines the algorithms of transparent bridging and source-route bridging to enable communication in mixed Ethernet/Token Ring environments.

Today, switching technology has emerged as the evolutionary heir to bridging-based internetworking solutions. Switching implementations now dominate applications in which bridging technologies were implemented in prior network designs. Superior throughput performance, higher port density, lower per-port cost, and greater flexibility have contributed to the emergence of switches as replacement technology for bridges and as complements to routing technology.

LINK-LAYER DEVICE OVERVIEW

Bridging and switching occur at the link layer, which controls data flow, handles transmission errors, provides physical (as opposed to logical) addressing, and manages access to the physical medium. Bridges provide these functions by using various link-layer protocols that dictate specific flow control, error handling, addressing, and media-access algorithms. Examples of popular link-layer protocols include Ethernet, Token Ring, and FDDI.

Bridges and switches are not complicated devices. They analyze incoming frames, make forwarding decisions based on information contained in the frames, and forward the frames toward the destination. In some cases, such as source-route bridging, the entire path to the destination is contained in each frame. In other cases, such as transparent bridging, frames are forwarded one hop at a time toward the destination.

Upper-layer protocol transparency is a primary advantage of both bridging and switching. Because both device types operate at the link layer, they are not required to examine upper-layer information. This means that they can rapidly forward traffic representing any network-layer protocol. It is not uncommon for a bridge to move AppleTalk, DECnet, TCP/IP, XNS, and other traffic between two or more networks.

Bridges are capable of filtering frames based on any Layer 2 fields. A bridge, for example, can be programmed to reject (not forward) all frames sourced from a particular network. Because link-layer information often includes a reference to an upper-layer protocol, bridges usually can filter on this parameter. Furthermore, filters can be helpful in dealing with unnecessary broadcast and multicast packets.

By dividing large networks into self-contained units, bridges and switches provide several advantages. Because only a certain percentage of traffic is forwarded, a bridge or switch diminishes the traffic experienced by devices on all connected segments. The bridge or switch will act as a firewall for some potentially damaging network errors, and both accommodate communication between a larger number of devices than would be supported on any single LAN connected to the bridge. Bridges and switches extend the effective length of a LAN, permitting the attachment of distant stations that were not previously permitted.

Although bridges and switches share most relevant attributes, several distinctions differentiate these technologies. Switches are significantly faster because they switch in hardware, while bridges switch in software and can interconnect LANs of unlike bandwidth. A 10-Mbps Ethernet LAN and a 100-Mbps Ethernet LAN, for example, can be connected using a switch. Switches also can support higher port densities than bridges. Some switches support cut-through switching, which reduces latency and delays in the network, while bridges support only store-and-forward traffic switching. Finally, switches reduce collisions on network segments because they provide dedicated bandwidth to each network segment.

TYPES OF BRIDGES

Bridges can be grouped into categories based on various product characteristics. Using one popular classification scheme, bridges are either *local* or *remote*. *Local* bridges provide a direct connection between multiple LAN segments in the same area. *Remote* bridges connect multiple LAN segments in different areas, usually over telecommunications lines. Figure 4–1 illustrates these two configurations.

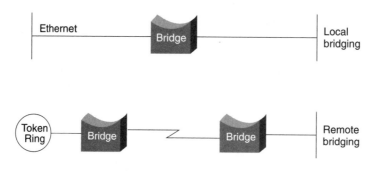

Figure 4–1
Local and remote bridges connect LAN segments in specific areas.

Remote bridging presents several unique internetworking challenges, one of which is the difference between LAN and WAN speeds. Although several fast WAN technologies now are establishing a presence in geographically dispersed internetworks, LAN speeds are often an order of magnitude faster than WAN speeds. Vast differences in LAN and WAN speeds can prevent users from running delay-sensitive LAN applications over the WAN.

Remote bridges cannot improve WAN speeds, but they can compensate for speed discrepancies through a sufficient buffering capability. If a LAN device capable of a 3-Mbps transmission rate wants to communicate with a device on a remote LAN, the local bridge must regulate the 3-Mbps data stream so that it does not overwhelm the 64-kbps serial link. This is done by storing the incoming data in on-board buffers and sending it over the serial link at a rate that the serial link can accommodate. This buffering can be achieved only for short bursts of data that do not overwhelm the bridge's buffering capability.

The Institute of Electrical and Electronic Engineers (IEEE) differentiates the OSI link layer into two separate sublayers: the *Media Access Control* (MAC) sublayer and the *Logical Link Control* (LLC) sublayer. The MAC sublayer permits and orchestrates media access, such as contention and token passing, while the LLC sublayer deals with framing, flow control, error control, and MAC-sublayer addressing.

Some bridges are *MAC-layer bridges*, which bridge between homogeneous networks (for example, IEEE 802.3 and IEEE 802.3), while other bridges can translate between different link-layer protocols (for example, IEEE 802.3 and IEEE 802.5). The basic mechanics of such a translation are shown in Figure 4–2.

Figure 4–2 illustrates an IEEE 802.3 host (Host A) formulating a packet that contains application information and encapsulating the packet in an IEEE 802.3-compatible frame for transit over the IEEE 802.3 medium to the bridge. At the bridge, the frame is stripped of its IEEE 802.3 header at the MAC sublayer of the link layer and is subsequently passed up to the LLC sublayer for further processing. After this processing, the packet is passed back down to an IEEE 802.5 implementation, which encapsulates the packet in an IEEE 802.5 header for transmission on the IEEE 802.5 network to the IEEE 802.5 host (Host B).

A bridge's translation between networks of different types is never perfect because one network likely will support certain frame fields and protocol functions not supported by the other network.

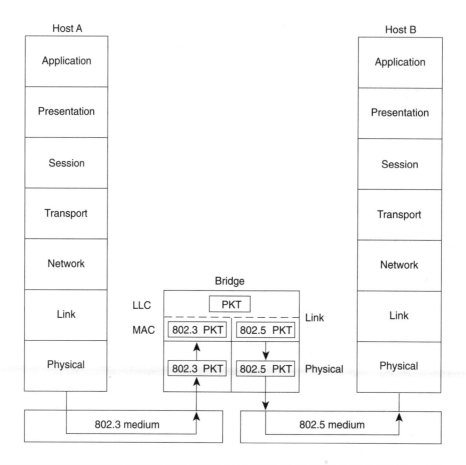

Figure 4–2
A MAC-layer bridge connects the IEEE 802.3 and IEEE 802.5 networks.

TYPES OF SWITCHES

Switches are data link-layer devices that, like bridges, enable multiple physical LAN segments to be interconnected into a single larger network. Similar to bridges, switches forward and flood traffic based on MAC addresses. Because switching is performed in hardware instead of in software, however, it is significantly faster. Switches use either store-and-forward switching or cut-through switching when forwarding traffic. Many types of switches exist, including ATM switches, LAN switches, and various types of WAN switches.

ATM Switch

Asynchronous Transfer Mode (ATM) switches provide high-speed switching and scalable bandwidths in the workgroup, the enterprise network backbone, and the wide area. ATM switches support voice, video, and data applications and are designed to switch fixed-size information units called *cells*, which are used in ATM communications. Figure 4–3 illustrates an enterprise network comprised of multiple LANs interconnected across an ATM backbone.

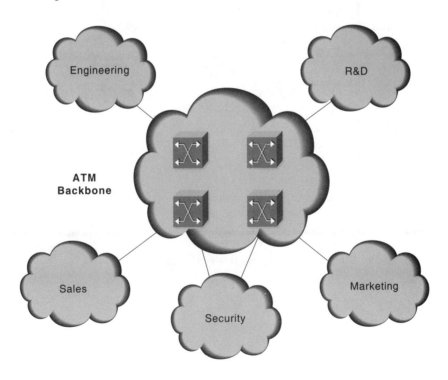

Figure 4–3
Multi-LAN networks can use an ATM-based backbone when switching cells.

LAN Switch

LAN switches are used to interconnect multiple LAN segments. LAN switching provides dedicated, collision-free communication between network devices, with support for multiple simultaneous conversations. LAN switches are designed to switch data frames at high speeds. Figure 4–4 illustrates a simple network in which a LAN switch interconnects a 10-Mbps and a 100-Mbps Ethernet LAN.

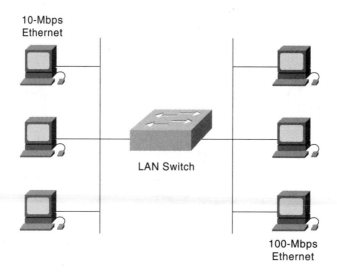

Figure 4–4
A LAN switch can link 10-Mbps and 100-Mbps Ethernet segments.

CHAPTER 5

Routing Basics

This chapter introduces the underlying concepts widely used in routing protocols. Topics summarized here include routing protocol components and algorithms. In addition, the role of routing protocols is briefly contrasted with the roles of routed or network protocols. Subsequent chapters in Part 6, "Routing Protocols," of this book address specific routing protocols in more detail, while the network protocols that use routing protocols are discussed in Part 5, "Network Protocols."

WHAT IS ROUTING?

Routing is the act of moving information across an internetwork from a source to a destination. Along the way, at least one intermediate node typically is encountered. Routing is often contrasted with bridging, which might seem to accomplish precisely the same thing to the casual observer. The primary difference between the two is that bridging occurs at Layer 2 (the link layer) of the OSI reference model, whereas routing occurs at Layer 3 (the network layer). This distinction provides routing and bridging with different information to use in the process of moving information from source to destination, so the two functions accomplish their tasks in different ways.

The topic of routing has been covered in computer science literature for more than two decades, but routing achieved commercial popularity as late as the mid-1980s. The primary reason for this time lag is that networks in the 1970s were fairly simple, homogeneous environments. Only relatively recently has large-scale internetworking become popular.

ROUTING COMPONENTS

Routing involves two basic activities: determining optimal routing paths and transporting information groups (typically called *packets*) through an internetwork. In the context of the routing process, the latter of these is referred to as *switching*. Although switching is relatively straightforward, path determination can be very complex.

Path Determination

A *metric* is a standard of measurement, such as path length, that is used by routing algorithms to determine the optimal path to a destination. To aid the process of path determination, routing algorithms initialize and maintain *routing tables*, which contain route information. Route information varies depending on the routing algorithm used.

Routing algorithms fill routing tables with a variety of information. Destination/next hop associations tell a router that a particular destination can be gained optimally by sending the packet to a particular router representing the "next hop" on the way to the final destination. When a router receives an incoming packet, it checks the destination address and attempts to associate this address with a next hop. Figure 5–1 depicts a sample destination/next hop routing table.

To reach network:	Send to:
27	Node A
57	Node B
17	Node C
24	Node A
52	Node A
16	Node B
26	Node A
. . .	. . .

Figure 5–1
Destination/next hop associations determine the data's optimal path.

Routing tables also can contain other information, such as data about the desirability of a path. Routers compare metrics to determine optimal routes, and these metrics differ depending on the design of the routing algorithm used. A variety of common metrics will be introduced and described later in this chapter.

Routers communicate with one another and maintain their routing tables through the transmission of a variety of *messages*. The *routing update* message is one such message that generally consists of all or a portion of a routing table. By analyzing routing updates from all other routers, a router can build a detailed picture of network topology. A *link-state advertisement*, another example of a message sent between routers, informs other routers of the state of the sender's links. Link information also can be used to build a complete picture of network topology to enable routers to determine optimal routes to network destinations.

Switching

Switching algorithms are relatively simple and are basically the same for most routing protocols. In most cases, a host determines that it must send a packet to another host. Having acquired a router's address by some means, the source host sends a packet addressed specifically to a router's physical (Media Access Control [MAC]-layer) address, this time with the protocol (network-layer) address of the destination host.

As it examines the packet's destination protocol address, the router determines that it either knows or does not know how to forward the packet to the next hop. If the router does not know how to forward the packet, it typically drops the packet. If the router knows how to forward the packet, however, it changes the destination physical address to that of the next hop and transmits the packet.

The next hop may, in fact, be the ultimate destination host. If not, the next hop is usually another router, which executes the same switching decision process. As the packet moves through the internetwork, its physical address changes, but its protocol address remains constant, as illustrated in Figure 5–2.

The preceding discussion describes switching between a source and a destination end system. The International Organization for Standardization (ISO) has developed a hierarchical terminology that is useful in describing this process. Using this terminology, network devices without the capability to forward packets between subnetworks are called *end systems* (ESs), whereas network devices with these capabilities are called *intermediate systems* (ISs). ISs are further divided into those that can communicate within routing domains (*intradomain ISs*) and those that communicate both within and between routing domains (*interdomain ISs*). A *routing domain* generally is considered to be a portion of an internetwork under common administrative authority that is regulated by a particular set of administrative guidelines.

Routing domains are also called *autonomous systems*. With certain protocols, routing domains can be divided into *routing areas*, but intradomain routing protocols are still used for switching both within and between areas.

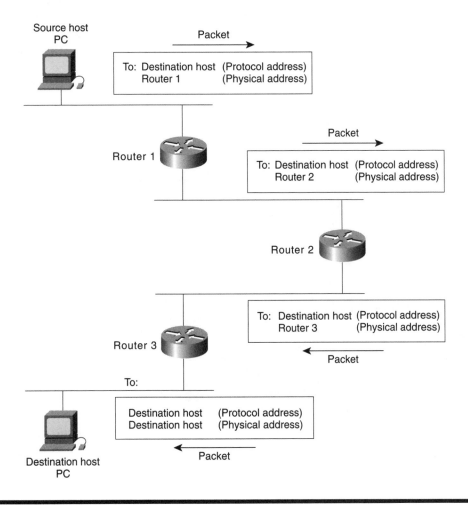

Figure 5–2
Numerous routers may come into play during the switching process.

ROUTING ALGORITHMS

Routing algorithms can be differentiated based on several key characteristics. First, the particular goals of the algorithm designer affect the operation of the resulting routing protocol. Second, various types of routing algorithms exist, and each algorithm has a different impact on network and router resources. Finally, routing algorithms use a variety of metrics that affect calculation of optimal routes. The following sections analyze these routing algorithm attributes.

Design Goals

Routing algorithms often have one or more of the following design goals:

- Optimality

- Simplicity and low overhead

- Robustness and stability

- Rapid convergence

- Flexibility

Optimality refers to the capability of the routing algorithm to select the best route, which depends on the metrics and metric weightings used to make the calculation. One routing algorithm, for example, may use a number of hops and delays, but may weight delay more heavily in the calculation. Naturally, routing protocols must define their metric calculation algorithms strictly.

Routing algorithms also are designed to be as simple as possible. In other words, the routing algorithm must offer its functionality efficiently, with a minimum of software and utilization overhead. Efficiency is particularly important when the software implementing the routing algorithm must run on a computer with limited physical resources.

Routing algorithms must be robust, which means that they should perform correctly in the face of unusual or unforeseen circumstances, such as hardware failures, high load conditions, and incorrect implementations. Because routers are located at network junction points, they can cause considerable problems when they fail. The best routing algorithms are often those that have withstood the test of time and have proven stable under a variety of network conditions.

In addition, routing algorithms must converge rapidly. Convergence is the process of agreement, by all routers, on optimal routes. When a network event causes routes either to go down or become available, routers distribute routing update messages that permeate networks, stimulating recalculation of optimal routes and eventually causing all routers to agree on these routes. Routing algorithms that converge slowly can cause routing loops or network outages.

In the routing loop displayed in Figure 5–3, a packet arrives at Router 1 at time t1. Router 1 already has been updated and thus knows that the optimal route to the destination calls for Router 2 to be the next stop. Router 1 therefore forwards the packet to Router 2, but because this router has not yet been updated, it believes that the optimal next hop is Router 1. Router 2 therefore forwards the packet back to Router 1, and the packet continues to bounce back and forth between the two routers until Router 2 receives its routing update or until the packet has been switched the maximum number of times allowed.

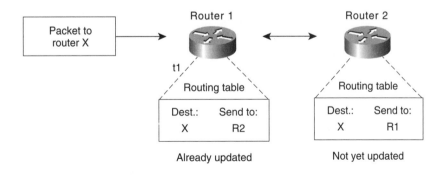

Figure 5–3
Slow convergence and routing loops can hinder progress.

Routing algorithms should also be flexible, which means that they should quickly and accurately adapt to a variety of network circumstances. Assume, for example, that a network segment has gone down. As they become aware of the problem, many routing algorithms will quickly select the next-best path for all routes normally using that segment. Routing algorithms can be programmed to adapt to changes in network bandwidth, router queue size, and network delay, among other variables.

Algorithm Types

Routing algorithms can be classified by type. Key differentiators include:

- Static versus dynamic
- Single-path versus multi-path
- Flat versus hierarchical
- Host-intelligent versus router-intelligent
- Intradomain versus interdomain
- Link state versus distance vector

Static Versus Dynamic

Static routing algorithms are hardly algorithms at all, but are table mappings established by the network administrator prior to the beginning of routing. These mappings do not change unless the network administrator alters them. Algorithms that use static routes are simple to design and work well in environments where network traffic is relatively predictable and where network design is relatively simple.

Because static routing systems cannot react to network changes, they generally are considered unsuitable for today's large, constantly changing networks. Most of the dominant routing algorithms in the 1990s are dynamic routing algorithms, which adjust to changing network circumstances by analyzing incoming routing update messages. If the message indicates that a network change has occurred, the routing software recalculates routes and sends out new routing update messages. These messages permeate the network, stimulating routers to rerun their algorithms and change their routing tables accordingly.

Dynamic routing algorithms can be supplemented with static routes where appropriate. A *router of last resort* (a router to which all unroutable packets are sent), for example, can be designated to act as a repository for all unroutable packets, ensuring that all messages are at least handled in some way.

Single-Path Versus Multipath

Some sophisticated routing protocols support multiple paths to the same destination. Unlike single-path algorithms, these multipath algorithms permit traffic multiplexing over multiple lines. The advantages of multipath algorithms are obvious: They can provide substantially better throughput and reliability.

Flat Versus Hierarchical

Some routing algorithms operate in a flat space, while others use routing hierarchies. In a flat routing system, the routers are peers of all others. In a hierarchical routing system, some routers form what amounts to a routing backbone. Packets from non-backbone routers travel to the backbone routers, where they are sent through the backbone until they reach the general area of the destination. At this point, they travel from the last backbone router through one or more non-backbone routers to the final destination.

Routing systems often designate logical groups of nodes, called domains, autonomous systems, or areas. In hierarchical systems, some routers in a domain can communicate with routers in other domains, while others can communicate only with routers within their domain. In very large networks, additional hierarchical levels may exist, with routers at the highest hierarchical level forming the routing backbone.

The primary advantage of hierarchical routing is that it mimics the organization of most companies and therefore supports their traffic patterns well. Most network communication occurs within small company groups (domains). Because intradomain routers need to know only about other routers within their domain, their routing algorithms can be simplified, and, depending on the routing algorithm being used, routing update traffic can be reduced accordingly.

Host-Intelligent Versus Router-Intelligent

Some routing algorithms assume that the source end-node will determine the entire route. This is usually referred to as *source routing*. In source-routing systems, routers merely act as store-and-forward devices, mindlessly sending the packet to the next stop.

Other algorithms assume that hosts know nothing about routes. In these algorithms, routers determine the path through the internetwork based on their own calculations. In the first system, the hosts have the routing intelligence. In the latter system, routers have the routing intelligence.

The trade-off between host-intelligent and router-intelligent routing is one of path optimality versus traffic overhead. Host-intelligent systems choose the better routes more often, because they typically discover all possible routes to the destination before the packet is actually sent. They then choose the best path based on that particular system's definition of "optimal." The act of determining all routes, however, often requires substantial discovery traffic and a significant amount of time.

Intradomain Versus Interdomain

Some routing algorithms work only within domains; others work within and between domains. The nature of these two algorithm types is different. It stands to reason, therefore, that an optimal intradomain-routing algorithm would not necessarily be an optimal interdomain-routing algorithm.

Link State Versus Distance Vector

Link-state algorithms (also known as *shortest path first* algorithms) flood routing information to all nodes in the internetwork. Each router, however, sends only the portion of the routing table that describes the state of its own links. Distance-vector algorithms (also known as *Bellman-Ford* algorithms) call for each router to send all or some portion of its routing table, but only to its neighbors. In essence, link-state algorithms send small updates everywhere, while distance-vector algorithms send larger updates only to neighboring routers.

Because they converge more quickly, link-state algorithms are somewhat less prone to routing loops than distance-vector algorithms. On the other hand, link-state algorithms require more CPU power and memory than distance-vector algorithms. Link-state algorithms, therefore, can be more expensive to implement and support. Despite their differences, however, both algorithm types perform well in most circumstances.

Routing Metrics

Routing tables contain information used by switching software to select the best route. But how, specifically, are routing tables built? What is the specific nature of the information they contain? How do routing algorithms determine that one route is preferable to others?

Routing algorithms have used many different metrics to determine the best route. Sophisticated routing algorithms can base route selection on multiple metrics, combining them in a single (hybrid) metric. All the following metrics have been used:

- Path Length
- Reliability
- Delay
- Bandwidth
- Load
- Communication Cost

Path length is the most common routing metric. Some routing protocols allow network administrators to assign arbitrary costs to each network link. In this case, path length is the sum of the costs associated with each link traversed. Other routing protocols define *hop count*, a metric that specifies the number of passes through internetworking products, such as routers, that a packet must take en route from a source to a destination.

Reliability, in the context of routing algorithms, refers to the dependability (usually described in terms of the bit-error rate) of each network link. Some network links might go down more often than others. After a network fails, certain network links might be repaired more easily or more quickly than other links. Any reliability factors can be taken into account in the assignment of the reliability ratings, which are arbitrary numeric values usually assigned to network links by network administrators.

Routing delay refers to the length of time required to move a packet from source to destination through the internetwork. Delay depends on many factors, including the bandwidth of intermediate network links, the port queues at each router along the way, network congestion on all intermediate network links, and the physical distance to be travelled. Because delay is a conglomeration of several important variables, it is a common and useful metric.

Bandwidth refers to the available traffic capacity of a link. All other things being equal, a 10-Mbps Ethernet link would be preferable to a 64-kbps leased line. Although bandwidth is a rating of the maximum attainable throughput on a link, routes through links with greater bandwidth do not necessarily provide better routes than routes through slower links. If, for example, a faster link is busier, the actual time required to send a packet to the destination could be greater.

Load refers to the degree to which a network resource, such as a router, is busy. Load can be calculated in a variety of ways, including CPU utilization and packets processed per second. Monitoring these parameters on a continual basis can be resource-intensive itself.

Communication cost is another important metric, especially because some companies may not care about performance as much as they care about operating expenditures. Even though line delay may be longer, they will send packets over their own lines rather than through the public lines that cost money for usage time.

NETWORK PROTOCOLS

Routed protocols are transported by routing protocols across an internetwork. In general, routed protocols in this context also are referred to as *network* protocols. These network protocols perform a variety of functions required for communication between user applications in source and destination devices, and these functions can differ widely among protocol suites. Network protocols occur at the upper four layers of the OSI reference model: the transport layer, the session layer, the presentation layer, and the application layer.

Confusion about the terms *routed protocol* and *routing protocol* is common. Routed protocols are protocols that are routed over an internetwork. Examples of such protocols are the Internet Protocol (IP), DECnet, AppleTalk, Novell NetWare, OSI, Banyan VINES, and Xerox Network System (XNS). Routing protocols, on the other hand, are protocols that implement routing algorithms. Put simply, routing protocols direct network protocols through an internetwork. Examples of these protocols include Interior Gateway Routing Protocol (IGRP), Enhanced Interior Gateway Routing Protocol (Enhanced IGRP), Open Shortest Path First (OSPF), Exterior Gateway Protocol (EGP), Border Gateway Protocol (BGP), Intermediate System to Intermediate System (IS-IS), and Routing Information Protocol (RIP). Routed and routing protocols are discussed in detail later in this book.

CHAPTER 6

Network Management Basics

This chapter describes functions common to most network management architectures and protocols. It also presents the five conceptual areas of management as defined by the International Organization for Standardization (ISO). Subsequent chapters in Part 7, "Network Management," of this book address specific network management technologies, protocols, and platforms in more detail.

WHAT IS NETWORK MANAGEMENT?

Network management means different things to different people. In some cases, it involves a solitary network consultant monitoring network activity with an outdated protocol analyzer. In other cases, network management involves a distributed database, auto-polling of network devices, and high-end workstations generating real-time graphical views of network topolgy changes and traffic. In general, network management is a service that employs a variety of tools, applications, and devices to assist human network managers in monitoring and maintaining networks.

A Historical Perspective

The early 1980s saw tremendous expansion in the area of network deployment. As companies realized the cost benefits and productivity gains created by network technology, they began to add networks and expand existing networks almost as rapidly as new network technologies and products were introduced. By the mid-1980s, certain companies were experiencing growing pains from deploying many different (and sometimes incompatible) network technologies.

The problems associated with network expansion affect both day-to-day network operation management and strategic network growth planning. Each new network technology requires its own set of experts. In the early 1980s, the staffing requirements alone for managing large, heterogeneous networks created a crisis for many organizations. An urgent need arose for automated network management (including what is typically called *network capacity planning*) integrated across diverse environments.

NETWORK MANAGEMENT ARCHITECTURE

Most network management architectures use the same basic structure and set of relationships. End stations (*managed devices*), such as computer systems and other network devices, run software that enables them to send alerts when they recognize problems (for example, when one or more user-determined thresholds are exceeded). Upon receiving these alerts, *management entities* are programmed to react by executing one, several, or a group of actions, including operator notification, event logging, system shutdown, and automatic attempts at system repair.

Management entities also can poll end stations to check the values of certain variables. Polling can be automatic or user-initiated, but *agents* in the managed devices respond to all polls. Agents are software modules that first compile information about the managed devices in which they reside, then store this information in a *management database*, and finally provide it (proactively or reactively) to management entities within *network management systems* (NMSs) via a *network management protocol*. Well-known network management protocols include the Simple Network Management Protocol (SNMP) and Common Management Information Protocol (CMIP). *Management proxies* are entities that provide management information on behalf of other entities. Figure 6–1 depicts a typical network management architecture.

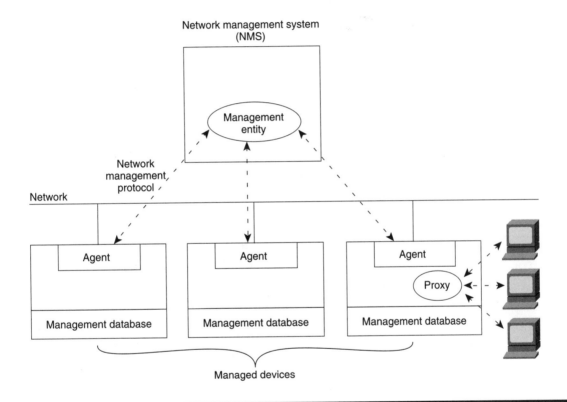

Figure 6–1
A typical network management architecture maintains many relationships.

ISO NETWORK MANAGEMENT MODEL

The ISO has contributed a great deal to network standardization. Their network management model is the primary means for understanding the major functions of network management systems. This model consists of five conceptual areas:

- Performance management

- Configuration management

- Accounting management

- Fault management

- Security management

Performance Management

The goal of *performance management* is to measure and make available various aspects of network performance so that internetwork performance can be maintained at an acceptable level. Examples of performance variables that might be provided include network throughput, user response times, and line utilization.

Performance management involves three main steps. First, performance data is gathered on variables of interest to network administrators. Second, the data is analyzed to determine normal (baseline) levels. Finally, appropriate performance thresholds are determined for each important variable so that exceeding these thresholds indicates a network problem worthy of attention.

Management entities continually monitor performance variables. When a performance threshold is exceeded, an alert is generated and sent to the network management system.

Each of the steps just described is part of the process to set up a reactive system. When performance becomes unacceptable because of an exceeded user-defined threshold, the system reacts by sending a message. Performance management also permits proactive methods: For example, network simulation can be used to project how network growth will affect performance metrics. Such simulation can alert administrators to impending problems so that counteractive measures can be taken.

Configuration Management

The goal of *configuration management* is to monitor network and system configuration information so that the effects on network operation of various versions of hardware and software elements can be tracked and managed.

Each network device has a variety of version information associated with it. An engineering workstation, for example, may be configured as follows:

- Operating system, Version 3.2

- Ethernet interface, Version 5.4

- TCP/IP software, Version 2.0

- NetWare software, Version 4.1

- NFS software, Version 5.1

- Serial communications controller, Version 1.1

- X.25 software, Version 1.0

- SNMP software, Version 3.1

Configuration management subsystems store this information in a database for easy access. When a problem occurs, this database can be searched for clues that may help solve the problem.

Accounting Management

The goal of *accounting management* is to measure network-utilization parameters so that individual or group uses on the network can be regulated appropriately. Such regulation minimizes network problems (because network resources can be apportioned based on resource capacities) and maximizes the fairness of network access across all users.

As with performance management, the first step toward appropriate accounting management is to measure utilization of all important network resources. Analysis of the results provides insight into current usage patterns, and usage quotas can be set at this point. Some correction, of course, will be required to reach optimal access practices. From this point, ongoing measurement of resource use can yield billing information, as well as information used to assess continued fair and optimal resource utilization.

Fault Management

The goal of *fault management* is to detect, log, notify users of, and (to the extent possible) automatically fix network problems to keep the network running effectively. Because faults can cause downtime or unacceptable network degradation, fault management is perhaps the most widely implemented of the ISO network management elements.

Fault management involves first determining symptoms and isolating the problem. Then the problem is fixed, and the solution is tested on all important subsystems. Finally, the detection and resolution of the problem is recorded.

Security Management

The goal of *security management* is to control access to network resources according to local guidelines so that the network cannot be sabotaged (intentionally or unintentionally) and sensitive information cannot be accessed by those without appropriate authorization. A security management subsystem, for example, can monitor users logging on to a network resource, refusing access to those who enter inappropriate access codes.

Security management subsystems work by partitioning network resources into authorized and unauthorized areas. For some users, access to any network resource is inappropriate, mostly because such users are usually company outsiders. For other (internal) network users, access to information originating from a particular department is inappropriate. Access to human resource files, for example, is inappropriate for most users outside the human resource department.

Security management subsystems perform several functions. They identify sensitive network resources (including systems, files, and other entities) and determine mappings between sensitive network resources and user sets. They also monitor access points to sensitive network resources and log inappropriate access to sensitive network resources.

PART 2

LAN Protocols

Part 2, "LAN Protocols," provides specifications and operational information about today's most important local area networking (LAN) media. Individual chapters discuss the following topics:

Ethernet Technologies—Explores the features, components, and operation of the Ethernet technologies, including Ethernet and IEEE 802.3, 100BaseT and 100VG-AnyLAN, and Gigabit Ethernet.

Fiber Distributed Data Interface (FDDI)—Explores FDDI architecture, specifications, transmission media, devices, fault-tolerant features, and frame format.

Token Ring/IEEE 802.5—Describes the operational components of Token Ring and IEEE 802.5 networks, and summarizes basic network operation.

CHAPTER 7

Ethernet Technologies

BACKGROUND

The term *Ethernet* refers to the family of local area network (LAN) implementations that includes three principal categories.

- *Ethernet and IEEE 802.3*—LAN specifications that operate at 10 Mbps over coaxial cable.

- *100-Mbps Ethernet*—A single LAN specification, also known as Fast Ethernet, that operates at 100 Mbps over twisted-pair cable.

- *1000-Mbps Ethernet*—A single LAN specification, also known as Gigabit Ethernet, that operates at 1000 Mbps (1 Gbps) over fiber and twisted-pair cables.

This chapter provides a high-level overview of each technology variant.

Ethernet has survived as an essential media technology because of its tremendous flexibility and its relative simplicity to implement and understand. Although other technologies have been touted as likely replacements, network managers have turned to Ethernet and its derivatives as effective solutions for a range of campus implementation requirements. To resolve Ethernet's limitations, innovators (and standards bodies) have created progressively larger Ethernet pipes. Critics might dismiss Ethernet as a technology that cannot scale, but its underlying transmission scheme continues to be one of the principal means of transporting data for contemporary campus applications. This chapter outlines the various Ethernet technologies that have evolved to date.

ETHERNET AND IEEE 802.3

Ethernet is a baseband LAN specification invented by Xerox Corporation that operates at 10 Mbps using carrier sense multiple access collision detect (CSMA/CD) to run over coaxial cable. Ethernet was created by Xerox in the 1970s, but the term is now often used to refer to all CSMA/CD LANs. Ethernet was designed to serve in networks with sporadic, occasionally heavy traffic requirements, and the IEEE 802.3 specification was developed in 1980 based on the original Ethernet technology. Ethernet Version 2.0 was jointly developed by Digital Equipment Corporation, Intel Corporation, and Xerox Corporation It is compatible with IEEE 802.3. Figure 7–1 illustrates an Ethernet network.

Ethernet and IEEE 802.3 are usually implemented in either an interface card or in circuitry on a primary circuit board. Ethernet cabling conventions specify the use of a transceiver to attach a cable to the physical network medium. The transceiver performs many of the physical-layer functions, including collision detection. The transceiver cable connects end stations to a transceiver.

IEEE 802.3 provides for a variety of cabling options, one of which is a specification referred to as 10Base5. This specification is the closest to Ethernet. The connecting cable is referred to as an attachment unit interface (AUI), and the network attachment device is called a media attachment unit (MAU), instead of a transceiver.

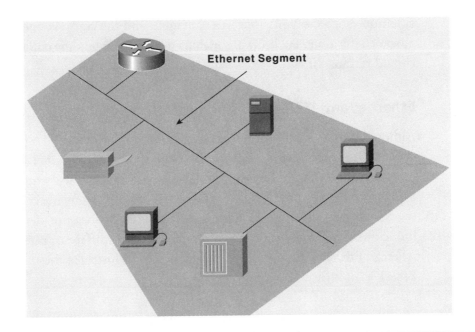

Figure 7–1
An Ethernet network runs CSMA/CD over coaxial cable.

Ethernet and IEEE 802.3 Operation

In Ethernet's broadcast-based environment, all stations see all frames placed on the network. Following any transmission, each station must examine every frame to determine whether that station is a destination. Frames identified as intended for a given station are passed to a higher-layer protocol.

Under the Ethernet CSMA/CD media-access process, any station on a CSMA/CD LAN can access the network at any time. Before sending data, CSMA/CD stations listen for traffic on the network. A station wanting to send data waits until it detects no traffic before it transmits.

As a contention-based environment, Ethernet allows any station on the network to transmit whenever the network is quiet. A collision occurs when two stations listen for traffic, hear none, and then transmit simultaneously. In this situation, both transmissions are damaged, and the stations must retransmit at some later time. Back-off algorithms determine when the colliding stations should retransmit.

Ethernet and IEEE 802.3 Service Differences

Although Ethernet and IEEE 802.3 are quite similar in many respects, certain service differences distinguish the two specifications. Ethernet provides services corresponding to Layers 1 and 2 of the OSI reference model, and IEEE 802.3 specifies the physical layer (Layer 1) and the channel-access portion of the link layer (Layer 2). In addition, IEEE 802.3 does not define a logical link-control protocol but does specify several different physical layers, whereas Ethernet defines only one. Figure 7–2 illustrates the relationship of Ethernet and IEEE 802.3 to the general OSI reference model.

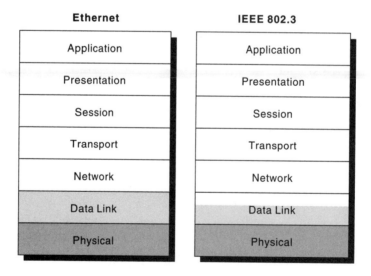

Figure 7–2

Ethernet and the IEEE 802.3 OSI reference model.

Each IEEE 802.3 physical-layer protocol has a three-part name that summarizes its characteristics. The components specified in the naming convention correspond to LAN speed, signaling method, and physical media type. Figure 7–3 illustrates how the naming convention is used to depict these components.

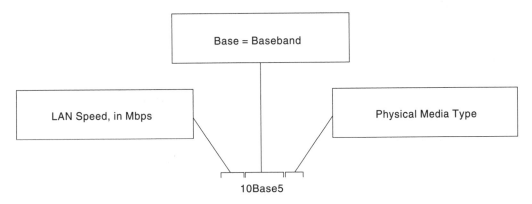

Figure 7–3
IEEE 802.3 components are named according to conventions.

Table 7–1 summarizes the differences between Ethernet and IEEE 802.3, as well as the differences between the various IEEE 802.3 physical-layer specifications.

Characteristic	Ethernet Value	10Base5	10Base2	IEEE 802.3 Values 10BaseT	10BaseFL	100BaseT
Data rate (Mbps)	10	10	10	10	10	100
Signaling method	Baseband	Baseband	Baseband	Baseband	Baseband	Baseband
Maximum segment length (m)	500	500	185	100	2,000	100
Media	50-ohm coax (thick)	50-ohm coax (thick)	50-ohm coax (thin)	Unshielded twisted-pair cable	Fiber-optic	Unshielded twisted-pair cable
Topology	Bus	Bus	Bus	Star	Point-to-point	Bus

Table 7–1
Comparison of Various IEEE 802.3 Physical-Layer Specifications

Ethernet and IEEE 802.3 Frame Formats

Figure 7–4 illustrates the frame fields associated with both Ethernet and IEEE 802.3 frames.

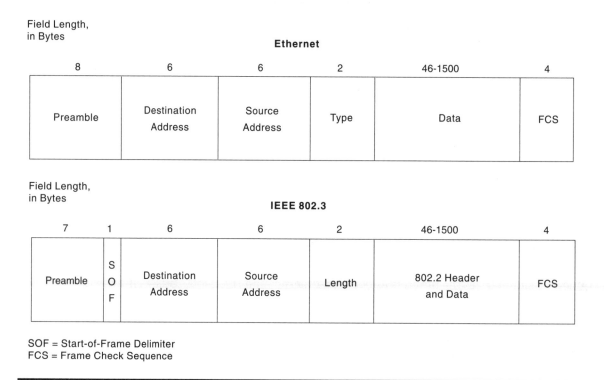

Figure 7–4
Various frame fields exist for both Ethernet and IEEE 802.3.

The Ethernet and IEEE 802.3 frame fields illustrated in Figure 7–4 are as follows:

- *Preamble*—The alternating pattern of ones and zeros tells receiving stations that a frame is coming (Ethernet or IEEE 802.3). The Ethernet frame includes an additional byte that is the equivalent of the Start-of-Frame field specified in the IEEE 802.3 frame.

- *Start-of-Frame (SOF)*—The IEEE 802.3 delimiter byte ends with two consecutive 1 bits, which serve to synchronize the frame-reception portions of all stations on the LAN. SOF is explicitly specified in Ethernet.

- *Destination and Source Addresses*—The first 3 bytes of the addresses are specified by the IEEE on a vendor-dependent basis. The last 3 bytes are specified by the Ethernet or IEEE 802.3 vendor. The source address is always a unicast (single-node) address. The destination address can be unicast, multicast (group), or broadcast (all nodes).

- *Type (Ethernet)*—The type specifies the upper-layer protocol to receive the data after Ethernet processing is completed.

- *Length (IEEE 802.3)*—The length indicates the number of bytes of data that follows this field.

- *Data (Ethernet)*—After physical-layer and link-layer processing is complete, the data contained in the frame is sent to an upper-layer protocol, which is identified in the Type field. Although Ethernet Version 2 does not specify any padding (in contrast to IEEE 802.3), Ethernet expects at least 46 bytes of data.

- *Data (IEEE 802.3)*—After physical-layer and link-layer processing is complete, the data is sent to an upper-layer protocol, which must be defined within the data portion of the frame, if at all. If data in the frame is insufficient to fill the frame to its minimum 64-byte size, padding bytes are inserted to ensure at least a 64-byte frame.

- *Frame Check Sequence (FCS)*—This sequence contains a 4-byte cyclic redundancy check (CRC) value, which is created by the sending device and is recalculated by the receiving device to check for damaged frames.

100-MBPS ETHERNET

100-Mbps Ethernet is a high-speed LAN technology that offers increased bandwidth to desktop users in the wiring center, as well as to servers and server clusters (sometimes called server farms) in data centers.

The IEEE Higher Speed Ethernet Study Group was formed to assess the feasibility of running Ethernet at speeds of 100 Mbps. The Study Group established several objectives for this new higher-speed Ethernet but disagreed on the access method. At issue was whether this new faster Ethernet would support CSMA/CD to access the network medium or some other access method.

The study group divided into two camps over this access-method disagreement: the Fast Ethernet Alliance and the 100VG-AnyLAN Forum. Each group produced a specification for running Ethernet (and Token Ring for the latter specification) at higher speeds: 100BaseT and 100VG-AnyLAN, respectively.

100BaseT is the IEEE specification for the 100-Mbps Ethernet implementation over unshielded twisted-pair (UTP) and shielded twisted-pair (STP) cabling. The Media Access Control (MAC) layer is compatible with the IEEE 802.3 MAC layer. Grand Junction, now a part of Cisco Systems Workgroup Business Unit (WBU), developed Fast Ethernet, which was standardized by the IEEE in the 802.3u specification.

100VG-AnyLAN is an IEEE specification for 100-Mbps Token Ring and Ethernet implementations over 4-pair UTP. The MAC layer is *not* compatible with the IEEE 802.3 MAC layer. 100VG-AnyLAN was developed by Hewlett-Packard (HP) to support newer time-sensitive applications, such as multimedia. A version of HP's implementation is standardized in the IEEE 802.12 specification.

100BaseT Overview

100BaseT uses the existing IEEE 802.3 CSMA/CD specification. As a result, 100BaseT retains the IEEE 802.3 frame format, size, and error-detection mechanism. In addition, it supports all applications and networking software currently running on 802.3 networks. 100BaseT supports dual speeds of 10 and 100 Mbps using 100BaseT fast link pulses (FLPs). 100BaseT hubs must detect dual speeds much like Token Ring 4/16 hubs, but adapter cards can support 10 Mbps, 100 Mbps, or both. Figure 7–5 illustrates how the 802.3 MAC sublayer and higher layers run unchanged on 100BaseT.

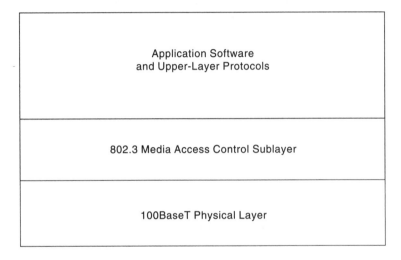

Figure 7–5
802.3 MAC and higher-layer protocols operate over 100BaseT.

100BaseT Signaling

100BaseT supports two signaling types:

- 100BaseX

- 4T+

Both signaling types are interoperable at the station and hub levels. The media-independent interface (MII), an AUI-like interface, provides interoperability at the station level. The hub provides interoperability at the hub level.

The 100BaseX signaling scheme has a convergence sublayer that adapts the full-duplex continuous signaling mechanism of the FDDI physical medium dependent (PMD) layer to the half-duplex, start-stop signaling of the Ethernet MAC sublayer. 100BaseTX's use of the existing FDDI specification has allowed quick delivery of products to market. 100BaseX is the signaling scheme used in the 100BaseTX and the 100BaseFX media types. Figure 7–6 illustrates how the 100BaseX convergence sublayer interfaces between the two signaling schemes.

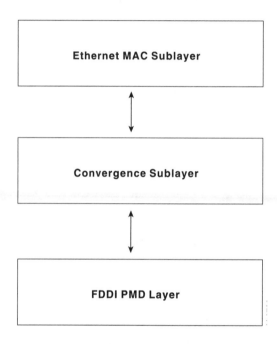

Figure 7–6
The 100BaseX convergence sublayer interfaces two signaling schemes.

The 4T+ signaling scheme uses one pair of wires for collision detection and the other three pairs to transmit data. It allows 100BaseT to run over existing Category 3 cabling if all four pairs are installed to the desktop. 4T+ is the signaling scheme used in the 100BaseT4 media type, and it supports half-duplex operation only. Figure 7–7 shows how 4T+ signaling requires all four UTP pairs.

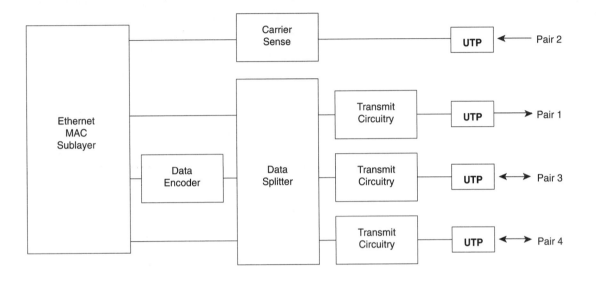

Figure 7–7
4T+ requires four UTP pairs.

100BaseT Hardware

Components used for a 100BaseT physical connection include the following:

- *Physical Medium*—This device carries signals between computers and can be one of three 100BaseT media types:
  - 100BaseTX
  - 100BaseFX
  - 100BaseT4

- *Medium-Dependent Interface (MDI)*—The MDI is a mechanical and electrical interface between the transmission medium and the physical-layer device.

- *Physical-Layer Device (PHY)*—The PHY provides either 10- or 100-Mbps operation and can be a set of integrated circuits (or a daughter board) on an Ethernet port, or an external device supplied with an MII cable that plugs into an MII port on a 100BaseT device (similar to a 10-Mbps Ethernet transceiver).

- *Media-Independent Interface (MII)*—The MII is used with a 100-Mbps external transceiver to connect a 100-Mbps Ethernet device to any of the three media types. The MII has a 40-pin plug and cable that stretches up to 0.5 meters.

Figure 7–8 depicts the 100BaseT hardware components.

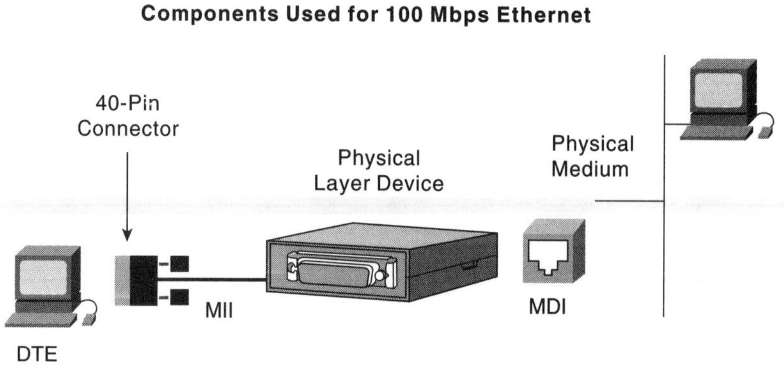

Components Used for 100 Mbps Ethernet

Figure 7–8
100BaseT requires several hardware components.

100BaseT Operation

100BaseT and 10BaseT use the same IEEE 802.3 MAC access and collision-detection methods, and they also have the same frame format and length requirements. The main difference between 100BaseT and 10BaseT (other than the obvious speed differential) is the network diameter. The 100BaseT maximum network diameter is 205 meters, which is approximately 10 times less than 10-Mbps Ethernet.

Reducing the 100BaseT network diameter is necessary because 100BaseT uses the same collision-detection mechanism as 10BaseT. With 10BaseT, distance limitations are defined so that a station knows while transmitting the smallest legal frame size (64 bytes) that a collision has taken place with another sending station that is located at the farthest point of the domain.

To achieve the increased throughput of 100BaseT, the size of the collision domain had to shrink. This is because the propagation speed of the medium has not changed, so a station transmitting 10 times faster must have a maximum distance that is 10 times less. As a result, any station knows within the first 64 bytes whether a collision has occurred with any other station.

100BaseT FLPs

100BaseT uses pulses, called FLPs, to check the link integrity between the hub and the 100BaseT device. FLPs are backward-compatible with 10BaseT normal-link pulses (NLPs). But FLPs contain more information than NLPs and are used in the autonegotiation process between a hub and a device on a 100BaseT network.

100BaseT Autonegotiation Option

100BaseT networks support an optional feature, called autonegotiation, that enables a device and a hub to exchange information (using 100BaseT FLPs) about their capabilities, thereby creating an optimal communications environment.

Autonegotiaton supports a number of capabilities, including speed matching for devices that support both 10- and 100-Mbps operation, full-duplex mode of operation for devices that support such communications, and an automatic signaling configuration for 100BaseT4 and 100BaseTX stations.

100BaseT Media Types

100BaseT supports three media types at the OSI physical layer (Layer 1):

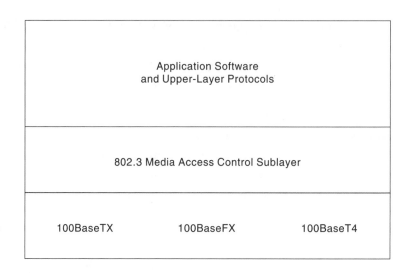

Figure 7–9
Three 100BaseT media types exist at the physical layer.

100BaseTX, 100BaseFX, and 100BaseT4. The three media types, which all interface with the IEEE 802.3 MAC layer, are shown in Figure 7–9. Table 7–2 compares key characteristics of the three 100BaseT media types.

100BaseTX

100BaseTX is based on the American National Standards Institutes (ANSI) Twisted Pair-Physical Medium Dependent (TP-PMD) specification. The ANSI TP-PMD supports UTP and STP cabling. 100BaseTX uses the 100BaseX signaling scheme over 2-pair Category 5 UTP or STP.

Characteristics	100BaseTX	100BaseFX	100BaseT4
Cable	Category 5 UTP, or Types 1 and 2 STP	62.5/125 micronmulti-mode fiber	Category 3, 4, or 5 UTP
Number of pairs or strands	2 pairs	2 strands	4 pairs
Connector	ISO 8877 (RJ-45) connector	Duplex media-interface connector (MIC)	ISO 8877 (RJ-45) connector
Maximum segment length	100 meters	400 meters	100 meters
Maximum network diameter	200 meters	400 meters	200 meters

Table 7–2
Characteristics of 100BaseT Media Types

The IEEE 802.3u specification for 100BaseTX networks allows a maximum of two repeater (hub) networks and a total network diameter of approximately 200 meters. A link segment, which is defined as a point-to-point connection between two Medium Independent Interface (MII) devices, can be up to 100 meters. Figure 7–10 illustrates these configuration guidelines.

100BaseFX

100BaseFX is based on the ANSI TP-PMD X3T9.5 specification for FDDI LANs. 100BaseFX uses the 100BaseX signaling scheme over two-strand multimode fiber-optic (MMF) cable. The IEEE 802.3u specification for 100BaseFX networks allows data terminal equipment (DTE)-to-DTE links of approximately 400 meters, or one repeater network of approximately 300 meters in length. Figure 7–11 illustrates these configuration guidelines.

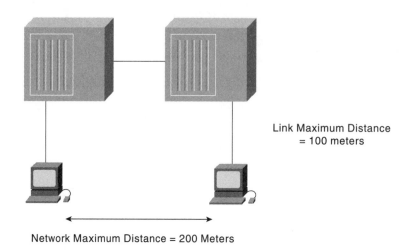

Link Maximum Distance
= 100 meters

Network Maximum Distance = 200 Meters

Figure 7–10

The 100BaseTX is limited to a link distance of 100 meters.

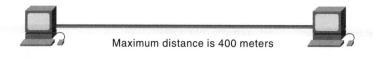

Maximum distance is 400 meters

Hub

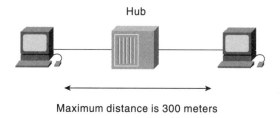

Maximum distance is 300 meters

Figure 7–11

The 100BaseFX DTE-to-DTE limit is 400 meters.

100BaseT4

100BaseT4 allows 100BaseT to run over existing Category 3 wiring, provided that all four pairs of cabling are installed to the desktop. 100BaseT4 uses the half-duplex 4T+ signaling scheme. The IEEE 802.3u specification for 100BaseT4 networks allows a maximum of two repeater (hub) networks and a total network diameter of approximately 200 meters. A link segment, which is defined as a point-to-point connection between two MII devices, can be up to 100 meters. Figure 7–12 illustrates these configuration guidelines.

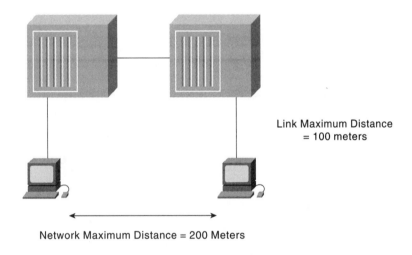

Link Maximum Distance = 100 meters

Network Maximum Distance = 200 Meters

Figure 7–12
The 100BaseT4 supports a maximum link distance of 100 meters.

100VG-AnyLAN

100VG-AnyLAN was developed by HP as an alternative to CSMA/CD for newer time-sensitive applications, such as multimedia. The access method is based on station demand and was designed as an upgrade path from Ethernet and 16-Mbps Token Ring. 100VG-AnyLAN supports the following cable types:

- 4-pair Category 3 UTP

- 2-pair Category 4 or 5 UTP

- STP

- Fiber optic

The IEEE 802.12 100VG-AnyLAN standard specifies the link-distance limitations, hub-configuration limitations, and maximum network-distance limitations. Link distances from node to hub are 100 meters (Category 3 UTP) or 150 meters (Category 5 UTP). Figure 7–13 illustrates the 100VG-AnyLAN link distance limitations.

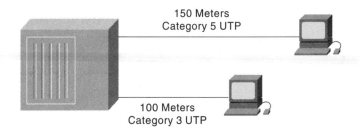

Figure 7–13

100VG-AnyLAN link-distance limitations differ for Category 3 and 5 UTP links.

100VG-Any LAN hubs are arranged in a hierarchical fashion. Each hub has at least one uplink port, and every other port can be a downlink port. Hubs can be cascaded three-deep if uplinked to other hubs, and cascaded hubs can be 100 meters apart (Category 3 UTP) or 150 meters apart (Category 5 UTP). Figure 7–14 shows the 100VG-AnyLAN hub configuration.

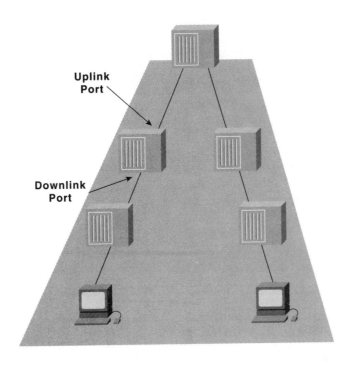

Figure 7–14
100VG-AnyLAN hubs are arranged hierarchically.

End-to-end network-distance limitations are 600 meters (Category 3 UTP) or 900 meters (Category 5 UTP). If hubs are located in the same wiring closet, end-to-end distances shrink to 200 meters (Category 3 UTP) and 300 meters (Category 5 UTP). Figure 7–15 shows the 100VG-AnyLAN maximum network-distance limitations.

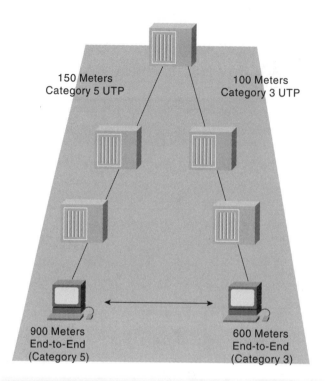

Figure 7–15
End-to-end distance limitations differ for 100VG-AnyLAN implementations.

100VG-AnyLAN Operation

100VG-AnyLAN uses a demand-priority access method that eliminates collisions and can be more heavily loaded than 100BaseT. The demand-priority access method is more deterministic than CSMA/CD because the hub controls access to the network.

The 100VG-AnyLAN standard calls for a level-one hub, or repeater, that acts as the root. This root repeater controls the operation of the priority domain. Hubs can be cascaded three-deep in a star topology. Interconnected hubs act as a single large repeater, with the root repeater polling each port in port order.

In general, under 100VG-AnyLAN demand-priority operation, a node wanting to transmit signals its request to the hub (or switch). If the network is idle, the hub immediately acknowledges the request and the node begins transmitting a packet to the hub. If more than one request is received at the same time, the hub uses a round-robin technique to acknowledge each request in turn. High-priority requests, such as time-sensitive videoconferencing applications, are serviced ahead of normal-priority requests. To ensure fairness to all stations, a hub does not grant priority access to a port more than twice in a row.

GIGABIT ETHERNET

Gigabit Ethernet is an extension of the IEEE 802.3 Ethernet standard. Gigabit Ethernet builds on the Ethernet protocol but increases speed tenfold over Fast Ethernet, to 1000 Mbps, or 1 Gbps. This MAC and PHY standard promises to be a dominant player in high-speed LAN backbones and server connectivity. Because Gigabit Ethernet significantly leverages on Ethernet, network managers will be able to leverage their existing knowledge base to manage and maintain Gigabit networks.

GIGABIT ETHERNET PROTOCOL ARCHITECTURE

To accelerate speeds from 100-Mbps Fast Ethernet to 1 Gbps, several changes need to be made to the physical interface. It has been decided that Gigabit Ethernet will look identical to Ethernet from the data link layer upward. The challenges involved in accelerating to 1 Gbps have been resolved by merging two technologies: IEEE 802.3 Ethernet and ANSI X3T11 Fibre Channel. Figure 7–16 shows how key components from each technology have been leveraged to form Gigabit Ethernet.

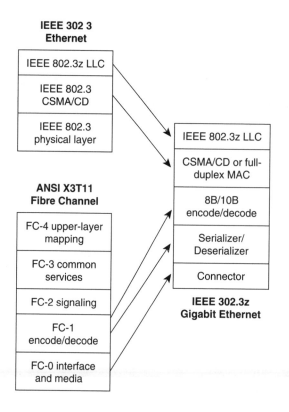

Figure 7–16

The Gigabit Ethernet protocol stack was developed from a combination of the Fibre Channel and IEEE 802.3 protocol stacks.

Leveraging these two technologies means that the standard can take advantage of the existing high-speed physical interface technology of Fibre Channel while maintaining the IEEE 802.3 Ethernet frame format, backward compatibility for installed media, and use of full- or half-duplex (via CSMA/CD).

A model of Gigabit Ethernet is shown in Figure 7–17.

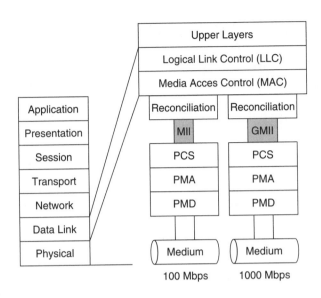

Figure 7-17
This diagram shows the architectural model of IEEE 802.3z Gigabit Ethernet. (Source: IEEE Media Access Control Parameters, Physical Layers, Repeater, and Management Parameters for 1000 Mbps Operation.)

The Physical Layer

The Gigabit Ethernet specification addresses three forms of transmission media: long-wave (LW) laser over single-mode and multimode fiber (to be known as 1000BaseLX), short-wave (SW) laser over multimode fiber (to be known as 1000BaseSX), and the 1000BaseCX medium, which allows for transmission over balanced shielded 150-ohm copper cable. The IEEE 802.3ab committee is examining the use of UTP cable for Gigabit Ethernet transmission (1000BaseT); that standard is expected sometime in 1999. The 1000BaseT draft standard will enable Gigabit Ethernet to extend to distances up to 100 meters over Category 5 UTP copper wiring, which constitutes the majority of the cabling inside buildings.

The Fibre Channel PMD specification currently allows for 1.062 gigabaud signaling in full-duplex. Gigabit Ethernet will increase this signaling rate to 1.25 Gbps. The 8B/10B encoding (to be discussed later) allows a data transmission rate of 1000 Mbps. The current connector type for Fibre Channel, and therefore for Gigabit Ethernet, is the SC connector for both single-mode and multimode fiber. The Gigabit Ethernet specification calls for media support for multimode fiber-optic cable, single-mode fiber-optic cable, and a special balanced shielded 150-ohm copper cable.

Long-Wave and Short-Wave Lasers over Fiber-Optic Media

Two standards of laser will be supported over fiber: 1000BaseSX (short-wave laser) and 1000BaseLX (long-wave laser). Short-wave and long-wave lasers will be supported over multimode fiber. There are two available types of multimode fiber: 62.5-millimeter and 50-millimeter diameter fibers. Long-wave lasers will be used for single-mode fiber because this fiber is optimized for long-wave laser transmission. There is no support for short-wave laser over single-mode fiber.

The key differences between the use of long-wave and short-wave laser technologies are cost and distance. Lasers over fiber-optic cable take advantage of variations in attenuation in a cable. At different wavelengths, "dips" in attenuation will be found over the cable. Short-wave and long-wave lasers take advantage of those dips and illuminate the cable at different wavelengths. Short-wave lasers are readily available because variations of these lasers are used in compact disc technology. Long-wave lasers take advantage of attenuation dips at longer wavelengths in the cable. The net result is that short-wave lasers will cost less, but transverse a shorter distance. In contrast, long-wave lasers will be more expensive but will transverse longer distances.

Single-mode fiber has traditionally been used in networking cable plants to achieve long distances. In Ethernet, for example, single-mode cable ranges reach up to 10 kilometers. Single-mode fiber, using a 9-micron core and

1300-nanometer laser, demonstrate the highest-distance technology. The small core and lower-energy laser elongate the wavelength of the laser and allow it to transverse greater distances. This enables single-mode fiber to reach the greatest distances of all media with the least reduction in noise.

Gigabit Ethernet will be supported over two types of multimode fiber: 62.5-micron and 50-micron diameter fibers. The 62.5-millimeter fiber is typically seen in vertical campus and building cable plants and has been used for Ethernet, Fast Ethernet, and FDDI backbone traffic. This type of fiber, however, has a lower modal bandwidth (the ability of the cable to transmit light), especially with short-wave lasers. This means that short-wave lasers over 62.5-micron fibers will be able to transverse shorter distances than long-wave lasers. The 50-micron fiber has significantly better modal bandwidth characteristics and will be able to transverse longer distances with short-wave lasers relative to 62.5-micron fiber.

150-Ohm Balanced Shielded Copper Cable (1000BaseCX)

For shorter cable runs (of 25 meters or less), Gigabit Ethernet will allow transmission over a special balanced 150-ohm cable. This is a new type of shielded cable; it is not UTP or IBM Type I or II. In order to minimize safety and interference concerns caused by voltage differences, transmitters and receivers will share a common ground. The return loss for each connector is limited to 20 dB to minimize transmission distortions. The connector type for 1000BaseCX will be a DB-9 connector. A new connector is being developed by Aero-Marine Products called the HSSDC (High-Speed Serial Data Connector), which will be included in the next revision of the draft.

The application for this type of cabling will be short-haul data-center interconnections and inter- or intrarack connections. Because of the distance limitation of 25 meters, this cable will not work for interconnecting data centers to riser closets.

The distances for the media supported under the IEEE 802.3z standard are shown in Figure 7–18.

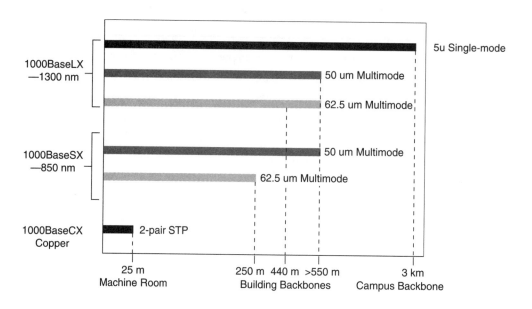

NB: Distances are draft targets; may change in final specification.

Figure 7–18

The Gigabit Ethernet draft specifies these distance specifications for Gigabit Ethernet.

The Serializer/Deserializer

The physical media attachment (PMA) sublayer for Gigabit Ethernet is identical to the PMA for Fibre Channel. The serializer/deserializer is responsible for supporting multiple encoding schemes and allowing presentation of those encoding schemes to the upper layers. Data entering the PHY will enter through the PMD and will need to support the encoding scheme appropriate to that medium. The encoding scheme for Fibre Channel is 8B/10B, designed specifically for fiber-optic cable transmission. Gigabit Ethernet will use a similar encoding scheme. The difference between Fibre Channel and Gigabit Ethernet, however, is that Fibre Channel utilizes a 1.062 gigabaud signaling, whereas Gigabit Ethernet will utilize 1.25 gigabaud signaling. A different encoding scheme will be required for transmission over UTP. This encoding will be performed by the UTP or 1000BaseT PHY.

8B/10B Encoding

The Fibre Channel FC1 layer describes the synchronization and the 8B/10B encoding scheme. FC1 defines the transmission protocol, including serial encoding and decoding to and from the physical layer, special characters, and error control. Gigabit Ethernet will use the same encoding/decoding as specified in the FC1 layer of Fibre Channel. The scheme used is the 8B/10B encoding. This is similar to the 4B/5B encoding used in FDDI; however, 4B/5B encoding was rejected for Fibre Channel because it lacks DC balance. The lack of DC balance can potentially result in data-dependent heating of lasers due to a transmitter sending more 1s than 0s, resulting in higher error rates.

Encoding data transmitted at high speeds provides some advantages:

- Encoding limits the effective transmission characteristics, such as ratio of 1s to 0s, on the error rate.

- Bit-level clock recovery of the receiver can be greatly improved by using data encoding.

- Encoding increases the possibility that the receiving station can detect and correct transmission or reception errors.

- Encoding can help distinguish data bits from control bits.

All these features have been incorporated into the Fibre Channel FC1 specification.

In Gigabit Ethernet, the FC1 layer will take decoded data from the FC2 layer, 8 bits at a time from the reconciliation sublayer (RS), which "bridges" the

Fibre Channel physical interface to the IEEE 802.3 Ethernet upper layers. Encoding takes place via an 8-bit to 10-bit character mapping. Decoded data comprises 8 bits with a control variable. This information is, in turn, encoded into a 10-bit transmission character.

Encoding is accomplished by providing each transmission character with a name, denoted as Zxx.y. Z is the control variable that can have two values: D for *data* and K for *special character*. The xx designation is the decimal value of the binary number composed of a subset of the decoded bits. The y designation is the decimal value of the binary number of remaining decoded bits. This implies that there are 256 possibilities for data (D designation) and 256 possibilities for special characters (K designation). However, only 12 Kxx.y values are valid transmission characters in Fibre Channel. When data is received, the transmission character is decoded into one of the 256 8-bit combinations.

Gigabit Ethernet Interface Carrier (GBIC)

The GBIC interface allows network managers to configure each Gigabit port on a port-by-port basis for short-wave and long-wave lasers, as well as for copper physical interfaces. This configuration allows switch vendors to build a single physical switch or switch module that the customer can configure for the required laser/fiber topology. As stated earlier, Gigabit Ethernet initially supports three key media: short-wave laser, long-wave laser, and short copper. In addition, fiber-optic cable comes in three types: multimode (62.5 um), multimode (50 um) and single-mode. A diagram for the GBIC function is provided in Figure 7–19.

In contrast, Gigabit Ethernet switches without GBICs either cannot support other lasers or need to be ordered customized to the laser types required. Note that the IEEE 802.3z committee provides the only GBIC specification. The 802.3ab committee may provide for GBICs as well.

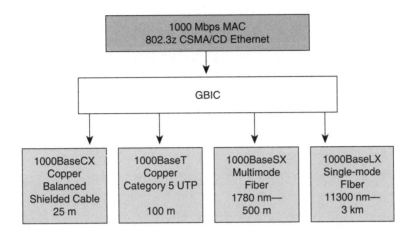

Figure 7–19
This diagram displays the function of the GBIC interface.

The MAC Layer

The MAC layer of Gigabit Ethernet is similar to those of standard Ethernet and Fast Ethernet. The MAC layer of Gigabit Ethernet will support both full-duplex and half-duplex transmission. The characteristics of Ethernet, such as collision detection, maximum network diameter, repeater rules, and so forth, will be the same for Gigabit Ethernet. Support for half-duplex Ethernet adds frame bursting and carrier extension, two functions not found in Ethernet and Fast Ethernet.

Half-Duplex Transmission

For half-duplex transmission, CSMA/CD will be utilized to ensure that stations can communicate over a single wire and that collision recovery can take place. Implementation of CSMA/CD for Gigabit Ethernet will be the same as for Ethernet and Fast Ethernet and will allow the creation of shared Gigabit Ethernet via hubs or half-duplex point-to-point connections.

Because the CSMA/CD protocol is delay sensitive, a bit-budget per-collision domain must be created. Note that delay sensitivity is of concern only when CSMA/CD is utilized; full-duplex operation has no such concerns. A collision domain is defined by the time of a valid minimum-length frame transmission. This transmission, in turn, governs the maximum separation between two end stations on a shared segment. As the speed of network operation increases, the minimum frame transmission time decreases, as does the maximum diameter of a collision domain. The bit budget of a collision domain is made up of the maximum signal delay time of the various networking components, such as repeaters, the MAC layer of the station, and the medium itself.

Acceleration of Ethernet to Gigabit speeds has created some challenges in terms of the implementation of CSMA/CD. At speeds greater than 100 Mbps, smaller packet sizes are smaller than the length of the slot-time in bits. (*Slot-time* is defined as the unit of time for Ethernet MAC to handle collisions.) To remedy the slot-time problem, carrier extension has been added to the Ethernet specification. Carrier extension adds bits to the frame until the frame meets the minimum slot-time required. In this way, the smaller packet sizes can coincide with the minimum slot-time and allow seamless operation with current Ethernet CSMA/CD.

Another change to the Ethernet specification is the addition of frame bursting. Frame bursting is an optional feature in which, in a CSMA/CD environment, an end station can transmit a burst of frames over the wire without having to relinquish control. Other stations on the wire defer to the burst transmission as long as there is no idle time on the wire. The transmitting station that is bursting onto the wire fills the interframe interval with extension bits such that the wire never appears free to any other end station.

It is important to point out that the issues surrounding half-duplex Gigabit Ethernet, such as frame size inefficiency (which in turn drives the need for carrier extension) as well as the signal round-trip time at Gigabit speeds, indicate that, in reality, half-duplex is not effective for Gigabit Ethernet.

IEEE 802.3x Full-Duplex Transmission

Full-duplex provides the means of transmitting and receiving simultaneously on a single wire. Full-duplex is typically used between two endpoints, such as between switches, between switches and servers, between switches and routers, and so on. Full-duplex has allowed bandwidth on Ethernet and Fast Ethernet networks to be easily and cost-effectively doubled from 10 Mbps to 20 Mbps and 100 Mbps to 200 Mbps, respectively. By using features such as Fast EtherChannel, "bundles" of Fast Ethernet connections can be grouped together to increase bandwidth up to 400%.

Full-duplex transmission will be utilized in Gigabit Ethernet to increase aggregate bandwidth from 1 Gbps to 2 Gbps for point-to-point links as well as to increase the distances possible for the particular media. Additionally, Gigabit EtherChannel "bundles" will allow creation of 8 Gbps connecting between switches. The use of full-duplex Ethernet eliminates collisions on the wire; therefore, CSMA/CD need not be utilized as a flow control or access medium. However, a full-duplex flow control method has been put forward in the standards committee with flow control as on optional clause. That standard is referred to as IEEE 802.3x; it formalizes full-duplex technology and is expected to be supported in future Gigabit Ethernet products. Because of the volume of full-duplex 100-Mbps network interface cards (NICs), it is unlikely that this standard will realistically apply to Fast Ethernet.

Optional 802.3x Flow Control

The optional flow control mechanism is set up between the two stations on the point-to-point link. If the receiving station at the end becomes congested, it can send back a frame called a *pause frame* to the source at the opposite end of the connection; the pause frame instructs that station to stop sending packets for a specific period of time. The sending station waits the requested time before sending more data. The receiving station can also send a frame back to the source with a time-to-wait of zero and instruct the source to begin sending data again. Figure 7–20 shows how IEEE 802.3x will work.

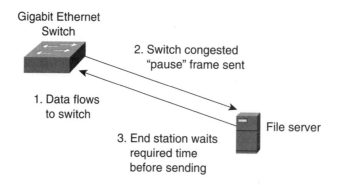

Gigabit Ethernet
Switch

2. Switch congested
"pause" frame sent

1. Data flows
to switch

3. End station waits
required time
before sending

File server

Figure 7-20

This figure presents an overview of the operation of the IEEE 802.3 flow control process.

This flow control mechanism was developed to match the sending and receiving device throughput. For example, a server can transmit to a client at a rate of 3000 pps. The client, however, may not be able to accept packets at that rate because of CPU interrupts, excessive network broadcasts, or multitasking within the system. In this example, the client would send a pause frame and request that the server hold transmission for a certain period. This mechanism, although separate from the IEEE 802.3z work, will complement Gigabit Ethernet by allowing Gigabit devices to participate in this flow-control mechanism.

The Logical Link Layer

Gigabit Ethernet has been designed to adhere to the standard Ethernet frame format, which maintains compatibility with the installed base of Ethernet and Fast Ethernet products and requires no frame translation. Figure 7-21 describes the IEEE 802.3/Ethernet frame format.

The original Xerox specification identified a Type field, which was utilized for protocol identification. The IEEE 802.3 specification eliminated the Type field, replacing it with the Length field. The Length field is used to identify the length in bytes of the data field. The protocol type in 802.3 frames are left to the data portion of the packet. The LLC is responsible for providing services to the network layer regardless of media type, such as FDDI, Ethernet, Token Ring, and so on.

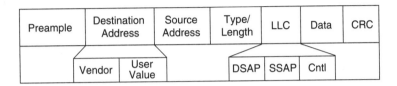

Figure 7–21
This figure shows the fields of the IEEE 802.3/Ethernet frame format.

In order to communicate between the MAC layer and the upper layers of the protocol stack, the Logical Link Control (LLC) layer of LLC protocol data units (or PDUs) makes use of three variable addresses to determine access into the upper layers via the LLC/PDU. Those addresses are the destination service access point (DSAP), source service access point (SSAP), and control variable. The DSAP address specifies a unique identifier within the station that provides protocol information for the upper layer. The SSAP provides the same information for the source address.

The LLC defines service access for protocols that conform to the Open System Interconnection (OSI) model for network protocols. Unfortunately, many protocols do not obey the rules for those layers. Therefore, additional information must be added to the LLC to provide information regarding those protocols. Protocols falling into this category include Internet Protocol (IP) and Internetwork Packet Exchange (IPX).

The method used to provide this additional protocol information is called a Subnetwork Access Protocol (SNAP) frame. A SNAP encapsulation is indicated by the SSAP and DSAP addresses being set to 0xAA. This address indicates that a SNAP header follows. The SNAP header is 5 bytes long: The first 3 bytes consist of the organization code, which is assigned by the IEEE; the second 2 bytes use the Type value set from the original Ethernet specifications.

MIGRATION TO GIGABIT ETHERNET

Several means can be used to deploy Gigabit Ethernet to increase bandwidth and capacity within the network. First, Gigabit Ethernet can be used to improve Layer 2 performance. Here, the throughput of Gigabit Ethernet is used to eliminate Layer 2 bottlenecks.

Scaling Bandwidth with Fast EtherChannel and Gigabit EtherChannel

Bandwidth requirements within the network core and between the network core and the wiring closet have placed significant demands on the network. Fast EtherChannel allows multiple Fast Ethernet ports to be bundled together and seen logically by the switches as a fat pipe. Fast EtherChannel allows the bundling of up to four ports, for an aggregate bandwidth of 800 Mbps. With support from NIC manufacturers such as Sun Microsystems, Intel, SGI, Compaq, and Adaptec, Fast EtherChannel can now be provided directly to high-end file servers. Figure 7–22 provides a possible Fast EtherChannel topology.

Scaling Router Backbones

Many large-scale networks use a meshed core of routers to form a redundant network backbone. This backbone typically consists of FDDI, Fast Ethernet, or ATM. However, as newer network designs heavily utilize switching with 100-Mbps links to these routers, a potential design bottleneck can be created. Although this is not currently a problem, the migration of services away from the workgroup and toward the enterprise can potentially lead to slower network performance.

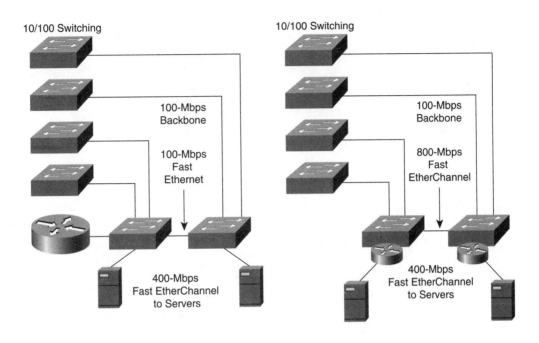

Figure 7–22
EtherChannel allows the bundling of up to four ports, for an aggregate bandwidth of 800 Mbps.

The solution demonstrated in Figure 7–23 uses Gigabit Ethernet switches that provide aggregation between routers in a routed backbone. Gigabit Ethernet and Gigabit switching are used to improve speed and capacity between the routers. Gigabit Ethernet switches are placed between the routers for improved throughput performance. By implementing this design, a fast Layer 2 aggregation is utilized, creating a high-speed core.

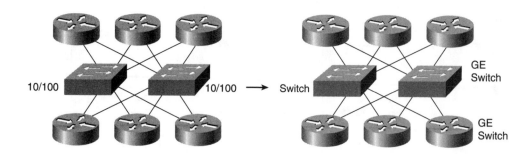

Figure 7–23
This design provides a scalable switching solution that increases throughput in a router backbone.

Scaling Wiring Closets

Gigabit Ethernet can also be used to aggregate traffic from wiring closets to the network core (see Figure 7–24). Gigabit Ethernet and Gigabit switching are used to aggregate traffic from multiple low-speed switches as a front end to the router. Low-speed switches can be connected either via Fast Ethernet or by a Gigabit Ethernet uplink while the switches provide dedicated 10-Mbps switching or group switching to individual users. The file servers are connected via Gigabit Ethernet for improved throughput performance. Keep in mind that as bandwidth requirements to the core or within the core increase, Gigabit EtherChannel can produce a fourfold increase in performance.

Gigabit Ethernet can also improve Layer 3 performance. This essentially means coupling Layer 2 performance with the benefits of Layer 3 routing. By using the switching paradigm as a road map, Gigabit switching and distributed Layer 3 services can improve the scalability and performance of campus intranets.

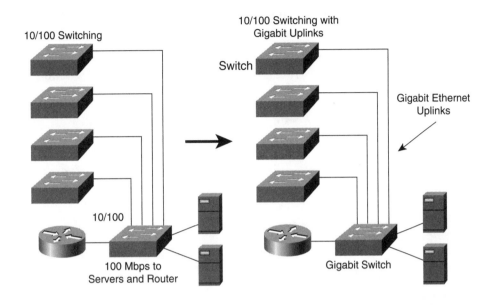

Figure 7–24
This design demonstrates the use of Gigabit Ethernet switching to improve data center applications.

GIGABIT ETHERNET CAMPUS APPLICATIONS

The key application of Gigabit Ethernet is expected to be use in the building backbone for interconnection of wiring closets. A Gigabit multilayer switch in the building data center aggregates the building's traffic and provides connection to servers via Gigabit Ethernet or Fast Ethernet. WAN connectivity can be provided by traditional routers or via ATM switching. Gigabit Ethernet can also be used for connecting buildings on the campus to a central multilayer Gigabit switch located at the campus data center. Servers located at the campus data center are also connected to the Gigabit multilayer switch that provides connectivity to the entire campus. Once again, Gigabit Ether-Channel can be utilized to significantly increase the bandwidth available within the campus backbone, to high-end wiring closets, or to high-end routers. Figure 7–25 illustrates potential multilayer Gigabit switching designs.

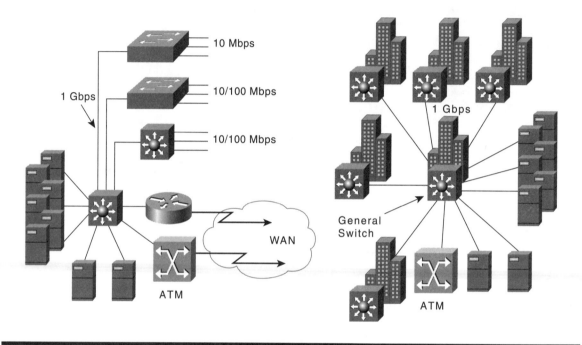

Figure 7–25

This design provides an example of a multilayer Gigabit switching environment.

CHAPTER 8

Fiber Distributed Data Interface (FDDI)

BACKGROUND

The Fiber Distributed Data Interface (FDDI) specifies a 100-Mbps token-passing, dual-ring LAN using fiber-optic cable. FDDI is frequently used as high-speed backbone technology because of its support for high bandwidth and greater distances than copper. It should be noted that relatively recently, a related copper specification, called Copper Distributed Data Interface (CDDI) has emerged to provide 100-Mbps service over copper. CDDI is the implementation of FDDI protocols over twisted-pair copper wire. This chapter focuses mainly on FDDI specifications and operations, but it also provides a high-level overview of CDDI.

FDDI uses a dual-ring architecture with traffic on each ring flowing in opposite directions (called *counter-rotating*). The dual-rings consist of a primary and a secondary ring. During normal operation, the primary ring is used for data transmission, and the secondary ring remains idle. The primary purpose of the dual rings, as will be discussed in detail later in this chapter, is to provide superior reliability and robustness. Figure 8–1 shows the counter-rotating primary and secondary FDDI rings.

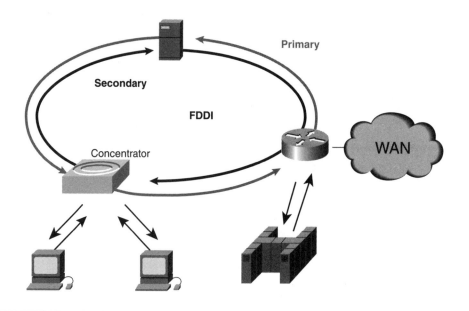

Figure 8–1
FDDI uses counter-rotating primary and secondary rings.

Standards

FDDI was developed by the American National Standards Institute (ANSI) X3T9.5 standards committee in the mid-1980s. At the time, high-speed engineering workstations were beginning to tax the bandwidth of existing local area networks (LANs) based on Ethernet and Token Ring. A new LAN media was needed that could easily support these workstations and their new distributed applications. At the same time, network reliability had become an increasingly important issue as system managers migrated mission-critical applications from large computers to networks. FDDI was developed to fill these needs. After completing the FDDI specification, ANSI submitted FDDI to the International Organization for Standardization (ISO), which created an international version of FDDI that is completely compatible with the ANSI standard version.

FDDI TRANSMISSION MEDIA

FDDI uses optical fiber as the primary transmission medium, but it also can run over copper cabling. As mentioned earlier, FDDI over copper is referred to as *Copper-Distributed Data Interface* (CDDI). Optical fiber has several advantages over copper media. In particular, security, reliability, and performance all are enhanced with optical fiber media because fiber does not emit electrical signals. A physical medium that does emit electrical signals (copper) can be tapped and therefore would permit unauthorized access to the data that is transiting the medium. In addition, fiber is immune to electrical interference from radio frequency interference (RFI) and electromagnetic interference (EMI). Fiber historically has supported much higher bandwidth (throughput potential) than copper, although recent technological advances have made copper capable of transmitting at 100 Mbps. Finally, FDDI allows two kilometers between stations using multi-mode fiber, and even longer distances using a single mode.

FDDI defines two types of optical fiber: single-mode and multi-mode. A *mode* is a ray of light that enters the fiber at a particular angle. Multi-mode fiber uses LED as the light-generating devices, while single-mode fiber generally uses lasers.

Multi-mode fiber allows multiple modes of light to propagate through the fiber. Because these modes of light enter the fiber at different angles, they will arrive at the end of the fiber at different times. This characteristic is known as *modal dispersion*. Modal dispersion limits the bandwidth and distances that can be accomplished using multi-mode fibers. For this reason, multi-mode fiber is generally used for connectivity within a building or within a relatively geographically contained environment.

Single-mode fiber allows only one mode of light to propagate through the fiber. Because only a single mode of light is used, modal dispersion is not present with single-mode fiber. Therefore, single-mode is capable of delivering considerably higher performance connectivity and over much larger distances, which is why it generally is used for connectivity between buildings and within environments that are more geographically dispersed.

Figure 8–2 depicts single-mode fiber using a laser light source and multi-mode fiber using a light-emitting diode (LED) light source.

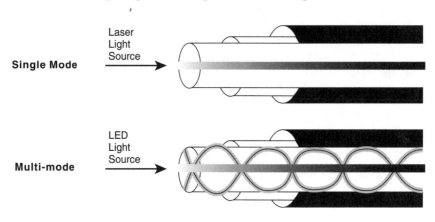

Figure 8–2
Light sources differ for single-mode and multi-mode fibers.

FDDI SPECIFICATIONS

FDDI specifies the physical and media-access portions of the OSI reference model. FDDI is not actually a single specification, but it is a collection of four separate specifications each with a specific function. Combined, these specifications have the capability to provide high-speed connectivity between upper-layer protocols such as TCP/IP and IPX, and media such as fiber-optic cabling.

FDDI's four specifications are the Media Access Control (MAC), Physical-Layer Protocol (PHY), Physical-Medium Dependent (PMD), and Station Management (SMT). The MAC specification defines how the medium is accessed, including frame format, token handling, addressing, algorithms for calculating cyclic redundancy check (CRC) value, and error-recovery mechanisms. The PHY specification defines data encoding/decoding procedures, clocking requirements, and framing, among other functions. The PMD specification defines the characteristics of the transmission medium, including fiber-optic links, power levels, bit-error rates, optical components, and connectors. The SMT specification defines FDDI station configuration, ring configuration, and ring control features, including station insertion and removal, initialization, fault isolation and recovery, scheduling, and statistics collection.

FDDI is similar to IEEE 802.3 Ethernet and IEEE 802.5 Token Ring in its relationship with the OSI model. Its primary purpose is to provide connectivity between upper OSI layers of common protocols and the media used to connect network devices. Figure 8–3 illustrates the four FDDI specifications and their relationship to each other and to the IEEE-defined Logical-Link Control (LLC) sublayer. The LLC sublayer is a component of Layer 2, the MAC layer, of the OSI reference model.

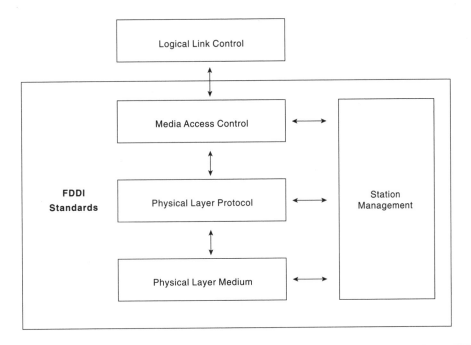

Figure 8–3
FDDI specifications map to the OSI hierarchical model.

FDDI STATION-ATTACHMENT TYPES

One of the unique characteristics of FDDI is that multiple ways actually exist by which to connect FDDI devices. FDDI defines three types of devices: single-attachment station (SAS), dual-attachment station (DAS), and a concentrator.

An SAS attaches to only one ring (the primary) through a concentrator. One of the primary advantages of connecting devices with SAS attachments is that the devices will not have any effect on the FDDI ring if they are disconnected or powered off. Concentrators will be discussed in more detail in the following discussion.

Each FDDI DAS has two ports, designated A and B. These ports connect the DAS to the dual FDDI ring. Therefore, each port provides a connection for both the primary and the secondary ring. As you will see in the next section, devices using DAS connections will affect the ring if they are disconnected or powered off. Figure 8–4 shows FDDI DAS A and B ports with attachments to the primary and secondary rings.

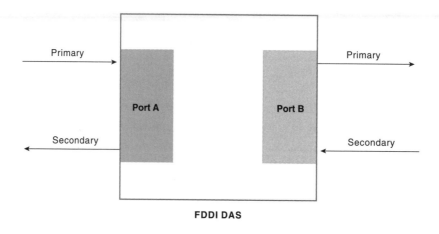

FDDI DAS

Figure 8–4
FDDI DAS ports attach to the primary and secondary rings.

An FDDI concentrator (also called a *dual-attachment concentrator* [DAC]) is the building block of an FDDI network. It attaches directly to both the primary and secondary rings and ensures that the failure or power-down of any SAS does not bring down the ring. This is particularly useful when PCs, or similar devices that are frequently powered on and off, connect to the ring. Figure 8–5 shows the ring attachments of an FDDI SAS, DAS, and concentrator.

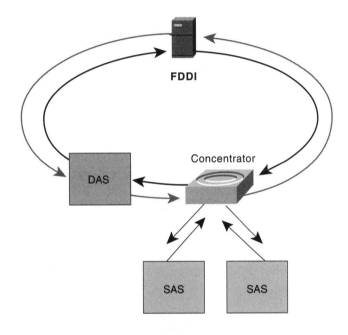

Figure 8–5
A concentrator attaches to both the primary and secondary rings.

FDDI FAULT TOLERANCE

FDDI provides a number of fault-tolerant features. In particular, FDDI's dual-ring environment, the implementation of the optical bypass switch, and dual-homing support make FDDI a resilient media technology.

Dual Ring

FDDI's primary fault-tolerant feature is the dual ring. If a station on the dual ring fails or is powered down, or if the cable is damaged, the dual ring is automatically *wrapped* (doubled back onto itself) into a single ring. When the ring is wrapped, the dual-ring topology becomes a single-ring topology. Data continues to be transmitted on the FDDI ring without performance impact during the wrap condition. Figure 8–6 and Figure 8–7 illustrate the effect of a ring wrapping in FDDI.

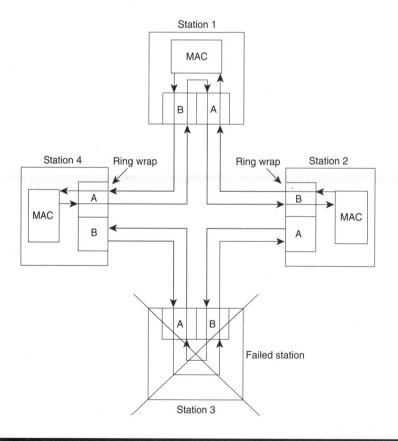

Figure 8–6

A ring recovers from a station failure by wrapping.

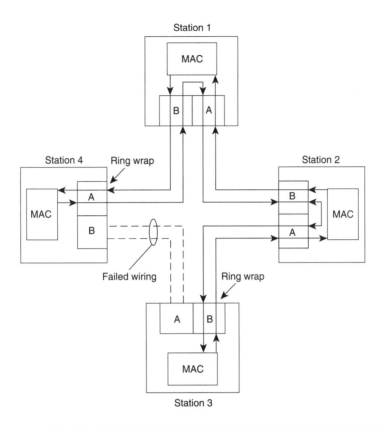

Figure 8–7
A ring also wraps to withstand a cable failure.

When a single station fails, as shown in Figure 8–6, devices on either side of the failed (or powered down) station wrap, forming a single ring. Network operation continues for the remaining stations on the ring. When a cable failure occurs, as shown in Figure 8–7, devices on either side of the cable fault wrap. Network operation continues for all stations.

It should be noted that FDDI truly provides fault-tolerance against a single failure only. When two or more failures occur, the FDDI ring segments into two or more independent rings that are unable to communicate with each other.

Optical Bypass Switch

An optical bypass switch provides continuous dual-ring operation if a device on the dual ring fails. This is used both to prevent ring segmentation and to eliminate failed stations from the ring. The optical bypass switch performs this function through the use of optical mirrors that pass light from the ring directly to the DAS device during normal operation. In the event of a failure of the DAS device, such as a power-off, the optical bypass switch will pass the light through itself by using internal mirrors and thereby maintain the ring's integrity. The benefit of this capability is that the ring will not enter a wrapped condition in the event of a device failure. Figure 8–8 shows the functionality of an optical bypass switch in an FDDI network.

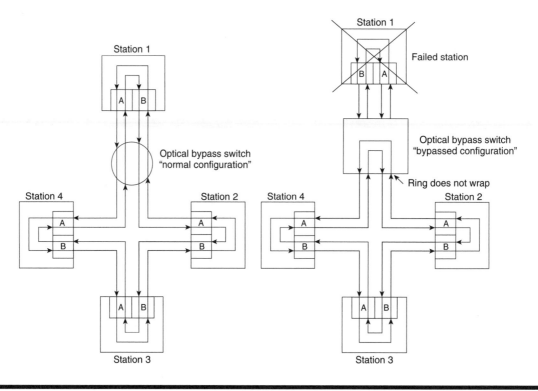

Figure 8–8
The optical bypass switch uses internal mirrors to maintain a network.

Dual Homing

Critical devices, such as routers or mainframe hosts, can use a fault-tolerant technique called *dual homing* to provide additional redundancy and to help guarantee operation. In dual-homing situations, the critical device is attached to two concentrators. Figure 8–9 shows a dual-homed configuration for devices such as file servers and routers.

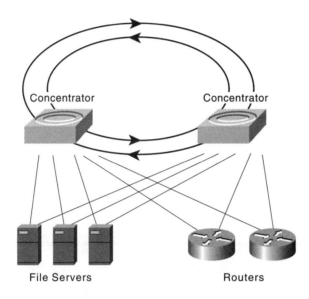

Figure 8–9
A dual-homed configuration guarantees operation.

One pair of concentrator links is declared the active link; the other pair is declared passive. The passive link stays in back-up mode until the primary link (or the concentrator to which it is attached) is determined to have failed. When this occurs, the passive link automatically activates.

FDDI FRAME FORMAT

The FDDI frame format is similar to the format of a Token Ring frame. This is one of the areas where FDDI borrows heavily from earlier LAN technologies, such as Token Ring. FDDI frames can be as large as 4,500 bytes. Figure 8–10 shows the frame format of an FDDI data frame and token.

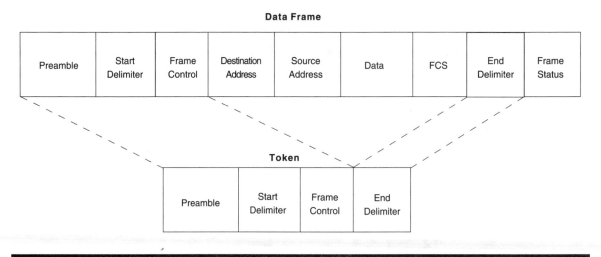

Figure 8–10
The FDDI frame is similar to that of a Token Ring frame.

FDDI Frame Fields

The following descriptions summarize the FDDI data frame and token fields illustrated in Figure 8–10.

- *Preamble*—A unique sequence that prepares each station for an upcoming frame.

- *Start Delimiter*—Indicates the beginning of a frame by employing a signaling pattern that differentiates it from the rest of the frame.

- *Frame Control*—Indicates the size of the address fields and whether the frame contains asynchronous or synchronous data, among other control information.

- *Destination Address*—Contains a unicast (singular), multicast (group), or broadcast (every station) address. As with Ethernet and Token Ring addresses, FDDI destination addresses are 6 bytes long.

- *Source Address*—Identifies the single station that sent the frame. As with Ethernet and Token Ring addresses, FDDI source addresses are 6 bytes long.

- *Data*—Contains either information destined for an upper-layer protocol or control information.

- *Frame Check Sequence (FCS)*—Filed by the source station with a calculated cyclic redundancy check value dependent on frame contents (as with Token Ring and Ethernet). The destination address recalculates the value to determine whether the frame was damaged in transit. If so, the frame is discarded.

- *End Delimiter*—Contains unique symbols, which cannot be data symbols, that indicate the end of the frame.

- *Frame Status*—Allows the source station to determine whether an error occurred and whether the frame was recognized and copied by a receiving station.

COPPER DISTRIBUTED DATA INTERFACE (CDDI)

Copper Distributed Data Interface (CDDI) is the implementation of FDDI protocols over twisted-pair copper wire. Like FDDI, CDDI provides data rates of 100 Mbps and uses a dual-ring architecture to provide redundancy. CDDI supports distances of about 100 meters from desktop to concentrator.

CDDI is defined by the ANSI X3T9.5 Committee. The CDDI standard is officially named the *Twisted-Pair Physical Medium Dependent* (TP-PMD) standard. It is also referred to as the *Twisted-Pair Distributed Data Interface* (TP-DDI), consistent with the term *Fiber-Distributed Data Interface* (FDDI). CDDI is consistent with the physical and media-access control layers defined by the ANSI standard.

The ANSI standard recognizes only two types of cables for CDDI: shielded twisted pair (STP) and unshielded twisted pair (UTP). STP cabling has a 150-ohm impedance and adheres to EIA/TIA 568 (IBM Type 1) specifications. UTP is data-grade cabling (Category 5) consisting of four unshielded pairs using tight-pair twists and specially developed insulating polymers in plastic jackets adhering to EIA/TIA 568B specifications.

Figure 8–11 illustrates the CDDI TP-PMD specification in relation to the remaining FDDI specifications.

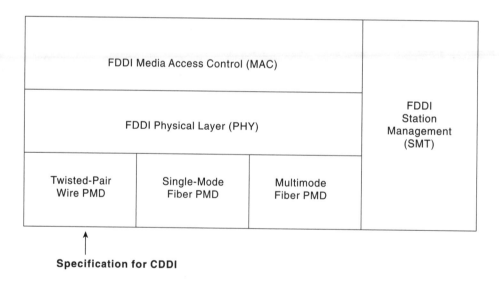

Figure 8–11
CDDI TP-PMD and FDDI specifications adhere to different standards.

CHAPTER 9

Token Ring/IEEE 802.5

BACKGROUND

The Token Ring network was originally developed by IBM in the 1970s. It is still IBM's primary local area network (LAN) technology and is second only to Ethernet/IEEE 802.3 in general LAN popularity. The related IEEE 802.5 specification is almost identical to and completely compatible with IBM's Token Ring network. In fact, the IEEE 802.5 specification was modeled after IBM Token Ring, and it continues to shadow IBM's Token Ring development. The term *Token Ring* generally is used to refer to both IBM's Token Ring network and IEEE 802.5 networks. This chapter addresses both Token Ring and IEEE 802.5.

Token Ring and IEEE 802.5 networks are basically compatible, although the specifications differ in minor ways. IBM's Token Ring network specifies a star, with all end stations attached to a device called a *multistation access unit* (MSAU). In contrast, IEEE 802.5 does not specify a topology, although virtually all IEEE 802.5 implementations are based on a star. Other differences exist, including media type (IEEE 802.5 does not specify a media type, although IBM Token Ring networks use twisted-pair wire) and routing information field size. Figure 9–1 summarizes IBM Token Ring network and IEEE 802.5 specifications.

	IBM Token Ring network	IEEE 802.5
Data rates	4.16 Mbps	4.16 Mbps
Stations/segment	260 (shielded twisted pair) 72 (unshielded twisted pair)	250
Topology	Star	Not specified
Media	Twisted pair	Not specified
Signaling	Baseband	Baseband
Access method	Token passing	Token passing
Encoding	Differential Manchester	Differential Manchester

Figure 9–1

Although dissimilar in some respects, IBM's Token Ring Network and IEEE 802.5 are generally compatible.

PHYSICAL CONNECTIONS

IBM Token Ring network stations are directly connected to MSAUs, which can be wired together to form one large ring (see Figure 9–2). Patch cables connect MSAUs to adjacent MSAUs, while lobe cables connect MSAUs to stations. MSAUs include bypass relays for removing stations from the ring.

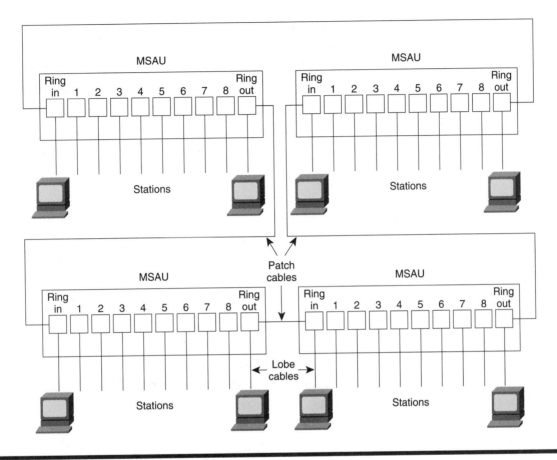

Figure 9–2
MSAUs can be wired together to form one large ring in an IBM Token Ring network.

TOKEN RING OPERATION

Token Ring and IEEE 802.5 are two principal examples of token-passing networks (FDDI being the other). Token-passing networks move a small frame, called a *token*, around the network. Possession of the token grants the right to transmit. If a node receiving the token has no information to send, it passes the token to the next end station. Each station can hold the token for a maximum period of time.

If a station possessing the token does have information to transmit, it seizes the token, alters one bit of the token, which turns the token into a start-of-frame sequence, appends the information it wants to transmit, and sends this information to the next station on the ring. While the information frame is circling the ring, no token is on the network (unless the ring supports *early token release*), which means that other stations wanting to transmit must wait. Therefore, collisions cannot occur in Token Ring networks. If early token release is supported, a new token can be released when frame transmission is complete.

The information frame circulates the ring until it reaches the intended destination station, which copies the information for further processing. The information frame continues to circle the ring and is finally removed when it reaches the sending station. The sending station can check the returning frame to see whether the frame was seen and subsequently copied by the destination.

Unlike CSMA/CD networks (such as Ethernet), token-passing networks are *deterministic*, which means that it is possible to calculate the maximum time that will pass before any end station will be able to transmit. This feature and several reliability features, which are discussed in the section "Fault-Management Mechanisms" later in this chapter, make Token Ring networks ideal for applications where delay must be predictable and robust network operation is important. Factory automation environments are examples of such applications.

PRIORITY SYSTEM

Token Ring networks use a sophisticated priority system that permits certain user-designated, high-priority stations to use the network more frequently. Token Ring frames have two fields that control priority: the *priority* field and the *reservation* field.

Only stations with a priority equal to or higher than the priority value contained in a token can seize that token. After the token is seized and changed to an information frame, only stations with a priority value higher than that of the transmitting station can reserve the token for the next pass around the network. When the next token is generated, it includes the higher priority of the reserving station. Stations that raise a token's priority level must reinstate the previous priority after their transmission is complete.

FAULT-MANAGEMENT MECHANISMS

Token Ring networks employ several mechanisms for detecting and compensating for network faults. One station in the Token Ring network, for example, is selected to be the *active monitor*. This station, which potentially can be any station on the network, acts as a centralized source of timing information for other ring stations and performs a variety of ring-maintenance functions. One of these functions is the removal of continuously circulating frames from the ring. When a sending device fails, its frame may continue to circle the ring. This can prevent other stations from transmitting their own frames and essentially can lock up the network. The active monitor can detect such frames, remove them from the ring, and generate a new token.

The IBM Token Ring network's star topology also contributes to overall network reliability. Because all information in a Token Ring network is seen by active MSAUs, these devices can be programmed to check for problems and selectively remove stations from the ring if necessary.

A Token Ring algorithm called *beaconing* detects and tries to repair certain network faults. Whenever a station detects a serious problem with the network (such as a cable break), it sends a beacon frame, which defines a failure domain. This domain includes the station reporting the failure, its *nearest active upstream neighbor* (NAUN), and everything in between. Beaconing initiates a process called *autoreconfiguration*, where nodes within the failure domain automatically perform diagnostics in an attempt to reconfigure the network around the failed areas. Physically, the MSAU can accomplish this through electrical reconfiguration.

FRAME FORMAT

Token Ring and IEEE 802.5 support two basic frame types: tokens and data/command frames. Tokens are 3 bytes in length and consist of a start delimiter, an access control byte, and an end delimiter. Data/command frames vary in size, depending on the size of the Information field. Data frames carry information for upper-layer protocols, while command frames contain control information and have no data for upper-layer protocols. Both formats are shown in Figure 9–3.

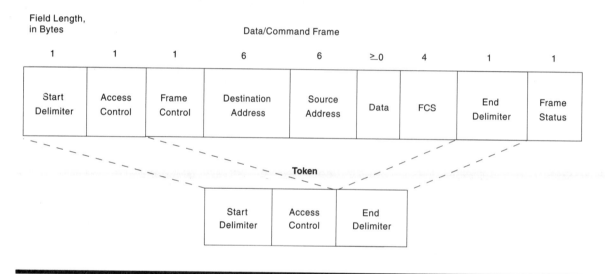

Figure 9–3
IEEE 802.5 and Token Ring specify tokens and data/command frames.

Token Frame Fields

The three token frame fields illustrated in Figure 9–3 are summarized in the descriptions that follow:

- *Start Delimiter*—Alerts each station of the arrival of a token (or data/command frame). This field includes signals that distinguish the byte from the rest of the frame by violating the encoding scheme used elsewhere in the frame.

- *Access-Control Byte*—Contains the Priority field (the most significant 3 bits) and Reservation field (the least significant 3 bits), as well as a token bit (used to differentiate a token from a data/command frame) and a monitor bit (used by the active monitor to determine whether a frame is circling the ring endlessly).

- *End Delimiter*—Signals the end of the token or data/command frame. This field also contains bits to indicate a damaged frame and identify the frame that is the last in a logical sequence.

Data/Command Frame Fields

Data/Command frames have the same three fields as Token Frames, plus several others. The Data/Command frame fields illustrated in Figure 9–3 are described in the following summaries:

- *Start Delimiter*—Alerts each station of the arrival of a token (or data/command frame). This field includes signals that distinguish the byte from the rest of the frame by violating the encoding scheme used elsewhere in the frame.

- *Access-Control Byte*—Contains the Priority field (the most significant 3 bits) and Reservation field (the least significant 3 bits), as well as a token bit (used to differentiate a token from a data/command frame) and a monitor bit (used by the active monitor to determine whether a frame is circling the ring endlessly).

- *Frame-Control Bytes*—Indicates whether the frame contains data or control information. In control frames, this byte specifies the type of control information.

- *Destination and Source Addresses*—Two 6-byte address fields identify the destination and source station addresses.

- *Data*—Length of field is limited by the ring token holding time, which defines the maximum time a station can hold the token.

- *Frame-Check Sequence (FCS)*—Filed by the source station with a calculated value dependent on the frame contents. The destination station recalculates the value to determine whether the frame was damaged in transit. If so, the frame is discarded.

- *End Delimiter*—Signals the end of the token or data/command frame. The end delimiter also contains bits to indicate a damaged frame and identify the frame that is the last in a logical sequence.

- *Frame Status*—A 1-byte field terminating a command/data frame. The Frame Status field includes the address-recognized indicator and frame-copied indicator.

PART 3

WAN Technologies

Part 3, "WAN Technologies," summarizes the specifications and operational characteristics of key wide-area network (WAN) technologies and protocols. Individual chapters discuss the following topics:

Frame Relay—Describes the operation and features of this high-speed WAN technology.

High-Speed Serial Interface (HSSI)—Defines HSSI and summarizes the use of HSSI technology in T3 WAN implementations.

Integrated Services Digital Network (ISDN)—Defines ISDN and summarizes the use of ISDN as a WAN technology.

Point-to-Point Protocol (PPP)—Defines PPP and describes the use of PPP to provide remote access in WAN environments.

Switched Multimegabit Data Service (SMDS)—Describes the features and operation of ADSL, a high-bandwidth dialup WAN technology.

Digital Subscriber Line—Describes the features and operation of SMDS, a high-speed WAN implementation.

Synchronous Data Link Control and Derivatives (SDLC)—Addresses the role of SDLC as a data-link layer protocol in IBM SNA networks and summarizes the operation of derivative protocols.

X.25—Covers the operation and features of X.25.

CHAPTER 10

Frame
Relay

BACKGROUND

Frame Relay is a high-performance WAN protocol that operates at the physical and data link layers of the OSI reference model. Frame Relay originally was designed for use across Integrated Services Digital Network (ISDN) interfaces. Today, it is used over a variety of other network interfaces as well. This chapter focuses on Frame Relay's specifications and applications in the context of WAN services.

Frame Relay is an example of a packet-switched technology. Packet-switched networks enable end stations to dynamically share the network medium and the available bandwidth. Variable-length packets are used for more efficient and flexible transfers. These packets then are switched between the various network segments until the destination is reached. Statistical multiplexing techniques control network access in a packet-switched network. The advantage of this technique is that it accommodates more flexibility and more efficient use of bandwidth. Most of today's popular LANs, such as Ethernet and Token Ring, are packet-switched networks.

Frame Relay often is described as a streamlined version of X.25, offering fewer of the robust capabilities, such as windowing and retransmission of last data, that are offered in X.25. This is because Frame Relay typically operates over WAN facilities that offer more reliable connection services and a higher degree of reliability than the facilities available during the late 1970s and early 1980s that served as the common platforms for X.25 WANs. As mentioned earlier, Frame Relay is strictly a Layer 2 protocol suite, whereas X.25 provides services at Layer 3 (the network layer) as well. This enables Frame Relay to offer higher performance and greater transmission efficiency than X.25 and makes Frame Relay suitable for current WAN applications, such as LAN interconnection.

Frame Relay Standardization

Initial proposals for the standardization of Frame Relay were presented to the Consultative Committee on International Telephone and Telegraph (CCITT) in 1984. Due to lack of interoperability and lack of complete standardization, however, Frame Relay did not experience significant deployment during the late 1980s.

A major development in Frame Relay's history occurred in 1990 when Cisco, Digital Equipment, Northern Telecom, and StrataCom formed a consortium to focus on Frame Relay technology development. This consortium developed a specification that conformed to the basic Frame Relay protocol that was being discussed in CCITT but extended the protocol with features that provide additional capabilities for complex internetworking environments. These Frame Relay extensions are referred to collectively as the Local Management Interface (LMI).

Since the consortium's specification was developed and published, many vendors have announced their support of this extended Frame Relay definition. ANSI and CCITT have subsequently standardized their own variations of the original LMI specification, and these standardized specifications now are more commonly used than the original version.

Internationally, Frame Relay was standardized by the International Telecommunications Union - Telecommunications Sector (ITU-T). In the United States, Frame Relay is an American National Standards Institute (ANSI) standard.

FRAME RELAY DEVICES

Devices attached to a Frame Relay WAN fall into two general categories: data terminal equipment (DTE) and data circuit-terminating equipment (DCE). DTEs generally are considered to be terminating equipment for a specific network and typically are located on the premises of a customer. In fact, they may be owned by the customer. Examples of DTE devices are terminals, personal computers, routers, and bridges.

DCEs are carrier-owned internetworking devices. The purpose of DCE equipment is to provide clocking and switching services in a network, which are the devices that actually transmit data through the WAN. In most cases, these are packet switches. Figure 10–1 shows the relationship between the two categories of devices.

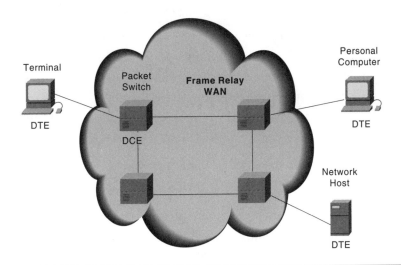

Figure 10–1
DCEs generally reside within carrier-operated WANs.

The connection between a DTE device and a DCE device consists of both a physical-layer component and a link-layer component. The physical component defines the mechanical, electrical, functional, and procedural specifications for the connection between the devices. One of the most commonly used physical-layer interface specifications is the recommended standard (RS)-232 specification. The link-layer component defines the protocol that establishes the connection between the DTE device, such as a router, and the DCE device, such as a switch. This chapter examines a commonly utilized protocol specification used in WAN networking—the Frame Relay protocol.

FRAME RELAY VIRTUAL CIRCUITS

Frame Relay provides connection-oriented data link layer communication. This means that a defined communication exists between each pair of devices and that these connections are associated with a connection identifier. This service is implemented by using a *Frame Relay virtual circuit*, which is a logical connection created between two data terminal equipment (DTE) devices across a Frame Relay packet-switched network (PSN).

Virtual circuits provide a bi-directional communications path from one DTE device to another and are uniquely identified by a data-link connection identifier (DLCI). A number of virtual circuits can be multiplexed into a single physical circuit for transmission across the network. This capability often can reduce the equipment and network complexity required to connect multiple DTE devices.

A virtual circuit can pass through any number of intermediate DCE devices (switches) located within the Frame Relay PSN.

Frame Relay virtual circuits fall into two categories: switched virtual circuits (SVCs) and permanent virtual circuits (PVCs).

Switched Virtual Circuits (SVCs)

Switched virtual circuits (SVCs) are temporary connections used in situations requiring only sporadic data transfer between DTE devices across the Frame Relay network. A communication session across an SVC consists of four operational states:

- *Call Setup*—The virtual circuit between two Frame Relay DTE devices is established.

- *Data Transfer*—Data is transmitted between the DTE devices over the virtual circuit.

- *Idle*—The connection between DTE devices is still active, but no data is transferred. If an SVC remains in an idle state for a defined period of time, the call can be terminated.

- *Call Termination*—The virtual circuit between DTE devices is terminated.

After the virtual circuit is terminated, the DTE devices must establish a new SVC if there is additional data to be exchanged. It is expected that SVCs will be established, maintained, and terminated using the same signaling protocols used in ISDN. Few manufacturers of Frame Relay DCE equipment, however, support Switched Virtual Connections. Therefore, their actual deployment is minimal in today's Frame Relay networks.

Permanent Virtual Circuits (PVCs)

Permanent virtual circuits (PVCs) are permanently established connections that are used for frequent and consistent data transfers between DTE devices across the Frame Relay network. Communication across a PVC does not require the call setup and termination states that are used with SVCs. PVCs always operate in one of the following two operational states:

- *Data Transfer*—Data is transmitted between the DTE devices over the virtual circuit.

- *Idle*—The connection between DTE devices is active, but no data is transferred. Unlike SVCs, PVCs will not be terminated under any circumstances due to being in an idle state.

DTE devices can begin transferring data whenever they are ready because the circuit is permanently established.

Data-Link Connection Identifier (DLCI)

Frame Relay virtual circuits are identified by data-link connection identifiers (DLCIs). DLCI values typically are assigned by the Frame Relay service provider (for example, the telephone company). Frame Relay DLCIs have local significance, which means that the values themselves are not unique in the Frame Relay WAN. Two DTE devices connected by a virtual circuit, for example, may use a different DLCI value to refer to the same connection. Figure 10–2 illustrates how a single virtual circuit may be assigned a different DLCI value on each end of the connection.

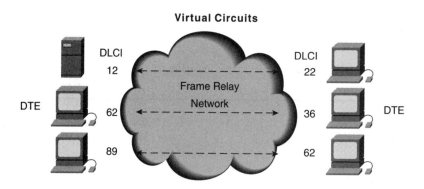

Figure 10–2
A single Frame Relay virtual circuit can be assigned different DLCIs on each end of a VC.

CONGESTION-CONTROL MECHANISMS

Frame Relay reduces network overhead by implementing simple congestion-notification mechanisms rather than explicit, per-virtual-circuit flow control. Frame Relay typically is implemented on reliable network media, so data integrity is not sacrificed because flow control can be left to higher-layer protocols. Frame Relay implements two congestion-notification mechanisms:

- Forward-explicit congestion notification (FECN)

- Backward-explicit congestion notification (BECN)

FECN and BECN each are controlled by a single bit contained in the Frame Relay frame header. The Frame Relay frame header also contains a *Discard Eligibility* (DE) bit, which is used to identify less important traffic that can be dropped during periods of congestion.

The FECN bit is part of the Address field in the Frame Relay frame header. The FECN mechanism is initiated when a DTE device sends Frame Relay frames into the network. If the network is congested, DCE devices (switches) set the value of the frames' FECN bit to 1. When the frames reach the destination DTE device, the Address field (with the FECN bit set) indicates that the frame experienced congestion in the path from source to destination. The DTE device can relay this information to a higher-layer protocol for processing. Depending on the implementation, flow-control may be initiated, or the indication may be ignored.

The BECN bit is part of the Address field in the Frame Relay frame header. DCE devices set the value of the BECN bit to 1 in frames traveling in the opposite direction of frames with their FECN bit set. This informs the receiving DTE device that a particular path through the network is congested. The DTE device then can relay this information to a higher-layer protocol for processing. Depending on the implementation, flow-control may be initiated, or the indication may be ignored.

Frame Relay Discard Eligibility (DE)

The Discard Eligibility (DE) bit is used to indicate that a frame has lower importance than other frames. The DE bit is part of the Address field in the Frame Relay frame header.

DTE devices can set the value of the DE bit of a frame to 1 to indicate that the frame has lower importance than other frames. When the network becomes congested, DCE devices will discard frames with the DE bit set before discarding those that do not. This reduces the likelihood of critical data being dropped by Frame Relay DCE devices during periods of congestion.

Frame Relay Error Checking

Frame Relay uses a common error-checking mechanism known as the *cyclic redundancy check* (CRC). The CRC compares two calculated values to determine whether errors occurred during the transmission from source to destination. Frame Relay reduces network overhead by implementing error checking rather than error correction. Frame Relay typically is implemented on reliable network media, so data integrity is not sacrificed because error correction can be left to higher-layer protocols running on top of Frame Relay.

FRAME RELAY LOCAL MANAGEMENT INTERFACE (LMI)

The Local Management Interface (LMI) is a set of enhancements to the basic Frame Relay specification. The LMI was developed in 1990 by Cisco Systems, StrataCom, Northern Telecom, and Digital Equipment Corporation. It offers a number of features (called *extensions*) for managing complex internetworks. Key Frame Relay LMI extensions include global addressing, virtual-circuit status messages, and multicasting.

The LMI global addressing extension gives Frame Relay *data-link connection identifier* (DLCI) values global rather than local significance. DLCI values become DTE addresses that are unique in the Frame Relay WAN. The global addressing extension adds functionality and manageability to Frame Relay internetworks. Individual network interfaces and the end nodes attached to them, for example, can be identified by using standard address-resolution and discovery techniques. In addition, the entire Frame Relay network appears to be a typical LAN to routers on its periphery.

LMI virtual circuit status messages provide communication and synchronization between Frame Relay DTE and DCE devices. These messages are used to periodically report on the status of PVCs, which prevents data from being sent into *black holes* (that is, over PVCs that no longer exist).

The LMI multicasting extension allows multicast groups to be assigned. *Multicasting* saves bandwidth by allowing routing updates and address-resolution messages to be sent only to specific groups of routers. The extension also transmits reports on the status of multicast groups in update messages.

FRAME RELAY NETWORK IMPLEMENTATION

A common private Frame Relay network implementation is to equip a T1 multiplexer with both Frame Relay and non-Frame Relay interfaces. Frame Relay traffic is forwarded out the Frame Relay interface and onto the data network. Non-Frame Relay traffic is forwarded to the appropriate application or service, such as a *private branch exchange* (PBX) for telephone service or to a video-teleconferencing application.

A typical Frame Relay network consists of a number of DTE devices, such as routers, connected to remote ports on multiplexer equipment via traditional point-to-point services such as T1, fractional T1, or 56 K circuits. An example of a simple Frame Relay network is shown in Figure 10–3.

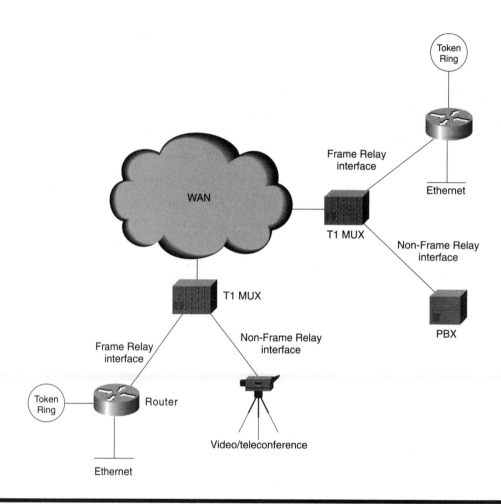

Figure 10–3

A simple Frame Relay network connects various devices to different services over a WAN.

The majority of Frame Relay networks deployed today are provisioned by service providers who intend to offer transmission services to customers. This is often referred to as a public Frame Relay service. Frame Relay is implemented in both public carrier-provided networks and in private enterprise networks. The following section examines the two methodologies for deploying Frame Relay.

Public Carrier-Provided Networks

In public carrier-provided Frame Relay networks, the Frame Relay switching equipment is located in the central offices of a telecommunications carrier. Subscribers are charged based on their network use but are relieved from administering and maintaining the Frame Relay network equipment and service.

Generally, the DCE equipment also is owned by the telecommunications provider. DCE equipment either will be customer-owned or perhaps owned by the telecommunications provider as a service to the customer.

The majority of today's Frame Relay networks are public carrier-provided networks.

Private Enterprise Networks

More frequently, organizations worldwide are deploying private Frame Relay networks. In private Frame Relay networks, the administration and maintenance of the network are the responsibilities of the enterprise (a private company). All the equipment, including the switching equipment, is owned by the customer.

FRAME RELAY FRAME FORMATS

To understand much of the functionality of Frame Relay, it is helpful to understand the structure of the Frame Relay frame. Figure 10–4 depicts the basic format of the Frame Relay frame, and Figure 10–5 illustrates the LMI version of the Frame Relay frame.

Flags indicate the beginning and end of the frame. Three primary components make up the Frame Relay frame: the header and address area, the user-data portion, and the frame-check sequence (FCS). The address area, which is 2 bytes in length, is comprised of 10 bits representing the actual circuit identifier and 6 bits of fields related to congestion management. This identifier commonly is referred to as the data-link connection identifier (DLCI). Each of these is discussed in the descriptions that follow.

Standard Frame Relay Frame

Standard Frame Relay frames consist of the fields illustrated in Figure 10–4.

Field Length, in Bytes

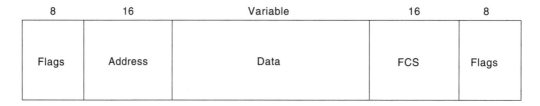

Figure 10–4
Five fields comprise the Frame Relay frame.

The following descriptions summarize the basic Frame Relay frame fields illustrated in Figure 10–4.

- *Flags*—Delimits the beginning and end of the frame. The value of this field is always the same and is represented either as the hexadecimal number 7E or the binary number 01111110.

- *Address*—Contains the following information:

  ○ DLCI: The 10-bit DLCI is the essence of the Frame Relay header. This value represents the virtual connection between the DTE device and the switch. Each virtual connection that is multiplexed onto the physical channel will be represented by a unique DLCI. The DLCI values have local significance only, which means that they are unique only to the physical channel on which they reside. Therefore, devices at opposite ends of a connection can use different DLCI values to refer to the same virtual connection.

○ Extended Address (EA): The EA is used to indicate whether the byte in which the EA value is 1 is the last addressing field. If the value is 1, then the current byte is determined to be the last DLCI octet. Although current Frame Relay implementations all use a two-octet DLCI, this capability does allow for longer DLCIs to be used in the future. The eighth bit of each byte of the Address field is used to indicate the EA.

○ C/R: The C/R is the bit that follows the most significant DLCI byte in the Address field. The C/R bit is not currently defined.

○ Congestion Control: This consists of the three bits that control the Frame Relay congestion-notification mechanisms. These are the FECN, BECN, and DE bits, which are the last three bits in the Address field.

Forward-explicit congestion notification (FECN) is a single bit field that can be set to a value of 1 by a switch to indicate to an end DTE device, such as a router, that congestion was experienced in the direction of the frame transmission from source to destination. The primary benefit of the use of the FECN and BECN fields is the ability of higher-layer protocols to react intelligently to these congestion indicators. Today, DECnet and OSI are the only higher-layer protocols that implement these capabilities.

Backward-explicit congestion notification (BECN) is a single bit field that, when set to a value of 1 by a switch, indicates that congestion was experienced in the network in the direction opposite of the frame transmission from source to destination.

Discard eligibility (DE) is set by the DTE device, such as a router, to indicate that the marked frame is of lesser importance relative to other frames being transmitted. Frames that are marked as "discard eligible" should be discarded before other frames in a congested network. This allows for a fairly basic prioritization mechanism in Frame Relay networks.

- *Data*—Contains encapsulated upper-layer data. Each frame in this variable-length field includes a user data or payload field that will vary in length up to 16,000 octets. This field serves to transport the higher-layer protocol packet (PDU) through a Frame Relay network.

- *Frame Check Sequence*—Ensures the integrity of transmitted data. This value is computed by the source device and verified by the receiver to ensure integrity of transmission.

LMI Frame Format

Frame Relay frames that conform to the LMI specifications consist of the fields illustrated in Figure 10–5.

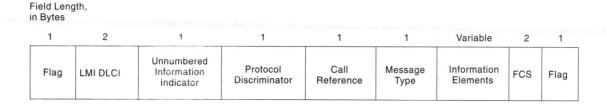

Figure 10–5
Nine fields comprise the Frame Relay that conforms to the LMI format.

The following descriptions summarize the fields illustrated in Figure 10–5.

- *Flag*—Delimits the beginning and end of the frame.

- *LMI DLCI*—Identifies the frame as an LMI frame instead of a basic Frame Relay frame. The LMI-specific DLCI value defined in the LMI consortium specification is DLCI = 1023.

- *Unnumbered Information Indicator*—Sets the poll/final bit to zero.

- *Protocol Discriminator*—Always contains a value indicating that the frame is an LMI frame.

- *Call Reference*—Always contains zeros. This field currently is not used for any purpose.

- *Message Type*—Labels the frame as one of the following message types:

  ○ Status-inquiry message: Allows a user device to inquire about the status of the network.
  ○ Status message: Responds to status-inquiry messages. Status messages include keep-alives and PVC status messages.

- *Information Elements*—Contains a variable number of individual information elements (IEs). IEs consist of the following fields:

  ○ IE Identifier: Uniquely identifies the IE.
  ○ IE Length: Indicates the length of the IE.
  ○ Data: Consists of one or more bytes containing encapsulated upper-layer data.

- *Frame Check Sequence (FCS)*—Ensures the integrity of transmitted data.

11

High-Speed Serial Interface

BACKGROUND

The *High-Speed Serial Interface* (HSSI) is a DTE/DCE interface developed by Cisco Systems and T3plus Networking to address the need for high-speed communication over WAN links. The HSSI specification is available to any organization wanting to implement HSSI.

HSSI is now in the American National Standards Institute (ANSI) Electronic Industries Association (EIA)/TIA TR30.2 committee for formal standardization. It has recently moved into the International Telecommunication Union Telecommunication Standardization Sector (ITU-T) (formerly the Consultative Committee for International Telegraph and Telephone [CCITT]) and the International Organization for Standardization (ISO), and is expected to be standardized by these bodies.

HSSI INTERFACE BASICS

HSSI defines both the electrical and the physical DTE/DCE interfaces. It therefore corresponds to the physical layer of the OSI reference model. HSSI technical characteristics are summarized in Table 11–1.

Characteristic	Value
Maximum signaling rate	52 Mbps
Maximum cable length	50 feet
Number of connector pins	50
Interface	DTE-DCE
Electrical technology	Differential ECL
Typical power consumption	610 mW
Topology	Point-to-point
Cable type	Shielded twisted-pair wire

Table 11–1
HSSI technical characteristics.

The maximum signaling rate of HSSI is 52 Mbps. At this rate, HSSI can handle the T3 speeds (45 Mbps) of many of today's fast WAN technologies, as well as the *Office Channel -1* (OC-1) speeds (52 Mbps) of the *synchronous digital hierarchy* (SDH). In addition, HSSI easily can provide high-speed connectivity between LANs, such as Token Ring and Ethernet.

The use of differential *emitter-coupled logic* (ECL) helps HSSI achieve high data rates and low noise levels. ECL has been used in Cray interfaces for years and is specified by the ANSI *High-Performance Parallel Interface* (HIPPI) communications standard for supercomputer LAN communications. ECL is off-the-shelf technology that permits excellent retiming on the receiver, resulting in reliable timing margins.

HSSI uses a subminiature, FCC-approved 50-pin connector that is smaller than its V.35 counterpart. To reduce the need for male-male and female-female adapters, HSSI cable connectors are specified as male. The HSSI cable uses the same number of pins and wires as the *Small Computer Systems Interface* 2 (SCSI-2) cable, but the HSSI electrical specification is tighter.

HSSI OPERATION

The flexibility of the HSSI clock and data-signaling protocol makes user (or vendor) bandwidth allocation possible. The DCE controls the clock by changing its speed or by deleting clock pulses. In this way, the DCE can allocate bandwidth between applications. A PBX, for example, may require a particular amount of bandwidth, a router another amount, and a channel extender a third amount. Bandwidth allocation is key to making T3 and other broadband services affordable and popular.

HSSI assumes a peer-to-peer intelligence in the DCE and DTE. The control protocol is simplified, with just two control signals required ("DTE available" and "DCE available"). Both signals must be asserted before the data circuit can be valid. The DCE and DTE are expected to be able to manage the networks behind their interfaces. Reducing the number of control signals improves circuit reliability by reducing the number of circuits that can fail.

Loopback Tests

HSSI provides four loopback tests, which are illustrated in Figure 11–1. The first provides a local cable test as the signal loops back after it reaches the DTE port. The second test reaches the line port of the local DCE. The third test reaches the line port of the remote DCE. Finally, the fourth test is a DCE-initiated test of the DTE's DCE port.

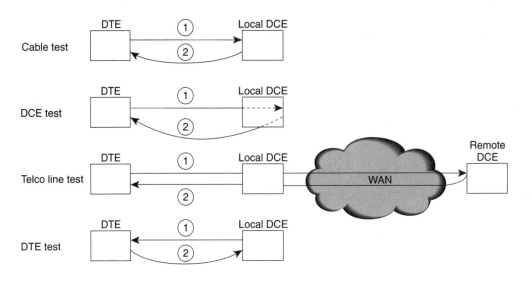

Figure 11–1

HSSI supports four loopback tests.

CHAPTER 12

Integrated Services Digital Network (ISDN)

BACKGROUND

Integrated Services Digital Network (ISDN) is comprised of digital telephony and data-transport services offered by regional telephone carriers. ISDN involves the digitization of the telephone network, which permits voice, data, text, graphics, music, video, and other source material to be transmitted over existing telephone wires. The emergence of ISDN represents an effort to standardize subscriber services, user/network interfaces, and network and inter-network capabilities. ISDN applications include high-speed image applications (such as Group IV facsimile), additional telephone lines in homes to serve the telecommuting industry, high-speed file transfer, and video conferencing. Voice service is also an application for ISDN. This chapter summarizes the underlying technologies and services associated with ISDN.

ISDN COMPONENTS

ISDN components include terminals, terminal adapters (TAs), network-termination devices, line-termination equipment, and exchange-termination equipment. ISDN terminals come in two types. Specialized ISDN terminals are referred to as *terminal equipment type 1* (TE1). Non-ISDN terminals, such as DTE, that predate the ISDN standards are referred to as *terminal equipment type 2* (TE2). TE1s connect to the ISDN network through a four-wire, twisted-pair digital link. TE2s connect to the ISDN network through a TA. The ISDN TA can be either a standalone device or a board inside the TE2. If the TE2 is implemented as a standalone device, it connects to the TA via a standard physical-layer interface. Examples include EIA/TIA-232-C (formerly RS-232-C), V.24, and V.35.

Beyond the TE1 and TE2 devices, the next connection point in the ISDN network is the *network termination type 1* (NT1) or *network termination type 2* (NT2) device. These are network-termination devices that connect the four-wire subscriber wiring to the conventional two-wire local loop. In North America, the NT1 is a *customer premises equipment* (CPE) device. In most other parts of the world, the NT1 is part of the network provided by the carrier. The NT2 is a more complicated device that typically is found in digital *private branch exchanges* (PBXs) and that performs Layer 2 and 3 protocol functions and concentration services. An NT1/2 device also exists as a single device that combines the functions of an NT1 and an NT2.

ISDN specifies a number of reference points that define logical interfaces between functional groupings, such as TAs and NT1s. ISDN reference points include the following:

- *R*—The reference point between non-ISDN equipment and a TA.

- *S*—The reference point between user terminals and the NT2.

- *T*—The reference point between NT1 and NT2 devices.

- *U*—The reference point between NT1 devices and line-termination equipment in the carrier network. The U reference point is relevant only in North America, where the NT1 function is not provided by the carrier network.

Figure 12–1 illustrates a sample ISDN configuration and shows three devices attached to an ISDN switch at the central office. Two of these devices are ISDN-compatible, so they can be attached through an S reference point to NT2 devices. The third device (a standard, non-ISDN telephone) attaches through the reference point to a TA. Any of these devices also could attach to an NT1/2 device, which would replace both the NT1 and the NT2. In addition, although they are not shown, similar user stations are attached to the far right ISDN switch.

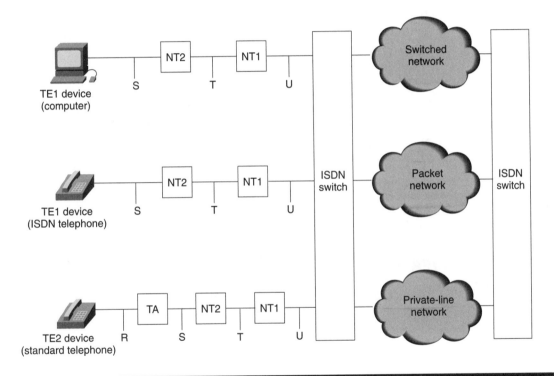

Figure 12–1
Sample ISDN configuration illustrates relationships between devices and reference points.

SERVICES

The ISDN *Basic Rate Interface* (BRI) service offers two *B channels* and one *D channel* (2B+D). BRI *B-channel service* operates at 64 kbps and is meant to carry user data; BRI *D-channel service* operates at 16 kbps and is meant to carry control and signaling information, although it can support user data transmission under certain circumstances. The D channel signaling protocol comprises Layers 1 through 3 of the OSI reference model. BRI also provides for framing control and other overhead, bringing its total bit rate to 192 kbps. The BRI physical-layer specification is *International Telecommunication Union Telecommunication Standardization Sector* (ITU-T) (formerly the *Consultative Committee for International Telegraph and Telephone* [CCITT]) I.430.

ISDN *Primary Rate Interface* (PRI) service offers 23 B channels and one D channel in North America and Japan, yielding a total bit rate of 1.544 Mbps (the PRI D channel runs at 64 Kbps). ISDN PRI in Europe, Australia, and other parts of the world provides 30 B channels plus one 64-Kbps D channel and a total interface rate of 2.048 Mbps. The PRI physical-layer specification is ITU-T I.431.

LAYER 1

ISDN physical-layer (Layer 1) frame formats differ depending on whether the frame is outbound (from terminal to network) or inbound (from network to terminal). Both physical-layer interfaces are shown in Figure 12–2).

The frames are 48 bits long, of which 36 bits represent data. The bits of an ISDN physical-layer frame are used as follows:

- *F*—Provides synchronization
- *L*—Adjusts the average bit value

- *E*—Ensures contention resolution when several terminals on a passive bus contend for a channel

- *A*—Activates devices

- *S*—Unassigned

- *B1, B2, and D*—Handles user data

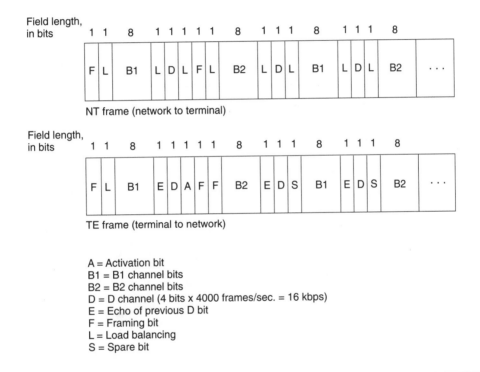

Figure 12–2
ISDN Physical-layer frame formats differ depending on their direction.

Multiple ISDN user devices can be physically attached to one circuit. In this configuration, collisions can result if two terminals transmit simultaneously. ISDN therefore provides features to determine link contention. When an NT receives a D bit from the TE, it echoes back the bit in the next E-bit position. The TE expects the next E bit to be the same as its last transmitted D bit.

Terminals cannot transmit into the D channel unless they first detect a specific number of ones (indicating "no signal") corresponding to a pre-established priority. If the TE detects a bit in the echo (E) channel that is different from its D bits, it must stop transmitting immediately. This simple technique ensures that only one terminal can transmit its D message at one time. After successful D-message transmission, the terminal has its priority reduced by requiring it to detect more continuous ones before transmitting. Terminals cannot raise their priority until all other devices on the same line have had an opportunity to send a D message. Telephone connections have higher priority than all other services, and signaling information has a higher priority than non-signaling information.

LAYER 2

Layer 2 of the ISDN signaling protocol is *Link Access Procedure, D channel (LAPD)*. LAPD is similar to *High-Level Data Link Control* (HDLC) and *Link Access Procedure, Balanced* (LAPB) (see Chapter 16, "Synchronous Data Link Control and Derivatives," and Chapter 17, "X.25," for more information on these protocols). As the expansion of the LAPD acronym indicates, this layer is used across the D channel to ensure that control and signaling information flows and is received properly. The LAPD frame format (see Figure 12–3) is very similar to that of HDLC and, like HDLC, LAPD uses *supervisory*, *information*, and *unnumbered* frames. The LAPD protocol is formally specified in ITU-T Q.920 and ITU-T Q.921.

The LAPD *Flag* and *Control* fields are identical to those of HDLC. The LAPD *Address* field can be either 1 or 2 bytes long. If the extended address bit of the first byte is set, the address is 1 byte; if it is not set, the address is 2 bytes. The first Address-field byte contains the *service access point identifier* (SAPI), which identifies the portal at which LAPD services are provided to Layer 3.

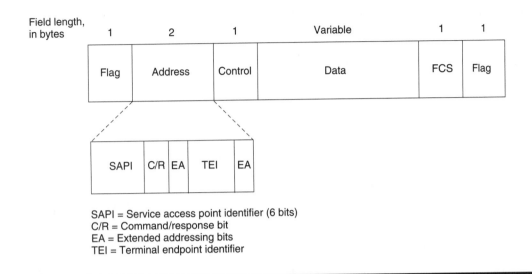

Figure 12–3
LAPD frame format is similar to HDLC and LAPB.

The C/R bit indicates whether the frame contains a command or a response. The *terminal end-point identifier* (TEI) field identifies either a single terminal or multiple terminals. A TEI of all ones indicates a broadcast.

LAYER 3

Two Layer 3 specifications are used for ISDN signaling: ITU-T (formerly CCITT) I.450 (also known as ITU-T Q.930) and ITU-T I.451 (also known as ITU-T Q.931). Together, these protocols support user-to-user, circuit-switched, and packet-switched connections. A variety of call-establishment, call-termination, information, and miscellaneous messages are specified, including SETUP, CONNECT, RELEASE, USER INFORMATION, CANCEL, STATUS, and DISCONNECT. These messages are functionally similar to those provided by the X.25 protocol (see Chapter 17 for more information). Figure 12–4, from ITU-T I.451, shows the typical stages of an ISDN circuit-switched call.

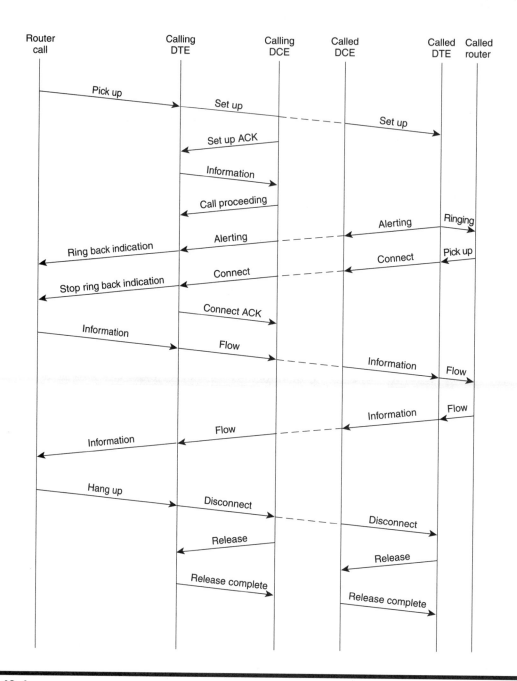

Figure 12–4

An ISDN circuit-switched call moves through various stages to its destination.

CHAPTER 13

Point-to-Point Protocol

BACKGROUND

The Point-to-Point Protocol (PPP) originally emerged as an encapsulation protocol for transporting IP traffic over point-to-point links. PPP also established a standard for the assignment and management of IP addresses, asynchronous (start/stop) and bit-oriented synchronous encapsulation, network protocol multiplexing, link configuration, link quality testing, error detection, and option negotiation for such capabilities as network-layer address negotiation and data-compression negotiation. PPP supports these functions by providing an extensible *Link Control Protocol* (LCP) and a family of *Network Control Protocols* (NCPs) to negotiate optional configuration parameters and facilities. In addition to IP, PPP supports other protocols, including Novell's Internetwork Packet Exchange (IPX) and DECnet. This chapter provides a summary of PPP's basic protocol elements and operations.

PPP COMPONENTS

PPP provides a method for transmitting datagrams over serial point-to-point links. PPP contains three main components:

- A method for encapsulating datagrams over serial links—PPP uses the *High-Level Data Link Control* (HDLC) protocol as a basis for encapsulating datagrams over point-to-point links. (See Chapter 16, "Synchronous Data Link Control and Derivatives," for more information on HDLC.)

- An extensible LCP to establish, configure, and test the data-link connection.

- A family of NCPs for establishing and configuring different network-layer protocols—PPP is designed to allow the simultaneous use of multiple network-layer protocols.

GENERAL OPERATION

To establish communications over a point-to-point link, the originating PPP first sends LCP frames to configure and (optionally) test the data-link. After the link has been established and optional facilities have been negotiated as needed by the LCP, the originating PPP sends NCP frames to choose and configure one or more network-layer protocols. When each of the chosen network-layer protocols has been configured, packets from each network-layer protocol can be sent over the link. The link will remain configured for communications until explicit LCP or NCP frames close the link, or until some external event occurs (for example, an inactivity timer expires or a user intervenes).

PHYSICAL-LAYER REQUIREMENTS

PPP is capable of operating across any DTE/DCE interface. Examples include EIA/TIA-232-C (formerly RS-232-C), EIA/TIA-422 (formerly RS-422), EIA/TIA-423 (formerly RS-423), and International Telecommunication Union Telecommunication Standardization Sector (ITU-T) (formerly CCITT) V.35. The only absolute requirement imposed by PPP is the provision of a duplex circuit, either dedicated or switched, that can operate in either an asynchronous or synchronous bit-serial mode, transparent to PPP link-layer frames. PPP does not impose any restrictions regarding transmission rate other than those imposed by the particular DTE/DCE interface in use.

PPP LINK LAYER

PPP uses the principles, terminology, and frame structure of the International Organization for Standardization (ISO) HDLC procedures (ISO 3309-1979), as modified by ISO 3309:1984/PDAD1 "Addendum 1: Start/stop transmission." ISO 3309-1979 specifies the HDLC frame structure for use in synchronous environments. ISO 3309:1984/PDAD1 specifies proposed modifications to ISO 3309-1979 to allow its use in asynchronous environments. The PPP control procedures use the definitions and control field encodings standardized in ISO 4335-1979 and ISO 4335-1979/Addendum 1-1979. The PPP frame format appears in Figure 13–1.

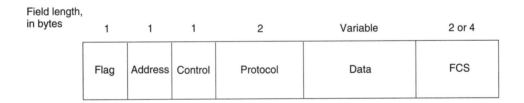

Figure 13–1
Six fields make up the PPP frame.

The following descriptions summarize the PPP frame fields illustrated in Figure 13–1:

- *Flag*—A single byte that indicates the beginning or end of a frame. The flag field consists of the binary sequence 01111110.

- *Address*—A single byte that contains the binary sequence 11111111, the standard broadcast address. PPP does not assign individual station addresses.

- *Control*—A single byte that contains the binary sequence 00000011, which calls for transmission of user data in an unsequenced frame. A connectionless link service similar to that of Logical Link Control (LLC) Type 1 is provided. (For more information about LLC types and frame types, refer to Chapter 16, "Synchronous Data Link Control and Derivatives.")

- *Protocol*—Two bytes that identify the protocol encapsulated in the information field of the frame. The most up-to-date values of the protocol field are specified in the most recent *Assigned Numbers Request for Comments* (RFC).

- *Data*—Zero or more bytes that contain the datagram for the protocol specified in the protocol field. The end of the information field is found by locating the closing flag sequence and allowing 2 bytes for the FCS field. The default maximum length of the information field is 1,500 bytes. By prior agreement, consenting PPP implementations can use other values for the maximum information field length.

- *Frame Check Sequence* (FCS)—Normally 16 bits (2 bytes). By prior agreement, consenting PPP implementations can use a 32-bit (4-byte) FCS for improved error detection.

The LCP can negotiate modifications to the standard PPP frame structure. Modified frames, however, always will be clearly distinguishable from standard frames.

PPP Link-Control Protocol

The PPP LCP provides a method of establishing, configuring, maintaining, and terminating the point-to-point connection. LCP goes through four distinct phases:

First, link establishment and configuration negotiation occurs. Before any network-layer datagrams (for example, IP) can be exchanged, LCP first must open the connection and negotiate configuration parameters. This phase is complete when a configuration-acknowledgment frame has been both sent and received.

This is followed by link-quality determination. LCP allows an optional link-quality determination phase following the link-establishment and configuration-negotiation phase. In this phase, the link is tested to determine whether the link quality is sufficient to bring up network-layer protocols. This phase is optional. LCP can delay transmission of network-layer protocol information until this phase is complete.

At this point, network-layer protocol configuration negotiation occurs. After LCP has finished the link-quality determination phase, network-layer protocols can be configured separately by the appropriate NCP and can be brought up and taken down at any time. If LCP closes the link, it informs the network-layer protocols so that they can take appropriate action.

Finally, link termination occurs. LCP can terminate the link at any time. This usually will be done at the request of a user but can happen because of a physical event, such as the loss of carrier or the expiration of an idle-period timer.

Three classes of LCP frames exist. Link-establishment frames are used to establish and configure a link. Link-termination frames are used to terminate a link, while link-maintenance frames are used to manage and debug a link.

These frames are used to accomplish the work of each of the LCP phases.

CHAPTER 14

Switched Multimegabit Data Service (SMDS)

BACKGROUND

Switched Multimegabit Data Service (SMDS) is a high-speed, packet-switched, datagram-based WAN networking technology used for communication over public data networks (PDNs). SMDS can use fiber- or copper-based media and supports speeds of 1.544 Mbps over Digital Signal level 1 (DS-1) transmission facilities, or 44.736 Mbps over Digital Signal level 3 (DS-3) transmission facilities. In addition, SMDS data units are large enough to encapsulate entire IEEE 802.3, IEEE 802.5, and Fiber-Distributed Data Interface (FDDI) frames. This chapter summarizes the operational elements of the SMDS environment and outlines the underlying protocol. A discussion of related technologies, such as Distributed Queue Dual Bus (DQDB) is also provided. The chapter closes with discussions of SMDS access classes and cell formats.

SMDS NETWORK COMPONENTS

SMDS networks feature several underlying entities to provide high-speed data service. These include *customer premises equipment* (CPE), *carrier equipment*, and the *subscriber network interface* (SNI). CPE is terminal equipment typically owned and maintained by the customer. CPE includes end devices, such as terminals and personal computers, and intermediate nodes, such as routers, modems, and multiplexers. Intermediate nodes, however, sometimes are provided by the SMDS carrier. Carrier equipment generally consists of high-speed WAN switches that must conform to certain network equipment specifications, such as those outlined by Bell Communications Research (Bellcore). These specifications define network operations, the interface between a local carrier network and a long-distance carrier network, and the interface between two switches inside a single carrier network.

The SNI is the interface between CPE and carrier equipment. This interface is the point at which the customer network ends and the carrier network begins. The function of the SNI is to render the technology and operation of the carrier SMDS network transparent to the customer. Figure 14–1 illustrates the relationship between these three components of an SMDS network.

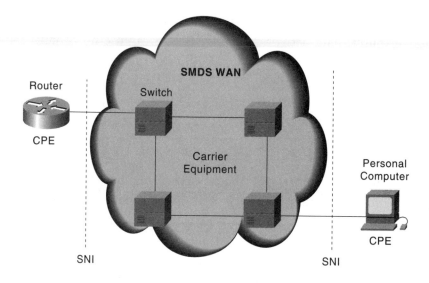

Figure 14–1

The SNI provides an interface between the CPE and the carrier equipment in SMDS.

SMDS INTERFACE PROTOCOL (SIP)

The SMDS Interface Protocol (SIP) is used for communications between CPE and SMDS carrier equipment. SIP provides connectionless service across the *subscriber-network interface* (SNI), allowing the CPE to access the SMDS network. SIP is based on the IEEE 802.6 *Distributed Queue Dual Bus (DQDB)* standard for cell relay across metropolitan-area networks (MANs). The DQDB was chosen as the basis for SIP because it is an open standard that supports all the SMDS service features. In addition, DQDB was designed for compatibility with current carrier transmission standards, and it is aligned with emerging standards for Broadband ISDN (BISDN), which will allow it to interoperate with broadband video and voice services. Figure 14–2 illustrates where SIP is used in an SMDS network.

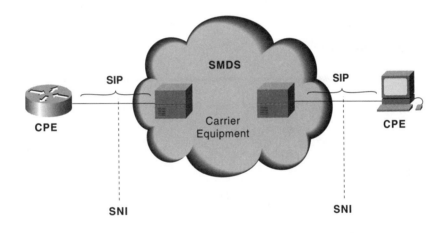

Figure 14–2
SIP provides connectionless service between the CPE and carrier equipment.

SIP Levels

SIP consists of three levels. *SIP Level 3* operates at the Media Access Control (MAC) sublayer of the data link layer of the OSI reference model. *SIP Level 2* operates at the MAC sublayer of the data link layer. *SIP Level 1* operates at the physical layer of the OSI reference model. Figure 14–3 illustrates how SIP maps to the OSI reference model, including the IEEE data link sublayers.

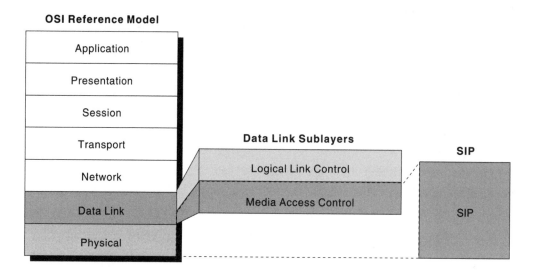

Figure 14–3
SIP provides services assoicated with the physical and data link layers of the OSI model.

SIP Level 3 begins operation when user information is passed to SIP Level 3 in the form of SMDS service data units (SDUs). SMDS SDUs then are encapsulated in a SIP Level 3 header and trailer. The resulting frame is called a Level 3 protocol data unit (PDU). SIP Level 3 PDUs then are subsequently passed to SIP Level 2.

SIP Level 2, which operates at the Media Access Control (MAC) sublayer of the data link layer, begins operating when it receives SIP Level 3 PDUs. The PDUs then are segmented into uniformly sized (53-octet) Level 2 PDUs, called cells. The cells are passed to SIP Level 1 for placement on the physical medium.

SIP Level 1 operates at the physical layer and provides the physical-link protocol that operates at DS-1 or DS-3 rates between CPE devices and the network. SIP Level 1 consists of the transmission system and Physical Layer Convergency Protocol (PLCP) sublayers. The *transmission system sublayer* defines the characteristics and method of attachment to a DS-1 or DS-3 transmission link. The PLCP specifies how SIP Level 2 cells are to be arranged relative to the DS-1 or DS-3 frame. PLCP also defines other management information.

DISTRIBUTED QUEUE DUAL BUS (DQDB)

The Distributed Queue Dual Bus (DQDB) is a data link layer communication protocol designed for use in metropolitan-area networks (MANs). DQDB specifies a network topology composed of two unidirectional logical buses that interconnect multiple systems. It is defined in the IEEE 802.6 DQDB standard.

An access DQDB describes just the operation of the DQDB protocol (in SMDS, SIP) across a user-network interface (in SMDS, across the SNI). Such operation is distinguished from the operation of a DQDB protocol in any other environment (for example, between carrier equipment within the SMDS PDN).

The access DQDB is composed of the basic SMDS network components:

- *Carrier equipment*—A switch in the SMDS network operates as one station on the bus.

- *CPE*—One or more CPE devices operate as stations on the bus.

- *SNI*—The SNI acts as the interface between the CPE and the carrier equipment.

Figure 14–4 depicts a basic access DQDB, with two CPE devices and one switch (carrier equipment) attached to the dual bus.

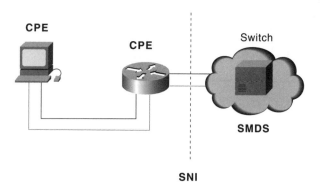

Figure 14–4

A basic access DQDB may consist of an end node, router, and a switch.

An SMDS access DQDB typically is arranged in a single-CPE configuration or a multi-CPE configuration.

A single-CPE access DQDB configuration consists of one switch in the carrier SMDS network and one CPE station at the subscriber site. Single-CPE DQDB configurations create a two-node DQDB subnetwork. Communication occurs only between the switch and the one CPE device across the SNI. No contention is on the bus because no other CPE devices attempt to access it.

A multi-CPE configuration consists of one switch in the carrier SMDS network and a number of interconnected CPE devices at the subscriber site (all belonging to the same subscriber). In multi-CPE configurations, local communication between CPE devices is possible. Some local communication will be visible to the switch serving the SNI, and some will not.

Contention for the bus by multiple devices requires the use of the DQDB distributed queuing algorithm, which makes implementing a multi-CPE configuration more complicated than implementing a single-CPE configuration.

SMDS ACCESS CLASSES

SMDS access classes enable SMDS networks to accommodate a broad range of traffic requirements and equipment capabilities. Access classes constrain CPE devices to a sustained or average rate of data transfer by establishing a maximum sustained information transfer rate and a maximum allowed degree of traffic *burstiness*. (Burstiness in this context is the propensity of a network to experience sudden increases in bandwidth demand.) SMDS access classes sometimes are implemented using a credit-management scheme. In this case, a credit-management algorithm creates and tracks a credit balance for each customer interface. As packets are sent into the network, the credit balance is decremented. New credits are allocated periodically, up to an established maximum. Credit management is used only on DS-3 rate SMDS interfaces, not on DS-1 rate interfaces.

Five access classes are supported for DS-3-rate access (corresponding to sustained information rates). Data rates supported are 4, 10, 16, 25, and 34 Mbps.

SMDS ADDRESSING OVERVIEW

SMDS protocol data units (PDUs) carry both a source and a destination address. SMDS addresses are 10-digit values resembling conventional telephone numbers.

The SMDS addressing implementation offers group addressing and security features.

SMDS group addresses allow a single address to refer to multiple CPE stations, which specify the group address in the Destination Address field of the PDU. The network makes multiple copies of the PDU, which are delivered to all members of the group. Group addresses reduce the amount of network resources required for distributing routing information, resolving addresses, and dynamically discovering network resources. SMDS group addressing is analogous to multicasting on LANs.

SMDS implements two security features: source address validation and address screening. *Source address validation* ensures that the PDU source address is legitimately assigned to the SNI from which it originated. Source address validation prevents address spoofing, in which illegal traffic assumes the source address of a legitimate device. *Address screening* allows a subscriber to establish a private virtual network that excludes unwanted traffic. If an address is disallowed, the data unit is not delivered.

SMDS Reference: SIP Level 3 PDU Format

Figure 14–5 illustrates the format of the SMDS Interface Protocol (SIP) Level 3 protocol data unit (PDU).

The following descriptions briefly summarize the function of the SIP Level 3 PDU fields illustrated in Figure 14–5:

- *X+*—Ensures that the SIP PDU format aligns with the DQDB protocol format. SMDS does not process or change the values in these fields, which may be used by systems connected to the SMDS network.

- *RSVD*—Consists of zeros.

- *BEtag*—Forms an association between the first and last segments of a segmented SIP Level 3 PDU. Both fields contain identical values and are used to detect a condition in which the last segment of one PDU and the first segment of the next PDU are both lost, which results in the receipt of an invalid Level 3 PDU.

- *BAsize*—Contains the buffer allocation size.

Field Length,
in Bytes

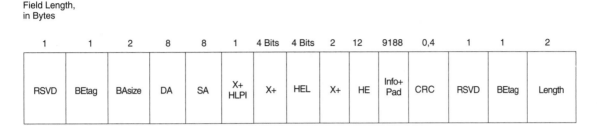

1	1	2	8	8	1	4 Bits	4 Bits	2	12	9188	0,4	1	1	2
RSVD	BEtag	BAsize	DA	SA	X+ HLPI	X+	HEL	X+	HE	Info+ Pad	CRC	RSVD	BEtag	Length

```
RSVD      =  Reserved
BEtag     =  Beginning-end Tag
BAsize    =  Buffer Allocation Size
DA        =  Destination Address
SA        =  Source Address
HLPI      =  Higher-layer Protocol Identifier
X+        =  Carried Across Network Unchanged
HEL       =  Header Extension Length
HE        =  Header Extension
Info+Pad  =  Information + Padding
             (to ensure that this field ends on a 32-bit boundary)
CRC       =  Cyclic Redundancy Check
```

Figure 14–5
SIP Level 3 protocol data unit consists of 15 fields.

- *Destination Address (DA)—*Consists of two parts:
  - Address Type: Occupies the four most significant bits of the field. The Address Type can be either 1100 or 1110. The former indicates a 60-bit individual address, while the latter indicates a 60-bit group address.
  - Address: The individual or group SMDS address for the destination. SMDS address formats are consistent with the North American Numbering Plan (NANP).
    The four most significant bits of the Destination Address subfield contain the value 0001 (the internationally defined country code for North America). The next 40 bits contain the binary-encoded value of the 10-digit SMDS address. The final 16 (least-significant) bits are populated with ones for padding.

- *Source Address (SA)*—Consists of two parts:

  ○ Address type: Occupies the four most significant bits of the field. The Source Address Type field can indicate only an individual address.

  ○ Address: Occupies the individual SMDS address of the source. This field follows the same format as the Address subfield of the Destination Address field.

- *Higher Layer Protocol Identifier (HLPI)*—Indicates the type of protocol encapsulated in the Information field. The value is not important to SMDS but can be used by certain systems connected to the network.

- *Header Extension Length (HEL)*—Indicates the number of 32-bit words in the Header Extension (HE) field. Currently, the field size for SMDS is fixed at 12 bytes. (Thus, the HEL value is always 0011.)

- *Header Extension (HE)*—Contains the SMDS version number. This field also conveys the carrier-selection value, which is used to select the particular interexchange carrier to carry SMDS traffic from one local carrier network to another.

- *Information and Padding (Info + Pad)*—Contains an encapsulated SMDS service data unit (SDU) and padding that ensures that the field ends on a 32-bit boundary.

- *Cyclic Redundancy Check (CRC)*—Contains a value used for error checking.

- *Length*—Indicates the length of the PDU.

SMDS REFERENCE: SIP LEVEL 2 CELL FORMAT

Figure 14–6 illustrates the format of the SMDS Interface Protocol (SIP) Level 2 cell format.

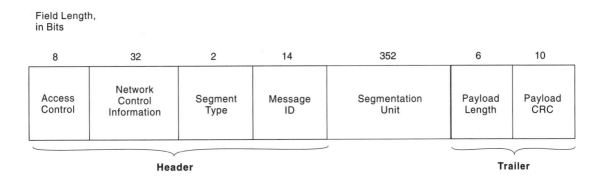

Figure 14-6
Seven fields comprise the SMDS SIP Level 2 cell.

The following descriptions briefly summarize the function of the SIP Level 2 PDU fields illustrated in Figure 14–6:

- *Access Control*—Contains different values, depending on the direction of information flow. If the cell was sent from a switch to a CPE device, only the indication of whether the Level 3 protocol data unit (PDU) contains information is important. If the cell was sent from a CPE device to a switch, and if the CPE configuration is multi-CPE, this field can carry request bits that indicate bids for cells on the bus going from the switch to the CPE device.

- *Network Control Information*—Contains a value indicating whether the PDU contains information.

- *Segment Type*—Indicates whether the cell is the first, last, or a middle cell from a segmented Level 3 PDU. Four possible Segment Type values exist:
  - 00: Continuation of message
  - 01: End of message
  - 10: Beginning of message
  - 11: Single-segment message

- *Message ID*—Associates Level 2 cells with a Level 3 PDU. The Message ID is the same for all of the segments of a given Level 3 PDU. In a multi-CPE configuration, Level 3 PDUs originating from different CPE devices must have a different Message ID. This allows the SMDS network receiving interleaved cells from different Level 3 PDUs to associate each Level 2 cell with the correct Level 3 PDU.

- *Segmentation Unit*—Contains the data portion of the cell. If the Level 2 cell is empty, this field is populated with zeros.

- *Payload Length*—Indicates how many bytes of a Level 3 PDU actually are contained in the Segmentation Unit field. If the Level 2 cell is empty, this field is populated with zeros.

- *Payload Cyclic Redundancy Check (CRC)*—Contains a CRC value used to detect errors in the following fields:

  - Segment Type
  - Message ID
  - Segmentation Unit
  - Payload Length
  - Payload CRC

The Payload CRC value does not cover the Access Control or the Network Control Information fields.

CHAPTER 15

Digital Subscriber Line

Digital Subscriber Line (DSL) technology is a modem technology that uses existing twisted-pair telephone lines to transport high-bandwidth data, such as multimedia and video, to service subscribers. The term *xDSL* covers a number of similar yet competing forms of DSL technologies, including ADSL, SDSL, HDSL, RADSL, and VDSL. xDSL is drawing significant attention from implementers and service providers because it promises to deliver high-bandwidth data rates to dispersed locations with relatively small changes to the existing telco infrastructure. xDSL services are dedicated, point-to-point, public network access over twisted-pair copper wire on the local loop ("last mile") between a network service provider's (NSP's) central office and the customer site, or on local loops created either intra-building or intra-campus. Currently the primary focus in xDSL is the development and deployment of ADSL and VDSL technologies and architectures. This chapter covers the characteristics and operations of ADSL and VDSL.

ASYMMETRIC DIGITAL SUBSCRIBER LINE (ADSL)

ADSL technology is asymmetric. It allows more bandwidth downstream—from an NSP's central office to the customer site—than upstream from the subscriber to the central office. This asymmetry, combined with always-on access (which eliminates call setup), makes ADSL ideal for Internet/intranet surfing, video-on-demand, and remote LAN access. Users of these applications typically download much more information than they send.

ADSL transmits more than 6 Mbps to a subscriber, and as much as 640 kbps more in both directions (shown in Figure 15–1). Such rates expand existing access capacity by a factor of 50 or more without new cabling. ADSL can literally transform the existing public information network from one limited to voice, text, and low-resolution graphics to a powerful, ubiquitous system capable of bringing multimedia, including full motion video, to every home this century.

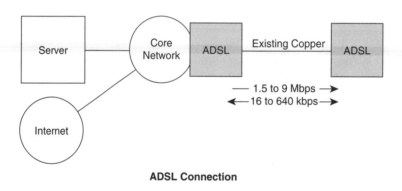

ADSL Connection

Figure 15–1
The components of a ADSL network include a telco and a CPE.

ADSL will play a crucial role over the next decade or more as telephone companies enter new markets for delivering information in video and multimedia formats. New broadband cabling will take decades to reach all prospective subscribers. Success of these new services will depend on reaching as many subscribers as possible during the first few years. By bringing movies, television, video catalogs, remote CD-ROMs, corporate LANs, and the Internet into homes and small businesses, ADSL will make these markets viable and profitable for telephone companies and application suppliers alike.

ADSL Capabilities

An ADSL circuit connects an ADSL modem on each end of a twisted-pair telephone line, creating three information channels—a high-speed downstream channel, a medium-speed duplex channel, and a basic telephone service channel. The basic telephone service channel is split off from the digital modem by filters, thus guaranteeing uninterrupted basic telephone service, even if ADSL fails. The high-speed channel ranges from 1.5 to 6.1 Mbps, and duplex rates range from 16 to 640 kbps. Each channel can be submultiplexed to form multiple lower-rate channels.

ADSL modems provide data rates consistent with North American T1 1.544 Mbps and European E1 2.048 Mbps digital hierarchies (see Figure 15–2) and can be purchased with various speed ranges and capabilities. The minimum configuration provides 1.5 or 2.0 Mbps downstream and a 16 kbps duplex channel; others provide rates of 6.1 Mbps and 64 kbps duplex. Products with downstream rates up to 8 Mbps and duplex rates up to 640 kbps are available today. ADSL modems accommodate Asynchronous Transfer Mode (ATM) transport with variable rates and compensation for ATM overhead, as well as IP protocols.

Downstream data rates depend on a number of factors, including the length of the copper line, its wire gauge, presence of bridged taps, and cross-coupled interference. Line attenuation increases with line length and frequency and decreases as wire diameter increases. Ignoring bridged taps, ADSL performs as shown in Table 15–1.

Downstream Bearer Channels	
n x 1.536 Mbps	1.536 Mbps
	3.072 Mbps
	4.608 Mbps
	6.144 Mbps
n x 2.048 Mbps	2.048 Mbps
	4.096 Mbps
Duplex Bearer Channels	
C Channel	16 Kbps
	64 Kbps
Optional Channels	160 Kbps
	384 Kbps
	544 Kbps
	576 Kbps

Figure 15–2
This chart shows the speeds for downstream bearer and duplex bearer channels.

Data Rate (Mbps)	Wire Gauge (AWG)	Distance (feet)	Wire Size (mm)	Distance (km)
1.5 or 2	24	18,000	0.5	5.5
1.5 or 2	26	15,000	0.4	4.6
6.1	24	12,000	0.5	3.7
6.1	26	9,000	0.4	2.7

Table 15-1
Claimed ADSL Physical-Media Performance

Although the measure varies from telco to telco, these capabilities can cover up to 95% of a loop plant, depending on the desired data rate. Customers beyond these distances can be reached with fiber-based digital loop carrier (DLC) systems. As these DLC systems become commercially available, telephone companies can offer virtually ubiquitous access in a relatively short time.

Many applications envisioned for ADSL involve digital compressed video. As a real-time signal, digital video cannot use link- or network-level error control procedures commonly found in data communications systems. ADSL modems therefore incorporate forward error correction that dramatically reduces errors caused by impulse noise. Error correction on a symbol-by-symbol basis also reduces errors caused by continuous noise coupled into a line.

ADSL Technology

ADSL depends on advanced digital signal processing and creative algorithms to squeeze so much information through twisted-pair telephone lines. In addition, many advances have been required in transformers, analog filters, and analog/digital (A/D) converters. Long telephone lines may attenuate signals at 1 MHz (the outer edge of the band used by ADSL) by as much as 90 dB, forcing analog sections of ADSL modems to work very hard to realize large dynamic ranges, separate channels, and maintain low noise figures. On the outside, ADSL looks simple—transparent synchronous data pipes at various data rates over ordinary telephone lines. The inside, where all the transistors work, is a miracle of modern technology. Figure 15–3 displays the ADSL transceiver-network end.

To create multiple channels, ADSL modems divide the available bandwidth of a telephone line in one of two ways—frequency-division multiplexing (FDM) or echo cancellation—as shown in Figure 15–4. FDM assigns one band for upstream data and another band for downstream data. The downstream path is then divided by time-division multiplexing into one or more high-speed channels and one or more low-speed channels. The upstream path is also multiplexed into corresponding low-speed channels. Echo cancellation assigns the upstream band to overlap the downstream, and separates the two by means of local echo cancellation, a technique well known in V.32 and V.34 modems. With either technique, ADSL splits off a 4 kHz region for basic telephone service at the DC end of the band.

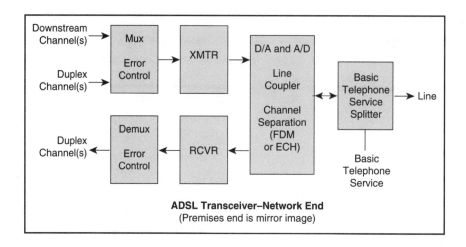

Figure 15–3

This diagram provides an overview of the devices that make up the ADSL transceiver–network end of the topology.

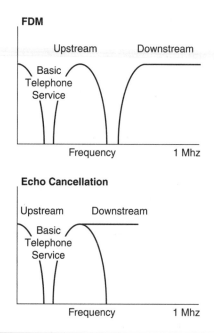

Figure 15–4

ADSL uses FDM and echo cancellation to divide the available bandwidth for services.

An ADSL modem organizes the aggregate data stream created by multiplexing downstream channels, duplex channels, and maintenance channels together into blocks, and attaches an error correction code to each block. The receiver then corrects errors that occur during transmission up to the limits implied by the code and the block length. The unit may, at the user's option, also create superblocks by interleaving data within subblocks; this allows the receiver to correct any combination of errors within a specific span of bits. This in turn allows for effective transmission of both data and video signals.

ADSL Standards and Associations

The American National Standards Institute (ANSI) Working Group T1E1.4 recently approved an ADSL standard at rates up to 6.1 Mbps (ANSI Standard T1.413). The European Technical Standards Institute (ETSI) contributed an annex to T1.413 to reflect European requirements. T1.413 currently embodies a single terminal interface at the premises end. Issue II, now under study by T1E1.4, will expand the standard to include a multiplexed interface at the premises end, protocols for configuration and network management, and other improvements.

The ATM Forum and the Digital Audio-Visual Council (DAVIC) have both recognized ADSL as a physical-layer transmission protocol for UTP media.

The ADSL Forum was formed in December 1994 to promote the ADSL concept and facilitate development of ADSL system architectures, protocols, and interfaces for major ADSL applications. The forum has more than 200 members, representing service providers, equipment manufacturers, and semiconductor companies throughout the world. At present, the Forum's formal technical work is divided into the following six areas, each of which is dealt with in a separate working group within the technical committee:

- ATM over ADSL (including transport and end-to-end architecture aspects)
- Packet over ADSL (this working group recently completed its work)

- CPE/CO (customer premises equipment/central office) configurations and interfaces

- Operations

- Network management

- Testing and interoperability

ADSL Market Status

ADSL modems have been tested successfully in more than 30 telephone companies, and thousands of lines have been installed in various technology trials in North America and Europe. Several telephone companies plan market trials using ADSL, principally for data access, but also including video applications for uses such as personal shopping, interactive games, and educational programming.

Semiconductor companies have introduced transceiver chipsets that are already being used in market trials. These chipsets combine off-the-shelf components, programmable digital signal processors, and custom ASICs (application-specific integrated circuits). Continued investment by these semiconductor companies has increased functionality and reduced chip count, power consumption, and cost, enabling mass deployment of ADSL-based services.

VERY-HIGH-DATA-RATE DIGITAL SUBSCRIBER LINE (VDSL)

It is becoming increasingly clear that telephone companies around the world are making decisions to include existing twisted-pair loops in their next-generation broadband access networks. Hybrid fiber coax (HFC), a shared-access medium well suited to analog and digital broadcast, comes up somewhat short when used to carry voice telephony, interactive video, and high-speed data communications at the same time. Fiber all the way to the home (FTTH) is still prohibitively expensive in a marketplace soon to be driven by competition rather than cost. An attractive alternative, soon to be commercially practical, is a combination of fiber cables feeding neighborhood optical network units (ONUs) and last-leg-premises connections by existing or new copper. This topology, which is often called fiber to the neighborhood (FTTN), encompasses fiber to the curb (FTTC) with short drops and fiber to the basement (FTTB), serving tall buildings with vertical drops.

One of the enabling technologies for FTTN is VDSL. In simple terms, VDSL transmits high-speed data over short reaches of twisted-pair copper telephone lines, with a range of speeds depending on actual line length. The maximum downstream rate under consideration is between 51 and 55 Mbps over lines up to 1000 feet (300 m) in length. Downstream speeds as low as 13 Mbps over lengths beyond 4000 feet (1500 m) are also common. Upstream rates in early models will be asymmetric, just like ADSL, at speeds from 1.6 to 2.3 Mbps. Both data channels will be separated in frequency from bands used for basic telephone service and Integrated Services Digital Network (ISDN), enabling service providers to overlay VDSL on existing services. At present the two high-speed channels are also separated in frequency. As needs arise for higher-speed upstream channels or symmetric rates, VDSL systems may need to use echo cancellation.

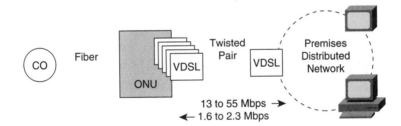

Figure 15–5
This diagram provides an overview of the devices in a VDSL network.

VDSL Projected Capabilities

Although VDSL has not achieved ADSL's degree of definition, it has advanced far enough that we can discuss realizable goals, beginning with data rate and range. Downstream rates derive from submultiples of the SONET (Synchronous Optical Network) and SDH (Synchronous Digital Hierarchy) canonical speed of 155.52 Mbps, namely 51.84 Mbps, 25.92 Mbps, and 12.96 Mbps. Each rate has a corresponding target range:

Target Range (Mbps)	Distance (feet)	Distance (meters)
12.96–13.8	4500	1500
25.92–27.6	3000	1000
51.84–55.2	1000	300

Upstream rates under discussion fall into three general ranges:

- 1.6–2.3 Mbps

- 19.2 Mbps

- Equal to downstream

Early versions of VDSL will almost certainly incorporate the slower asymmetric rate. Higher upstream and symmetric configurations may only be possible for very short lines. Like ADSL, VDSL must transmit compressed video, a real-time signal unsuited to error retransmission schemes used in data communications. To achieve error rates compatible with those of compressed video, VDSL will have to incorporate forward error correction (FEC) with sufficient interleaving to correct all errors created by impulsive noise events of some specified duration. Interleaving introduces delay, on the order of 40 times the maximum length correctable impulse.

Data in the downstream direction will be broadcast to every CPE on the premises or be transmitted to a logically separated hub that distributes data to addressed CPE based on cell or time-division multiplexing (TDM) within the data stream itself. Upstream multiplexing is more difficult. Systems using a passive network termination (NT) must insert data onto a shared medium, either by a form of TDM access (TDMA) or a form of frequency-division multiplexing (FDM). TDMA may use a species of token control called cell grants passed in the downstream direction from the ONU modem, or contention, or both (contention for unrecognized devices, cell grants for recognized devices). FDM gives each CPE its own channel, obviating a Media Access Control (MAC) protocol, but either limiting data rates available to any one CPE or requiring dynamic allocation of bandwidth and inverse multiplexing at each CPE. Systems using active NTs transfer the upstream collection problem to a logically separated hub that would use (typically) Ethernet or ATM protocols for upstream multiplexing.

Migration and inventory considerations dictate VDSL units that can operate at various (preferably all) speeds with automatic recognition of a newly connected device to a line or a change in speed. Passive network interfaces need to have hot insertion, where a new VDSL premises unit can be put on the line without interfering with the operation of other modems.

VDSL Technology

VDSL technology resembles ADSL to a large degree, although ADSL must face much larger dynamic ranges and is considerably more complex as a result. VDSL must be lower in cost and lower in power, and premises VDSL units may have to implement a physical-layer MAC for multiplexing upstream data.

Line Code Candidates

Four line codes have been proposed for VDSL:

- *CAP (carrierless amplitude modulation/phase modulation)*—A version of suppressed carrier quadrature amplitude modulation (QAM). For passive NT configurations, CAP would use quadrature phase shift keying (QPSK) upstream and a type of TDMA for multiplexing (although CAP does not preclude an FDM approach to upstream multiplexing).

- *DMT (discrete multitone)*—A multicarrier system using discrete fourier transforms to create and demodulate individual carriers. For passive

NT configurations, DMT would use FDM for upstream multiplexing (although DMT does not preclude a TDMA multiplexing strategy).

- *DWMT (discrete wavelet multitone)*—A multicarrier system using wavelet transforms to create and demodulate individual carriers. DWMT also uses FDM for upstream multiplexing, but also allows TDMA.

- *SLC (simple line code)*—A version of four-level baseband signaling that filters the based band and restores it at the receiver. For passive NT configurations, SLC would most likely use TDMA for upstream multiplexing, although FDM is possible.

Channel Separation

Early versions of VDSL will use frequency division multiplexing to separate downstream from upstream channels and both of them from basic telephone service and ISDN (shown in Figure 15–6). Echo cancellation may be required for later-generation systems featuring symmetric data rates. A rather substantial distance, in frequency, will be maintained between the lowest data channel and basic telephone service to enable very simple and cost-effective basic telephone service splitters. Normal practice would locate the downstream channel above the upstream channel. However, the DAVIC specification reverses this order to enable premises distribution of VDSL signals over coaxial cable systems.

Forward Error Control

FEC will no doubt use a form of Reed Soloman coding and optional interleaving to correct bursts of errors caused by impulse noise. The structure will be very similar to ADSL, as defined in T1.413. An outstanding question is whether FEC overhead (in the range of 8%) will be taken from the payload capacity or added as an out-of-band signal. The former reduces payload capacity but maintains nominal reach, whereas the latter retains the nominal payload but suffers a small reduction in reach. ADSL puts FEC overhead out of band.

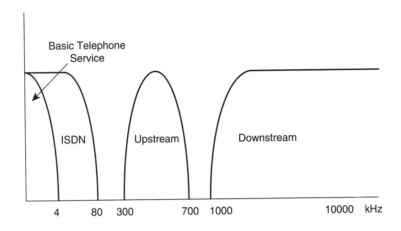

Basic Telephone
Service

ISDN   Upstream   Downstream

4   80   300   700 1000   10000   kHz

Figure 15–6
Early versions of VDSL will use FDM to separate downstream from upstream channels and both of them from basic telphone service and ISDN, as this example shows.

Upstream Multiplexing

If the premises VDSL unit comprises the network termination (an active NT), then the means of multiplexing upstream cells or data channels from more than one CPE into a single upstream becomes the responsibility of the premises network. The VDSL unit simply presents raw data streams in both directions. As illustrated in Figure 15–7, one type of premises network involves a star connecting each CPE to a switching or multiplexing hub; such a hub could be integral to the premises VDSL unit.

In a passive NT configuration, each CPE has an associated VDSL unit. (A passive NT does not conceptually preclude multiple CPE per VDSL, but then the question of active versus passive NT becomes a matter of ownership, not a matter of wiring topology and multiplexing strategies.) Now the upstream channels for each CPE must share a common wire. Although a collision-detection system could be used, the desire for guaranteed bandwidth indicates one of two solutions. The first invokes a cell-grant protocol in which downstream frames generated at the ONU or farther up the network contain a few bits that grant access to specific CPE during a specified period subsequent to receiving a frame. A granted CPE can send one upstream cell during this period. The transmitter in the CPE must turn on, send a preamble to condition the ONU receiver, send the cell, and then turn itself off. The protocol must insert enough silence to let line ringing clear. One construction of this protocol uses 77 octet intervals to transmit a single 53-octet cell.

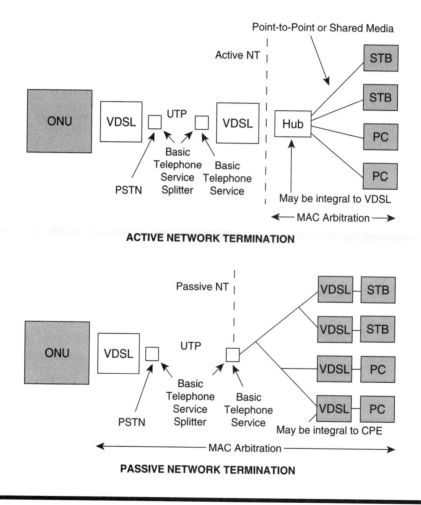

Figure 15–7

This figure shows examples of termination methods in passive and active networks.

The second method divides the upstream channel into frequency bands and assigns one band to each CPE. This method has the advantage of avoiding any MAC with its associated overhead (although a multiplexor must be built in to the ONU), but either restricts the data rate available to any one CPE or imposes a dynamic inverse multiplexing scheme that lets one CPE send more than its share for a period. The latter would look a great deal like a MAC protocol, but without the loss of bandwidth associated with carrier detect and clear for each cell.

VDSL Issues

VDSL is still in the definition stage; some preliminary products exist, but not enough is known yet about telephone line characteristics, radio frequency interface emissions and susceptibility, upstream multiplexing protocols, and information requirements to frame a set of definitive, standardizable properties. One large unknown is the maximum distance that VDSL can reliably realize for a given data rate. This is unknown because real line characteristics at the frequencies required for VDSL are speculative, and items such as short bridged taps or unterminated extension lines in homes, which have no effect on telephony, ISDN, or ADSL, may have very detrimental affects on VDSL in certain configurations. Furthermore, VDSL invades the frequency ranges of amateur radio, and every above-ground telephone wire is an antenna that both radiates and attracts energy in amateur radio bands. Balancing low signal levels to prevent emissions that interfere with amateur radio with higher signals needed to combat interference by amateur radio could be the dominant factor in determining line reach.

A second dimension of VDSL that is far from clear is the services environment. It can be assumed that VDSL will carry information in ATM cell format for video and asymmetric data communications, although optimum downstream and upstream data rates have not been ascertained. What is more difficult to assess is the need for VDSL to carry information in non-ATM formats (such as conventional Plesiochronous Digital Hierarchy [PDH] structures) and the need for symmetric channels at broadband rates (above T1/E1).

VDSL will not be completely independent of upper-layer protocols, particularly in the upstream direction, where multiplexing data from more than one CPE may require knowledge of link-layer formats (that is, ATM or not).

A third difficult subject is premises distribution and the interface between the telephone network and CPE. Cost considerations favor a passive network interface with premises VDSL installed in CPE and upstream multiplexing handled similarly to LAN buses. System management, reliability, regulatory constraints, and migration favor an active network termination, just like ADSL and ISDN, that can operate like a hub, with point-to-point or shared-media distribution to multiple CPE on-premises wiring that is independent and physically isolated from network wiring.

However, costs cannot be ignored. Small ONUs must spread common equipment costs, such as fiber links, interfaces, and equipment cabinets, over a small number of subscribers compared to HFC. VDSL therefore has a much lower cost target than ADSL because VDSL may connect directly from a wiring center or cable modems, which also have much lower common equipment costs per user. Furthermore, VDSL for passive NTs may (only *may*) be more expensive than VDSL for active NTs, but the elimination of any other premises network electronics may make it the most cost-effective solution, and highly desired, despite the obvious benefits of an active NT. Stay tuned.

Standards Status

At present five standards organizations/forums have begun work on VDSL:

- *T1E1.4*—The U.S. ANSI standards group T1E1.4 has just begun a project for VDSL, making a first attack on system requirements that will evolve into a system and protocol definition.

- *ETSI*—The ETSI has a VDSL standards project, under the title High-Speed Metallic Access Systems, and has compiled a list of objective, problems, and requirements. Among its preliminary findings are the need for an active NT and payloads in multiples of SDH virtual container VC-12, or 2.3 Mbps. ETSI works very closely with T1E1.4 and the ADSL Forum, with significant overlapping attendees.

- *DAVIC*—DAVIC has taken the earliest position on VDSL. Its first specification due to be finalized will define a line code for downstream data, another for upstream data, and a MAC for upstream multiplexing based on TDMA over shared wiring. DAVIC is only specifying VDSL for a single downstream rate of 51.84 Mbps and a single upstream rate of 1.6 Mbps over 300 m or less of copper. The proposal assumes, and is driven to a large extent by, a passive NT, and further assumes premises distribution from the NT over new coaxial cable or new copper wiring.

- *The ATM Forum*—The ATM Forum has defined a 51.84 Mbps interface for private network UNIs and a corresponding transmission technology. It has also taken up the question of CPE distribution and delivery of ATM all the way to premises over the various access technologies described above.

- *The ADSL Forum*—The ADSL Forum has just begun consideration of VDSL. In keeping with its charter, the forum will address network, protocol, and architectural aspects of VDSL for all prospective applications, leaving line code and transceiver protocols to T1E1.4 and ETSI and higher-layer protocols to organizations such as the ATM Forum and DAVIC.

VDSL's Relationship with ADSL

VDSL has an odd technical resemblance to ADSL. VDSL achieves data rates nearly 10 times greater than those of ADSL (shown in Figure 15–8), but ADSL is the more complex transmission technology, in large part because ADSL must contend with much larger dynamic ranges than VDSL. However, the two are essentially cut from the same cloth. ADSL employs advanced transmission techniques and forward error correction to realize data rates from 1.5 to 9 Mbps over twisted pair, ranging to 18,000 feet; VDSL employs the same advanced transmission techniques and forward error correction to realize data rates from 13 to 55 Mbps over twisted pair, ranging to 4,500 feet. Indeed, the two can be considered a continuum, a set of transmission tools that delivers about as much data as theoretically possible over varying distances of existing telephone wiring.

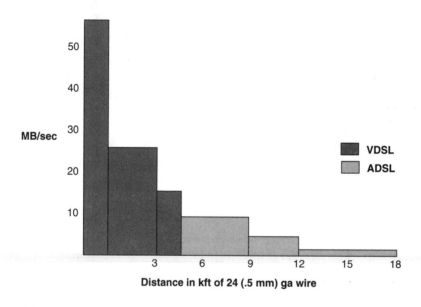

Figure 15–8
This chart provides a comparison of transfer rates between ADSL and VDSL.

VDSL is clearly a technology suitable for a full-service network (assuming that *full service* does not imply more than two high-definition television [HDTV] channels over the highest-rate VDSL). It is equally clear that telephone companies cannot deploy ONUs overnight, even if all the technology were available. ADSL may not be a full-service network technology, but it has the singular advantage of offering service over lines that exist today, and ADSL products are closer in time than VDSL. Many new services being contemplated today—such as videoconferencing, Internet access, video on demand, and remote LAN access—can be delivered at speeds at or below

T1/E1 rates. For such services, ADSL/VDSL provides an ideal combination for network evolution. On the longest lines, ADSL delivers a single channel. As line length shrinks, either from natural proximity to a central office or deployment of fiber-based access nodes, ADSL and VDSL simply offer more channels and capacity for services that require rates above T1/E1 (such as digital live television and virtual CD-ROM access).

CHAPTER 16

Synchronous Data Link Control and Derivatives

BACKGROUND

IBM developed the Synchronous Data Link Control (SDLC) protocol in the mid-1970s for use in Systems Network Architecture (SNA) environments. SDLC was the first link-layer protocol based on synchronous, bit-oriented operation. This chapter provides a summary of SDLC's basic operational characteristics and outlines several derivative protocols.

After developing SDLC, IBM submitted it to various standards committees. The International Organization for Standardization (ISO) modified SDLC to create the High-Level Data Link Control (HDLC) protocol. The International Telecommunication Union–Telecommunication Standardization Sector (ITU-T; formerly CCITT) subsequently modified HDLC to create Link Access Procedure (LAP), and then Link Access Procedure, Balanced (LAPB). The Institute of Electrical and Electronic Engineers (IEEE) modified HDLC to create IEEE 802.2. Each of these protocols has become important in its own domain, but SDLC remains the primary SNA link-layer protocol for WAN links.

215

SDLC TYPES AND TOPOLOGIES

SDLC supports a variety of link types and topologies. It can be used with point-to-point and multipoint links, bounded and unbounded media, half-duplex and full-duplex transmission facilities, and circuit-switched and packet-switched networks.

SDLC identifies two types of network nodes: primary and secondary. *Primary* nodes control the operation of other stations, called *secondaries*. The primary polls the secondaries in a predetermined order, and secondaries can then transmit if they have outgoing data. The primary also sets up and tears down links and manages the link while it is operational. *Secondary* nodes are controlled by a primary, which means that secondaries can send information to the primary only if the primary grants permission.

SDLC primaries and secondaries can be connected in four basic configurations:

- *Point-to-point*—Involves only two nodes, one primary and one secondary.

- *Multipoint*—Involves one primary and multiple secondaries.

- *Loop*—Involves a loop topology, with the primary connected to the first and last secondaries. Intermediate secondaries pass messages through one another as they respond to the requests of the primary.

- *Hub go-ahead*—Involves an inbound and an outbound channel. The primary uses the outbound channel to communicate with the secondaries. The secondaries use the inbound channel to communicate with the primary. The inbound channel is daisy-chained back to the primary through each secondary.

SDLC FRAME FORMAT

The SDLC frame is shown in Figure 16–1.

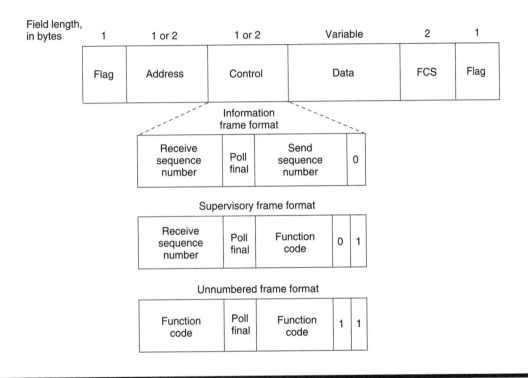

Figure 16–1
Six fields comprise the SDLC frame.

The following descriptions summarize the fields illustrated in Figure 16–1:

- *Flag*—Initiates and terminates error checking.

- *Address*—Contains the SDLC address of the secondary station, which indicates whether the frame comes from the primary or secondary. This address can contain a specific address, a group address, or a broadcast address. A primary is either a communication source or a destination, which eliminates the need to include the address of the primary.

- *Control*—Employs three different formats, depending on the type of SDLC frame used:

  - *Information (I) frame*: Carries upper-layer information and some control information. This frame sends and receives sequence numbers, and the poll final (P/F) bit performs flow and error control. The send-sequence number refers to the number of the frame to be sent next. The receive-sequence number provides the number of the frame to be received next. Both sender and receiver maintain send- and receive-sequence numbers.

    A primary station uses the P/F bit to tell the secondary whether it requires an immediate response. A secondary station uses the P/F bit to tell the primary whether the current frame is the last in its current response.

  - *Supervisory (S) frame*: Provides control information. An S frame can request and suspend transmission, reports on status, and acknowledge receipt of I frames. S frames do not have an information field.

  - *Unnumbered (U) frame*: Supports control purposes and is not sequenced. A U frame can be used to initialize secondaries. Depending on the function of the U frame, its control field is 1 or 2 bytes. Some U frames have an information field.

- *Data*—Contains a path information unit (PIU) or exchange identification (XID) information.

- *Frame Check Sequence (FCS)*—Precedes the ending flag delimiter and is usually a cyclic redundancy check (CRC) calculation remainder. The CRC calculation is redone in the receiver. If the result differs from the value in the original frame, an error is assumed.

A typical SDLC-based network configuration is shown in Figure 16–2. As illustrated, an IBM establishment controller (formerly called a cluster controller) in a remote site connects to dumb terminals and to a Token Ring network. In a local site, an IBM host connects (via channel-attached techniques) to an IBM front-end processor (FEP), which also can have links to local Token Ring LANs and an SNA backbone. The two sites are connected through an SDLC-based 56-kbps leased line.

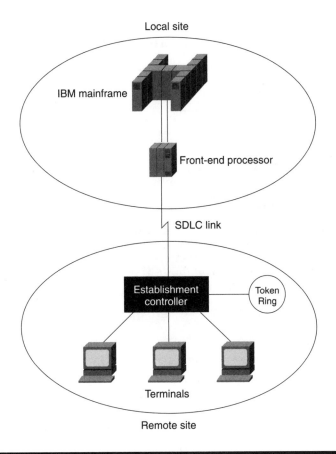

Figure 16–2
An SDLC line links local and remote sites over a serial line.

DERIVATIVE PROTOCOLS

Despite the fact that it omits several features used in SDLC, HDLC is generally considered to be a compatible superset of SDLC. LAP is a subset of HDLC and was created to ensure ongoing compatibility with HDLC, which had been modified in the early 1980s. IEEE 802.2 is a modification of HDLC for LAN environments. Qualified Logical Link Control (QLLC) is a link-layer protocol defined by IBM that enables SNA data to be transported across X.25 networks.

High-Level Data Link Control (HDLC)

HDLC shares the frame format of SDLC, and HDLC fields provide the same functionality as those in SDLC. Also, as in SDLC, HDLC supports synchronous, full-duplex operation.

HDLC differs from SDLC in several minor ways, however. First, HDLC has an option for a 32-bit checksum. Also, unlike SDLC, HDLC does not support the loop or hub go-ahead configurations.

The major difference between HDLC and SDLC is that SDLC supports only one transfer mode, whereas HDLC supports three:

- *Normal response mode* (NRM)—This transfer mode is also used by SDLC. In this mode, secondaries cannot communicate with a primary until the primary has given permission.

- *Asynchronous response mode* (ARM)—This transfer mode enables secondaries to initiate communication with a primary without receiving permission.

- *Asynchronous balanced mode* (ABM)—ABM introduces the *combined* node, which can act as a primary or a secondary, depending on the situation. All ABM communication occurs between multiple combined nodes. In ABM environments, any combined station can initiate data transmission without permission from any other station.

Link-Access Procedure, Balanced (LAPB)

LAPB is best known for its presence in the X.25 protocol stack. LAPB shares the same frame format, frame types, and field functions as SDLC and HDLC. Unlike either of these, however, LAPB is restricted to the ABM transfer mode and is appropriate only for combined stations. Also, LAPB circuits can be established by either the data terminal equipment (DTE) or the data circuit-terminating equipment (DCE). The station initiating the call is determined to be the primary, and the responding station is the secondary. Finally, LAPB use of the P/F bit is somewhat different from that of the other protocols. For details on LAPB, see Chapter 17, "X.25."

IEEE 802.2

IEEE 802.2 is often referred to as the *Logical Link Control* (LLC). It is extremely popular in LAN environments, where it interoperates with protocols such as IEEE 802.3, IEEE 802.4, and IEEE 802.5. IEEE 802.2 offers three types of service.

- *Type 1* provides unacknowledged connectionless service, which means that LLC Type 1 does not confirm data transfers. Because many upper-layer protocols, such as *Transmission Control Protocol/Internet Protocol* (TCP/IP), offer reliable data transfer that can compensate for unreliable lower-layer protocols, Type 1 is a commonly used service.

- *Type 2* provides connection-oriented service. LLC Type 2 (often called *LLC2*) service establishes logical connections between sender and receiver and is therefore connection oriented. LLC2 acknowledges data upon receipt and is used in IBM communication systems.

- *Type 3* provides acknowledged connectionless service. Although LLC Type 3 service supports acknowledged data transfer, it does not establish logical connections. As a compromise between the other two

LLC services, LLC Type 3 is useful in factory-automation environments where error detection is important but context storage space (for virtual circuits) is extremely limited.

End stations can support multiple LLC service types. A Class I device supports only Type 1 service. A Class II device supports both Type 1 and Type 2 service. Class III devices support both Type 1 and Type 3 services, and Class IV devices support all three types of service.

Upper-layer processes use IEEE 802.2 services through service access points (SAPs). The IEEE 802.2 header begins with a destination service access point (DSAP) field, which identifies the receiving upper-layer process. In other words, after the receiving node's IEEE 802.2 implementation completes its processing, the upper-layer process identified in the DSAP field receives the remaining data. Following the DSAP address is the *source service access point* (SSAP) address, which identifies the sending upper-layer process.

Qualified Logical-Link Control (QLLC)

QLLC provides the data link control capabilities that are required to transport SNA data across X.25 networks. Together, QLLC and X.25 replace SDLC in the SNA protocol stack. QLLC uses the packet-level layer (Layer 3) of the X.25 protocol stack. To indicate that a Layer 3 X.25 packet must be handled by QLLC, a special bit called the *qualifier bit*, in the general format identifier (GFI) of the Layer 3 X.25 packet-level header is set to one. The SNA data is carried as user data in Layer 3 X.25 packets. For more information about the X.25 protocol stack, see Chapter 17, "X.25."

X.25

BACKGROUND

X.25 is an International Telecommunication Union–Telecommunication Standardization Sector (ITU-T) protocol standard for WAN communications that defines how connections between user devices and network devices are established and maintained. X.25 is designed to operate effectively regardless of the type of systems connected to the network. It is typically used in the packet-switched networks (PSNs) of common carriers, such as the telephone companies. Subscribers are charged based on their use of the network. The development of the X.25 standard was initiated by the common carriers in the 1970s. At that time, there was a need for WAN protocols capable of providing connectivity across public data networks (PDNs). X.25 is now administered as an international standard by the ITU-T. This chapter covers the basic functions and components of X.25.

X.25 DEVICES AND PROTOCOL OPERATION

X.25 network devices fall into three general categories: data terminal equipment (DTE), data circuit-terminating equipment (DCE), and packet switching

exchange (PSE). Data terminal equipment devices are end systems that communicate across the X.25 network. They are usually terminals, personal computers, or network hosts, and are located on the premises of individual
subscribers. DCE devices are communications devices, such as modems and
packet switches, that provide the interface between DTE devices and a PSE
and are generally located in the carrier's facilities. PSEs are switches that com-
pose the bulk of the carrier's network. They transfer data from one DTE
device to another through the X.25 PSN. Figure 17–1 illustrates the relationships between the three types of X.25 network devices.

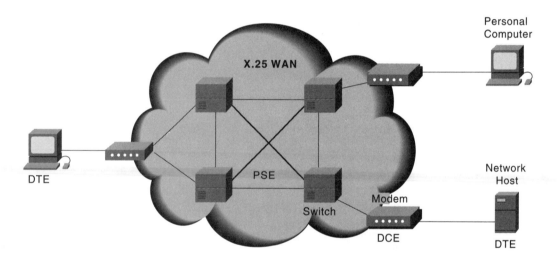

Figure 17–1
DTEs, DCEs, and PSEs make up an X.25 network.

Packet Assembler/Disassembler (PAD)

The packet assembler/disassembler (PAD) is a device commonly found in X.25
networks. PADs are used when a DTE device, such as a character-mode terminal, is too simple to implement the full X.25 functionality. The PAD is
located between a DTE device and a DCE device, and it performs three primary functions: buffering, packet assembly, and packet disassembly. The PAD

buffers data sent to or from the DTE device. It also assembles outgoing data into packets and forwards them to the DCE device. (This includes adding an X.25 header.) Finally, the PAD disassembles incoming packets before forwarding the data to the DTE. (This includes removing the X.25 header.) Figure 17–2 illustrates the basic operation of the PAD when receiving packets from the X.25 WAN.

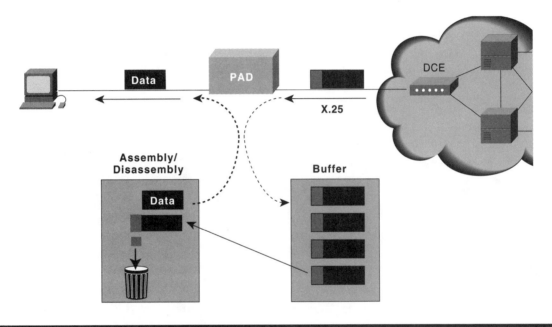

Figure 17–2
The PAD buffers, assembles, and disassembles data packets.

X.25 Session Establishment

X.25 sessions are established when one DTE device contacts another to request a communication session. The DTE device that receives the request can either accept or refuse the connection. If the request is accepted, the two systems begin full-duplex information transfer. Either DTE device can terminate the connection. After the session is terminated, any further communication requires the establishment of a new session.

X.25 Virtual Circuits

A virtual circuit is a logical connection created to ensure reliable communication between two network devices. A virtual circuit denotes the existence of a logical, bidirectional path from one DTE device to another across an X.25 network. Physically, the connection can pass through any number of intermediate nodes, such as DCE devices and PSEs. Multiple virtual circuits (logical connections) can be multiplexed onto a single physical circuit (a physical connection). Virtual circuits are demultiplexed at the remote end, and data is sent to the appropriate destinations. Figure 17–3 illustrates four separate virtual circuits being multiplexed onto a single physical circuit.

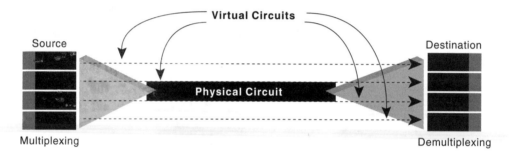

Figure 17–3

Virtual circuits can be multiplexed onto a single physical circuit.

Two types of X.25 virtual circuits exist: switched and permanent. Switched virtual circuits (SVCs) are temporary connections used for sporadic data transfers. They require that two DTE devices establish, maintain, and terminate a session each time the devices need to communicate. Permanent virtual circuits (PVCs) are permanently established connections used for frequent and consistent data transfers. PVCs do not require that sessions be established and terminated. Therefore, DTEs can begin transferring data whenever necessary, because the session is always active.

The basic operation of an X.25 virtual circuit begins when the source DTE device specifies the virtual circuit to be used (in the packet headers) and then sends the packets to a locally connected DCE device. At this point, the local DCE device examines the packet headers to determine which virtual circuit to use and then sends the packets to the closest PSE in the path of that virtual circuit. PSEs (switches) pass the traffic to the next intermediate node in the path, which may be another switch or the remote DCE device.

When the traffic arrives at the remote DCE device, the packet headers are examined and the destination address is determined. The packets are then sent to the destination DTE device. If communication occurs over an SVC and neither device has additional data to transfer, the virtual circuit is terminated.

THE X.25 PROTOCOL SUITE

The X.25 protocol suite maps to the lowest three layers of the OSI reference model. The following protocols are typically used in X.25 implementations: Packet-Layer Protocol (PLP), Link Access Procedure, Balanced (LAPB), and those among other physical-layer serial interfaces (such as EIA/TIA-232, EIA/TIA-449, EIA-530, and G.703). Figure 17–4 maps the key X.25 protocols to the layers of the OSI reference model.

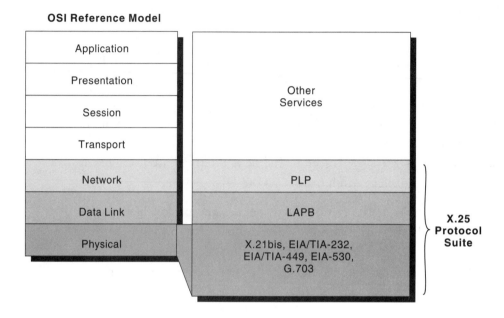

Figure 17–4

Key X.25 protocols map to the three lower layers of the OSI reference model.

Packet-Layer Protocol (PLP)

PLP is the X.25 network-layer protocol. PLP manages packet exchanges between DTE devices across virtual circuits. PLPs also can run over Logical-Link Control 2 (LLC2) implementations on LANs and over Integrated Services Digital Network (ISDN) interfaces running Link Access Procedure on the D channel (LAPD).

The PLP operates in five distinct modes: call setup, data transfer, idle, call clearing, and restarting.

Call setup mode is used to establish SVCs between DTE devices. A PLP uses the X.121 addressing scheme to set up the virtual circuit. The call setup mode is executed on a per-virtual circuit basis, which means that one virtual circuit can be in call-setup mode while another is in data-transfer mode. This mode is used only with SVCs, not with PVCs.

Data-transfer mode is used for transferring data between two DTE devices across a virtual circuit. In this mode, PLP handles segmentation and reassembly, bit padding, and error and flow control. This mode is executed on a per-virtual circuit basis and is used with both PVCs and SVCs.

Idle mode is used when a virtual circuit is established but data transfer is not occurring. It is executed on a per-virtual circuit basis and is used only with SVCs.

Call-clearing mode is used to end communication sessions between DTE devices and to terminate SVCs. This mode is executed on a per-virtual circuit basis and is used only with SVCs.

Restarting mode is used to synchronize transmission between a DTE device and a locally connected DCE device. This mode is not executed on a per-virtual circuit basis. It affects all the DTE device's established virtual circuits.

Four types of PLP packet fields exist:

- *General Format Identifier (GFI)*—Identifies packet parameters, such as whether the packet carries user data or control information, what kind of windowing is being used, and whether delivery confirmation is required.

- *Logical Channel Identifier (LCI)*—Identifies the virtual circuit across the local DTE/DCE interface.

- *Packet Type Identifier (PTI)*—Identifies the packet as one of 17 different PLP packet types.

- *User Data*—Contains encapsulated upper-layer information. This field is present only in data packets. Otherwise, additional fields containing control information are added.

Link Access Procedure, Balanced (LAPB)

LAPB is a data link-layer protocol that manages communication and packet framing between DTE and DCE devices. LAPB is a bit-oriented protocol which ensures that frames are correctly ordered and error free.

Three types of LAPB frames exist: information, supervisory, and unnumbered. The *information frame* (I-frame) carries upper-layer information and some control information. I-frame functions include sequencing, flow control, and error detection and recovery. I-frames carry send and receive sequence numbers. The *supervisory frame* (S-frame) carries control information. S-frame functions include requesting and suspending transmissions, reporting on status, and acknowledging the receipt of I-frames. S-frames carry only receive sequence numbers. The *unnumbered frame* (U-frame) carries control information. U-frame functions include link setup and disconnection, as well as error reporting. U-frames carry no sequence numbers.

The X.21bis Protocol

X.21bis is a physical-layer protocol used in X.25 that defines the electrical and mechanical procedures for using the physical medium. X.21bis handles the activation and deactivation of the physical medium connecting DTE and DCE devices. It supports point-to-point connections, speeds up to 19.2 kbps, and synchronous, full-duplex transmission over four-wire media. Figure 17–5 shows the format of the PLP packet and its relationship to the LAPB frame and the X.21bis frame.

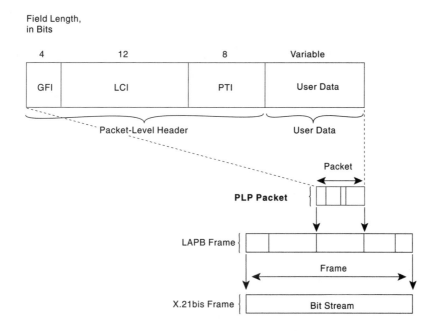

Figure 17–5
The PLP packet is encapsulated within the LAPB frame and the X.21bis frame.

LAPB FRAME FORMAT

LAPB frames include a header, encapsulated data, and a trailer. Figure 17–6 illustrates the format of the LAPB frame and its relationship to the PLP packet and the X.21bis frame.

The following descriptions summarize the fields illustrated in Figure 17–6:

- *Flag*—Delimits the beginning and end of the LAPB frame. Bit stuffing is used to ensure that the flag pattern does not occur within the body of the frame.

- *Address*—Indicates whether the frame carries a command or a response.

- *Control*—Qualifies command and response frames and indicates whether the frame is an I-frame, an S-frame, or a U-frame. In addition, this field contains the frame's sequence number and its function (for example, whether receiver-ready or disconnect). Control frames vary in length depending on the frame type.

- *Data*—Contains upper-layer data in the form of an encapsulated PLP packet.

- *FCS*—Handles error checking and ensures the integrity of the transmitted data.

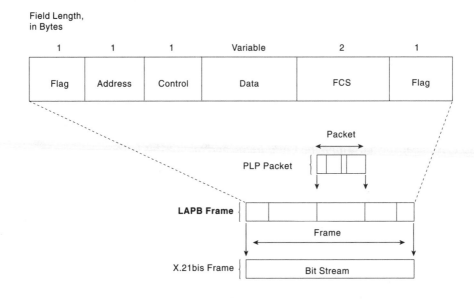

Figure 17–6
An LAPB frame includes a header, a trailer, and encapsulated data.

X.121 Address Format

X.121 addresses are used by the X.25 PLP in call-setup mode to establish SVCs. Figure 17–7 illustrates the format of an X.121 address.

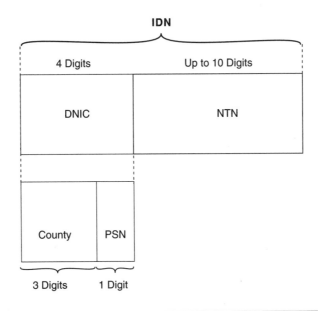

Figure 17–7
The X.121 address includes an IDN field.

The X.121 Address field includes the International Data Number (IDN), which consists of two fields: the Data Network Identification Code (DNIC) and the National Terminal Number (NTN).

DNIC is an optional field that identifies the exact PSN in which the destination DTE device is located. This field is sometimes omitted in calls within the same PSN. The DNIC has two subfields: Country and PSN. The Country sub-field specifies the country in which the destination PSN is located. The PSN field specifies the exact PSN in which the destination DTE device is located.

The NTN identifies the exact DTE device in the PSN for which a packet is destined. This field varies in length.

CHAPTER 18

Multiservice Access Technologies

Multiservice networking is emerging as a strategically important issue for enterprise and public service provider infrastructures alike. The proposition of multiservice networking is the combination of all types of communications, all types of data, voice, and video over a single packet-cell-based infrastructure. The benefits of multiservice networking are reduced operational costs, higher performance, greater flexibility, integration and control, and faster new application and service deployment.

A key issue often confused in multiservice networking is the degree to which Layer 2 switching and services are mixed with Layer 3 switching and services. An intelligent multiservice network fully integrates both, taking advantage of the best of each; most multiservice offerings in the marketplace are primarily Layer 2 based, from traditional circuit switching technology suppliers.

THE IMPORTANCE OF VOICE OVER IP

Of the key emerging technologies for data, voice, and video integration, voice over IP (Internet Protocol) is arguably very important. The most quality of service (QoS) sensitive of all traffic, voice is the true test of the engineering and quality of a network. Demand for Voice over IP is leading the movement for QoS in IP environments, and will ultimately lead to use of the Internet for fax, voice telephony, and video telephony services. Voice over IP will ultimately be a key component of the migration of telephony to the LAN infrastructure.

Significant advances in technology have been made over the past few years that enable the transmission of voice traffic over traditional public networks such as Frame Relay (Voice over Frame Relay) as well as Voice over the Internet through the efforts of the Voice over IP Forum and the Internet Engineering Task Force (IETF). Additionally, the support of Asynchronous Transfer Mode (ATM) for different traffic types and the ATM Forum's recent completion of the Voice and Telephony over ATM specification will quicken the availability of industry-standard solutions.

PACKET VOICE

All packet voice systems follow a common model, as shown in Figure 18–1. The packet voice transport network, which may be IP based, Frame Relay, or ATM, forms the traditional "cloud." At the edges of this network are devices or components that can be called *voice agents*. It is the mission of these devices to change the voice information from its traditional telephony form to a form suitable for packet transmission. The network then forwards the packet data to a voice agent serving the destination or called party.

This voice agent connection model shows that there are two issues in packet voice networking that must be explored to ensure that packet voice services meet user needs. The first issue is voice coding—how voice information is transformed into packets, and how the packets are used to re-create the voice. Another issue is the signaling associated with identifying who the calling party is trying to call and where the called party is in the network.

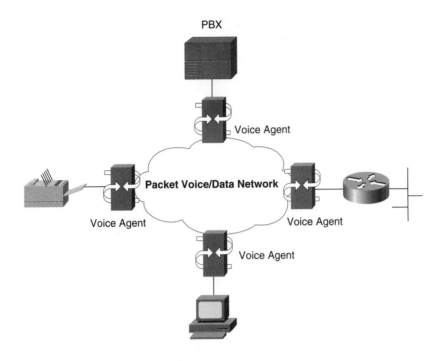

Figure 18–1
This diagram displays the packet voice model.

PACKET VOICE TRANSPORT

Integrating voice and data networks should include an evaluation of these three packet voice transport technologies:

- Voice over ATM (VoATM)
- Voice over Frame Relay (VoFR)
- Voice over IP (VoIP)

There are two basic models for integrating voice over data—transport and translate—as shown in Figure 18–2. Transport is the transparent support of voice over the existing data network. Simulation of tie lines over ATM using circuit emulation is a good example.

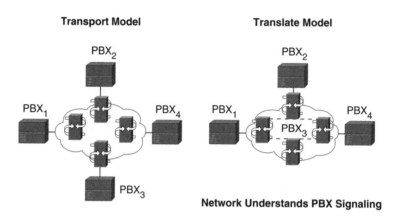

Figure 18–2
There are two basic models for transporting over a data network.

Translate is the translation of traditional voice functions by the data infrastructure. An example is the interpretation of voice signaling and the creation of switched virtual circuits (SVCs) within ATM. Translate networking is more complex than transport networking, and its implementation is a current topic for many of the standards committees.

Voice over ATM

The ATM Forum and the ITU have specified different classes of services to represent different possible traffic types for VoATM.

Designed primarily for voice communications, constant bit rate (CBR) and variable bit rate (VBR) classes have provisions for passing real-time traffic and are suitable for guaranteeing a certain level of service. CBR, in particular, allows the amount of bandwidth, end-to-end delay, and delay variation to be specified during the call setup.

Designed principally for bursty traffic, unspecified bit rate (UBR) and available bit rate (ABR) are more suitable for data applications. UBR, in particular, makes no guarantees about the delivery of the data traffic.

The method of transporting voice channels through an ATM network is dependent on the nature of the traffic. Different ATM adaptation types have been developed for different traffic types, each with its benefits and detriments. ATM Adaptation Layer 1 (AAL1) is the most common adaptation layer used with CBR services.

Unstructured AAL1 takes a continuous bit stream and places it within ATM cells. This is a common method of supporting a full E1 byte stream from end to end. The problem with this approach is that a full E1 may be sent, regardless of the actual number of voice channels in use. (An EI is a wide-area digital transmission scheme used predominantly in Europe that carries data at a rate of 2.048 Mbps.)

Structured AAL1 contains a pointer in the payload that allows the digital signal level 0 (DS0) structure to be maintained in subsequent cells. This allows network efficiencies to be gained by not using bandwidth for unused DS0s. (A DS0 is a framing specification used in transmitting digital signals over a single channel at 64 kbps on a T1 facility.)

The remapping option allows the ATM network to terminate structured AAL1 cells and remap DS0s to the proper destinations. This eliminates the need for permanent virtual circuits (PVCs) between every possible source/destination combination. The major difference from the above approach is that a PVC is not built across the network from edge to edge.

VoATM Signaling

Figure 18–3 describes the transport method, in which voice signaling is carried through the network transparently. PVCs are created for both signaling and voice transport. First, a signaling message is carried transparently over the signaling PVC from end station to end station. Second, coordination between the end systems allow the selection of a PVC to carry the voice communication between end stations.

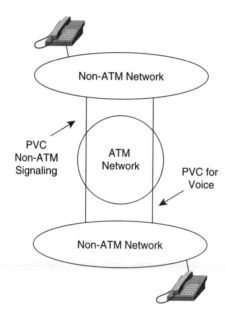

Figure 18–3

The VoATM signaling transport model describes the transport method, in which voice signaling is carried through the network transparently.

At no time is the ATM network participating in the interpretation of the signaling that takes place between end stations. However, as a value-added feature, some products are capable of understanding channel associated signaling (CAS) and can prevent the sending of empty voice cells when the end stations are on-hook.

Figure 18–4 shows the translate model. In this model, the ATM network interprets the signaling from both non-ATM and ATM network devices. PVCs are created between the end stations and the ATM network. This contrasts with the previous model, in which the PVCs are carried transparently across the network.

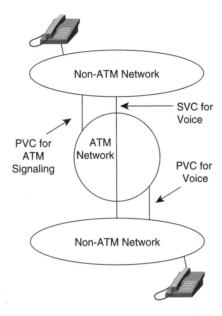

Figure 18–4
In the VoATM signaling translate model, the ATM network interprets the signaling from both non-ATM and ATM network devices.

A signaling request from an end station causes the ATM network to create an SVC with the appropriate QoS to the desired end station. The creation of an SVC versus the prior establishment of PVCs is clearly more advantageous for three reasons:

- SVCs are more efficient users of bandwidth than PVCs.

- QoS for connections do not need to be constant, as with PVCs.

- The ability to switch calls within the network can lead to the elimination of the tandem private branch exchange (PBX) and potentially the edge PBX. (A PBX is a digital or analog telephone switchboard located on the subscriber premises and used to connect private and public telephone networks.)

VoATM Addressing

ATM standards support both private and public addressing schemes. Both schemes involve addresses that are 20 bytes in length (shown in Figure 18–5).

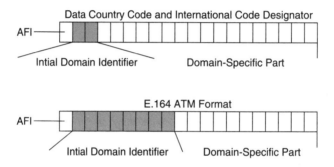

Figure 18–5
ATM supports a 20-byte addressing format.

The Authority and Format Identifier (AFI) identifies the particular addressing format employed. Three identifiers are currently specified: data country code (DCC), international code designator (ICD), and E.164. Each is administered by a standards body. The second part of the address is the initial domain identifier (IDI). This address uniquely identifies the customer's network. The E.164 scheme has a longer IDI that corresponds to the 15-digit ISDN network number. The final portion, the domain-specific part (DSP), identifies logical groupings and ATM end stations.

In a transport model you don't need to be aware of the underlying addressing used by the voice network. However, in the translate model, the ability to communicate from a non-ATM network device to an ATM network device implies a level of address mapping. Fortunately, ATM supports the E.164 addressing scheme, which is employed by telephone networks throughout the world.

VoATM Routing

ATM uses a private network-to-network interface (PNNI), a hierarchical link-state routing protocol that is scalable for global usage. In addition to determining reachability and routing within an ATM network, it is also capable of call setup.

A virtual circuit (VC) call request causes a connection with certain QoS requirements to be requested through the ATM network. The route through the network is determined by the source ATM switch based on what it determines is the best path through the network, based on the PNNI protocol and the QoS request. Each switch along the path is checked to determine whether it has the appropriate resources for the connection.

When the connection is established, voice traffic flows between end stations as if a leased line existed between the two. This specification spells out routing in private networks. Within carrier networks, the switch-to-switch protocol is B-ICI. Current research and development of integrated non-ATM and ATM routing will yield new capabilities to build translate level voice and ATM networks.

VoATM and Delay

ATM has several mechanisms for controlling delay and delay variation. The QoS capabilities of ATM allow the specific request of constant bit rate traffic with bandwidth and delay variation guarantees. The use of VC queues allows each traffic stream to be treated uniquely. Priority can be given for the transmission of voice traffic. The use of small, fixed-size cells reduces queuing delay and the delay variation associated with variable-sized packets.

VOICE OVER FRAME RELAY

Voice over Frame Relay enables a network to carry live voice traffic (for example, telephone calls and faxes) over a Frame Relay network. Frame Relay is a common and inexpensive transport that is provided by most of the large telcos.

VoFR Signaling

Historically, Frame Relay call setup has been proprietary by vendor. This has meant that products from different vendors would not interoperate. Frame Relay Forum FRF.11 establishes a standard for call setup, coding types, and packet formats for VoFR, and will provide the basis for interoperability between vendors in the future.

VoFR Addressing

Address mapping is handled through static tables—dialed digits mapped to specific PVCs. How voice is routed depends on which routing protocol is chosen to establish PVCs and the hardware used in the Frame Relay network. Routing can be based on bandwidth limits, hops, delay, or some combination, but most routing implementations are based on maximizing bandwidth utilization.

The two extremes for designing a VoFR network are

- A full mesh of voice and data PVCs to minimize the number of network transit hops and maximize the ability to establish different QoS. A network designed in this fashion minimizes delay and improves voice quality, but represents the highest network cost.

- Most Frame Relay providers charge based on the number of PVCs used. To reduce costs, both data and voice segments can be configured to use the same PVC, thereby reducing the number of PVCs required. In this design, the central site switch re-routes voice calls. This design has the potential of creating a transit hop when voice needs to go from one remote to another remote office. However, it avoids the compression and decompression that occurs when using a tandem PBX.

A number of mechanisms can minimize delay and delay variation on a Frame Relay network. The presence of long data frames on a low-speed Frame Relay link can cause unacceptable delays for time-sensitive voice frames. To reduce this problem, some vendors implement smaller frame sizes to help reduce delay and delay variation. FRF.12 proposes an industry standard approach to do this, so products from different vendors will be able to interoperate and consumers will know what type of voice quality to expect.

Methods for prioritizing voice frames over data frames also help reduce delay and delay variation. This, and the use of smaller frame sizes, are vendor-specific implementations. To ensure voice quality, the committed information rate (CIR) on each PVC should be set to ensure that voice frames are not discarded. Future Frame Relay networks will provide SVC signaling for call setup, and may also allow Frame Relay DTEs to request a QoS for a call. This will enhance VoFR quality in the future.

VOICE OVER IP

VoIP's appeal is based on its capability to facilitate voice and data convergence at an application layer. Increasingly, VoIP is being seen as the ideal last-mile solution for cable, DSL, and wireless networks because it allows service providers to bundle their offerings.

VoIP also offers service providers the ability to provision standalone local loop bypass and long distance arbitrage services. To provide a VoIP solution, signaling, routing, and addressing must be addressed.

VoIP Signaling

VoIP signaling has three distinct areas: signaling from the PBX to the router, signaling between routers, and signaling from the router to the PBX. The corporate intranet appears as a trunk line to the PBX, which signals the corporate intranet to seize a trunk. Signaling from the PBX to the intranet may be any of the common signaling methods used to seize a trunk line, such as fax expansion module (FXS) or E&M signaling. In the future, digital signaling such as common channel signaling (CCS) or Q signaling (QSIG) will become available. The PBX then forwards the dialed digits to the router in the same manner in which the digits would be forwarded to a telco switch.

Within the router the dial plan mapper maps the dialed digits to an IP address and signals a Q.931 call establishment request to the remote peer that is indicated by the IP address. Meanwhile, the control channel is used to set up the Real-Time Control Protocol (RTCP) audio streams, and the Resource Reservation Protocol (RSVP) is used to request a guaranteed QoS.

When the remote router receives the Q.931 call request, it signals a line seizure to the PBX. After the PBX acknowledges, the router forwards the dialed digits to the PBX and signals a call acknowledgment to the originating router.

In connectionless network architectures such as IP, the responsibility for session establishment and signaling is with the end stations. To successfully emulate voice services across an IP network, enhancements to the signaling stacks are required.

For example, an H.323 agent is added to the router for standards-based support of the audio and signaling streams. The Q.931 protocol is used for call establishment and teardown between H.323 agents or end stations. RTCP is used to establish the audio channels themselves. A reliable session-oriented protocol, Transmission Control Protocol (TCP), is deployed between end stations to carry the signaling channels. Real-Time Transport Protocol (RTP), which is built on top of User Datagram Protocol (UDP), is used for transport of the real-time audio stream. RTP uses UDP as a transport mechanism because it has lower delay than TCP and because actual voice traffic, unlike data traffic or signaling, tolerates low levels of loss and cannot effectively exploit retransmission.

Table 18–1 depicts the relationship between the ISO reference model and the protocols used in IP voice agents.

ISO Protocol Layer	ITU H.323 Standard
Presentation	G.711,G.729, G.729a, G.726, G.728, G.723.1
Session	H.323, H.245, H.225, RTCP
Transport	RTP, UDP
Network	IP, RSVP, WFQ
Link	RFC 1717 (PPP/ML), Frame, ATM, X.25, public IP networks (including the Internet), circuit-switched leased-line networks

Table 18–1
The ISO Reference Model and H.323 Standards

VoIP Addressing

An existing corporate intranet should have an IP addressing plan in place. To the IP numbering scheme, the voice interfaces appear as additional IP hosts, either as an extension of the existing scheme or with new IP addresses.

Translation of dial digits from the PBX to an IP host address is performed by the dial plan mapper. The destination telephone number, or some portion of the number, is mapped to the destination IP address. When the number is received from the PBX, the router compares the number to those mapped in the routing table. If a match is found, the call is routed to the IP host. After the connection is established, the corporate intranet connection is transparent to the subscriber.

VoIP Routing

One of the strengths of IP is the maturity and sophistication of its routing protocols. A modern routing protocol, such as Enhanced Interior Gateway Routing Protocol (EIGRP), is able to consider delay when calculating the best path. These are also fast converging routing protocols, which allow voice traffic to take advantage of the self-healing capabilities of IP networks. Advanced features, such as policy routing and access lists, make it possible to create highly sophisticated and secure routing schemes for voice traffic.

RSVP can be automatically invoked by VoIP gateways to ensure that voice traffic is able to use the best path through the network. This can include segments of arbitrary media, such as switched LANs or ATM networks. Some of the most interesting developments in IP routing are tag switching and other IP switching disciplines. Tag switching provides a way of extending IP routing, policy, and RSVP functionality over ATM and other high-speed transports. Another benefit of tag switching is its traffic engineering capabilities, which are needed for the efficient use of network resources. Traffic engineering can be used to shift traffic load based on different predicates, such as time of day.

VoIP and Delay

Routers and specifically IP networks offer some unique challenges in controlling delay and delay variation. Traditionally, IP traffic has been treated as "best effort," meaning that incoming IP traffic is allowed to be transmitted on a first-come, first-served basis. Packets have been variable in nature, allowing large file transfers to take advantage of the efficiency associated with larger packet sizes. These characteristics have contributed to large delays and large delay variations in packet delivery. RSVP allows network managers to reserve resources in the network by end station. The network manager can then allocate queues for different types of traffic, helping to reduce the delay and delay variation inherent in current IP networks.

The second part of supporting delay-sensitive voice traffic is to provide a means of prioritizing the traffic within the router network. RFC 1717 breaks down large packets into smaller packets at the link layer. This reduces the problems of queuing delay and delay variation by limiting the amount of time a voice packet must wait in order to gain access to the trunk.

Weighted fair queuing, or priority queuing, allows the network to put different traffic types into specific QoS queues. This is designed to prioritize the transmittal of voice traffic over data traffic. This reduces the potential of queuing delay.

APPLYING PACKET VOICE

In today's networking, there are several attractive alternatives both to conventional public telephony and to leased lines. Among the most interesting are networking technologies based on a different kind of voice transmission, called packet voice. Packet voice appears to a network as data; thus it can be transported over networks normally reserved for data, where costs are often far less than in voice networks. Packet voice uses less transmission bandwidth than conventional voice, so more can be carried on a given connection. Whereas telephony requires as much as 64,000 bits per second (bps), packet voice often needs less than 10,000 bps. For many companies, there is sufficient reserve capacity on national and international data networks to transport considerable voice traffic, making voice essentially free.

Packet voice networks can be used in two broad contexts, differentiated by geography or by the types of users to be served. The economics and technology of the network may be unaffected by these factors, but there may be legal constraints in some areas for some combinations of these two contexts, and network users or operators should be aware of them.

Telecommunications is regulated within countries by national administrations, or arms of the governments, based on local regulations. In some countries, such as the United States, there may be multiple levels of regulatory authority. In all cases, treaties define the international connection rules, rates, and so forth. It is important for any business planning to use or build a packet voice network to ensure that it is operating in conformance with all laws and regulations in all the areas the network serves. This normally requires some direct research, but the current state of the regulations can be summarized as follows:

- Within a national administration or telephony jurisdiction, it is almost always proper for a business to employ packet voice to support its own voice calling among its own sites.

  In such applications, it is normally expected that some of the calls transported on the packet voice network will have originated in the public phone network. Such outside calling over packet voice is uniformly tolerated in a regulatory sense, on the basis that the calls are from employees, customers, or suppliers and represent the company's business.

- When a packet voice connection is made between national administrations to support the activities of a single company—to connect two or more company locations in multiple countries—the application is uniformly tolerated in a regulatory sense.

  In such a situation, an outside call placed from a public phone network in one country and terminated in a company site within another via packet voice may be a technical violation of national monopolies or treaties on long-distance service. Where such a call is between company employees or between employees and suppliers or customers, such a technical violation is unlikely to attract official notice.

- When a packet voice network is used to connect public calls within a company, the packet voice provider is technically providing a local or national telephone service and is subject to regulation as such.

- When a packet voice network is used to connect public calls between countries, the packet voice provider is subject to the national regulations in the countries involved and also to any treaty provisions for international calling to which any of the countries served are signatories.

Thus, it is safe to say that companies could employ packet voice networking for any applications where traditional leased-line, PBX-to-PBX networking could be legally employed. In fact, a good model for deploying packet voice without additional concerns about regulatory matters is to duplicate an existing PBX trunk network or tie-line network using packet voice facilities.

CHAPTER 19

Virtual Private Networks (VPNs)

Virtual private network is defined as customer connectivity deployed on a shared infrastructure with the same policies as a private network. The shared infrastructure can leverage a service provider IP, Frame Relay, or ATM backbone, or the Internet. There are three types of VPNs, which align with how businesses and organizations use VPNs

- *Access VPN*—Provides remote access to a corporate intranet or extranet over a shared infrastructure with the same policies as a private network. Access VPNs enable users to access corporate resources whenever, wherever, and however they require. Access VPNs encompass analog, dial, ISDN, Digital Subscriber Line (DSL), mobile IP, and cable technologies to securely connect mobile users, telecommuters, or branch offices.

- *Intranet VPN*—Links corporate headquarters, remote offices, and branch offices over a shared infrastructure using dedicated connections. Businesses enjoy the same policies as a private network, including security, quality of service (QoS), manageability, and reliability.

- *Extranet VPN*—Links customers, suppliers, partners, or communities of interest to a corporate intranet over a shared infrastructure using dedicated connections. Businesses enjoy the same policies as a private network, including security, QoS, manageability, and reliability.

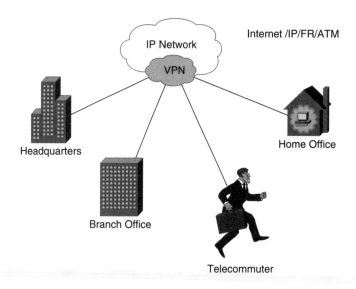

Figure 19–1
This figure provides a logical topology view of a VPN.

CISCO SYSTEMS VPNS

Currently there are no standards outlining the software and hardware components of a VPN. Every vendor that provides a VPN service performs it in a method that is best supported by its own hardware platforms and software applications. The following sections of this chapter discuss the Cisco Systems implementation of VPN services.

The Cisco Systems VPN Design

Cisco's end-to-end hardware and Cisco IOS software networking products provide sophisticated security for sensitive private transmissions over the public infrastructure, QoS through traffic differentiation, reliability for mission-critical applications, scalability for supporting large bandwidth of data, and comprehensive network management to enable a complete access VPN solution.

The following sections discuss how Cisco network access servers (NASs) and routers with Cisco IOS software provide new functionality with virtual dialup services. This functionality is based on the L2F protocol Internet Engineering Task Force (IETF) draft request for comments (RFC). The L2F protocol focuses on providing a standards-based tunneling mechanism for transporting link-layer frames—for example, High-Level Data Link Control (HDLC), async Point-to-Point Protocol (PPP), Serial Line Internet Protocol (SLIP), or PPP Integrated Services Digital Network (ISDN)—of higher-layer protocols. Using such tunnels, it is possible to divorce the location of the initial dialup server from the location at which the dialup protocol connection is terminated and the location at which access to the network is provided (usually a corporate gateway).

Tunneling Defined

A key component of the virtual dialup service is tunneling, a vehicle for encapsulating packets inside a protocol that is understood at the entry and exit points of a given network. These entry and exit points are defined as tunnel interfaces. The tunnel interface itself is similar to a hardware interface, but is configured in software.

Figure 19–2 shows the format in which a packet would traverse the network within a tunnel.

IP/UDP	L2F	PPP (Data)
Carrier Protocol	Encapsulating Protocol	Passenger Protocol

Figure 19–2
This is an overview of a tunneling packet format.

Tunneling involves three types of protocols.

- The *passenger protocol* is the protocol being encapsulated; in a dialup scenario, this protocol could be PPP, SLIP, or text dialog.

- The *encapsulating protocol* is used to create, maintain, and tear down the tunnel. Cisco supports several encapsulating protocols, including the L2F protocol, which is used for virtual dialup services.

- The *carrier protocol* is used to carry the encapsulated protocol; IP is the first carrier protocol used by the L2F protocol because of its robust routing capabilities, ubiquitous support across different media, and deployment within the Internet.

No dependency exists between the L2F protocol and IP. In subsequent releases of the L2F functionality, Frame Relay, X.25 virtual circuits (VCs), and Asynchronous Transfer Mode (ATM) switched virtual circuits (SVCs) could be used as a direct Layer 2 carrier protocol for the tunnel.

Tunneling has evolved to become one of the key components in defining and using VPNs. Cisco Systems provides virtual dialup service through a telecommuting form of a VPN.

Cisco's Virtual Dialup Services

The following terms are defined to fully describe the virtual dialup service that Cisco provides in its Cisco IOS software:

- *Remote user*—The client who is dialing ISDN/Public Switched Telephone Network (PSTN) from either home or a remote location.

- *NAS*—The telecommuting device that terminates the dialup calls either over analog (basic telephone service) or digital (ISDN) circuits.

- *Internet service provider (ISP)*—The ISP, which supplies the dialup services, can provide for services itself through the NAS or can deliver the dialup remote user to a designated corporate gateway.

- *Corporate gateway*—The destination router that provides access to the services the remote user is requesting. The services could be a corporation or even another ISP.

Remote users (using either asynchronous PPP or ISDN) access the corporate LAN as if they were dialed directly into the corporate gateway, although their physical dialup is through the ISP NAS. Figure 19–2 gives a topological view of how these conventions would be deployed within a virtual dialup service.

Cisco's L2F Implementation

The key management requirements of service that are provided by Cisco's L2F implementation are as follows:

- Neither the remote end system nor its corporate hosts should require any special software to use this service in a secure manner.

- Authentication as provided by dialup PPP, Challenge Handshake Authentication Protocol (CHAP), or Password Authentication Protocol (PAP), including Terminal Access Controller Access Control System Plus (TACACS+) and Remote Authentication Dial-In User Service (RADIUS) solutions, as well as support for smart cards and one-time passwords; the authentication will be manageable by the user independently of the ISP.

• Addressing will be as manageable as dedicated dialup solutions; the address will be assigned by the remote user's respective corporation, and not by the ISP.

• Authorization will be managed by the corporation's remote users, as it would be in a direct dialup solution.

• Accounting will be performed by both the ISP (for billing purposes) and by the user (for chargeback and auditing).

These requirements are primarily achieved based on the functionality provided by tunneling the remote user directly to the corporate location using the L2F protocol. In the case of PPP, all Link Control Protocol (LCP) and Network Control Protocol (NCP) negotiations take place at the remote user's corporate location. PPP is allowed to flow from the remote user and terminate at the corporate gateway. Figure 19–3 illustrates this process.

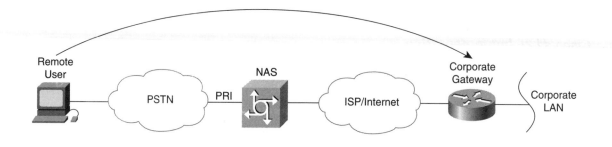

Figure 19–3
The remote client establishes a PPP connection with the corporate network to complete the virtual dialup topology.

End-to-End Virtual Dialup Process

To illustrate how the virtual dialup service works, the following example describes what might happen when a remote user initiates access. Figure 19–4 gives a step-by-step flow of this end-to-end process.

The remote user initiates a PPP connection to an ISP over the PSTN or natively over ISDN. The NAS accepts the connection, and the PPP link is established. (See Figure 19–4, step 1.)

The ISP authenticates the end system/user using CHAP or PAP. Only the username field is interpreted to determine whether the user requires a virtual dialup service. It is expected that usernames will be structured (for example, *smith@cisco.com*) or that the ISP will maintain a database mapping users to services. In the case of virtual dialup, the mapping will name a specific endpoint, the corporate gateway. At the time of the first release, this endpoint is the IP address of the corporate gateway known to the public ISP network. (See Figure 19–4, step 2.)

Note that if permitted by the organization's security policy, the authorization of the dial-in user at the NAS can be performed only on a domain name within the username field and not on every individual username. This setup can substantially reduce the size of the authorization database.

If a virtual dialup service is not required, traditional access to the Internet may be provided by the NAS. All address assignment and authentication would be performed locally by the ISP in this situation.

If no tunnel connection currently exists to the desired corporate gateway, one is initiated. The details of such tunnel creation are outside the scope of this specification; L2F requires only that the tunnel media provide point-to-point connectivity. Obvious examples of such media are the User Datagram Protocol (UDP), Frame Relay, ATM, and X.25 VCs. Cisco supports UDP in its first release of the virtual dialup service. Based on UDP using a carrier protocol of IP, any media supporting IP will support the virtual dialup functionality. (See Figure 19–4, step 3.)

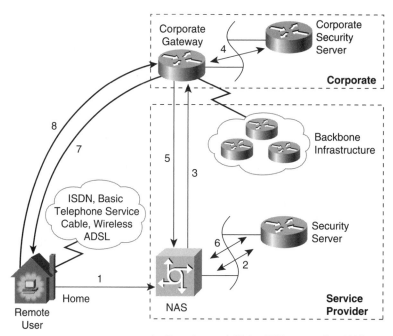

1. Remote user initiates PPP connection, NAS accepts call.
2. NAS identifies remote user.
3. NAS initiates L2F tunnel to desired corporate gateway.
4. Corporate gateway authenticates remote user and accepts or declines tunnel.
5. Corporate gateway confirms acceptance of call and L2F tunnel.
6. NAS logs acceptance/traffic optional.
7. Corporate gateway exchanges PPP negotiations with remote user. IP address can be assigned by corporate gateway at this point.
8. End-to-end data tunneled from remote user and corporate gateway.

Figure 19–4

Eight steps are required for communications between a remote VPN client and a corporate LAN.

When the tunnel connection is established, the NAS allocates an unused multiplex ID (MID) and sends a connect indication to notify the corporate gateway of this new dialup session. The MID identifies a particular connection within the tunnel. Each new connection is assigned a MID that is currently unused within the tunnel. The corporate gateway either accepts the connection or rejects it. Rejection may include a reason indication, which may be displayed to the dialup user, after which the call should be disconnected.

The initial setup notification may include the authentication information required to allow the corporate gateway to authenticate the user and decide to accept or decline the connection. In the case of CHAP, the setup packet includes the challenge, username, and raw password; for PAP, it includes username and clear text password. The corporate gateway can be configured to use this information to complete its authentication, avoiding an additional cycle of authentication. Note that the authentication takes place at the corporate customer, allowing the corporation to impose its own security and corporate policy on the remote users accessing its network. In this way, the organization does not have to fully trust the authentication that was performed by the ISP. (See Figure 19–4, step 4.)

If the corporate gateway accepts the connection, it creates a virtual interface for PPP in a manner analogous to what it would use for a direct-dialed connection. With this virtual interface in place, link-layer frames can pass over this tunnel in both directions. (See Figure 19–4, step 5.) Frames from the remote user are received at the NAS, stripped of any link framing or transparency bytes, encapsulated in L2F, and forwarded over the appropriate tunnel. In the first release, the carrier protocol used by the L2F protocol within the tunnel is IP, requiring the frames to also be encapsulated within IP.

The corporate gateway accepts these frames, strips L2F, and processes the frames as normal incoming frames for the appropriate interface and protocol. The virtual interface behaves very much like a hardware interface, except that the hardware in this case is physically located at the ISP NAS. The reverse traffic direction behaves analogously, with the corporate gateway encapsulating the packet in L2F, and the NAS stripping L2F encapsulation before transmitting it out the physical interface to the remote user.

In addition, the NAS can optionally log the acceptance of the call and any relevant information with respect to the type of services provided to the remote user, such as duration of call, packets/bytes transferred, and protocol ports accessed. (See Figure 19–4, step 6.)

At this point, the connectivity is a point-to-point PPP connection whose endpoints are the remote user's networking application on one end and the termination of this connectivity into the corporate gateway's PPP support on the other. Because the remote user has become simply another dialup client of the corporate gateway access server, client connectivity can now be managed using traditional mechanisms with respect to further authorization, address negotiation, protocol access, accounting, and filtering. (See Figure 19–4, steps 7 and 8.)

Because L2F connection notifications for PPP clients contain sufficient information for a corporate gateway to authenticate and initialize its LCP state machine, the remote user is not required to be queried for CHAP authentication a second time, nor is the client required to undergo multiple rounds of LCP negotiation and convergence. These techniques are intended to optimize connection setup and are not intended to circumvent any functions required by the PPP specification.

Highlights of Virtual Dialup Service

The following sections discuss some of the significant differences between the standard Internet access service and the virtual dialup service with respect to authentication, address allocation, authorization, and accounting. It should be noted that the functionality provided by Cisco's network access servers are intended to provide for both the virtual dialup and traditional dialup services.

Authentication/Security

In a traditional dialup scenario, the ISP using a NAS in conjunction with a security server follows an authentication process by challenging the remote user for both the username and password. If the remote user passes this phase, the authorization phase can begin.

For the virtual dialup service, the ISP pursues authentication to the extent required to discover the user's apparent identity (and by implication, the user's desired corporate gateway). No password interaction is performed at this point. As soon as the corporate gateway is determined, a connection is initiated with the authentication information gathered by the ISP. The corporate gateway completes the authentication by either accepting or rejecting the connection. (For example, the connection is rejected in a PAP request in which the username or password is found to be incorrect.) When the connection is accepted, the corporate gateway can pursue another phase of authentication at the PPP layer. These additional authentication activities are outside the scope of the specification, but might include proprietary PPP extensions or textual challenges carried within a TCP/IP Telnet session.

For each L2F tunnel established, L2F tunnel security generates a unique random key to resist spoofing attacks. Within the L2F tunnel, each multiplexed session maintains a sequence number to prevent the duplication of packets.

Cisco provides the flexibility of allowing users to implement compression at the client end. In addition, encryption on the tunnel can be done using IP security (IPsec).

Authorization

When providing a traditional dialup service, the ISP is required to maintain per-user profiles defining the authorization. Thus a security server could interact with the NAS to provide policy-based usage to connecting users, based on their authentication. These policy statements can range from simple source/destination filters for a handful of sites to complex algorithms that determine specific applications, time of day access, and a long list of permitted or denied destinations. This process can become burdensome to the ISP, especially if providing access to remote users on behalf of corporations that require constant change to this policy.

In a virtual dialup service, the burden of providing detailed authorization based on policy statements is given directly to the remote user's corporation. By allowing end-to-end connectivity between remote users and their corporate gateway, all authorization can be performed as if the remote users are dialed into the corporate location directly. This setup frees the ISP from having to maintain a large database of individual user profiles based on many different corporations. More importantly, the virtual dialup service becomes more secure for the corporations using it because it allows the corporations to quickly react to changes in their remote user community.

Address Allocation

For a traditional Internet service, the user accepts that the IP address may be allocated dynamically from a pool of service provider addresses. This model often means that remote users have little or no access to their corporate network's resources because firewalls and security policies deny access to the corporate network from external IP addresses.

For the virtual dialup service, the corporate gateway can exist behind the corporate firewall and allocate addresses that are internal (and, in fact, can be RFC 1597 addresses, or non-IP addresses). Because L2F tunnels operate exclusively at the frame layer, the actual policies of such address management are irrelevant to correct virtual dialup service; for all purposes of PPP protocol handling, the dialin user appears to have connected at the corporate gateway.

Accounting

The requirement that both the NAS and the corporate gateway provide accounting data can mean that they may count packets, octets, and connection start and stop times.

Because virtual dialup is an access service, accounting of connection attempts (in particular, failed connection attempts) is of significant interest. The corporate gateway can reject new connections based on the authentication information gathered by the ISP, with corresponding logging. For cases in which the corporate gateway accepts the connection and then continues with further authentication, the corporate gateway might subsequently disconnect the client. For such scenarios, the disconnection indication back to the ISP can also include a reason.

Because the corporate gateway can decline a connection based on the authentication information collected by the ISP, accounting can easily draw a distinction between a series of failed connection attempts and a series of brief successful connections. Without this facility, the corporate gateway must always accept connection requests, and would need to exchange numerous PPP packets with the remote system.

PART 4

Bridging and Switching

Part 4, "Bridging and Switching," addresses key technologies influencing bridging and switching implementations. Individual chapters discuss the following topics:

Asynchronous Transfer Mode (ATM) Switching—Explores ATM technology, including components, connection types, addressing, multicasting challenges, and LAN Emulation (LANE).

Data-Link Switching (DLSw)—Defines and describes the operation of DLSw as implemented for the transport of SNA and NetBIOS traffic over IP WANs.

LAN Switching—Discusses LAN switching origins, benefits, operations, types, and applications.

Tag Switching—Discusses tag switching, including TDP, tag-allocation methods, and the different routing modules.

Mixed-Media Bridging—Defines and describes translational bridging and source-route transparent bridging, and uncovers key implementation challenges.

Source-Route Bridging (SRB)—Surveys SRB concepts, standards, route-discovery process, and the RIF frame format.

Transparent Bridging—Summarizes transparent bridging operations, bridging loops, and the spanning-tree algorithm.

CHAPTER ◼ 20

Asynchronous Transfer Mode (ATM) Switching

BACKGROUND

Asynchronous Transfer Mode (ATM) is an International Telecommunication Union–Telecommunication Standardization Sector (ITU-T) standard for cell relay wherein information for multiple service types, such as voice, video, or data, is conveyed in small, fixed-size cells. ATM networks are connection oriented. This chapter provides summaries of ATM protocols, services, and operation. Figure 20–1 illustrates a private ATM network and a public ATM network carrying voice, video, and data traffic.

Standards

ATM is based on the efforts of the ITU-T Broadband Integrated Services Digital Network (BISDN) standard. It was originally conceived as a high-speed transfer technology for voice, video, and data over public networks. The ATM Forum extended the ITU-T's vision of ATM for use over public *and* private networks. The ATM Forum has released work on the following specifications:

- User-to-Network Interface (UNI) 2.0

- UNI 3.0

- UNI 3.1

- Public-Network Node Interface (P-NNI)

- LAN Emulation (LANE)

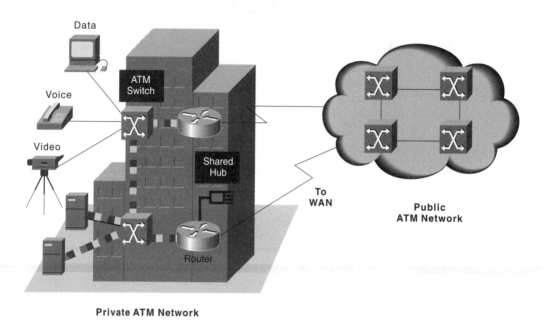

Figure 20–1
A private ATM network and a public ATM network both can carry voice, video, and data traffic.

ATM DEVICES AND THE NETWORK ENVIRONMENT

ATM is a cell-switching and multiplexing technology that combines the benefits of circuit switching (guaranteed capacity and constant transmission delay) with those of packet switching (flexibility and efficiency for intermittent traffic). It provides scalable bandwidth from a few megabits per second (Mbps) to many gigabits per second (Gbps). Because of its asynchronous nature, ATM is more efficient than synchronous technologies, such as time-division multiplexing (TDM).

With TDM, each user is assigned to a time slot, and no other station can send in that time slot. If a station has a lot of data to send, it can send only when its time slot comes up, even if all other time slots are empty. If, however, a station has nothing to transmit when its time slot comes up, the time slot is sent empty and is wasted. Because ATM is asynchronous, time slots are available on demand with information identifying the source of the transmission contained in the header of each ATM cell.

ATM Cell Basic Format

ATM transfers information in fixed-size units called *cells*. Each cell consists of 53 octets, or bytes. The first 5 bytes contain cell-header information, and the remaining 48 contain the "payload" (user information). Small fixed-length cells are well suited to transferring voice and video traffic because such traffic is intolerant of delays that result from having to wait for a large data packet to download, among other things. Figure 20–2 illustrates the basic format of an ATM cell.

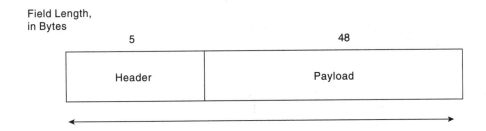

Figure 20–2
An ATM cell consists of a header and payload data.

ATM Devices

An ATM *network* is made up of an ATM *switch* and ATM *endpoints*. An ATM switch is responsible for cell transit through an ATM network. The job of an ATM switch is well defined: It accepts the incoming cell from an ATM endpoint or another ATM switch. It then reads and updates the cell-header information and quickly switches the cell to an output interface toward its destination. An ATM endpoint (or end system) contains an ATM network interface adapter. Examples of ATM endpoints are workstations, routers, digital service units (DSUs), LAN switches, and video coder-decoders (CODECs). Figure 20–3 illustrates an ATM network made up of ATM switches and ATM endpoints.

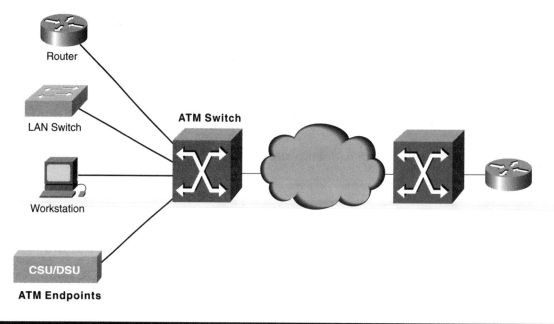

Figure 20–3
An ATM network comprises ATM switches and endpoints.

ATM Network Interfaces

An ATM network consists of a set of ATM switches interconnected by point-to-point ATM links or interfaces. ATM switches support two primary types of interfaces: UNI and NNI. The UNI connects ATM end systems (such as hosts and routers) to an ATM switch. The NNI connects two ATM switches.

Depending on whether the switch is owned and located at the customer's premises or publicly owned and operated by the telephone company, UNI and NNI can be further subdivided into public and private UNIs and NNIs. A private UNI connects an ATM endpoint and a private ATM switch. Its public counterpart connects an ATM endpoint or private switch to a public switch. A private NNI connects two ATM switches within the same private organization. A public one connects two ATM switches within the same public organization.

An additional specification, the Broadband Interexchange Carrier Interconnect (B-ICI), connects two public switches from different service providers. Figure 20–4 illustrates the ATM interface specifications for private and public networks.

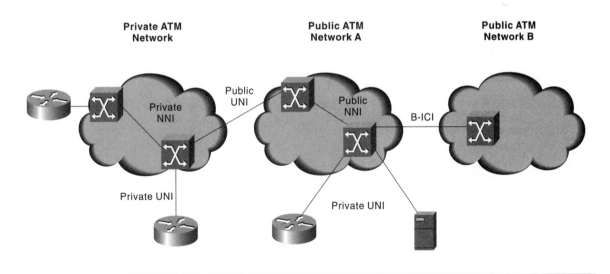

Figure 20–4
ATM interface specifications differ for private and public networks.

ATM CELL-HEADER FORMAT

An ATM cell header can be one of two formats: UNI or the NNI. The UNI header is used for communication between ATM endpoints and ATM switches in private ATM networks. The NNI header is used for communication between ATM switches. Figure 20–5 depicts the basic ATM cell format, the ATM UNI cell-header format, and the ATM NNI cell-header format.

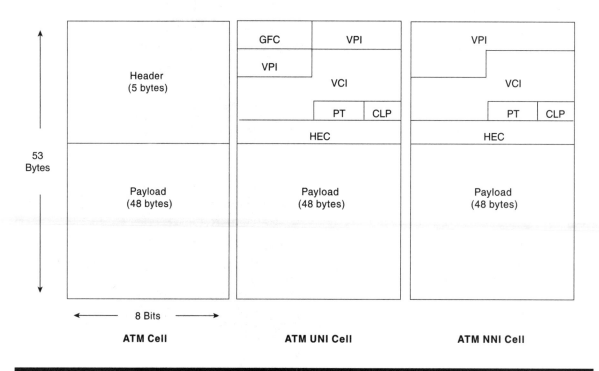

Figure 20–5

An ATM cell, ATM UNI cell, and ATM NNI cell header each contain 48 bytes of payload.

Unlike the UNI, the NNI header does not include the Generic Flow Control (GFC) field. Additionally, the NNI header has a Virtual Path Identifier (VPI) field that occupies the first 12 bits, allowing for larger trunks between public ATM switches.

ATM Cell-Header Fields

In addition to GFC and VPI header fields, several others are used in ATM cell-header fields. The following descriptions summarize the ATM cell-header fields illustrated in Figure 20–5:

- *Generic Flow Control (GFC)*—Provides local functions, such as identifying multiple stations that share a single ATM interface. This field is typically not used and is set to its default value.

- *Virtual Path Identifier (VPI)*—In conjunction with the VCI, identifies the next destination of a cell as it passes through a series of ATM switches on the way to its destination.

- *Virtual Channel Identifier (VCI)*—In conjunction with the VPI, identifies the next destination of a cell as it passes through a series of ATM switches on the way to its destination.

- *Payload Type (PT)*—Indicates in the first bit whether the cell contains user data or control data. If the cell contains user data, the second bit indicates congestion, and the third bit indicates whether the cell is the last in a series of cells that represent a single AAL5 frame.

- *Congestion Loss Priority (CLP)*—Indicates whether the cell should be discarded if it encounters extreme congestion as it moves through the network. If the CLP bit equals 1, the cell should be discarded in preference to cells with the CLP bit equal to zero.

- *Header Error Control (HEC)*—Calculates checksum only on the header itself.

ATM Services

Three types of ATM services exist: permanent virtual circuits (PVC), switched virtual circuits (SVC), and connectionless service (which is similar to SMDS).

A PVC allows direct connectivity between sites. In this way, a PVC is similar to a leased line. Among its advantages, a PVC guarantees availability of a connection and does not require call setup procedures between switches. Disadvantages of PVCs include static connectivity and manual setup.

An SVC is created and released dynamically and remains in use only as long as data is being transferred. In this sense, it is similar to a telephone call. Dynamic call control requires a signaling protocol between the ATM endpoint and the ATM switch. The advantages of SVCs include connection flexibility and call setup that can be handled automatically by a networking device. Disadvantages include the extra time and overhead required to set up the connection.

ATM Virtual Connections

ATM networks are fundamentally connection oriented, which means that a virtual channel (VC) must be set up across the ATM network prior to any data transfer. (A virtual channel is roughly equivalent to a virtual circuit.)

Two types of ATM connections exist: *virtual paths*, which are identified by virtual path identifiers, and *virtual channels*, which are identified by the combination of a VPI and a *virtual channel identifier* (VCI).

A virtual path is a bundle of virtual channels, all of which are switched transparently across the ATM network on the basis of the common VPI. All VCIs and VPIs, however, have only local significance across a particular link and are remapped, as appropriate, at each switch.

A transmission path is a bundle of VPs. Figure 20–6 illustrates how VCs concatenate to create VPs, which, in turn, concatenate to create a transmission path.

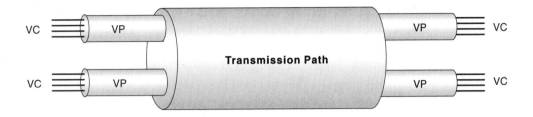

Figure 20–6
VCs concatenate to create VPs.

ATM SWITCHING OPERATIONS

The basic operation of an ATM switch is straightforward: The cell is received across a link on a known VCI or VPI value. The switch looks up the connection value in a local translation table to determine the outgoing port (or ports) of the connection and the new VPI/VCI value of the connection on that link. The switch then retransmits the cell on that outgoing link with the appropriate connection identifiers. Because all VCIs and VPIs have only local significance across a particular link, these values are remapped, as necessary, at each switch.

ATM REFERENCE MODEL

The ATM architecture uses a logical model to describe the functionality it supports. ATM functionality corresponds to the physical layer and part of the data link layer of the OSI reference model.

The ATM reference model is composed of the following planes, which span all layers:

- *Control*—This plane is responsible for generating and managing signaling requests.

- *User*—This plane is responsible for managing the transfer of data.

- *Management*— This plane contains two components:

  - *Layer management* manages layer-specific functions, such as the detection of failures and protocol problems.
  - *Plane management* manages and coordinates functions related to the complete system.

The ATM reference model is composed of the following ATM layers:

- *Physical layer*—Analogous to the physical layer of the OSI reference model, the ATM physical layer manages the medium-dependent transmission.

- *ATM layer*—Combined with the ATM adaptation layer, the ATM layer is roughly analogous to the data link layer of the OSI reference model. The ATM layer is responsible for establishing connections and passing cells through the ATM network. To do this, it uses information in the header of each ATM cell.

- *ATM adaptation layer (AAL)*—Combined with the ATM layer, the AAL is roughly analogous to the data link layer of the OSI model. The AAL is responsible for isolating higher-layer protocols from the details of the ATM processes.

Finally, the higher layers residing above the AAL accept user data, arrange it into packets, and hand it to the AAL. Figure 20–7 illustrates the ATM reference model.

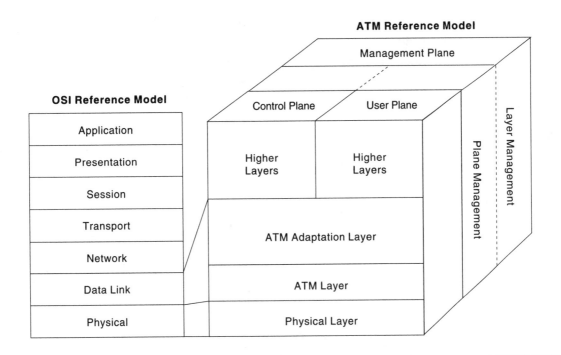

Figure 20-7
The ATM reference model relates to the lowest two layers of the OSI reference model.

The ATM Physical Layer

The ATM physical layer has four functions: Bits are converted into cells, the transmission and receipt of bits on the physical medium are controlled, ATM cell boundaries are tracked, and cells are packaged into the appropriate types of frames for the physical medium.

The ATM physical layer is divided into two parts: the physical medium-dependent (PMD) sublayer and the transmission-convergence (TC) sublayer.

The PMD sublayer provides two key functions. First, it synchronizes transmission and reception by sending and receiving a continuous flow of bits with associated timing information. Second, it specifies the physical media for the physical medium used, including connector types and cable. Examples of physical medium standards for ATM include Synchronous Optical Network/ Synchronous Digital Hierarchy (SONET/SDH), DS-3/E3, 155 Mbps over multimode fiber (MMF) using the 8B/10B encoding scheme, and 155 Mbps 8B/10B over shielded twisted-pair (STP) cabling.

The TC sublayer has four functions: cell dilineation, header error-control (HEC) sequence generation and verification, cell-rate decoupling, and transmission-frame adaptation. The cell delineation function maintains ATM cell boundaries, allowing devices to locate cells within a stream of bits. HEC sequence generation and verification generates and checks the header error-control code to ensure valid data. Cell-rate decoupling maintains synchronization and inserts or suppresses idle (unassigned) ATM cells to adapt the rate of valid ATM cells to the payload capacity of the transmission system. Transmission-frame adaptation packages ATM cells into frames acceptable to the particular physical-layer implementation.

ATM Adaptation Layers: AAL1

AAL1, a connection-oriented service, is suitable for handling circuit-emulation applications, such as voice and video conferencing. Circuit-emulation service also accommodates the attachment of equipment currently using leased lines to an ATM backbone network. AAL1 requires timing synchronization between the source and destination. For this reason, AAL1 depends on a medium, such as SONET, that supports clocking. The AAL1 process prepares a cell for transmission in three steps. First, synchronous samples (for example, 1 byte of data at a sampling rate of 125 microseconds) are inserted into the Payload field. Second, Sequence Number (SN) and Sequence Number Protection (SNP) fields are added to provide information that the receiving AAL1 uses to verify that it has received cells in the correct order. Third, the remainder of the Payload field is filled with enough single bytes to equal 48 bytes. Figure 20–8 illustrates how AAL1 prepares a cell for transmission.

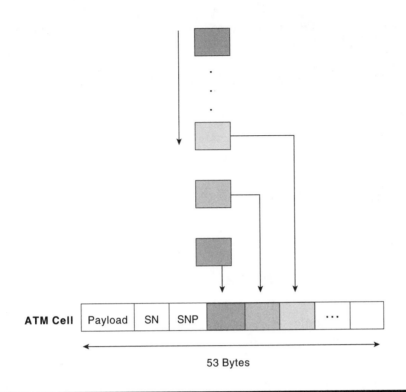

ATM Cell | Payload | SN | SNP | ... |

53 Bytes

Figure 20–8
AAL1 prepares a cell for transmission so that the cells retain their order.

ATM Adaptation Layers: AAL3/4

AAL3/4 supports both connection-oriented and connectionless data. It was designed for network service providers and is closely aligned with Switched Multimegabit Data Service (SMDS). AAL3/4 is used to transmit SMDS packets over an ATM network.

AAL3/4 prepares a cell for transmission in four steps. First, the convergence sublayer (CS) creates a protocol data unit (PDU) by prepending a beginning/end tag header to the frame and appending a length field as a trailer. Second, the segmentation and reassembly (SAR) sublayer fragments the PDU and prepends a header to it. Then, the SAR sublayer appends a CRC-10 trailer to each PDU fragment for error control. Finally, the completed SAR PDU becomes the Payload field of an ATM cell to which the ATM layer prepends the standard ATM header.

An AAL 3/4 SAR PDU header consists of Type, Sequence Number, and Multiplexing Identifier fields. Type fields identify whether a cell is the beginning, continuation, or end of a message. Sequence number fields identify the order in which cells should be reassembled. The Multiplexing Identifier field determines which cells from different traffic sources are interleaved on the same virtual circuit connection (VCC) so that the correct cells are reassembled at the destination.

ATM Adaptation Layers: AAL5

AAL5 is the primary AAL for data and supports both connection-oriented and connectionless data. It is used to transfer most non-SMDS data, such as classical IP over ATM and LAN Emulation (LANE). AAL5 also is known as the simple and efficient adaptation layer (SEAL) because the SAR sublayer simply accepts the CS-PDU and segments it into 48-octet SAR-PDUs without adding any additional fields.

AAL5 prepares a cell for transmission in three steps. First, the CS sublayer appends a variable-length pad and an 8-byte trailer to a frame. The pad ensures that the resulting PDU falls on the 48-byte boundary of an ATM cell. The trailer includes the length of the frame and a 32-bit cyclic redundancy check (CRC) computed across the entire PDU. This allows the AAL5 receiving process to detect bit errors, lost cells, or cells that are out of sequence. Second, the SAR sublayer segments the CS-PDU into 48-byte blocks. A header and trailer are not added (as is in AAL3/4), so messages cannot be interleaved. Finally, the ATM layer places each block into the Payload field of an ATM cell. For all cells except the last, a bit in the Payload Type (PT) field is set to zero to indicate that the cell is not the last cell in a series that represents a single frame. For the last cell, the bit in the PT field is set to one.

ATM Addressing

The ITU-T standard is based on the use of E.164 addresses (similar to telephone numbers) for public ATM (BISDN) networks. The ATM Forum extended ATM addressing to include private networks. It decided on the subnetwork or overlay model of addressing, in which the ATM layer is responsible for mapping network-layer addresses to ATM addresses. This subnetwork model is an alternative to using network-layer protocol addresses (such as IP and IPX) and existing routing protocols (such as IGRP and RIP). The ATM Forum defined an address format based on the structure of the OSI network service access point (NSAP) addresses.

Subnetwork Model of Addressing

The subnetwork model of addressing decouples the ATM layer from any existing higher-layer protocols, such as IP or IPX. Therefore, it requires an entirely new addressing scheme and routing protocol. Each ATM system must be assigned an ATM address, in addition to any higher-layer protocol addresses. This requires an ATM address resolution protocol (ATM ARP) to map higher-layer addresses to their corresponding ATM addresses.

NSAP Format ATM Addresses

The 20-byte NSAP-format ATM addresses are designed for use within private ATM networks, whereas public networks typically use E.164 addresses, which are formatted as defined by ITU-T. The ATM Forum has specified an NSAP encoding for E.164 addresses, which is used for encoding E.164 addresses within private networks, but this address can also be used by some private networks.

Such private networks can base their own (NSAP format) addressing on the E.164 address of the public UNI to which they are connected and can take the address prefix from the E.164 number, identifying local nodes by the lower-order bits.

All NSAP-format ATM addresses consist of three components: the authority and format identifier (AFI), the initial domain identifier (IDI), and the domain specific part (DSP). The AFI identifies the type and format of the IDI, which, in turn, identifies the address allocation and administrative authority. The DSP contains actual routing information.

Three formats of private ATM addressing differ by the nature of the AFI and IDI. In the NSAP-encoded E.164 format, the IDI is an E.164 number. In the DCC format, the IDI is a data country code (DCC), which identifies particular countries, as specified in ISO 3166. Such addresses are administered by the ISO National Member Body in each country. In the ICD format, the IDI is an international code designator (ICD), which is allocated by the ISO 6523 registration authority (the British Standards Institute). ICD codes identify particular international organizations.

The ATM Forum recommends that organizations or private-network service providers use either the DCC or ICD formats to form their own numbering plan.

Figure 20–9 illustrates the three formats of ATM addresses used for private networks.

ATM Address Fields

The following descriptions summarize the fields illustrated in Figure 20–9:

- *AFI*—Identifies the type and format of the address (E.164, ICD, or DCC).

- *DCC*—Identifies particular countries.

- *High-Order Domain Specific Part (HO-DSP)*—Combines the routing domain (RD) and area indentifier (AREA) of the NSAP addresses. The ATM Forum combined these fields to support a flexible, multilevel addressing hierarchy for prefix-based routing protocols.

- *End System Identifier (ESI)*—Specifies the 48-bit MAC address, as administered by the Institute of Electrical and Electronic Engineers (IEEE).

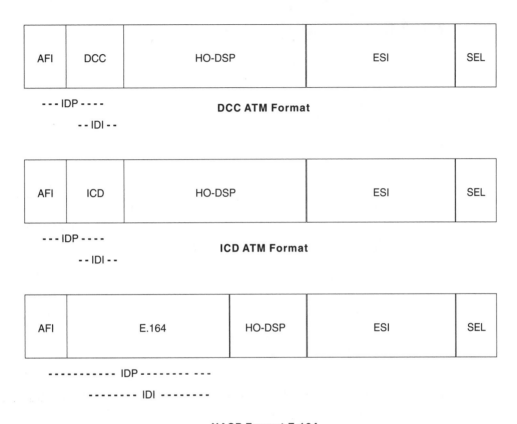

Figure 20–9
Three formats of ATM addresses are used for private networks.

- *Selector (SEL)*—Used for local multiplexing within end stations and has no network significance.

- *ICD*—Identifies particular international organizations.

- *E.164*—Indicates the BISDN E.164 address.

ATM CONNECTIONS

ATM supports two types of connections: point-to-point and point-to-multipoint.

Point-to-point connects two ATM end systems and can be unidirectional (one-way communication) or bidirectional (two-way communication). Point-to-multipoint connects a single-source end system (known as the root node) to multiple destination end systems (known as leaves). Such connections are unidirectional only. Root nodes can transmit to leaves, but leaves cannot transmit to the root or each other on the same connection. Cell replication is done within the ATM network by the ATM switches where the connection splits into two or more branches.

It would be desirable in ATM networks to have bidirectional multipoint-to-multipoint connections. Such connections are analogous to the broadcasting or multicasting capabilities of shared-media LANs, such as Ethernet and Token Ring. A broadcasting capability is easy to implement in shared-media LANs, where all nodes on a single LAN segment must process all packets sent on that segment. Unfortunately, a multipoint-to-multipoint capability cannot be implemented by using AAL5, which is the most common AAL to transmit data across an ATM network. Unlike AAL3/4, with its Message Identifier (MID) field, AAL5 does not provide a way within its cell format to interleave cells from different AAL5 packets on a single connection. This means that all AAL5 packets sent to a particular destination across a particular connection must be received in sequence; otherwise, the destination reassembly process will be unable to reconstruct the packets. This is why AAL5 point-to-multipoint connections can be only unidirectional. If a leaf node were to transmit an AAL5 packet onto the connection, for example, it would be received by both the root node and all other leaf nodes. At these nodes, the packet sent by the leaf could be interleaved with packets sent by the root and possibly other leaf nodes, precluding the reassembly of any of the interleaved packets.

ATM AND MULTICASTING

ATM requires some form of multicast capability. AAL5 (which is the most common AAL for data) currently does not support interleaving packets, so it does not support multicasting.

If a leaf node transmitted a packet onto an AAL5 connection, the packet can get intermixed with other packets and be improperly reassembled. Three methods have been proposed for solving this problem: VP multicasting, multicast server, and overlaid point-to-multipoint connection.

Under the first solution, a multipoint-to-multipoint VP links all nodes in the multicast group, and each node is given a unique VCI value within the VP. Interleaved packets hence can be identified by the unique VCI value of the source. Unfortunately, this mechanism would require a protocol to uniquely allocate VCI values to nodes, and such a protocol mechanism currently does not exist. It is also unclear whether current SAR devices could easily support such a mode of operation.

A multicast server is another potential solution to the problem of multicasting over an ATM network. In this scenario, all nodes wanting to transmit onto a multicast group set up a point-to-point connection with an external device known as a multicast server (perhaps better described as a *resequencer* or *serializer*). The multicast server, in turn, is connected to all nodes wanting to receive the multicast packets through a point-to-multipoint connection. The multicast server receives packets across the point-to-point connections and then retransmits them across the point-to-multipoint connection—but only after ensuring that the packets are serialized (that is, one packet is fully transmitted prior to the next being sent). In this way, cell interleaving is precluded.

An overlaid point-to-multipoint connection is the third potential solution to the problem of multicasting over an ATM network. In this scenario, all nodes in the multicast group establish a point-to-multipoint connection with each other node in the group and, in turn, become leaves in the equivalent connections of all other nodes. Hence, all nodes can both transmit to and receive from all other nodes. This solution requires each node to maintain a connection for each transmitting member of the group, whereas the multicast-server mechanism requires only two connections. This type of connection would also require a registration process for informing the nodes that join a group of the other nodes in the group so that the new nodes can form the point-to-multipoint connection. The other nodes must know about the new node so that they can add the new node to their own point-to-multipoint connections. The multicast-server mechanism is more scalable in terms of connection resources but has the problem of requiring a centralized resequencer, which is both a potential bottleneck and a single point of failure.

ATM QUALITY OF SERVICE (QoS)

ATM supports QoS guarantees comprising of traffic contract, traffic shaping, and traffic policing.

A *traffic contract* specifies an envelope that describes the intended data flow. This envelope specifies values for peak bandwidth, average sustained bandwidth, and burst size, among others. When an ATM end system connects to an ATM network, it enters a contract with the network, based on QoS parameters.

Traffic shaping is the use of queues to constrain data bursts, limit peak data rate, and smooth jitters so that traffic will fit within the promised envelope. ATM devices are responsible for adhering to the contract by means of traffic shaping. ATM switches can use *traffic policing* to enforce the contract The switch can measure the actual traffic flow and compare it against the agreed-upon traffic envelope. If the switch finds that traffic is outside of the agreed-upon parameters, it can set the cell-loss priority (CLP) bit of the offending cells. Setting the CLP bit makes the cell *discard eligible*, which means that any switch handling the cell is allowed to drop the cell during periods of congestion.

ATM Signaling and Connection Establishment

When an ATM device wants to establish a connection with another ATM device, it sends a signaling-request packet to its directly connected ATM switch. This request contains the ATM address of the desired ATM endpoint, as well as any QoS parameters required for the connection.

ATM signaling protocols vary by the type of ATM link, which can be either UNI signals or NNI signals. UNI is used between an ATM end system and ATM switch across ATM UNI, and NNI is used across NNI links.

The ATM Forum UNI 3.1 specification is the current standard for ATM UNI signaling. The UNI 3.1 specification is based on the Q.2931 public network signaling protocol developed by the ITU-T. UNI signaling requests are carried in a well-known default connection: VPI = 0, VPI = 5.

Standards currently exist only for ATM UNI signaling, but standardization work is continuing on NNI signaling.

The ATM Connection-Establishment Process

ATM signaling uses the *one-pass* method of connection setup that is used in all modern telecommunication networks, such as the telephone network. An ATM connection setup proceeeds in the following manner. First, the source end system sends a connection-signaling request. The connection request is propagated through the network. As a result, connections are set up through the network. The connection request reaches the final destination, which either accepts or rejects the connection request.

Connection-Request Routing and Negotiation

Routing of the connection request is governed by an ATM routing protocol (which routes connections based on destination and source addresses), traffic, and the QoS parameters requested by the source end system. Negotiating a connection request that is rejected by the destination is limited because call routing is based on parameters of initial connection; changing parameters might, in turn, affect the connection routing. Figure 20–10 highlights the one-pass method of ATM connection establishment.

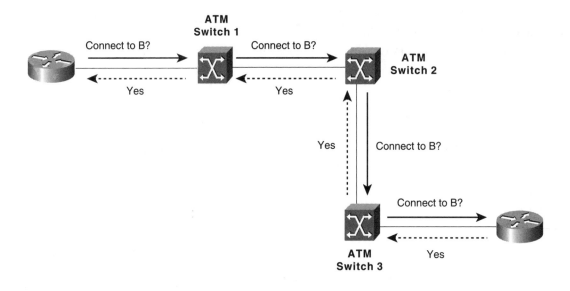

Figure 20–10
ATM devices establish connections through the one-pass method.

ATM CONNECTION-MANAGEMENT MESSAGES

A number of connection-management message types, including setup, call proceeding, connect, and release, are used to establish and tear down an ATM connection. The source end system sends a setup message (including the destination end-system address and any traffic QoS parameters) when it wants to set up a connection. The ingress switch sends a call proceeding message back to the source in response to the setup message. The destination end system next sends a connect message if the connection is accepted. The destination end system sends a release message back to the source end system if the connection is rejected, thereby clearing the connection.

Connection-management messages are used to establish an ATM connection in the following manner. First, a source end system sends a setup message, which is forwarded to the first ATM switch (ingress switch) in the network. This switch sends a call proceeding message and invokes an ATM routing protocol. The signaling request is propagated across the network. The exit switch (called the *egress* switch) that is attached to the destination end system receives the setup message. The egress switch forwards the setup message to the end system across its UNI, and the ATM end system sends a connect message if the connection is accepted. The connect message traverses back through the network along the same path to the source end system, which sends a connect acknowledge message back to the destination to acknowledge the connection. Data transfer can then begin.

LAN EMULATION (LANE)

LANE is a standard defined by the ATM Forum that gives to stations attached via ATM the same capabilities they normally obtain from legacy LANs, such as Ethernet and Token Ring. As the name suggests, the function of the LANE protocol is to emulate a LAN on top of an ATM network. Specifically, the LANE protocol defines mechanisms for emulating either an IEEE 802.3 Ethernet or an 802.5 Token Ring LAN. The current LANE protocol does not define a separate encapsulation for FDDI. (FDDI packets must be mapped into either Ethernet or Token Ring emulated LANs [ELANs] by using existing translational bridging techniques.) Fast Ethernet (100BaseT) and IEEE 802.12 (100VG-AnyLAN) both can be mapped unchanged because they use the same packet formats. Figure 20–11 compares a physical LAN and an ELAN.

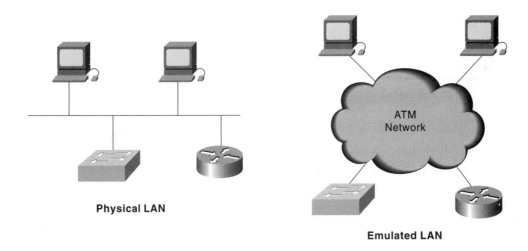

Figure 20–11
ATM networks can emulate a physical LAN.

The LANE protocol defines a service interface for higher-layer (that is, network-layer) protocols that is identical to that of existing LANs. Data sent across the ATM network is encapsulated in the appropriate LAN MAC packet format. Simply put, the LANE protocols make an ATM network look and behave like an Ethernet or Token Ring LAN—albeit one operating much faster than an actual Ethernet or Token Ring LAN network.

It is important to note that LANE does not attempt to emulate the actual MAC protocol of the specific LAN concerned (that is, CSMA/CD for Ethernet or token passing for IEEE 802.5). LANE requires no modifications to higher-layer protocols to enable their operation over an ATM network. Because the LANE service presents the same service interface of existing MAC protocols to network-layer drivers (such as an NDIS- or ODI-like driver interface), no changes are required in those drivers.

The LANE Protocol Architecture

The basic function of the LANE protocol is to resolve MAC addresses to ATM addresses. The goal is to resolve such address mappings so that LANE end systems can set up direct connections between themselves and then forward data. The LANE protocol is deployed in two types of ATM-attached equipment: ATM network interface cards (NICs) and internetworking and LAN switching equipment.

ATM NICs implement the LANE protocol and interface to the ATM network but present the current LAN service interface to the higher-level protocol drivers within the attached end system. The network-layer protocols on the end system continue to communicate as if they were on a known LAN by using known procedures. However, they are able to use the vastly greater bandwidth of ATM networks.

The second class of network gear to implement LANE consists of ATM-attached LAN switches and routers. These devices, together with directly attached ATM hosts equipped with ATM NICs, are used to provide a virtual LAN (VLAN) service in which ports on the LAN switches are assigned to particular VLANs independently of physical location. Figure 20–12 shows the LANE protocol architecture implemented in ATM network devices.

NOTES

The LANE protocol does not directly affect ATM switches. LANE, as with most of the other ATM internetworking protocols, builds on the overlay model. As such, the LANE protocols operate transparently over and through ATM switches, using only standard ATM signaling procedures.

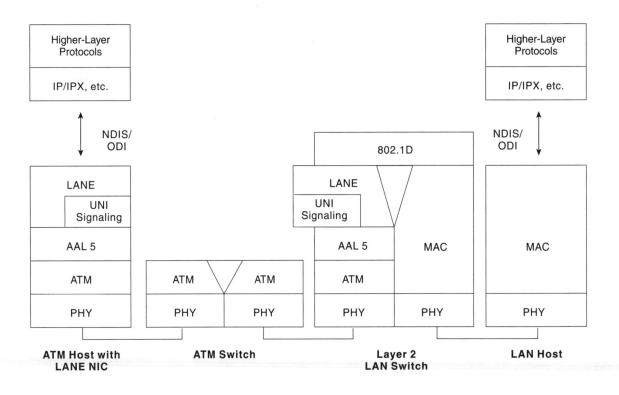

Figure 20–12
LANE protocol architecture can be implemented in ATM network devices.

LANE Components

The LANE protocol defines the operation of a single ELAN or VLAN. Although multiple ELANs can simultaneously exist on a single ATM network, an ELAN emulates either an Ethernet or a Token Ring and consists of the following components:

- *LAN emulation client (LEC)*—The LEC is an entity in an end system that performs data forwarding, address resolution, and registration of MAC addresses with the LAN emulation server (LES). The LEC also provides a standard LAN interface to higher-level protocols on legacy

LANs. An ATM end system that connects to multiple ELANs has one LEC per ELAN.

- *LES*—The LES provides a central control point for LECs to forward registration and control information. (Only one LES exists per ELAN.)

- *Broadcast and unknown server (BUS)*—The BUS is a multicast server that is used to flood unknown destination address traffic and to forward multicast and broadcast traffic to clients within a particular ELAN. Each LEC is associated with only one BUS per ELAN.

- *LAN emulation configuration server (LECS)*—The LECS maintains a database of LECs and the ELANs to which they belong. This server accepts queries from LECs and responds with the appropriate ELAN identifier, namely the ATM address of the LES that serves the appropriate ELAN. One LECS per administrative domain serves all ELANs within that domain.

Figure 20–13 illustrates the components of an ELAN.

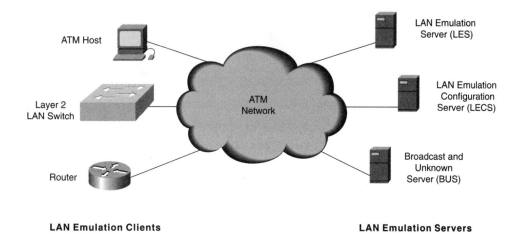

Figure 20–13
An ELAN consists of clients, and servers, and various intermediate nodes.

LAN Emulation Connection Types

The Phase 1 LANE entities communicate with each other by using a series of ATM VCCs. LECs maintain separate connections for data transmission and control traffic. The LANE data connections are data-direct VCC, multicast send VCC, and multicast forward VCC.

Data-direct VCC is a bidirectional point-to-point VCC set up between two LECs that want to exchange data. Two LECs typically use the same data-direct VCC to carry all packets between them rather than opening a new VCC for each MAC address pair. This technique conserves connection resources and connection setup latency.

Multicast send VCC is a bidirectional point-to-point VCC set up by the LEC to the BUS.

Multicast forward VCC is a unidirectional VCC set up to the LEC from the BUS. It typically is a point-to-multipoint connection, with each LEC as a leaf.

Figure 20–14 shows the LANE data connections.

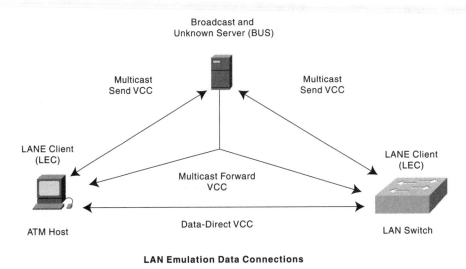

LAN Emulation Data Connections

Figure 20–14
LANE data connections use a series of VCLs to link a LAN switch and ATM hosts.

Control connections include configuration-direct VCC, control-direct VCC, and control-distribute VCC. Configuration-direct VCC is a bidirectional point-to-point VCC set up by the LEC to the LECS. Control-direct VCC is a bidirectional VCC set up by the LEC to the LES. Control-distribute VCC is a unidirectional VCC set up from the LES back to the LEC (this is typically a point-to-multipoint connection). Figure 20–15 illustrates LANE control connections.

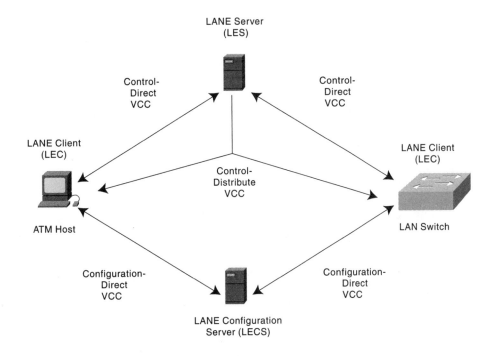

LAN Emulation Control Connections

Figure 20–15
LANE control connections link the LES, LECS, LAN switch, and ATM host.

LANE Operation

The operation of a LANE system and components is best understood by examining these stages of LEC operation: intialization and configuration, joining and registering with the LES, finding and joining the BUS, and data transfer.

Initialization and Configuration

Upon initialization, an LEC finds the LECs to obtain required configuration information. It begins this process when the LEC obtains its own ATM address, which typically occurs through address registration.

The LEC must then determine the location of the LECS. To do this, the LEC first must locate the LECS by one of the following methods: by using a defined ILMI procedure to determine the LECS address, by using a well-known LECS address, or by using a well-known permanent connection to the LECS (VPI = 0, VCI = 17).

When the LECS is found, the LEC sets up a configuration-direct VCC to the LECS and sends a LE_CONFIGURE_REQUEST. If a matching entry is found, the LECS returns a LE_CONFIGURE_RESPONSE to the LEC with the configuration information it requires to connect to its target ELAN, including the following: ATM address of the LES, type of LAN being emulated, maximum packet size on the ELAN, and ELAN name (a text string for display purposes).

Joining and Registering with the LES

When an LEC joins the LES and registers its own ATM and MAC addresses, it does so by following three steps:

   1. After the LEC obtains the LES address, the LEC optionally clears the connection to the LECS, sets up the control-direct VCC to the LES, and sends an LE_JOIN_REQUEST on that VCC. This allows the LEC to register its own MAC and ATM addresses with the LES and

(optionally) any other MAC addresses for which it is proxying. This information is maintained so that no two LECs will register the same MAC or ATM address.

2. After receipt of the LE_JOIN_REQUEST, the LES checks with the LECS via its open connection, verifies the request, and confirms the client's membership.

3. Upon successful verification, the LES adds the LEC as a leaf of its point-to-multipoint control-distribute VCC and issues the LEC a successful LE_JOIN_RESPONSE that contains a unique LAN Emulation Client ID (LECID). The LECID is used by the LEC to filter its own broadcasts from the BUS.

Finding and Joining the BUS

After the LEC has successfully joined the LECS, its first task is to find the BUS/s ATM address to join the broadcast group and become a member of the emulated LAN.

First, the LEC creates an LE_ARP_REQUEST packet with the MAC address 0xFFFFFFFF. Then the LEC sends this special LE_ARP packet on the control-direct VCC to the LES. The LES recognizes that the LEC is looking for the BUS and responds with the BUS's ATM address on the control-distribute VCC.

When the LEC has the BUS's ATM address, it joins the BUS by first creating a signaling packet with the BUS's ATM address and setting up a multicast-send VCC with the BUS. Upon receipt of the signaling request, the BUS adds the LEC as a leaf on its point-to-multipoint multicast forward VCC. The LEC is now a member of the ELAN and is ready for data transfer.

Data Transfer

The final state, data transfer, involves resolving the ATM address of the destination LEC and actual data transfer, which might include the flush procedure.

When a LEC has a data packet to send to an unknown-destination MAC address, it must discover the ATM address of the destination LEC through which the particular address can be reached. To accomplish this, the LEC first sends the data frame to the BUS (via the multicast send VCC) for distribution to all LECs on the ELAN via the multicast forward VCC. This is done because resolving the ATM address might take some time, and many network protocols are intolerant of delays.

The LEC then sends a LAN Emulation Address Resolution Protocol Request (LE_ARP_Request) control frame to the LES via a control-direct VCC.

If the LES knows the answer, it responds with the ATM address of the LEC that owns the MAC address in question. If the LES does not know the answer, it floods the LE_ARP_REQUEST to some or all LECs (under rules that parallel the BUS's flooding of the actual data frame, but over control-direct and control-distribute VCCs instead of the multicast send or multicast forward VCCs used by the BUS). If bridge/switching devices with LEC software participating in the ELAN exist, they translate and forward the ARP on their LAN interfaces.

In the case of actual data transfer, if an LE_ARP is received, the LEC sets up a data-direct VCC to the destination node and uses this for data transfer rather than the BUS path. Before it can do this, however, the LEC might need to use the LANE flush procedure, which ensures that all packets previously sent to the BUS were delivered to the destination prior to the use of the data-direct VCC. In the flush procedure, a control cell is sent down the first transmission path following the last packet. The LEC then waits until the destination acknowledges receipt of the flush packet before using the second path to send packets.

CHAPTER 21

Data-Link Switching

BACKGROUND

Data-link switching (DLSw) provides a means of transporting IBM Systems Network Architecture (SNA) and network basic input/output system (NetBIOS) traffic over an IP network. It serves as an alternative to source-route bridging (SRB), a protocol for transporting SNA and NetBIOS traffic in Token Ring environments that was widely deployed prior to the introduction of DLSw. In general, DLSw addresses some of the shortcomings of SRB for certain communication requirements—particularly in WAN implementations. This chapter contrasts DLSw with SRB, summarizes underlying protocols, and provides a synopsis of normal protocol operations.

DLSw initially emerged as a proprietary IBM solution in 1992. It was first submitted to the IETF as RFC 1434 in 1993. DLSw is now documented in detail by IETF RFC 1795, which was submitted in April 1995. DLSw was jointly developed by the Advanced Peer-to-Peer Networking (APPN) Implementors Workshop (AIW) and the Data-Link Switching Related Interest Group (DLSw RIG).

RFC 1795 describes three primary functions of DLSw;

- The Switch-to-Switch Protocol (SSP) is the protocol maintained between two DLSw nodes or routers.

- The termination of SNA data-link control (DLC) connections helps to reduce the likelihood of link-layer timeouts across WANs.

- The local mapping of DLC connections to a DLSw circuit.

Each of these functions is discussed in detail in this chapter. Figure 21–1 illustrates a generalized DLSw environment.

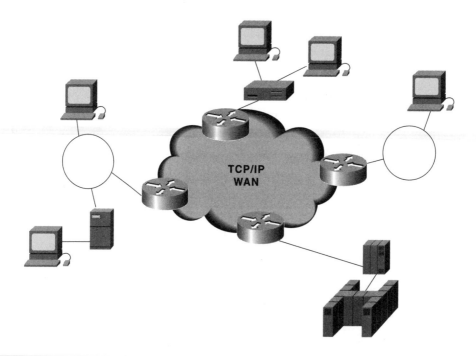

Figure 21–1
A DLSw circuit facilitates SNA connectivity over an IP WAN.

DLSw Contrasted with Source-Route Bridging

The principal difference between SRB and DLSw involves support of local termination. SNA and NetBIOS traffic rely on link-layer acknowledgments and keep-alive messages to ensure the integrity of connections and the delivery of data. For connection-oriented data, the local DLSw node or router terminates data-link control. Therefore, link-layer acknowledgments and keep-alive messages do not have to traverse a WAN. By contrast, DLC for SRB is handled on an end-to-end basis, which results in increased potential for DLC timeouts over WAN connections.

Although SRB has been a viable solution for many environments, several issues limit the usefulness of SRB for transport of SNA and NetBIOS in WAN implementations. Chief among them are the following constraints:

- SRB hop-count limitation of seven hops

- Broadcast traffic handling (from SRB explorer frames or NetBIOS name queries)

- Unnecessary traffic forwarding (acknowledgments and keep-alives)

- Lack of flow control and prioritization

Figure 21–2 illustrates the basic end-to-end nature of an SRB connection over a WAN link.

Local termination of DLC connections by DLSw provides a number of advantages over SRB-based environments. DLSw local termination eliminates the requirement for link-layer acknowledgments and keep-alive messages to flow across a WAN. In addition, local termination reduces the likelihood of link-layer timeouts across WANs. Similarly, DLSw ensures that the broadcast of search frames is controlled by the DLSw when the location of a target system is discovered. Figure 21–3 illustrates the flow of information and the use of local acknowledgment in a DLSw environment.

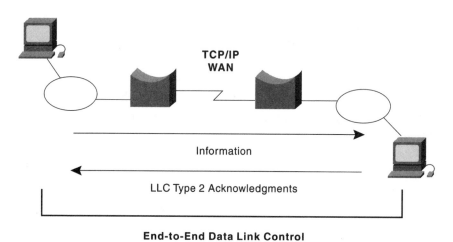

End-to-End Data Link Control

Figure 21–2

SRB provides an end-to-end connection over an IP WAN.

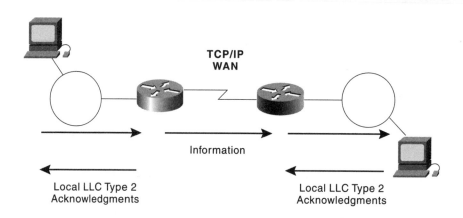

Figure 21–3

DLSw uses local acknowledgment to control data flow.

DLSw SNA Support

One of the advantages inherent with DLSw is that DLSw supplies broader device and media support than previously available with SRB. DLSw accommodates a number of typical SNA environments and provides for IEEE 802.2-compliant LAN support, which includes support for SNA Physical Unit (PU) 2, PU 2.1, and PU 4 systems and NetBIOS-based systems.

DLSw provides for Synchronous Data Link Control (SDLC) support, covering PU 2 (primary or secondary) and PU 2.1 systems. With SDLC-attached systems, each SDLC PU is presented to the DLSw Switch-to-Switch Protocol (SSP) as a unique Media Access Control (MAC)/service access point (SAP) address pair. With Token Ring–attached systems, a DLSw node appears as a source-route bridge. Remote Token Ring systems accessed via a DLSw node are seen as attached to an adjacent ring. This apparent adjacent ring is known as a virtual ring created within each DLSw node. Figure 21–4 illustrates various IBM nodes connected to a TCP/IP WAN through DLSw devices, which, in this case, are routers.

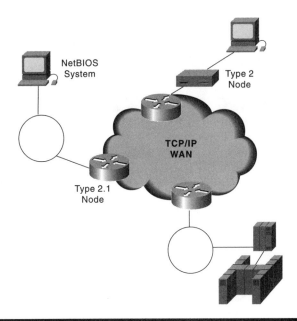

Figure 21–4
SNA nodes connect through TCP/IP WAN via DLSw.

DLSw SWITCH-TO-SWITCH PROTOCOL (SSP)

SSP is a protocol used between DLSw nodes (routers) to establish connections, locate resources, forward data, and handle flow control and error recovery. This is truly the essence of DLSw. In general, SSP does not provide for full routing between nodes because this is generally handled by common routing protocols such as RIP, OSPF, or IGRP/EIGRP. Instead, SSP switches packets at the SNA data link layer. It also encapsulates packets in TCP/IP for transport over IP-based networks and uses TCP as a means of reliable transport between DLSw nodes. Figure 21–5 illustrates where SSP falls in the overall SNA architecture, as well as its relationship to the OSI reference model.

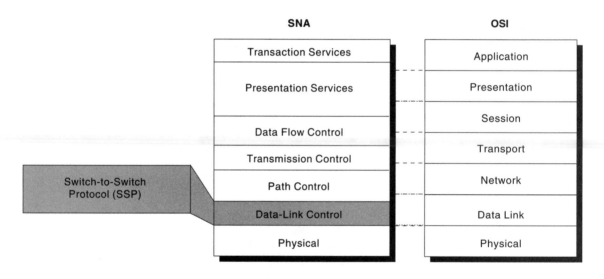

Figure 21–5
SSP maps to the data link components of SNA and the OSI reference model.

DLSw OPERATION

DLSw involves several operational stages. Two DLSw partners establish two TCP connections with each other. TCP connections provide the foundation for the DLSw communication. Because TCP provides for reliable and guaranteed delivery of IP traffic, it ensures the delivery and integrity of the traffic that is being encapsulated in the IP protocol, which, in this case, is SNA and NetBIOS traffic. After a connection is established, the DLSw partners exchange a list of supported capabilities. This is particularly vital when the DLSw partners are manufactured by different vendors. Next, the DLSw partners establish circuits between SNA or NetBIOS end systems, and information frames can flow over the circuit.

DLSw Processes

The overall DLSw operational process can be broken into three basic components: capabilities exchange, circuit establishment, and flow control. In the context of DLSw, *capabilities exchange* involves the trading of information about capabilities associated with a DLSw session. This exchange of information is negotiated when the session is initiated and during the course of session operations. *Circuit establishment* in DLSw occurs between end systems. It includes locating the target end system and setting up data-link control connections between each end system and its local router. DLSw *flow control* enables the establishment of independent, unidirectional flow control between partners. Each process in discussed in the sections that follow.

DLSw Capabilities Exchange

DLSw capabilities exchange is based on a switch-to-switch control message that describes the capabilities of the sending data-link switch. A capabilities exchange control message is sent after the switch-to-switch connection is established or during run time if certain operational parameters that must be communicated to the partner switch have changed. During the capabilities exchange, a number of capabilities are identified and negotiated. Capabilities exchanged between DLSw partners include the following:

- DLSw version number

- Initial pacing window size (receive window size)

- NetBIOS support

- List of supported link SAPs (LSAPs)

- Number of TCP sessions supported

- MAC address lists

- NetBIOS name lists

- Search frames support

DLSw Circuit Establishment

The process of circuit establishment between a pair of end systems in DLSw involves locating the target end system and setting up data-link control (DLC) connections between each end system and its local router. The specifics of circuit establishment differ based on traffic type.

One of the primary functions of DLSw is to provide a transport mechanism for SNA traffic. SNA circuit establishment involves several distinct stages. First, SNA devices on a LAN find other SNA devices by sending an explorer frame with the MAC address of the target SNA device. When a DLSw internetworking node receives an explorer frame, that node sends a "canureach" frame to each of its DLSw partners. The function of this frame is to query each of the DLSw partners to see whether it can locate the device in question. If one of the DLSw partners can reach the specified MAC address, the partner replies with an icanreach frame, which indicates that a specific DLSw partner can provide a communications path to the device in question. After the canureach and icanreach frames have been exchanged, the two DLSw partners establish a circuit that consists of a DLC connection between each router and the locally attached SNA end system (for a total of two connections) and a TCP connection between the DLSw partners. The resulting circuit is uniquely identified by the source and destination circuit IDs. Each SNA DLSw circuit ID includes a MAC address, a link-service access point (LSAP), and the DLC port ID. Circuit priority is negotiated at circuit setup time.

NetBIOS circuit establishment parallels SNA circuit establishment, with a few differences. First, with NetBIOS circuit establishment, DLSw nodes send a name query with a NetBIOS name (not a canureach frame specifying a MAC address). Similarly, the DLSw nodes establishing a NetBIOS circuit send a name recognized frame (not an icanreach frame).

DLSw Flow Control

DLSw flow control involves *adaptive pacing* between DLSw routers. During the flow-control negotiation, two independent, unidirectional flow-control mechanisms are established between DLSw partners. Adaptive pacing employs a windowing mechanism that dynamically adapts to buffer availability. Windows can be incremented, decremented, halved, or reset to zero. This allows the DLSw nodes to control the pace of traffic forwarded through the network to ensure integrity and delivery of all data.

DLSw Flow-Control Indicators

Granted units (the number of units that the sender has permission to send) are incremented with a flow-control indication (one of several possible indicators) from the receiver. DLSw flow control provides for the following indicator functions:

- *Repeat*—Increments granted units by the current window size.

- *Increment*—Increases the window size by one and increases granted units by the new window size.

- *Decrement*—Decrements window size by one and increments granted units by the new window size.

- *Reset*—Decreases window to zero and sets granted units to zero, which stops all transmission in one direction until an increment flow-control indicator is sent.

- *Half*—Cuts the current window size in half and increments granted units by the new window size.

Flow-control indicators and flow-control acknowledgments can be piggybacked on information frames or sent as independent flow-control messages. Reset indicators are always sent as independent messages.

Adaptive-Pacing Examples

Examples of adaptive-pacing criteria include buffer availability, transport utilization, outbound queue length, and traffic priority. Examples of how each can be used to influence pacing follow:

- *Buffer availability*—If memory buffers in a DLSw node are critically low, the node can decrement the window size to reduce the flow of traffic. As buffer availability increases, the node then can increase the window size to increase traffic flow between the DLSw partners.

- *Transport utilization*—If the link between two DLSw partners reaches a high level of utilization, the window size can be reduced to lower the level of link utilization and to prevent packet loss between the nodes.

- *Outbound queue length*—Traffic forwarded by a DLSw node typically is placed into an outbound queue, which is a portion of memory dedicated to traffic being forwarded by one device to another. If this queue reaches a specified threshold or perhaps becomes full, the number of granted units can be reduced until the queue utilization is reduced to a satisfactory level.

- *Traffic priority*—One of the unique capabilities of the SSP is the ability to prioritize specific traffic. These priorities are identified by the circuit-priority field in the DLSw message frame. By providing a varying number of granted units to specific DLSw circuits, the nodes can maintain different levels of priority to each circuit.

DLSw MESSAGE FORMATS

Two message header formats are exchanged between DLSw nodes:

- Control

- Information

The control message header is used for all messages except information frames (Iframes) and independent flow-control messages (IFCMs), which are sent in information header format.

Figure 21–6 illustrates the format of the DLSw control and information fields. These fields are discussed in detail in the subsequent descriptions.

The following fields are illustrated in Figure 21–6 (fields in the first 16 bytes of all DLSw message headers are the same):

- *Version Number*—When set to 0x31 (ASCII 1), indicates a decimal value of 49, which identifies this device as utilizing DLSw version 1. This will allow future interoperability between DLSw nodes using different versions of the DLSw standard. Currently, all devices utilize DLSw version 1, so this field will always have the decimal value of 49.

- *Header Length*—When set to 0x48 for control messages, indicates a decimal value of 72 bytes. This value is set to 0x10 for information and independent flow control messages, indicating a decimal value of 16 bytes.

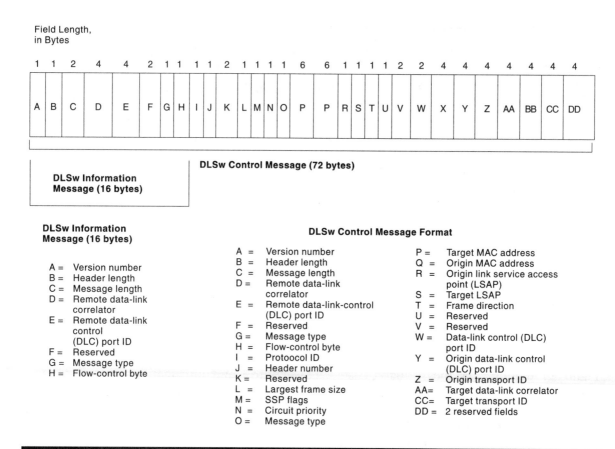

Figure 21–6

DLSw control and information frames have their first 16 bytes in common.

- *Message Length*—Defines the number of bytes within the data field following the header.

- *Remote Data-Link Correlator*—Works in tandem with the remote DLC port ID to form a 64-bit circuit ID that identifies the DLC circuit within a single DLSw node. The circuit ID is unique in a single DLSw node and is assigned locally. An end-to-end circuit is identified by a pair of circuit IDs that, along with the data-link IDs, uniquely identifies a single end-to-end circuit. Each DLSw node must keep a table of these circuit ID pairs: one for the local end of the circuit and the other for the remote end of the circuit. The remote data-link correlator is set equal to the target data-link correlator if the Frame Direction field is set to 0x01. It is equal to the origin data-link correlator if the Frame Direction field is set to 0x02.

- *Remote DLC Port ID*—Works in tandem with the remote data-link correlator to form a 64-bit circuit ID that identifies the DLC circuit within a single DLSw node. The circuit ID is unique in a single DLSw node and is assigned locally. The end-to-end circuit is identified by a pair of circuit IDs that, along with the data-link IDs, uniquely identifies a single end-to-end circuit. Each DLSw device must keep a table of these circuit ID pairs: one for the local end of the circuit and the other for the remote end of the circuit. The remote DLC Port ID is set equal to the target DLC Port ID if the Frame Direction field is set to 0x01. It is equal to the origin DLC Port ID if the Frame Direction field is set to 0x02.

- *Message Type*—Indicates a specific DLSw message type. The value is specified in two different fields (offset 14 and 23 decimal) of the control message header. Only the first field is used when parsing a received SSP message. The second field is ignored by new implementations on reception but is retained for backward compatibility with RFC 1434 implementations and can be used in future versions, if needed.

- *Flow-Control Byte*—Carries the flow-control indicator, flow-control acknowledgment, and flow-control operator bits.

- *Protocol ID*—When set to 0x42, indicates a decimal value of 66.

- *Header Number*—When set to 0x01, indicates a value of 1.

- *Largest Frame Size*—Carries the largest frame size bits across the DLSw connection. This field is implemented to ensure that the two end-stations always negotiate a frame size to be used on a circuit that does not require DLSw partners to resegment frames.

- *SSP Flags*—Contains additional information about the SSP message. Flag definitions (bit 7 is the most significant bit, and bit 0 is the least significant bit of the octet) are shown in Table 21-1.

Bit Position	Name	Meaning
7	SSPex	1 = Explorer message (canureach or icanreach)
6 through 0	Reserved	None. Reserved fields are set to 0 upon transmission and are ignored upon receipt.

Table 21-1
SSP Flag Definitions

- *Circuit Priority*—Provides for unsupported, low, medium, high, and highest circuit priorities in the three low-order bits of this byte. At circuit start time, each circuit endpoint provides priority information to its circuit partner. The initiator of the circuit chooses which circuit priority is effective for the life of the circuit. If the priority is not implemented by the nodes, the unsupported priority is used.

- *Target MAC Address*—Combines with the target link SAP, origin MAC address, and origin SAP to define a logical end-to-end association called a data-link ID.

- *Origin MAC Address*—Serves as the MAC address of the origin end station.

- *Origin LSAP*—Serves as the SAP of the source device. The SAP is used to logically identify the traffic being transmitted.

- *Target LSAP*—Serves as the SAP of the destination device.

- *Frame Direction*—Contains the value 0x01 for frames sent from the origin DLSw to the target DLSw node, or 0x02 for frames sent from the target DLSw to the origin DLSw node.

- *DLC Header Length*—When set to 0 for SNA and 0x23 for NetBIOS datagrams, indicates a length of 35 bytes. The NetBIOS header includes the following information:

  - Access Control (AC) field
  - Frame Control (FC) field
  - Destination MAC address (DA)
  - Source MAC address (SA)
  - Routing Information (RI) field (padded to 18 bytes)
  - Destination service access point (DSAP)
  - Source SAP (SSAP)
  - LLC control field (UI)

- *Origin DLC Port ID*—Works in tandem with the origin data-link correlator to form a 64-bit circuit ID that identifies the DLC circuit within a single DLSw node. The circuit ID is unique in a single DLSw node and is assigned locally. The end-to-end circuit is identified by a pair of circuit IDs that, along with the data-link IDs, uniquely identifies a single end-to-end circuit. Each DLSw node must keep a table of these circuit ID pairs: one for the local end of the circuit and one for the remote end of the circuit.

- *Origin Data-Link Correlator*—Works in tandem with the origin DLC port ID to form a 64-bit circuit ID that identifies the DLC circuit within a single DLSw node. The circuit ID is unique in a single DLSw and is assigned locally. The end-to-end circuit is identified by a pair of circuit IDs that, along with the data-link IDs, uniquely identify a single end-to-end circuit. Each DLSw node must keep a table of these circuit ID pairs: one for the local end of the circuit and one for the remote end of the circuit.

- *Origin Transport ID*—Identifies the individual TCP/IP port on a DLSw node. Values have only local significance. Each DLSw node must reflect the values, along with the associated values for the DLC port ID and the data-link correlator, when returning a message to a DLSw partner.

- *Target Data-Link Correlator*—Works in tandem with the target DLC port ID to form a 64-bit circuit ID that identifies the DLC circuit within a single DLSw node. The circuit ID is unique in a single DLSw node and is assigned locally. The end-to-end circuit is identified by a pair of circuit IDs that, along with the data-link IDs, uniquely identifies a single end-to-end circuit. Each DLSw node must keep a table of these circuit ID pairs: one for the local end of the circuit and one for the remote end of the circuit.

- *Transport ID*—Identifies the individual TCP/IP port on a DLSw node. Values have only local significance. Each DLSw node must reflect the values, along with the associated values for the DLC port ID and the data-link correlator, when returning a message to a DLSw partner.

CHAPTER 22

LAN Switching

BACKGROUND

A LAN switch is a device that provides much higher port density at a lower cost than traditional bridges. For this reason, LAN switches can accommodate network designs featuring fewer users per segment, thereby increasing the average available bandwidth per user. This chapter provides a summary of general LAN switch operation and maps LAN switching to the OSI reference model.

The trend toward fewer users per segment is known as *microsegmentation*. Microsegmentation allows the creation of private or dedicated segments, that is, one user per segment. Each user receives instant access to the full bandwidth and does not have to contend for available bandwidth with other users. As a result, collisions (a normal phenomenon in shared-medium networks employing hubs) do not occur. A LAN switch forwards frames based on either the frame's Layer 2 address (Layer 2 LAN switch), or in some cases, the frame's Layer 3 address (multi-layer LAN switch). A LAN switch is also called a frame switch because it forwards Layer 2 frames, whereas an ATM switch forwards cells. Although Ethernet LAN switches are most common,

Token Ring and FDDI LAN switches are becoming more prevalent as network utilization increases.

Figure 22–1 illustrates a LAN switch providing dedicated bandwidth to devices, and it illustrates the relationship of Layer 2 LAN switching to the OSI data link layer:

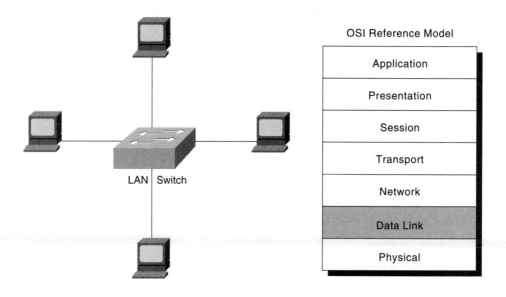

Figure 22–1
A LAN switch is a data link layer device.

History

The earliest LAN switches were developed in 1990. They were Layer 2 devices dedicated to solving bandwidth issues. Recent LAN switches are evolving to multi-layer devices capable of handling protocol issues involved in high-bandwidth applications that historically have been solved by routers. Today, LAN switches are being used to replace hubs in the wiring closet because user applications are demanding greater bandwidth.

LAN SWITCH OPERATION

LAN switches are similar to transparent bridges in functions such as learning the topology, forwarding, and filtering. These switches also support several new and unique features, such as dedicated communication between devices, multiple simultaneous conversation, full-duplex communication, and media-rate adaption.

Dedicated collision-free communication between network devices increases file-transfer throughput. Multiple simultaneous conversations can occur by forwarding, or switching, several packets at the same time, thereby increasing network capacity by the number of conversations supported. Full-duplex communication effectively doubles the throughput, while with media-rate adaption, the LAN switch can translate between 10 and 100 Mbps, allowing bandwidth to be allocated as needed.

Deploying LAN switches requires no change to existing hubs, network interface cards (NICs), or cabling.

LAN Switching Forwarding

LAN switches can be characterized by the forwarding method they support. In the store-and-forward switching method, error checking is performed and erroneous frames are discarded. With the cut-through switching method, latency is reduced by eliminating error checking.

With the store-and-forward switching method, the LAN switch copies the entire frame into its onboard buffers and computes the cyclic redundancy check (CRC). The frame is discarded if it contains a CRC error or if it is a *runt* (less than 64 bytes including the CRC) or a *giant* (more than 1518 bytes including the CRC). If the frame does not contain any errors, the LAN switch looks up the destination address in its forwarding, or switching, table and determines the outgoing interface. It then forwards the frame toward its destination.

With the cut-through switching method, the LAN switch copies only the destination address (the first 6 bytes following the preamble) into its onboard buffers. It then looks up the destination address in its switching table, determines the outgoing interface, and forwards the frame toward its destination. A cut-through switch provides reduced latency because it begins to forward the frame as soon as it reads the destination address and determines the outgoing interface.

Some switches can be configured to perform cut-through switching on a per-port basis until a user-defined error threshold is reached, when they automatically will change to store-and-forward mode. When the error rate falls below the threshold, the port automatically changes back to store-and-forward mode.

LAN Switching Bandwidth

LAN switches also can be characterized according to the proportion of bandwidth allocated to each port. Symmetric switching provides evenly distributed bandwidth to each port, while asymmetric switching provides unlike, or unequal, bandwidth between some ports.

An asymmetric LAN switch provides switched connections between ports of unlike bandwidths, such as a combination of 10BaseT and 100BaseT. This type of switching is also called *10/100 switching*. Asymmetric switching is optimized for client-server traffic flows where multiple clients simultaneously communicate with a server, requiring more bandwidth dedicated to the server port to prevent a bottleneck at that port.

A symmetric switch provides switched connections between ports with the same bandwidth, such as all 10BaseT or all 100BaseT. Symmetric switching is optimized for a reasonably distributed traffic load, such as in a peer-to-peer desktop environment.

A network manager must evaluate the needed amount of bandwidth for connections between devices to accommodate the data flow of network-based applications when deciding to select an asymmetric or symmetric switch.

LAN SWITCH AND THE OSI MODEL

LAN switches can be categorized according to the OSI layer at which they filter and forward, or switch, frames. These categories are: Layer 2, Layer 2 with Layer 3 features, or multi-layer.

A Layer 2 LAN switch is operationally similar to a multiport bridge but has a much higher capacity and supports many new features, such as full-duplex operation. A Layer 2 LAN switch performs switching and filtering based on the OSI data link layer (Layer 2) MAC address. As with bridges, it is completely transparent to network protocols and user applications.

A Layer 2 LAN switch with Layer 3 features can make switching decisions based on more information than just the Layer 2 MAC address. Such a switch might incorporate some Layer 3 traffic-control features, such as broadcast and multicast traffic management, security through access lists, and IP fragmentation.

A multi-layer switch makes switching and filtering decisions on the basis of OSI data link layer (Layer 2) and OSI network-layer (Layer 3) addresses. This type of switch dynamically decides whether to switch (Layer 2) or route (Layer 3) incoming traffic. A multi-layer LAN switch switches within a workgroup and routes between different workgroups.

CHAPTER 23

Tag Switching

BACKGROUND

Rapid changes in the type (and quantity) of traffic handled by the Internet and the explosion in the number of Internet users is putting an unprecedented strain on the Internet's infrastructure. This pressure is mandating new traffic-management solutions. *Tag switching* is aimed at resolving many of the challenges facing an evolving Internet and high-speed data communications in general. This chapter summarizes basic tag-switching operation, architecture, and implementation environments. Tag switching currently is addressed by a series of Internet drafts, which include:

- "Tag Distribution Protocol," P. Doolan, B. Davie, D. Katz

- "Tag Switching Architecture Overview," Y. Rekhter, B. Davie, D. Katz

- "Use of Flow Label for Tag Switching," F. Baker, Y. Rekhter

- "Use of Tag Switching With ATM," B. Davie, P. Doolan, J. Lawrence, K. McCloghrie

- "Tag Switching: Tag Stack Encoding," E. Rosen, D. Tappan, D. Farinacci

TAG-SWITCHING ARCHITECTURE

Tag switching relies on two principal components: forwarding and control. The forwarding component uses the tag information (tags) carried by packets and the tag-forwarding information maintained by a tag switch to perform packet forwarding. The control component is responsible for maintaining correct tag-forwarding information among a group of interconnected tag switches. Details about tag switching's forwarding and control mechanisms follow.

Forwarding Component

The forwarding paradigm employed by tag switching is based on the notion of *label swapping*. When a packet with a tag is received by a tag switch, the switch uses the tag as an index in its Tag Information Base (TIB). Each entry in the TIB consists of an incoming tag and one or more subentries (of the form outgoing tag, outgoing interface, outgoing link-level information). If the switch finds an entry with the incoming tag equal to the tag carried in the packet, then, for each component in the entry, the switch replaces the tag in the packet with the outgoing tag, replaces the link-level information (such as the MAC address) in the packet with the outgoing link-level information, and forwards the packet over the outgoing interface.

From the above description of the forwarding component, we can make several observations. First, the forwarding decision is based on the exact-match algorithm using a fixed-length, fairly short tag as an index. This enables a simplified forwarding procedure, relative to longest-match forwarding traditionally used at the network layer.

This, in turn, enables higher forwarding performance (higher packets per second). The forwarding procedure is simple enough to allow a straightforward hardware implementation. A second observation is that the forwarding decision is independent of the tag's forwarding granularity. The same forwarding algorithm, for example, applies to both unicast and multicast: a unicast entry would have a single (outgoing tag, outgoing interface, outgoing link-level information) subentry, while a multicast entry might have one or more sub-entries. This illustrates how the same forwarding paradigm can be used in tag switching to support different routing functions.

The simple forwarding procedure is thus essentially decoupled from the control component of tag switching. New routing (control) functions can readily be deployed without disturbing the forwarding paradigm. This means that it is not necessary to re-optimize forwarding performance (by modifying either hardware or software) as new routing functionality is added.

Tag Encapsulation

Tag information can be carried in a packet in a variety of ways:

- As a small "shim" tag header inserted between the Layer 2 and the network-layer headers

- As part of the Layer 2 header, if the Layer 2 header provides adequate semantics (such as ATM)

- As part of the network-layer header (such as using the Flow Label field in IPv6 with appropriately modified semantics)

As a result, tag switching can be implemented over any media type, including point-to-point links, multi-access links, and ATM. The tag-forwarding component is independent of the network-layer protocol. Use of control component(s) specific to a particular network-layer protocol enables the use of tag switching with different network-layer protocols.

Control Component

Essential to tag switching is the notion of binding between a tag and network-layer routing (routes). Tag switching supports a wide range of forwarding granularities to provide good scaling characteristics while also accommodating diverse routing functionality. At one extreme, a tag could be associated (bound) to a group of routes (more specifically to the network-layer reachability information of the routes in the group). At the other extreme, a tag could be bound to an individual application flow (such as an RSVP flow), or it could be bound to a multicast tree.

The control component is responsible for creating tag bindings and then distributing the tag-binding information among tag switches.

The control component is organized as a collection of modules, each designed to support a particular routing function. To support new routing functions, new modules can be added. The following describes some of the modules.

DESTINATION-BASED ROUTING

With destination-based routing, a router makes a forwarding decision based on the destination address carried in a packet and the information stored in the Forwarding Information Base (FIB) maintained by the router. A router constructs its FIB by using the information the router receives from routing protocols, such as OSPF and BGP.

To support destination-based routing with tag switching, a tag switch participates in routing protocols and constructs its FIB by using the information it receives from these protocols. In this way, it operates much like a router.

Three permitted methods accommodate tag allocation and Tag Information Base (TIB) management:

- Downstream tag allocation

- Downstream tag allocation on demand

- Upstream tag allocation

In all cases, a tag switch allocates tags and binds them to address prefixes in its FIB. In downstream allocation, the tag that is carried in a packet is generated and bound to a prefix by the switch at the downstream end of the link (with respect to the direction of data flow). In upstream allocation, tags are allocated and bound at the upstream end of the link. On-demand allocation means that tags are allocated and distributed by the downstream switch only when requested to do so by the upstream switch.

Downstream tag allocation on demand and upstream tag allocation are most useful in ATM networks. In downstream allocation, a switch is responsible for creating tag bindings that apply to incoming data packets, and receiving tag bindings for outgoing packets from its neighbors. In upstream allocation, a switch is responsible for creating tag bindings for outgoing tags, such as tags that are applied to data packets leaving the switch, and receiving bindings for incoming tags from its neighbors. Operational differences are outlined in the following summaries.

Downstream Tag Allocation

With downstream tag allocation, the switch allocates a tag for each route in its FIB, creates an entry in its TIB with the incoming tag set to the allocated tag, and then advertises the binding between the (incoming) tag and the route to other adjacent tag switches. The advertisement can be accomplished by either piggybacking the binding on top of the existing routing protocols, or by using a separate Tag-Distribution Protocol (TDP). When a tag switch receives tag-binding information for a route, and that information was originated by the next hop for that route, the switch places the tag (carried as part of the binding information) into the outgoing tag of the TIB entry associated with the route. This creates the binding between the outgoing tag and the route.

Downstream Tag Allocation on Demand

For each route in its FIB, the switch identifies the next hop for that route. It then issues a request (via TDP) to the next hop for a tag binding for that route. When the next hop receives the request, it allocates a tag, creates an entry in its TIB with the incoming tag set to the allocated tag, and then returns the binding between the (incoming) tag and the route to the switch that sent the original request. When the switch receives the binding information, the switch creates an entry in its TIB, and sets the outgoing tag in the entry to the value received from the next hop.

Upstream Tag Allocation

With upstream tag allocation, a tag switch allocates a tag for each route in its FIB whose next hop is reachable via one of these interfaces (if it has one or more point-to-point interfaces), creates an entry in its TIB with the outgoing tag set to the allocated tag, and then advertises to the next hop (via TDP) the binding between the (outgoing) tag and the route. When a tag switch that is the next hop receives the tag-binding information, the switch places the tag (carried as part of the binding information) into the incoming tag of the TIB entry associated with the route.

After a TIB entry is populated with both incoming and outgoing tags, the tag switch can forward packets for routes bound to the tags by using the tag-switching forwarding algorithm.

When a tag switch creates a binding between an outgoing tag and a route, the switch, in addition to populating its TIB, also updates its FIB with the binding information. This enables the switch to add tags to previously untagged packets. Observe that the total number of tags that a tag switch must maintain can be no greater than the number of routes in the switch's FIB. Moreover, in some cases, a single tag could be associated with a group of routes rather than with a single route. Thus, much less state is required than would be the case if tags were allocated to individual flows.

In general, a tag switch will try to populate its TIB with incoming and outgoing tags for all reachable routes, allowing all packets to be forwarded by simple label swapping. Tag allocation thus is driven by topology (routing), not traffic.The existence of a FIB entry causes tag allocations, not the arrival of data packets.

The use of tags associated with routes, rather than flows, also means that there is no need to perform flow-classification procedures for all the flows to determine whether to assign a tag to a flow. That simplifies the overall routing scheme and creates a more robust and stable environment.

When tag switching is used to support destination-based routing, it does not eliminate the need for normal network-layer forwarding. First of all, to add a tag to a previously untagged packet requires normal network-layer forwarding. This function can be performed by the first hop router, or by the first router on the path that is able to participate in tag switching. In addition, whenever a tag switch aggregates a set of routes into a single tag and the routes do not share a common next hop, the switch must perform network-layer forwarding for packets carrying that tag. The number of places, however, where routes are aggregated is smaller than the total number of places where forwarding decisions must be made. In addition, aggregation often is applied to a subset of the routes maintained by a tag switch. As a result, a packet usually can be forwarded by using the tag-switching algorithm.

HIERARCHICAL ROUTING

The IP routing architecture models a network as a collection of routing domains. Within a domain, routing is provided via interior routing (such as OSPF), while routing across domains is provided via exterior routing (such as BGP). All routers within domains that carry transit traffic, however, (such as domains formed by Internet Service Providers) must maintain information provided by exterior routing, not just interior routing.

Tag switching allows the decoupling of interior and exterior routing so that only tag switches at the border of a domain are required to maintain routing information provided by exterior routing. All other switches within the domain maintain routing information provided by the domain's interior routing, which usually is smaller than the exterior-routing information. This, in turn, reduces the routing load on non-border switches and shortens routing convergence time.

To support this functionality, tag switching allows a packet to carry not one, but a set of tags organized as a stack. A tag switch either can swap the tag at the top of the stack, pop the stack, or swap the tag and push one or more tags into the stack. When a packet is forwarded between two (border) tag switches in different domains, the tag stack in the packet contains just one tag.

When a packet is forwarded within a domain, however, the tag stack in the packet contains not one, but two tags (the second tag is pushed by the domain's ingress-border tag switch). The tag at the top of the stack provides packet forwarding to an appropriate egress-border tag switch, while the next tag in the stack provides correct packet forwarding at the egress switch. The stack is popped by either the egress switch or by the penultimate switch (with respect to the egress switch).

The control component used in this scenario is similar to the one used with destination-based routing. The only essential difference is that, in this scenario, the tag-binding information is distributed both among physically adjacent tag switches and among border tag switches within a single domain.

FLEXIBLE ROUTING USING EXPLICIT ROUTES

One of the fundamental properties of destination-based routing is that the only information from a packet that is used to forward the packet is the destination address. Although this property enables highly scalable routing, it also limits the capability to influence the actual paths taken by packets. This limits the ability to evenly distribute traffic among multiple links, taking the load off highly utilized links and shifting it towards less-utilized links. For Internet Service Providers (ISPs) who support different classes of service, destination-based routing also limits their capability to segregate different classes with respect to the links used by these classes. Some of the ISPs today use Frame Relay or ATM to overcome the limitations imposed by destination-based routing. Tag switching, because of the flexible granularity of tags, is able to overcome these limitations without using either Frame Relay or ATM. To provide forwarding along the paths that are different from the paths determined by the destination-based routing, the control component of tag switching allows installation of tag bindings in tag switches that do not correspond to the destination-based routing paths.

MULTICAST ROUTING

In a multicast routing environment, multicast routing procedures (such as Protocol-Independent Multicast [PIM]) are responsible for constructing spanning trees, with receivers as leaves. Multicast forwarding is responsible for forwarding multicast packets along these spanning trees.

Tag switches support multicast by utilizing data link-layer multicast capabilities, such as those provided by Ethernet. All tag switches that are part of a given multicast tree on a common subnetwork must agree on a common tag to be used for forwarding a multicast packet to all downstream switches on that subnetwork. This way, the packet will be multicast at the data link layer over the subnetwork. Tag switches that belong to a common multicast tree on a common data-link subnetwork agree on the tag switch that is responsible for allocating a tag for the tree. Tag space is partitioned into nonoverlapping regions for all the tag switches connected to a common data-link subnetwork. Each tag switch claims a region of the tag space and announces this region to its neighbors. Conflicts are resolved based on the IP address of the contending switches. Multicast tags are associated with interfaces on a tag switch rather than with a tag switch as a whole. Therefore, the switch maintains TIBs associated with individual interfaces rather than a single TIB for the entire switch. Tags enable the receiving switch to identify both a particular multicast group and the upstream tag switch (the previous hop) that sent the packet.

Two possible ways exist to create binding between tags and multicast trees (routes). For a set of tag switches that share a common data-link subnetwork, the tag switch that is upstream with respect to a particular multicast tree allocates a tag, binds the tag to a multicast route, and then advertises the binding to all the downstream switches on the subnetwork. This method is similar to destination-based upstream tag allocation. One tag switch that is downstream with respect to a particular multicast tree allocates a tag, binds the tag to a multicast route, and advertises the binding to all the switches, both downstream and upstream, on the subnetwork. Usually, the first tag switch to join the group is the one that performs the allocation.

TAG SWITCHING WITH ATM

Because the tag-switching forwarding paradigm is based on label swapping, as is ATM forwarding, tag-switching technology can be applied to ATM switches by implementing the control component of tag switching. The tag information needed for tag switching can be carried in the ATM VCI field. If two levels of tagging are needed, then the ATM VPI field could be used as well, although the size of the VPI field limits the size of networks in which this would be practical. The VCI field, however, is adequate for most applications of one level of tagging.

To obtain the necessary control information, the switch acts as a peer in network-layer routing protocols, such as OSPF and BGP. Moreover, if the switch must perform routing information aggregation, then to support destination-based unicast routing the switch performs network-layer forwarding for some fraction of the traffic as well. Supporting the destination-based routing function with tag switching on an ATM switch might require the switch to maintain not one, but several tags associated with a route (or a group of routes with the same next hop). This is necessary to avoid the interleaving of packets that arrive from different upstream tag switches but are sent concurrently to the same next hop. Either the downstream tag allocation on demand or the upstream tag allocation scheme could be used for the tag allocation and TIB maintenance procedures with ATM switches.

Therefore, an ATM switch can support tag switching, but at the minimum, it must implement network-layer routing protocols and the tag-switching control component on the switch. It also might need to support some network-layer forwarding.

Implementing tag switching on an ATM switch would simplify integration of ATM switches and routers. An ATM switch capable of tag switching would appear as a router to an adjacent router. That would provide a scalable alternative to the "overlay" model and remove the necessity for ATM addressing, routing, and signalling schemes. Because destination-based forwarding is topology-driven rather than traffic-driven, application of this approach to ATM switches does not involve high call-setup rates, nor does it depend on the longevity of flows.

Implementing tag switching on an ATM switch does not preclude the capability to support a traditional ATM control plane (such as PNNI) on the same switch. The two components, tag switching and the ATM control plane, would operate independently with VPI/VCI space and other resources partitioned so that the components do not interact.

QUALITY OF SERVICE

An important proposed tag-switching capability is quality of service (QoS) support. Two mechanisms are needed to provide a range of QoS to packets passing through a router or a tag switch:

- Classification of packets into different classes

- Handling of packets via appropriate QoS characteristics (such as bandwidth and loss)

Tag switching provides an easy way to mark packets as belonging to a particular class after they have been classified the first time.

Initial classification would be done by using information carried in the network-layer or higher-layer headers. A tag corresponding to the resultant class then would be applied to the packet. Tagged packets could be handled efficiently by the tag-switching routers in their path without needing to be reclassified. The actual packet scheduling and queueing is largely orthogonal: the key point here is that tag switching enables simple logic to be used to find the state that identifies how the packet should be scheduled.

The exact use of tag switching for QoS purposes depends a great deal on how QoS is deployed. If RSVP is used to request a certain QoS for a class of packets, then it would be necessary to allocate a tag corresponding to each RSVP session for which state is installed at a tag switch. This might be done by TDP or by extension of RSVP.

IP SWITCHING

IP switching is a related technology that combines ATM Layer 2 switching with Layer 3 routing. In this way, it is another a type of multi-layer switching. IP switching typically allocates a label per source/destination packet flow. An IP switch processes the initial packets of a flow by passing them to a standard router module that is part of the IP switch.

When an IP switch has seen enough packets go by on a flow to consider it long-lived, the IP switch sets up labels for the flow with its neighboring IP switches or edge routers such that subsequent packets for the flow can be label-switched at high-speed (such as in an ATM switching fabric), bypassing the slower router module. IP switching gateways are responsible for converting packets from non-labeled to labeled formats, and from packet media to ATM.

CHAPTER 24

Mixed-Media Bridging

BACKGROUND

Transparent bridges are found predominantly in Ethernet networks, and source-route bridges (SRBs) are found almost exclusively in Token Ring networks. Both transparent bridges and SRBs are popular, so it is reasonable to ask whether a method exists to directly bridge between them. Several solutions have evolved.

Translational bridging provides a relatively inexpensive solution to some of the many problems involved with bridging between transparent bridging and SRB domains. Translational bridging first appeared in the mid- to late-1980s but has not been championed by any standards organization. As a result, many aspects of translational bridging are left to the implementor.

In 1990, IBM addressed some of the weaknesses of translational bridging by introducing source-route transparent (SRT) bridging. SRT bridges can forward traffic from both transparent and source-route end nodes and form a common spanning tree with transparent bridges, thereby allowing end stations of each type to communicate with end stations of the same type in a network of arbitrary topology. SRT is specified in the IEEE 802.1d Appendix C.

Ultimately, the goal of connecting transparent bridging and SRB domains is to allow communication between transparent bridges and SRB end stations. This chapter describes the technical problems that must be addressed by algorithms attempting to do this and presents two possible solutions: translational bridging and SRT bridging.

TRANSLATION CHALLENGES

Many challenges are associated with allowing end stations from the Ethernet/transparent bridging domain to communicate with end stations from the SRB/Token Ring domain:

- *Incompatible bit ordering*—Although both Ethernet and Token Ring support 48-bit Media Access Control (MAC) addresses, the internal hardware representation of these addresses differ. In a serial bit stream representing an address, Token Ring considers the first bit encountered to be the high-order bit of a byte. Ethernet, on the other hand, considers the first bit encountered to be the low-order bit.

- *Embedded MAC addresses*—In some cases, MAC addresses actually are carried in the data portion of a frame. The *Address Resolution Protocol* (ARP), a popular protocol in *Transmission Control Protocol/Internet Protocol* (TCP/IP) networks, for example, places hardware addresses in the data portion of a link-layer frame. Conversion of addresses that might or might not appear in the data portion of a frame is difficult because they must be handled on a case by case basis.

- *Incompatible maximum transfer unit (MTU) sizes*—Token Ring and Ethernet support different maximum frame sizes. Ethernet's MTU is approximately 1500 bytes, whereas Token Ring frames can be much larger. Because bridges are not capable of frame fragmentation and reassembly, packets that exceed the MTU of a given network must be dropped.

- *Handling of frame-status bit actions*—Token Ring frames include three frame-status bits: A, C, and E. The purpose of these bits is to tell the frame's source whether the destination saw the frame (A bit set), copied the frame (C bit set), or found errors in the frame (E bit set). Because Ethernet does not support these bits, the question of how to deal with them is left to the Ethernet-Token Ring bridge manufacturer.

- *Handling of exclusive Token Ring functions*—Certain Token Ring bits have no corollary in Ethernet. Ethernet, for example, has no priority mechanism, whereas Token Ring does. Other Token Ring bits that must be thrown out when a Token Ring frame is converted to an Ethernet frame include the token bit, the monitor bit, and the reservation bits.

- *Handling of explorer frames*—Transparent bridges do not inherently understand what to do with SRB explorer frames. Transparent bridges learn about the network's topology through analysis of the source address of incoming frames. They have no knowledge of the SRB route-discovery process.

- *Handling of routing information field (RIF) information within Token Ring frames*—The SRB algorithm places routing information in the RIF field. The transparent-bridging algorithm has no RIF equivalent, and the idea of placing routing information in a frame is foreign to transparent bridging.

- *Incompatible spanning-tree algorithms*—Transparent bridging and SRB both use the spanning-tree algorithm to try to avoid loops, but the particular algorithms employed by the two bridging methods are incompatible.

- *Handling of frames without route information*—SRBs expect all inter-LAN frames to contain route information. When a frame without an RIF field (including transparent bridging configuration and topology-change messages as well as MAC frames sent from the transparent-bridging domain) arrives at an SRB bridge, it is ignored.

TRANSLATIONAL BRIDGING

Because there has been no real standardization in how communication between two media types should occur, no single translational bridging implementation can be called correct. The following describes several popular methods for implementing translational bridging.

Translational bridges reorder source and destination address bits when translating between Ethernet and Token Ring frame formats. The problem of embedded MAC addresses can be solved by programming the bridge to check for various types of MAC addresses, but this solution must be adapted with each new type of embedded MAC address. Some translational-bridging solutions simply check for the most popular embedded addresses. If translational-bridging software runs in a multiprotocol router, the router can successfully route these protocols and avoid the problem entirely.

The RIF field has a subfield that indicates the largest frame size that can be accepted by a particular SRB implementation. Translational bridges that send frames from the transparent-bridging domain to the SRB domain usually set the MTU size field to 1,500 bytes to limit the size of Token Ring frames entering the transparent-bridging domain. Some hosts cannot correctly process this field, in which case translational bridges are forced to drop those frames that exceed Ethernet's MTU size.

Bits representing Token Ring functions that have no Ethernet corollary typically are thrown out by translational bridges.Token Ring's priority, reservation, and monitor bits, for example, (contained in the access-control byte) are discarded. Token Ring's frame status bits (contained in the byte following the ending delimiter, which follows the data field) are treated differently depending on the bridge manufacturer. Some bridge manufacturers simply ignore the bits. Others have the bridge set the C bit (to indicate that the frame has been copied) but not the A bit (which indicates that the destination station recognizes the address). In the former case, a Token Ring source node determines whether the frame it sent has become lost. Proponents of this approach suggest that reliability mechanisms, such as the tracking of lost frames, are better left for implementation in Layer 4 of the OSI model. Proponents of the "set the C bit approach" contend that this bit must be set to track lost frames but that the A bit cannot be set because the bridge is not the final destination.

Translational bridges can create a software gateway between the two domains. To the SRB end stations, the translational bridge has a ring number and bridge number associated with it, and so it looks like a standard SRB. The ring number, in this case, actually reflects the entire transparent-bridging domain. To the transparent-bridging domain, the translational bridge is simply another transparent bridge.

When bridging from the SRB domain to the transparent-bridging domain, SRB information is removed. RIFs usually are cached for use by subsequent return traffic. When bridging from the transparent bridging to the SRB domain, the translational bridge can check the frame to see if it has a unicast destination. If the frame has a multicast or broadcast destination, it is sent into the SRB domain as a spanning-tree explorer. If the frame has a unicast address, the translational bridge looks up the destination in the RIF cache. If a path is found, it is used, and the RIF information is added to the frame; otherwise, the frame is sent as a spanning-tree explorer. Because the two spanning-tree implementations are not compatible, multiple paths between the SRB and the transparent-bridging domains typically are not permitted. Figures 24–2 through 24–3 illustrate frame conversions that can take place in translational bridging.

Figure 24–1 illustrates the frame conversion between IEEE 802.3 and Token Ring. The destination and source addresses (DASA), service-access point

(SAP), Logical-Link Control (LLC) information, and data are passed to the corresponding fields of the destination frame. The destination and source address bits are reordered. When bridging from IEEE 802.3 to Token Ring, the length field of the IEEE 802.3 frame is removed. When bridging from Token Ring to IEEE 802.3, the access-control byte and RIF are removed. The RIF can be cached in the translational bridge for use by return traffic.

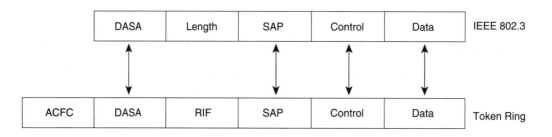

Figure 24–1
Four fields remain the same in frame conversion between IEEE 802.3 and Token Ring.

Figure 24–2 illustrates the frame conversion between Ethernet Type II and Token Ring Subnetwork Access Protocol (SNAP). (SNAP adds vendor and type codes to the data field of the Token Ring frame.) The destination and source addresses, type information, and data are passed to the corresponding fields of the destination frame, and the DASA bits are reordered. When bridging from Token Ring SNAP to Ethernet Type II, the RIF information, SAP, LLC information, and vendor code are removed. The RIF can be cached in the translational bridge for use by return traffic. When bridging from Ethernet Type II to Token Ring SNAP, no information is removed.

Figure 24–3 illustrates the frame conversion between Ethernet Type II "0x80D5" format and Token Ring. (Ethernet Type II "0x80D5" carries IBM SNA data in Ethernet frames.) The DASA, SAP, LLC information, and data are passed to the corresponding fields of the destination frame, and the destination and source address bits are reordered. When bridging from Ethernet Type II "0x80D5" to Token Ring, the type and 80D5 header fields are removed. When bridging from Token Ring to Ethernet Type II "0x80D5," the RIF is removed. The RIF can be cached in the translational bridge for use by return traffic.

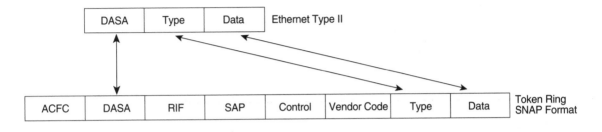

Figure 24–2
Three fields remain the same in frame conversion between Ethernet Type II and Token Ring SNAP.

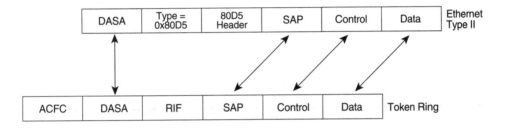

Figure 24–3
Four fields remain the same in frame conversion between Ethernet Type II "0x80D5" format and Token Ring.

SOURCE-ROUTE TRANSPARENT BRIDGING

SRT bridges combine implementations of the transparent-bridging and SRB algorithms. SRT bridges use the *routing information indicator* (RII) bit to distinguish between frames employing SRB and frames employing transparent bridging. If the RII bit is 1, a RIF is present in the frame, and the bridge uses the SRB algorithm. If the RII bit is 0, a RIF is not present, and the bridge uses transparent bridging.

As with translational bridges, SRT bridges are not perfect solutions to the problems of mixed-media bridging. SRT bridges still must deal with the Ethernet/Token Ring incompatibilities described earlier. SRT bridging is likely to require hardware upgrades to SRBs to allow them to handle the increased burden of analyzing every packet. Software upgrades to SRBs also might be required. Furthermore, in environments of mixed SRT bridges, transparent bridges, and SRBs, source routes chosen must traverse whatever SRT bridges and SRBs are available. The resulting paths potentially can be substantially inferior to spanning-tree paths created by transparent bridges. Finally, mixed SRB/SRT bridging networks lose the benefits of SRT bridging, so users feel compelled to execute a complete cutover to SRT bridging at considerable expense. Still, SRT bridging permits the coexistence of two incompatible environments and allows communication between SRB and transparent-bridging end nodes.

CHAPTER 25

Source-Route
Bridging (SRB)

BACKGROUND

The source-route bridging (SRB) algorithm was developed by IBM and proposed to the IEEE 802.5 committee as the means to bridge between all LANs. Since its initial proposal, IBM has offered a new bridging standard to the IEEE 802 committee: the source-route transparent (SRT) bridging solution. SRT bridging eliminates pure SRBs entirely, proposing that the two types of LAN bridges be transparent bridges and SRT bridges. Although SRT bridging has achieved support, SRBs are still widely deployed. SRT is covered in Chapter 24, "Mixed-Media Bridging." This chapter summarizes the basic SRB frame-forwarding algorithm and describes SRB frame fields.

SRB ALGORITHM

SRBs are so named because they assume that the complete source-to-destination route is placed in all inter-LAN frames sent by the source. SRBs store and forward the frames as indicated by the route appearing in the appropriate frame field. Figure 25–1 illustrates a sample SRB network.

In Figure 25–1, assume that Host X wants to send a frame to Host Y. Initially, Host X does not know whether Host Y resides on the same or a different LAN. To determine this, Host X sends out a test frame. If that frame returns to Host X without a positive indication that Host Y has seen it, Host X must assume that Host Y is on a remote segment.

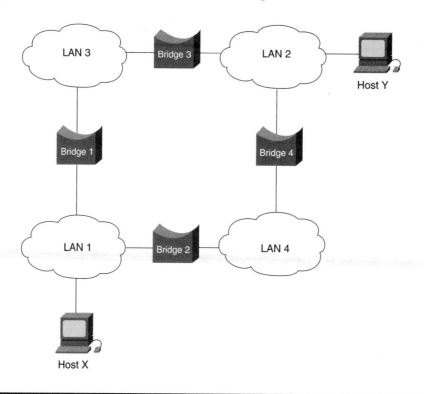

Figure 25–1

An SRB network contains LANs and bridges.

To determine the exact remote location of Host Y, Host X sends an *explorer* frame. Each bridge receiving the explorer frame (Bridges 1 and 2, in this example) copies the frame onto all outbound ports. Route information is added to the explorer frames as they travel through the internetwork. When Host X's explorer frames reach Host Y, Host Y replies to each individually, using the accumulated route information. Upon receipt of all response frames, Host X chooses a path based on some predetermined criteria.

In the example in Figure 25–1, this process will yield two routes:

- LAN 1 to Bridge 1 to LAN 3 to Bridge 3 to LAN 2
- LAN 1 to Bridge 2 to LAN 4 to Bridge 4 to LAN 2

Host X must select one of these two routes. The IEEE 802.5 specification does not mandate the criteria Host X should use in choosing a route, but it does make several suggestions, including the following:

- First frame received
- Response with the minimum number of hops
- Response with the largest allowed frame size
- Various combinations of the preceding criteria

In most cases, the path contained in the first frame received is used.

After a route is selected, it is inserted into frames destined for Host Y in the form of a *routing information field* (RIF). An RIF is included only in those frames destined for other LANs. The presence of routing information within the frame is indicated by setting the most significant bit within the Source Address field, called the *routing information indicator* (RII) bit.

FRAME FORMAT

The IEEE 802.5 RIF is structured as shown in Figure 25–2.

The RIF illustrated in Figure 25–2 consists of two main fields: *Routing Control* and *Routing Designator*. These fields are described in the summaries that follow.

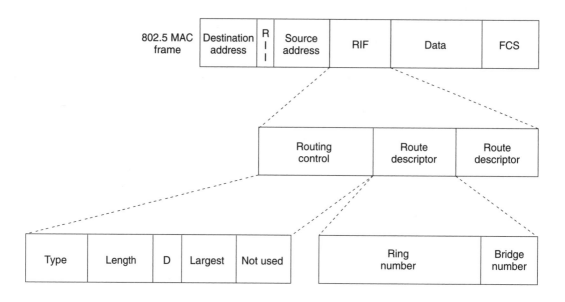

Figure 25–2

A IEEE 802.5 RIF is present in frames destined for other LANs.

Routing Control Field

The Routing Control field consists of four subfields: Type, Length, D bit, and Largest frame. The fields are summarized in the following list:

- *Type*—Consists of three possible types of routing controls:

  - Specifically routed—Used when the source node supplies the route in the RIF header. The bridges route the frame by using the route designator field(s).
  - All paths explorer—Used to find a remote node. The route is collected as the frame traverses the network. Bridges add to the frame their bridge number and ring number onto which the frame is forwarded. (The first bridge also adds the ring number of the first ring.) The target destination will receive as many frames as routes to that destination.

- Spanning-tree explorer—Used to find a remote node. Only bridges in the spanning tree forward the frame, adding their bridge number and attached ring number as it is forwarded. The spanning-tree explorer reduces the number of frames sent during the discovery process.

- *Length*—Indicates the total length (in bytes) of the RIF. The value can range from 2 to 30 bytes.

- *D Bit*—Indicates and controls the direction (forward or reverse) the frame traverses. The D bit affects whether bridges read the ring number/bridge number combinations in the route designators from right to left (forward) or left to right (reverse).

- *Largest Frame*—Indicates the largest frame size that can be handled along a designated route. The source initially sets the largest frame size, but bridges can lower it if they cannot accommodate the requested size.

Routing Designator Fields

Each routing designator field consists of two subfields:

- *Ring Number* (12 bits)—Assigns value that must be unique within the bridged network.

- *Bridge Number* (4 bits)—Assigns value that follows the ring number. This number does not have to be unique unless it is parallel with another bridge connecting two rings.

Bridges add to the frame their bridge number and the ring number onto which the frame is forwarded. (The first bridge also adds the ring number of the first ring.)

Routes are alternating sequences of ring and bridge numbers that start and end with ring numbers. A single RIF can contain more than one routing designator field. The IEEE specifies a maximum of 14 routing designator fields (a maximum of 13 bridges or hops, because the last bridge number always equals zero).

Until recently, IBM specified a maximum of eight Routing Designator fields (a maximum of seven bridges or hops), and most bridge manufacturers followed IBM's implementation. Newer IBM bridge software programs combined with new LAN adapters support 13 hops.

CHAPTER 26

Transparent Bridging

BACKGROUND

Transparent bridges were first developed at Digital Equipment Corporation (Digital) in the early 1980s. Digital submitted its work to the Institute of Electrical and Electronic Engineers (IEEE), which incorporated the work into the IEEE 802.1 standard. Transparent bridges are very popular in Ethernet/IEEE 802.3 networks. This chapter provides an overview of transparent bridging's handling of traffic and protocol components.

TRANSPARENT BRIDGING OPERATION

Transparent bridges are so named because their presence and operation are transparent to network hosts. When transparent bridges are powered on, they learn the network's topology by analyzing the source address of incoming frames from all attached networks. If, for example, a bridge sees a frame arrive on Line 1 from Host A, the bridge concludes that Host A can be reached through the network connected to Line 1. Through this process, transparent bridges build a table, such as the one in Figure 26–1.

Host address	Network number
15	1
17	1
12	2
13	2
18	1
9	1
14	3
.	.
.	.
.	.

Figure 26–1
Transparent bridges build a table that determines a host's accessibility.

The bridge uses its table as the basis for traffic forwarding. When a frame is received on one of the bridge's interfaces, the bridge looks up the frame's destination address in its internal table. If the table contains an association between the destination address and any of the bridge's ports aside from the one on which the frame was received, the frame is forwarded out the indicated port. If no association is found, the frame is flooded to all ports except the inbound port. Broadcasts and multicasts also are flooded in this way.

Transparent bridges successfully isolate intrasegment traffic, thereby reducing the traffic seen on each individual segment. This usually improves network response times, as seen by the user. The extent to which traffic is reduced and response times are improved depends on the volume of intersegment traffic relative to the total traffic, as well as the volume of broadcast and multicast traffic.

Bridging Loops

Without a bridge-to-bridge protocol, the transparent-bridge algorithm fails when multiple paths of bridges and local area networks (LANs) exist between any two LANs in the internetwork. Figure 26–2 illustrates such a bridging loop.

Suppose Host A sends a frame to Host B. Both bridges receive the frame and correctly conclude that Host A is on Network 2. Unfortunately, after Host B receives two copies of Host A's frame, both bridges again will receive the frame on their Network 1 interfaces because all hosts receive all messages on broadcast LANs. In some cases, the bridges will change their internal tables to indicate that Host A is on Network 1. If so, when Host B replies to Host A's frame, both bridges will receive and subsequently drop the replies because their tables will indicate that the destination (Host A) is on the same network segment as the frame's source.

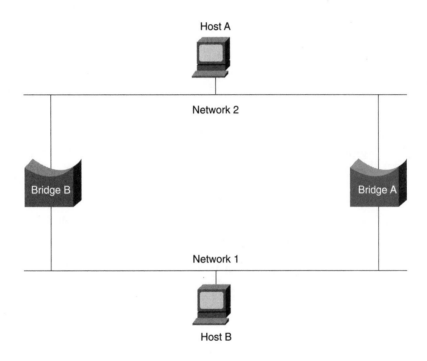

Figure 26–2
Bridging loops can result in inaccurate forwarding and learning in transparent bridging environments.

In addition to basic connectivity problems, the proliferation of broadcast messages in networks with loops represents a potentially serious network problem. Referring again to Figure 26–2, assume that Host A's initial frame is a broadcast. Both bridges will forward the frames endlessly, using all available network bandwidth and blocking the transmission of other packets on both segments.

A topology with loops, such as that shown in Figure 26–2, can be useful as well as potentially harmful. A loop implies the existence of multiple paths through the internetwork, and a network with multiple paths from source to destination can increase overall network fault tolerance through improved topological flexibility.

Spanning-Tree Algorithm (STA)

The spanning-tree algorithm (STA) was developed by Digital Equipment Corporation, a key Ethernet vendor, to preserve the benefits of loops while eliminating their problems. Digital's algorithm subsequently was revised by the IEEE 802 committee and published in the IEEE 802.1d specification The Digital algorithm and the IEEE 802.1d algorithm are not compatible.

The STA designates a loop-free subset of the network's topology by placing those bridge ports that, if active, would create loops into a standby (blocking) condition. Blocking bridge ports can be activated in the event of primary link failure, providing a new path through the internetwork.

The STA uses a conclusion from graph theory as a basis for constructing a loop-free subset of the network's topology. Graph theory states the following:

> For any connected graph consisting of nodes and edges
> connecting pairs of nodes, a spanning tree of edges maintains the
> connectivity of the graph but contains no loops.

Figure 26–3 illustrates how the STA eliminates loops. The STA calls for each bridge to be assigned a unique identifier. Typically, this identifier is one of the bridge's *Media Access Control* (MAC) addresses, plus a priority. Each port in every bridge also is assigned a unique identifier (within that bridge), which is typically its own MAC address. Finally, each bridge port is associated with a path cost, which represents the cost of transmitting a frame onto a LAN through that port. In Figure 26–3, path costs are noted on the lines emanating from each bridge. Path costs are usually defaulted but can be assigned manually by network administrators.

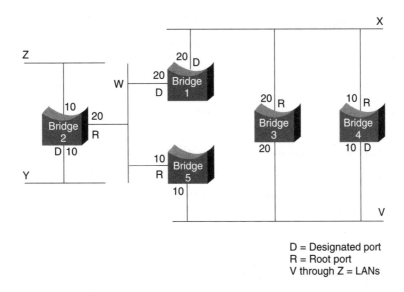

D = Designated port
R = Root port
V through Z = LANs

Figure 26–3
STA-based bridges use designated and root ports to eliminate loops.

The first activity in spanning-tree computation is the selection of the *root bridge*, which is the bridge with the lowest-value bridge identifier. In Figure 26–3, the root bridge is Bridge 1. Next, the *root port* on all other bridges is determined. A bridge's root port is the port through which the root bridge can be reached with the least aggregate path cost, a value that is called the *root path cost*.

Finally, *designated bridges* and their *designated ports* are determined. A designated bridge is the bridge on each LAN that provides the minimum root path cost. A LAN's designated bridge is the only bridge allowed to forward frames to and from the LAN for which it is the designated bridge. A LAN's designated port is the port that connects it to the designated bridge.

In some cases, two or more bridges can have the same root path cost. In Figure 26–3, for example, Bridges 4 and 5 can both reach Bridge 1 (the root bridge) with a path cost of 10. In this case, the bridge identifiers are used again, this time to determine the designated bridges. Bridge 4's LAN V port is selected over Bridge 5's LAN V port.

Using this process, all but one of the bridges directly connected to each LAN are eliminated, thereby removing all two-LAN loops. The STA also eliminates loops involving more than two LANs, while still preserving connectivity. Figure 26–4 shows the results of applying the STA to the network shown in Figure 26–3. Figure 26–4 shows the tree topology more clearly. Comparing this figure to the pre-spanning-tree figure shows that the STA has placed both Bridge 3's and Bridge 5's ports to LAN V in standby mode.

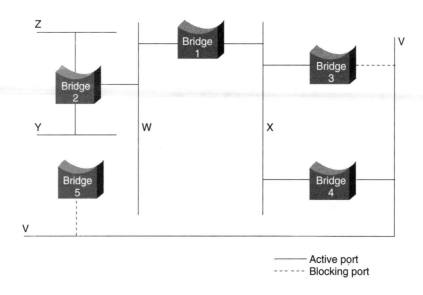

Figure 26–4

Creates a loop-free tree topology. A STA-based transparent-bridge network.

The spanning-tree calculation occurs when the bridge is powered up and whenever a topology change is detected. The calculation requires communication between the spanning-tree bridges, which is accomplished through configuration messages (sometimes called *bridge protocol data units*, or *BPDUs*). Configuration messages contain information identifying the bridge that is presumed to be the root (root identifier) and the distance from the sending bridge to the root bridge (root path cost). Configuration messages also contain the bridge and port identifier of the sending bridge, as well as the age of information contained in the configuration message.

Bridges exchange configuration messages at regular intervals (typically one to four seconds). If a bridge fails (causing a topology change), neighboring bridges will detect the lack of configuration messages and initiate a spanning-tree recalculation.

All transparent-bridge topology decisions are made locally. Configuration messages are exchanged between neighboring bridges, and no central authority exists on network topology or administration.

FRAME FORMAT

Transparent bridges exchange *configuration* messages and *topology-change* messages. Configuration messages are sent between bridges to establish a network topology. Topology-change messages are sent after a topology change has been detected to indicate that the STA should be rerun.

Figure 26–5 illustrates the IEEE 802.1d configuration-message format.

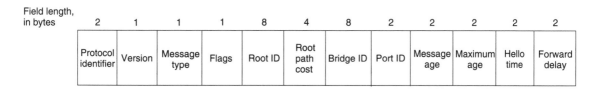

Field length, in bytes	2	1	1	1	8	4	8	2	2	2	2	2
	Protocol identifier	Version	Message type	Flags	Root ID	Root path cost	Bridge ID	Port ID	Message age	Maximum age	Hello time	Forward delay

Figure 26–5
Twelve fields comprise the transparent-bridge configuration message.

The fields of the transparent bridge configuration message are as follows:

- *Protocol Identifier*—Contains the value zero.

- *Version*—Contains the value zero.

- *Message Type*—Contains the value zero.

- *Flag*—Contains 1 byte, of which only the first two bits are used. The topology-change (TC) bit signals a topology change. The topology-change acknowledgment (TCA) bit is set to acknowledge receipt of a configuration message with the TC bit set.

- *Root ID*—Identifies the root bridge by listing its 2-byte priority followed by its 6-byte ID.

- *Root Path Cost*—Contains the cost of the path from the bridge sending the configuration message to the root bridge.

- *Bridge ID*—Identifies the priority and ID of the bridge sending the message.

- *Port ID*—Identifies the port from which the configuration message was sent. This field allows loops created by multiple attached bridges to be detected and handled.

- *Message Age*—Specifies the amount of time since the root sent the configuration message on which the current configuration message is based.

- *Maximum Age*—Indicates when the current configuration message should be deleted.

- *Hello Time*—Provides the time period between root bridge configuration messages.

- *Forward Delay*—Provides the length of time that bridges should wait before transitioning to a new state after a topology change. If a bridge transitions too soon, not all network links might be ready to change their state, and loops can result.

Topology-change messages consist of only 4 bytes, which include a *Protocol-Identifier* field, which contains the value zero; a *Version* field, which contains the value zero; and a *Message-Type* field, which contains the value 128.

PART 5

Network Protocols

Part 5, "Network Protocols," summarizes the principal components of today's most widely implemented networking protocols. Individual chapters discuss the following topics:

AppleTalk—Covers the entire AppleTalk protocol suite.

DECnet—Covers the DECnet Phase IV and DECnet/OSI (DECnet Phase V) protocol suites.

IBM Systems Network Architectures (SNA) Protocols—Summarizes the fundamentals of IBM SNA protocol components and operations, including hierarchical and peer-based environments.

Internet Protocols—Surveys common Internet protocols, including IP, TCP, UDP, ICMP, and ARP—and summarizes well-known application-layer protocols.

NetWare Protocols—Covers the NetWare protocol suite, emphasizing IPX and SAP.

Open Systems Interconnection (OSI) Protocols—Describes the features and operations of the ISO OSI protocol suite.

Banyan VINES—Describes the Banyan VINES protocol family.

Xerox Network Systems (XNS)—Describes the XNS protocol suite.

CHAPTER 27

AppleTalk

BACKGROUND

AppleTalk, a protocol suite developed by Apple Computer in the early 1980s, was developed in conjunction with the Macintosh computer. AppleTalk's purpose was to allow multiple users to share resources, such as files and printers. The devices that supply these resources are called *servers*, while the devices that make use of these resources (such as a user's Macintosh computer) are referred to as *clients*. Hence, AppleTalk is one of the early implementations of a distributed client-server networking system. This chapter provides a summary of AppleTalk's network architecture.

AppleTalk was designed with a transparent network interface. That is, the interaction between client computers and network servers requires little interaction from the user. In addition, the actual operations of the AppleTalk protocols are invisible to end users, who see only the result of these operations. Two versions of AppleTalk exist: AppleTalk Phase 1 and AppleTalk Phase 2.

AppleTalk Phase 1, which is the first AppleTalk specification, was developed in the early 1980s strictly for use in local workgroups. Phase 1 therefore has two key limitations: Its network segments can contain no more than 127 hosts and 127 servers, and it can support only nonextended networks. Extended and nonextended networks will be discussed in detail later in this chapter.

AppleTalk Phase 2, which is the second enhanced AppleTalk implementation, was designed for use in larger internetworks. Phase 2 addresses the key limitations of AppleTalk Phase 1 and features a number of improvements over Phase 1. In particular, Phase 2 allows any combination of 253 hosts or servers on a single AppleTalk network segment and supports both nonextended and extended networks.

APPLETALK NETWORK COMPONENTS

AppleTalk networks are arranged hierarchically. Four basic components form the basis of an AppleTalk network: *sockets*, *nodes*, *networks*, and *zones*. Figure 27–1 illustrates the hierarchical organization of these components in an AppleTalk internetwork. Each of these concepts is summarized in the sections that follow.

Sockets

An AppleTalk socket is a unique, addressable location in an AppleTalk node. It is the logical point at which upper-layer AppleTalk software processes and the network-layer Datagram-Delivery Protocol (DDP) interact. These upper-layer processes are known as *socket clients*. Socket clients own one or more sockets, which they use to send and receive datagrams. Sockets can be assigned statically or dynamically. Statically assigned sockets are reserved for use by certain protocols or other processes. Dynamically assigned sockets are assigned by DDP to socket clients upon request. An AppleTalk node can contain up to 254 different socket numbers. Figure 27–2 illustrates the relationship between the sockets in an AppleTalk node and DDP at the network layer.

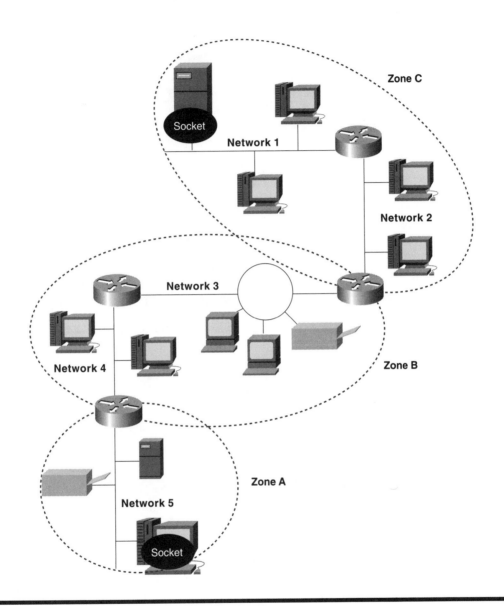

Figure 27–1
The AppleTalk internetwork consists of a hierarchy of components.

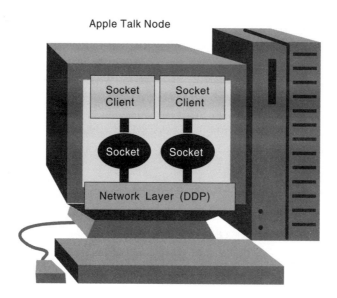

Apple Talk Node

Figure 27–2

Socket clients use sockets to send and receive datagrams.

Nodes

An AppleTalk node is a device that is connected to an AppleTalk network. This device might be a Macintosh computer, a printer, an IBM PC, a router, or some other similar device. Within each AppleTalk node exist numerous software processes called sockets. As discussed earlier, the function of these sockets is to identify the software processes running in the device. Each node in an AppleTalk network belongs to a single network and a specific zone.

Networks

An AppleTalk network consists of a single logical cable and multiple attached nodes. The logical cable is comprised of either a single physical cable or multiple physical cables interconnected by using bridges or routers. AppleTalk networks can be nonextended or extended. Each is discussed briefly in the following sections.

Nonextended Networks

A *nonextended* AppleTalk network is a physical-network segment that is assigned only a single network number, which can range between 1 and 1,024. Network 100 and Network 562, for example, are both valid network numbers in a nonextended network. Each node number in a nonextended network must be unique, and a single nonextended network segment cannot have more than one AppleTalk Zone configured on it. (A zone is a logical group of nodes or networks.) AppleTalk Phase 1 supports only nonextended networks, but as a rule, nonextended network configurations are no longer used in new networks because they have been superseded by extended networks. Figure 27–3 illustrates a nonextended AppleTalk network.

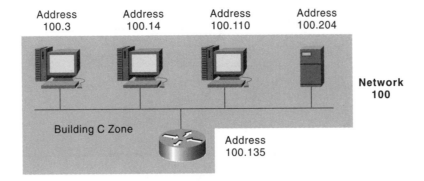

Figure 27–3
A nonextended network is assigned only one network number.

Extended Networks

An *extended* AppleTalk network is a physical-network segment that can be assigned multiple network numbers. This configuration is known as a *cable range*. AppleTalk cable ranges can indicate a single network number or multiple consecutive network numbers. The cable ranges Network 3-3 (unary) and Network 3-6, for example, are both valid in an extended network. Just as in other protocol suites, such as TCP/IP and IPX, each combination of network number and node number in an extended network must be unique, and its address must be unique for identification purposes. Extended networks can have multiple AppleTalk zones configured on a single network segment, and nodes on extended networks can belong to any single zone associated with the extended network. Extended network configurations have, as a rule, replaced nonextended network configurations. Figure 27–4 illustrates an extended network.

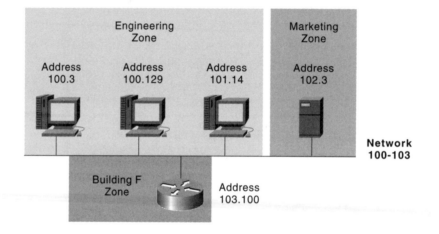

Figure 27–4

An extended network can be assigned multiple network numbers.

Zones

An AppleTalk *zone* is a logical group of nodes or networks that is defined when the network administrator configures the network. The nodes or networks need not be physically contiguous to belong to the same AppleTalk zone. Figure 27–5 illustrates an AppleTalk internetwork composed of three noncontiguous zones.

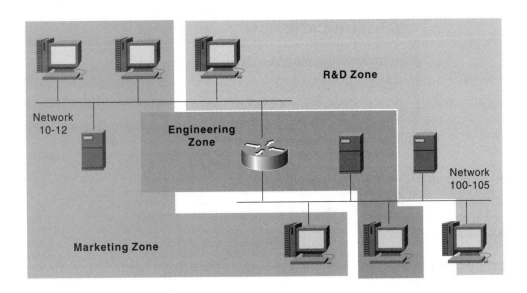

Figure 27–5
Nodes or networks in the same zone need not be physically contiguous.

APPLETALK PHYSICAL AND DATA LINK LAYERS

As with other popular protocol suites, such as TCP/IP and IPX, the AppleTalk architecture maintains media-access dependencies on such lower-layer protocols as Ethernet, Token Ring, and FDDI. Four main media-access implementations exist in the AppleTalk protocol suite: EtherTalk, LocalTalk, TokenTalk, and FDDITalk.

These data link-layer implementations perform address translation and other functions that allow proprietary AppleTalk protocols to communicate over industry-standard interfaces, which include IEEE 802.3 (using EtherTalk), Token Ring/IEEE 802.5 (using TokenTalk), and FDDI (using FDDITalk). In addition, AppleTalk implements its own network interface, known as Local-Talk. Figure 27–6 illustrates how the AppleTalk media-access implementations map to the OSI reference model.

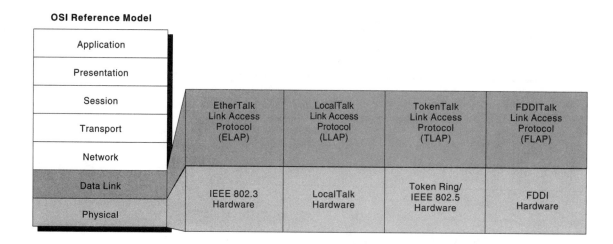

Figure 27–6

AppleTalk media-access maps to the bottom two layers of the OSI reference model.

EtherTalk

EtherTalk extends the data link layer to enable the AppleTalk protocol suite to operate atop a standard IEEE 802.3 implementation. EtherTalk networks are organized exactly as IEEE 802.3 networks, supporting the same speeds and segment lengths, as well as the same number of active network nodes. This allows AppleTalk to be deployed over any of the thousands of Ethernet-based networks in existence today. Communication between the upper-layer protocols of the AppleTalk architecture and the Ethernet protocols is handled by the EtherTalk Link-Access Protocol (ELAP).

EtherTalk Link-Access Protocol

The *EtherTalk Link-Access Protocol* (ELAP) handles the interaction between the proprietary AppleTalk protocols and the standard IEEE 802.3 data link layer. Upper-layer AppleTalk protocols do not recognize standard IEEE 802.3 hardware addresses, so ELAP uses the *Address-Mapping Table* (AMT) maintained by the *AppleTalk Address-Resolution Protocol* (AARP) to properly address transmissions.

ELAP handles the interaction between upper-layer protocols of AppleTalk and the data link layer by encapsulating or enclosing the data inside the protocol units of the 802.3 data link layer. ELAP performs three levels of encapsulation when transmitting DDP packets:

- Subnetwork-Access Protocol (SNAP) header

- IEEE 802.2 Logical Link-Control (LLC) header

- IEEE 802.3 header

This process of encapsulation performed by the ELAP is detailed in the following section.

ELAP Data-Transmission Process

ELAP uses a specific process to transmit data across the physical medium. First, ELAP receives a DDP packet that requires transmission. Next, it finds the protocol address specified in the DDP header and checks the AMT to find the corresponding IEEE 802.3 hardware address. ELAP then prepends three different headers to the DDP packet, beginning with the SNAP and 802.2 LLC headers. The third header is the IEEE 802.3 header. When prepending this header to the packet, the hardware address taken from the AMT is placed in the Destination Address field. The final result, an IEEE 802.3 frame, is placed on the physical medium for transmission to the destination.

LocalTalk

LocalTalk, which is a proprietary data link-layer implementation developed by Apple Computer for its AppleTalk protocol suite, was designed as a cost-effective network solution for connecting local workgroups. LocalTalk hardware typically is built into Apple products, which are easily connected by using inexpensive twisted-pair cabling. LocalTalk networks are organized in a bus topology, which means that devices are connected to each other in series. Network segments are limited to a 300-meter span with a maximum of 32 active nodes, and multiple LocalTalk networks can be interconnected by using routers or other similar intermediate devices. The communication between the data link-layer protocol LocalTalk and upper-layer protocols is the LocalTalk Link-Access Protocol (LLAP).

LocalTalk Link-Access Protocol

The *LocalTalk Link-Access Protocol* (LLAP) is the media-access protocol used in LocalTalk networks to provide best-effort, error-free delivery of frames between AppleTalk nodes. This means that delivery of datagrams is not guaranteed by the LLAP; such a function is performed only by higher-layer protocols in the AppleTalk architecture. LLAP is responsible for regulating node access to the physical media and dynamically acquiring data link-layer node addresses.

Regulating Node Access to the Physical Media

LLAP implements a media-access scheme known as *carrier-sense multiple access, collision avoidance* (CSMA/CA), whereby nodes check the link to see if it is in use. The link must be idle for a certain random period of time before a node can begin transmitting data. LLAP uses data exchanges known as *handshakes* to avoid *collisions* (that is, simultaneous transmissions by two or more nodes). A successful handshake between nodes effectively reserves the link for their use. If two nodes transmit a handshake simultaneously, the transmissions collide. In this case, both transmissions are damaged, causing the packets to be discarded. The handshake exchange is not completed, and the sending nodes infer that a collision occurred. When the collision occurs, the device will remain idle for a random period of time and then retry its transmission. This process is similar to the access mechanism used with Ethernet technology.

Acquiring Node Addresses

LLAP acquires data link-layer node addresses dynamically. The process allows a unique data link-layer address to be assigned without permanently assigning the address to the node. When a node starts up, LLAP assigns the node a randomly chosen node identifier (node ID). The uniqueness of this node ID is determined by the transmission of a special packet that is addressed to the randomly chosen node ID. If the node receives a reply to this packet, the node ID is not unique. The node therefore is assigned another randomly chosen node ID and will send out another packet addressed to that node until no reply returns. If the acquiring node does not receive a reply to the first query, it makes a number of subsequent attempts. If there is still no reply after these attempts, the node ID is considered unique, and the node uses this node ID as its data link-layer address.

TokenTalk

TokenTalk extends the data link layer to allow the AppleTalk protocol suite to operate atop a standard IEEE 802.5/Token Ring implementation. Token-Talk networks are organized exactly as IEEE 802.5/Token Ring networks, supporting the same speeds and the same number of active network nodes. Communication between the data link-layer protocols used with Token Ring and upper-layer protocols is the TokenTalk Link-Access Protocol (TLAP).

TokenTalk Link-Access Protocol

The *TokenTalk Link-Access Protocol* (TLAP) handles the interaction between the proprietary AppleTalk protocols and the standard IEEE 802.5 data-link layer. Upper-layer AppleTalk protocols do not recognize standard IEEE 802.5 hardware addresses, so TLAP uses the AMT maintained by the AARP to properly address transmissions. TLAP performs three levels of encapsulation when transmitting DDP packets:

- Subnetwork-Access Protocol (SNAP) header

- IEEE 802.2 Logical Link-Control (LLC) header

- IEEE 802.5 header

TLAP Data Transmission Process

TLAP data transmission involves a number of steps to transmit data across the physical medium. When TLAP receives a DDP packet that requires transmission, it finds the protocol address specified in the DDP header and then checks the AMT to find the corresponding IEEE 802.5/Token Ring hardware address. Next, TLAP prepends three different headers to the DDP packet, beginning with the SNAP and 802.2 LLC headers. When the third header, IEEE 802.5/Token Ring, is prepended to the packet, the hardware address received from the AMT is placed in the Destination Address field. The final result, an IEEE 802.5/Token Ring frame, is placed on the physical medium for transmission to the destination.

FDDITalk

FDDITalk extends the data link layer to allow the AppleTalk protocol suite to operate atop a standard ANSI FDDI implementation. FDDITalk networks are organized exactly as FDDI networks, supporting the same speeds and the same number of active network nodes.

FDDITalk Link-Access Protocol

The *FDDITalk Link-Access Protocol* (FLAP) handles the interaction between the proprietary AppleTalk protocols and the standard FDDI data link layer. Upper-layer AppleTalk protocols do not recognize standard FDDI hardware addresses, so FLAP uses the AMT maintained by the AARP to properly address transmissions. FLAP performs three levels of encapsulation when transmitting DDP packets:

- Subnetwork-Access Protocol (SNAP) header

- IEEE 802.2 Logical Link Control (LLC) header

- FDDI header

FLAP Data-Transmission Process

As with TLAP, FLAP involves a multi-stage process to transmit data across the physical medium. When FLAP receives a DDP packet requiring transmission, it finds the protocol address specified in the DDP header and then checks the AMT to find the corresponding FDDI hardware address. FLAP then prepends three different headers to the DDP packet, beginning with the SNAP and 802.2 LLC headers. When the third header, the FDDI header, is prepended to the packet, the hardware address received from the AMT is placed in the Destination Address field. The final result, an FDDI frame, is placed on the physical medium for transmission to the destination.

NETWORK ADDRESSES

AppleTalk utilizes addresses to identify and locate devices on a network in a manner similar to the process utilized by such common protocols as TCP/IP and IPX. These addresses, which are assigned dynamically as discussed in the following section, are composed of three elements:

- *Network number*—A 16-bit value that identifies a specific AppleTalk network (either nonextended or extended).

- *Node number*—An 8-bit value that identifies a particular AppleTalk node attached to the specified network.

- *Socket number*—An 8-bit number that identifies a specific socket running on a network node.

AppleTalk addresses usually are written as decimal values separated by a period. For example, 10.1.50 means Network 10, Node 1, Socket 50. This also might be represented as 10.1, socket 50. Figure 27–7 illustrates the AppleTalk network address format.

Field Length,
in Bits:

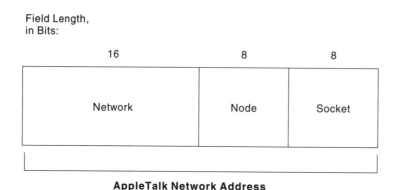

AppleTalk Network Address

Figure 27-7

The AppleTalk network address consists of three distinct numbers.

Network-Address Assignment

One of the unique characteristics of AppleTalk is the dynamic nature of device addresses. It is not necessary to statically define an address to an Apple-Talk device. Rather, AppleTalk nodes are assigned addresses dynamically when they first attach to a network.

When an AppleTalk network node starts up, it receives a provisional network-layer address. The network portion of the provisional address (the first 16 bits) is selected from the *startup range*, which is a reserved range of network addresses (values 65280 to 65534). The node portion (the next 8 bits) of the provisional address is chosen randomly.

Using the *Zone-Information Protocol (ZIP)*, the node communicates with a router attached to the network. The router replies with the valid cable range for the network to which the node is attached. Next, the node selects a valid network number from the cable range supplied by the router and then randomly chooses a node number. A broadcast message is used to determine whether the selected address is in use by another node.

If the address is not being used (that is, no other node responds to the broadcast within a specific period of time), the node has successfully been assigned an address. If, however, another node is using the address, that node responds to the broadcast with a message indicating that the address is in use. The new node must choose another address and repeat the process until it selects an address that is not in use.

AppleTalk Address-Resolution Protocol (AARP)

AppleTalk Address-Resolution Protocol (AARP) is a network-layer protocol in the AppleTalk protocol suite that associates AppleTalk network addresses with hardware addresses. AARP services are used by other AppleTalk protocols. When an AppleTalk protocol has data to transmit, for example, it specifies the network address of the destination. It is the job of AARP to find the hardware address that is associated with the device using that network address.

AARP uses a request-response process to learn the hardware address of other network nodes. Because AARP is a media-dependent protocol, the method used to request a hardware address from a node varies depending on the data link-layer implementation. Typically, a broadcast message is sent to all AppleTalk nodes on the network.

Address-Mapping Table

Each AppleTalk node contains an Address-Mapping Table (AMT), where hardware addresses are associated with network addresses. Each time AARP resolves a network and hardware address combination, the mapping is recorded in the AMT.

Over time, the potential for an AMT entry to become invalid increases. For this reason, each AMT entry typically has a timer associated with it. When AARP receives a packet that verifies or changes the entry, the timer is reset.

If the timer expires, the entry is deleted from the AMT. The next time an AppleTalk protocol wants to communicate with that node, another AARP request must be transmitted to discover the hardware address.

Address Gleaning

In certain implementations, incoming DDP packets are examined to learn the hardware and network addresses of the source node. DDP then can place this information in the AMT. This is one way in which a device, such as a router, workstation, or server, can discover devices within an AppleTalk network.

This process of obtaining address mappings from incoming packets is known as *address gleaning*. Address gleaning is not widely used, but in some situations it can reduce the number of AARP requests that must be transmitted.

AARP Operation

The AppleTalk Address-Resolution Protocol (AARP) maps hardware addresses to network addresses. When an AppleTalk protocol has data to send, it passes the network address of the destination node to AARP. It is the job of AARP to supply the hardware address associated with that network address.

AARP checks the AMT to see whether the network address is already mapped to a hardware address. If the addresses are already mapped, the hardware address is passed to the inquiring AppleTalk protocol, which uses it to communicate with the destination. If the addresses are not mapped, AARP transmits a broadcast requesting the node using the network address in question supply its hardware address.

When the request reaches the node using the network address, that node replies with its hardware address. If no node exists with the specified network address, no response is sent. After a specified number of retries, AARP assumes that the protocol address is not in use and returns an error to the inquiring AppleTalk protocol. If a response is received, the hardware address is associated to the network address in the AMT. The hardware address then is passed to the inquiring AppleTalk protocol, which uses it to communicate with the destination node.

DATAGRAM DELIVERY PROTOCOL (DDP) OVERVIEW

The Datagram Delivery Protocol (DDP) is the primary network-layer routing protocol in the AppleTalk protocol suite that provides a best-effort connectionless datagram service between AppleTalk sockets. As with protocols such as TCP, no virtual circuit or connection is established between two devices. The function of guaranteeing delivery instead is handled by upper-layer protocols of the AppleTalk protocol suite. These upper-layer protocols will be discussed later in this chapter.

DDP performs two key functions: packet transmission and receipt.

- *Transmission of packets*—DDP receives data from socket clients, creates a DDP header by using the appropriate destination address, and passes the packet to the data link-layer protocol.

- *Reception of packets*—DDP receives frames from the data link layer, examines the DDP header to find the destination address, and routes the packet to the destination socket.

DDP maintains the cable range of the local network and the network address of a router attached to the local network in every AppleTalk node. In addition to this information, AppleTalk routers must maintain a routing table by using the Routing Table Maintenance Protocol (RTMP).

DDP Transmission Process

DDP operates much like any routing protocol. Packets are addressed at the source, passed to the data link layer, and transmitted to the destination. When DDP receives data from an upper-layer protocol, it determines whether the source and destination nodes are on the same network by examining the network number of the destination address. If the destination network number is within the cable range of the local network, the packet is encapsulated in a DDP header and is passed to the data link layer for transmission to the destination node. If the destination network number is not within the cable range of the local network, the packet is encapsulated in a DDP header and is passed to the data link layer for transmission to a router. Intermediate routers use their routing tables to forward the packet toward the destination network. When the packet reaches a router attached to the destination network, the packet is transmitted to the destination node.

AppleTalk Transport Layer

The transport layer in AppleTalk implements reliable internetwork data-transport services that are transparent to upper layers. Transport-layer functions typically include flow control, multiplexing, virtual circuit management, and error checking and recovery.

Five key implementations exist at the transport layer of the AppleTalk protocol suite:

- Routing Table Maintenance Protocol (RTMP)
- Name-Binding Protocol (NBP)
- AppleTalk Update-Based Routing Protocol (AURP)
- AppleTalk Transaction Protocol (ATP)
- AppleTalk Echo Protocol (AEP)

Each of these protocol implementations are addressed briefly in the discussions that follow.

Routing Table Maintenance Protocol (RTMP) Overview

The *Routing Table Maintenance Protocol* (RTMP) is a transport-layer protocol in the AppleTalk protocol suite that establishes and maintains routing tables in AppleTalk routers.

RTMP is based on the Routing Information Protocol (RIP), and as with RIP, RTMP uses hop count as a routing metric. *Hop count* is calculated as the number of routers or other intermediate nodes through which a packet must pass to travel from the source network to the destination network.

RTMP Routing Tables

RTMP is responsible for establishing and maintaining routing tables for AppleTalk routers. These routing tables contain an entry for each network that a packet can reach.

Routers periodically exchange routing information to ensure that the routing table in each router contains the most current information, and that the information is consistent across the internetwork. An RTMP routing table contains the following information about each of the destination networks known to the router:

- Network cable range of the destination network

- Distance in hops to the destination network

- Router port that leads to the destination network

- Address of the next hop router

- Current state of the routing-table entry (good, suspect, or bad)

Figure 27–8 illustrates a typical RTMP routing table.

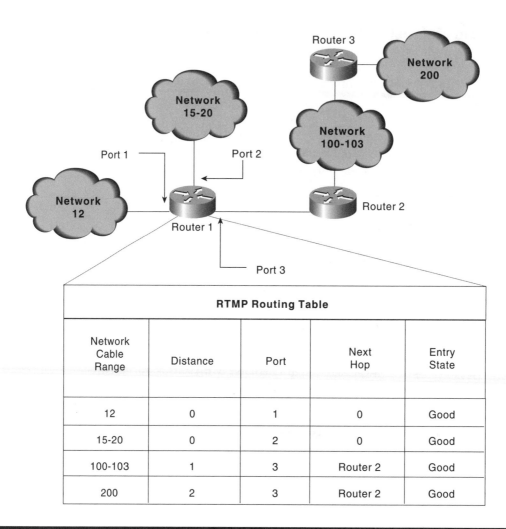

Figure 27–8

An RTMP routing table contains information about each destination network known to the router.

Name-Binding Protocol (NBP) Overview

The *Name-Binding Protocol (NBP)* is a transport-layer protocol in the Apple-Talk protocol suite that maps the addresses used at lower layers to AppleTalk names. Socket clients within AppleTalk nodes are known as *Network-Visible*

Entities (NVEs). An NVE is a network-addressable resource, such as a print service, that is accessible over the internetwork. NVEs are referred to by character strings known as *entity names*. NVEs also have a zone and various attributes, known as *entity types*, associated with them.

Two key reasons exist for using entity names rather than addresses at the upper layers. First, network addresses are assigned to nodes dynamically and, therefore, change regularly. Entity names provide a consistent way for users to refer to network resources and services, such as a file server. Second, using names instead of addresses to refer to resources and services preserves the transparency of lower-layer operations to end-users.

Name Binding

Name binding is the process of mapping NVE entity names with network addresses. Each AppleTalk node maps the names of its own NVEs to their network addresses in a names table. The combination of all the names tables in all internetwork nodes is known as the *names directory*, which is a distributed database of all name-to-address mappings. Name binding can occur when a node is first started up or dynamically, immediately before the named entity is accessed.

NBP performs the following four functions: name lookup, name recognition, name confirmation, and name deletion. *Name lookup* is used to learn the network address of an NVE before the services in that NVE are accessed. NBP checks the names directory for the name-to-address mapping. *Name registration* allows a node to create its names table. NBP confirms that the name is not in use and then adds the name-to-address mappings to the table. *Name confirmation* is used to verify that a mapping learned by using a name lookup is still accurate. *Name deletion* is used to remove an entry from the names table in such instances as when the node is powered off.

AppleTalk Update-Based Routing Protocol (AURP)

The *AppleTalk Update-Based Routing Protocol* (AURP) is a transport-layer protocol in the AppleTalk protocol suite that allows two or more AppleTalk internetworks to be interconnected through a *Transmission-Control Protocol/Internet Protocol* (TCP/IP) network to form an AppleTalk WAN. AURP encapsulates packets in User-Datagram Protocol (UDP) headers, allowing them to be transported transparently through a TCP/IP network. An AURP implementation has two components: exterior routers and AURP tunnels.

Exterior routers connect a local AppleTalk internetwork to an AURP tunnel. Exterior routers convert AppleTalk data and routing information to AURP and perform encapsulation and de-encapsulation of AppleTalk traffic. An exterior router functions as an AppleTalk router in the local network and as an end node in the TCP/IP network. When exterior routers first attach to an AURP tunnel, they exchange routing information with other exterior routers. Thereafter, exterior routers send routing information only under the following circumstances:

- When a network is added to or removed from the routing table

- When the distance to a network is changed

- When a change in the path to a network causes the exterior router to access that network through its local internetwork rather than through the tunnel, or through the tunnel rather than through the local internetwork

An AURP tunnel functions as a single, virtual data link between remote AppleTalk internetworks. Any number of physical nodes can exist in the path between exterior routers, but these nodes are transparent to the AppleTalk networks. Two kinds of AURP tunnels exist: *point-to-point tunnels* and *multipoint tunnels*. A point-to-point AURP tunnel connects only two exterior routers. A multipoint AURP tunnel connects three or more exterior routers. Two kinds of multipoint tunnels also exist. A fully connected multipoint tunnel enables all connected exterior routers to send packets to one another. With a partially connected multipoint tunnel, one or more exterior routers are aware only of some, not all, the other exterior routers. Figure 27–9 illustrates two AppleTalk LANs connected via a point-to-point AURP tunnel.

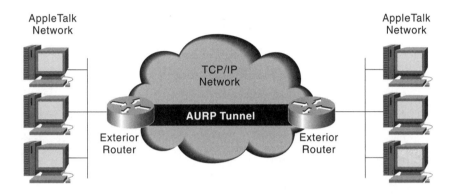

Figure 27–9
An AURP tunnel acts as a virtual link between remote networks.

AURP Encapsulation

When exchanging routing information or data through an AURP tunnel, AppleTalk packets must be converted from RTMP, ZIP, and (in the Cisco implementation) Enhanced IGRP to AURP. The packets then are encapsulated in User-Datagram Protocol (UDP) headers for transport across the TCP/IP network. The conversion and encapsulation are performed by exterior routers, which receive AppleTalk routing information or data packets that must be sent to a remote AppleTalk internetwork. The exterior router converts the packets to AURP packets, and these packets then are encapsulated in UDP headers and sent into the tunnel (that is, the TCP/IP network).

The TCP/IP network treats the packets as normal UDP traffic. The remote exterior router receives the UDP packets and removes the UDP header information. The AURP packets then are converted back into their original format, whether as routing information or data packets. If the AppleTalk packets contain routing information, the receiving exterior router updates its routing tables accordingly. If the packets contain data destined for an Apple-Talk node on the local network, the traffic is sent out the appropriate interface.

AppleTalk Transaction Protocol (ATP)

The *AppleTalk Transaction Protocol* (ATP) is a transport-layer protocol in the AppleTalk protocol suite that handles transactions between two Apple-Talk sockets. A transaction consists of transaction requests and transaction responses, which are exchanged by the involved socket clients.

The requesting socket client sends a transaction request asking that the receiving client perform some action. Upon receiving the request, the client performs the requested action and returns the appropriate information in a transaction response. In transmitting transaction requests and responses, ATP performs most of the important transport-layer functions, including acknowledgment and retransmission, packet sequencing, and segmentation and reassembly.

Several session-layer protocols run over ATP, including the *AppleTalk Session Protocol* (ASP) and the *Printer-Access Protocol* (PAP). These two upper-layer AppleTalk protocols are discussed later in this chapter.

Responding devices behave differently depending on which of two types of transaction services is being used: *At-Least-Once* (ALO) or *Exactly-Once* (XO) transactions. ALO transactions are used when repetition of the transaction request is the same as executing it once. If a transaction response is lost, the source will retransmit its request. This does not adversely affect protocol operations, because repetition of the request is the same as executing it once. XO transactions are used when repetition of the transaction request might adversely affect protocol operations. Receiving devices keep a list of every recently received transaction so that duplicate requests are not executed more than once.

AppleTalk Echo Protocol (AEP)

The *AppleTalk Echo Protocol* (AEP) is a transport-layer protocol in the AppleTalk protocol suite that generates packets that test the reachability of network nodes. AEP can be implemented in any AppleTalk node and has the statically assigned socket number 4 (the Echoer socket).

To test the reachability of a given node, an AEP request packet is passed to the DDP at the source. DDP addresses the packet appropriately, indicating in the Type field that the packet is an AEP request. When the packet is received by the destination, DDP examines the Type field and sees that it is an AEP request. In this process, the packet is copied, changed to an AEP reply (by changing a field in the AEP packet), and returned to the source node.

APPLETALK UPPER-LAYER PROTOCOLS

AppleTalk implements services at the session, presentation, and application layers of the OSI model. Four key implementations at the session layer are included in the AppleTalk protocol suite. (The session layer establishes, manages, and terminates communication sessions between presentation-layer entities).

Communication sessions consist of service requests and service responses that occur between applications located in different network devices. These requests and responses are coordinated by protocols implemented at the session layer.

The session-layer protocol implementations supported by AppleTalk include the *AppleTalk Data-Stream Protocol* (ADSP), *Zone-Information Protocol* (ZIP), *AppleTalk Session Protocol* (ASP), and *Printer-Access Protocol* (PAP).

The *AppleTalk Filing Protocol* (AFP) is implemented at the presentation and application layers of the AppleTalk protocol suite. In general, the presentation layer provides a variety of coding and conversion functions that are applied to application-layer data. The application layer interacts with software applications (which are outside the scope of the OSI model) that implement a communicating component. Application-layer functions typically include identifying communication partners, determining resource availability, and synchronizing communication. Figure 27–10 illustrates how the upper layers of the AppleTalk protocol suite map to the OSI model.

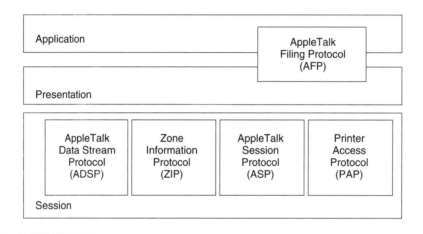

Figure 27–10
AppleTalk upper layer protocols map to three layers of the OSI model.

AppleTalk Data-Stream Protocol (ADSP)

The *AppleTalk Data-Stream Protocol* (ADSP) is a session-layer protocol in the AppleTalk protocol suite that establishes and maintains full-duplex communication between two AppleTalk sockets. ADSP guarantees that data is correctly sequenced and that packets are not duplicated. ADSP also implements a flow-control mechanism that allows a destination to slow source transmissions by reducing the size of the advertised receive window. ADSP runs directly on top of the DDP.

Zone-Information Protocol (ZIP)

The Zone-Information Protocol (ZIP) is a session-layer protocol in the AppleTalk protocol suite that maintains network number-to-zone name mappings in AppleTalk routers. ZIP is used primarily by AppleTalk routers. Other network nodes, however, use ZIP services at startup to choose their zone. ZIP maintains a *zone-information table* (ZIT) in each router. ZITs are lists maintained by ZIP that map specific network numbers to one or more zone names. Each ZIT contains a network number-to-zone name mapping for every network in the internetwork. Figure 27–11 illustrates a basic ZIT.

Network Number	Zones
10	Marketing
20-25	Documentation, Training
50	Finance
100-120	Engineering
100-120	Facilities, Administration

Figure 27–11
Zone-information tables assist in zone identification.

AppleTalk Session Protocol (ASP)

The *AppleTalk Session Protocol (ASP)* is a session-layer protocol in the AppleTalk protocol suite that establishes and maintains sessions between AppleTalk clients and servers. ASP allows a client to establish a session with a server and to send commands to that server. Multiple client sessions to a single server can be maintained simultaneously. ASP uses many of the services provided by lower-layer protocols, such as ATP and NBP.

Printer-Access Protocol (PAP) Overview

The *Printer-Access Protocol* (PAP) is a session-layer protocol in the AppleTalk protocol suite that allows client workstations to establish connections with servers, particularly printers. A session between a client workstation and a server is initiated when the workstation requests a session with a particular server. PAP uses the NBP to learn the network address of the requested server and then opens a connection between the client and server. Data is exchanged between client and server using the ATP. When the communication is complete, PAP terminates the connection. Servers implementing PAP can support multiple simultaneous connections with clients. This allows a print server, for example, to process jobs from several different workstations at the same time.

AppleTalk Filing Protocol (AFP)

The *AppleTalk Filing Protocol* (AFP) permits AppleTalk workstations to share files across a network. AFP performs functions at the presentation and application layers of the AppleTalk protocol suite. This protocol preserves the transparency of the network by allowing users to manipulate remotely stored files in exactly the same manner as locally stored files. AFP uses the services provided by the ASP, the ATP, and the AEP.

AppleTalk Protocol Suite

Figure 27–12 illustrates the entire AppleTalk protocol suite and how it maps to the OSI reference model.

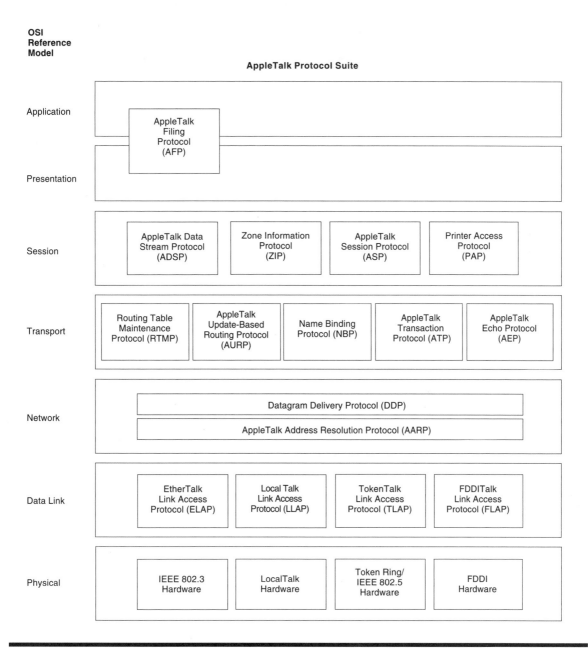

Figure 27–12
The AppleTalk protocol suite maps to every layer of the OSI model.

DDP Packet Format

The following descriptions summarize the fields associated with the DDP packets. This packet has two forms:

- *Short DDP Packet*—The short format is used for transmissions between two nodes on the same network segment in a nonextended network only. This format is seldom used in new networks.

- *Extended DDP Packet*—The extended format is used for transmissions between nodes with different network numbers (in a nonextended network), and for any transmissions in an extended network.

Figure 27–13 illustrates the format of the extended DDP packet.

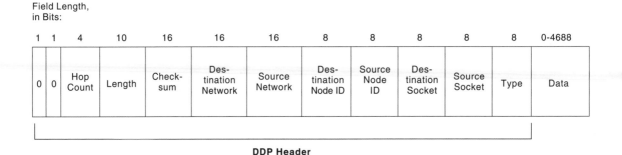

Field Length, in Bits:

1	1	4	10	16	16	16	8	8	8	8	8	0-4688
0	0	Hop Count	Length	Check-sum	Des-tination Network	Source Network	Des-tination Node ID	Source Node ID	Des-tination Socket	Source Socket	Type	Data

DDP Header

Figure 27–13
An extended DDP packet consists of 13 fields.

The extended DDP packet fields illustrated in Figure 25-13 are summarized in the discussion the follows:

- *Hop Count*—Counts the number of intermediate devices through which the packet has passed. At the source, this field is set to zero. Each intermediate node through which the packet passes increases the value of this field by one. The maximum number of hops is 15.

- *Length*—Indicates the total length, in bytes, of the DDP packet.

- *Checksum*—Contains a checksum value used to detect errors. If no checksum is performed, the bits in this optional field are set to zero.

- *Destination Network*—Indicates the 16-bit destination network number.

- *Source Network*—Indicates the 16-bit source network number.

- *Destination Node ID*—Indicates the 8-bit destination node ID.

- *Source Node ID*—Indicates the 8-bit source node ID.

- *Destination Socket*—Indicates the 8-bit destination socket number.

- *Source Socket*—Indicates the 8-bit source socket number.

- *Type*—Indicates the upper-layer protocol to which the information in the data field belongs.

- *Data*—Contains data from an upper-layer protocol.

CHAPTER 28

DECnet

BACKGROUND

DECnet is a group of data-communications products, including a protocol suite, developed and supported by Digital Equipment Corporation (Digital). The first version of DECnet, released in 1975, allowed two directly attached PDP-11 minicomputers to communicate. In more recent years, Digital has included support for nonproprietary protocols, but DECnet remains the most important of Digital's network product offerings. This chapter provides a summary of the DECnet protocol suite, Digital's networking architectures, and the overall operation of DECnet traffic management.

Figure 28–1 illustrates a DECnet internetwork with routers interconnecting two LANs that contain workstations and VAXs.

Several versions of DECnet have been released. The first allowed two directly attached minicomputers to communicate.

Subsequent releases expanded the DECnet functionality by adding support for additional proprietary and standard protocols, while remaining compatible with the immediately preceding release. This means the protocols are backward-compatible. Currently, two versions of DECnet are in wide use: DECnet Phase IV and DECnet/OSI.

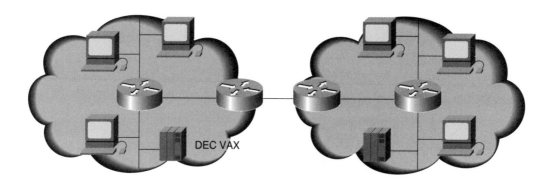

Figure 28–1
In a DECnet-based internetwork routers interconnect workstations and VAXs.

DECnet Phase IV is the most widely implemented version of DECnet. However, DECnet/OSI is the most recent release. DECnet Phase IV is based on the Phase IV Digital Network Architecture (DNA), and it supports proprietary Digital protocols and other proprietary and standard protocols. DECnet Phase IV is backward-compatible with DECnet Phase III, the version that preceded it.

DECnet/OSI (also called DECnet Phase V) is backward-compatible with DECnet Phase IV and is the most recent version of DECnet. This version is based on the DECnet/OSI DNA. DECnet/OSI supports a subset of the OSI protocols, multiple proprietary DECnet protocols, and other proprietary and standard protocols.

DECNET PHASE IV DIGITAL NETWORK ARCHITECTURE (DNA)

The *Digital Network Architecture* (DNA) is a comprehensive layered network architecture that supports a large set of proprietary and standard protocols. The Phase IV DNA is similar to the architecture outlined by the OSI reference model. As with the OSI reference model, the Phase IV DNA utilizes a layered approach, whereby specific layer functions provide services to protocol layers above it and depend on protocol layers below it. Unlike the OSI model, however, the Phase IV DNA is comprised of eight layers. Figure 28–2 illustrates how the eight layers of the Phase IV DNA relate to the OSI reference model.

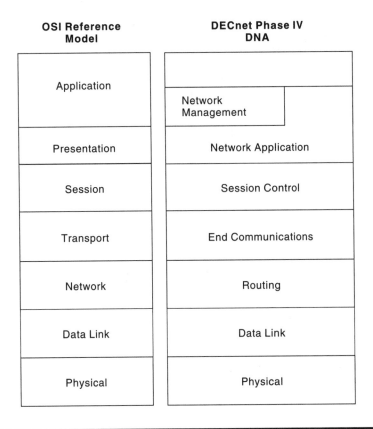

Figure 28–2
Phase IV consists of eight layers that map to the OSI layers.

The following section details the functionality and role of each of these layers and identifies the similarities between the Phase IV DNA architecture and the OSI reference model.

Phase IV DNA Layers

The DECnet Phase IV DNA defines an eight-layer model, as illustrated in Figure 28–2. The *user layer* represents the user-network interface, supporting user services and programs with a communicating component. The user layer corresponds roughly to the OSI application layer. The *network management layer* represents the user interface to network-management information. This layer interacts with all the lower layers of the DNA and corresponds roughly with the OSI application layer. The *network application layer* provides various network applications, such as remote file access and virtual terminal access. This layer corresponds roughly to the OSI presentation and application layers. The *session control layer* manages logical link connections between end nodes and corresponds roughly to the OSI session layer. The *end communications layer* handles flow control, segmentation, and reassembly functions and corresponds roughly to the OSI transport layer. The *routing layer* performs routing and other functions, and corresponds roughly to the OSI network layer. The *data link layer* manages physical network channels and corresponds to the OSI data link layer. The *physical layer* manages hardware interfaces and determines the electrical and mechanical functions of the physical media, and this layer corresponds to the OSI physical layer.

Phase IV DECnet Addressing

DECnet addresses are not associated with the physical networks to which the nodes are connected. Instead, DECnet locates hosts using area/node address pairs. An area's value ranges from 1 to 63, inclusive. Likewise, a node address can be between 1 and 1,023, inclusive. Therefore, each area can have 1,023 nodes, and approximately 65,000 nodes can be addressed in a DECnet network. Areas can span many routers, and a single cable can support many areas. Therefore, if a node has several network interfaces, it uses the same area/node address for each interface. Figure 28–3 illustrates a sample DECnet network with several addressable entities.

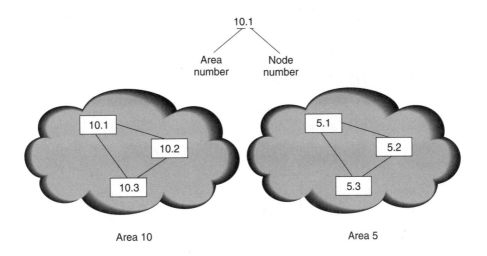

Figure 28–3
DECnet locates hosts using area/node address pairs.

DECnet hosts do not use manufacturer-assigned Media Access Control (MAC)-layer addresses. Instead, network-level addresses are embedded in the MAC-layer address according to an algorithm that multiplies the area number by 1,024 and adds the node number to the product. The resulting 16-bit decimal address is converted to a hexadecimal number and appended to the address AA00.0400 in byte-swapped order, with the least-significant byte first. For example, DECnet address 12.75 becomes 12363 (base 10), which equals 304B (base 16). After this byte-swapped address is appended to the standard DECnet MAC address prefix, the address is AA00.0400.4B30.

DECNET/OSI DIGITAL NETWORK ARCHITECTURE (DNA)

The DECnet/OSI (DECnet Phase V) DNA is very similar to the architecture outlined by the OSI reference model. DECnet Phase V utilizes a layered approach that achieves a high degree of flexibility in terms of support for upper-layer protocol suites. As the following section discusses, DECnet OSI actually allows for the support of multiple protocol suites.

DECnet/OSI DNA Implementations

The DECnet/OSI DNA defines a layered model that implements three protocol suites: OSI, DECnet, and Transmission Control Protocol/Internet Protocol (TCP/IP). The OSI implementation of DECnet/OSI conforms to the seven-layer OSI reference model and supports many of the standard OSI protocols. The Digital implementation of DECnet/OSI provides backward compatibility with DECnet Phase IV and supports multiple proprietary Digital protocols. The TCP/IP implementation of DECnet/OSI supports the lower-layer TCP/IP protocols and enables the transmission of DECnet traffic over TCP transport protocols. Figure 28–4 illustrates the three DECnet/OSI implementations:

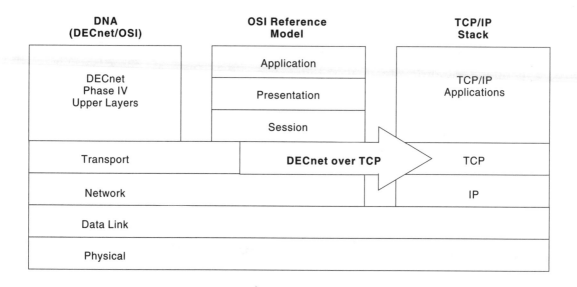

Figure 28–4

The OSI, DECnet, and TCP are all supported by DECnet/OSI DNA.

DECNET MEDIA ACCESS

DECnet Phase IV and DECnet/OSI support a variety of media-access implementations at the physical and data link layers. This has contributed to the relatively wide acceptance of DECnet in the computer networking industry. As explained in the following sections, both DECnet Phase IV and Phase V can support many of the common physical and data-link technologies in use today.

At the physical layer, DECnet Phase IV and DECnet/OSI support most of the popular physical implementations, including Ethernet/IEEE 802.3, Token Ring/IEEE 802.5, and Fiber Distributed Data Interface (FDDI). In addition, DECnet/OSI supports Frame Relay and X.21bis.

At the data link layer, DECnet Phase IV and DECnet/OSI support IEEE 802.2 Logical Link Control (LLC), Link-Access Procedure, Balanced (LAPB), Frame Relay, and High-Level Data Link Control (HDLC). Both DECnet Phase IV and DECnet/OSI also support the proprietary Digital data-link protocol, Digital Data Communications Message Protocol (DDCMP), which provides point-to-point and multipoint connections; full-duplex or half-duplex communication over synchronous and asynchronous channels; and error correction, sequencing, and management.

DECNET ROUTING

DECnet routing occurs at the routing layer of the DNA in DECnet Phase IV and at the network layer of the OSI model in DECnet/OSI. The routing implementations in both DECnet Phase IV and DECnet/OSI, however, are similar.

DECnet Phase IV routing is implemented by the DECnet Routing Protocol (DRP), which is a relatively simple and efficient protocol whose primary function is to provide optimal path determination through a DECnet Phase IV network. Figure 28–5 provides a sample DECnet network to illustrate how the routing function is performed in a DECnet Phase IV network.

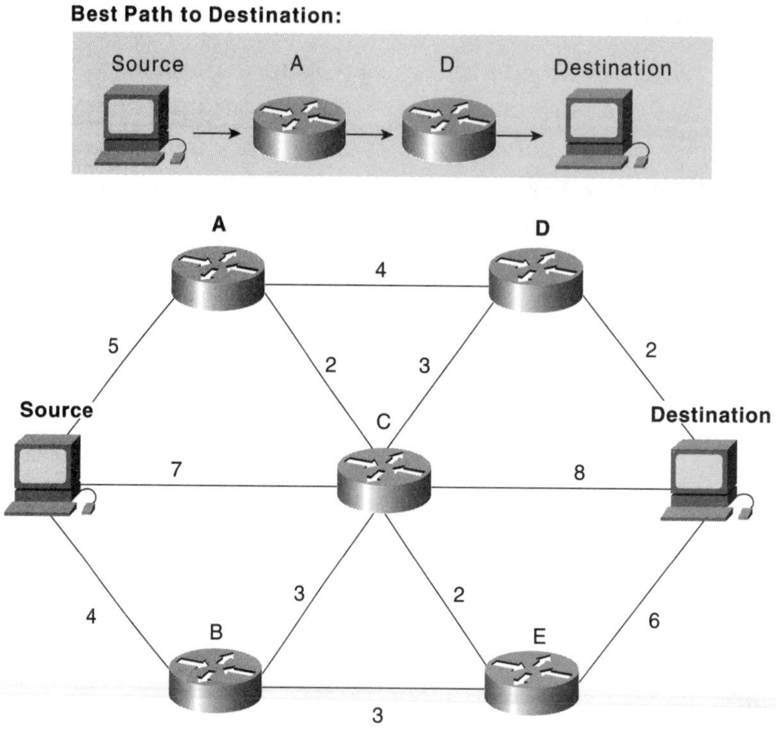

Best Path to Destination:

Figure 28–5
The DRP determines the optimal route through a DECnet Phase IV network.

DECnet routing decisions are based on cost, an arbitrary measure assigned by network administrators to be used in comparing various paths through an internetwork environment. Costs typically are based on hop count or media bandwidth, among other measures. The lower the cost, the better the path. When network faults occur, the DRP uses cost values to recalculate the best paths to each destination.

DECnet/OSI routing is implemented by the standard OSI routing protocols (ISO 8473, ISO 9542, and ISO 10589) and by DRP. Detailed information on the OSI routing protocols can be found in Chapter 41, "Open Systems Interconnection (OSI) Routing Protocol."

DECNET END-COMMUNICATIONS LAYER

DECnet Phase IV supports a single transport protocol at the DNA end-communications layer, the Network-Services Protocol (NSP).

Network-Services Protocol

The *Network-Services Protocol* (NSP) is a proprietary, connection-oriented, end-communications protocol developed by Digital that is responsible for creating and terminating connections between nodes, performing message fragmentation and reassembly, and managing error control.

NSP also manages two types of flow control: a simple start/stop mechanism in which the receiver tells the sender when to terminate and resume data transmission, and a more complex scheme in which the receiver tells the sender how many messages it can accept.

DECNET/OSI TRANSPORT LAYER

DECnet/OSI supports NSP, three standard OSI transport protocols, and the Transmission Control Protocol (TCP).

DECnet/OSI supports Transport Protocol classes (TP) 0, TP2, and TP4. TP0 is the simplest OSI connection-oriented transport protocol. Of the classic transport-layer functions, it performs only segmentation and reassembly. This means that TP0 will note the smallest maximum-size protocol data unit (PDU) supported by the underlying subnetworks, and will break the transport packet into smaller pieces that are not too big for network transmission. TP2 can multiplex and demultiplex data streams over a single virtual circuit. This capability makes TP2 particularly useful over public data networks (PDNs), where each virtual circuit incurs a separate charge. As with TP0 and TP1, TP2 also segments and reassembles PDUs, while TP3 combines the features of TP1 and TP2. TP4, the most popular OSI transport protocol, is similar to the Internet protocol suite's TCP and, in fact, was based on that model. In addition to

TP3's features, TP4 provides reliable transport service and assumes a network in which problems are not detected.

Request For Comments (RFC) 1006 and RFC 1006 Extensions define an implementation of OSI transport-layer protocols atop the TCP. RFC 1006 defines the implementation of OSI Transport Protocol class 0 (TP0) on top of TCP. RFC 1006 Extensions define the implementation of Transport Protocol class 2 (TP2) on top of TCP.

DECNET PHASE IV UPPER LAYERS

The DECnet Phase IV DNA specifies four upper layers to provide user interaction services, network-management capabilities, file transfer, and session management. Specifically, these are referred to as the user layer, network-management layer, network-application layer, and session-control layer. The upper layers of the DECnet Phase IV architecture are discussed in more detail in the following sections.

User Layer

The DNA user layer supports user services and programs that interact with user applications. The end user interacts directly with these applications, and the applications use the services and programs provided by the user layer.

Network-Management Layer

The network-management protocol widely used in DECnet networks is the proprietary Digital Network Information and Control Exchange (NICE) protocol. NICE is a command-response protocol. Commands, which request an action, are issued to a managed node or process; responses, in the form of actions, are returned by those nodes or processes. NICE performs a variety of network management-related functions and can be used to transfer an operating system from a local system into a remote system, as well as enable an unattended remote system to dump its memory to the local system. Protocols using NICE can examine or change certain characteristics of the network. NICE supports an event logger that automatically tracks important network events, such as an adjacency change or a circuit-state change. NICE supports functions that accommodate hardware and node-to-node loop tests.

Certain network management functions can use the *Maintenance Operations Protocol* (MOP), a collection of functions that can operate without the presence of the DNA layers between the network-management and data link layers. This allows access to nodes that exist in a state where only data link layer services are available or operational.

Network-Application Layer

Data-Access Protocol (DAP), a proprietary Digital protocol, is used by DECnet Phase IV at the network-application layer. DAP supports remote file access and remote file transfer, services that are used by network-management layer and user-layer applications. Other proprietary Digital protocols operating at the network-application layer include MAIL, which allows the exchange of mail messages, and CTERM, which allows remote interactive terminal access.

Session-Control Layer

The *Session-Control Protocol* (SCP) is the DECnet Phase IV session-control layer protocol that performs a number of functions. In particular, SCP requests a logical link from an end device, receives logical-link requests from end devices, accepts or rejects logical-link requests, translates names to addresses, and terminates logical links.

DECNET/OSI UPPER LAYERS

The DECnet/OSI DNA is based on the OSI reference model. DECnet/OSI supports two protocol suites at each of the upper layers: the OSI protocols and the DECnet Phase IV protocols (for backward compatibility). DECnet/OSI supports functionality in the application, presentation and session layers.

Application Layer

DECnet/OSI implements the standard OSI application-layer implementations, as well as standard application-layer processes such as *Common Management-Information Protocol (CMIP)* and *File Transfer, Access, and Management (FTAM)*, among others. DECnet/OSI also supports all the protocols implemented by DECnet Phase IV at the user and network-management layers of the DNA, such as the *Network Information and Control Exchange (NICE)* protocol.

The OSI application layer includes actual applications, as well as application service elements (ASEs). ASEs allows easy communication from applications to lower layers. The three most important ASEs are Association Control Service Element (ACSE), Remote Operations Service Element (ROSE), and Reliable Transfer Service Element (RTSE). ACSE associates application names with one another in preparation for application-to-application communications. ROSE implements a generic request-reply mechanism that permits remote operations in a manner similar to that of remote procedure calls (RPCs). RTSE aids reliable delivery by making session-layer constructs easy to use.

Presentation Layer

DECnet/OSI implements all the standard OSI presentation-layer implementations. DECnet/OSI also supports all the protocols implemented by DECnet Phase IV at the network-application layer of the DNA. The most important of these is the *Data-Access Protocol (DAP)*.

The OSI presentation layer typically is just a pass-through protocol for information from adjacent layers. Although many people believe that Abstract Syntax Notation 1 (ASN.1) is OSI's presentation-layer protocol, ASN.1 is used for expressing data formats in a machine-independent format. This allows communication between applications on diverse computer systems (ESs) in a manner transparent to the applications.

Session Layer

DECnet/OSI implements all the standard OSI session-layer implementations. DECnet/OSI also supports all the protocols implemented by DECnet Phase IV at the session-control layer of the DNA. The primary session-control layer protocol is the Session-Control Protocol (SCP). The OSI session-layer protocol turns the data streams provided by the lower four layers into sessions by implementing various control mechanisms. These mechanisms include accounting, conversation control, and session-parameter negotiation. Session-conversation control is implemented by use of a token, the possession of which provides the right to communicate. The token can be requested, and ESs can be granted priorities that provide for unequal token use.

Figure 28–6 illustrates the complete DECnet Phase IV and DECnet/OSI protocol suites, including the implementation of DECnet/OSI over TCP.

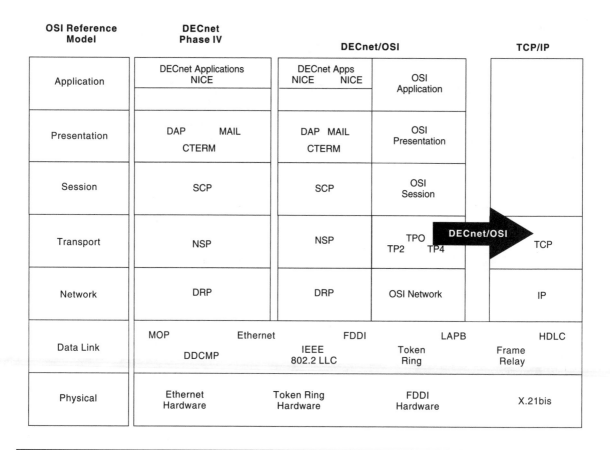

Figure 28–6

DECnet Phase IV and DECnet/OSI support the same data link and physical layer specifications.

29

IBM Systems Network Architecture (SNA) Protocols

BACKGROUND

IBM networking today consists of essentially two separate architectures that branch, more or less, from a common origin. Before contemporary networks existed, IBM's *Systems Network Architecture* (SNA) ruled the networking landscape, so it often is referred to as traditional or legacy SNA.

With the rise of personal computers, workstations, and client/server computing, the need for a peer-based networking strategy was addressed by IBM with the creation of *Advanced Peer-to-Peer Networking* (APPN) and *Advanced Program-to-Program Computing* (APPC).

Although many of the legacy technologies associated with mainframe-based SNA have been brought into APPN-based networks, real differences exist. This chapter discusses each branch of the IBM networking environment, beginning with legacy SNA environments and following with a discussion of AAPN. The chapter closes with summaries of the IBM Basic-Information Unit (BIU) and Path-Information Unit (PIU).

NOTES

IBM-based routing strategies are covered in a separate chapter. Refer to Chapter 37, "IBM Systems Network Architecture (SNA) Routing" for details about IBM routing protocols.

TRADITIONAL SNA ENVIRONMENTS

SNA was developed in the 1970s with an overall structure that parallels the OSI reference model. With SNA, a mainframe running *Advanced Communication Facility/Virtual Telecommunication Access Method* (ACF/VTAM) serves as the hub of an SNA network. ACF/VTAM is responsible for establishing all sessions and for activating and deactivating resources. In this environment, resources are explicitly predefined, thereby eliminating the requirement for broadcast traffic and minimizing header overhead. The underlying architecture and key components of traditional SNA networking are summarized in the sections that follow.

IBM SNA Architecture

IBM SNA-model components map closely to the OSI reference model. The descriptions that follow outline the role of each SNA component in providing connectivity among SNA entities.

- *Data-link control (DLC)*—Defines several protocols, including the *Synchronous Data Link Control* (SDLC) protocol for hierarchical communication, and the Token Ring Network communication protocol for LAN communication between peers

- *Path control*—Performs many OSI network-layer functions, including routing and datagram *segmentation and reassembly (SAR)*

- *Transmission control*—Provides a reliable end-to-end connection service, as well as encrypting and decrypting services

- *Data flow control*—Manages request and response processing, determines whose turn it is to communicate, groups messages together, and interrupts data flow on request

- *Presentation services*—Specifies data-transformation algorithms that translate data from one format to another, coordinate resource sharing, and synchronize transaction operations

- *Transaction services*—Provides application services in the form of programs that implement distributed processing or management services

---

NOTES

SNA does not define specific protocols for its physical control layer. The physical control layer is assumed to be implemented via other standards.

Figure 29–1 illustrates how these elements of the IBM SNA model map to the general ISO OSI networking model.

A key construct defined within the overall SNA network model is the *path control network*, which is responsible for moving information between SNA nodes and facilitating internetwork communication between nodes on different networks. The path control network environment uses functions provided by the path control and data-link control (DLC). The path control network is a subset of the IBM transport network.

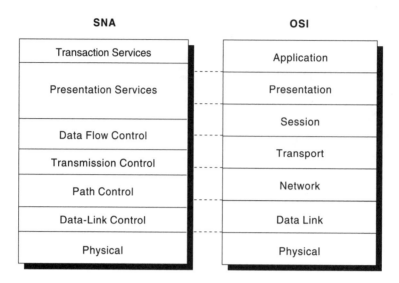

Figure 29–1
IBM SNA maps to all seven levels of the OSI model.

IBM SNA Physical Entities

Traditional SNA physical entities assume one of the following four forms: *hosts, communications controllers, establishment controllers,* and *terminals.* Hosts in SNA control all or part of a network and typically provide computation, program execution, database access, directory services, and network management. (An example of a host device within a traditional SNA environment is an S/370 mainframe.) Communications controllers manage the physical network and control communication links. In particular, communications controllers—also called *front-end processors* (FEPs)—are relied upon to route data through a traditional SNA network. (An example of a communications controller is a 3745.) Establishment controllers are commonly called *cluster controllers.* These devices control input and output operations of attached devices, such as terminals. (An example of an establishment controller is a 3174.) Terminals, also referred to as workstations, provide the user interface to the network. (A typical example would be a 3270. Figure 29–2 illustrates each of these physical entities in the context of a generalized SNA network diagram.)

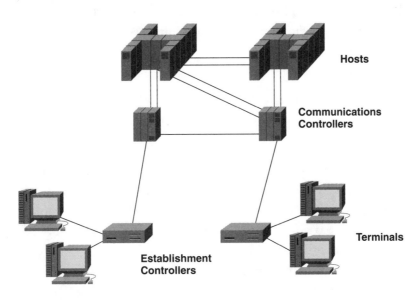

Figure 29–2
SNA physical entities can assume one of four forms.

IBM SNA Data-Link Control

The SNA *data-link control* (DLC) layer supports a number of media, each of which is designed to provide access to devices and users with differing requirements. SNA-supported media types include mainframe channels, SDLC, X.25, and Token Ring, among other media.

A standard SNA mainframe channel attachment provides a parallel-data channel that uses *direct memory access* (DMA) data-movement techniques. A mainframe channel connects IBM hosts to each other and to communications controllers via multiwire cables. Each cable can be up to several hundred feet in length. A standard mainframe channel can transfer data at rate of 3 to 4.5 Mbps.

IBM's Enterprise Systems Connection (ESCON) mainframe attachment environment permits higher throughput and can cover greater physical distances. In general, ESCON transfers data at 18 Mbps and supports a point-to-point connection, ranging up to several kilometers, and transfers. To allow higher data rates and longer distances, ESCON uses optical fiber for its network medium.

SDLC has been widely implemented in SNA networks to interconnect communications and establishment controllers and to move data via telecommunications links.

X.25 networks have long been implemented for WAN interconnections. In general, an X.25 network is situated between two SNA nodes and is treated as a single link. SNA implements X.25 as the access protocol, and SNA nodes are considered adjacent to one another in the context of X.25 networks. To interconnect SNA nodes over an X.25-based WAN, SNA requires DLC-protocol capabilities that X.25 does not provide. Several specialized DLC protocols are employed to fill the gap, such as the physical services header, Qualified Logical Link Control (QLLC) and Enhanced Logical Link Control (ELLC).

Token Ring networks are the primary SNA DLC method for providing media access to LAN-based devices. Token Ring, as supported by IBM, is virtually the same as the IEEE 802.5 link-access protocol running under IEEE 802.2 Logical Link Control Type 2 (LLC2).

In addition to the basic suite of media types, IBM added support for several other widely implemented media, including IEEE 802.3/Ethernet, Fiber-Distributed Data Interface (FDDI), and Frame Relay.

Figure 29–3 illustrates how the various media generally fit into an SNA network.

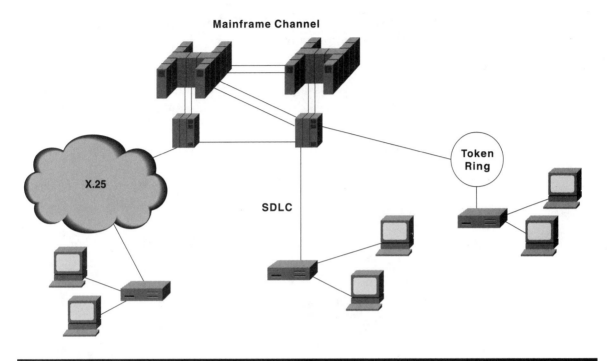

Figure 29–3
SNA has evolved to support a variety of media.

IBM Network Addressable Units (NAUs)

SNA defines three essential Network Addressable Units (NAUs): *logical units*, *physical units*, and *control points*. Each plays an important role in establishing connections between systems in an SNA network.

Logical units (LUs) function as end-user access ports into an SNA network. LUs provide users with access to network resources, and they manage the transmission of information between end users.

Physical units (PUs) are used to monitor and control attached network links and other network resources associated with a particular node. PUs are implemented on hosts by SNA access methods, such as the virtual telecommunication access method (VTAM). PUs also are implemented within communications controllers by network control programs (NCPs).

Control points (CPs) manage SNA nodes and their resources. CPs generally are differentiated from PUs in that CPs determine which actions must be taken, while PUs cause actions to occur. An example of a CP is the SNA system services control point (SSCP). An SSCP can be the CP residing in a PU 5 node or an SSCP as implemented under an SNA access method, such as VTAM.

IBM SNA Nodes

Traditional SNA nodes belong to one of two categories: *subarea nodes* and *peripheral nodes*. SNA subarea nodes provide all network services, including intermediate node routing and address mapping between local and network-wide addresses. No relationship exists between SNA node types and actual physical devices. Two subarea nodes are of particular interest: *node type 4* and *node type 5*.

Node type 4 (T4) usually is contained within a communications controller, such as a 3745. An example of a T4 node is an NCP, which routes data and controls flow between a front-end processor and other network resources.

Node type 5 (T5) usually is contained in a host, such as a S/370 mainframe. An example of a T5 node is the VTAM resident within an IBM mainframe. A VTAM controls the logical flow of data through a network, provides the interface between application subsystems and a network, and protects application subsystems from unauthorized access.

SNA peripheral nodes use only local addressing and communicate with other nodes through subarea nodes. Node type 2 (T2) is generally the peripheral node type of interest, although SNA does specify a node type 1 peripheral node. T2 typically resides in intelligent terminals (such as a 3270) or establishment controllers (such as a 3174). Node Type 1 (T1) is now obsolete, but when implemented, it resided in unintelligent terminals. Figure 29–4 illustrates the various SNA nodes and their relationships to each other.

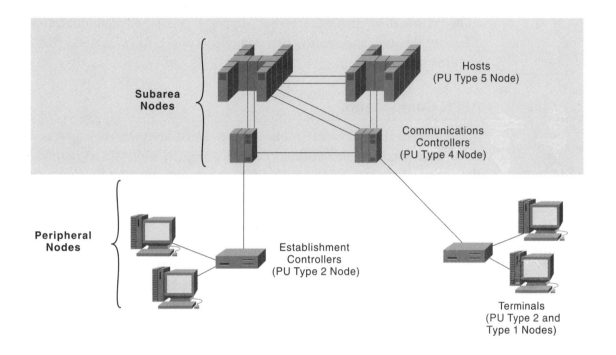

Figure 29–4
Peripheral nodes communicate with other nodes through subarea nodes.

IBM PEER-BASED NETWORKING

Changes in networking and communications requirements caused IBM to evolve (and generally overhaul) many of the basic design characteristics of SNA. The emergence of peer-based networking entities (such as routers) resulted in a number of significant changes in SNA. Internetworking among SNA peers hinges on several IBM-developed networking components.

Advanced Peer-to-Peer Networking (APPN) represents IBM's second-generation SNA. In creating APPN, IBM moved SNA from a hierarchical, mainframe-centric environment to a peer-based networking environment. At the heart of APPN is an IBM architecture that supports peer-based communications, directory services, and routing between two or more APPC systems that are not directly attached.

APPN Components

In addition to the APPN environment, peer-based SNA networking specifies three additional key networking concepts: *logical units* (LUs), *Advanced Program-to-Program Computing* (APPC), and *node type* 2.1. Each plays an important role in the establishment of communication among SNA peers within the context of an SNA-based peer internetwork.

Logical Unit (LU) 6.2 governs peer-to-peer communications in an SNA environment. In addition, LU 6.2 supports general communication between programs in a distributed processing environment and between both similar and dissimilar node types. APPC enables SNA applications to communicate directly with peer SNA applications, and it provides a set of programming conventions and protocols that implement LU 6.2. Node type 2.1s (T2.1) are logical entities that permit direct communication among peripheral nodes capable of supporting T2.1. The T2.1 entity facilitates point-to-point communications by providing data-transport support for peer-level communications supported by APPC. In addition, a T2.1 contains a Peripheral Node Control Point (PNCP) that combines the traditional functions of a physical unit (PU) and control point (CP).

IBM APPN Node Types

Under APPN, peer-based communication occurs among several well-defined node types. These nodes can be broken down into three basic types: *low-entry nodes* (LENs), *end nodes* (ENs), and *network nodes* (NNs).

The low-entry network (LEN) node is a pre-APPN era peer-to-peer node. A LEN node participates in APPN networking by taking advantage of services provided by an adjacent network node (NN). The CP of the LEN node manages local resources but does not establish a CP-to-CP session with the adjacent NN. Before a session can start, session partners must be defined for a LEN node, and the LEN node must be defined for its service-providing adjacent NN.

An end node EN contains a subset of full APPN support. An end node accesses the network through an adjacent NN and uses the routing services of the same adjacent NN. To communicate on a network, an EN establishes a CP-to-CP session with an adjacent NN and uses the CP-to-CP session to register resources, request directory services, and request routing information.

A network node (NN) contains full APPN functionality. The CP in an NN manages the resources of the NN, as well as the attached ENs and LEN nodes. In addition, the CP in an NN establishes CP-to-CP sessions with adjacent ENs and NNs and maintains the network topology and directory databases created and updated by gathering information dynamically from adjacent NNs and ENs.

Figure 29–5 illustrates where each of these peers types might be found in a generalized APPN environment.

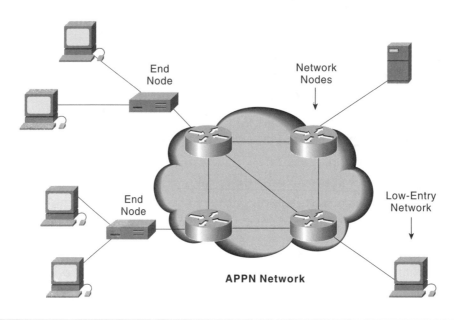

Figure 29–5
APPN supports several well-defined node types.

IBM APPN Services

Basic APPN services fall into four general categories: configuration, directors, topology, and routing and session services. Each is summarized in the sections that follow.

IBM APPN Configuration Services

APPN configuration services are responsible for activating connections to the APPN network. Connection activation involves establishing a connection, establishing a session, and selecting an adjacency option.

The connect phase of connection activation enables the initial establishment of communications between nodes. This initial communication involves exchanging characteristics and establishing roles, such as primary versus secondary. Connection establishment is accomplished by the transmission of *exchange identification* type 3 (XID3) frames between nodes.

During session establishment, CP-to-CP sessions are established with an adjacent EN or NN. Minimally, each node must establish at least one pair of CP-to-CP sessions with one adjacent node. An EN can establish a maximum of one pair of CP-to-CP sessions but can be attached to more than one NN. Between NNs, pairs of CP-to-CP sessions with all adjacent nodes or a subset of adjacent nodes can be established. The minimum requirement is a single pair of sessions to one adjacent NN, which ensures proper topology updating.

Adjacency among APPN nodes is determined by using CP-to-CP sessions. Two configurable options are available for determining node adjacency. A node can be specified as adjacent to a single node or as logically adjacent to every possible adjacent node. Selecting an adjacency option for a specific situation depends on a given network's connectivity requirements. The reduction in CP-to-CP sessions associated with single-node adjacency can reduce network overhead associated with topology updates, as well as the number of buffers required to distribute topology updates. Reducing the number of adjacent nodes, however, also increases the time required to synchronize routers.

IBM APPN Directory Services

Directory services are intended to help network devices locate service providers. These services are essential to establishing a session between end users. Directory services in APPN call for each NN to maintain a directory of local resources and a network directory that associate end users with NNs providing service. A distributed directory service then is formed from the collection of individual NN network directories. This section summarizes the nature of APPN databases, node-directory service handling, and the role of a centralized directory service.

The local and network directory databases support three service-entry types: *configured entries*, *registered entries*, and *cached entries*. Configured database entries usually are local low-entry network nodes that must be configured because no CP-to-CP session can be established over which to exchange information. Other nodes might be configured to reduce broadcast traffic, which is generated as part of the discovery process. Registered entries are local resource entries about which an end node has informed its associated network node server when CP-to-CP sessions are established. A registered entry is added by an NN to its local directory. Cached database entries are directory entries created as session requests and received by an NN. The total number of cached entries permitted can be controlled through user configurations to manage memory requirements.

The end-node directory service-negotiation process involves several steps. An EN first sends a LOCATE request to the NN providing network services. The local and network directory databases next are searched to determine whether the destination end user is already known. If the destination end-user is known, a single directed LOCATE request is sent to ensure its current availability. If the destination end-user is not found in the existing databases, the NN sends a LOCATE request to adjacent ENs to determine whether the destination end user is a local resource. If the destination is not local, the NN sends a broadcast LOCATE request to all adjacent NNs for propagation throughout the network. A message is sent back to the originating NN indicating that the destination is found when the NN providing network services for the destination end-user locates the end-user resource. Finally, both origin and destination NNs cache the information.

Directory services for LEN nodes are handled by a proxy service process. First, a LEN node sends a bind session (BIND) request for attached resources. This contrasts with the LOCATE request sent by ENs. To receive any directory services, an NN must provide proxy services for a LEN node. When a proxy service NN is linked to the LEN node, the NN broadcasts LOCATE requests as needed for the LEN node.

A central directory service usually exists within an ACF/VTAM and usually is implemented to help minimize LOCATE broadcasts. This kind of database can be used to maintain a centrally located directory for an entire network because it contains configured, registered, and cached entries. Under a centralized directory service process, an NN sends a directed LOCATE broadcast to the central directory server, which then searches the central database and broadcasts when necessary.

IBM APPN Topology and Routing Services

In an APPN network topology, network nodes are connected by *transmission groups* (TGs). Each TG consists of a single link, and all NNs maintain a network-topology database that contains a complete picture of all NNs and TGs in the network. Transmission groups are discussed in Chapter 37, "IBM Systems Network Architecture (SNA) Routing."

A network's topology database is updated by information received in a *topology-database update* (TDU) message. These TDU messages flow over CP-to-CP sessions whenever a change occurs in the network, such as when a node or link becomes active or inactive, when congestion occurs, or when resources are limited.

The network-topology database contains information used when calculating routes with a particular *class of service* (COS). This information includes NN and TG connectivity and status, and NN and TG characteristics, such as TG capacity.

APPN's routing services function uses information from directory and topology databases to determine a route based on COS. Route determination starts when an end node first receives a session request from a logical unit. A LOCATE request is sent from the EN to its NN to request destination information and to obtain a route through the network. The NN then identifies the properties associated with the requested level of service. The identified properties are compared to properties of each TG and NN in the network, and all routes that meet the specified criteria are cached as applicable. Each EN, NN, and TG in the network is assigned a weight based on COS properties, such as capacity, cost, security, and delay. Properties also can be user-defined. Finally, a least-cost path is determined by totaling the weights on the paths that meet the routing criteria.

IBM APPN Session Services

Following route establishment, the APPN session-establishment process varies depending on the node type. If the originating end user is attached to an EN, a LOCATE reply containing the location of the destination and route is returned to the originating EN by the NN adjacent to the destination EN. The originating EN then sends a BIND on a session route. If originating, the end user is attached to a LEN node that sends a BIND to its adjacent NN. The adjacent NN converts the LEN BIND to APPN BIND and sends a BIND on the session path.

NOTES

A BIND is a specific type of request message sent from one LU to another LU. A BIND carries the route being used for a session. It specifies NNs and TGs, a unique session identifier for each TG, the transmission priority for the session, and window information to support adaptive pacing to limit traffic on the network.

BASIC INFORMATION UNIT (BIU) FORMAT

IBM SNA NAUs employ basic information units (BIUs) to exchange requests and responses. Figure 29–6 illustrates the BIU format.

BIU Fields

The following field descriptions summarize the content of the BIU, as illustrated in Figure 29-6:

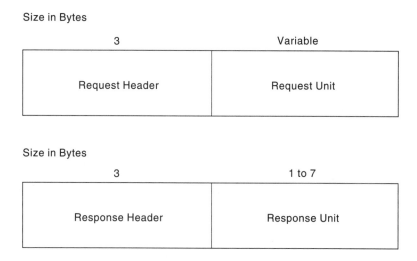

Figure 29–6
A basic information unit (BIU) can be either a request or response.

- *Request Header*—Identifies the type of data in the associated request units. This header provides information about the format of the data and specifies protocols for the session. Only NAUs use Request Header information.

- *Request Unit*—Contains either end-user data or SNA commands. End-user data is sent in data-request units. SNA commands are sent in command-request units that control the network and contain information exchanged between end users.

- *Response Header*—Identifies the type of data associated with the response unit. The request/response indicator bit distinguishes a response header from a request header. A receiving NAU indicates whether the response being returned to the request sender is positive or negative by setting the *response-type indicator* (RTI) bit in the response header.

- *Response Unit*—Contains information about the request indicating either a positive or negative response. Positive responses to command requests usually contain a 1- to 3-byte response unit that identifies the command request. Positive responses to data requests contain response headers but no response unit.

  Negative response units are 4 to 7 bytes long and always are returned with a negative response. A receiving NAU returns a negative response to the requesting NAU under one of three conditions:

  ○ Sender violates SNA protocol
  ○ Receiver does not understand the transmission
  ○ Unusual condition, such as a path failure, occurs

  When a negative response is transmitted, the first 4 bytes of a response unit contain data that explains why the request is unacceptable. The receiving NAU sends up to 3 additional bytes that identify the rejected request.

PATH INFORMATION UNIT (PIU) FORMAT

The path information unit (PIU) is an SNA message unit formed by path-control elements by adding a transmission header to a BIU. Figure 29–7 illustrates the PIU format.

PIU Fields

The following field descriptions summarize the content of the PIU, as illustrated in Figure 29-7:

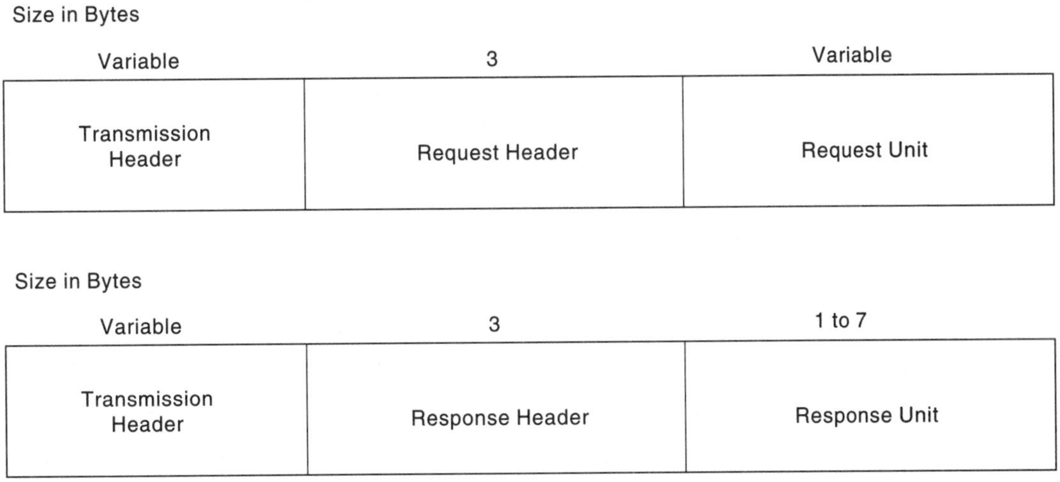

Size in Bytes

Variable	3	Variable
Transmission Header	Request Header	Request Unit

Size in Bytes

Variable	3	1 to 7
Transmission Header	Response Header	Response Unit

Figure 29–7
The path information unit (PIU) requests and responses each consist of three fields.

- *Transmission Header*—Routes message units through the network. This header contains routing information for traditional SNA subarea networking. Transmission-header formats are differentiated by the *format identification* (FID) type. Path control uses the FID types to route data among SNA nodes.

  Three FID types are implemented in PIUs:

  ○ FID0 is used to route data between adjacent subarea nodes for non-SNA devices. FID0 generally is rendered obsolete by the FID4 bit set to indicate whether a device is an SNA or non-SNA device.

- FID1 is used to route data between adjacent subarea nodes when one or both of the nodes do not support explicit and virtual route protocols.
- FID2 is used to route data between a subarea boundary node and an adjacent peripheral node, or between adjacent type 2.1 nodes.

In general, the transmission header is used to route data between adjacent subarea nodes when both the subarea nodes support explicit and virtual route protocols.

- *Request Header*—Identifies the type of data in the associated request units. This header provides information about the format of the data and specifies protocols for the session. Only NAUs use request header information.

- *Request Unit*—Contains either end-user data or SNA commands. End-user data is sent in data-request units. SNA commands are sent in command-request units that control the network and contain information exchanged between end-users.

- *Response Header*—Identifies the type of data associated with a response unit. The request/response indicator bit distinguishes a response header from a request header. A receiving NAU indicates whether the response being returned to the request sender is positive or negative by setting the RTI bit in the response header.

- *Response Unit*—Contains information about the request indicating either a positive or negative response. Positive responses to command requests usually contain a 1- to 3-byte response unit that identifies the command request. Positive responses to data requests contain response headers but no response unit.

Negative response units are 4 to 7 bytes long and always are returned with a negative response. A receiving NAU returns a negative response to the requesting NAU under one of three conditions: The sender violates SNA protocol, a receiver does not understand the transmission, or an unusual condition, such as a path failure, occurs.

When a negative response is transmitted, the first 4 bytes of a response unit contain data that explains why the request is unacceptable. The receiving NAU sends up to 3 additional bytes that identify the rejected request.

CHAPTER 30

Internet Protocols

BACKGROUND

The Internet protocols are the world's most popular open-system (nonproprietary) protocol suite because they can be used to communicate across any set of interconnected networks and are equally well suited for LAN and WAN communications. The Internet protocols consist of a suite of communication protocols, of which the two best known are the Transmission Control Protocol (TCP) and the Internet Protocol (IP). The Internet protocol suite not only includes lower-layer protocols (such as TCP and IP), but it also specifies common applications such as electronic mail, terminal emulation, and file transfer. This chapter provides a broad introduction to specifications that comprise the Internet protocols. Discussions include IP addressing and key upper-layer protocols used in the Internet. Specific routing protocols are addressed individually in Part 6, "Routing Protocols."

Internet protocols were first developed in the mid-1970s, when the Defense Advanced Research Projects Agency (DARPA) became interested in establishing a packet-switched network that would facilitate communication between dissimilar computer systems at research institutions. With the goal of heterogeneous connectivity in mind, DARPA funded research by Stanford University and Bolt, Beranek, and Newman (BBN). The result of this development effort was the Internet protocol suite, completed in the late 1970s.

TCP/IP later was included with Berkeley Software Distribution (BSD) UNIX and has since become the foundation on which the Internet and the World Wide Web (WWW) are based.

Documentation of the Internet protocols (including new or revised protocols) and policies are specified in technical reports called Request For Comments (RFCs), which are published and then reviewed and analyzed by the Internet community. Protocol refinements are published in the new RFCs. To illustrate the scope of the Internet protocols, Figure 30–1 maps many of the protocols of the Internet protocol suite and their corresponding OSI layers. This chapter addresses the basic elements and operations of these and other key Internet protocols.

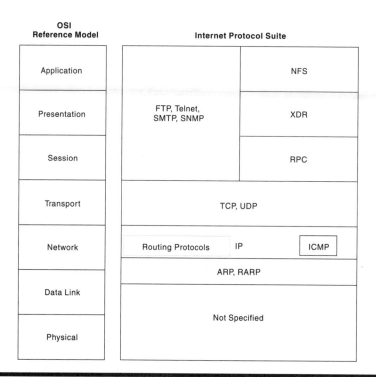

Figure 30–1

Internet protocols span the complete range of OSI model layers.

INTERNET PROTOCOL (IP)

The Internet Protocol (IP) is a network-layer (Layer 3) protocol that contains addressing information and some control information that enables packets to be routed. IP is documented in RFC 791 and is the primary network-layer protocol in the Internet protocol suite. Along with the Transmission Control Protocol (TCP), IP represents the heart of the Internet protocols. IP has two primary responsibilities: providing connectionless, best-effort delivery of datagrams through an internetwork; and providing fragmentation and reassembly of datagrams to support data links with different maximum-transmission unit (MTU) sizes.

IP Packet Format

An IP packet contains several types of information, as illustrated in Figure 30–2.

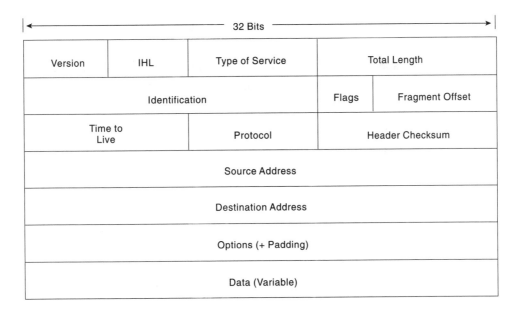

Figure 30–2
Fourteen fields comprise an IP packet.

The following discussion describes the IP packet fields illustrated in Figure 30–2:

- *Version*—Indicates the version of IP currently used.

- *IP Header Length (IHL)*—Indicates the datagram header length in 32-bit words.

- *Type-of-Service*—Specifies how an upper-layer protocol would like a current datagram to be handled, and assigns datagrams various levels of importance.

- *Total Length*—Specifies the length, in bytes, of the entire IP packet, including the data and header.

- *Identification*—Contains an integer that identifies the current datagram. This field is used to help piece together datagram fragments.

- *Flags*—Consists of a 3-bit field of which the two low-order (least-significant) bits control fragmentation. The low-order bit specifies whether the packet can be fragmented. The middle bit specifies whether the packet is the last fragment in a series of fragmented packets. The third or high-order bit is not used.

- *Fragment Offset*—Indicates the position of the fragment's data relative to the beginning of the data in the original datagram, which allows the destination IP process to properly reconstruct the original datagram.

- *Time-to-Live*—Maintains a counter that gradually decrements down to zero, at which point the datagram is discarded. This keeps packets from looping endlessly.

- *Protocol*—Indicates which upper-layer protocol receives incoming packets after IP processing is complete.

- *Header Checksum*—Helps ensure IP header integrity.

- *Source Address*—Specifies the sending node.

- *Destination Address*—Specifies the receiving node.

- *Options*—Allows IP to support various options, such as security.

- *Data*—Contains upper-layer information.

IP Addressing

As with any other network-layer protocol, the IP addressing scheme is integral to the process of routing IP datagrams through an internetwork. Each IP address has specific components and follows a basic format. These IP addresses can be subdivided and used to create addresses for subnetworks, as discussed in more detail later in this chapter.

Each host on a TCP/IP network is assigned a unique 32-bit logical address that is divided into two main parts: the network number and the host number. The network number identifies a network and must be assigned by the Internet Network Information Center (InterNIC) if the network is to be part of the Internet. An Internet Service Provider (ISP) can obtain blocks of network addresses from the InterNIC and can itself assign address space as necessary. The host number identifies a host on a network and is assigned by the local network administrator.

IP Address Format

The 32-bit IP address is grouped eight bits at a time, separated by dots, and represented in decimal format (known as *dotted decimal notation*). Each bit in the octet has a binary weight (128, 64, 32, 16, 8, 4, 2, 1). The minimum value for an octet is 0, and the maximum value for an octet is 255. Figure 30–3 illustrates the basic format of an IP address.

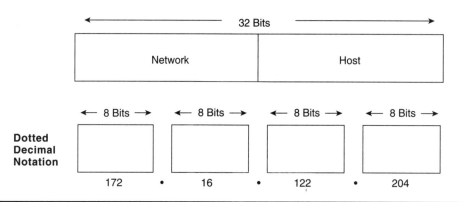

Figure 30–3

An IP address consists of 32 bits, grouped into four octets.

IP Address Classes

IP addressing supports five different address classes: A, B,C, D, and E. Only classes A, B, and C are available for commercial use. The left-most (high-order) bits indicate the network class. Table 30-1 provides reference information about the five IP address classes.

IP Address Class	Format	Purpose	High-Order Bit(s)	Address Range	No. Bits Network/Host	Max. Hosts
A	N.H.H.H[1]	Few large organizations	0	1.0.0.0 to 126.0.0.0	7/24	16,777, 214[2] ($2^{24}-2$)
B	N.N.H.H	Medium-size organizations	1, 0	128.1.0.0 to 191.254.0.0	14/16	65, 543 ($2^{16}-2$)
C	N.N.N.H	Relatively small organizations	1, 1, 0	192.0.1.0 to 223.255.254.0	22/8	245 ($2^{8}-2$)
D	N/A	Multicast groups (RFC 1112)	1, 1, 1, 0	224.0.0.0 to 239.255.255.255	N/A (not for commercial use)	N/A
E	N/A	Experimental	1, 1, 1, 1	240.0.0.0 to 254.255.255.255	N/A	N/A

1. N = Network number, H = Host number.
2. One address is reserved for the broadcast address, and one address is reserved for the network.

Table 30-1

Reference Information About the Five IP Address Classes

Figure 30–4 illustrates the format of the commercial IP address classes. (Note the high-order bits in each class.)

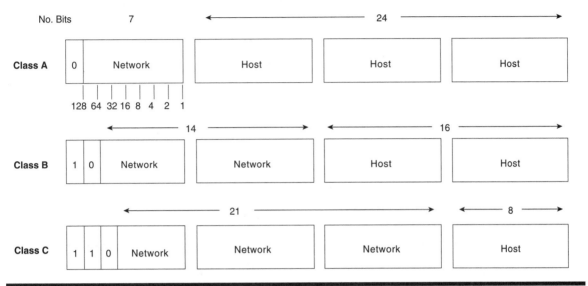

Figure 30–4
IP address formats A, B, and C are available for commercial use.

The class of address can be determined easily by examining the first octet of the address and mapping that value to a class range in the following table. In an IP address of 172.31.1.2, for example, the first octet is 172. Because 172 falls between 128 and 191, 172.31.1.2 is a Class B address. Figure 30–5 summarizes the range of possible values for the first octet of each address class.

IP Subnet Addressing

IP networks can be divided into smaller networks called subnetworks (or subnets). Subnetting provides the network administrator with several benefits, including extra flexibility, more efficient use of network addresses, and the capability to contain broadcast traffic (a broadcast will not cross a router).

Address Class	First Octet in Decimal	High-Order Bits
Class A	1 – 126	0
Class B	128 – 191	10
Class C	192 – 223	110
Class D	224 – 239	1110
Class E	240 – 254	1111

Figure 30–5
A range of possible values exists for the first octet of each address class.

Subnets are under local administration. As such, the outside world sees an organization as a single network and has no detailed knowledge of the organization's internal structure.

A given network address can be broken up into many subnetworks. For example, 172.16.1.0, 172.16.2.0, 172.16.3.0, and 172.16.4.0 are all subnets within network 171.16.0.0. (All 0s in the host portion of an address specifies the entire network.)

IP Subnet Mask

A subnet address is created by "borrowing" bits from the host field and designating them as the subnet field. The number of borrowed bits varies and is specified by the subnet mask. Figure 30–6 shows how bits are borrowed from the host address field to create the subnet address field.

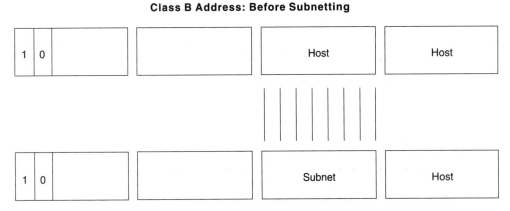

Figure 30–6

Bits are borrowed from the host address field to create the subnet address field.

Subnet masks use the same format and representation technique as IP addresses. The subnet mask, however, has binary 1s in all bits specifying the network and subnetwork fields, and binary 0s in all bits specifying the host field. Figure 30–7 illustrates a sample subnet mask.

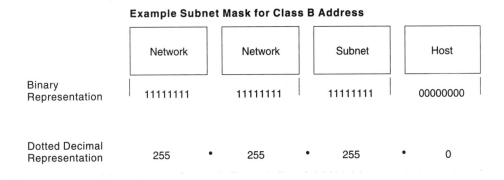

Figure 30–7

A sample subnet mask consists of all binary 1s and 0s.

Subnet mask bits should come from the high-order (left-most) bits of the host field, as Figure 30–8 illustrates. Details of Class B and C subnet mask types follow. Class A addresses are not discussed in this chapter because they generally are subnetted on an 8-bit boundary.

128	64	32	16		8	4	2	1		
1	0	0	0		0	0	0	0	=	128
1	1	0	0		0	0	0	0	=	192
1	1	1	0		0	0	0	0	=	224
1	1	1	1		0	0	0	0	=	240
1	1	1	1		1	0	0	0	=	248
1	1	1	1		1	1	0	0	=	252
1	1	1	1		1	1	1	0	=	254
1	1	1	1		1	1	1	1	=	255

Figure 30–8
Subnet mask bits come from the high-order bits of the host field.

Various types of subnet masks exist for Class B and C subnets.

The default subnet mask for a Class B address that has no subnetting is 255.255.0.0, while the subnet mask for a Class B address 171.16.0.0 that specifies eight bits of subnetting is 255.255.255.0. The reason for this is that eight bits of subnetting or $2^8 - 2$ (1 for the network address and 1 for the broadcast address) = 254 subnets possible, with $2^8 - 2 = 254$ hosts per subnet.

The subnet mask for a Class C address 192.168.2.0 that specifies five bits of subnetting is 255.255.255.248. With five bits available for subnetting, $2^5 - 2 = 30$ subnets possible, with $2^3 - 2 = 6$ hosts per subnet.

The reference charts shown in table 30–2 and table 30–3 can be used when planning Class B and C networks to determine the required number of subnets and hosts, and the appropriate subnet mask.

Number of Bits	Subnet Mask	Number of Subnets	Number of Hosts
2	255.255.192.0	2	16382
3	255.255.224.0	6	8190
4	255.255.240.0	14	4094
5	255.255.248.0	30	2046
6	255.255.252.0	62	1022
7	255.255.254.0	126	510
8	255.255.255.0	254	254
9	255.255.255.128	510	126
10	255.255.255.192	1022	62
11	255.255.255.224	2046	30
12	255.255.255.240	4094	14
13	255.255.255.248	8190	6
14	255.255.255.252	16382	2

Table 30-2
Class B Subnetting Reference Chart

Number of Bits	Subnet Mask	Number of Subnets	Number of Hosts
2	255.255.255.192	2	62
3	255.255.255.224	6	30
4	255.255.255.240	14	14
5	255.255.255.248	30	6
6	255.255.255.252	62	2

Table 30-3
Class C Subnetting Reference Chart

How Subnet Masks are Used to Determine the Network Number

The router performs a set process to determine the network (or more specifically, the subnetwork) address. First, the router extracts the IP destination address from the incoming packet and retrieves the internal subnet mask. It then performs a *logical AND* operation to obtain the network number. This causes the host portion of the IP destination address to be removed, while the destination network number remains. The router then looks up the destination network number and matches it with an outgoing interface. Finally, it forwards the frame to the destination IP address. Specifics regarding the logical AND operation are discussed in the following section.

Logical AND Operation

Three basic rules govern logically "ANDing" two binary numbers. First, 1 "ANDed" with 1 yields 1. Second, 1 "ANDed" with 0 yields 0. Finally, 0 "ANDed" with 0 yields 0. The truth table provided in table 30–4 illustrates the rules for logical AND operations.

Input	Input	Output
1	1	1
1	0	0
0	1	0
0	0	0

Table 30-4
Rules for Logical AND Operations

Two simple guidelines exist for remembering logical AND operations: Logically "ANDing" a 1 with a 1 yields the original value, and logically "ANDing" a 0 with any number yields 0.

Figure 30–9 illustrates that when a logical AND of the destination IP address and the subnet mask is performed, the subnetwork number remains, which the router uses to forward the packet.

		Network	Subnet	Host
Destination IP Address	171.16.1.2		00000001	00000010
Subnet Mask	255.255.255.0		11111111	00000000
			00000001	00000000
			1	0

Figure 30–9
Applying a logical AND the destination IP address and the subnet mask produces the subnetwork number.

ADDRESS RESOLUTION PROTOCOL (ARP) OVERVIEW

For two machines on a given network to communicate, they must know the other machine's physical (or MAC) addresses. By broadcasting Address Resolution Protocols (ARPs) a host can dynamically discover the MAC-layer address corresponding to a particular IP network-layer address.

After receiving a MAC-layer address, IP devices create an ARP cache to store the recently acquired IP-to-MAC address mapping, thus avoiding having to broadcast ARPS when they want to recontact a device. If the device does not respond within a specified time frame, the cache entry is flushed.

In addition to the Reverse Address Resolution Protocol (RARP) is used to map MAC-layer addresses to IP addresses. RARP, which is the logical inverse of ARP, might be used by diskless workstations that do not know their IP addresses when they boot. RARP relies on the presence of a RARP server with table entries of MAC-layer-to-IP address mappings.

INTERNET ROUTING

Internet routing devices traditionally have been called gateways. In today's terminology, however, the term gateway refers specifically to a device that performs application-layer protocol translation between devices. Interior gateways refer to devices that perform these protocol functions between machines or networks under the same administrative control or authority, such as a corporation's internal network. These are known as autonomous systems. Exterior gateways perform protocol functions between independent networks.

Routers within the Internet are organized hierarchically. Routers used for information exchange within autonomous systems are called interior routers, which use a variety of Interior Gateway Protocols (IGPs) to accomplish this purpose. The Routing Information Protocol (RIP) is an example of an IGP.

Routers that move information between autonomous systems are called exterior routers. These routers use an exterior gateway protocol to exchange information between autonomous systems. The Border Gateway Protocol (BGP) is an example of an exterior gateway protocol.

NOTES

Specific routing protocols, including BGP and RIP, are addressed in individual chapters presented in Part 6 later in this book.

IP Routing

IP routing protocols are dynamic. Dynamic routing calls for routes to be calculated automatically at regular intervals by software in routing devices. This contrasts with static routing, where routers are established by the network administrator and do not change until the network administrator changes them.

An IP routing table, which consists of destination address/next hop pairs, is used to enable dynamic routing. An entry in this table, for example, would be interpreted as follows: To get to network 172.31.0.0, send the packet out Ethernet interface 0 (E0).

IP routing specifies that IP datagrams travel through internetworks one hop at a time. The entire route is not known at the onset of the journey, however. Instead, at each stop, the next destination is calculated by matching the destination address within the datagram with an entry in the current node's routing table.

Each node's involvement in the routing process is limited to forwarding packets based on internal information. The nodes do not monitor whether the packets get to their final destination, nor does IP provide for error reporting back to the source when routing anomalies occur. This task is left to another Internet protocol, the Internet Control-Message Protocol (ICMP), which is discussed in the following section.

INTERNET CONTROL MESSAGE PROTOCOL (ICMP)

The *Internet Control Message Protocol* (ICMP) is a network-layer Internet protocol that provides message packets to report errors and other information regarding IP packet processing back to the source. ICMP is documented in RFC 792.

ICMP Messages

ICMPs generate several kinds of useful messages, including Destination Unreachable, Echo Request and Reply, Redirect, Time Exceeded, and Router Advertisement and Router Solicitation. If an ICMP message cannot be delivered, no second one is generated. This is to avoid an endless flood of ICMP messages.

When an ICMP destination-unreachable message is sent by a router, it means that the router is unable to send the package to its final destination. The router then discards the original packet. Two reasons exist for why a destination might be unreachable. Most commonly, the source host has specified a nonexistent address. Less frequently, the router does not have a route to the destination.

Destination-unreachable messages include four basic types: network unreachable, host unreachable, protocol unreachable, and port unreachable. *Network-unreachable messages* usually mean that a failure has occurred in the routing or addressing of a packet. *Host-unreachable messages* usually indicates delivery failure, such as a wrong subnet mask. *Protocol-unreachable messages* generally mean that the destination does not support the upper-layer protocol specified in the packet. *Port-unreachable messages* imply that the TCP socket or port is not available.

An ICMP echo-request message, which is generated by the ping command, is sent by any host to test node reachability across an internetwork. The ICMP echo-reply message indicates that the node can be successfully reached.

An ICMP Redirect message is sent by the router to the source host to stimulate more efficient routing. The router still forwards the original packet to the destination. ICMP redirects allow host routing tables to remain small because it is necessary to know the address of only one router, even if that router does not provide the best path. Even after receiving an ICMP Redirect message, some devices might continue using the less-efficient route.

An ICMP Time-exceeded message is sent by the router if an IP packet's Time-to-Live field (expressed in hops or seconds) reaches zero. The Time-to-Live field prevents packets from continuously circulating the internetwork if the internetwork contains a routing loop. The router then discards the original packet.

ICMP Router-Discovery Protocol (IDRP)

IDRP uses Router-Advertisement and Router-Solicitation messages to discover the addresses of routers on directly attached subnets. Each router periodically multicasts Router-Advertisement messages from each of its interfaces. Hosts then discover addresses of routers on directly attached subnets by listening for these messages. Hosts can use Router-Solicitation messages to request immediate advertisements rather than waiting for unsolicited messages.

IRDP offers several advantages over other methods of discovering addresses of neighboring routers. Primarily, it does not require hosts to recognize routing protocols, nor does it require manual configuration by an administrator.

Router-Advertisement messages enable hosts to discover the existence of neighboring routers but not which router is best to reach a particular destination. If a host uses a poor first-hop router to reach a particular destination, it receives a Redirect message identifying a better choice.

TRANSMISSION CONTROL PROTOCOL (TCP)

The TCP provides reliable transmission of data in an IP environment. TCP corresponds to the transport layer (Layer 4) of the OSI reference model. Among the services TCP provides are stream data transfer, reliability, efficient flow control, full-duplex operation, and multiplexing.

With stream data transfer, TCP delivers an unstructured stream of bytes identified by sequence numbers. This service benefits applications because they do not have to chop data into blocks before handing it off to TCP. Instead, TCP groups bytes into segments and passes them to IP for delivery.

TCP offers reliability by providing connection-oriented, end-to-end reliable packet delivery through an internetwork. It does this by sequencing bytes with a forwarding acknowledgment number that indicates to the destination the next byte the source expects to receive. Bytes not acknowledged within a specified time period are retransmitted. The reliability mechanism of TCP allows devices to deal with lost, delayed, duplicate, or misread packets. A time-out mechanism allows devices to detect lost packets and request retransmission.

TCP offers efficient flow control, which means that, when sending acknowledgments back to the source, the receiving TCP process indicates the highest sequence number it can receive without overflowing its internal buffers.

Full-duplex operation means that TCP processes can both send and receive at the same time.

Finally, TCP's multiplexing means that numerous simultaneous upper-layer conversations can be multiplexed over a single connection.

TCP Connection Establishment

To use reliable transport services, TCP hosts must establish a connection-oriented session with one another. Connection establishment is performed by using a "three-way handshake" mechanism.

A three-way handshake synchronizes both ends of a connection by allowing both sides to agree upon initial sequence numbers. This mechanism also guarantees that both sides are ready to transmit data and know that the other side is ready to transmit as well. This is necessary so that packets are not transmitted or retransmitted during session establishment or after session termination.

Each host randomly chooses a sequence number used to track bytes within the stream it is sending and receiving. Then, the three-way handshake proceeds in the following manner:

The first host (Host A) initiates a connection by sending a packet with the initial sequence number (X) and SYN bit set to indicate a connection request. The second host (Host B) receives the SYN, records the sequence number X, and replies by acknowledging the SYN (with an ACK = X + 1). Host B includes its own initial sequence number (SEQ = Y). An ACK = 20 means the host has received bytes 0 through 19 and expects byte 20 next. This technique is called *forward acknowledgment*. Host A then acknowledges all bytes Host B sent with a forward acknowledgment indicating the next byte Host A expects to receive (ACK = Y + 1). Data transfer then can begin.

Positive Acknowledgment and Retransmission (PAR)

A simple transport protocol might implement a reliability-and-flow-control technique where the source sends one packet, starts a timer, and waits for an acknowledgment before sending a new packet. If the acknowledgment is not received before the timer expires, the source retransmits the packet. Such a technique is called *positive acknowledgment and retransmission* (PAR).

By assigning each packet a sequence number, PAR enables hosts to track lost or duplicate packets caused by network delays that result in premature retransmission. The sequence numbers are sent back in the acknowledgments so that the acknowledgments can be tracked.

PAR is an inefficient use of bandwidth, however, because a host must wait for an acknowledgment before sending a new packet, and only one packet can be sent at a time.

TCP Sliding Window

A *TCP sliding window* provides more efficient use of network bandwidth than PAR because it enables hosts to send multiple bytes or packets before waiting for an acknowledgment.

In TCP, the receiver specifies the current window size in every packet. Because TCP provides a byte-stream connection, window sizes are expressed in bytes. This means that a window is the number of data bytes that the sender is allowed to send before waiting for an acknowledgment. Initial window sizes are indicated at connection setup but might vary throughout the data transfer to provide flow control. A window size of zero, for instance, means "Send no data."

In a TCP sliding-window operation, for example, the sender might have a sequence of bytes to send (numbered 1 to 10) to a receiver who has a window size of five. The sender then would place a window around the first five bytes and transmit them together. It would then wait for an acknowledgment.

The receiver would respond with an ACK = 6, indicating that it has received bytes 1 to 5 and is expecting byte 6 next. In the same packet, the receiver would indicate that its window size is 5. The sender then would move the sliding window five bytes to the right and transmit bytes 6 to 10. The receiver would respond with an ACK = 11, indicating that it is expecting sequenced byte 11 next. In this packet, the receiver might indicate that its window size is 0 (because, for example, its internal buffers are full). At this point, the sender cannot send any more bytes until the receiver sends another packet with a window size greater than 0.

TCP Packet Format

Figure 30–10 illustrates the fields and overall format of a TCP packet.

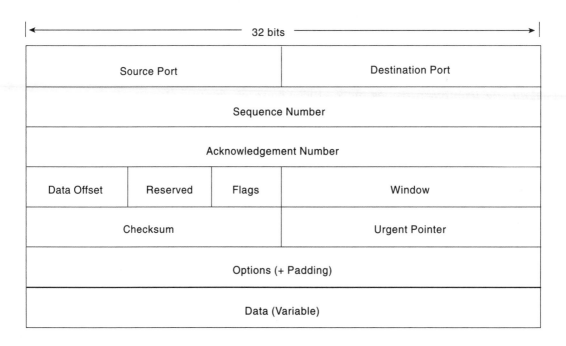

Figure 30–10
Twelve fields comprise a TCP packet.

TCP Packet Field Descriptions

The following descriptions summarize the TCP packet fields illustrated in Figure 30–10:

- *Source Port and Destination Port*—Identifies points at which upper-layer source and destination processes receive TCP services.

- *Sequence Number*—Usually specifies the number assigned to the first byte of data in the current message. In the connection-establishment phase, this field also can be used to identify an initial sequence number to be used in an upcoming transmission.

- *Acknowledgment Number*—Contains the sequence number of the next byte of data the sender of the packet expects to receive.

- *Data Offset*—Indicates the number of 32-bit words in the TCP header.

- *Reserved*—Remains reserved for future use.

- *Flags*—Carries a variety of control information, including the SYN and ACK bits used for connection establishment, and the FIN bit used for connection termination.

- *Window*—Specifies the size of the sender's receive window (that is, the buffer space available for incoming data).

- *Checksum*—Indicates whether the header was damaged in transit.

- *Urgent Pointer*—Points to the first urgent data byte in the packet.

- *Options*—Specifies various TCP options.

- *Data*—Contains upper-layer information.

USER DATAGRAM PROTOCOL (UDP)

The User Datagram Protocol (UDP) is a connectionless transport-layer protocol (Layer 4) that belongs to the Internet protocol family. UDP is basically an interface between IP and upper-layer processes. UDP protocol ports distinguish multiple applications running on a single device from one another.

Unlike the TCP, UDP adds no reliability, flow-control, or error-recovery functions to IP. Because of UDP's simplicity, UDP headers contain fewer bytes and consume less network overhead than TCP.

UDP is useful in situations where the reliability mechanisms of TCP are not necessary, such as in cases where a higher-layer protocol might provide error and flow control.

UDP is the transport protocol for several well-known application-layer protocols, including Network File System (NFS), Simple Network Management Protocol (SNMP), Domain Name System (DNS), and Trivial File Transfer Protocol (TFTP).

The UDP packet format contains four fields, as shown in Figure 30–11. These include source and destination ports, length, and checksum fields.

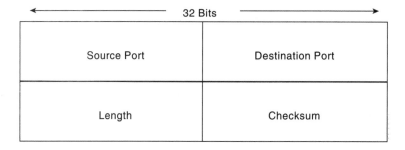

Figure 30–11
A UDP packet consists of four fields.

Source and destination ports contain the 16-bit UDP protocol port numbers used to demultiplex datagrams for receiving application-layer processes. A length field specifies the length of the UDP header and data. Checksum provides an (optional) integrity check on the UDP header and data.

INTERNET PROTOCOLS APPLICATION-LAYER PROTOCOLS

The Internet protocol suite includes many application-layer protocols that represent a wide variety of applications, including the following:

- *File Transfer Protocol (FTP)*—Moves files between devices

- *Simple Network-Management Protocol (SNMP)*—Primarily reports anomalous network conditions and sets network threshold values

- *Telnet*—Serves as a terminal emulation protocol

- *X Windows*—Serves as a distributed windowing and graphics system used for communication between X terminals and UNIX workstations

- *Network File System (NFS), External Data Representation (XDR), and Remote Procedure Call (RPC)*—Work together to enable transparent access to remote network resources

- *Simple Mail Transfer Protocol (SMTP)*—Provides electronic mail services

- *Domain Name System (DNS)*—Translates the names of network nodes into network addresses

Table 30-5 lists these higher-layer protocols and the applications that they support.

Application	Protocols
File transfer	FTP
Network management	SNMP
Terminal emulation	Telnet
Distributed file services	NFS, XDR, RPC, X Windows
Electronic mail	SMTP
Distributed naming services	DNS

Table 30-5
Higher-Layer Protocols and Their Applications

CHAPTER 31

NetWare Protocols

BACKGROUND

NetWare is a network operating system (NOS) that provides transparent remote file access and numerous other distributed network services, including printer sharing and support for various applications such as electronic mail transfer and database access. NetWare specifies the upper five layers of the OSI reference model and as such, runs on virtually any media-access protocol (Layer 2). Additionally, NetWare runs on virtually any kind of computer system, from PCs to mainframes. This chapter summarizes the principal communications protocols that support NetWare.

NetWare was developed by Novell, Inc., and introduced in the early 1980s. It was derived from Xerox Network Systems (XNS), which was created by Xerox Corporation in the late 1970s, and is based on a client-server architecture. Clients (sometimes called *workstations*) request services, such as file and printer access, from servers.

NetWare's client-server architecture supports remote access that is transparent to users through remote procedure calls. A remote procedure call begins when the local computer program running on the client sends a procedure call to the remote server. The server then executes the remote procedure call and returns the requested information to the local client.

Figure 31–1 illustrates the NetWare protocol suite, the media-access protocols on which NetWare runs, and the relationship between the NetWare protocols and the OSI reference model. This chapter addresses the elements and operations of these protocol components.

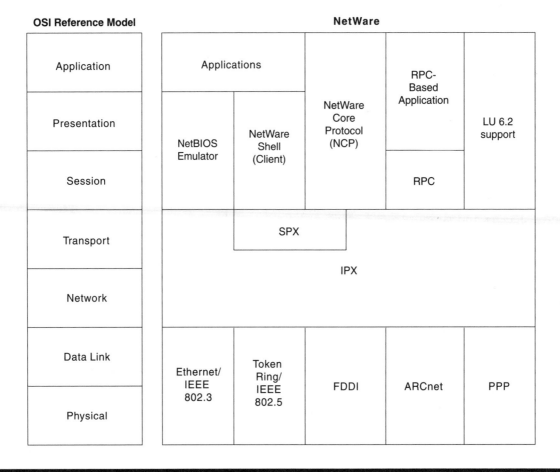

Figure 31–1
The NetWare protocol suite maps to all OSI layers.

NETWARE MEDIA ACCESS

The NetWare suite of protocols supports several media-access (Layer 2) protocols, including Ethernet/IEEE 802.3, Token Ring/IEEE 802.5, Fiber Distributed Data Interface (FDDI), and Point-to-Point Protocol (PPP). Figure 31–2 highlights NetWare's breadth of media-access support.

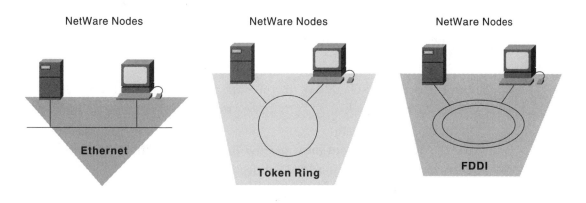

Figure 31–2
NetWare supports most common media-access protocols.

INTERNETWORK PACKET EXCHANGE (IPX) OVERVIEW

Internetwork Packet Exchange (IPX) is the original NetWare network-layer (Layer 3) protocol used to route packets through an internetwork. IPX is a connectionless datagram-based network protocol and, as such, is similar to the Internet Protocol found in TCP/IP networks.

IPX uses the services of a dynamic distance vector-routing protocol (Routing Information Protocol [RIP]) or a link-state routing protocol (NetWare Link-State Protocol [NLSP]). IPX RIP sends routing updates every 60 seconds. To make best-path routing decisions, IPX RIP uses a "tick" as the metric, which in principle is the delay expected when using a particular length. One tick is 1/18th of a second. In the case of two paths with an equal tick count, IPX RIP uses the hop count as a tie breaker. (A *hop* is the passage of a packet through a router.) IPX's RIP is not compatible with RIP implementations used in other networking environments.

As with other network addresses, Novell IPX network addresses must be unique. These addresses are represented in hexadecimal format and consist of two parts: a network number and a node number. The IPX network number, which is assigned by the network administrator, is 32 bits long. The node number, which usually is the Media Access Control (MAC) address for one of the system's network interface cards (NICs), is 48 bits long.

IPX's use of a MAC address for the node number enables the system to send nodes to predict what MAC address to use on a data link. (In contrast, because the host portion of an IP network address has no correlation to the MAC address, IP nodes must use the Address-Resolution Protocol [ARP] to determine the destination MAC address.)

IPX ENCAPSULATION TYPES

Novell NetWare IPX supports multiple encapsulation schemes on a single router interface, provided that multiple network numbers are assigned. Encapsulation is the process of packaging upper-layer protocol information and data into a frame. NetWare supports the following four encapsulation schemes:

- *Novell Proprietary*—Also called "802.3 raw" or Novell Ethernet_802.3, Novell proprietary serves as the initial encapsulation scheme Novell uses. It includes an Institute of Electrical and Electronic Engineers (IEEE) 802.3 Length field but not an IEEE 802.2 (LLC) header. The IPX header immediately follows the 802.3 Length field.

- *802.3*—Also called Novell_802.2, 802.3 is the standard IEEE 802.3 frame format.

- *Ethernet Version 2*—Also called Ethernet-II or ARPA, Ethernet Version 2 includes the standard Ethernet Version 2 header, which consists of Destination and Source Address fields followed by an EtherType field.

- *SNAP*—Also called Ethernet_SNAP, SNAP extends the IEEE 802.2 header by providing a type code similar to that defined in the Ethernet Version 2 specification.

Figure 31–3 illustrates these encapsulation types.

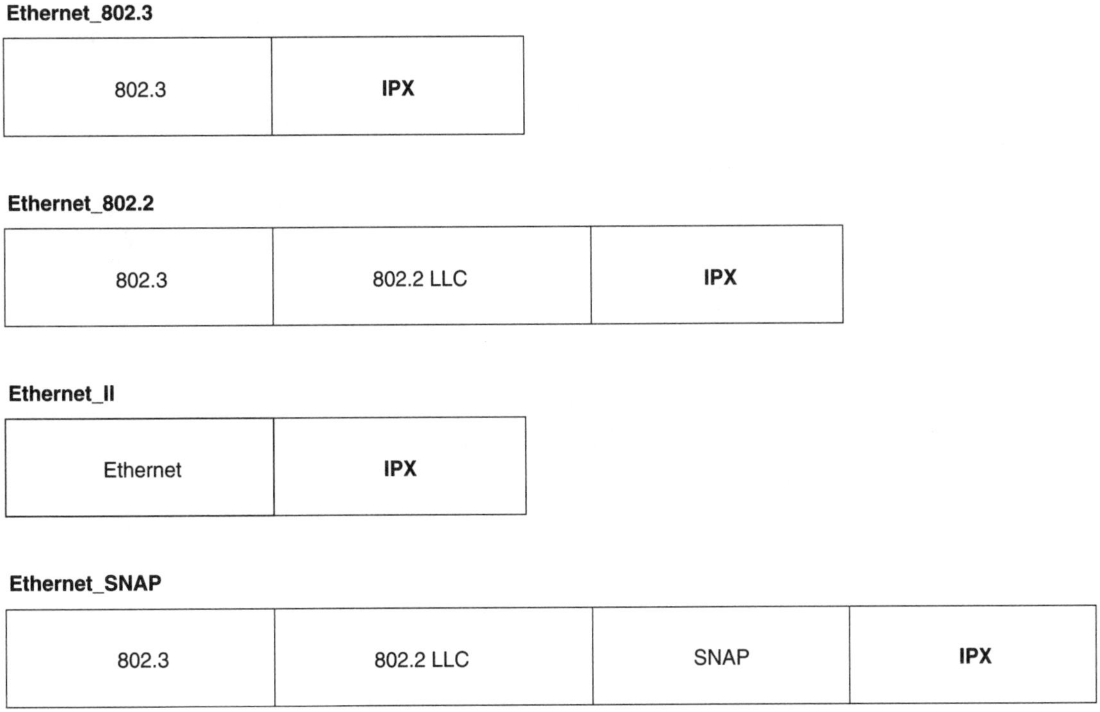

Ethernet_802.3

802.3	IPX

Ethernet_802.2

802.3	802.2 LLC	IPX

Ethernet_II

Ethernet	IPX

Ethernet_SNAP

802.3	802.2 LLC	SNAP	IPX

Figure 31–3
Four IPX encapsulation types exist.

SERVICE ADVERTISEMENT PROTOCOL (SAP)

The *Service Advertisement Protocol* (SAP) is an IPX protocol through which network resources, such as file servers and print servers, advertise their addresses and the services they provide. Advertisements are sent via SAP every 60 seconds. Services are identified by a hexadecimal number, which is called a SAP identifier (for example, 4 = file server, and 7 = print server).

A SAP operation begins when routers listen to SAPs and build a table of all known services along with their network address. Routers then send their SAP table every 60 seconds. Novell clients can send a query requesting a particular file, printer, or gateway service. The local router responds to the query with the network address of the requested service, and the client then can contact the service directly.

SAP is pervasive in current networks based on NetWare 3.11 and earlier but is utilized less frequently in NetWare 4.0 networks because workstations can locate services by consulting a NetWare Directory Services (NDS) Server. SAP, however, still is required in NetWare 4.0 networks for workstations when they boot up to locate an NDS server.

SAP Filters

Using the SAP identifier, SAP advertisements can be filtered on a router's input or output port, or from a specific router. SAP filters conserve network bandwidth and are especially useful in large Novell installations where hundreds of SAP services exist.

In general, the use of SAP filters is recommended for services that are not required for a particular network. Remote sites, for example, probably do not need to receive SAP advertising print services located at a central site. A SAP output filter at the central site (preferred) or a SAP input filter that uses the SAP identifier for a print server at the remote site prevents the router from including print services in SAP updates.

NETWARE TRANSPORT LAYER

The *Sequenced Packet Exchange* (SPX) protocol is the most common Net-Ware transport protocol at Layer 4 of the OSI model. SPX resides atop IPX in the NetWare Protocol Suite. SPX is a reliable, connection-oriented protocol that supplements the datagram service provided by the IPX, NetWare's network-layer (Layer 3) protocol. SPX was derived from the Xerox Networking Systems (XNS) Sequenced Packet Protocol (SPP). Novell also offers Internet Protocol support in the form of the User Datagram Protocol (UDP). IPX datagrams are encapsulated inside UDP/IP headers for transport across an IP-based internetwork.

NETWARE UPPER-LAYER PROTOCOLS AND SERVICES

NetWare supports a wide variety of upper-layer protocols, including *NetWare Shell, NetWare Remote Procedure Call, NetWare Core Protocol,* and *Network Basic Input/Output System.*

The NetWare shell runs clients (often called workstations in the NetWare community) and intercepts application input/output (I/O) calls to determine whether they require network access for completion. If the application request requires network access, the NetWare shell packages the request and sends it to lower-layer software for processing and network transmission. If the application request does not require network access, the request is passed to the local I/O resources. Client applications are unaware of any network access required for completion of application calls.

NetWare Remote Procedure Call (NetWare RPC) is another more general redirection mechanism similar in concept to the NetWare shell supported by Novell.

NetWare Core Protocol (NCP) is a series of server routines designed to satisfy application requests coming from, for example, the NetWare shell. The services provided by NCP include file access, printer access, name management, accounting, security, and file synchronization.

NetWare also supports the *Network Basic Input/Output System* (NetBIOS) session-layer interface specification from IBM and Microsoft. NetWare's NetBIOS emulation software allows programs written to the industry-standard NetBIOS interface to run within NetWare system.

NetWare Application-Layer Services

NetWare application-layer services include *NetWare message-handling service* (NetWare MHS), *Btrieve, NetWare loadable modules* (NLMs), and *IBM Logical Unit* (LU) *6.2 network-addressable units* (NAUs). NetWare MHS is a message-delivery system that provides electronic mail transport. Btrieve is Novell's implementation of the binary tree (btree) database-access mechanism. NLMs are add-on modules that attach into a NetWare system. NLMs currently available from Novell and third parties include alternate protocol stacks, communication services, and database services. In terms of IBM LU 6.2 NAU support, NetWare allows peer-to-peer connectivity and information exchange across IBM networks. NetWare packets are encapsulated within LU 6.2 packets for transit across an IBM network.

IPX PACKET FORMAT

The IPX packet is the basic unit of Novell NetWare internetworking. Figure 31–4 illustrates the format of a NetWare IPX packet.

The following descriptions summarize the IPX packet fields illustrated in Figure 31–4:

- *Checksum*—Indicates that the checksum is not used when this 16-bit field is set to 1s (FFFF).

- *Packet Length*—Specifies the length, in bytes, of a complete IPX datagram. IPX packets can be any length, up to the media maximum-transmission unit (MTU) size (no packet fragmentation allowed).

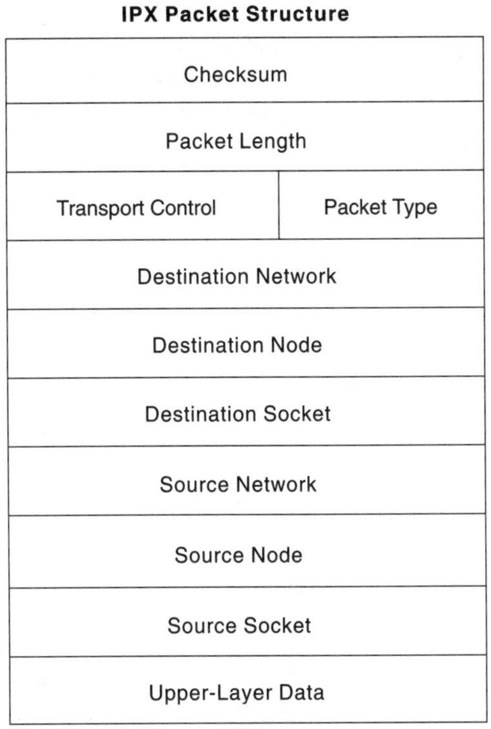

IPX Packet Structure

Checksum
Packet Length

Transport Control	Packet Type

Destination Network
Destination Node
Destination Socket
Source Network
Source Node
Source Socket
Upper-Layer Data

Figure 31–4
A NetWare IPX packet consists of eleven fields.

- *Transport Control*—Indicates the number of routers through which the packet has passed. When this value reaches 16, the packet is discarded under the assumption that a routing loop might be occurring.

- *Packet Type*—Specifies which upper-layer protocol should receive the packet's information. It has two common values:

  ○ 5: Specifies Sequenced Packet-Exchange (SPX)
  ○ 17: Specifies NetWare Core Protocol (NCP)

- *Destination Network, Destination Node, and Destination Socket*— Specify destination information.

- *Source Network, Source Node, and Source Socket*—Specifies source information.

- *Upper-Layer Data*—Contains information for upper-layer processes.

CHAPTER 32

Open System Interconnection (OSI) Protocols

BACKGROUND

The Open System Interconnection (OSI) protocol suite is comprised of numerous standard protocols that are based on the OSI reference model. These protocols are part of an international program to develop data-networking protocols and other standards that facilitate multivendor equipment interoperability. The OSI program grew out of a need for international networking standards and is designed to facilitate communication between hardware and software systems despite differences in underlying architectures.

The OSI specifications were conceived and implemented by two international standards organizations: the International Organization for Standardization (ISO) and the International Telecommunication Union-Telecommunication Standardization Sector (ITU-T). This chapter provides a summary of the OSI protocol suite and illustrates its mapping to the general OSI reference model.

OSI NETWORKING PROTOCOLS

Figure 32–1 illustrates the entire OSI protocol suite and its relation to the layers of the OSI reference model. Each component of this protocol suite is discussed briefly in this chapter. The OSI routing protocols are addressed in more detail in Chapter 41, "Open Systems Interconnection (OSI) Routing Protocols."

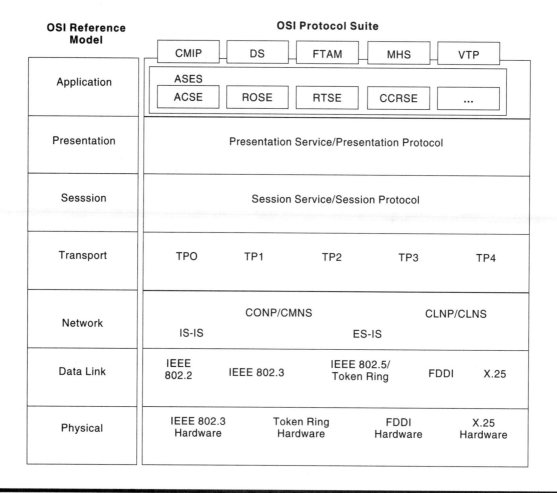

Figure 32–1

The OSI protocol suite maps to all layers of the OSI reference model.

OSI Physical and Data Link layers

The OSI protocol suite supports numerous standard media-access protocols at the physical and data link layers. The wide variety of media-access protocols supported in the OSI protocol suite allows other protocol suites to exist easily alongside OSI on the same network media. Supported media-access protocols include IEEE 802.2 LLC, IEEE 802.3, Token Ring/IEEE 802.5, Fiber Distributed Data Interface (FDDI), and X.25.

OSI Network Layer

The OSI protocol suite specifies two routing protocols at the network layer: End System-to-Intermediate System (ES-IS) and Intermediate System-to-Intermediate System (IS-IS). In addition, the OSI suite implements two types of network services: connectionless service and connection-oriented service.

OSI-Layer Standards

In addition to the standards specifying the OSI network-layer protocols and services, the following documents describe other OSI network-layer specifications:

- ISO 8648—This standard defines the internal organization of the network layer (IONL), which divides the network layer into three distinct sublayers to support different subnetwork types.

- ISO 8348—This standard defines network-layer addressing and describes the connection-oriented and connectionless services provided by the OSI network layer.

- ISO TR 9575—This standard describes the framework, concepts, and terminology used in relation to OSI routing protocols.

OSI Connectionless Network Service

OSI connectionless network service is implemented by using the Connectionless Network Protocol (CLNP) and Connectionless Network Service (CLNS). CLNP and CLNS are described in the ISO 8473 standard.

CLNP is an OSI network-layer protocol that carries upper-layer data and error indications over connectionless links. CLNP provides the interface between the Connectionless Network Service (CLNS) and upper layers.

CLNS provides network-layer services to the transport layer via CLNP.

CLNS does not perform connection setup or termination because paths are determined independently for each packet that is transmitted through a network. This contrasts with Connection-Mode Network Service (CMNS).

In addition, CLNS provides best-effort delivery, which means that no guarantee exists that data will not be lost, corrupted, misordered, or duplicated. CLNS relies on transport-layer protocols to perform error detection and correction.

OSI Connection-Oriented Network Service

OSI connection-oriented network service is implemented by using the Connection-Oriented Network Protocol (CONP) and Connection-Mode Network Service (CMNS).

CONP is an OSI network-layer protocol that carries upper-layer data and error indications over connection-oriented links. CONP is based on the X.25 Packet-Layer Protocol (PLP) and is described in the ISO 8208 standard, "X.25 Packet-Layer Protocol for DTE."

CONP provides the interface between CMNS and upper layers. It is a network-layer service that acts as the interface between the transport layer and CONP and is described in the ISO 8878 standard.

CMNS performs functions related to the explicit establishment of paths between communicating transport-layer entities. These functions include connection setup, maintenance, and termination, and CMNS also provides a mechanism for requesting a specific quality of service (QOS). This contrasts with CLNS.

Network–Layer Addressing

OSI network-layer addressing is implemented by using two types of hierarchical addresses: network service access-point addresses and network-entity titles.

A network service-access point (NSAP) is a conceptual point on the boundary between the network and the transport layers. The NSAP is the location at which OSI network services are provided to the transport layer. Each transport-layer entity is assigned a single NSAP, which is individually addressed in an OSI internetwork using NSAP addresses.

Figure 32–2 illustrates the format of the OSI NSAP address, which identifies individual NSAPs.

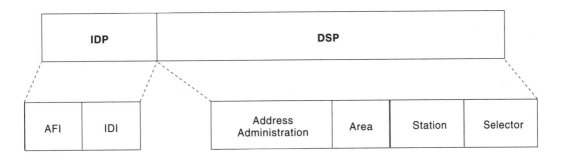

Figure 32–2
The OSI NSAP address is assigned to each transport-layer entity.

NSAP Address Fields

Two NSAP Address fields exist: the Initial Domain Part (IDP) and the Domain-Specific Part (DSP).

The IDP field is divided into two parts: the Authority Format Identifier (AFI) and the Initial Domain Identifier (IDI). The AFI provides information about the structure and content of the IDI and DSP fields, such as whether the IDI is of variable length and whether the DSP uses decimal or binary notation. The IDI specifies the entity that can assign values to the DSP portion of the NSAP address.

The DSP is subdivided into four parts by the authority responsible for its administration. The Address Administration fields allow for the further administration of addressing by adding a second authority identifier and by delegating address administration to subauthorities. The Area field identifies the specific area within a domain and is used for routing purposes. The Station field identifies a specific station within an area and also is used for routing purposes. The Selector field provides the specific n-selector within a station and, much like the other fields, is used for routing purposes. The reserved n-selector 00 identifies the address as a network entity title (NET).

End-System NSAPs

An OSI end system (ES) often has multiple NSAP addresses, one for each transport entity that it contains. If this is the case, the NSAP address for each transport entity usually differs only in the last byte (called the *n-selector*). Figure 32–3 illustrates the relationship between a transport entity, the NSAP, and the network service.

A network-entity title (NET) is used to identify the network layer of a system without associating that system with a specific transport-layer entity (as an NSAP address does). NETs are useful for addressing intermediate systems (ISs), such as routers, that do not interface with the transport layer. An IS can have a single NET or multiple NETs, if it participates in multiple areas or domains.

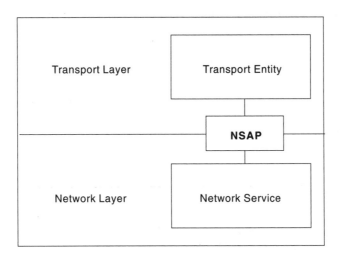

Figure 32–3
The NSAP provides a linkage between a transport entity and a network service.

OSI Protocols Transport Layer

The OSI protocol suite implements two types of services at the transport layer: connection-oriented transport service and connectionless transport service.

Five connection-oriented transport-layer protocols exist in the OSI suite, ranging from Transport Protocol Class 0 through Transport Protocol Class 4. Connectionless transport service is supported only by Transport Protocol Class 4.

Transport Protocol Class 0 (TP0), the simplest OSI transport protocol, performs segmentation and reassembly functions. TP0 requires connection-oriented network service.

Transport Protocol Class 1 (TP1) performs segmentation and reassembly and offers basic error recovery. TP1 sequences protocol data units (PDUs) and will retransmit PDUs or reinitiate the connection if an excessive number of PDUs are unacknowledged. TP1 requires connection-oriented network service.

Transport Protocol Class 2 (TP2) performs segmentation and reassembly, as well as multiplexing and demultiplexing data streams over a single virtual circuit. TP2 requires connection-oriented network service.

Transport Protocol Class 3 (TP3) offers basic error recovery and performs segmentation and reassembly, in addition to multiplexing and demultiplexing data streams over a single virtual circuit. TP3 also sequences PDUs and retransmits them or reinitiates the connection if an excessive number are unacknowledged. TP3 requires connection-oriented network service.

Transport Protocol Class 4 (TP4) TP4 offers basic error recovery, performs segmentation and reassembly, and supplies multiplexing and demultiplexing of data streams over a single virtual circuit. TP4 sequences PDUs and retransmits them or reinitiates the connection if an excessive number are unacknowledged. TP4 provides reliable transport service and functions with either connection-oriented or connectionless network service. It is based on the Transmission Control Protocol (TCP) in the Internet Protocols suite and is the only OSI protocol class that supports connectionless network service.

OSI Protocols Session Layer

The session-layer implementation of the OSI protocol suite consists of a session protocol and a session service. The session protocol allows session-service users (SS-users) to communicate with the session service. An *SS-user* is an entity that requests the services of the session layer. Such requests are made at Session-Service Access Points (SSAPs), and SS-users are uniquely identified by using an SSAP address. Figure 32–4 shows the relationship between the SS-user, the SSAP, the session protocol, and the session service.

Session service provides four basic services to SS-users. First, it establishes and terminates connections between SS-users and synchronizes the data exchange between them. Second, it performs various negotiations for the use of session-layer tokens, which must be possessed by the SS-user to begin communicating. Third, it inserts synchronization points in transmitted data that allow the session to be recovered in the event of errors or interruptions.

Finally, it allows SS-users to interrupt a session and resume it later at a specific point.

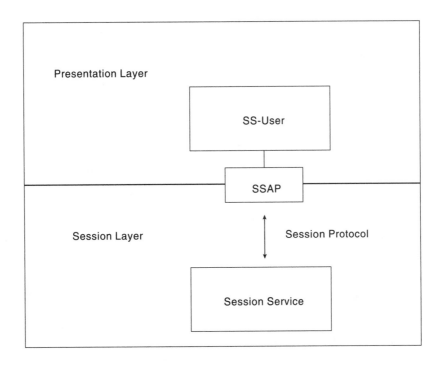

Figure 32-4
Session layer functions provide service to presentation layer functions via a SSAP.

Session service is defined in the ISO 8326 standard and in the ITU-T X.215 recommendation. The session protocol is defined in the ISO 8327 standard and in the ITU-T X.225 recommendation. A connectionless version of the session protocol is specified in the ISO 9548 standard.

OSI Protocols Presentation Layer

The presentation-layer implementation of the OSI protocol suite consists of a presentation protocol and a presentation service. The presentation protocol allows presentation-service users (PS-users) to communicate with the presentation service.

A PS-user is an entity that requests the services of the presentation layer. Such requests are made at Presentation-Service Access Points (PSAPs). PS-users are uniquely identified by using PSAP addresses.

Presentation service negotiates transfer syntax and translates data to and from the transfer syntax for PS-users, which represent data using different syntaxes. The presentation service is used by two PS-users to agree upon the transfer syntax that will be used. When a transfer syntax is agreed upon, presentation-service entities must translate the data from the PS-user to the correct transfer syntax.

The OSI presentation-layer service is defined in the ISO 8822 standard and in the ITU-T X.216 recommendation. The OSI presentation protocol is defined in the ISO 8823 standard and in the ITU-T X.226 recommendation. A connectionless version of the presentation protocol is specified in the ISO 9576 standard.

OSI Protocols Application Layer

The application-layer implementation of the OSI protocol suite consists of various application entities. An application entity is the part of an application process that is relevant to the operation of the OSI protocol suite. An application entity is composed of the user element and the application service element (ASE).

The user element is the part of an application entity that uses ASEs to satisfy the communication needs of the application process. The ASE is the part of an application entity that provides services to user elements and, therefore, to application processes. ASEs also provide interfaces to the lower OSI layers.

Figure 32–5 portrays the composition of a single application process (composed of the application entity, the user element, and the ASEs) and its relation to the PSAP and presentation service.

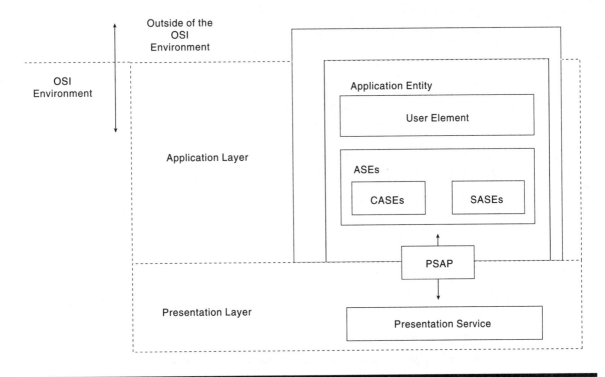

Figure 32–5
An application process relies on the PSAP and presentation service.

ASEs fall into one of the two following classifications: Common-Application Service Elements (CASEs) and Specific-Application Service Elements (SASEs). Both of these might be present in a single application entity.

Common-Application Service Elements (CASEs)

Common-Application Service Elements (CASEs) are ASEs that provide services used by a wide variety of application processes. In many cases, multiple CASEs are used by a single application entity. The following four CASEs are defined in the OSI specification:

- *Association Control Service Element* (ACSE)—Creates associations between two application entities in preparation for application-to-application communication

- *Remote Operations Service Element* (ROSE)—Implements a request-reply mechanism that permits various remote operations across an application association established by the ACSE

- *Reliable Transfer Service Element* (RTSE)—Allows ASEs to reliably transfer messages while preserving the transparency of complex lower-layer facilities

- *Commitment, Concurrence, and Recovery Service Elements* (CCRSE)—Coordinates dialogues between multiple application entities.

Specific-Application Service Elements (SASEs)

Specific-Application Service Elements are ASEs that provide services used only by a specific application process, such as file transfer, database access, and order-entry, among others.

OSI Protocols Application Processes

An application process is the element of an application that provides the interface between the application itself and the OSI application layer. Some of the standard OSI application processes include the following:

- *Common Management-Information Protocol (CMIP)*—Performs network management functions, allowing the exchange of management information between ESs and management stations. CMIP is specified in the ITU-T X.700 recommendation and is functionally similar to the Simple Network-Management Protocol (SNMP) and NetView.

- *Directory Services (DS)*—Serves as a distributed directory that is used for node identification and addressing in OSI internetworks. DS is specified in the ITU-T X.500 recommendation.

- *File Transfer, Access, and Management (FTAM)*—Provides file-transfer service and distributed file-access facilities.

- *Message Handling System (MHS)*—Provides a transport mechanism for electronic messaging applications and other applications by using store-and-forward services.

- *Virtual Terminal Protocol (VTP)*—Provides terminal emulation that allows a computer system to appear to a remote ES as if it were a directly attached terminal.

CHAPTER 33

Banyan VINES

BACKGROUND

Banyan Virtual Integrated Network Service (VINES) implements a distributed network-operating system based on a proprietary protocol family derived from the Xerox Corporation's Xerox Network Systems (XNS) protocols. VINES uses a client-server architecture in which clients request certain services, such as file and printer access, from servers. This chapter provides a summary of VINES communications protocols. The VINES protocol stack is illustrated in Figure 33–1.

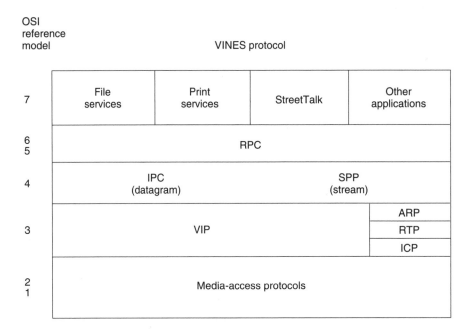

Figure 33–1
The VINES protocol stack consists of five separate levels.

MEDIA ACCESS

The lower two layers of the VINES stack are implemented with a variety of well-known media-access mechanisms, including High-Level Data Link Control (HDLC), X.25, Ethernet, and Token Ring.

NETWORK LAYER

VINES uses the *VINES Internetwork Protocol* (VIP) to perform Layer 3 activities (including internetwork routing). VINES also supports its own *Address-Resolution Protocol* (ARP), its own version of the *Routing Information Protocol* (RIP)—called the *Routing Table Protocol* (RTP)—and the *Internet Control Protocol* (ICP), which provides exception handling and special routing cost information. ARP, ICP, and RTP packets are encapsulated in a VIP header.

VINES Internetwork Protocol (VIP)

VINES network-layer addresses are 48-bit entities subdivided into network (32 bits) and subnetwork (16 bits) portions. The network number is better described as a server number because it is derived directly from the server's *key* (a hardware module that identifies a unique number and the software options for that server). The subnetwork portion of a VINES address is better described as a host number because it is used to identify hosts on VINES networks. Figure 33–2 illustrates the VINES address format.

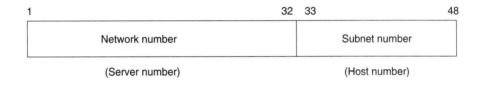

Figure 33–2
A VINES address consists of a network number and a subnet number.

The network number identifies a VINES logical network, which is represented as a two-level tree with the root at a *service node*. Service nodes, which are usually servers, provide address resolution and routing services to *clients*, which represent the leaves of the tree. The service node assigns VIP addresses to clients.

When a client is powered on, it broadcasts a request for servers, and all servers that hear the request respond. The client chooses the first response and requests a subnetwork (host) address from that server. The server responds with an address consisting of its own network address (derived from its key) concatenated with a subnetwork (host) address of its own choosing. Client subnetwork addresses typically are assigned sequentially, starting with 8001H. Server subnetwork addresses are always 1. Figure 33–3 illustrates the VINES address-selection process.

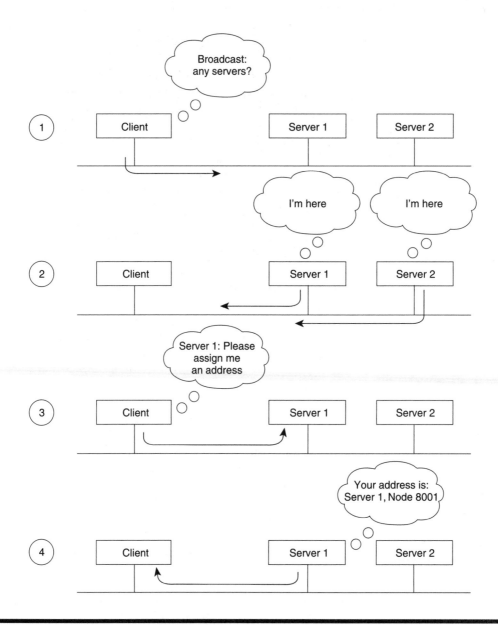

Figure 33–3

VINES moves through four steps in selecting an address.

Dynamic address assignment is not unique in the industry (AppleTalk also uses this process), but it certainly is not as common as static address assignment. Because addresses are chosen exclusively by a particular server (whose address is unique as a result of the hardware key), very little chance exists for duplicating an address. This is fortunate, because duplicate addresses could cause potentially devastating problems for *Internet Protocol* (IP) and other networks.

In the VINES network scheme, all servers with multiple interfaces are essentially routers. Clients always choose their own server as a first-hop router, even if another server on the same cable provides a better route to the ultimate destination. Clients can learn about other routers by receiving redirect messages from their own server. Because clients rely on their servers for first-hop routing, VINES servers maintain routing tables to help them find remote nodes.

VINES routing tables consist of host/cost pairs, where the *host* corresponds to a network node that can be reached, and *cost* corresponds to a delay (expressed in milliseconds) to get to that node. RTP helps VINES servers find neighboring clients, servers, and routers.

Periodically, all clients advertise both their network-layer and their MAC-layer addresses with the equivalent of a *hello* packet, which indicates that the client is still operating and network-ready. The servers themselves send routing updates to other servers periodically to alert other routers to changes in node addresses and network topology.

When a VINES server receives a packet, it checks to see whether the packet is destined for another server or whether it is a broadcast. If the current server is the destination, the server handles the request appropriately. If another server is the destination, the current server either forwards the packet directly (if the server is a neighbor) or routes it to the next server in line. If the packet is a broadcast, the current server checks to see whether the packet came from the least-cost path. If not, the packet is discarded. If so, the packet is forwarded on all interfaces except the one on which it was received. This approach helps diminish the number of broadcast storms, a common problem in other network environments. Figure 33–4 illustrates the VINES routing algorithm.

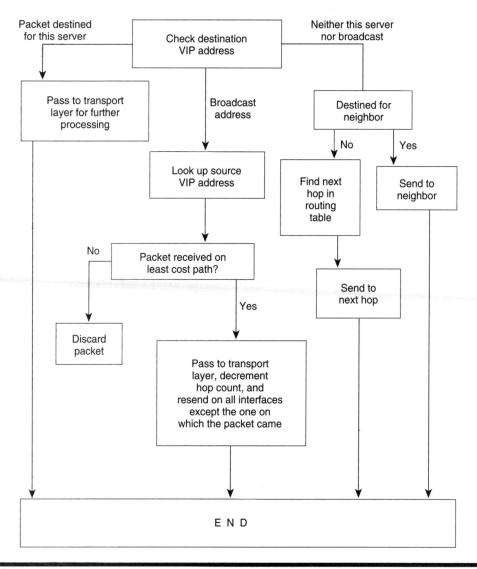

Figure 33–4
The VINES routing algorithm determines the appropriate path to a destination.

Figure 33–5 illustrates the VIP packet format.

Field length, in bytes	2	2	1	1	4	2	4	2	Variable
	Check-sum	Packet length	Trans-port control	Protocol type	Destination network number	Destination subnetwork number	Source network number	Source subnetwork number	Data

Figure 33–5
A VIP packet consists of nine individual fields.

The fields of a VIP packet include the *checksum, packet length, transport control, protocol type, destination network number, destination subnetwork number, source network number,* and *source subnetwork number.*

The checksum field is used to detect packet corruption. The packet-length field indicates the length of the entire VIP packet.

The transport-control field consists of several subfields. If the packet is a broadcast packet, two subfields are provided: *class* (bits 1 through 3) and *hop count* (bits 4 through 7). If the packet is not a broadcast packet, four subfields are provided: *error, metric, redirect,* and *hop count.* The class subfield specifies the type of node that should receive the broadcast. For this purpose, nodes are broken into various categories according to the type of node and the type of link on which the node is found. By specifying the type of nodes to receive broadcasts, the class subfield reduces the disruption caused by broadcasts. The hop-count subfield represents the number of hops (router traversals) the packet has been through. The error subfield specifies whether the ICP protocol should send an exception-notification packet to the packet's source if a packet turns out to be unroutable. The metric subfield is set to one by a transport entity when it must learn the routing cost of moving packets between a service node and a neighbor. The redirect subfield specifies whether the router should generate a redirect, when appropriate.

The *protocol-type* field indicates the network- or transport-layer protocol for which the metric or exception-notification packet is destined.

Finally, *destination network number, destination subnetwork number, source network number,* and *source subnetwork number* all provide VIP address information.

Routing-Table Protocol (RTP)

RTP distributes network-topology information. Routing-update packets are broadcast periodically by both client and service nodes. These packets inform neighbors of a node's existence and also indicate whether the node is a client or a service node. In each routing-update packet, service nodes include, in each routing update packet, a list of all known networks and the cost factors associated with reaching those networks.

Two routing tables are maintained: a *table of all known networks* and a *table of neighbors*. For service nodes, the table of all known networks contains an entry for each known network except the service node's own network. Each entry contains a network number, a routing metric, and a pointer to the entry for the next hop to the network in the table of neighbors. The table of neighbors contains an entry for each neighbor service node and client node. Entries include a network number, a subnetwork number, the media-access protocol (for example, Ethernet) used to reach that node, a local area network (LAN) address (if the medium connecting the neighbor is a LAN), and a neighbor metric.

RTP specifies four packet types: *routing update, routing request, routing response,* and *routing redirect*. Routing update is issued periodically to notify neighbors of an entity's existence. Routing requests are exchanged by entities when they must learn the network's topology quickly. Routing responses contain topological information and are used by service nodes to respond to routing-request packets. A *routing-redirect* packet provides better path information to nodes using inefficient paths.

RTP packets have a 4-byte header that consists of the following 1-byte fields: *operation type*, which indicates the packet type; *node type*, which indicates whether the packet came from a service node or a nonservice node; *controller type*, which indicates whether the controller in the node transmitting the RTP packet has a multibuffer controller; and *machine type*, which indicates whether the processor in the RTP sender is fast or slow.

Both the controller-type and the machine-type fields are used for pacing.

Address Resolution Protocol (ARP)

Address-Resolution Protocol (ARP) entities are classified as either *address-resolution clients* or *address-resolution services*. *Address-resolution clients* usually are implemented in client nodes, whereas *address-resolution services* typically are provided by service nodes.

ARP packets have an 8-byte header that consists of a 2-byte *packet type*, a 4-byte *network number*, and a 2-byte *subnetwork number*. Four packet types exist: a *query request*, which is a request for an ARP service; a *service response*, which is a response to a query request; an *assignment request*, which is sent to an ARP service to request a VINES internetwork address; and an *assignment response*, which is sent by the ARP service as a response to the assignment request. The network-number and subnet-number fields have meaning only in an assignment-response packet.

ARP clients and services implement the following algorithm when a client starts up. First, the client broadcasts query-request packets. Then, each service that is a neighbor of the client responds with a service-response packet. The client then issues an assignment-request packet to the first service that responded to its query-request packet. The service responds with an assignment-response packet that contains the assigned internetwork address.

Internet Control Protocol (ICP)

The Internet Control Protocol (ICP) defines *exception-notification* and *metric-notification* packets. *Exception-notification* packets provide information about network-layer exceptions; *metric-notification* packets contain information about the final transmission used to reach a client node.

Exception notifications are sent when a VIP packet cannot be routed properly and the error subfield in the VIP header's transport control field is enabled. These packets also contain a field identifying the particular exception by its error code.

ICP entities in service nodes generate metric-notification messages when the metric subfield in the VIP header's transport-control field is enabled, and the destination address in the service node's packet specifies one of the service node's neighbors.

TRANSPORT LAYER

VINES provides three transport-layer services: unreliable-datagram service, reliable-message service, and data-stream service.

Unreliable-datagram service sends packets that are routed on a best-effort basis but not acknowledged at the destination.

Reliable-message service is a virtual-circuit service that provides reliable sequenced and acknowledged delivery of messages between network nodes. A reliable message can be transmitted in a maximum of four VIP packets.

Data-stream service supports the controlled flow of data between two processes. The data-stream service is an acknowledged virtual-circuit service that supports the transmission of messages of unlimited size.

UPPER-LAYER PROTOCOLS

As a distributed network, VINES uses the *remote procedure call* (RPC) model for communication between clients and servers. RPC is the foundation of distributed-service environments. The *NetRPC* protocol (Layers 5 and 6) provides a high-level programming language that allows access to remote services in a manner transparent to both the user and the application.

At Layer 7, VINES offers file-service and print-service applications, as well as *StreetTalk*, which provides a globally consistent name service for an entire internetwork.

VINES also provides an integrated applications-development environment under several operating systems, including DOS and Unix. This development environment allows third parties to develop both clients and services that run in the VINES environment.

CHAPTER 34

Xerox Network Systems (XNS)

BACKGROUND

The Xerox Network Systems (XNS) protocols were created by Xerox Corporation in the late 1970s and early 1980s. They were designed to be used across a variety of communication media, processors, and office applications. Several XNS protocols resemble the Internet Protocol (IP) and Transmission-Control Protocol (TCP) entities developed by the Defense Advanced Research Projects Agency (DARPA) for the U.S. Department of Defense (DoD).

Because of its availability and early entry into the market, XNS was adopted by most of the early LAN companies, including Novell, Inc., Ungermann-Bass, Inc. (now a part of Tandem Computers), and 3Com Corporation. Each of these companies has since made various changes to the XNS protocols. Novell added the Service Advertisement Protocol (SAP) to permit resource advertisement and modified the OSI Layer 3 protocols (which Novell renamed IPX, for Internetwork Packet Exchange) to run on IEEE 802.3 rather than Ethernet networks. Ungermann-Bass modified RIP to support delay as well as hop count and made other small changes. Over time, the XNS implementations for PC networking have become more popular than XNS as it was designed by Xerox. This chapter presents a summary of the XNS protocol stack in the context of the OSI reference model.

XNS HIERARCHY OVERVIEW

Although the XNS design objectives are the same as those for the OSI reference model, the XNS concept of a protocol hierarchy is somewhat different from that provided by the OSI reference model, as Figure 34–1 illustrates.

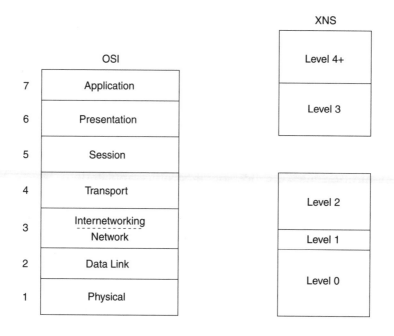

Figure 34–1
Xerox adopted a five-layer model of packet communication.

As illustrated in Figure 34–1, Xerox provided a five-level model of packet communications. Level 0 corresponds roughly to OSI Layers 1 and 2, handling link access and bit-stream manipulation. Level 1 corresponds roughly to the portion of OSI Layer 3 that pertains to network traffic. Level 2 corresponds to the portion of OSI Layer 3 that pertains to internetwork routing, and to OSI Layer 4, which handles interprocess communication. Levels 3 and 4 correspond roughly to the upper two layers of the OSI model, handling data structuring, process-to-process interaction and applications. XNS has no protocol corresponding to OSI Layer 5 (the session layer).

MEDIA ACCESS

Although XNS documentation mentions X.25, Ethernet, and High-Level Data Link Control (HDLC), XNS does not expressly define what it refers to as a Level 0 protocol. As with many other protocol suites, XNS leaves media access an open issue, implicitly allowing any such protocol to host the transport of XNS packets over a physical medium.

NETWORK LAYER

The XNS network-layer protocol is called the *Internet Datagram Protocol* (IDP). IDP performs standard Layer 3 functions, including logical addressing and end-to-end datagram delivery across an internetwork. Figure 34–2 illustrates the format of an IDP packet.

The following descriptions summarize the IDP packet fields illustrated in Figure 34–2:

- *Checksum*—A 16-bit field that helps gauge the integrity of the packet after it traverses the internetwork.

- *Length*—A 16-bit field that carries the complete length (including the checksum) of the current datagram.

- *Transport Control*—An 8-bit field that contains the *hop count* and *maximum packet lifetime* (MPL) subfields. The hop-count subfield is initialized to zero by the source and incremented by one as the datagram passes through a router. When the hop-count field reaches 16, the datagram is discarded on the assumption that a routing loop is occurring. The MPL subfield provides the maximum amount of time, in seconds, that a packet can remain on the internetwork.

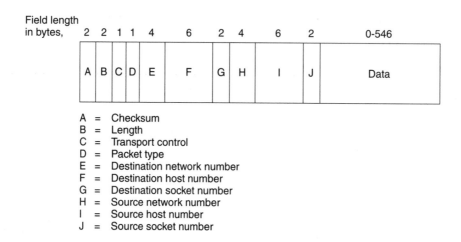

Field length in bytes,

A = Checksum
B = Length
C = Transport control
D = Packet type
E = Destination network number
F = Destination host number
G = Destination socket number
H = Source network number
I = Source host number
J = Source socket number

Figure 34–2
Eleven fields comprise an IDP packet.

- *Packet Type*—An 8-bit field that specifies the format of the data field.

- *Destination Network Number*—A 32-bit field that uniquely identifies the destination network in an internetwork.

- *Destination Host Number*—A 48-bit field that uniquely identifies the destination host.

- *Destination Socket Number*—A 16-bit field that uniquely identifies a socket (process) within the destination host.

- *Source Network Number*—A 32-bit field that uniquely identifies the source network in an internetwork.

- *Source Host Number*—A 48-bit field that uniquely identifies the source host.

- *Source Socket Number*—A16-bit field that uniquely identifies a socket (process) within the source host.

IEEE 802 addresses are equivalent to host numbers, so that hosts that are connected to more than one IEEE 802 network have the same address on each segment. This makes network numbers redundant but nevertheless useful for routing. Certain socket numbers are *well known*, which means that the service performed by the software using them is statically defined. All other socket numbers are reusable.

XNS supports Ethernet Version 2.0 encapsulation for Ethernet, and three types of encapsulation for Token Ring: 3Com, SubNet Access Protocol (SNAP), and Ungermann-Bass.

XNS supports *unicast* (point-to-point), *multicast*, and *broadcast* packets. Multicast and broadcast addresses are further divided into *directed* and *global* types. Directed multicasts deliver packets to members of the multicast group on the network specified in the destination multicast network address. Directed broadcasts deliver packets to all members of a specified network. Global multicasts deliver packets to all members of the group within the entire internetwork, whereas global broadcasts deliver packets to all internetwork addresses. One bit in the host number indicates a single versus a multicast address. Conversely, all ones in the host field indicate a broadcast address.

To route packets in an internetwork, XNS uses the RIP dynamic routing scheme. Today, RIP is the most commonly used *Interior Gateway Protocol* (IGP) in the Internet community. For more information about RIP, see Chapter 44, "Routing Information Protocol (RIP)."

TRANSPORT LAYER

OSI transport-layer functions are implemented by several protocols. Each of the following protocols is described in the XNS specification as a Level 2 protocol.

The *Sequenced-Packet Protocol (SPP)* provides reliable, connection-based, flow-controlled packet transmission on behalf of client processes. It is similar in function to the Internet Protocol suite's *Transmission-Control Protocol (TCP)* and the OSI protocol suite's *Transport Protocol 4 (TP4)*. For more information about TCP, see Chapter 30, "Internet Protocols." For more information about TP4, see Chapter 32, "Open System Interconnection (OSI) Protocols."

Each SPP packet includes a *sequence number*, which is used to order packets and to determine whether any have been duplicated or missed. SPP packets also contain two 16-bit *connection identifiers*. One connection identifier is specified by each end of the connection, and together, the two connection identifiers uniquely identify a logical connection between client processes.

SPP packets cannot be longer than 576 bytes. Client processes can negotiate use of a different packet size during connection establishment, but SPP does not define the nature of this negotiation.

The *Packet Exchange Protocol* (PEP) is a request-response protocol designed to have greater reliability than simple datagram service (as provided by IDP, for example) but less reliability than SPP. PEP is functionally similar to the Internet Protocol suite's *User Datagram Protocol* (UDP). For more information about UDP, see Chapter 30. PEP is single-packet based, providing retransmissions but no duplicate-packet detection. As such, it is useful in applications where request-response transactions can be repeated without damaging data, or where reliable transfer is executed at another layer.

The *Error Protocol* (EP) can be used by any client process to notify another client process that a network error has occurred. This protocol is used, for example, in situations where an SPP implementation has identified a duplicate packet.

UPPER-LAYER PROTOCOLS

XNS offers several upper-layer protocols. The *Printing Protocol* provides print services, the *Filing Protocol* provides file-access services, and the *Clearinghouse Protocol* provides name services. Each of these three protocols runs on top of the *Courier Protocol*, which provides conventions for data structuring and process interaction.

XNS also defines Level 4 protocols, which are application protocols, but because they have little to do with actual communication functions, the XNS specification does not include any pertinent definitions.

The Level 2 *Echo Protocol* is used to test the reachability of XNS network nodes and to support functions such as that provided by the ping command found in Unix and other environments.

PART 6

Routing Protocols

Part 6, "Routing Protocols," summarizes the characteristics and operations of contemporary routing protocols. Individual chapters discuss the following topics:

Border Gateway Protocol (BGP)—Describes the operation of BGP, an exterior gateway protocol in the Internet Protocol suite.

Enhanced Interior Gateway Routing Protocol (Enhanced IGRP)—Describes the characteristics and operation of Enhanced IGRP.

IBM Systems Network Architecture (SNA) Routing—Provides descriptions of IBM SNA routing components and operations in subarea and APPN routing environments.

Interior Gateway Routing Protocol (IGRP)—Describes the characteristics and operations of IGRP.

Internet Protocol (IP) Multicast—Describes IP multicast and outlines basic operations of various supporting protocols.

NetWare Link Services Protocol (NLSP)—Describes the components, features, and operations of Novell NLSP.

Open Systems Interconnection (OSI) Routing—Covers the features and operations of the OSI routing protocols: ES-IS, IS-IS, Integrated IS-IS, and IDRP.

Open Shortest Path First (OSPF)—Discusses the components and operations of this link-state, interior-gateway routing protocol.

Resource Reservation Protocol (RSVP)—Provides descriptions of RSVP functional components and operational characteristics.

Routing Information Protocol (RIP)—Describes the features and operations of this distance-vector Internet routing protocol.

Simple Multicast Routing Protocol (SMRP)—Defines and describes SMRP and outlines its basic operations.

CHAPTER 35

Border Gateway Protocol (BGP)

BACKGROUND

Routing involves two basic activities: determination of optimal routing paths and the transport of information groups (typically called packets) through an internetwork. The transport of packets through an internetwork is relatively straightforward. Path determination, on the other hand, can be very complex. One protocol that addresses the task of path determination in today's networks is the *Border Gateway Protocol* (BGP). This chapter summarizes the basic operations of BGP and provides a description of its protocol components.

BGP performs interdomain routing in Transmission-Control Protocol/ Internet Protocol (TCP/IP) networks. BGP is an exterior gateway protocol (EGP), which means that it performs routing between multiple autonomous systems or domains and exchanges routing and reachability information with other BGP systems.

BGP was developed to replace its predecessor, the now obsolete *Exterior Gateway Protocol* (EGP), as the standard exterior gateway-routing protocol used in the global Internet. BGP solves serious problems with EGP and scales to Internet growth more efficiently.

NOTES

EGP is a particular instance of an exterior gateway protocol (also EGP)—the two should not be confused.

Figure 35–1 illustrates core routers using BGP to route traffic between autonomous systems.

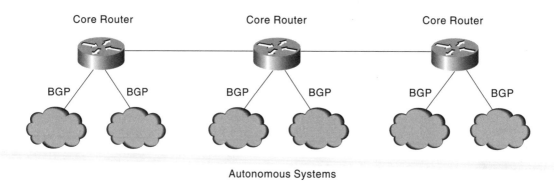

Figure 35–1

Core routers can use BGP to route traffic between autonomous systems.

BGP is specified in several *Request For Comments* (RFCs):

- RFC 1771—Describes BGP4, the current version of BGP

- RFC 1654—Describes the first BGP4 specification

- RFC 1105, RFC 1163, and RFC 1267—Describes versions of BGP prior to BGP4

BGP OPERATION

BGP performs three types of routing: *interautonomous system routing*, *intra-autonomous system routing*, and *pass-through autonomous system routing*.

Interautonomous system routing occurs between two or more BGP routers in different autonomous systems. Peer routers in these systems use BGP to maintain a consistent view of the internetwork topology. BGP neighbors communicating between autonomous systems must reside on the same physical network. The Internet serves as an example of an entity that uses this type of routing because it is comprised of autonomous systems or administrative domains. Many of these domains represent the various institutions, corporations, and entities that make up the Internet. BGP is frequently used to provide path determination to provide optimal routing within the Internet.

Intra-autonomous system routing occurs between two or more BGP routers located within the same autonomous system. Peer routers within the same autonomous system use BGP to maintain a consistent view of the system topology. BGP also is used to determine which router will serve as the connection point for specific external autonomous systems. Once again, the Internet provides an example of interautonomous system routing. An organization, such as a university, could make use of BGP to provide optimal routing within its own administrative domain or autonomous system. The BGP protocol can provide both inter- and intra-autonomous system routing services.

Pass-through autonomous system routing occurs between two or more BGP peer routers that exchange traffic across an autonomous system that does not run BGP. In a pass-through autonomous system environment, the BGP traffic did not originate within the autonomous system in question and is not destined for a node in the autonomous system. BGP must interact with whatever intra-autonomous system routing protocol is being used to successfully transport BGP traffic through that autonomous system. Figure 35–2 illustrates a pass-through autonomous system environment:

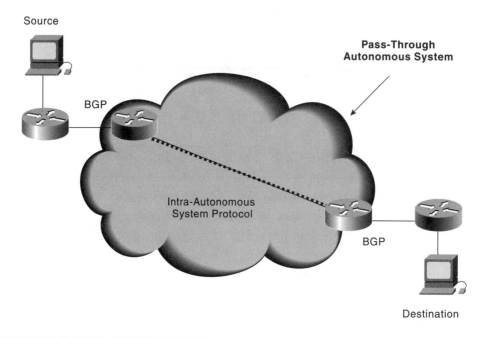

Figure 35–2

In pass-through autonomous system routing, BGP pairs with another intra-autonomous system-routing protocol.

BGP ROUTING

As with any routing protocol, BGP maintains routing tables, transmits routing updates, and bases routing decisions on routing metrics. The primary function of a BGP system is to exchange network-reachability information, including information about the list of autonomous system paths, with other BGP systems. This information can be used to construct a graph of autonomous system connectivity from which routing loops can be pruned and with which autonomous system-level policy decisions can be enforced.

Each BGP router maintains a routing table that lists all feasible paths to a particular network. The router does not refresh the routing table, however.

Instead, routing information received from peer routers is retained until an incremental update is received.

BGP devices exchange routing information upon initial data exchange and after incremental updates. When a router first connects to the network, BGP routers exchange their entire BGP routing tables. Similarly, when the routing table changes, routers send the portion of their routing table that has changed. BGP routers do not send regularly scheduled routing updates, and BGP routing updates advertise only the optimal path to a network.

BGP uses a single routing metric to determine the best path to a given network. This metric consists of an arbitrary unit number that specifies the degree of preference of a particular link. The BGP metric typically is assigned to each link by the network administrator. The value assigned to a link can be based on any number of criteria, including the number of autonomous systems through which the path passes, stability, speed, delay, or cost.

BGP MESSAGE TYPES

Four BGP message types are specified in RFC 1771, *A Border Gateway Protocol 4 (BGP-4)*: open message, update message, notification message, and keep-alive message.

The *open message* opens a BGP communications session between peers and is the first message sent by each side after a transport-protocol connection is established. Open messages are confirmed using a keep-alive message sent by the peer device and must be confirmed before updates, notifications, and keep-alives can be exchanged.

An *update message* is used to provide routing updates to other BGP systems, allowing routers to construct a consistent view of the network topology. Updates are sent using the Transmission-Control Protocol (TCP) to ensure reliable delivery. Update messages can withdraw one or more unfeasible routes from the routing table and simultaneously can advertise a route while withdrawing others.

The *notification message* is sent when an error condition is detected. Notifications are used to close an active session and to inform any connected routers of why the session is being closed.

The keep-alive message notifies BGP peers that a device is active. Keep-alives are sent often enough to keep the sessions from expiring.

BGP PACKET FORMATS

The sections that follow summarize BGP open, updated, notification, and keep-alive message types, as well as the basic BGP header format. Each is illustrated with a format drawing, and the fields shown are defined.

Header Format

All BGP message types use the basic packet header. Open, update, and notification messages have additional fields, but keep-alive messages use only the basic packet header. Figure 35–3 illustrates the fields used in the BGP header. The section that follows summarizes the function of each field.

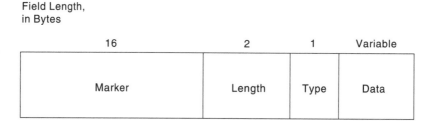

Figure 35–3
A BGP packet header consists of four fields.

BGP Packet-Header Fields

Each BGP packet contains a header whose primary purpose is to identify the function of the packet in question. The following descriptions summarize the function of each field in the BGP header illustrated in Figure 35-3.

- *Marker*—Contains an authentication value that the message receiver can predict.

- *Length*—Indicates the total length of the message in bytes.

- *Type*—Specifies the message type as one of the following:

  ○ Open
  ○ Update
  ○ Notification
  ○ Keep-alive

- *Data*—Contains upper-layer information in this optional field.

Open Message Format

BGP open messages are comprised of a BGP header and additional fields. Figure 35–4 illustrates the additional fields used in BGP open messages.

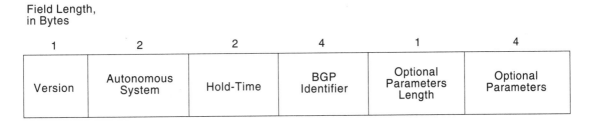

Figure 35–4
A BGP open message consists of six fields.

BGP Open Message Fields

BGP packets in which the type field in the header identifies the packet to be a BGP open message packet include the following fields. These fields provide the exchange criteria for two BGP routers to establish a peer relationship.

- *Version*—Provides the BGP version number so that the recipient can determine whether it is running the same version as the sender.

- *Autonomous System*—Provides the autonomous system number of the sender.

- *Hold-Time*—Indicates the maximum number of seconds that can elapse without receipt of a message before the transmitter is assumed to be nonfunctional.

- *BGP Identifier*—Provides the BGP identifier of the sender (an IP address), which is determined at startup and is identical for all local interfaces and all BGP peers.

- *Optional Parameters Length*—Indicates the length of the optional parameters field (if present).

- *Optional Parameters*—Contains a list of optional parameters (if any). Only one optional parameter type is currently defined: authentication information.

  Authentication information consists of the following two fields:

  ○ Authentication code: Indicates the type of authentication being used.
  ○ Authentication data: Contains data used by the authentication mechanism (if used).

Update Message Format

BGP update messages are comprised of a BGP header and additional fields. Figure 35–5 illustrates the additional fields used in BGP update messages.

Field Length,
in Bytes

2	Variable	2	Variable	Variable
Unfeasible Routes Length	Withdrawn Routes	Total Path Attribute Length	Path Attributes	Network Layer Reachability Information

Figure 35–5
A BGP update message contains five fields.

BGP Update Message Fields

BGP packets in which the type field in the header identifies the packet to be a BGP update message packet include the following fields. Upon receiving an update message packet, routers will be able to add or delete specific entries from their routing tables to ensure accuracy. Update messages consist of the following packets:

- *Unfeasible Routes Length*—Indicates the total length of the withdrawn routes field or that the field is not present.

- *Withdrawn Routes*—Contains a list of IP address prefixes for routes being withdrawn from service.

- *Total Path Attribute Length*—Indicates the total length of the path attributes field or that the field is not present.

- *Path Attributes*—Describes the characteristics of the advertised path. The following are possible attributes for a path:

  - Origin: Mandatory attribute that defines the origin of the path information
  - AS Path: Mandatory attribute composed of a sequence of autonomous system path segments
  - Next Hop: Mandatory attribute that defines the IP address of the border router that should be used as the next hop to destinations listed in the network layer reachability information field
  - Mult Exit Disc: Optional attribute used to discriminate between multiple exit points to a neighboring autonomous system
  - Local Pref: Discretionary attribute used to specify the degree of preference for an advertised route
  - Atomic Aggregate: Discretionary attribute used to disclose information about route selections
  - Aggregator: Optional attribute that contains information about aggregate routes

- *Network Layer Reachability Information*—Contains a list of IP address prefixes for the advertised routes

Notification Message Format

Figure 35–6 illustrates the additional fields used in BGP notification messages.

BGP Notification Message Fields

BGP packets in which the type field in the header identifies the packet to be a BGP notification message packet include the following fields. This packet is used to indicate some sort of error condition to the peers of the originating router.

Field Length,
in Bytes

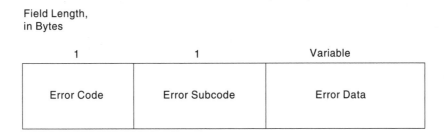

Figure 35–6
A BGP notification message consists of three fields.

- *Error Code*—Indicates the type of error that occurred. The following are the error types defined by the field:

  - Message Header Error: Indicates a problem with a message header, such as unacceptable message length, unacceptable marker field value, or unacceptable message type.
  - Open Message Error: Indicates a problem with an open message, such as unsupported version number, unacceptable autonomous system number or IP address, or unsupported authentication code.
  - Update Message Error: Indicates a problem with an update message, such as a malformed attribute list, attribute list error, or invalid next-hop attribute.
  - Hold Time Expired: Indicates that the hold-time has expired, after which time a BGP node will be considered nonfunctional.
  - Finite State Machine Error: Indicates an unexpected event.
  - Cease: Closes a BGP connection at the request of a BGP device in the absence of any fatal errors.

- *Error Subcode*—Provides more specific information about the nature of the reported error.

- *Error Data*—Contains data based on the error code and error subcode fields. This field is used to diagnose the reason for the notification message.

36

Enhanced IGRP

BACKGROUND

The Enhanced Internet Gateway Routing Protocol (IGRP) represents an evolution from its predecessor IGRP (refer to Chapter 38, "Internet Gateway Routing Protocol)." This evolution resulted from changes in networking and the demands of diverse, large-scale internetworks. Enhanced IGRP integrates the capabilities of link-state protocols into distance-vector protocols. It incorporates the *Diffusing-Update Algorithm* (DUAL) developed at SRI International by Dr. J.J. Garcia-Luna-Aceves.

Enhanced IGRP provides compatibility and seamless interoperation with IGRP routers. An automatic-redistribution mechanism allows IGRP routes to be imported into Enhanced IGRP, and vice versa, so it is possible to add Enhanced IGRP gradually into an existing IGRP network. Because the metrics for both protocols are directly translatable, they are as easily comparable as if they were routes that originated in their own Autonomous Systems (ASs). In addition, Enhanced IGRP treats IGRP routes as external routes and provides a way for the network administrator to customize them.

This chapter provides an overview of the basic operations and protocol characteristics of Enhanced IGRP.

ENHANCED IGRP CAPABILITIES AND ATTRIBUTES

Key capabilities that distinguish Enhanced IGRP from other routing protocols include fast convergence, support variable-length subnet mask, support for partial updates, and support for multiple network-layer protocols.

A router running Enhanced IGRP stores all its neighbors' routing tables so that it can quickly adapt to alternate routes. If no appropriate route exists, Enhanced IGRP queries its neighbors to discover an alternate route. These queries propagate until an alternate route is found.

Its support for variable-length subnet masks permits routes to be automatically summarized on a network number boundary. In addition, Enhanced IGRP can be configured to summarize on any bit boundary at any interface.

Enhanced IGRP does not make periodic updates. Instead, it sends partial updates only when the metric for a route changes. Propagation of partial updates is automatically bounded so that only those routers that need the information are updated. As a result of these two capabilities, Enhanced IGRP consumes significantly less bandwidth than IGRP.

Enhanced IGRP includes support for AppleTalk, IP, and Novell NetWare. The AppleTalk implementation redistributes routes learned from the Routing Table Maintenance Protocol (RTMP). The IP implementation redistributes routes learned from OSPF, Routing Information Protocol (RIP), IS-IS, Exterior Gateway Protocol (EGP), or Border Gateway Protocol (BGP). The Novell implementation redistributes routes learned from Novell RIP or Service Advertisement Protocol (SAP).

UNDERLYING PROCESSES AND TECHNOLOGIES

To provide superior routing performance, Enhanced IGRP employs four key technologies that combine to differentiate it from other routing technologies: *neighbor discovery/recovery*, *reliable transport protocol (RTP)*, *DUAL finite-state machine*, and *protocol-dependent modules*.

Neighbor discovery/recovery is used by routers to dynamically learn about other routers on their directly attached networks. Routers also must discover when their neighbors become unreachable or inoperative. This process is achieved with low overhead by periodically sending small hello packets. As long as a router receives hello packets from a neighboring router, it assumes that the neighbor is functioning, and the two can exchange routing information.

Reliable Transport Protocol (RTP) is responsible for guaranteed, ordered delivery of Enhanced IGRP packets to all neighbors. It supports intermixed transmission of multicast or unicast packets. For efficiency, only certain Enhanced IGRP packets are transmitted reliably. On a multiaccess network that has multicast capabilities, such as Ethernet, it is not necessary to send hello packets reliably to all neighbors individually. For that reason, Enhanced IGRP sends a single multicast hello packet containing an indicator that informs the receivers that the packet need not be acknowledged. Other types of packets, such as updates, indicate in the packet that acknowledgment is required. RTP contains a provision for sending multicast packets quickly when unacknowledged packets are pending, which helps ensure that convergence time remains low in the presence of varying speed links.

DUAL finite-state machine embodies the decision process for all route computations by tracking all routes advertised by all neighbors. DUAL uses distance information to select efficient, loop-free paths and selects routes for insertion in a routing table based on feasible successors. A *feasible successor* is a neighboring router used for packet forwarding that is a least-cost path to a destination that is guaranteed not to be part of a routing loop. When a neighbor changes a metric, or when a topology change occurs, DUAL tests for feasible successors. If one is found, DUAL uses it to avoid recomputing the route unnecessarily. When no feasible successors exist but neighbors still advertise the destination, a recomputation (also known as a diffusing computation) must occur to determine a new successor. Although recomputation is not processor-intensive, it does affect convergence time, so it is advantageous to avoid unnecessary recomputations.

Protocol-dependent modules are responsible for network-layer protocol-specific requirements. The IP-Enhanced IGRP module, for example, is responsible for sending and receiving Enhanced IGRP packets that are encapsulated in IP. Likewise, IP-Enhanced IGRP is also responsible for parsing Enhanced IGRP packets and informing DUAL of the new information that has been received. IP-Enhanced IGRP asks DUAL to make routing decisions, the results of which are stored in the IP routing table. IP-Enhanced IGRP is responsible for redistributing routes learned by other IP routing protocols.

ROUTING CONCEPTS

Enhanced IGRP relies on four fundamental concepts: neighbor tables, topology tables, route states, and route tagging. Each of these is summarized in the discussions that follow.

Neighbor Tables

When a router discovers a new neighbor, it records the neighbor's address and interface as an entry in the *neighbor table*. One neighbor table exists for each protocol-dependent module. When a neighbor sends a hello packet, it advertises a hold time, which is the amount of time a router treats a neighbor as reachable and operational. If a hello packet is not received within the hold time, the hold time expires and DUAL is informed of the topology change.

The neighbor-table entry also includes information required by RTP. Sequence numbers are employed to match acknowledgments with data packets, and the last sequence number received from the neighbor is recorded so that out-of-order packets can be detected. A transmission list is used to queue packets for possible retransmission on a per-neighbor basis. Round-trip timers are kept in the neighbor-table entry to estimate an optimal retransmission interval.

Topology Tables

The *topology table* contains all destinations advertised by neighboring routers. The protocol-dependent modules populate the table, and the table is acted on by the DUAL finite-state machine. Each entry in the topology table includes the destination address and a list of neighbors that have advertised the destination. For each neighbor, the entry records the advertised metric, which the neighbor stores in its routing table. An important rule that distance vector protocols must follow is that if the neighbor advertises this destination, it must use the route to forward packets.

The metric that the router uses to reach the destination is also associated with the destination. The metric that the router uses in the routing table, and to advertise to other routers, is the sum of the best advertised metric from all neighbors, plus the link cost to the best neighbor.

Route States

A topology-table entry for a destination can exist in one of two states: active or passive. A destination is in the passive state when the router is not performing a recomputation, or in the active state when the router is performing a recomputation. If feasible successors are always available, a destination never has to go into the active state, thereby avoiding a recomputation.

A recomputation occurs when a destination has no feasible successors. The router initiates the recomputation by sending a query packet to each of its neighboring routers. The neighboring router can send a reply packet, indicating it has a feasible successor for the destination, or it can send a query packet, indicating that it is participating in the recomputation. While a destination is in the active state, a router cannot change the destination's routing-table information. After the router has received a reply from each neighboring router, the topology-table entry for the destination returns to the passive state, and the router can select a successor.

Route Tagging

Enhanced IGRP supports internal and external routes. Internal routes originate within an Enhanced IGRP AS. Therefore, a directly attached network that is configured to run Enhanced IGRP is considered an internal route and is propagated with this information throughout the Enhanced IGRP AS. External routes are learned by another routing protocol or reside in the routing table as static routes. These routes are tagged individually with the identity of their origin.

External routes are tagged with the following information:

- Router ID of the Enhanced IGRP router that redistributed the route
- AS number of the destination
- Configurable administrator tag
- ID of the external protocol
- Metric from the external protocol
- Bit flags for default routing

Route tagging allows the network administrator to customize routing and maintain flexible policy controls. Route tagging is particularly useful in transit ASs, where Enhanced IGRP typically interacts with an interdomain routing protocol that implements more global policies, resulting in a very scalable, policy-based routing.

ENHANCED IGRP PACKET TYPES

Enhanced IGRP uses the following packet types: hello and acknowledgment, update, and query and reply.

Hello packets are multicast for neighbor discovery/recovery and do not require acknowledgment. An *acknowledgment* packet is a hello packet that has no data. Acknowledgment packets contain a non-zero acknowledgment number and always are sent by using a unicast address.

Update packets are used to convey reachability of destinations. When a new neighbor is discovered, unicast update packets are sent so that the neighbor can build up its topology table. In other cases, such as a link-cost change, updates are multicast. Updates always are transmitted reliably.

Query and reply packets are sent when a destination has no feasible successors. *Query* packets are always multicast. Reply packets are sent in response to query packets to instruct the originator not to recompute the route because feasible successors exist. *Reply* packets are unicast to the originator of the query. Both query and reply packets are transmitted reliably.

CHAPTER 37

IBM Systems Network Architecture (SNA) Routing

BACKGROUND

IBM's networking architecture has evolved considerably as computing in general has evolved away from domination by centralized computing solutions to peer-based computing. Today, IBM Systems Network Architecture (SNA) routing involves two separate kinds of environments, although a number of key concepts are central to all SNA routing situations. This chapter addresses functions and services that make both SNA subarea routing and Advanced Peer-to-Peer Networking (APPN) routing possible. Topics covered include session connections, transmission groups, explicit and virtual routes, and class of service (COS). Refer to Chapter 29, "IBM Systems Network Architecture (SNA) Protocols," for general information about traditional IBM SNA and APPN. Figure 37–1 illustrates the concepts addressed in this chapter in the context of a traditional SNA environment.

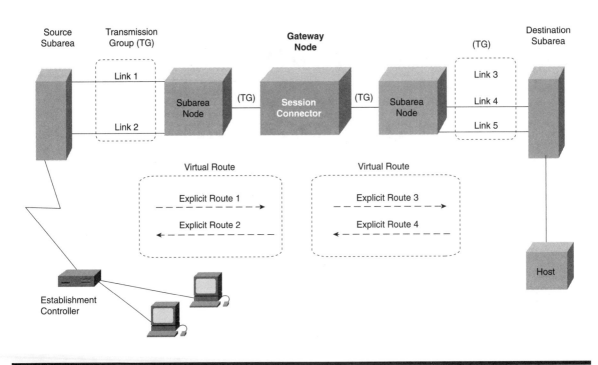

Figure 37–1
SNA routing relies on transmission groups to interconnect subarea entities.

IBM SNA SESSION CONNECTORS

IBM SNA session connectors are used to bridge address spaces when sessions traverse multiple address spaces. Three types of session connectors exist: *boundary functions*, *SNA network interconnection (SNI) gateways*, and *APPN intermediate routing functions*. Boundary functions reside in subarea nodes and map between subarea and peripheral address spaces. SNI gateways act as bridges between SNA networks, accepting data from one network and transmitting it to the appropriate destination in another network. SNI gateways are transparent to end point network attachment units (NAUs). APPN intermediate nodes perform intermediate routing within APPN networks.

Refer to Figure 37–1 for the relative position of a session connector in a traditional SNA environment.

IBM SNA Transmission Groups (TGs)

IBM SNA transmission groups (TGs) are logical connections formed between adjacent IBM SNA nodes that are used to pass SNA session traffic. TGs are comprised of one or more SNA links and their assigned transmission priorities. Multi-link TGs, which provide added reliability and bandwidth, are used to bundle multiple physical links into a single logical SNA link. Multi-link TGs are supported only between T4 nodes. TG sequence numbers are used to resequence out-of-order messages at each hop. Four transmission priorities are supported at each transmission group: low, medium, high, and network-service traffic (the highest priority). Refer to Figure 37–1 for an illustration of the relationship of TGs with respect to other common SNA routing components within the context of a subarea routing environment.

IBM SNA Explicit and Virtual Routes

Routes between subareas assume either an *explicit* or *virtual* route form. Explicit routes are the physical connections between two subarea nodes and serve as the ordered sequences of subareas and connecting transmission groups. Explicit routes are unidirectional, and two explicit routes are required to create a full-duplex path. Virtual routes are two-way logical connections formed between two subarea nodes. A virtual route flows over both an explicit route and a reverse explicit route that follows the same physical path. Virtual routes do not cross network boundaries; instead, they use an SNA network interconnect session connector to bridge two virtual routes. Virtual routes include values defining transmission priority and global flow control, which is provided by pacing, where a receiver with sufficient buffer space grants pacing windows to the sender. Each pacing window enables the sender to transmit a certain amount of information before the sender must request the next pacing window. Refer to Figure 37–1 for an illustration of the relationship between explicit routes and virtual routes, and their relative position in the context of an SNA subarea routing environment.

IBM SNA CLASS OF SERVICE (COS)

The IBM SNA class-of-service function designates the transport network characteristics of a given session. Depending on user requirements, different COSs can be specified in an SNA network. COS provides the mechanism to determine all SNA routes and describes acceptable service levels for a session. COS also specifies the collection of session characteristics, including response time, security, and availability. In addition, COS can be established automatically when logging in, or manually (by the user) when the session is initiated. Each COS name is associated with a list of virtual routes that meet the desired service-level requirement. Relevant information for a given session is captured in COS subarea and APPN tables. The differences between COS implementation in subarea and APPN routing are summarized in the following sections.

COS in Subarea Routing

In subarea routing, the user defines COS support required for a particular session. Specific virtual routes are mapped to identified services, while COS characteristics are associated with the underlying explicit routes. The *System Services Control Point* (SSCP) uses the COS table to provide information on virtual routes and transmission priority to the path-control function. Path control in turn selects a virtual route and transmission priority for use in a session. Figure 37–2 illustrates the subarea routing COS table-entry format.

Subarea routing COS table entries include COS *name, virtual-route number* (VRN), and *subarea transmission priority* (TRPI).

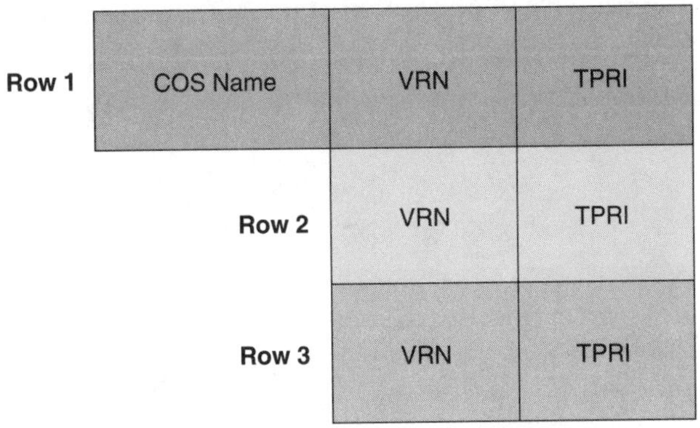

Row 1	COS Name	VRN	TPRI
Row 2		VRN	TPRI
Row 3		VRN	TPRI

Figure 37–2
A subarea routing COS table holds data on virtual routes and transmission priorities.

COS name is a standard name, such as SEC3, that is agreed upon by conventions.

The VRN identifies a specific route between subareas. Up to eight virtual-route numbers can be assigned between two subarea nodes. Each virtual route can be assigned with up to three different transmission priorities, and up to 24 virtual routes are possible between two subareas.

TPRI identifies the priority of logical unit-to-logical unit (LU-to-LU) session data flowing over an explicit route. Users can select one of three priorities for each virtual route: 0 (lowest), 1, or 2 (highest).

COS in APPN Routing

COS in APPN is defined explicitly with COS table parameters. COS is more granular in APPN than subarea SNA. In particular, COS for APPN allows a route to be defined based on capacity, cost, security, propagation delay, and user-defined characteristics. It extends service to end nodes (ENs) and is not limited to communications controllers, as in subarea SNA. APPN COS permits the topology database to maintain a tree for every COS that tracks all routes and costs. APPN COS also provides a configuration option to control memory dedicated to COS trees. Figure 37–3 illustrates the APPN routing COS table-entry format.

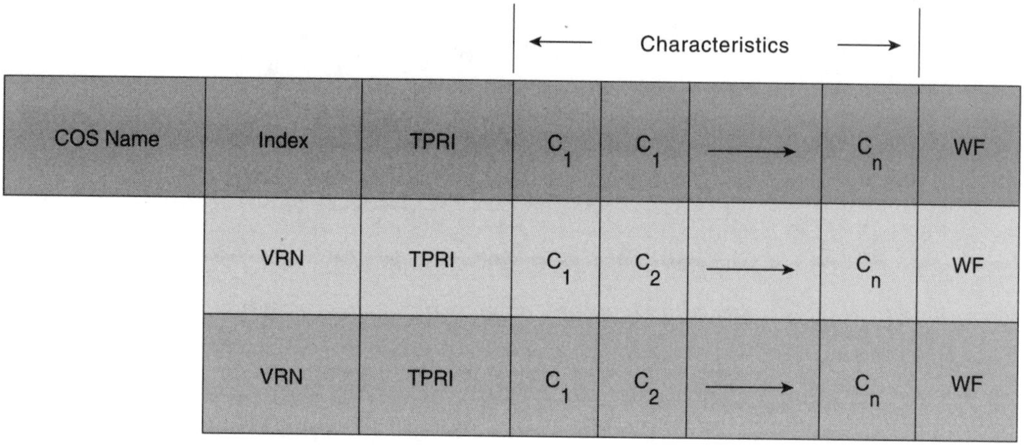

Figure 37–3
An APPN routing COS table can include special character returns and route weighting information.

APPN routing COS table entries include COS name, index, APPN Transmission Priority (TPRI), characteristics, and APPN COS Weighted Field (WF).

The COS name is a standard name, such as SEC3, that is agreed upon by conventions.

The index field entry enables computed weight values for route components to be stored and retrieved. This entry points to the entry in the COS weight array where the weights for the COS are stored.

APPN TPRI identifies the priority of LU-to-LU session data flowing over an explicit route. It specifies only one TPRI field for each COS table entry. APPN TPRI requires that traffic over a given session with the same COS in a particular APPN network flow with the same transmission priority.

Node and transmission group (TG) characteristics consist of a user-specified list of characteristics acceptable for identified COS. Each row defines either a set of node characteristics or a set of TG characteristics. Entries can include security, cost per connect time, and available capacity. The field representing a characteristic contains a range of acceptable values.

The APPN COS WF enables *routes-selection services* (RSS) to assign a weight to a given possible route component (node or TG). WF is used by RSS to determine relative desirability of a particular route component. The WF can contain a constant or the name of a function that RSS uses in weight calculation.

IBM SNA SUBAREA ROUTING

SNA logical areas and node addressing are two central components of traditional routing in SNA environments. This section addresses these topics in the context of traditional SNA networking.

SNA networks are divided into logical areas: *subareas* and *domains*. Subareas consist of a subarea node and its attached peripherals. Domains consist of a *system services control point* (SSCP) and the network resources that it can control. SSCPs in different domains can cooperate with one another to compensate for host processor failures. Figure 37–4 illustrates the relationship between subareas and domains in the context of SNA subarea routing.

Node addresses are categorized as *subarea-* and *peripheral-node addresses*. Subarea-node addresses are global and must be unique within the entire network. These addresses are assigned to NAUs when activated. Subarea-node addresses generally consist of a subarea portion and an element portion. All NAUs within a given subarea share the same subarea address but have different element addresses.

Peripheral-node addresses, which are considered local addresses, differ depending on whether the node is T2 or T2.1. T2 addresses refer to NAUs and are statically assigned, while T2.1 addresses are dynamically assigned for the duration of a session and identify the session rather than the NAU. Peripheral-node addresses are referred to as local form-session identifiers.

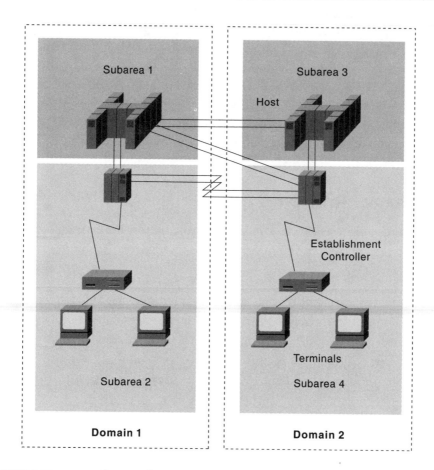

Figure 37–4
Subareas exist within domains in SNA subarea routing.

IBM ADVANCED PEER-TO-PEER NETWORKING (APPN) ROUTING

APPN routing is dynamic and is based on a least-weight path calculated from input received from all APPN network nodes. Each APPN network node is responsible for reporting changes in its local topology (that is, the node itself and the attached links). Topology information is passed until all APPN nodes receive it. When a node receives data it already has, it stops forwarding the data to other nodes. Duplicate information is recognized via a check of update sequence numbers. Figure 37–5 illustrates where APPN network nodes fit into the general scheme of an APPN environment with ENs and low-entry network (LEN) nodes.

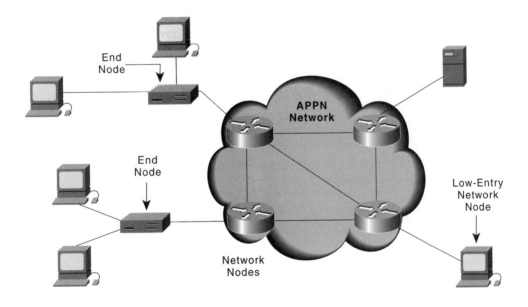

Figure 37–5
APPN network nodes link to ENs, LENs, and other network nodes.

Several underlying functions and capabilities enable APPN routing. These include Node Type 2.1 routing, Dependent Logical-Unit Requester/Server (DLUR/S) routing, connections networks, and border nodes.

IBM APPN Node Type 2.1 Routing

Node Type 2.1 routing involves routing traffic between one or more APPN network nodes. Two node Type 2.1 routing processes are supported: *Intermediate Session Routing* (ISR) and *High-Performance Routing* (HPR).

Intermediate Session Routing

The ISR process involves *bind session* BIND requests and responses flowing from network node to network node. In this environment, session connectors are built and used in place of routing tables in APPN. With ISR, a map is generated of the session identifier and port from one side of a node to the other. A unique session identifier in the session connector header is swapped for an outgoing identifier and then is sent out from the appropriate port.

ISR-supported subarea SNA features include node-to-node error and flow-control processing, as well as session switching around network failures. Node-to-node error and flow-control processing are considered redundant and unnecessary because these processes reduce end-to-end throughput.

High Performance Routing

The *High-Performance Routing* (HPR) protocol, an alternative to ISR, is based on two key components: *Rapid-Transport Protocol* (RTP) and *Automatic Network Routing* (ANR). RTP is a reliable, connection-oriented protocol that ensures delivery and manages end-to-end network error and flow control. RTP creates new routes following a network failure. ANR is a connectionless service that is responsible for node-to-node source-routed service.

The RTP layer is invoked only at the edges of an APPN network. In intermediate nodes, only the ANR layer is invoked. RTP nodes establish RTP connections to carry session data. All traffic for a single session flows over the same RTP-to-RTP connection and is multiplexed with traffic from other sessions using the same connection. Figure 37–6 illustrates the overall architecture of an HPR-based routing environment.

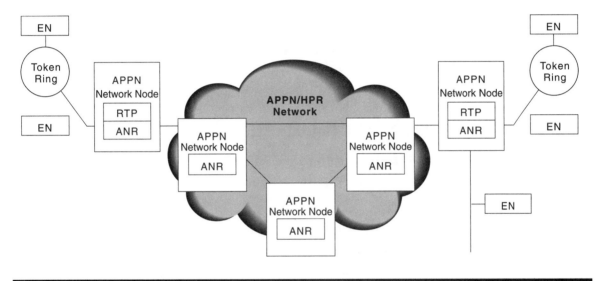

Figure 37–6
RTP is supported only in APPN edge network nodes.

A typical HPR routing process involves several stages. First, a route is selected while it is using ISR. To establish a connection between the edge RTP nodes, either an existing RTP-to-RTP connection is used or a Route-Services Request (RSR) is sent. The returned Route-Services Reply (RSP) carries information showing forward and reverse paths through the network.

Paths represent the forward and reverse port lists and include the port identifier used in each ANR node. These lists are carried on every message, eliminating the need for routing tables or session connectors in the ANR nodes.

HPR provides for link-failure recovery. If a link fails and an alternate path exists between the RTP end points for a particular COS, a new RTP-to RTP connection can be selected and a session can be moved without disruption. If a connection does not exist along the new path, RSR and RSP messages are sent to obtain the new port lists. Sending a new BIND is not required because the session is not disrupted.

Flow control in an HRP environment uses a technique called *adaptive rate-based (ARB)* flow control. ARB flow control monitors and controls the amount of traffic introduced into the network. Under ARB flow control, the sending and receiving RTP nodes exchange messages at regular intervals. Traffic introduced into the network is modified to adapt to network conditions.

IBM APPN DLUR/S Routing

The *Dependent Logical-Unit Requester/Server* (DLUR/S) is an APPN feature that allows legacy SNA traffic to flow on an APPN network.

Under DLUR/S, a client/server relationship is established between a *Dependent Logical-Unit Server* (DLUS) and a *Dependent Logical-Unit Requester (DLUR)*. A DLUS is typically an ACF/UTAM4.2 entity, a DLUR is typically a router. A pair of LU 6.2 sessions is established between the DLUR and DLUS. These LU 6.2 sessions transport legacy SNA control messages. Those messages not recognized in an APPN environment are encapsulated on the LU 6.2 session. Messages then are de-encapsulated by DLUR and passed to the legacy SNA LU. The DLU session initiation is then passed to the DLUS and is processed by the DLUS as legacy traffic. The DLUS sends a message to the application host, and the application host sends the BIND. Finally, legacy SNA data flows natively with APPN traffic.

IBM APPN Connection Network

An IBM APPN connection network is a logical construct used to provide direct connectivity between APPN ENs without the configuration overhead of defining direct connections between every pair of ENs. In general, the process of creating a connection network starts when a LOCATE request is received from an EN.

A network node (NN) then is used to locate the destination specified in the LOCATE request. If the NN sees that the two ENs (source and destination) are attached to the same transport medium (such as Token Ring), a *virtual node* (VN) is used to connect the two end points and form a connection network. The NN defines the session path as a direct connection from EN1 to VN to EN2, and then traffic is permitted to flow.

IBM APPN Border Node

A border node is an APPN entity that enables multiple APPN networks to interconnect. Presently, border nodes are implemented only in ACF/VTAM and OS/400. Border nodes are responsible for tying directories and topology databases together for connected networks and rebuilding BIND requests to show separate routes in each network.

With border nodes, topology and directory databases in NNs are reduced to sizes required for individual subnetworks rather than the composite network. In addition, cross-network sessions are routed through the border node. Figure 37–7 illustrates the position of border nodes (ACF/VTAM and OS/400 devices) in an multi-network APPN environment:

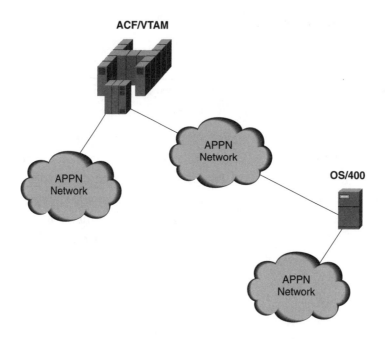

Figure 37–7
Border nodes (ACF/VTAM and OS/400 devices) can connect APPN networks.

CHAPTER 38

Interior Gateway Routing Protocol

BACKGROUND

The Interior Gateway Routing Protocol (IGRP) is a routing protocol that was developed in the mid-1980s by Cisco Systems, Inc. Cisco's principal goal in creating IGRP was to provide a robust protocol for routing within an autonomous system (AS).

In the mid-1980s, the most popular intra-AS routing protocol was the *Routing Information Protocol* (RIP). Although RIP was quite useful for routing within small- to moderate-sized, relatively homogeneous internetworks, its limits were being pushed by network growth. In particular, RIP's small hop-count limit (16) restricted the size of internetworks, and its single metric (hop count) did not allow for much routing flexibility in complex environments. The popularity of Cisco routers and the robustness of IGRP have encouraged many organizations with large internetworks to replace RIP with IGRP.

Cisco's initial IGRP implementation worked in Internet Protocol (IP) networks. IGRP was designed to run in any network environment, however, and Cisco soon ported it to run in OSI Connectionless-Network Protocol (CLNP) networks. Cisco developed Enhanced IGRP in the early 1990s to improve the operating efficiency of IGRP. This chapter discusses IGRP's basic design and implementation. Enhanced IGRP is discussed in Chapter 36, "Enhanced IGRP."

IGRP PROTOCOL CHARACTERISTICS

IGRP is a *distance-vector* interior gateway protocol (IGP). Distance-vector routing protocols call for each router to send all or a portion of its routing table in a routing-update message at regular intervals to each of its neighboring routers. As routing information proliferates through the network, routers can calculate distances to all nodes within the internetwork.

Distance-vector routing protocols are often contrasted with link-state routing protocols, which send local connection information to all nodes in the internetwork. For a discussion of *Open Shortest Path First* (OSPF) and *Intermediate System-to-Intermediate System* (IS-IS), two popular link-state routing algorithms, see Chapter 42, "Open Shortest Path First (OSPF)," and Chapter 41, "Open Systems Interconnection (OSI) Routing Protocol," respectively.

IGRP uses a combination (vector) of metrics. *Internetwork delay, bandwidth, reliability,* and *load* are all factored into the routing decision. Network administrators can set the weighting factors for each of these metrics. IGRP uses either the administrator-set or the default weightings to automatically calculate optimal routes.

IGRP provides a wide range for its metrics. Reliability and load, for example, can take on any value between 1 and 255; bandwidth can take on values reflecting speeds from 1,200 bps to 10 gigabits per second, while delay can take on any value from 1 to 2 to the 24th power. Wide metric ranges allow satisfactory metric setting in internetworks with widely varying performance characteristics. Most importantly, the metric components are combined in a user-definable algorithm. As a result, network administrators can influence route selection in an intuitive fashion.

To provide additional flexibility, IGRP permits multipath routing. Dual equal-bandwidth lines can run a single stream of traffic in round-robin fashion, with automatic switchover to the second line if one line goes down. Also, multiple paths can be used even if the metrics for the paths are different. If, for example, one path is three times better than another because its metric is three times lower, the better path will be used three times as often. Only routes with metrics that are within a certain range of the best route are used as multiple paths.

Stability Features

IGRP provides a number of features that are designed to enhance its stability. These include *hold-downs*, *split horizons*, and *poison-reverse updates*.

Hold-downs are used to prevent regular update messages from inappropriately reinstating a route that might have gone bad. When a router goes down, neighboring routers detect this via the lack of regularly scheduled update messages. These routers then calculate new routes and send routing update messages to inform their neighbors of the route change. This activity begins a wave of triggered updates that filter through the network. These triggered updates do not instantly arrive at every network device, so it is therefore possible for a device that has yet to be informed of a network failure to send a regular update message (indicating that a route that has just gone down is still good) to a device that has just been notified of the network failure. In this case, the latter device would contain (and potentially advertise) incorrect routing information. Hold-downs tell routers to hold down any changes that might affect routes for some period of time. The hold-down period usually is calculated to be just greater than the period of time necessary to update the entire network with a routing change.

Split horizons derive from the premise that it is never useful to send information about a route back in the direction from which it came. Figure 38–1 illustrates the split-horizon rule. Router 1 (R1) initially advertises that it has a route to Network A. There is no reason for Router 2 (R2) to include this route in its update back to R1 because R1 is closer to Network A. The split-horizon rule says that R2 should strike this route from any updates it sends to R1. The split-horizon rule helps prevent routing loops. Consider, for example, the case where R1's interface to Network A goes down. Without split horizons, R2 continues to inform R1 that it can get to Network A (through R1). If R1 does not have sufficient intelligence, it actually might pick up R2's route as an alternative to its failed direct connection, causing a routing loop. Although hold-downs should prevent this, split horizons are implemented in IGRP because they provide extra algorithm stability.

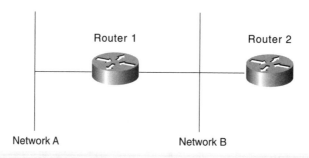

Figure 38–1

The split horizons rule helps protect against routing loops.

Split horizons should prevent routing loops between adjacent routers, but poison-reverse updates are necessary to defeat larger routing loops. Increases in routing metrics generally indicate routing loops. Poison-reverse updates then are sent to remove the route and place it in hold-down. In Cisco's implementation of IGRP, poison-reverse updates are sent if a route metric has increased by a factor of 1.1 or greater.

Timers

IGRP maintains a number of timers and variables containing time intervals. These include an update timer, an invalid timer, a hold-time period, and a flush timer. The *update* timer specifies how frequently routing update messages should be sent. The IGRP default for this variable is 90 seconds. The *invalid* timer specifies how long a router should wait in the absence of routing-update messages about a specific route before declaring that route invalid. The IGRP default for this variable is three times the update period. The *hold-time variable* specifies the hold-down period. The IGRP default for this variable is three times the update timer period plus 10 seconds. Finally, the *flush* timer indicates how much time should pass before a route should be flushed from the routing table. The IGRP default is seven times the routing update period.

CHAPTER 39

Internet Protocol (IP) Multicast

BACKGROUND

Internet Protocol (IP) multicast is a routing technique that allows IP traffic to be sent from one source or multiple sources and delivered to multiple destinations. Instead of sending individual packets to each destination, a single packet is sent to a multicast group, which is identified by a single IP destination group address. IP multicast routing arose because unicast and broadcast techniques do not handle the requirements of new applications efficiently. Multicast addressing, for example, supports the transmission of a single IP datagram to multiple hosts. This chapter focuses on the leading multicast routing options. Figure 39–1 illustrates the general nature of a multicast environment.

Figure 39–1
IP multicast provides a means to deliver high-bandwidth traffic to multiple destinations.

INTERNET GROUP-MEMBERSHIP PROTOCOL (IGMP)

A principle component of IP multicast is the Internet Group-Membership Protocol (IGMP). IGMP relies on Class D IP addresses for the creation of multicast groups and is defined in RFC 1112. IGMP is used to dynamically register individual hosts in a multicast group with a Class D address. Hosts identify group memberships by sending IGMP messages, and traffic is sent to all members of that multicast group. Under IGMP, routers listen to IGMP messages and periodically send out queries to discover which groups are active or inactive on particular LANs. Routers communicate with each other by using one or more protocols to build multicast routes for each group.

IP MULTICAST ROUTING PROTOCOLS

Several routing protocols are used to discover multicast groups and to build routes for each group. These include Protocol-Independent Multicast (PIM), Distance-Vector Multicast Routing Protocol (DVMRP), and Multicast Open Shortest Path First (MOSPF). The following table summarizes the unicast requirements needed and flooding algorithms used for each protocol. Table 39-1 summarizes the multicast routing option.

Protocol	Unicast Protocol Requirements	Flooding Algorithm
PIM-dense mode	Any	Reverse path flooding (RPF)
PIM-sparse mode	Any	RPF
DVMRP	Internal, RIP-like routing protocol	RPF
MOSPF	Open Shortest Path First (OSPF)	Shortest-path first (SPF)

Table 39-1
Summary of Multicast Routing Options

Protocol-Independent Multicast (PIM)

Protocol-Independent Multicast (PIM) is addressed in an Internet draft RFC (under discussion by the IETF Multicast Routing Working Group). It includes two different modes of behavior for dense and sparse traffic environments: *dense* mode and *sparse* mode.

The PIM dense mode uses a process of reverse path flooding that is similar to the DVMRP. Differences exist, however, between dense mode PIM and DVMRP. PIM, for example, does not require a particular unicast protocol to determine which interface leads back to the source of a data stream. DVMRP employs its own unicast protocol, while PIM uses whatever unicast protocol the internetwork is using.

The PIM sparse mode is optimized for internetworks with many data streams but relatively few LANs. It defines a rendezvous point that is then used as a registration point to facilitate the proper routing of packets.

When a sender wants to transmit data, the first-hop router (with respect to the source) node sends data to the rendezvous point. When a receiver wants to receive data, the last-hop router (with respect to the receiver) registers with the rendezvous point. A data stream then can flow from the sender to the rendezvous point and to the receiver. Routers in the path optimize the path and automatically remove any unnecessary hops, even at the rendezvous point.

Distance-Vector Multicast Routing Protocol (DVMRP)

The Distance-Vector Multicast Routing Protocol (DVMRP) uses a reverse path-flooding technique and is used as the basis for the Internet's multicast backbone (MBONE). DVMRP is defined in RFC 1075 and has certain some shortcomings. In particular, DVMRP is notorious for poor network scaling, resulting from reflooding, particularly with versions that do not implement pruning. DVMRP's flat unicast routing mechanism also affects its capability to scale.

The reverse path-flooding operation involves a router sending a copy of a packet out to all paths (except the path back to the origin) upon the packet's receipt. Routers then send a prune message back to the source to stop a data stream if the router is attached to a LAN that does not want to receive a particular multicast group.

Reflooding and *DVMRP unicast* are used in DVMRP path-flooding operations. In reflooding, DVMRP routers periodically reflood an attached network to reach new hosts. The flooding mechanism uses an algorithm that takes into account the frequency of flooding and the time required for a new multicast group member to receive the data stream. DVMRP unicast is used to determine which interface leads back to the source of a data stream. It is unique to DVMRP but is similar to RIP in that it is based on hop count. The

DVMRP unicast environment permits the use of a different path than the path used for multicast traffic.

Multicast Open Shortest Path First (MOSPF)

The Multicast Open Shortest Path First (MOSPF) is an extension of OSPF. In general, MOSPF employs a unicast routing protocol that requires each router in a network to be aware of all available links.

An MOSPF router calculates routes from the source to all possible group members for a particular multicast group. MOSPF routers include multicast information in OSPF link states. MOSPF calculates the routes for each source/multicast group pair when the router receives traffic for that pair, and routes are cached until a topology change occurs. MOSPF then recalculates the topology.

Several MOSPF implementation issues have been identified and require consideration. First, MOSPF works only in internetworks that use OSPF. In addition, MOSPF is best suited for environments with relatively few active source/group pairs. MOSPF can take up significant router CPU bandwidth in environments that have many active source/group pairs or that are unstable.

CHAPTER 40

NetWare Link-Services Protocol (NLSP)

BACKGROUND

The *NetWare Link-Services Protocol (NLSP)* is a link-state routing protocol from Novell designed to overcome some of the limitations associated with the IPX Routing Information Protocol (RIP) and its companion protocol, the Service Advertisement Protocol (SAP). NLSP is based on the OSI Intermediate System-to-Intermediate System (IS-IS) protocol and was designed to replace RIP and SAP, Novell's original routing protocols that were designed when internetworks were local and relatively small. As such, RIP and SAP are not well-suited for today's large, global internetworks. This chapter summarizes the routing processes and protocol components of NLSP.

As compared to RIP and SAP, NLSP provides improved routing, better efficiency, and scalability. In addition, NLSP-based routers are backward-compatible with RIP-based routers. NLSP-based routers use a reliable delivery protocol, so delivery is guaranteed. Furthermore, NLSP facilitates improved routing decisions because NLSP-based routers store a complete map of the network, not just next-hop information such as RIP-based routers use. Routing information is transmitted only when the topology has changed, not every 60 seconds as RIP-based routers do, regardless of whether the topology has changed. Additionally, NLSP-based routers send service-information updates only when services change, not every 60 seconds as SAP does.

NLSP is efficient in several ways. It is particularly useful over a WAN link because its support of IPX header compression makes it possible to reduce the size of packets. NLSP also supports multicast addressing so that routing information is sent only to other NLSP routers, not to all devices as RIP does.

In addition, NLSP supports load balancing across parallel paths and improves link integrity. It periodically checks links for connectivity and for the data integrity of routing information. If a link fails, NLSP switches to an alternate link and updates the network-topology databases stored in each node when connectivity changes occur anywhere in the routing area.

In terms of scalability, NLSP can support up to 127 hops (RIP supports only 15 hops) and permits hierarchical addressing of network nodes, which allows networks to contain thousands of LANs and servers.

NLSP Hierarchical Routing

NLSP supports hierarchal routing with area, domain, and global internetwork components. An area is a collection of connected networks that all have the same area address. A domain is a collection of areas that belong to the same organization. A global internetwork is a collection of domains that usually belong to different organizations but with an arms-length relationship. Areas can be linked to create routing domains, and domains can be linked to create a global internetwork.

NLSP supports three levels of hierarchical routing: *Level 1*, *Level 2*, and *Level 3* routing. A Level 1 router connects network segments within a given routing area. A Level 2 router connects areas and also acts as a Level 1 router within its own area. A Level 3 router connects domains and also acts as a Level 2 router within its own domain. Figure 40–1 illustrates the three routing levels NLSP defines.

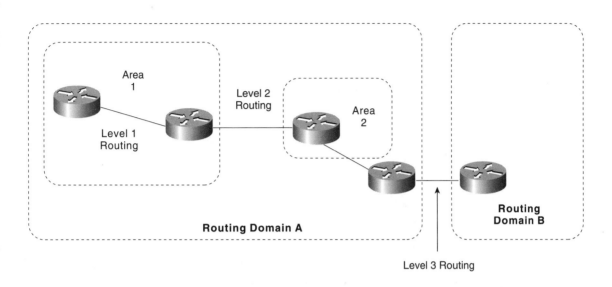

Figure 40-1
NLSP defines three routing levels.

Hierarchical Routing Efficiencies

Hierarchical routing simplifies the process of enlarging a network by reducing the amount of information that every router must store and process to route packets within a domain. A Level 1 router is required to keep detailed information only about its own area instead of storing link-state information for every router and network segment in its domain. To exchange traffic with other areas, a Level 1 router must only find the nearest Level 2 router. Between areas, Level 2 routers advertise the area address(es) only for their respective areas, not their entire link-state databases. Level 3 routers perform similarly between domains.

NLSP Adjacencies

By exchanging hello packets, a router determines the reachability of its neighbors and uses this information to establish adjacency. *Adjacency* is a record that a router keeps about the state of its connectivity with a neighbor and the attributes of the neighboring router. The router stores these records in its adjacency database.

Adjacency-establishment procedures vary depending upon whether the router is establishing and maintaining adjacencies over a WAN or a LAN.

Establishing router adjacency over a WAN involves first establishing the underlying data-link connection (details depend upon the medium). The routers then exchange identities by using the IPX WAN Version 2 protocol and determine certain operational characteristics of the link. Hello packets are exchanged and the routers update their adjacency databases. The routers then exchange both link-state packets (LSPs) describing the state of their links and IPX data packets over the link. To maintain a WAN link, the router maintains a state variable indicating whether the link is up, down, or initializing for each adjacency. If the router does not hear from a neighbor within the time specified in a holding timer, the router generates a message indicating that the link is down and deletes the adjacency.

WAN Hello packets enable routers to discover each other's identity, decide whether they are in the same routing area, and determine whether other routers and links are operational. A router sends Hello packets when the circuit is first established, when a timer expires, or when the contents of the next Hello to be transmitted are different than the contents of the previous Hello transmitted by this system (and one or more seconds have elapsed since the previous Hello). Hello packets are sent as long as the circuit exists.

Establishing a New WAN Adjacency

A typical startup procedure between two routers (A and B) on a WAN link begins with the link in the down state. Router A sends a WAN Hello indicating the down state to Router B, which changes its state for the link to Initializing. Router B sends a WAN Hello with a field indicating Initializing to Router A. Router A then changes its state for the link to initializing and sends a WAN Hello with a field indicating this to Router B. Router B changes its state for the link to the up state and sends a WAN Hello with a field indicating its new state. Finally, Router A changes its state for the link to Up.

Maintaining Adjacencies over LANs

When a broadcast circuit, such as an 802.3 Ethernet and 802.5 Token Ring, is enabled on a router, the router begins sending and accepting Hello packets from other routers on the LAN and starts the Designated Router election process.

The Designated Router represents the LAN as a whole in the link-state database, makes routing decisions on behalf of the whole, and originates LSPs on behalf of the LAN. This ensures that the size of the link-state databases that each router must construct and to manage to stay within reasonable limits.

Periodically, every router sends a multicast Hello packet on the LAN. The router with the highest priority (a configurable parameter) becomes the Level 1 Designated Router on the LAN. In case of a tie, the router with the higher MAC address wins.

Sending LAN Hello Packets

Hello packets enable routers on the broadcast circuit to discover the identity of the other Level 1 routers in the same routing area on that circuit. The packets are sent immediately when any circuit has been enabled to a special multicast destination address. Routers listen on this address for arriving Hello packets.

NLSP OPERATION

An NLSP router extracts certain information from the adjacency database and adds locally derived information. Using this information, the router constructs a link-state packet (LSP) that describes its immediate neighbors. All

LSPs constructed by all routers in the routing area make up the link-state database for the area.

The NLSP specification intends that each router maintain a copy of the link-state database and keep these copies synchronized with each other. The link-state database is synchronized by reliably propagating LSPs throughout the routing area when a router observes a topology change. Two methods ensure that accurate topology-change information is propagated: *flooding* and *receipt confirmation*.

Flooding is instigated when a router detects a topology change. When such a change is detected, the router constructs a new LSP and transmits it to each of its neighbors. Such LSPs are directed packets on a WAN and multicast packets on a LAN. Upon receiving an LSP, the router uses the sequence number in the packet to decide whether the packet is newer than the current copy stored in its database. If it is a newer LSP, the router retransmits it to all its neighbors (except on the circuit over which the LSP was received).

The receipt-confirmation process is different for LANs and WANs. On WANs, a router receiving an LSP replies with an acknowledgment. On LANs, no explicit acknowledgment occurs, but the Designated Router periodically multicasts a packet called a complete sequence number packet (CSNP) that contains all the LSP identifiers and sequence numbers it has in its database for the entire area. This ensures that other routers can detect whether they are out of synchronization with the Designated Router.

NLSP HIERARCHICAL ADDRESSING

NLSP supports a hierarchical addressing scheme. Each routing area is identified by two 32-bit quantities: a *network address* and a *mask*. This pair of numbers is called an *area address*. Expressed in hexadecimal, an example of an area address follows:

- 01234500—This number is the network address for this routing area. Every network number within that area starts with the identification code 012345.

- FFFFFF00—This number is the mask that identifies how much of the network address refers to the area itself and how much refers to individual networks within the area.

In the example area address above, the first 24 bits (012345) identify the routing area. The remaining 8 bits are used to identify individual network numbers within the routing area (for example, 012345AB, 012345C1, 01234511). Figure 40–2 highlights the above addressing concepts with three different networks in a single area.

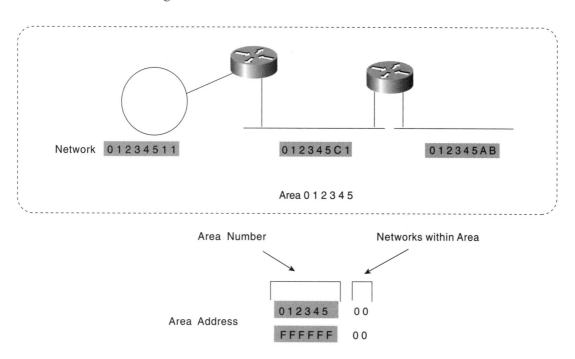

Figure 40–2
NLSP addresses consist of a network address and a mask.

A routing area can have as many as three different area addresses, each with a different mask. Having more than one area address allows the routing area to be reorganized without interrupting operations. Any combination of area addresses can be used within a domain.

NLSP HELLO PACKETS

Two types of NLSP Hello packets exist: WAN Hello and Level 1 LAN Hello packets.

WAN Hello Packet

Figure 40–3 illustrates the fields of a WAN Hello packet.

WAN Hello Packet Fields

The following WAN hello packet field descriptions summarize each field illustrated in Figure 40-3.

- *Protocol ID*—Identifies the NLSP routing layer with the 0x83 hex number.

- *Length Indicator*—Determines the number of bytes in the fixed portion of the header.

- *Minor Version*—Contains 1 possible decimal value and is ignored on receipt.

- *Reserved*—Contains no decimal values and is ignored on receipt.

- *Packet Type (5 bits)*—Contains 17 possible decimal values.

- *Major Version*—Contains 1 possible decimal value.

- *Reserved*—Contains no decimal values and is ignored on receipt.

- *State (2 bits)*—Sends the router's state associated with the link (0 = Up, 1 = Initializing, 2 = Down).

WAN Hello	Number of Bytes
Protocol ID	1
Length Indicator	1
Minor Version	1
Reserved	1
Reserved / Packet Type	1
Major Version	1
Reserved	2
Reserved / State / Cct Type	1
Source ID	6
Holding Time	2
Packet Length	2
Local WAN Circuit ID	1
Variable Length Fields	Variable

Figure 40–3
Fourteen fields make up a WAN Hello packet.

- *Circuit Type (Cct type)*—Consists of 2 bits. This field can have one of the following values:

  ○ 0 = Reserved value, ignore entire packet
  ○ 1 = Level 1 routing only

- ○ 2 = Level 2 routing only (sender uses this link for Level 2 routing)
- ○ 3 = Both Level 1 and Level 2 (sender is a Level 2 router and uses this link for Level 1 and Level 2 traffic)

- *Source ID*—Serves as the system identifier of the sending router.

- *Holding Time*—Contains the holding timer, in seconds, to be used for the sending router.

- *Packet Length*—Determines the entire length of the packet, in bytes, including the NLSP header.

- *Local WAN Circuit ID*—Acts as a unique identifier assigned to this circuit when it is created by the router.

- *Variable Length Field*—Consists of a series of optional fields.

NLSP LAN Hello Packets

Figure 40–4 illustrates the fields of a LAN Level 1 Hello packet.

Level 1 LAN Hello Packet Fields

The following Level 1 LAN Hello packet field descriptions summarize each field illustrated in Figure 40-4:

- *Protocol ID*—Identifies the NLSP routing layer with the 0x83 hex number.

- *Length Indicator*—Determines the number of bytes in the fixed portion of the header (up to and including the LAN ID field).

- *Minor Version*—Contains 1 possible decimal value and is ignored on receipt.

- *Reserved*—Contains no possible decimal values and is ignored on receipt.

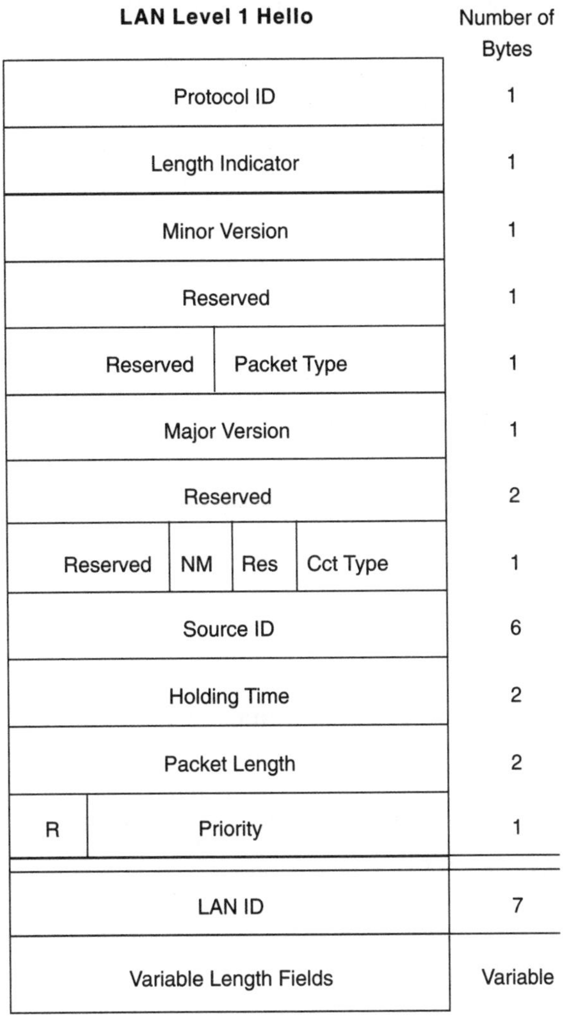

LAN Level 1 Hello

Field	Number of Bytes
Protocol ID	1
Length Indicator	1
Minor Version	1
Reserved	1
Reserved / Packet Type	1
Major Version	1
Reserved	2
Reserved / NM / Res / Cct Type	1
Source ID	6
Holding Time	2
Packet Length	2
R / Priority	1
LAN ID	7
Variable Length Fields	Variable

Figure 40–4

A LAN Level 1 Hello packet consists of 16 fields.

- *Packet Type* (5 bits)—Contains 15 possible decimal values.
- *Major Version*—Contains 1 possible decimal value.

- *Reserved*—Contains no possible decimal values and is ignored on receipt.

- *No Multicast (NM) (1 bit)*—Indicates, when set to 1, that the packet sender cannot receive traffic addressed to a multicast address. (Future packets on this LAN must be sent to the broadcast address.)

- *Circuit Type (Cct Type) (2 bits)*—Can have one of the following values:

  ○ 0 = Reserved value, ignore entire packet
  ○ 1 = Level 1 routing only
  ○ 2 = Level 2 routing only (sender uses this link for Level 2 routing)
  ○ 3 = Both Level 1 and Level 2 (sender is a Level 2 router and uses this link for Level 1 and Level 2 traffic)

- *Source ID*—Contains the system ID of the sending router.

- *Holding Time*—Contains the holding timer, in seconds, to be used for the sending router.

- *Packet Length*—Determines the entire length of the packet, in bytes, including the NLSP header.

- *R*—Contains no possible decimal values and is ignored on receipt.

- *Priority (7 bits)*—Serves as the priority associated with being the LAN Level 1 Designated Router. (Higher numbers have higher priority.)

- *LAN ID*—Contains the system ID (6 bytes) of the LAN Level 1 Designated Router, followed by a field assigned by that Designated Router.

- *Variable Length Fields*—Consists of a series of optional fields.

CHAPTER 41

Open Systems Interconnection (OSI) Routing Protocol

BACKGROUND

The International Organization for Standardization (ISO) developed a complete suite of routing protocols for use in the Open Systems Interconnection (OSI) protocol suite. These include *Intermediate System-to-Intermediate Systems* (IS-IS), *End System-to-Intermediate System* (ES-IS), and *Interdomain Routing Protocol* (IDRP). This chapters addresses the basic operations of each of these protocols.

IS-IS is based on work originally done at Digital Equipment Corporation (Digital) for DECnet/OSI (DECnet Phase V). IS-IS originally was developed to route in ISO *Connectionless Network Protocol* (CLNP) networks. A version has since been created that supports both CLNP and *Internet Protocol* (IP) networks; this version usually is referred to as *Integrated IS-IS* (it also has been called *Dual IS-IS)*.

OSI routing protocols are summarized in several ISO documents, including ISO 10589, which defines IS-IS. The American National Standards Institute (ANSI) X3S3.3 (network and transport layers) committee was the motivating force behind ISO standardization of IS-IS. Other ISO documents include ISO 9542 (which defines ES-IS) and ISO 10747 (which defines IDRP).

OSI Networking Terminology

The world of OSI networking uses some specific terminology, such as *end system* (ES), which refers to any nonrouting network nodes, and *intermediate system* (IS), which refers to a router. These terms form the basis for the ES-IS and IS-IS OSI protocols. The ES-IS protocol enables ESs and ISs to discover each other. The IS-IS protocol provides routing between ISs. Other important OSI networking terms include *area*, *domain*, *Level 1 routing*, and *Level 2 routing*. An area is a group of contiguous networks and attached hosts that is specified to be an area by a network administrator or manager. A domain is a collection of connected areas. Routing domains provide full connectivity to all end systems within them. Level 1 routing is routing within a Level 1 area, while Level 2 routing is routing between Level 1 areas. Figure 41–1 illustrates the relationship between areas and domains and depicts the levels of routing between the two.

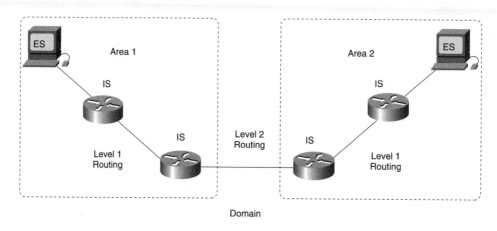

Figure 41–1

Areas exist within a larger domain and use Level 2 routing to communicate.

END SYSTEM-TO-INTERMEDIATE SYSTEM (ES-IS)

End System-to-Intermediate System (ES-IS) is an OSI protocol that defines how end systems (hosts) and intermediate systems (routers) learn about each other, a process known as *configuration*. Configuration must happen before routing between ESs can occur.

ES-IS is more of a *discovery* protocol than a routing protocol. It distinguishes between three different types of subnetworks: *point-to-point subnetworks*, *broadcast subnetworks*, and *general-topology subnetworks*. Point-to-point subnetworks, such as WAN serial links, provide a point-to-point link between two systems. Broadcast subnetworks, such as Ethernet and IEEE 802.3, direct a single physical message to all nodes on the subnetwork. General-topology subnetworks, such as X.25, support an arbitrary number of systems. Unlike broadcast subnetworks, however, the cost of an *n*-way transmission scales directly with the subnetwork size on a general-topology subnetwork. Figure 41–2 illustrates the three types of ES-IS subnetworks.

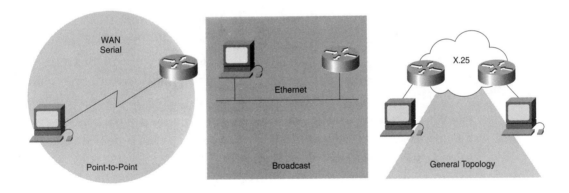

Figure 41–2
ES-IS can be deployed in point-to-point, broadcast, and general topology subnetworks.

ES-IS Configuration

ES-IS configuration is the process whereby ESs and ISs discover each other so that routing between ESs can occur. ES-IS configuration information is transmitted at regular intervals through two types of messages: *ES hello messages* (ESHs) and *IS hello messages* (ISHs). ESHs are generated by ESs and sent to every IS on the subnetwork. ISHs are generated by ISs and sent to all ESs on the subnetwork. These hello messages primarily are intended to convey the subnetwork and network-layer addresses of the systems that generate them. Where possible, ES-IS attempts to send configuration information simultaneously to many systems. On broadcast subnetworks, ES-IS hello messages are sent to all ISs through a special multicast address that designates all end systems. When operating on a general-topology subnetwork, ES-IS generally does not transmit configuration information because of the high cost of multicast transmissions.

ES-IS Addressing Information

The ES-IS configuration protocol conveys both OSI network-layer and OSI subnetwork addresses. OSI network-layer addresses identify either the network service-access point (NSAP), which is the interface between OSI Layer 3 and Layer 4, or the network entity title (NET), which is the network-layer entity in an OSI IS. OSI subnetwork addresses, or *subnetwork point-of-attachment addresses* (SNPAs) are the points at which an ES or IS is physically attached to a subnetwork. The SNPA address uniquely identifies each system attached to the subnetwork. In an Ethernet network, for example, the SNPA is the 48-bit Media-Access Control (MAC) address. Part of the configuration information transmitted by ES-IS is the NSAP-to-SNPA or NET-to-SNPA mapping.

INTERMEDIATE SYSTEM-TO-INTERMEDIATE SYSTEM (IS-IS)

Intermediate System-to-Intermediate System (IS-IS) is an OSI link-state hierarchical routing protocol that floods the network with link-state information to build a complete, consistent picture of network topology. To simplify router design and operation, IS-IS distinguishes between Level 1 and Level 2 ISs. Level 1 ISs communicate with other Level 1 ISs in the same area. Level 2 ISs route between Level 1 areas and form an intradomain routing backbone. Hierarchical routing simplifies backbone design because Level 1 ISs only need to know how to get to the nearest Level 2 IS. The backbone routing protocol also can change without impacting the intra-area routing protocol.

OSI Routing Operation

Each ES lives in a particular area. OSI routing begins when the ESs discovers the nearest IS by listening to ISH packets. When an ES wants to send a packet to another ES, it sends the packet to one of the ISs on its directly attached network. The router then looks up the destination address and forwards the packet along the best route. If the destination ES is on the same subnetwork, the local IS will know this from listening to ESHs and will forward the packet appropriately. The IS also might provide a *redirect* (RD) message back to the source to tell it that a more direct route is available. If the destination address is an ES on another subnetwork in the same area, the IS will know the correct route and will forward the packet appropriately. If the destination address is an ES in another area, the Level 1 IS sends the packet to the nearest Level 2 IS. Forwarding through Level 2 ISs continues until the packet reaches a Level 2 IS in the destination area. Within the destination area, ISs forward the packet along the best path until the destination ES is reached.

Link-state update messages help ISs learn about the network topology. First, each IS generates an update specifying the ESs and ISs to which it is connected, as well as the associated metrics. The update then is sent to all neighboring ISs, which forward (flood) it to their neighbors, and so on. (Sequence numbers terminate the flood and distinguish old updates from new ones.) Using these updates, each IS can build a complete topology of the network. When the topology changes, new updates are sent.

IS-IS Metrics

IS-IS uses a single required default metric with a maximum path value of 1,024. The metric is arbitrary and typically is assigned by a network administrator. Any single link can have a maximum value of 64, and path links are calculated by summing link values. Maximum metric values were set at these levels to provide the granularity to support various link types while at the same time ensuring that the shortest-path algorithm used for route computation will be reasonably efficient. IS-IS also defines three optional metrics (costs): delay, expense, and error. The delay cost metric reflects the amount of delay on the link. The expense cost metric reflects the communications cost associated with using the link. The error cost metric reflects the error rate of the link. IS-IS maintains a mapping of these four metrics to the *quality-of-service* (QoS) option in the CLNP packet header. IS-IS uses these mappings to compute routes through the internetwork.

IS-IS Packet Formats

IS-IS uses three basic packet formats: *IS-IS hello packets, link-state packets* (LSPs), and *sequence-numbers packets (SNPs)*. Each of the three IS-IS packets has a complex format with the following three different logical parts. The first part consists of an 8-byte fixed header shared by all three packet types. The second part is a packet-type-specific portion with a fixed format. The third part is also packet-type-specific but of variable length. Figure 41–3 illustrates the logical format of IS-IS packets. Figure 41–4 shows the common header fields of the IS-IS packets.

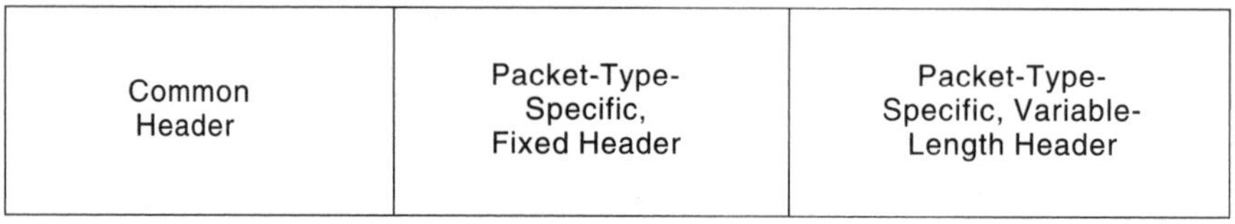

Common Header	Packet-Type-Specific, Fixed Header	Packet-Type-Specific, Variable-Length Header

Figure 41–3
IS-IS packets consist of three logical headers.

Field Length,
in Bytes

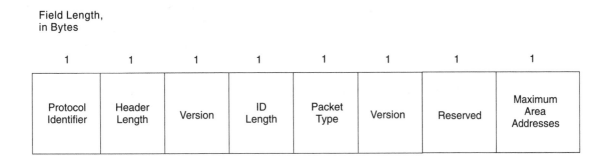

Figure 41–4
IS-IS packets consist of eight fields.

The following descriptions summarize the fields illustrated in Figure 41-4:

- *Protocol Identifier*—Identifies the IS-IS protocol and contains the constant 131.

- *Header Length*—Contains the fixed header length. The length always is equal to 8 bytes but is included so that IS-IS packets do not differ significantly from CLNP packets.

- *Version*—Contains a value of 1 in the current IS-IS specification.

- *ID Length*—Specifies the size of the ID portion of an NSAP address. If the field contains a value between 1 and 8 inclusive, the ID portion of an NSAP address is that number of bytes. If the field contains a value of zero, the ID portion of an NSAP address is 6 bytes. If the field contains a value of 255 (all ones), the ID portion of an NSAP address is zero bytes.

- *Packet Type*—Specifies the type of IS-IS packet (hello, LSP, or SNP).

- *Version*—Repeats after the packet type field.

- *Reserved*—Is ignored by the receiver and is equal to 0.

- *Maximum Area Addresses*—Specifies the number of addresses permitted in this area.

Following the common header, each packet type has a different additional fixed portion, followed by a variable portion.

INTEGRATED IS-IS

Integrated IS-IS is a version of the OSI IS-IS routing protocol that uses a single routing algorithm to support more network-layer protocols than just CLNP. Integrated IS-IS sometimes is called Dual IS-IS, named after a version designed for IP and CLNP networks. Several fields are added to IS-IS packets to allow IS-IS to support additional network layers. These fields inform routers about the reachability of network addresses from other protocol suites and other information required by a specific protocol suite. Integrated IS-IS implementations send only one set of routing updates, which is more efficient than two separate implementations.

Integrated IS-IS represents one of two ways of supporting multiple network-layer protocols in a router; the other is the *ships-in-the-night* approach. Ships-in-the-night routing advocates the use of a completely separate and distinct routing protocol for each network protocol so that the multiple routing protocols essentially exist independently. Essentially, the different types of routing information pass like ships in the night. Integrated routing has the capability to route multiple network-layer protocols through tables calculated by a single routing protocol, thus saving some router resources. Integrated IS-IS uses this approach.

INTERDOMAIN ROUTING PROTOCOL (IDRP)

The Interdomain Routing Protocol is an OSI protocol that specifies how routers communicate with routers in different domains. IDRP is designed to operate seamlessly with CLNP, ES-IS, and IS-IS. IDRP is based on the Border

Gateway Protocol (BGP), an interdomain routing protocol that originated in the IP community. IDRP features include the following:

- Support for CLNP quality of service (QOS)

- Loop suppression by keeping track of all RDs traversed by a route

- Reduction of route information and processing by using confederations, the compression of RD path information, and other means

- Reliability by using a built-in reliable transport

- Security by using cryptographic signatures on a per-packet basis

- Route servers

IDRP Terminology

IDRP introduces several environment-specific terms. These include *border intermediate system* (BIS), *routing domain* (RD), *routing-domain identifier* (RDI), *routing-information base* (RIB), and *confederation*. A BIS is an IS that participates in interdomain routing and, as such, uses IDRP. An RD is a group of ESs and ISs that operate under the same set of administrative rules and share a common routing plan. An RDI is a unique RD identifier. A RIB is a routing database used by IDRP that is built by each BIS from information received from within the RD and from other BISs. A RIB contains the set of routes chosen for use by a particular BIS. A confederation is a group of RDs that appears to RDs outside the confederation as a single RD. The confederation's topology is not visible to RDs outside the confederation. Confederations must be nested within one another and help reduce network traffic by acting as internetwork firewalls. Figure 41–5 illustrates the relationship between IDRP entities.

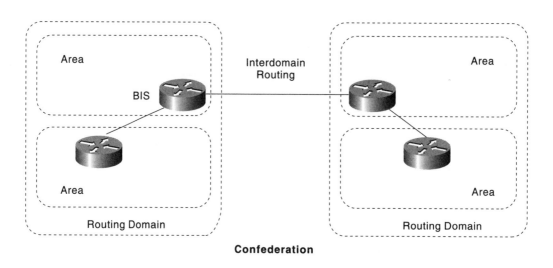

Figure 41–5
Domains communicate via border intermediate systesm (BISs).

IDRP Routing

An IDRP route is a sequence of RDIs, some of which can be confederations. Each BIS is configured to know the RD and the confederations to which it belongs. It learns about other BISs, RDs, and confederations through information exchanges with each neighbor. As with distance-vector routing, routes to a particular destination accumulate outward from the destination. Only routes that satisfy a BIS's local policies and have been selected for use will be passed on to other BISs. Route recalculation is partial and occurs when one of three events occurs: an incremental routing update with new routes is received, a BIS neighbor goes down, or a BIS neighbor comes up.

CHAPTER 42

Open Shortest Path First (OSPF)

BACKGROUND

Open Shortest Path First (OSPF) is a routing protocol developed for Internet Protocol (IP) networks by the interior gateway protocol (IGP) working group of the Internet Engineering Task Force (IETF). The working group was formed in 1988 to design an IGP based on the shortest path first (SPF) algorithm for use in the Internet. Similar to the Interior Gateway Routing Protocol (IGRP), OSPF was created because in the mid-1980s, the Routing Information Protocol (RIP) was increasingly unable to serve large, heterogeneous internetworks. This chapter examines the OSPF routing environment, underlying routing algorithm, and general protocol components.

OSPF was derived from several research efforts, including Bolt, Beranek, Newman's (BBN's) SPF algorithm developed in 1978 for the ARPANET (a landmark packet-switching network developed in the early 1970s by BBN), Dr. Radia Perlman's research on fault-tolerant broadcasting of routing information (1988), BBN's work on area routing (1986), and an early version of OSI's Intermediate System-to-Intermediate System (IS-IS) routing protocol.

OSPF has two primary characteristics. The first is that the protocol is open, which means that its specification is in the public domain. The OSPF specification is published as Request For Comments (RFC) 1247. The second principal characteristic is that OSPF is based on the SPF algorithm, which sometimes is referred to as the *Dijkstra* algorithm, named for the person credited with its creation.

OSPF is a *link-state* routing protocol that calls for the sending of *link-state advertisements* (LSAs) to all other routers within the same hierarchical area. Information on attached interfaces, metrics used, and other variables is included in OSPF LSAs. As OSPF routers accumulate link-state information, they use the SPF algorithm to calculate the shortest path to each node.

As a link-state routing protocol, OSPF contrasts with RIP and IGRP, which are distance-vector routing protocols. Routers running the distance-vector algorithm send all or a portion of their routing tables in routing-update messages to their neighbors.

ROUTING HIERARCHY

Unlike RIP, OSPF can operate within a hierarchy. The largest entity within the hierarchy is the *autonomous system* (AS), which is a collection of networks under a common administration that share a common routing strategy. OSPF is an intra-AS (interior gateway) routing protocol, although it is capable of receiving routes from and sending routes to other ASs.

An AS can be divided into a number of *areas*, which are groups of contiguous networks and attached hosts. Routers with multiple interfaces can participate in multiple areas. These routers, which are called *area border routers*, maintain separate topological databases for each area.

A *topological database* is essentially an overall picture of networks in relationship to routers. The topological database contains the collection of LSAs received from all routers in the same area. Because routers within the same area share the same information, they have identical topological databases.

The term *domain* sometimes is used to describe a portion of the network in which all routers have identical topological databases. Domain is frequently used interchangeably with AS.

An area's topology is invisible to entities outside the area. By keeping area topologies separate, OSPF passes less routing traffic than it would if the AS were not partitioned.

Area partitioning creates two different types of OSPF routing, depending on whether the source and destination are in the same or different areas. Intra-area routing occurs when the source and destination are in the same area; interarea routing occurs when they are in different areas.

An OSPF *backbone* is responsible for distributing routing information between areas. It consists of all area border routers, networks not wholly contained in any area, and their attached routers. Figure 42–1 shows an example of an internetwork with several areas.

In the figure, Routers 4, 5, 6, 10, 11, and 12 make up the backbone. If Host H1 in Area 3 wants to send a packet to Host H2 in area 2, the packet is sent to Router 13, which forwards the packet to Router 12, which sends the packet to Router 11. Router 11 then forwards the packet along the backbone to area border Router 10, which sends the packet through two intra-area routers (Router 9 and Router 7) to be forwarded to Host H2.

The backbone itself is an OSPF area, so all backbone routers use the same procedures and algorithms to maintain routing information within the backbone that any area router would. The backbone topology is invisible to all intra-area routers, as are individual area topologies to the backbone.

Areas can be defined in such a way that the backbone is not contiguous. In this case, backbone connectivity must be restored through *virtual links*. *Virtual links* are configured between any backbone routers that share a link to a nonbackbone area and function as if they were direct links.

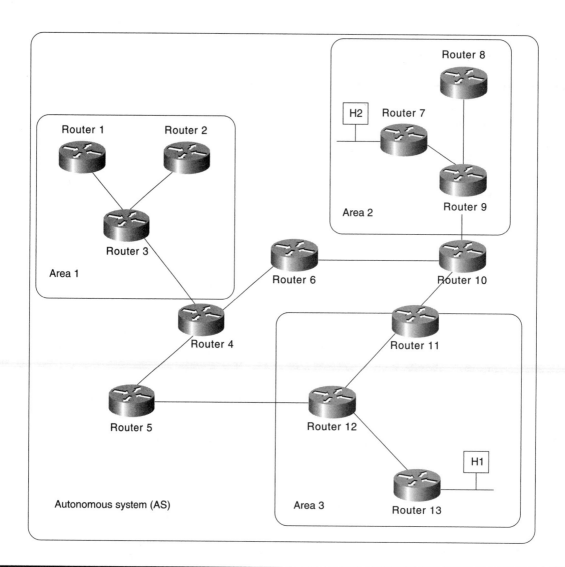

Figure 42–1

An OSPF AS consists of multiple areas linked by routers.

AS border routers running OSPF learn about exterior routes through exterior gateway protocols (EGPs), such as Exterior Gateway Protocol (EGP) or Border Gateway Protocol (BGP), or through configuration information. For more information about these protocols, see Chapter 35, "Border Gateway Protocol (BGP)."

SPF ALGORITHM

The shortest path first (SPF) routing algorithm is the basis for OSPF operations. When an SPF router is powered up, it initializes its routing-protocol data structures and then waits for indications from lower-layer protocols that its interfaces are functional.

After a router is assured that its interfaces are functioning, it uses the OSPF Hello protocol to acquire *neighbors*, which are routers with interfaces to a common network. The router sends hello packets to its neighbors and receives their hello packets. In addition to helping acquire neighbors, hello packets also act as keep-alives to let routers know that other routers are still functional.

On *multiaccess networks* (networks supporting more than two routers), the Hello protocol elects a *designated router* and a backup designated router. Among other things, the designated router is responsible for generating LSAs for the entire multiaccess network. Designated routers allow a reduction in network traffic and in the size of the topological database.

When the link-state databases of two neighboring routers are synchronized, the routers are said to be *adjacent*. On multiaccess networks, the designated router determines which routers should become adjacent. Topological databases are synchronized between pairs of adjacent routers. Adjacencies control the distribution of routing-protocol packets, which are sent and received only on adjacencies.

Each router periodically sends an LSA to provide information on a router's adjacencies or to inform others when a router's state changes. By comparing established adjacencies to link states, failed routers can be detected quickly and the network's topology altered appropriately. From the topological database generated from LSAs, each router calculates a shortest-path tree, with itself as root. The shortest-path tree, in turn, yields a routing table.

PACKET FORMAT

All OSPF packets begin with a 24-byte header, as illustrated in Figure 42–2.

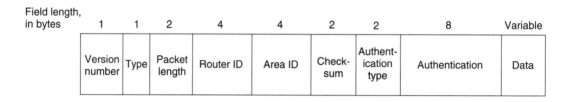

Figure 42–2
OSPF packets consist of nine fields.

The following descriptions summarize the header fields illustrated in figure 42-2.

- *Version Number*—Identifies the OSPF version used.

- *Type*—Identifies the OSPF packet type as one of the following:

  ○ Hello: Establishes and maintains neighbor relationships.
  ○ Database Description: Describes the contents of the topological database. These messages are exchanged when an adjacency is initialized.
  ○ Link-state Request: Requests pieces of the topological database from neighbor routers. These messages are exchanged after a router discovers (by examining database-description packets) that parts of its topological database are out of date.
  ○ Link-state Update: Responds to a link-state request packet. These messages also are used for the regular dispersal of LSAs. Several LSAs can be included within a single link-state update packet.

- ○ Link-state Acknowledgment: Acknowledges link-state update packets.

- *Packet Length*—Specifies the packet length, including the OSPF header, in bytes.

- *Router ID*—Identifies the source of the packet.

- *Area ID*—Identifies the area to which the packet belongs. All OSPF packets are associated with a single area.

- *Checksum*—Checks the entire packet contents for any damage suffered in transit.

- *Authentication Type*—Contains the authentication type. All OSPF protocol exchanges are authenticated. The Authentication Type is configurable on per-area basis.

- *Authentication*—Contains authentication information.

- *Data*—Contains encapsulated upper-layer information.

ADDITIONAL OSPF FEATURES

Additional OSPF features include *equal-cost, multipath routing,* and routing based on upper-layer *type-of-service* (TOS) requests. TOS-based routing supports those upper-layer protocols that can specify particular types of service. An application, for example, might specify that certain data is urgent. If OSPF has high-priority links at its disposal, these can be used to transport the urgent datagram.

OSPF supports one or more metrics. If only one metric is used, it is considered to be arbitrary, and TOS is not supported. If more than one metric is used, TOS is optionally supported through the use of a separate metric (and, therefore, a separate routing table) for each of the eight combinations created by the three IP TOS bits (the *delay, throughput,* and *reliability* bits). If, for example, the IP TOS bits specify low delay, low throughput, and high reliability, OSPF calculates routes to all destinations based on this TOS designation.

IP subnet masks are included with each advertised destination, enabling *variable-length subnet masks*. With variable-length subnet masks, an IP network can be broken into many subnets of various sizes. This provides network administrators with extra network-configuration flexibility.

CHAPTER 43

Resource Reservation Protocol (RSVP)

BACKGROUND

The Resource Reservation Protocol (RSVP) is a network-control protocol that enables Internet applications to obtain special qualities of service (QoSs) for their data flows. RSVP is not a routing protocol; instead, it works in conjunction with routing protocols and installs the equivalent of dynamic access lists along the routes that routing protocols calculate. RSVP occupies the place of a transport protocol in the OSI model seven-layer protocol stack. RSVP originally was conceived by researchers at the University of Southern California (USC) Information Sciences Institute (ISI) and Xerox Palo Alto Research Center. The Internet Engineering Task Force (IETF) is now working toward standardization through an RSVP working group. RSVP operational topics discussed in this chapter include data flows, quality of service, session startup, reservation style, and soft state implementation. Figure 43–1 illustrates an RSVP environment.

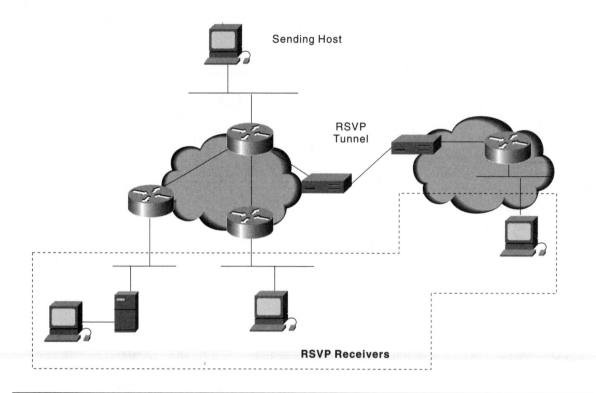

Figure 43-1
In RSVP, host information is delivered to receivers over data flows.

RSVP DATA FLOWS

In RSVP, a data flow is a sequence of messages that have the same source, destination (one or more), and quality of service. QoS requirements are communicated through a network via a *flow specification*, which is a data structure used by internetwork hosts to request special services from the internetwork. A flow specification often guarantees how the internetwork will handle some of its host traffic.

RSVP supports three traffic types: *best-effort*, *rate-sensitive*, and *delay-sensitive*. The type of data-flow service used to support these traffic types depends on QoS implemented. The following sections address these traffic types and associated services. For information regarding QoS, refer to the appropriate section later in this chapter.

Best-effort traffic is traditional IP traffic. Applications include file transfer, such as mail transmissions, disk mounts, interactive logins, and transaction traffic. The service supporting best-effort traffic is called *best-effort service*.

Rate-sensitive traffic is willing to give up timeliness for guaranteed rate. Rate-sensitive traffic, for example, might request 100 kbps of bandwidth. If it actually sends 200 kbps for an extended period, a router can delay traffic. Rate-sensitive traffic is not intended to be run over a circuit-switched network; however, it usually is associated with an application that has been ported from a circuit-switched network (such as ISDN) and is running on a datagram network (IP).

An example of such an application is H.323 videoconferencing, which is designed to run on ISDN (H.320) or ATM (H.310) but is found on the Internet. H.323 encoding is a constant rate or nearly constant rate, and it requires a constant transport rate. The RSVP service supporting rate-sensitive traffic is called *guaranteed bit-rate service*.

Delay-sensitive traffic is traffic that requires timeliness of delivery and varies its rate accordingly. MPEG-II video, for example, averages about 3 to 7 Mbps depending on the amount of change in the picture. As an example, 3 Mbps might be a picture of a painted wall, although 7 Mbps would be required for a picture of waves on the ocean. MPEG-II video sources send key and delta frames. Typically, one or two key frames per second describe the whole picture, and 13 or 28 frames describe the change from the key frame. Delta frames are usually substantially smaller than key frames. As a result, rates vary quite a bit from frame to frame. A single frame, however, requires delivery within a frame time or the CODEC is unable to do its job. A specific priority must be negotiated for delta-frame traffic. RSVP services supporting delay-sensitive traffic are referred to as *controlled-delay service* (non-real time service) and *predictive service* (real-time service).

RSVP Data Flows Process

RSVP data flows are generally characterized by *sessions*, over which data packets flow. A session is a set of data flows with the same unicast or multicast destination, and RSVP treats each session independently. RSVP supports both unicast and multicast sessions (where a session is some number of senders talking to some number of receivers), whereas a flow always originates with a single sender. Data packets in a particular session are directed to the same IP destination address or a generalized destination port. The IP destination address can be the group address for multicast delivery or the unicast address of a single receiver. A generalized destination port can be defined by a UDP/TCP destination port field, an equivalent field in another transport protocol, or some application-specific information.

RSVP data distribution is handled via either multicasts or unicasts. Multicast traffic involves a copy of each data packet forwarded from a single sender toward multiple destinations. Unicast traffic features a session involving a single receiver. Even if the destination address is unicast, there might be multiple receivers, distinguished by a generalized port. Multiple senders also might exist for a unicast destination, in which case, RSVP can set up reservations for multipoint-to-point transmission.

Each RSVP sender and receiver can correspond to a unique Internet host. A single host, however, can contain multiple logical senders and receivers, distinguished by generalized ports.

RSVP QUALITY OF SERVICE (QoS)

In the context of RSVP, quality of service (QoS) is an attribute specified in flow specifications that is used to determine the way in which data interchanges are handled by participating entities (routers, receivers, and senders). RSVP is used to specify the QoS by both hosts and routers. Hosts use RSVP to request a QoS level from the network on behalf of an application data stream. Routers use RSVP to deliver QoS requests to other routers along the path(s) of the data stream. In doing so, RSVP maintains the router and host state to provide the requested service.

RSVP SESSION START-UP

To initiate an RSVP multicast session, a receiver first joins the multicast group specified by an IP destination address by using the Internet Group-Membership Protocol (IGMP). In the case of a unicast session, unicast routing serves the function that IGMP, coupled with Protocol-Independent Multicast (PIM), serves in the multicast case. After the receiver joins a group, a potential sender starts sending RSVP path messages to the IP destination address. The receiver application receives a path message and starts sending appropriate reservation-request messages specifying the desired flow descriptors using RSVP. After the sender application receives a reservation-request message, the sender starts sending data packets.

RSVP RESERVATION STYLE

Reservation style refers to a set of control options that specify a number of supported parameters. RSVP supports two major classes of reservation: *distinct reservations* and *shared reservations*. Distinct reservations install a flow for each relevant sender in each session. A shared reservation is used by a set of senders that are known not to interfere with each other. Figure 43–2 illustrates distinct and shared RSVP reservation-style types in the context of their scope. Each supported reservation style/scope combination is described following the illustration.

Wildcard-Filter (WF) Style

The *wildcard-filter (WF) style* specifies a shared reservation with a wildcard scope. With a WF-style reservation, a single reservation is created into which flows from all upstream senders are mixed. Reservations can be thought of as a shared pipe whose size is the largest of the resource requests for that link from all receivers, independent of the number of senders. The reservation is propagated upstream toward all sender hosts and is automatically extended to new senders as they appear.

Scope	Reservations	
	Distinct	Shared
Explicit	Fixed-Filter (FF) Style	Shared-Explicit (SE) Style
Wildcard	None Defined	Wildcard-Filter (WF) Style

Figure 43–2
RSVP supports both distinct reservations and shared reservations.

Fixed-Filter (FF) Style

The *fixed-filter (FF) style* specifies a distinct reservation with an explicit scope. With an FF-style reservation, a distinct reservation request is created for data packets from a particular sender. The reservation scope is determined by an explicit list of senders. The total reservation on a link for a given session is the total of the FF reservations for all requested senders. FF reservations that are requested by different receivers but select the same sender, however, must be merged to share a single reservation in a given node.

Shared-Explicit (SE) Style

The *shared-explicit (SE) style* reservation specifies a shared reservation environment with an explicit reservation scope. The SE style creates a single reservation into which flows from all upstream senders are mixed. As in the case of an FF reservation, the set of senders (and therefore the scope) is specified explicitly by the receiver making the reservation.

RSVP Reservation Style Implications

WF and SE are both shared reservations that are appropriate for multicast applications in which application-specific constraints make it unlikely that multiple data sources will transmit simultaneously. An example might be audio-conferencing, where a limited number of people talk at once. Each receiver might issue a WF or SE reservation request twice for one audio channel (to allow some over-speaking). The FF style creates independent reservations for the flows from different senders. The FF style is more appropriate for video signals. Unfortunately, it is not possible to merge shared reservations with distinct reservations.

RSVP Soft State Implementation

In the context of an RSVP, a *soft state* refers to a state in routers and end nodes that can be updated by certain RSVP messages. The soft state characteristic permits an RSVP network to support dynamic group membership changes and adapt to changes in routing. In general, the soft state is maintained by an RSVP-based network to enable the network to change states without consultation with end points. This contrasts with a circuit-switch architecture in which an end point places a call and, in the event of a failure, places a new call.

RSVP protocol mechanisms provide a general facility for creating and maintaining a distributed reservation state across a mesh of multicast and unicast delivery paths.

To maintain a reservation state, RSVP tracks a soft state in router and host nodes. The RSVP soft state is created and periodically refreshed by path and reservation-request messages. The state is deleted if no matching refresh messages arrive before the expiration of a cleanup timeout interval. The soft state also can be deleted as the result of an explicit teardown message. RSVP periodically scans the soft state to build and forward path and reservation-request refresh messages to succeeding hops.

When a route changes, the next path message initializes the path state on the new route. Future reservation-request messages establish a reservation state. The state on the now-unused segment is timed out. (The RSVP specification requires initiation of new reservations through the network two seconds after a topology change.)

When state changes occur, RSVP propagates those changes from end to end within an RSVP network without delay. If the received state differs from the stored state, the stored state is updated. If the result modifies the refresh messages to be generated, refresh messages are generated and forwarded immediately.

RSVP OPERATIONAL MODEL

Under RSVP, resources are reserved for simple data streams (that is, unidirectional data flows). Each sender is logically distinct from a receiver, but any application can act as a sender and receiver. Receivers are responsible for requesting resource reservations. Figure 43–3 illustrates this general operational environment, while the subsequent section provides an outline of the specific sequence of events.

General RSVP Protocol Operation

The RSVP resource-reservation process initiation begins when an RSVP daemon consults the local routing protocol(s) to obtain routes. A host sends IGMP messages to join a multicast group and RSVP messages to reserve resources along the delivery path(s) from that group. Each router that is capable of participating in resource reservation passes incoming data packets to a packet classifier and then queues them as necessary in a packet scheduler. The RSVP packet classifier determines the route and QoS class for each packet.

The RSVP scheduler allocates resources for transmission on the particular data link layer medium used by each interface. If the data link layer medium has its own QoS management capability, the packet scheduler is responsible for negotiation with the data-link layer to obtain the QoS requested by RSVP.

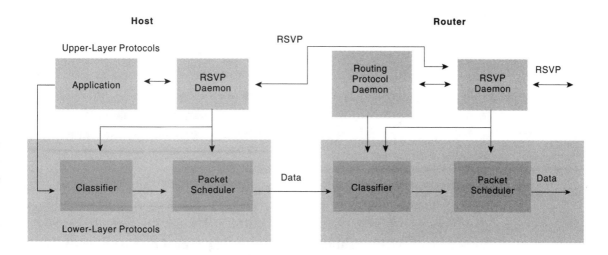

Figure 43–3
The RSVP operational environment reserves resources for unidirectional data flows.

The scheduler itself allocates packet-transmission capacity on a QoS-passive medium, such as a leased line, and also can allocate other system resources, such as CPU time or buffers. A QoS request, typically originating in a receiver host application, is passed to the local RSVP implementation as an RSVP daemon.

The RSVP protocol then is used to pass the request to all the nodes (routers and hosts) along the reverse data path(s) to the data source(s). At each node, the RSVP program applies a local decision procedure called admission control to determine whether it can supply the requested QoS. If admission control succeeds, the RSVP program sets the parameters of the packet classifier and scheduler to obtain the desired QoS. If admission control fails at any node, the RSVP program returns an error indication to the application that originated the request.

RSVP Tunneling

It is impossible to deploy RSVP or any new protocol at the same moment throughout the entire Internet. Indeed, RSVP might never be deployed everywhere. RSVP therefore must provide correct protocol operation even when two RSVP-capable routers are joined by an arbitrary cloud of non-RSVP routers. An intermediate cloud that does not support RSVP is unable to perform resource reservation, so service guarantees cannot be made. If, however, such a cloud has sufficient excess capacity, it can provide acceptable and useful real-time service.

To support connection of RSVP networks through non-RSVP networks, RSVP supports tunneling, which occurs automatically through non-RSVP clouds. Tunneling requires RSVP and non-RSVP routers to forward path messages toward the destination address by using a local routing table. When a path message traverses a non-RSVP cloud, the path-message copies carry the IP address of the last RSVP-capable router. Reservation-request messages are forwarded to the next upstream RSVP-capable router.

Two arguments have been offered in defense of implementing tunneling in an RSVP environment. First, RSVP will be deployed sporadically rather than universally. Second, by implementing congestion control in situations known to be highly congested, tunneling can be made more effective.

Sporadic, or piecemeal, deployment means that some parts of the network will actively implement RSVP before others parts. If RSVP is required end to end, no benefit is achievable without nearly universal deployment, which is unlikely unless early deployment shows substantial benefits.

Weighted Fair-Queuing Solution

Having the technology to enforce effective resource reservation (such as Cisco's weighted fair-queuing scheme) in a location that presents a bottleneck can have real positive effects. Tunneling presents a risk only when the bottleneck is within a non-RSVP domain and the bottleneck cannot be avoided. Figure 43–4 illustrates an RSVP environment featuring a tunnel between RSVP-based networks.

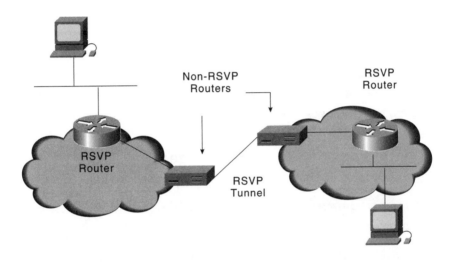

Figure 43–4
An RSVP environment can feature a tunnel between RSVP-based networks.

RSVP MESSAGES

RSVP supports four basic message types: *reservation-request messages, path messages, error* and *confirmation messages,* and *teardown messages.* Each of these is described briefly in the sections that follow.

Reservation-Request Messages

A reservation-request message is sent by each receiver host toward the senders. This message follows in reverse the routes that the data packets use, all the way to the sender hosts. A reservation-request message must be delivered to the sender hosts so that the hosts can set up appropriate traffic-control parameters for the first hop. RSVP does not send any positive acknowledgment messages.

Path Messages

An RSVP path message is sent by each sender forward along the unicast or multicast routes provided by the routing protocol(s). A path message is used to store the path state in each node. The path state is used to route reservation-request messages in the reverse direction.

Error and Confirmation Messages

Three error and confirmation message forms exist: *path-error* messages, *reservation-request error* messages, and *reservation-request acknowledgment* messages.

Path-error messages result from path messages and travel toward senders. Path-error messages are routed hop-by-hop using the path state. At each hop, the IP destination address is the unicast address of the previous hop.

Reservation-request error messages result from reservation-request messages and travel toward the receiver. Reservation-request error messages are routed hop-by-hop using the reservation state. At each hop, the IP destination address is the unicast address of the next-hop node. Information carried in error messages can include the following:

- Admission failure

- Bandwidth unavailable

- Service not supported

- Bad flow specification

- Ambiguous path

Reservation-request acknowledgment messages are sent as the result of the appearance of a reservation-confirmation object in a reservation-request message. This acknowledgment message contains a copy of the reservation confirmation. An acknowledgment message is sent to the unicast address of a receiver host, and the address is obtained from the reservation-confirmation object. A reservation-request acknowledgment message is forwarded to the receiver hop-by-hop (to accommodate the hop-by-hop integrity-check mechanism).

Teardown Messages

RSVP teardown messages remove the path and reservation state without waiting for the cleanup timeout period. Teardown messages can be initiated by an application in an end system (sender or receiver) or a router as the result of state timeout. RSVP supports two types of teardown messages: *path-teardown* messages and *reservation-request teardown* messages. Path-teardown messages delete the path state (which deletes the reservation state), travel toward all receivers downstream from the point of initiation, and are routed like path messages. Reservation-request teardown messages delete the reservation state, travel toward all matching senders upstream from the point of teardown initiation, and are routed like corresponding reservation-request messages.

RSVP PACKET FORMAT

Figure 43–5 illustrates the RSVP packet format. The summaries that follow outline the header and object fields illustrated in Figure 43-5.

RSVP Message Header Fields

Field Length,
in Bits

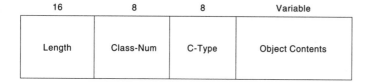

RSVP Object Fields

Field Length,
in Bits

16	8	8	Variable
Length	Class-Num	C-Type	Object Contents

Figure 43–5
An RSVP packet format consists of message headers and object fields.

RSVP Message Header Fields

RSVP message-header fields are comprised of the following:

- *Version*—4-bit field indicating the protocol version number (currently version 1).

- *Flags*—4-bit field with no flags currently defined.

- *Type*—8-bit field with 6 possible (integer) values, as shown in table 43-1.

- *Checksum*—16-bit field representing a standard TCP/UDP checksum over the contents of the RSVP message, with the checksum field replaced by zero.

Value	Message Type
1	Path
2	Reservation-request
3	Path-error
4	Reservation-request error
5	Path-teardown
6	Reservation-teardown
7	Reservation-request acknowledgment

Table 43–1
RSVP Message Type Field Values

- *Length*—16-bit field representing the length of this RSVP packet in bytes, including the common header and the variable-length objects that follow. If the More Fragment (MF) flag is set or the fragment offset field is non-zero, this is the length of the current fragment of a larger message.

- *Send TTL*—8-bit field indicating the IP time-to-live (TTL) value with which the message was sent.

- *Message ID*—32-bit field providing a label shared by all fragments of one message from a given next/previous RSVP hop.

- *More Fragments (MF) Flag*—Low-order bit of a 1-byte word with the other 7 high-order bits specified as reserved. MF is set on for all but the last fragment of a message.

- *Fragment Offset*—24-bit field representing the byte offset of the fragment in the message

RSVP Object Fields

RSVP object fields are comprised of the following:

- *Length*—16-bit field containing the total object length in bytes (must always be a multiple of 4 and be at least 4).

- *Class-Num*—Identifies the object class. Each object class has a name. An RSVP implementation must recognize the classes listed in Table 43-2.

The high-order bit of the Class-Num determines what action a node should take if it does not recognize the Class-Num of an object.

- *C-Type*—Object type, unique within Class-Num. The maximum object content length is 65528 bytes. Class-Num and C-Type fields (together with the flag bit) can be used together as a 16-bit number to define a unique type for each object.

- *Object Contents*—The Length, Clas-Num, and C-Type fields specify the form of the object content. Refer to Table 43-2 for definitions of the classes of objects that can be included in the object contents.

Object Class	Description
Null	Contains a Class-Num of zero, and its C-Type is ignored. Its length must be at least 4 but can be any multiple of 4. A null object can appear anywhere in a sequence of objects, and its contents will be ignored by the receiver.
Session	Contains the IP destination address and possibly a generalized destination port to define a specific session for the other objects that follow (required in every RSVP message).
RSVP Hop	Carries the IP address of the RSVP-capable node that sent this message.
Time Values	If present, contains values for the refresh period and the state TTL to override the default values.
Style	Defines the reservation style plus style-specific information that is not a flow-specification or filter-specification object (included in a reservation-request message).
Flow Specification	Defines a desired QoS (included in a reservation-request message).
Filter Specification	Defines a subset of session-data packets that should receive the desired QoS (specified by a flow-specification object within a reservation-request message).
Sender Template	Contains a sender IP address and perhaps some additional demultiplexing information to identify a sender (included in a path message).
Sender TSPEC	Defines the traffic characteristics of a sender's data stream (included in a path message).
Adspec	Carries advertising data in a path message.
Error Specification	Specifies an error (included in a path-error or reservation-request error message).
Policy Data	Carries information that will enable a local policy module to decide whether an associated reservation is administratively permitted (included in a path or reservation-request message).
Integrity	Contains cryptographic data to authenticate the originating node and perhaps to verify the contents of this reservation-request message.
Scope	An explicit specification of the scope for forwarding a reservation-request message.
Reservation Confirmation	Carries the IP address of a receiver that requested a confirmation. Can appear in either a reservation-request or reservation-request acknowledgment.

Table 43–2
RSVP Object Classes

CHAPTER 44

Routing Information Protocol (RIP)

BACKGROUND

The Routing Information Protocol (RIP) is a distance-vector protocol that uses hop count as its metric. RIP is widely used for routing traffic in the global Internet and is an *interior gateway protocol* (IGP), which means that it performs routing within a single autonomous system. Exterior gateway protocols, such as the Border Gateway Protocol (BGP), perform routing between different autonomous systems. The original incarnation of RIP was the Xerox protocol, GWINFO. A later version, known as *routed* (pronounced "route dee"), shipped with Berkeley Standard Distribution (BSD) Unix in 1982. RIP itself evolved as an Internet routing protocol, and other protocol suites use modified versions of RIP. The AppleTalk Routing Table Maintenance Protocol (RTMP) and the Banyan VINES Routing Table Protocol (RTP), for example, both are based on the Internet Protocol (IP) version of RIP. The latest enhancement to RIP is the RIP 2 specification, which allows more information to be included in RIP packets and provides a simple authentication mechanism.

IP RIP is formally defined in two documents: Request For Comments (RFC) 1058 and 1723. RFC 1058 (1988) describes the first implementation of RIP, while RFC 1723 (1994) updates RFC 1058. RFC 1058 enables RIP messages to carry more information and security features.

This chapter summarizes the basic capabilities and features associated with RIP. Topics include the routing-update process, RIP routing metrics, routing stability, and routing timers.

ROUTING UPDATES

RIP sends routing-update messages at regular intervals and when the network topology changes. When a router receives a routing update that includes changes to an entry, it updates its routing table to reflect the new route. The metric value for the path is increased by one, and the sender is indicated as the next hop. RIP routers maintain only the best route (the route with the lowest metric value) to a destination. After updating its routing table, the router immediately begins transmitting routing updates to inform other network routers of the change. These updates are sent independently of the regularly scheduled updates that RIP routers send.

RIP ROUTING METRIC

RIP uses a single routing metric (hop count) to measure the distance between the source and a destination network. Each hop in a path from source to destination is assigned a hop-count value, which is typically 1. When a router receives a routing update that contains a new or changed destination-network entry, the router adds one to the metric value indicated in the update and enters the network in the routing table. The IP address of the sender is used as the next hop.

RIP prevents routing loops from continuing indefinitely by implementing a limit on the number of hops allowed in a path from the source to a destination. The maximum number of hops in a path is 15. If a router receives a routing update that contains a new or changed entry, and if increasing the metric

value by one causes the metric to be infinity (that is, 16), the network destination is considered unreachable.

RIP STABILITY FEATURES

To adjust for rapid network-topology changes, RIP specifies a number of stability features that are common to many routing protocols. RIP, for example,
implements the split-horizon and hold-down mechanisms to prevent incorrect
routing information from being propagated. In addition, the RIP hop-count
limit prevents routing loops from continuing indefinitely.

RIP TIMERS

RIP uses numerous timers to regulate its performance. These include a
routing-update timer, a *route timeout*, and a *route-flush timer*. The routing-update timer clocks the interval between periodic routing updates. Generally, it is set to 30 seconds, with a small random number of seconds added
each time the timer is reset to prevent collisions. Each routing-table entry has
a route-timeout timer associated with it. When the route-timeout timer
expires, the route is marked invalid but is retained in the table until the
route-flush timer expires.

PACKET FORMATS

The following section focuses on the IP RIP and IP RIP 2 packet formats illustrated in Figures 44–1 and 44–2. Each illustration is followed by descriptions
of the fields illustrated.

RIP Packet Format

Figure 44–1 illustrates the IP RIP packet format.

Field Length,
in Bytes

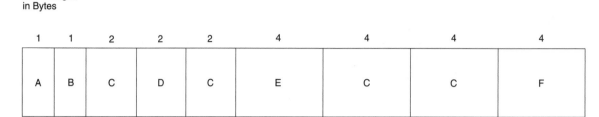

A = Command
B = Version Number
C = Zero
D = Address Family Identifier
E = Address
F = Metric

Figure 44–1

An IP RIP packet consists of nine fields.

The following descriptions summarize the IP RIP packet-format fields illustrated in Figure 44–1:

- *Command*—Indicates whether the packet is a request or a response. The request asks that a router send all or part of its routing table. The response can be an unsolicited regular routing update or a reply to a request. Responses contain routing table entries. Multiple RIP packets are used to convey information from large routing tables.

- *Version Number*—Specifies the RIP version used. This field can signal different potentially incompatible versions.

- *Zero*—Not used.

- *Address-Family Identifier (AFI)*—Specifies the address family used. RIP is designed to carry routing information for several different protocols. Each entry has an address-family identifier to indicate the type of address being specified. The AFI for IP is 2.

- *Address*—Specifies the IP address for the entry.

- *Metric*—Indicates how many internetwork hops (routers) have been traversed in the trip to the destination. This value is between 1 and 15 for a valid route, or 16 for an unreachable route.

NOTES

Up to 25 occurrences of the AFI, address, and metric fields are permitted in a single IP RIP packet. (Up to 25 destinations can be listed in a single RIP packet.)

RIP 2 Packet Format

The RIP 2 specification (described in RFC 1723) allows more information to be included in RIP packets and provides a simple authentication mechanism. Figure 44–2 shows the IP RIP 2 packet format.

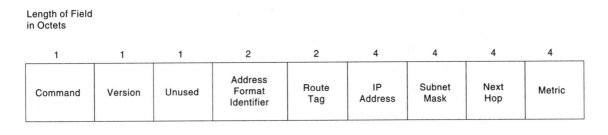

Figure 44–2
An IP RIP 2 packet consists of fields similar to those of an IP RIP packet.

The following descriptions summarize the IP RIP 2 packet format fields illustrated in figure 44–2:

- *Command*—Indicates whether the packet is a request or a response. The request asks that a router send all or a part of its routing table. The response can be an unsolicited regular routing update or a reply to a request. Responses contain routing-table entries. Multiple RIP packets are used to convey information from large routing tables.

- *Version*—Specifies the RIP version used. In a RIP packet implementing any of the RIP 2 fields or using authentication, this value is set to 2.

- *Unused*—Value set to zero.

- *Address-Family Identifier (AFI)*—Specifies the address family used. RIP is designed to carry routing information for several different protocols. Each entry has an address-family identifier to indicate the type of address specified. The address-family identifier for IP is 2. If the AFI for the first entry in the message is 0xFFFF, the remainder of the entry contains authentication information. Currently, the only authentication type is simple password.

- *Route Tag*—Provides a method for distinguishing between internal routes (learned by RIP) and external routes (learned from other protocols).

- *IP Address*—Specifies the IP address for the entry.

- *Subnet Mask*—Contains the subnet mask for the entry. If this field is zero, no subnet mask has been specified for the entry.

- *Next Hop*—Indicates the IP address of the next hop to which packets for the entry should be forwarded.

- *Metric*—Indicates how many internetwork hops (routers) have been traversed in the trip to the destination. This value is between 1 and 15 for a valid route, or 16 for an unreachable route.

NOTES

Up to 25 occurrences of the AFI, address, and metric fields are permitted in a single IP RIP packet. That is, up to 25 routing table entries can be listed in a single RIP packet. If the AFI specifies an authenticated message, only 24 routing table entries can be specified.

CHAPTER 45

Simple Multicast Routing Protocol (SMRP)

BACKGROUND

The *Simple Multicast Routing Protocol (SMRP)* is a transport-layer protocol developed to route multimedia data streams over AppleTalk networks. It supports Apple Computer's QuickTime Conferencing (QTC) technology. SMRP provides connectionless, best-effort delivery of multicast datagrams and relies on underlying network-layer protocols for services. In particular, SMRP facilitates the transmission of data from a single source to multiple destinations. This chapter focuses on the functional elements and protocol operations of SMRP. Figure 45–1 illustrates a generalized SMRP environment.

In creating SMRP, Apple borrowed a number of strategies and concepts from other protocols and technologies. In doing so, many terms were adapted to have specific meanings in Apple's SMRP environment. Table 45–1 provides a summary of SMRP-specific terms and definitions. These terms are used throughout this chapter.

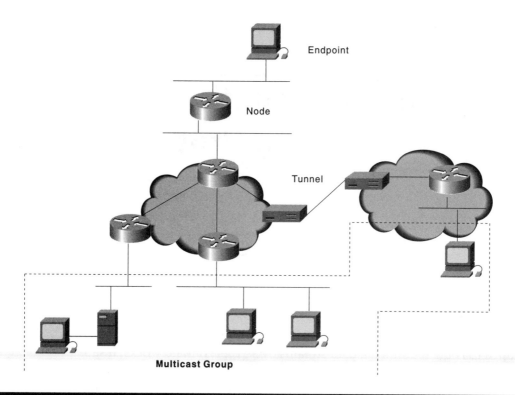

Figure 45–1
A generalized SMRP environment runs from a multicast group to an endpoint.

Term	Definition
Adjacent endpoint	In relation to a node or endpoint, an endpointendpoint on the same local network or a node connected through a tunnel.
Adjacent node	In relation to a node or endpoint, a node on the same local network.
Child endpoint	An adjacent endpoint to which a node sends multicast data.
Child node	In relation to a member node of a group, a neighbor node farther from the creator endpoint.
Child port	In relation to a group, a port that is the interface to one or more child nodes.
Creator endpoint	The endpoint that requested creation of the group, and the source of data forwarded to the group.

Table 45–1
SMRP-Specific Terms and Definitions

Term	Definition
Creator node	The primary node that created the group.
Designated node	An SMRP router that has been designated as a primary or secondary node.
Destination tree	The spanning tree rooted on a local network with paths directed toward the local network.
Distribution tree	The active subset of a source tree that is used to forward multicast data for a group.
endpoint	A nonrouting source or destination of multicast packets.
Group	A set of recipient endpoints or a multicast address.
Join	Term for the process of becoming a member of a group.
Joining path	A path on the destination tree for a local network used to reach a creator node and constructed using the SMRP distance-vector algorithm.
Leave	Term for the process of relinquishing membership in a group.
Local net	A shared-access data link and its associated network-layer protocol. A LAN might support more than one local net.
Member endpoint	An endpoint that is a member of the group.
Member node	A node that is on the distribution tree of a group.
Neighbor node	In relation to a member node of a group, an adjacent node that is on the distribution tree for the group.
Node	A router implementing SMRP.
Parent port	In relation to a group, the port that is the interface to the parent node.
Parent node	In relation to a member node of a group, the neighbor node closer to the creator endpoint.
Port	A local network or tunnel interface on an SMRP router.
Port parent	The address of the node that is responsible for handling group requests.
Primary node	The node on a local network responsible for creating groups.
Reverse path	The reverse of a joining path, a path on the source tree for a local net used to forward multicast data.
Secondary node	The node ready to take over for a disappearing primary node.

Continues

Table 45–1
SMRP-Specific Terms and Definitions

Term	Definition
Source tree	The spanning tree rooted on a local network with paths directed away from the local network.
Spanning tree	A connected set of paths using local networks between all nodes on an internetwork with only one path between any two nodes.
Tunnel	A point-to-point connection between nodes on nonadjacent networks through routers not implementing SMRP.

Table 45–1
SMRP-Specific Terms and Definitions, continued

SMRP MULTICAST TRANSPORT SERVICES

SMRP is designed to enable routers and end stations to exchange multicast packets over network-layer protocols. SMRP provides the capability to manage multicast address assignment and enables a single source to send data addressed to a unique multicast group address. Receivers join this group if they are interested in receiving data for this group. In support of these functions, SMRP involves a number of services. The discussions that follow focus on the key processes and technologies that enable SMRP services, including address management, the Multcast Transaction Protocol (MTP), node management, multicast route management, data forwarding, and topology management.

SMRP Multicast Address Management

SMRP addressing is based on the local network of a creator endpoint. An SMRP address consists of two parts: a 3-byte network number and a 1-byte socket number. Each local network is configured with a range of unique network numbers.

In network number mapping, network numbers must be assigned to local nets for SMRP and must be unique throughout an entire internetwork. Each local net can be assigned any contiguous range of 3-byte network numbers. The number of multicast groups available for a local net is the number of network numbers assigned times 254. Network numbers can be configured or can be mapped from the network number of underlying network-layer protocols. Unique network number ranges can be reserved for supported network protocols.

In the case of multicast address mapping, SMRP multicast addresses must be mapped to network-layer multicast addresses, and these in turn are mapped to data link layer multicast addresses. For each network-layer type, a block of multicast addresses must be obtained for SMRP. In the best case, these addresses will map directly. In most cases, a direct mapping is not possible, and more than one SMRP multicast address is mapped to a single network-layer multicast address.

The manner in which multicast addresses are mapped to network-layer addresses is network-layer dependent. When SMRP transport-layer multicast addresses do not map directly to network-layer multicast addresses, filtering of the SMRP multicast addresses is required. When network-layer multicast addresses do not map directly to data link layer multicast addresses, the network layer is expected to filter out multicast addresses that have not been subscribed.

Network-layer multicast addresses are preset for *AllEndpoints*, *AllNodes*, and *AllEntities* addresses. AllEndpoints messages sent to this multicast address are relayed to all endpoints on a network. AllNodes messages sent to this multicast address are relayed to all SMRP routing nodes on a network, and AllEntities messages sent to this multicast address are relayed to all endpoints and all SMRP routing nodes on a network.

SMRP Multicast Transaction Protocol (MTP)

SMRP involves a multicast transaction protocol (MTP) that provides for three transaction types: node, endpoint, and simultaneously node/endpoint. Communications between adjacent nodes and between nodes and endpoints occurs through request/response transactions.

Responses always are unicast. MTP provides for the retransmission of requests and/or responses in case of network errors. Only hello and designated node-request packets are sent as multicast messages; all others are unicast. Endpoint-to-node requests are sent as multicasts, while node-to-endpoint requests are sent either as unicasts or multicasts.

The basic MTP design as implemented in SMRP routers uses two queues for all transactions: a request queue and a response queue. The request-queue entries are deleted after the router processes the response that it received. The response is processed, when matched with a request, using a callback specified in the entry.

After response processing, the request is discarded. If the request is unanswered, an internally generated reject response, with the error MCNoResponse, is sent to the callback. Requests can be sent to a unicast address or the AllNodes or AllEndpoints multicast address, depending on the context. Unless explicitly redirected, requests are sent to the AllNodes multicast.

The response-queue entries are created upon receipt of a request packet. The entry is referenced during all processing of the request, and the processed entry remains in the queue until it expires and is deleted from the queue. If a duplicate request is received, it is ignored if the SMRP router is still processing the original request, or if a duplicate response is generated if processing is complete. Responses always are unicast to the requestor. Some received requests require an SMRP routing node to generate additional requests. In this case, the original request(s) will be processed by the callback handler of the routing node's request entry.

SMRP Node Management

SMRP relies on a number of node relationships, including *designated nodes*, *adjacent nodes*, and *tunnel nodes*, to permit transport of multicast datagrams.

Designated nodes are SMRP routers that have been specified as primary or secondary nodes. A designated primary node is responsible for allocating group addresses. A primary node is required for each local network with SMRP nodes. A designated secondary node is required if a local network has more than one node. The secondary is used to maintain a copy of the Group Creation table, and it becomes the primary node if the primary node for a network fails.

The basic process of primary- and secondary-node determination begins at startup, when a node first tries to become the designated secondary node on each local net. If successful, the node then tries to become the designated primary node. Transactions are initiated by either a primary-node request or a secondary-node request. No response to the request indicates that the negotiation succeeded, while a positive response indicates that the negotiation failed. If two nodes try to become the designated primary node or the designated secondary node at the same time, the node with the lower network-layer unicast address becomes the designated node. A primary node then sends add-group entry packets and remove-group entry packets to the secondary node for a local network to maintain an identical Group Creation table.

In relation to a specific node or endpoint, an adjacent node exists on the same local network. Nodes periodically send out hello packets on each port. If a hello packet is not received from an adjacent node within a certain interval of time, the nodes's adjacency state is changed to Not Operational, and associated routes are marked unreachable. Notify packets are sent to each adjacent node whenever the state of a port in the node changes to a different operational state. Each node maintains an entry in the Node table for each an adjacent node. The table entry is allocated the first time it receives a packet from adjacent node. Table entries include the time of the most recent hello packet and its state.

Tunnel nodes are point-to-point connections between nodes on nonadjacent networks through routers not implementing SMRP. Two distinct tunnel nodes are defined: tunnels between nodes and tunnels between a node and an endpoint.

Tunnel nodes are maintained as entries in the Adjacent Node table in every node in the same way as for other adjacent nodes with respect to the use of hello packets and notify packets. Similarly, SMRP enables tunnel nodes to join and leave groups in the same manner as any other adjacent node.

NOTES

Cisco does not support tunnel nodes. SMRP, however, can be enabled to run network-layer tunnels between nonadjacent nodes.

SMRP Multicast Routes

SMRP relies on a spanning tree-based forwarding scheme to determine routing paths for multicast traffic. This route-determination process relies on the use of a distance-vector algorithm. A node sends distance-vector request packets to adjacent nodes at startup time and when routes change. The distance specified in the vector is the number of hops needed to reach a particular network number range. Nodes contain a vector for each entry in the Network Route table and send as many packets as necessary to send all the vectors. When routes change, each node sends distance-vector request packets to every adjacent node.

When a route is received on a port, the port-parent address must be set for the route for all ports. Because the group address is bound to the network address, the port-parent address also is used if a node is to handle a request for specified groups. When the port-parent address is the node's own address, the node is responsible for the request. Equal path nodes decide which node is responsible for a request by determining which node has the highest network address.

When a distance-vector request with entries for unknown local networks is received by a node, network ranges for associated local networks are added to Network Route table for the node, with a received distance incremented by one. The adjacent node that sent the distance-vector packet then becomes the parent node for the local network. The table entry is updated if a distance-vector packet is received for known local networks, and the distance-vector packet plus one is less than the entry in the Node Route table. A tie breaker is used if a distance-vector packet is received from an adjacent node with the same distance to a local network. The tie breaker is determined to be the adjacent node with a higher network-layer unicast address. That node is identified as the parent node for the local network.

SMRP Multicast Group Management

In SMRP, multicast group participation is managed via a process involving negotiations among endpoints and nodes. An endpoint attempts to join a group by contacting a node on a local network. Any contacted node is responsible for joining the distribution tree for the group by activating paths to an existing distribution tree. Nodes leave a distribution tree for a group by deactivating paths whenever no more member endpoints for the group exist on those paths. Four basic processes are required to manage SMRP groups: *creating*, *joining*, *leaving*, and *deleting*.

An endpoint sends a create-group request to the designated primary node when it wants to start sending data to a group. The primary node then assigns an unused group address and allocates an entry in the Group Creation table. The primary node finally returns the group address to the creator endpoint and sends an add-group request to the secondary node, if it exists.

Endpoints send requests to initiate joining a multicast group. The parent node for a group on a local network responds to endpoint-join group request packets. (A node determines whether it is the parent node by examining the network number in the group address.) When the parent node for a group gets a join-group request packet and that node is not yet a member of the group, the node forwards the join request toward the creator node of the group. Eventually the join-group request packet reaches a member node or the creator node for the group, and a join-group confirm packet is sent back along the reverse path. The member or creator node adds a child port to the Group Forwarding table if the join was received on that port. When data arrives in the reverse path, it is forwarded to all child ports. When the creator node receives the first join request for a group, it forwards the request to the creator endpoint to enable it to start sending data.

To leave a multicast group, endpoints send leave-group request packets on their local net. The parent node for the group on a local net returns a leave-group confirm packet to the endpoint and sends out a group-member request packet on the child port. If the parent node does not get a group-member confirm packet on the child port from a member node or endpoint, the parent node removes that port from the entry. If the parent node has no child ports left in the entry, it sets the state of the entry to Leaving and sends a leave-group request packet up the distribution tree to its parent node. Each respective parent node removes the entry from its Group Forwarding table when it receives the leave-group confirm packet.

The endpoint sends a delete-group request when it wants to stop sending data to the group. Only the designated primary node responds to this request.

Forwarding Multicast Datagrams

SMRP data forwarding involves nodes forwarding multicast datagrams on active paths of the source tree for a particular group. An active path has member endpoints on it for the group, or is a path needed as a transit path to reach other active paths. The subset of active paths for the source tree is the distribution tree for the group. Data forwarding under SMRP involves a series of negotiations among endpoints and nodes. In general, nodes receive multicast datagrams when endpoints send data to a group. The creator endpoint can send data packets with a network-layer multicast address to its local network after it receives a join request from the creator node. Parent nodes on the local network receive this multicast and forward the packet to all child ports in the forwarding table for the group. A node multicasts a packet on a local network only if it is the parent node for the group on that local network and if the data was received on the parent port for the group. Nodes also forward data to adjacent tunnel nodes that are members of the group. In the case of an SMRP tunnel, multicast datagrams are encapsulated in a unicast network-layer packet.

Handling SMRP Topology Changes

Topology maps are maintained by SMRP entities to manage path or membership changes within an SMRP environment. SMRP anticipates a number of typical topology changes and defines specific techniques for handling them.

Disappearing Member Endpoints

To detect disappearing member endpoints, nodes periodically send a group-member request packet to each active child port. Each member node and endpoint returns a group-member confirmation packet to the parent node. If no group-member confirmation packets are received by the parent node, the node sends a leave-group request packet to its parent node and then deletes the group entry.

Stranded Groups

To detect stranded groups, creator nodes periodically send a group-creator request packet to the creator endpoint. If after a number of retries no group-creator confirm packets are received by the creator node, the group is deleted. Network route tables are kept up to date by nodes sending distance-vector packets to their adjacent nodes when routes change. This allows nodes to change multicast group routing based on changes in topology.

SMRP TRANSACTION EXAMPLE

A typical SMRP-based transaction session involves a Macintosh workstation creating a group, other Macintosh workstations joining the group, and data being sent to the group members.

In a typical SMRP transaction session, a Macintosh (call this system Creator-Mac) first sends a create-group request to all nodes on a particular network. The primary router (Primary) for the local network assigns an unused group address and returns that address to the Creator-Mac. A Macintosh on a distant network (called Member-Mac) finds the Creator-Mac via the Name-Binding Protocol (NBP).

Creator-Mac then responds with the group address via an NBP response. The Member-Mac sends a join-group request to all nodes. A remote router (say Router M) with a valid route to the group and a correct port parent sends a join-group request toward the Primary.

The Primary finally receives the join-group request and sends it to the Creator-Mac. It also adds the incoming port to the group in the forwarding table. The Creator-Mac confirms the join-group request and sends data to the group. The Primary receives the data and forwards it to the group's child ports.

Finally, the data is received by Router M, which looks up the group in the forwarding table and forwards the multicast data. The Member-Mac then receives data for the group.

SMRP PACKET FORMAT

Figure 45–2 illustrates the general SMRP packet format.

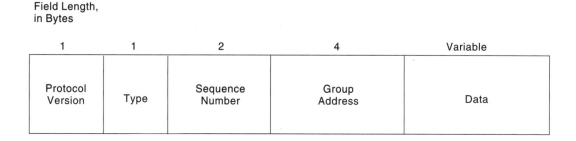

Figure 45-2
A general SMRP packet consists of five fields.

The following descriptions summarize the SMRP packet fields illustrated in Figure 45-2:

- *Protocol Version*—Indicates the version of SMRP.

- *Type*—Consists of 2 subfields. The first 2 bits modify the packet type specified by the bottom 6 bits in order to identify whether a packet is a transaction packet, and if so, what type of transaction.

- *Sequence Number*—Matches responses to requests in transactions in order to avoid duplicate requests and responses. All packet types are transaction packets and will have a nonzero sequence number (with the exception of multicast data packets and hello packets whose sequence numbers are set to zero).

- *Group Address*—Serves as the designated primary node and assigns group addresses for all multicast sources on the local network. A particular local network can be assigned more than one network number, but multiple network numbers must be in a contiguous range. Nodes must configure network numbers that are unique to each local network and each primary node to prevent collisions of multicast addresses. When a primary node assigns a new group address, it arbitrarily assigns any unused group address for its network number.

- *Data*—Varies depending on SMRP packet type. Table 45–3 summarizes data characteristics based on packet type.

Packet Type	Data Carried	Size
Multicast Data	Data	Variable, depending on network-layer datagram size
Hello	Port state	2 bytes
Notify	Port state	1 byte
Designated Node	None	0 bytes
Distance Vector	Multicast vector	8 bytes
Create Group	None	0 bytes
Delete Group	None	0 bytes
Join Group	None	0 bytes
Add Group Entry	Network-layer unicast address	Variable, depending on network-layer address format
Remove Group Entry	None	0 bytes
Leave Group	None	0 bytes
Creator Request	None	0 bytes
Member Request	None	0 bytes
Reject	Error indication	Short integer ranging from −7700 to −7710, depending on errors

Table 45–3
Data Characteristics Based on Packet Type

CHAPTER 46

Quality of Service (QoS) Networking

NETWORK QoS DEFINED

QoS refers to the capability of a network to provide better service to selected network traffic over various technologies, including Frame Relay, Asynchronous Transfer Mode (ATM), Ethernet and 802.1 networks, SONET, and IP-routed networks that may use any or all of these underlying technologies. Primary goals of QoS include dedicated bandwidth, controlled jitter and latency (required by some real-time and interactive traffic), and improved loss characteristics. QoS technologies provide the elemental building blocks that will be used for future business applications in campus, WAN, and service provider networks. This chapter outlines the features and benefits of the QoS provided by the Cisco IOS QoS.

The Cisco IOS QoS software enables complex networks to control and predictably service a variety of networked applications and traffic types. Almost any network can take advantage of QoS for optimum efficiency, whether it is a small corporate network, an Internet service provider, or an enterprise network. The Cisco IOS QoS software provides these benefits:

- *Control over resources*—You have control over which resources (bandwidth, equipment, wide-area facilities, and so on) are being used. For example, you can limit the bandwidth consumed over a backbone link by FTP transfers or give priority to an important database access.

- *More efficient use of network resources*—Using Cisco's network analysis management and accounting tools, you will know what your network is being used for and that you are servicing the most important traffic to your business.

- *Tailored services*—The control and visibility provided by QoS enables Internet service providers to offer carefully tailored grades of service differentiation to their customers.

- *Coexistence of mission-critical applications*—Cisco's QoS technologies make certain that your WAN is used efficiently by mission-critical applications that are most important to your business; that bandwidth and minimum delays required by time-sensitive multimedia and voice applications are available; and that other applications using the link get their fair service without interfering with mission-critical traffic.

- *Foundation for a fully integrated network in the future*—Implementing Cisco QoS technologies in your network now is a good first step toward the fully integrated multimedia network needed in the near future.

BASIC QOS ARCHITECTURE

The basic architecture introduces the three fundamental pieces for QoS implementation (see Figure 46–1):

- QoS within a single network element (for example, queuing, scheduling, and traffic shaping tools)

- QoS signaling techniques for coordinating QoS from end to end between network elements

- QoS policy, management, and accounting functions to control and administer end-to-end traffic across a network

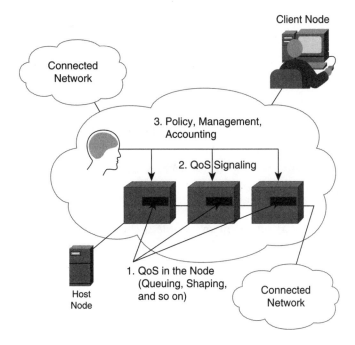

Figure 46–1
A basic QoS implementation has three main components.

End-to-End QoS Levels

Service levels refer to the actual end-to-end QoS capabilities, meaning the ability of a network to deliver service needed by specific network traffic from end to end or edge to edge. The services differ in their level of "QoS strictness," which describes how tightly the service can be bound by specific bandwidth, delay, jitter, and loss characteristics.

Three basic levels of end-to-end QoS can be provided across a heterogeneous network, as shown in Figure 46–2:

- *Best-effort service*—Also known as lack of QoS, best-effort service is basic connectivity with no guarantees.

- *Differentiated service (also called soft QoS)*—Some traffic is treated better than the rest (faster handling, more bandwidth on average, lower loss rate on average). This is a statistical preference, not a hard and fast guarantee.

- *Guaranteed service (also called hard QoS)*—An absolute reservation of network resources for specific traffic.

Deciding which type of service is appropriate to deploy in the network depends on several factors:

- The application or problem the customer is trying to solve. Each of the three types of service is appropriate for certain applications. This does not imply that a customer must migrate to differentiated and then to guaranteed service (although many probably eventually will). A differentiated service—or even best-effort service—may be appropriate depending on the customer application requirements.

- The rate at which customers can realistically upgrade their infrastructures. There is a natural upgrade path from the technology needed to provide differentiated services to that needed to provide guaranteed services, which is a superset of that needed for differentiated services.

- The cost of implementing and deploying guaranteed service is likely to be more than that for a differentiated service.

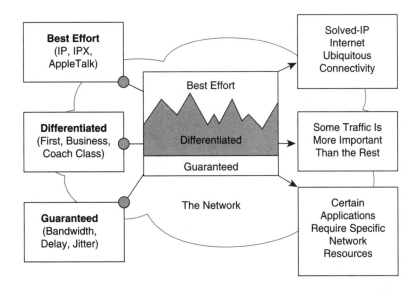

Figure 46–2
The three levels of end-to-end QoS are best-effort service, differentiated service, and guaranteed service.

Congestion Management Tools

One way network elements handle an overflow of arriving traffic is to use a queuing algorithm to sort the traffic, and then determine some method of prioritizing it onto an output link. Cisco IOS software includes the following queuing tools:

- First-in, first-out (FIFO) queuing
- Priority queuing (PQ)

- Custom queuing (CQ)

- Weighted fair queuing (WFQ)

Each queuing algorithm was designed to solve a specific network traffic problem and has a particular effect on network performance, as described in the following sections.

FIFO: Basic Store-and-Forward Capability

In its simplest form, FIFO queuing involves storing packets when the network is congested and forwarding them in order of arrival when the network is no longer congested. FIFO is the default queuing algorithm in some instances, thus requiring no configuration, but it has several shortcomings. Most importantly, FIFO queuing makes no decision about packet priority; the order of arrival determines bandwidth, promptness, and buffer allocation. Nor does it provide protection against ill-behaved applications (sources). Bursty sources can cause long delays in delivering time-sensitive application traffic, and potentially to network control and signaling messages. FIFO queuing was a necessary first step in controlling network traffic, but today's intelligent networks need more sophisticated algorithms. Cisco IOS software implements queuing algorithms that avoid the shortcomings of FIFO queuing.

PQ: Prioritizing Traffic

PQ ensures that important traffic gets the fastest handling at each point where it is used. It was designed to give strict priority to important traffic. Priority queuing can flexibly prioritize according to network protocol (for example IP, IPX, or AppleTalk), incoming interface, packet size, source/destination address, and so on. In PQ, each packet is placed in one of four queues—high, medium, normal, or low—based on an assigned priority. Packets that are not classified by this priority-list mechanism fall into the normal queue; see Figure 46–3. During transmission, the algorithm gives higher-priority queues absolute preferential treatment over low-priority queues.

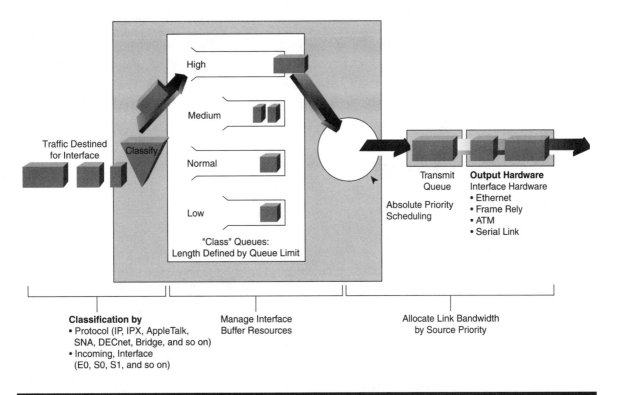

Figure 46-3
Priority queuing places data into four levels of queues: high, medium, normal, and low.

PQ is useful for making sure that mission-critical traffic traversing various WAN links gets priority treatment. For example, Cisco uses PQ to ensure that important Oracle-based sales reporting data gets to its destination ahead of other, less-critical traffic. PQ currently uses static configuration and thus does not automatically adapt to changing network requirements.

CQ: Guaranteeing Bandwidth

CQ was designed to allow various applications or organizations to share the network among applications with specific minimum bandwidth or latency requirements. In these environments, bandwidth must be shared proportionally between applications and users. You can use the Cisco CQ feature to provide guaranteed bandwidth at a potential congestion point, ensuring the specified traffic a fixed portion of available bandwidth and leaving the remaining bandwidth to other traffic. Custom queuing handles traffic by assigning a specified amount of queue space to each class of packets and then servicing the queues in a round-robin fashion; see Figure 46–4.

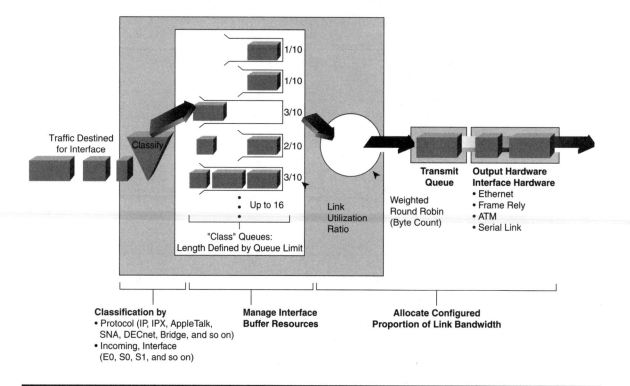

Figure 46–4

Custom queuing handles traffic by assigning a specified amount of queue space to each class of packets and then servicing up to 17 queues in a round-robin fashion.

As an example, encapsulated Systems Network Architecture (SNA) requires a guaranteed minimum level of service. You could reserve half of available bandwidth for SNA data, and allow the remaining half to be used by other protocols such as IP and Internetwork Packet Exchange (IPX).

The queuing algorithm places the messages in one of 17 queues (queue 0 holds system messages such as keepalives, signaling, and so on), and is emptied with weighted priority. The router services queues 1 through 16 in round-robin order, dequeuing a configured byte count from each queue in each cycle. This feature ensures that no application (or specified group of applications) achieves more than a predetermined proportion of overall capacity when the line is under stress. Like PQ, CQ is statically configured and does not automatically adapt to changing network conditions.

WFQ: Cisco's Intelligent Queuing Tool for Today's Networks

For situations in which it is desirable to provide consistent response time to heavy and light network users alike without adding excessive bandwidth, the solution is WFQ. WFQ is one of Cisco's premier queuing techniques. It is a flow-based queuing algorithm that does two things simultaneously: It schedules interactive traffic to the front of the queue to reduce response time, and it fairly shares the remaining bandwidth among high-bandwidth flows.

WFQ ensures that queues do not starve for bandwidth, and that traffic gets predictable service. Low-volume traffic streams—which comprise the majority of traffic—receive preferential service, transmitting their entire offered loads in a timely fashion. High-volume traffic streams share the remaining capacity proportionally between them, as shown in Figure 46–5.

WFQ is designed to minimize configuration effort and automatically adapts to changing network traffic conditions. In fact, WFQ does such a good job for most applications that it has been made the default queuing mode on most serial interfaces configured to run at or below E1 speeds (2.048 Mbps).

WFQ is efficient in that it uses whatever bandwidth is available to forward traffic from lower-priority flows if no traffic from higher-priority flows is present. This is different from time-division multiplexing (TDM), which simply carves up the bandwidth and lets it go unused if no traffic is present for a particular traffic type. WFQ works with both of Cisco's primary QoS signaling techniques—IP precedence and Resource Reservation Protocol (RSVP), described later in this chapter—to help provide differentiated QoS as well as guaranteed services.

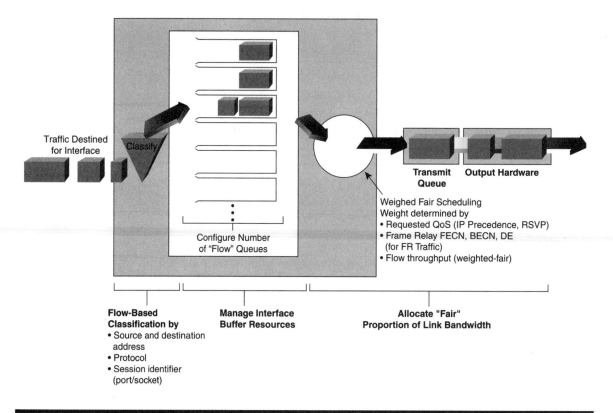

Figure 46–5

With WFQ, if multiple high-volume conversations are active, their transfer rates and interarrival periods are made much more predictable.

The WFQ algorithm also addresses the problem of round-trip delay variability. If multiple high-volume conversations are active, their transfer rates and interarrival periods are made much more predictable. WFQ greatly enhances algorithms such as the SNA Logical Link Control (LLC) and the Transmission Control Protocol (TCP) congestion control and slow-start features. The result is more predictable throughput and response time for each active flow, as shown in Figure 46–6.

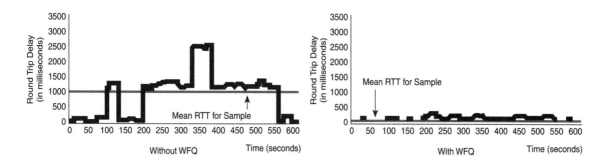

Figure 46–6
This diagram shows an example of interactive traffic delay (128-kbps Frame Relay WAN link).

Cooperation Between WFQ and QoS Signaling Technologies

WFQ is IP precedence aware; that is, it is able to detect higher-priority packets marked with precedence by the IP forwarder and can schedule them faster, providing superior response time for this traffic. The IP Precedence field has values between 0 (the default) and 7. As the precedence value increases, the algorithm allocates more bandwidth to that conversation to make sure that it is served more quickly when congestion occurs. WFQ assigns a weight to each flow, which determines the transmit order for queued packets. In this scheme, lower weights are served first. IP precedence serves as a divisor to this weighting factor. For instance, traffic with an IP Precedence field value of 7 gets a lower weight than traffic with an IP Precedence field value of 3, and thus has priority in the transmit order.

For example, if you have one flow at each precedence level on an interface, each flow will get precedence + 1 parts of the link, as follows:

$$1 + 2 + 3 + 4 + 5 + 6 + 7 + 8 = 36$$

and the flows will get $8/_{36}$, $7/_{36}$, $6/_{36}$, and $5/_{36}$ of the link, and so on. However, if you have 18 precedence − 1 flows and 1 of each of the others, the formula looks like this:

$$1 + 18 \times 2 + 3 + 4 + 5 + 6 + 7 + 8 = 36 - 2 + 18 \times 2 = 70$$

and the flows will get $8/_{70}$, $7/_{70}$, $6/_{70}$, $5/_{70}$, $4/_{70}$, $3/_{70}$, $2/_{70}$, and $1/_{70}$ of the link, and 18 of the flows will get approximately $2/_{70}$ of the link.

WFQ is also RSVP aware; RSVP uses WFQ to allocate buffer space and schedule packets, and guarantees bandwidth for reserved flows. Additionally, in a Frame Relay network, the presence of congestion is flagged by the forward explicit congestion notification (FECN) and backward explicit congestion notification (BECN) bits. WFQ weights are affected by Frame Relay discard eligible (DE), FECN, and BECN bits when the traffic is switched by the Frame Relay switching module. When congestion is flagged, the weights used by the algorithm are altered so that the conversation encountering the congestion transmits less frequently.

Congestion Avoidance Tools

Congestion avoidance techniques monitor network traffic loads in an effort to anticipate and avoid congestion at common network bottlenecks, as opposed to congestion management techniques that operate to control congestion after it occurs. The primary Cisco IOS congestion avoidance tool is weighted random early detection.

WRED: Avoiding Congestion

The random early detection (RED) algorithms are designed to avoid congestion in internetworks before it becomes a problem. RED works by monitoring traffic load at points in the network and stochastically discarding packets if the congestion begins to increase. The result of the drop is that the source detects the dropped traffic and slows its transmission. RED is primarily designed to work with TCP in IP internetwork environments.

WRED Cooperation with QoS Signaling Technologies

WRED combines the capabilities of the RED algorithm with IP precedence. This combination provides for preferential traffic handling for higher-priority packets. It can selectively discard lower-priority traffic when the interface starts to get congested and provide differentiated performance characteristics for different classes of service. See Figure 46–7. WRED is also RSVP aware, and can provide an integrated services controlled-load QoS.

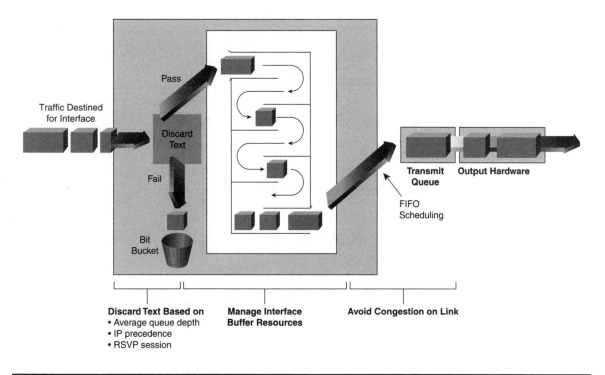

Figure 46–7
WRED provides a method that stochastically discards packets if the congestion begins to increase.

D-WRED: Delivering High-Speed Differentiated Traffic on the 7500 Platform

Cisco IOS software also provides distributed weighted random early detection (D-WRED), a high-speed version of WRED that runs on VIP-distributed processors. The D-WRED algorithm provides functionality beyond what WRED provides, such as minimum and maximum queue depth thresholds and drop capabilities for each class of service.

Traffic Shaping and Policing Tools

Cisco's QoS software solutions include two traffic shaping tools—generic traffic shaping (GTS) and Frame Relay traffic shaping (FRTS)—to manage traffic and congestion on the network.

GTS: Controlling Outbound Traffic Flow

GTS provides a mechanism to control the traffic flow on a particular interface. It reduces outbound traffic flow to avoid congestion by constraining specified traffic to a particular bit rate (also known as the token bucket approach), while queuing bursts of the specified traffic. Thus, traffic adhering to a particular profile can be shaped to meet downstream requirements, eliminating bottlenecks in topologies with data-rate mismatches. Figure 46–8 illustrates GTS.

GTS applies on a per-interface basis, can use access lists to select the traffic to shape, and works with a variety of Layer 2 technologies, including Frame Relay, ATM, Switched Multimegabit Data Service (SMDS), and Ethernet.

On a Frame Relay subinterface, GTS can be set up to adapt dynamically to available bandwidth by integrating BECN signals, or set up simply to shape to a prespecified rate. GTS can also be configured on an ATM/AIP (ATM Interface Processor) interface card to respond to RSVP signaled over statically configured ATM permanent virtual circuits (PVCs).

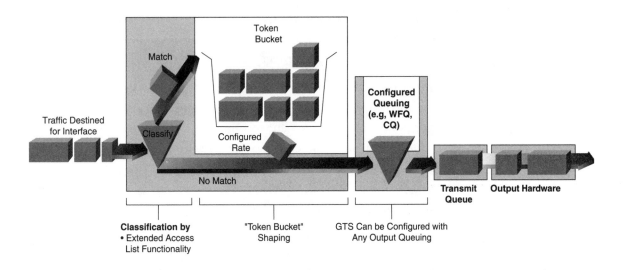

Figure 46–8
Generic traffic shaping is applied on a per-interface basis.

FRTS: Managing Frame Relay Traffic

FRTS provides parameters that are useful for managing network traffic congestion. These include committed information rate (CIR), FECN and BECN, and the DE bit. For some time, Cisco has provided support for FECN for DECnet, BECN for SNA traffic using direct LLC2 encapsulation via RFC 1490, and DE bit support. The FRTS feature builds on this Frame Relay support with additional capabilities that improve the scalability and performance of a Frame Relay network, increasing the density of virtual circuits and improving response time.

For example, you can configure rate enforcement—a peak rate configured to limit outbound traffic—to either the CIR or some other defined value, such as the excess information rate (EIR), on a per-virtual-circuit (VC) basis.

You can also define priority and custom queuing at the VC or subinterface level. This allows for finer granularity in the prioritization and queuing of traffic and provides more control over the traffic flow on an individual VC. If you combine CQ with the per-VC queuing and rate enforcement capabilities, you enable Frame Relay VCs to carry multiple traffic types such as IP, SNA, and IPX, with bandwidth guaranteed for each traffic type.

FRTS can eliminate bottlenecks in Frame Relay networks with high-speed connections at the central site and low-speed connections at the branch sites. You can configure rate enforcement to limit the rate at which data is sent on the VC at the central site. You can also use rate enforcement with the existing data-link connection identifier (DLCI) prioritization feature to further improve performance in this situation. FRTS applies only to Frame Relay PVCs and switched virtual circuits (SVCs).

Using information contained in BECN-tagged packets received from the network, FRTS can also dynamically throttle traffic. With BECN-based throttling, packets are held in the router's buffers to reduce the data flow from the router into the Frame Relay network. The throttling is done on a per-VC basis and the transmission rate is adjusted based on the number of BECN-tagged packets received.

FRTS also provides a mechanism for sharing media by multiple VCs. Rate enforcement allows the transmission speed used by the router to be controlled by criteria other than line speed, such as the CIR or EIR. The rate enforcement feature can also be used to preallocate bandwidth to each VC, creating a virtual TDM network. Finally, with the Cisco's FRTS feature, you can integrate StrataCom ATM Foresight closed loop congestion control to actively adapt to downstream congestion conditions.

Link Efficiency Mechanisms

Currently, Cisco IOS software offers two link efficiency mechanisms—Link Fragmentation and Interleaving (LFI) and Real-Time Protocol Header Compression (RTP-HC)—which work with queuing and traffic shaping to improve the efficiency and predictability of the application service levels.

LFI: Fragmenting and Interleaving IP Traffic

Interactive traffic (Telnet, voice over IP, and the like) is susceptible to increased latency and jitter when the network processes large packets (for example LAN-to-LAN FTP transfers traversing a WAN link), especially as they are queued on slower links. The Cisco IOS LFI feature reduces delay and jitter on slower-speed links by breaking up large datagrams and interleaving low-delay traffic packets with the resulting smaller packets; see Figure 46–9.

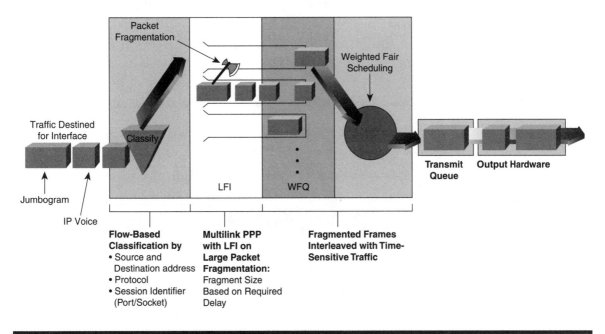

Figure 46–9

By dividing large datagrams with the LFI feature, delay is reduced on slower speed links.

LFI was designed especially for lower-speed links in which serialization delay is significant. LFI requires that multilink Point-to-Point Protocol (PPP) be configured on the interface with interleaving turned on. A related IETF Draft, called Multiclass Extensions to Multilink PPP (MCML) implements almost the same function as LFI.

RTP Header Compression: Increasing Efficiency of Real-Time Traffic

Real-Time Transport Protocol is a host-to-host protocol used for carrying newer multimedia application traffic, including packetized audio and video, over an IP network. Real-Time Transport Protocol provides end-to-end network transport functions intended for applications transmitting real-time requirements, such as audio, video, or simulation data over multicast or unicast network services. Real-Time Transport Protocol header compression increases efficiency for many of the newer voice over IP or multimedia applications that take advantage of Real-Time Transport Protocol, especially on slow links. Figure 46–10 illustrates Real-Time Transport Protocol header compression.

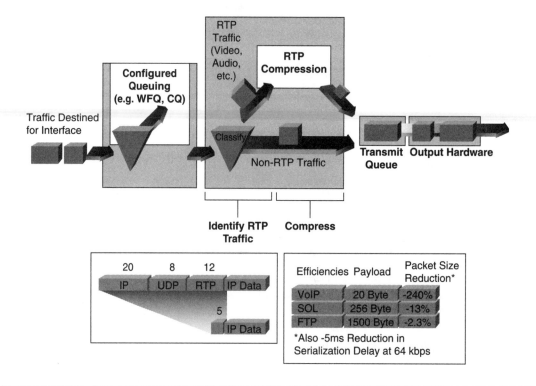

Figure 46–10

This diagram illustrates Real-Time Transport Protocol header compression.

For compressed-payload audio applications, the RTP packet has a 40-byte header and typically a 20- to 150-byte payload. Given the size of the IP/UDP/Real-Time Transport Protocol header combination, it is inefficient to transmit an uncompressed header. Real-Time Transport Protocol header compression helps Real-Time Transport Protocol run more efficiently—especially over lower-speed links—by compressing the Real-Time Transport Protocol/UDP/IP header from 40 bytes to 2 to 5 bytes. This is especially beneficial for smaller packets (such as IP voice traffic) on slower links (385 kbps and below), where RTP header compression can reduce overhead and transmission delay significantly. Real-Time Transport Protocol header compression reduces line overhead for multimedia Real-Time Transport Protocol traffic with a corresponding reduction in delay, especially for traffic that uses short packets relative to header length.

RTP header compression is supported on serial lines using Frame Relay, High-Level Data Link Control (HDLC), or PPP encapsulation. It is also supported over ISDN interfaces. A related IETF Draft, called Compressed RTP (CRTP), defines essentially the same functionality.

QOS SIGNALING

Think of QoS signaling as a form of network communication. It provides a way for an end station or a network element to signal certain requests to a neighbor. For example, an IP network can use part of the IP packet header to request special handling of priority or time-sensitive traffic. QoS signaling is useful for coordinating the traffic handling techniques described earlier in this chapter and has a key role in configuring successful end-to-end QoS across your network.

True end-to-end QoS requires that every element in the network path—switch, router, firewall, host, client, and so on—deliver its part of QoS, and it all must be coordinated with QoS signaling. However, the challenge is finding a robust QoS signaling solution that can operate end-to-end over heterogeneous network infrastructures. Although many viable QoS signaling solutions provide QoS at some places in the infrastructure, they often have limited scope across the network, as shown in Figure 46–11.

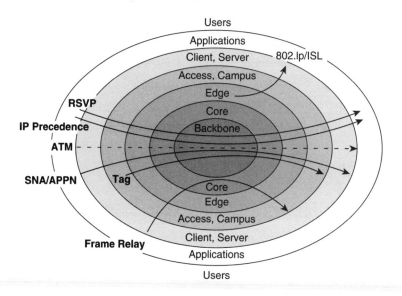

Figure 46–11

QoS signaling solutions provide QoS at some places in the infrastructure; they often have limited scope across the network.

Cisco IOS software takes advantage of the end-to-end nature of IP to meet this challenge by overlaying Layer 2 technology-specific QoS signaling solutions with the Layer 3 IP QoS signaling methods of RSVP and IP precedence.

This section focuses on IP precedence and RSVP because both of these methods take advantage of the end-to-end nature of IP. As the majority of applications converge on the use of IP as the primary networking protocol, IP precedence and RSVP provide a powerful combination for QoS signaling—IP precedence signals for differentiated QoS, and RSVP for guaranteed QoS.

IP Precedence: Signaling Differentiated QoS

IP precedence utilizes the three precedence bits in the IPv4 header's ToS (Type of Service) field to specify class of service for each packet, as shown in Figure 46–12. You can partition traffic in up to six classes of service using IP precedence (two others are reserved for internal network use). The queuing technologies throughout the network can then use this signal to provide the appropriate expedited handling.

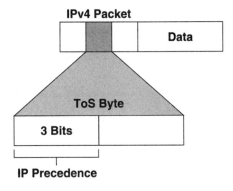

Figure 46–12
This diagram shows the IP precedence ToS field in an IP packet header.

Features such as policy-based routing and committed access rate (CAR) can be used to set precedence based on extended access-list classification. This allows considerable flexibility for precedence assignment, including assignment by application or user, or by destination and source subnet, and so on. Typically this functionality is deployed as close to the edge of the network (or administrative domain) as possible, so that each subsequent network element can provide service based on the determined policy.

IP precedence can also be set in the host or network client, and this signaling can be used optionally; however, this can be overridden by policy within the network. IP precedence enables service classes to be established using existing network queuing mechanisms (for example, WFQ or WRED), with no changes to existing applications or complicated network requirements. Note that this same approach is easily extended to IPv6 using its Priority field.

RSVP: GUARANTEEING QoS

RSVP is an IETF Internet Standard (RFC 2205) protocol for allowing an application to dynamically reserve network bandwidth. RSVP enables applications to request a specific QoS for a data flow, as shown in Figure 46–13. Cisco's implementation also allows RSVP to be initiated within the network, using configured proxy RSVP. Network managers can thereby take advantage of the benefits of RSVP in the network, even for non-RSVP-enabled applications and hosts.

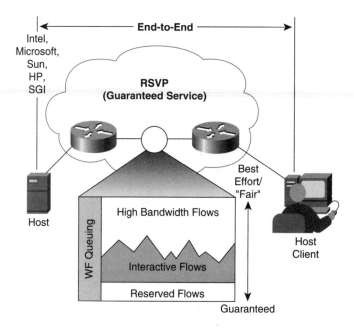

Figure 46–13

This figure shows RSVP implemented in a Cisco-based router network.

Hosts and routers use RSVP to deliver QoS requests to the routers along the paths of the data stream and to maintain router and host state to provide the requested service, usually bandwidth and latency. RSVP uses a mean data rate, the largest amount of data the router will keep in queue, and minimum QoS to determine bandwidth reservation.

WFQ or WRED acts as the workhorse for RSVP, setting up the packet classification and scheduling required for the reserved flows. Using WFQ, RSVP can deliver an integrated services guaranteed service. Using WRED, it can deliver a controlled load service. WFQ continues to provide its advantageous handling of nonreserved traffic by expediting interactive traffic and fairly sharing the remaining bandwidth between high-bandwidth flows, and WRED provides its commensurate advantages for non-RSVP flow traffic. RSVP can be deployed in existing networks with a software upgrade.

Tag Switching: Allowing Flexible Traffic Engineering

Cisco's tag switching feature contains the mechanisms to interoperate with and take advantage of both RSVP and IP precedence signaling. The tag switching header contains a 3-bit field that can be used as a traffic prioritization signal. It can also be used to map particular flows and classes of traffic along engineered tag switching paths to obtain the required QoS through the tag switching portion of a network.

CISCO'S QOS POLICY, MANAGEMENT, AND ACCOUNTING CAPABILITIES

Cisco IOS software provides technologies that enable policy control, management, and accounting of the QoS techniques described in this chapter. The following sections provide an overview of these technologies.

QoS Policy Control

The QoS policy control architecture is being developed as a key initial piece of the CiscoAssure policy networking initiative. This initiative leverages standards-based QoS policy control protocols and mechanisms to implement QoS policy from a single console interface.

At the infrastructure level, packet classification is a key capability for each policy technique that allows the appropriate packets traversing a network element or particular interface to be selected for QoS. These packets can then be marked for the appropriate IP precedence in some cases, or identified as an RSVP. Policy control also requires integration with underlying data link-layer network technologies or non-IP protocols.

SNA ToS

SNA ToS in conjunction with data-link switching plus (DLSw+), allows mapping of traditional SNA class of service (CoS) into IP differentiated service. This feature takes advantage of both QoS signaling and pieces of the architecture. DLSW+ opens four TCP sessions and maps each SNA ToS traffic into a different session. Each session is marked by IP precedence. Cisco's congestion control technologies (CQ, PQ, and WFQ) act on these sessions to provide a bandwidth guarantee or other improved handling across an intranet, as shown in Figure 46–14. This provides a migration path for traditional SNA customers onto an IP-based intranet, while preserving the performance characteristics expected of SNA.

Thus, traditional mainframe-based, mission-critical applications can take advantage of evolving IP intranets and extranets without sacrificing the QoS capabilities historically provided by SNA networking.

QoS Policy Setting with Policy-Based Routing (PBR)

Cisco IOS PBR allows you to classify traffic based on extended access list criteria, set IP precedence bits, and even route to specific traffic-engineered paths that may be required to allow a specific QoS through the network. By setting precedence levels on incoming traffic and using them in combination with the queuing tools described earlier in this chapter, you can create differentiated service. These tools provide powerful, simple, and flexible options for implementing QoS policies in your network.

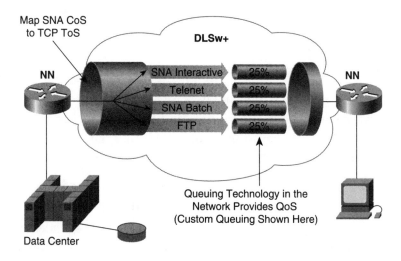

Figure 46–14
SNA ToS, in conjunction with DLSw, allows mapping of SNA CoS into IP differentiated services.

You can also set up PBR as a way to route packets based on configured policies. Some applications or traffic can benefit from QoS-specific routing-transferring stock records to a corporate office (for example, on a higher-bandwidth, higher-cost link for a short time), while transmitting routine application data such as e-mail over a lower-bandwidth, lower-cost link. PBR can be used to direct packets to take different paths than the path derived from the routing protocols. It provides a more flexible mechanism for routing packets, complementing the existing mechanisms provided by routing protocols.

CAR: Managing Access Bandwidth Policy and Performing Policing

Similar in some ways to PBR, the CAR feature allows you to classify and police traffic on an incoming interface. It also allows specification of policies for handling traffic that exceeds a certain bandwidth allocation. CAR looks at traffic received on an interface, or a subset of that traffic selected by access list criteria, compares its rate to that of a configured token bucket, and then takes action based on the result (for example, drop or rewrite IP precedence).

QoS for Packetized Voice

One of the most promising uses for IP networks is to allow sharing of voice traffic with the traditional data and LAN-to-LAN traffic. Typically, this can help reduce transmission costs by reducing the number of network connections, sharing existing connections and infrastructure, and so on.

Cisco has a wide range of voice networking products and technologies, including a number of voice over IP (VoIP) solutions. To provide the required voice quality, however, QoS capability must be added to the traditional data-only network. Cisco IOS software QoS features give VoIP traffic the service it needs, while providing the traditional data traffic with the service it needs as well.

Figure 46–15 shows a business that has chosen to reduce some of its voice costs by combining voice traffic onto its existing IP network. Voice traffic at each office is digitized on voice modules on 3600 processors. This traffic is then routed via H.323 Gatekeeper, which also requests specific QoS for the voice traffic. In this case, IP precedence is set to high for the voice traffic. WFQ is enabled on all the router interfaces for this network. WFQ automatically expedites the forwarding of high-precedence voice traffic out each interface, reducing delay and jitter for this traffic.

Because the IP network was originally handling LAN-to-LAN traffic, many datagrams traversing the network are large 1500-byte packets. On slow links (below T1/E1 speeds), voice packets may be forced to wait behind one of these large packets, adding tens or even hundreds of milliseconds to the delay.

LFI is used in conjunction with WFQ to break up these "jumbograms" and interleave the voice traffic to reduce this delay as well as jitter.

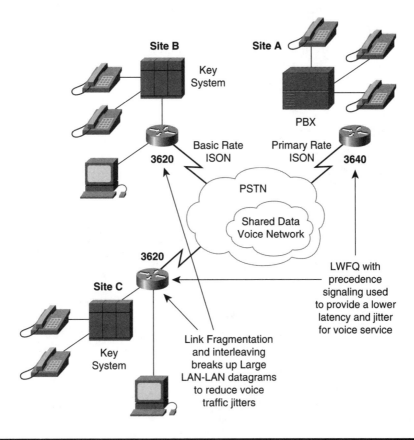

Figure 46–15
This diagram provides an overview of a QoS VoIP solution.

QoS for Streaming Video

One of the most significant challenges for IP-based networks, which have traditionally provided only best-effort service, has been to provide some type of service guarantees for different types of traffic. This has been a particular challenge for streaming video applications, which often require a significant amount of reserved bandwidth to be useful.

In the network shown in Figure 46–16, RSVP is used in conjunction with ATM PVCs to provide guaranteed bandwidth to a mesh of locations. RSVP is configured from within Cisco IOS to provide paths from the router networks, at the edges, and through the ATM core. Simulation traffic then uses these guaranteed paths to meet the constraints of geographically distributed real-time simulation. Video-enabled machines at the various sites also use this network to do live videoconferencing.

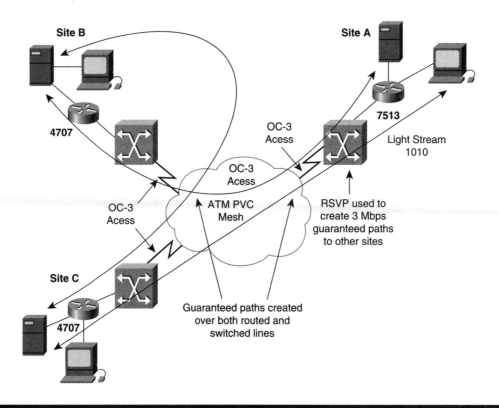

Figure 46–16
The network diagram shows the use of RSVP in a meshed ATM environment.

In this instance, OC-3 ATM links are configured with multiple 3 Mbps PVCs connecting to various remote sites. RSVP ensures that QoS from this PVC is extended to the appropriate application across the local routed network. In the future, Cisco IOS will extend this RSVP capability to dynamically set up ATM SVCs. This will reduce configuration complexity and add a great degree of automatic configuration.

QoS Looking Forward

In a continued evolution toward end-to-end services, Cisco is expanding QoS interworking to operate more seamlessly across heterogeneous link-layer technologies, and working closely with host platform partners to ensure inter-operation between networks and end systems.

PART 7

Internet Access Technologies

Part 7, "Internet Access Technologies," provides information on technologies used for accessing the Internet. Individual chapters discuss the following topics:

Security Technologies—Presents an overview of security technologies, including those needed when connecting to the Internet, information on different kinds of networks and their security requirements, and information on establishing a security perimeter.

Directory-Enabled Networking—Provides information on directory enabling a network and using schemata.

Network Caching Technologies—Explains the basics of network caching, including the use of Cisco's network-based shared caching.

CHAPTER 47

Security Technologies

With the rapid growth of interest in the Internet, network security has become a major concern to companies throughout the world. The fact that the information and tools needed to penetrate the security of corporate networks are widely available has increased that concern.

Because of this increased focus on network security, network administrators often spend more effort protecting their networks than on actual network setup and administration. New tools that probe for system vulnerabilities, such as the Security Administrator Tool for Analyzing Networks (SATAN), assist in these efforts, but these tools only point out areas of weakness instead of providing a means to protect networks. Thus, as a network administrator, you must constantly try to keep abreast of the large number of security issues confronting you in today's world. This chapter describes many of the security issues that arise when connecting a private network to the Internet.

SECURITY ISSUES WHEN CONNECTING TO THE INTERNET

When you connect your private network to the Internet, you are physically connecting your network to more than 50,000 unknown networks and all their users. Although such connections open the door to many useful applications and provide great opportunities for information sharing, most private networks contain some information that should not be shared with outside users on the Internet. In addition, not all Internet users are involved in lawful activities. These two statements foreshadow the key questions behind most security issues on the Internet:

- How do you protect confidential information from those who do not explicitly need to access it?

- How do you protect your network and its resources from malicious users and accidents that originate outside your network?

Protecting Confidential Information

Confidential information can reside in two states on a network. It can reside on physical storage media, such as a hard drive or memory, or it can reside in transit across the physical network wire in the form of packets. These two information states present multiple opportunities for attacks from users on your internal network, as well as those users on the Internet. We are primarily concerned with the second state, which involves network security issues. The following are five common methods of attack that present opportunities to compromise the information on your network:

- Network packet sniffers

- IP spoofing

- Password attacks

- Distribution of sensitive internal information to external sources

- Man-in-the-middle attacks

When protecting your information from these attacks, your concern is to prevent the theft, destruction, corruption, and introduction of information that can cause irreparable damage to sensitive and confidential information. This section describes these common methods of attack and provides examples of how your information can be compromised.

Network Packet Sniffers

Because networked computers communicate serially (one information piece is sent after another), large information pieces are broken into smaller pieces. (The information stream would be broken into smaller pieces even if networks communicated in parallel. The overriding reason for breaking streams into network packets is that computers have limited intermediate buffers.) These smaller pieces are called *network packets*. Several network applications distribute network packets in *clear text*; that is, the information sent across the network is not encrypted. (Encryption is the transformation, or scrambling, of a message into an unreadable format by using a mathematical algorithm.) Because the network packets are not encrypted, they can be processed and understood by any application that can pick them up off the network and process them.

A network protocol specifies how packets are identified and labeled, which enables a computer to determine whether a packet is intended for it. Because the specifications for network protocols, such as TCP/IP, are widely published, a third party can easily interpret the network packets and develop a packet sniffer. (The real threat today results from the numerous freeware and shareware packet sniffers that are available, which do not require the user to understand anything about the underlying protocols.) A *packet sniffer* is a software application that uses a network adapter card in promiscuous mode (a mode in which the network adapter card sends all packets received on the physical network wire to an application for processing) to capture all network packets that are sent across a local-area network.

Because several network applications distribute network packets in clear text, a packet sniffer can provide its user with meaningful and often sensitive information, such as user account names and passwords. If you use networked databases, a packet sniffer can provide an attacker with information that is queried from the database, as well as the user account names and passwords used to access the database. One serious problem with acquiring user account names and passwords is that users often reuse their login names and passwords across multiple applications.

In addition, many network administrators use packet sniffers to diagnose and fix network-related problems. Because in the course of their usual and necessary duties these network administrators (such as those in the Payroll Department) work during regular employee hours, they can potentially examine sensitive information distributed across the network.

Many users employ a single password for access to all accounts and applications. If an application is run in client/server mode and authentication information is sent across the network in clear text, then it is likely that this same authentication information can be used to gain access to other corporate resources. Because attackers know and use human characteristics (attack methods known collectively as *social engineering attacks*), such as using a single password for multiple accounts, they are often successful in gaining access to sensitive information.

IP Spoofing

An *IP spoofing attack* occurs when an attacker outside your network pretends to be a trusted computer either by using an IP address that is within the range of IP addresses for your network or by using an authorized external IP address that you trust and to which you wish to provide access to specified resources on your network.

Normally, an IP spoofing attack is limited to the injection of data or commands into an existing stream of data passed between a client and server application or a peer-to-peer network connection. To enable bidirectional communication, the attacker must change all routing tables to point to the spoofed IP address. Another approach the attacker could take is to simply not worry about receiving any response from the applications. If an attacker is attempting to get a system to mail him or her a sensitive file, application responses are unimportant.

However, if an attacker manages to change the routing tables to point to the spoofed IP address, he can receive all the network packets that are addressed to the spoofed address and reply just as any trusted user can. Like packet sniffers, IP spoofing is not restricted to people who are external to the network.

Password Attacks

Password attacks can be implemented using several different methods, including brute-force attacks, Trojan horse programs (discussed later in the chapter), IP spoofing, and packet sniffers. Although packet sniffers and IP spoofing can yield user accounts and passwords, password attacks usually refer to repeated attempts to identify a user account and/or password; these repeated attempts are called brute-force attacks.

Often a brute-force attack is performed using a program that runs across the network and attempts to log in to a shared resource, such as a server. When an attacker successfully gains access to a resource, he or she has the same rights as the user whose account has been compromised to gain access to that resource. If this account has sufficient privileges, the attacker can create a back door for future access, without concern for any status and password changes to the compromised user account.

Distribution of Sensitive Information

Controlling the distribution of sensitive information is at the core of a network security policy. Although such an attack may not seem obvious to you, the majority of computer break-ins that organizations suffer are at the hands of disgruntled present or former employees. At the core of these security breaches is the distribution of sensitive information to competitors or others who will use it to your disadvantage. An outside intruder can use password and IP spoofing attacks to copy information, and an internal user can easily place sensitive information on an external computer or share a drive on the network with other users.

For example, an internal user could place a file on an external FTP server without ever leaving his or her desk. The user could also e-mail an attachment that contains sensitive information to an external user.

Man-in-the-Middle Attacks

A man-in-the-middle attack requires that the attacker have access to network packets that come across the networks. An example of such a configuration could be someone who is working for your Internet service provider (ISP), who can gain access to all network packets transferred between your network and any other network. Such attacks are often implemented using network packet sniffers and routing and transport protocols. The possible uses of such attacks are theft of information, hijacking of an ongoing session to gain access to your internal network resources, traffic analysis to derive information about your network and its users, denial of service, corruption of transmitted data, and introduction of new information into network sessions.

Protecting Your Network: Maintaining Internal Network System Integrity

Although protecting your information may be your highest priority, protecting the integrity of your network is critical in your ability to protect the information it contains. A breach in the integrity of your network can be extremely costly in time and effort, and it can open multiple avenues for continued attacks. This section covers the five methods of attack that are commonly used to compromise the integrity of your network:

- Network packet sniffers
- IP spoofing
- Password attacks

- Denial-of-service attacks

- Application layer attacks

When considering what to protect within your network, you are concerned with maintaining the integrity of the physical network, your network software, any other network resources, and your reputation. This integrity involves the verifiable identity of computers and users, proper operation of the services that your network provides, and optimal network performance; all these concerns are important in maintaining a productive network environment. This section describes the previously mentioned attacks and provide examples of how they can be used to compromise your network's integrity.

Network Packet Sniffers

As mentioned earlier, network packet sniffers can yield critical system information, such as user account information and passwords. When an attacker obtains the correct account information, he or she has the run of your network. In a worst-case scenario, an attacker gains access to a system-level user account, which the attacker uses to create a new account that can be used at any time as a back door to get into your network and its resources. The attacker can modify system-critical files, such as the password for the system administrator account, the list of services and permissions on file servers, and the login information for other computers that contain confidential information.

Packet sniffers provide information about the topology of your network that many attackers find useful. This information, such as what computers run which services, how many computers are on your network, which computers have access to others, and so on can be deduced from the information contained within the network packets that are distributed across your network as part of necessary daily operations.

In addition, a network packet sniffer can be modified to interject new information or change existing information in a network packet. By doing so, the attacker can cause network connections to shut down prematurely, as well as change critical information within the packet. Imagine what could happen if an attacker modified the information being transmitted to your accounting system. The effects of such attacks can be difficult to detect and very costly to correct.

IP Spoofing

IP spoofing can yield access to user accounts and passwords, and it can also be used in other ways. For example, an attacker can emulate one of your internal users in ways that prove embarrassing for your organization; the attacker could send e-mail messages to business partners that appear to have originated from someone within your organization. Such attacks are easier when an attacker has a user account and password, but they are possible by combining simple spoofing attacks with knowledge of messaging protocols.

Password Attacks

Just as with packet sniffers and IP spoofing attacks, a brute-force password attack can provide access to accounts that can be used to modify critical network files and services. An example that compromises your network's integrity is an attacker modifying the routing tables for your network. By doing so, the attacker ensures that all network packets are routed to him or her before they are transmitted to their final destination. In such a case, an attacker can monitor all network traffic, effectively becoming a man in the middle.

Denial-of-Service Attacks

Denial-of-service attacks are different from most other attacks because they are not targeted at gaining access to your network or the information on your network. These attacks focus on making a service unavailable for normal use, which is typically accomplished by exhausting some resource limitation on the network or within an operating system or application.

When involving specific network server applications, such as a Hypertext Transfer Protocol (HTTP) server or a File Transfer Protocol (FTP) server, these attacks can focus on acquiring and keeping open all the available connections supported by that server, effectively locking out valid users of the server or service. Denial-of-service attacks can also be implemented using common Internet protocols, such as TCP and Internet Control Message Protocol (ICMP). Most denial-of-service attacks exploit a weakness in the overall architecture of the system being attacked rather than a software bug or security hole. However, some attacks compromise the performance of your network by flooding the network with undesired, and often useless, network packets and by providing false information about the status of network resources.

Application-Layer Attacks

Application-layer attacks can be implemented using several different methods. One of the most common methods is exploiting well-known weaknesses in software commonly found on servers, such as sendmail, PostScript, and FTP. By exploiting these weaknesses, attackers can gain access to a computer with the permissions of the account running the application, which is usually a privileged system-level account.

Trojan horse program attacks are implemented using programs that an attacker substitutes for common programs. These programs may provide all the functionality that the normal program provides, but also include other features that are known to the attacker, such as monitoring login attempts to capture user account and password information. These programs can capture sensitive information and distribute it back to the attacker. They can also modify application functionality, such as applying a blind carbon copy to all e-mail messages so that the attacker can read all of your organization's e-mail.

One of the oldest forms of application-layer attacks is a Trojan horse program that displays a screen, banner, or prompt that the user believes is the valid login sequence. The program then captures the information that the user types in and stores or e-mails it to the attacker. Next, the program either forwards the information to the normal login process (normally impossible on modern systems) or simply sends an expected error to the user (for example, Bad Username/Password Combination), exits, and starts the normal login sequence. The user, believing that he or she has incorrectly entered the password (a common mistake experienced by everyone), retypes the information and is allowed access.

One of the newest forms of application-layer attacks exploits the openness of several new technologies: the Hypertext Markup Language (HTML) specification, Web browser functionality, and HTTP. These attacks, which include Java applets and ActiveX controls, involve passing harmful programs across the network and loading them through a user's browser.

Users of ActiveX controls may be lulled into a false sense of security by the Authenticode technology promoted by Microsoft. However, attackers have already discovered how to utilize properly signed and bug-free ActiveX controls to make them act as Trojan horses. This technique uses VBScript to direct the controls to perform their dirty work, such as overwriting files and executing other programs.

These new forms of attack are different in two respects:

- They are initiated not by the attacker but by the user who selects the HTML page that contains the harmful applet or script stored using the <OBJECT>, <APPLET>, or <SCRIPT> tags.

- Their attacks are no longer restricted to certain hardware platforms and operating systems because of the portability of the programming languages involved.

TRUSTED, UNTRUSTED, AND UNKNOWN NETWORKS

As a network manager creates a network security policy, each network that makes up the topology must be classified as one of three types of networks:

- Trusted

- Untrusted

- Unknown

Trusted Networks

Trusted networks are the networks inside your network security perimeter. These networks are the ones you are trying to protect. Often, you or someone in your organization administers the computers that comprise these networks, and your organization controls their security measures. Usually, trusted networks are within the security perimeter.

When you set up the firewall server, you explicitly identify the type of networks that are attached to the firewall server through network adapter cards. After the initial configuration, the trusted networks include the firewall server and all networks behind it.

One exception to this general rule is the inclusion of virtual private networks (VPNs), which are trusted networks that transmit data across an untrusted network infrastructure. For the purposes of our discussion, the network packets that originate on a VPN are considered to originate from within your internal perimeter network. This origin is logical because of how VPNs are established. For communications that originate on a VPN, security mechanisms must exist by which the firewall server can authenticate the origin, data integrity, and other security principles contained within the network traffic according to the same security principles enforced on your trusted networks.

Untrusted Networks

Untrusted networks are the networks that are known to be outside your security perimeter. They are untrusted because they are outside your control. You have no control over the administration or security policies for these sites. They are the private, shared networks from which you are trying to protect your network. However, you still need and want to communicate with these networks even though they are untrusted.

When you set up the firewall server, you explicitly identify the untrusted networks from which that firewall can accept requests. Untrusted networks are outside the security perimeter and external to the firewall server.

Unknown Networks

Unknown networks are networks that are neither trusted nor untrusted. They are unknown quantities to the firewall because you cannot explicitly tell the firewall server that the network is a trusted or an untrusted network. Unknown networks exist outside your security perimeter. By default, all non-trusted networks are considered unknown networks, and the firewall applies the security policy that is applied to the Internet node in the user interface, which represents all unknown networks. However, you can identify unknown networks below the Internet node and apply more specialized policies to those untrusted networks.

ESTABLISHING A SECURITY PERIMETER

When you define a network security policy, you must define procedures to safeguard your network and its contents and users against loss and damage. From this perspective, a network security policy plays a role in enforcing the overall security policy defined by an organization.

A critical part of an overall security solution is a network firewall, which monitors traffic crossing network perimeters and imposes restrictions according to security policy. Perimeter routers are found at any network boundary, such as between private networks, intranets, extranets, or the Internet. Firewalls most commonly separate internal (private) and external (public) networks.

A network security policy focuses on controlling the network traffic and usage. It identifies a network's resources and threats, defines network use and responsibilities, and details action plans for when the security policy is violated. When you deploy a network security policy, you want it to be strategically enforced at defensible boundaries within your network. These strategic boundaries are called *perimeter networks*.

Perimeter Networks

To establish your collection of perimeter networks, you must designate the networks of computers that you wish to protect and define the network security mechanisms that protect them. To have a successful network security perimeter, the firewall server must be the gateway for *all* communications between trusted networks and untrusted and unknown networks.

Each network can contain multiple perimeter networks. When describing how perimeter networks are positioned relative to each other, three types of perimeter networks are present: the outermost perimeter, internal perimeters, and the innermost perimeter. Figure 47–1 depicts the relationships among the various perimeters. Note that the multiple internal perimeters are relative to a particular asset, such as the internal perimeter that is just inside the firewall server.

The outermost perimeter network identifies the separation point between the assets that you control and the assets that you do not control—usually, this point is the router that you use to separate your network from your ISP's network. Internal perimeter networks represent additional boundaries where you have other security mechanisms in place, such as intranet firewalls and filtering routers.

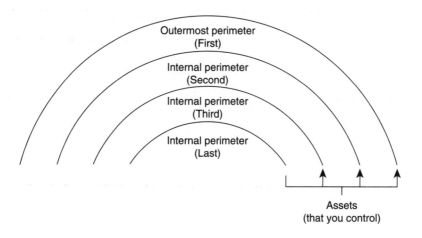

Figure 47–1
There are three types of perimeter networks: outermost, internal, and innermost.

Figure 47–2 depicts two perimeter networks (an outermost perimeter network and an internal perimeter network) defined by the placement of the internal and external routers and the firewall server.

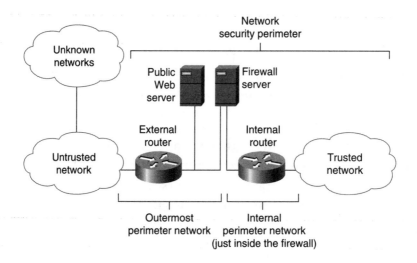

Figure 47–2
The diagram is an example of a two-perimeter network security design.

Positioning your firewall between an internal and external router provides little additional protection from attacks on either side, but it greatly reduces the amount of traffic the firewall server must evaluate, which can increase the firewall's performance. From the perspective of users on an external network, the firewall server represents all accessible computers on the trusted network. It defines the point of focus, or choke point, through which all communications between the two networks must pass.

The outermost perimeter network is the most insecure area of your network infrastructure. Normally, this area is reserved for routers, firewall servers, and public Internet servers, such as HTTP, FTP, and Gopher servers. This area of the network is the easiest area to gain access to, and therefore, it is the most frequently attacked, usually in an attempt to gain access to the internal networks. Sensitive company information that is for internal use only should *not* be placed on the outermost perimeter network. Following this precaution helps avoid having your sensitive information stolen or damaged.

Developing Your Security Design

The design of the perimeter network and security policies requires the following subjects to be addressed.

Knowing Your Enemy

Knowing your enemy refers to knowing attackers or intruders. Consider who might want to circumvent your security measures and identify their motivations. Determine what they might want to do and the damage that they could cause to your network.

Security measures can never make it impossible for a user to perform unauthorized tasks with a computer system; they can only make it harder. The goal is to make sure the network security controls are beyond the attacker's ability or motivation.

Counting the Cost

Security measures almost always reduce convenience, especially for sophisticated users. Security can delay work and create expensive administrative and educational overhead. Security can use significant computing resources and require dedicated hardware.

When you design your security measures, understand their costs and weigh those costs against the potential benefits. To do that, you must understand the costs of the measures themselves and the costs and likelihoods of security breaches. If you incur security costs out of proportion to the actual dangers, you have done yourself a disservice.

Identifying Your Assumptions

Every security system has underlying assumptions. For example, you might assume that your network is not tapped, or that attackers know less than you do, that they are using standard software, or that a locked room is safe. Be sure to examine and justify your assumptions. Any hidden assumption is a potential security hole.

Controlling Your Secrets

Most security is based on secrets. Passwords and encryption keys, for example, are secrets. Too often, though, the secrets are not really all that secret. The most important part of keeping secrets is knowing the areas you need to protect. What knowledge would enable someone to circumvent your system? You should jealously guard that knowledge and assume that everything else is known to your adversaries. The more secrets you have, the harder it will be to keep them all. Security systems should be designed so that only a limited number of secrets need to be kept.

Remembering Human Factors

Many security procedures fail because their designers do not consider how users will react to them. For example, because they can be difficult to remember, automatically generated "nonsense" passwords are often found written on the undersides of keyboards. For convenience, a "secure" door that leads to the system's only tape drive is sometimes propped open. For expediency, unauthorized modems are often connected to a network to avoid onerous dial-in security measures.

If your security measures interfere with essential use of the system, those measures will be resisted and perhaps circumvented. To get compliance, you must make sure that users can get their work done, and you must sell your security measures to users. Users must understand and accept the need for security.

Any user can compromise system security, at least to some degree. Passwords, for instance, can often be found simply by calling legitimate users on the telephone, claiming to be a system administrator, and asking for them. If your users understand security issues, and if they understand the reasons for your security measures, they are far less likely to make an intruder's life easier.

At a minimum, users should be taught never to release passwords or other secrets over unsecured telephone lines (especially cellular telephones) or e-mail. Users should be wary of people who call them on the telephone and ask questions. Some companies have implemented formalized network security training for their employees so that employees are not allowed access to the Internet until they have completed a formal training program.

Knowing Your Weaknesses

Every security system has vulnerabilities. You should understand your system's weak points and know how they could be exploited. You should also know the areas that present the greatest danger and prevent access to them immediately. Understanding the weak points is the first step toward turning them into secure areas.

Limiting the Scope of Access

You should create appropriate barriers in your system so that if intruders access one part of the system, they do not automatically have access to the rest of the system. The security of a system is only as good as the weakest security level of any single host in the system.

Understanding Your Environment

Understanding how your system normally functions, knowing what is expected and what is unexpected, and being familiar with how devices are usually used will help you detect security problems. Noticing unusual events can help you catch intruders before they can damage the system. Auditing tools can help you detect those unusual events.

Limiting Your Trust

You should know exactly which software you rely on, and your security system should not have to rely on the assumption that all software is bug-free.

Remembering Physical Security

Physical access to a computer (or a router) usually gives a sufficiently sophisticated user total control over that computer. Physical access to a network link usually allows a person to tap that link, jam it, or inject traffic into it. It makes no sense to install complicated software security measures when access to the hardware is not controlled.

Making Security Pervasive

Almost any change you make in your system may have security effects. This is especially true when new services are created. Administrators, programmers, and users should consider the security implications of every change they make. Understanding the security implications of a change takes practice; it requires lateral thinking and a willingness to explore every way a service could potentially be manipulated.

CHAPTER 48

Directory-Enabled Networking

Directory services are the cornerstone for creating intelligent networks. A directory service is a physically distributed, logically centralized repository of infrequently changing data that is used to manage the entire enterprise networking environment. Today, the computing environment that must be managed includes not only the computers themselves, but also the network devices that connect them. Extending networks to include directory services is a response to the new, more demanding requirements for network management by means of the directory.

A traditional directory service provides a means for locating and identifying users and available resources in a distributed system. Directory services also provide the foundation for adding, modifying, removing, renaming, and managing system components without disrupting the services provided by other system components. Today's directory services are used to do the following:

- Store information about system components in a distributed manner. The directory is replicated among several servers so that a user or service needing access to the directory can query a local server for the information.

- Support white pages (by attribute, such as name, for example, "find the phone number for James Smith") and yellow pages (by classification, for example, "find all color printers on the third floor") lookup.

- Allow single-user logon to services, resources, and applications.

- Enable a location-independent point of administration and management. Note that administrative tools do not have to be centrally located and managed.

- Replicate data to provide consistent access. Modifications made to any replica of the directory are propagated around the network so that any application accessing the directory anywhere sees consistent information after the change is propagated.

Rapid Internet growth over the past several years has created the need for more robust, scalable, and secure directory services. As PCs become more powerful, people are finding more ways to fully utilize the power of their computers. Residential customers desire rich multimedia services, such as data and video. Corporate customers are looking to telcos and service providers for powerful, yet affordable, services. Users want a reliable, easy-to-use, friendly service.

A fundamental shift toward bandwidth-intensive and isochronous network applications is occurring. Current directory services technology is not designed to meet the ever-increasing demands of today's public and private network applications because current directory services were built mainly to accommodate administrative needs. The directory must be transformed from a "dumb warehouse" to an authoritative, distributed, intelligent repository of information for services and applications. The directory is the foundation for an intelligent infrastructure. Bandwidth-intensive and isochronous network applications require that the devices that lie on a path through the network between source and end device be configured appropriately if they are to function properly. This configuration is often dynamic, taking place on demand when a particular user logs on to the network from any of a number of possible locations. Only when management information about the users, network devices, and services involved is available in a single, authoritative location is it possible to actually manage this new class of applications.

THE PURPOSE AND SCOPE OF DIRECTORY-ENABLED NETWORKING

This section defines the problem domains, information model, usage, and detailed directory schema for integrating networks with directory services. Cisco Systems and Microsoft Corporation have introduced an initiative to define a rational, usable model for enhancing networks via integration with the directory service. In these networks, the network resources (devices, operating systems, management tools, and applications) use the directory service to

- Publish information about themselves

- Discover other resources

- Obtain information about other resources

The directory service becomes the hub around which the distributed system turns; the degree of cooperation among network components and distributed applications is dramatically enhanced. The result is a network in which service to users is predictable and repeatable, security is strengthened, and management is easier.

This section defines an environment for directory-enabled networks. The environment defined here provides the basis for network equipment vendors, directory service providers, software developers, common carriers, and end users to develop the interoperating components that will comprise next-generation networks.

Networks, the Universe, and You

Administrative needs and the tools that service them have evolved as distributed systems have evolved. Today's directory services were designed to provide central management of security and contact information in a network with a relatively small number of relatively large computers. Network management has been the province of more specialized tools, each with its own information store. Application management has been addressed as an afterthought, when it has been addressed at all.

Convergence of the information stores holding the universe of management information has been difficult. The result is an environment in which vertical management tools have proliferated. Lack of integration and the sheer complexity of the tools themselves has become a barrier to the deployment of new applications.

Administrators need a level of control over their networks that is currently unavailable. Streaming multimedia, use of public networks and the attendant security concerns, and rapidly growing user communities present a tremendous challenge.

Simply managing individual devices is no longer sufficient. Network administrators need to define and manage *policies* to control the network and its resources in a distributed, yet logically centralized, manner. In general terms, policies define what resources a given consumer can use in the context of a given application or service. Inability to easily manage policies is a significant barrier to deployment of leading-edge distributed applications.

Defining and managing policies requires a common store of well-defined information about the network and its resources—users, applications, devices, protocols, and media—and the relationships among these elements. This is information *about the network* as well as the information traditionally viewed as defining the network (for example, routing tables). At issue is where to store policy and other information that needs to be applied across components in a way that makes it usable by a broad range of consumers.

A scalable, secure directory service that presents a logically centralized view of physically distributed information is the logical place to store the meta-information essential to creating and managing a next-generation network. The specification for the integration of directory services and network services defines the information model and schema to make this possible.

Directory Service and Network Management

Network elements typically have a dynamic state and a persistent state. Dynamic state is well addressed by network management protocols. However, there is no standard way to describe and store persistent state. Moreover, existing tools and applications focus on managing individual network elements rather than the entire network. This specification defines a standard schema for storing persistent state *and* an information model for describing the relationships among objects representing users, applications, network elements, and network services (see Figure 48–1). Network management protocols (such as SNMP, CMIP, and HMMP) are used to talk *to* the network elements. The network schema extensions for the directory service are used to talk *about* network elements.

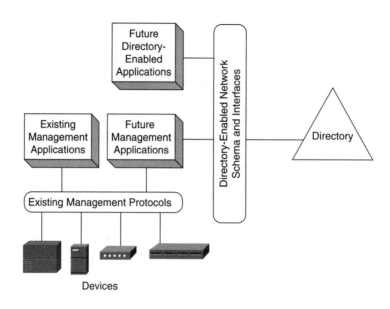

Figure 48–1

This figure displays a high-level overview of the directory-enabled network schema.

The integration of the network infrastructure with the directory service allows the applications and users to discover the existence of devices and relationships by querying the directory service, rather than contacting the individual devices and aggregating the results. Exposing network elements in the directory enhances manageability and usability while reducing the load on the network. The end user and administrator experience is enhanced because there is a single, authoritative place to obtain the information of interest.

The Common Information Model (CIM)

CIM is an object-oriented conceptual model for the information required to manage many common aspects of complex computer systems, defined by the Desktop Management Task Force (DMTF).

Ongoing development of CIM is part of an industrywide initiative for enabling enterprise management of devices and applications. A primary goal of CIM is the presentation of a consistent view of the managed environment, independent of the various protocols and data formats supported by those devices and applications. Many network infrastructure and management software providers have accepted CIM as an information model for enterprise management tools.

The schema for network integration defined in this specification and CIM are complementary. The extended schema is primarily concerned with the expression and management of policy in both enterprise and service provider networks. CIM is primarily concerned with the management of individual components in the context of the enterprise. The enhanced, integrated network and directory service and CIM have many information needs in common.

The schema for integrating networks and the directory service incorporates concepts from both X.500 and CIM. The use of CIM promotes synergy between integrated, enhanced network and directory applications and management applications that use CIM:

- CIM and applications written to use CIM are natural sources of information for the directory.

- The directory is a natural source of information for CIM and applications written to use CIM, and adds models for defining and enforcing policy.

- Network applications integrated with the directory benefit from CIM, and CIM applications benefit from network applications integrated with the directory, with minimal effort on the application developer's part because the directory-enabled network schema is an extension of the CIM schema. Thus, there is no need for cumbersome information mapping.

THE EXTENDED SCHEMA AND OTHER DEVICE SCHEMATA

Schemata defined by SNMP (MIBs), DMTF CIM, and so on are intended primarily to address the details of individual devices. The intent of the integrated, extended schema is to leverage the information exposed by existing schemata and management frameworks, not to replace them.

This specification exposes network element information and relationships gathered from the network with existing protocols and schemata using the widely available and well-understood protocol Lightweight Directory Access Protocol (LDAP), without imposing LDAP on the devices themselves.

Network Applications Integrated with the Directory and Other Network Protocols

The schema and information model defined augments existing network services and associated protocols, such as Domain Name System (DNS), Dynamic Host Configuration Protocol (DHCP), and RADIUS.

The directory provides a common store for network information; the information model describes the relationships that can be represented in the directory. The usage model defines how existing network services and protocols work with the elements in the information model to accomplish specific goals, such as coordinating IP address allocation across multiple DHCP servers, establishing and propagating remote access login policy, and so on.

Deliverables

A set of specifications in a vacuum is not helpful in building actual products. Completeness requires one or more implementations illustrating the use and deployment of the information model and detailed schema defined by this specification.

Deliverables in the Near Term

The participants in the open process will deliver an integrated network and directory environment consisting of

- Abstractions of the eight major network objects—device, protocol, media, service, application, profile, policy, and user—with additional subsidiary classes as needed refined into a set of abstract classes in a schema that addresses a well-defined set of problem domains
- A usage model for the schema within the selected problem domains
- Vendor-specific products based on the foundation schema and information model described in this document

Deliverables in the Longer Term

The longer-term deliverables are a rich set of interoperable products and tools based on the schema and usage models, refined through an open process of industry review and the evolving needs of network consumers.

The Directory-Enabled Networking Vision

The vision for enhancing networking through integration with the directory service is to provide network-enabled applications appropriate information from the directory. Eventually, intelligent network applications will transparently leverage the network on behalf of the user. The development of intelligent networks can be achieved through the following steps:

1. Relying on a robust directory service
2. Adding a standards-based schema for modeling network elements and services
3. Adding protocols for accessing, managing, and manipulating directory information

The goal of work in developing directory-enabled networks is to

- Provide support for applications that have the ability to leverage the network infrastructure transparently on behalf of the end user

- Provide a robust, extensible foundation for building network-centric applications

- Enable end-to-end network services on a per-user basis

- Enable networkwide service creation and provisioning

- Enable networkwide management

The focus is on providing management of the network as a system, not a set of disparate components. Using directory services to define the relationship among components allows the network manager to manage the network as a system. Vendors have adopted de facto and open industry standards to tie these services into its enterprise management systems. Key standards include DNS, DHCP, and LDAP. DNS and DHCP provide a critical foundation for tying system names, IP addresses, users, systems, and other services together in a more seamless and easily managed fashion. LDAP provides access to information about systems, users, services, and resources from a wide variety of vendors' network directories in an industry-standard fashion.

CHAPTER 49

Network Caching Technologies

Although the volume of Web traffic on the Internet is staggering, a large percentage of that traffic is redundant—multiple users at any given site request much of the same content. This means that a significant percentage of the WAN infrastructure carries the identical content (and identical requests for it) day after day. Eliminating a significant amount of recurring telecommunications charges offers an enormous savings opportunity for enterprise and service provider customers.

Web caching performs the local storage of Web content to serve these redundant user requests more quickly, without sending the requests and the resulting content over the WAN.

GROWTH OF WEB CONTENT

Data networking is growing at a dizzying rate. More than 80% of Fortune 500 companies have Web sites. More than half of these companies have implemented intranets and are putting graphically rich data onto the corporate

WANs. The number of Web users is expected to increase by a factor of five in the next three years. The resulting uncontrolled growth of Web access requirements is straining all attempts to meet the bandwidth demand.

CACHING

Caching is the technique of keeping frequently accessed information in a location close to the requester. A Web cache stores Web pages and content on a storage device that is physically or logically closer to the user—this is closer and faster than a Web lookup. By reducing the amount of traffic on WAN links and on overburdened Web servers, caching provides significant benefits to ISPs, enterprise networks, and end users. There are two key benefits:

- *Cost savings due to WAN bandwidth reduction*—ISPs can place cache engines at strategic points on their networks to improve response times and lower the bandwidth demand on their backbones. ISPs can station cache engines at strategic WAN access points to serve Web requests from a local disk rather than from distant or overrun Web servers.

  In enterprise networks, the dramatic reduction in bandwidth usage due to Web caching allows a lower-bandwidth (lower-cost) WAN link to serve the same user base. Alternatively, the organization can add users or add more services that use the freed bandwidth on the existing WAN link.

- *Improved productivity for end users*—The response of a local Web cache is often three times faster than the download time for the same content over the WAN. End users see dramatic improvements in response times, and the implementation is completely transparent to them.

Other benefits include

- *Secure access control and monitoring*—The cache engine provides network administrators with a simple, secure method to enforce a sitewide access policy through URL filtering.

- *Operational logging*—Network administrators can learn which URLs receive hits, how many requests per second the cache is serving, what percentage of URLs are served from the cache, and other related operational statistics.

Web caching works as follows:

1. A user accesses a Web page.
2. While the page is being transmitted to the user, the caching system saves the page and all its associated graphics on a local storage device. That content is now cached.
3. Another user (or the original user) accesses that Web page later in the day.
4. Instead of sending the request over the Internet, the Web cache system delivers the Web page from local storage. This process speeds download time for the user, and reduces bandwidth demand on the WAN link.
5. The important task of ensuring that data is up-to-date is addressed in a variety of ways, depending on the design of the system.

Browser-Based Client Caching

Internet browser applications allow an individual user to cache Web pages (that is, images and HTML text) on his or her local hard disk. A user can configure the amount of disk space devoted to caching. Figure 49–1 shows the cache configuration window for Netscape Navigator.

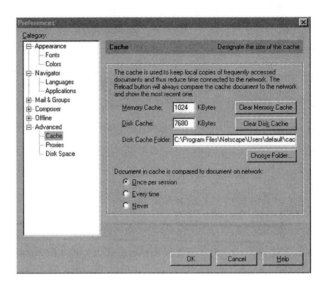

Figure 49-1

You use the cache configuration window to configure the amount of disk space devoted to caching in Netscape Navigator.

This setup is useful in cases where a user accesses a site more than once. The first time the user views a Web site, that content is saved as files in a subdirectory on that computer's hard disk. The next time the user points to this Web site, the browser gets the content from the cache without accessing the network. The user notices that the elements of the page—especially larger Web graphics such as buttons, icons, and images—appear much more quickly than they did the first time the page was opened.

This method serves this user well, but does not benefit other users on the same network who might access the same Web sites. In Figure 49-2, the fact that User A has cached a popular page has no effect on the download time of this page for Users B and C.

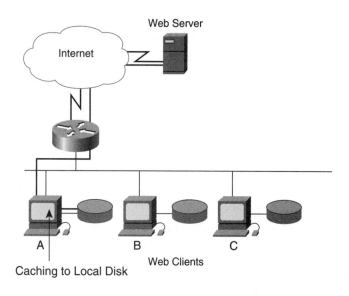

Figure 49-2
This figure demonstrates the benefits gained by a single node using browser caching.

Attempts at a Caching Solution on the Network Level

To limit bandwidth demand caused by the uncontrolled growth of Internet use, vendors have developed applications that extend local caching to the network level. The two current types of network-level caching products are proxy servers and network caches:

- *Proxy servers* are software applications that run on general-purpose hardware and operating systems. A proxy server is placed on hardware that is physically between a client application, such as a Web browser, and a Web server. The proxy acts as a gatekeeper that receives all packets destined for the Web server and examines each packet to determine whether it can fulfill the requests itself; if it can't, it forwards the request to the Web server. Proxy servers can also be used to filter requests, for example, to prevent employees from accessing a specific set of Web sites.

Unfortunately, proxy servers are not optimized for caching, and they fail under heavy network loads. In addition, because the proxy is in the path of all user traffic (it's a "bump in the cable"), two problems arise: All traffic is slowed to allow the proxy to examine each packet, and failure of the proxy software or hardware causes all users to lose network access. Further, proxies require configuration of each user's browser—an unacceptable option for service providers and large enterprises. Expensive hardware is required to compensate for low software performance and the lack of scalability of proxy servers.

- In response to these shortcomings, some vendors have created *network caches*. These caching-focused software applications are designed to improve performance by enhancing the caching software and eliminating the other slow aspects of proxy server implementations. However, because network caches run under general-purpose operating systems (such as UNIX or Windows NT) that involve very high per-process context overhead, they cannot scale to large numbers of simultaneous processes in a graceful fashion. This is especially true for networking caching systems that can have many thousands of simultaneous and short-lived transactions.

Cisco's Network-Based Shared Caching

The cache engine was designed from the ground up as a loosely coupled, multinode network system optimized to provide robust shared network caching. The cache engine solution comprises the Web Cache Control Protocol (a standard feature of Cisco IOS software) and one or more Cisco cache engines that store the data in the local network.

The Web Cache Control Protocol defines the communication between the cache engine and the router. Using the Web Cache Control Protocol, the router directs only Web requests to the cache engine (rather than to the intended server). The router also determines cache engine availability, and redirects requests to new cache engines as they are added to an installation.

The Cisco cache engine is a single-purpose network appliance that stores and retrieves content using highly optimized caching and retrieval algorithms. (See Figure 49–3.)

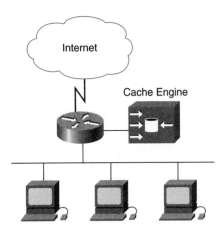

Figure 49–3
This figure shows a Cisco cache engine connected to a Cisco IOS router.

Cache Engine Operation

Using the Web Cache Control Protocol, the Cisco IOS router routes requests for TCP port 80 (HTTP traffic) over a local subnet to the cache engine. The cache engine is dedicated solely to content management and delivery. Because only Web requests are routed to the cache engine, no other user traffic is affected by the caching process—Web caching is done "off to the side." For non-Web traffic, the router functions entirely in its traditional role.

The cache engine works as follows (see Figure 49–4):

1. A client requests Web content in the normal fashion.
2. The router, running the Web Cache Control Protocol, intercepts TCP port 80 Web traffic and routes it to the cache engine. The client is not involved in this transaction, and no changes to the client or browser are required.
3. If the cache engine does not have the requested content, it sends the request to the Internet or intranet in the normal fashion. The content returns to, and is stored at, the cache engine.
4. The cache engine returns the content to the client. Upon subsequent requests for the same content, the cache engine fulfills the request from local storage.

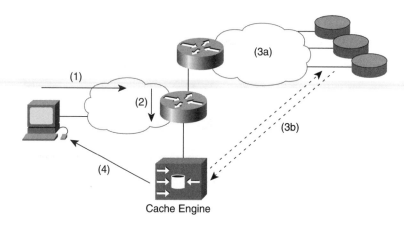

Figure 49–4
This figure provides an overview of the operation of the cache engine.

Transparency

Because the router redirects packets destined for Web servers to the cache engine, the cache engine operates transparently to clients. Clients do not need to configure their browsers to be in proxy server mode. This is a compelling feature for ISPs and large enterprises, for whom uniform client configuration is extremely expensive and difficult to implement. In addition, the operation of the cache engine is transparent to the network—the router operates entirely in its normal role for non-Web traffic. This transparent design is a requirement for a system to offer networkwide scalability, fault tolerance, and fail-safe operation.

Hierarchical Use

Because the Cisco cache engine is transparent to the user and to network operation, customers can place cache engines in several network locations in a hierarchical fashion. For example, if an ISP places a large cache farm at its main point of access to the Internet, then all its points of presence (POPs) benefit. (See Figure 49–5.) Client requests hit the cache farm and are fulfilled from its storage. To further improve service to clients, the ISP should deploy cache farms at its POPs. Then, when the client at a POP accesses the Internet, the request is diverted to the POP cache farm. If the POP cache farm is unable to fulfill the request from local storage, it makes a normal Web request. This request is routed to the cache farm at the main access point. If the request is filled by that cache farm, the traffic on the main Internet access link is avoided, the Web servers experience lower demand, and the user still experiences improved performance. As shown in Figure 49–6, enterprise networks can apply this architecture to benefit in the same ways.

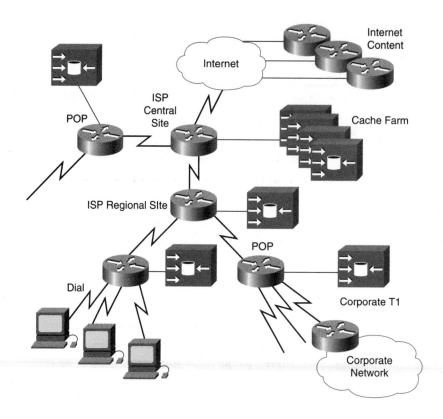

Figure 49-5

This figure shows example of how to perform a hierarchical implementation of cache engines (ISP).

High Performance

The cache engine uses thread-oriented, real-time file system management and networking stack software designed solely for its role as a caching and retrieval system, eliminating the file fragmentation and long directory searches associated with general-purpose file system management design. The cache engine's secure, real-time, embedded operating system has none of the process context overhead of general-purpose operating systems such as UNIX or Windows NT; this overhead slows file access and adds to the communications load. General-purpose operating systems cannot scale to large numbers of simultaneous processes in a graceful fashion—this is especially true of a shared network cache system that can have many thousands of simultaneous, short-lived transactions. The result is an extremely high-performance, scalable cache engine.

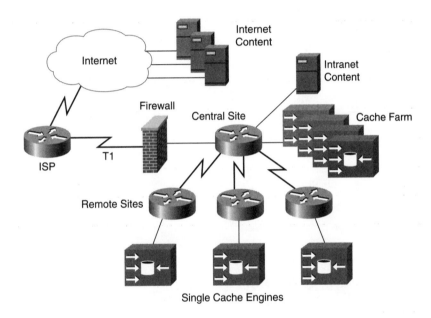

Figure 49–6
This figure shows an example of how to perform a hierarchical implementation of cache engines (enterprise).

PART 8

Network Management

Part 8, "Network Management," outlines the functions provided by several widely deployed network-management environments. Individual chapters discuss the following topics:

IBM Network Management—Covers the basics of IBM network management for SNA and APPN

Remote Monitoring (RMON)—Covers the features and functions of this standardized monitoring specification

Simple Network Management Protocol (SNMP)—Discusses SNMP, the widely used Internet network-management protocol

CHAPTER 50

IBM Network Management

BACKGROUND

IBM network management refers to any architecture used to manage IBM Systems Network Architecture (SNA) networks or Advanced Peer-to-Peer Networking (APPN) networks. IBM network management is part of the IBM Open-Network Architecture (ONA) and is performed centrally by using management platforms such as NetView and others. It is divided into five functions that are similar to the network management functions specified under the Open System Interconnection (OSI) model. This chapter summarizes the IBM network management functional areas, ONA network management architecture, and management platforms. Figure 50–1 illustrates a basic managed IBM network.

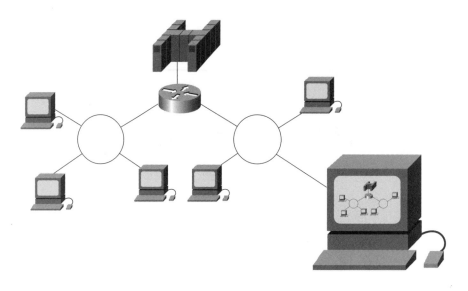

Figure 50–1
IBM network management handles SNA or APPN networks.

IBM NETWORK-MANAGEMENT FUNCTIONAL AREAS

IBM divides network management into the following five user-based functions: *configuration management*, *performance and accountant management*, *problem management*, *operations management*, and *change management*.

IBM Configuration Management

IBM configuration management controls information describing the physical and logical characteristics of network resources, as well as the relationships between those resources. A central management system stores data in a configuration management-databases and might include information such as system software or microcode version numbers; serial numbers of hardware or software; physical locations of network devices; and names, addresses, and telephone numbers of contacts. As might be expected, IBM configuration management corresponds closely to OSI configuration management.

Configuration-management facilities aid in maintaining an inventory of network resources and in ensuring that network-configuration changes are reflected in the configuration-management database. Configuration management also provides information that is used by problem-management and change-management systems. Problem-management systems use this information to compare version differences and to locate, identify, and check the characteristics of network resources. Change-management systems use the information to analyze the effect of changes and to schedule changes at times of minimal network impact.

IBM Performance and Accounting Management

IBM performance and accounting management provides information about the performance of network resources. The functions of the performance- and accounting-management facilities include monitoring response times of systems; measuring availability of resources; measuring the use of resources; and tuning, tracking, and controlling network performance. The information gathered by the performance- and accounting-management functions is useful for determining whether network performance goals are being met and whether problem-determination procedures should be initiated based on performance. IBM performance and accounting management performs functions similar to those handled by OSI performance management and OSI accounting management.

IBM Problem Management

IBM problem management is similar to OSI fault management in that it handles error conditions that cause users to lose the full functionality of a network resource. Problem management is performed in five steps: problem determination, problem diagnosis, problem bypass and recovery, problem resolution, and problem tracking and control. Problem determination consists of detecting a problem and completing the steps necessary for beginning problem diagnosis, such as isolating the problem to a particular subsystem. Problem diagnosis consists of determining the precise cause of the problem and the action required to solve it. Problem bypass and recovery consists of attempts to bypass the problem, either partially or completely. It provides only a temporary solution and relies on problem resolution to solve the problem permanently. Problem resolution consists of efforts to eliminate the problem. It usually begins after problem diagnosis is complete and often involves corrective action, such as the replacement of failed hardware or software. Problem tracking and control consists of tracking each problem until final resolution is reached. Vital information describing the problem is recorded in a problem database.

IBM Operations Management

IBM operations management consists of managing distributed network resources from a central site, using two sets of functions: operations-management services and common-operations services. Operations-management services provide the capability to control remote resources centrally using the following functions: resource activation and deactivation, command cancellation, and clock setting. Operations-management services can be initiated automatically in response to certain system-problem notifications.

Common-operations services allow for the management of resources not explicitly addressed by other management areas, using specialized communication through new, more capable applications. Common-operations services offer two important services, the execute command and resource-management service. The execute command provides a standardized means of executing remote commands. Resource-management service provides a way to transport information in a context-independent manner.

IBM Change Management

Change management tracks network changes and maintains change files at remote nodes. Network changes occur primarily for two reasons: changing user requirement and problem circumvention. Changing user requirements include hardware and software upgrades, new applications and services, and other factors that constantly change the needs of network users. Problem circumvention is needed to deal with unexpected changes resulting from the failure of hardware, software, or other network components. Change management attempts to minimize problems by promoting orderly network changes and managing change files, which log network changes. IBM change management is similar in some respects to OSI accounting management.

IBM NETWORK-MANAGEMENT ARCHITECTURES

Two of the most well-known IBM network-management architectures are the *Open-Network Architecture* (ONA) and *SystemView*.

Open-Network Architecture (ONA)

The Open-Network Architecture (ONA) is a generalized network-management architecture that defines four key management entities: the focal point, collection point, entry point, and service point.

The focal point is a management entity that provides support for centralized network-management operations. It responds to end-station alerts, maintains management databases, and provides a user interface for the network-management operator. Three kinds of focal points exist: primary, secondary, and nested. The primary focal points performs all focal-point functions. The secondary focal point acts as a backup for primary focal points and is used when primary focal points fail. The nested focal point provides distributed management support in large networks. Nested focal points are responsible for forwarding critical information to more global focal points.

Collection points relay information from self-contained SNA subnetworks to focal points. They are commonly used to forward data from IBM peer-to-peer networks into the ONA hierarchy.

An entry point is an SNA device that can implement ONA for itself and other devices. Most standard SNA devices are capable of being entry points.

A service point is a system that provides access into ONA for non-SNA devices and is essentially a gateway into ONA. Service points are capable of sending management information about non-SNA systems to focal points, receiving commands from focal points, translating commands into a format acceptable to non-SNA devices, and forwarding commands to non-SNA devices for execution.

Figure 50–2 illustrates the relationships between the different ONA management entities.

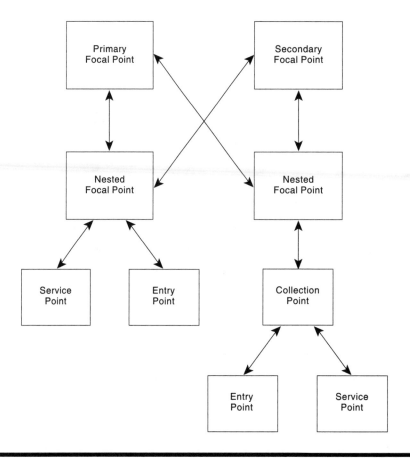

Figure 50–2

The four types of focal points link to one another within the ONA environment.

SystemView

SystemView is a blueprint for creating management applications that are capable of managing multivendor information systems. SystemView describes how applications that manage heterogeneous networks operate with other management systems. It is the official systems-management strategy of the IBM Systems-Application Architecture.

IBM Network-Management Platforms

IBM network management is implemented on several platforms, including *NetView*, *LAN Network Manager* (LNM), and *Simple Network Management Protocol* (SNMP).

NetView

NetView is a comprehensive IBM enterprise network-management platform that provides centralized SNA network-management services. It is used on IBM mainframes and is part of the ONA. NetView consists of the *command-control facility, hardware monitor, session monitor, help function, status monitor, performance monitor*, and *distribution monitor*. The command-control facility provides network control by issuing basic operator and file-access commands to Virtual Telecommunications Access Method (VTAM) applications, controllers, operating systems, and NetView/PC (an interface between NetView and non-SNA devices). The hardware-monitor function monitors the network and automatically alerts the network operator when hardware errors occur. The session monitor acts as a VTAM performance monitor and provides software-problem determination and configuration management. The help function provides help for NetView users and includes a browse facility, a help-desk facility, and a library of commonly encountered network operation situations. The status monitor summarizes and presents network status information. The performance-monitor function monitors the performance of front-end processors (FEPs), the Network Control Program (NCP), and other attached resources. The distribution manager plans, schedules, and tracks the distribution of data, software, and microcode in SNA environments.

LAN Network Manager (LNM)

The LAN Network Manager (LNM) is an IBM network-management application that controls Token Ring LANs from a central support site. LNM is an OS/2 Extended Edition-based product that interoperates with IBM NetView (which is aware of such LNM activities as alarms) and other IBM management software.

Simple Network Management Protocol (SNMP)

IBM network management can be implemented by using SNMP. Refer to Chapter 52, "Simple Network Management Protocol (SNMP)" for details about SNMP implementation.

CHAPTER 51

Remote Monitoring (RMON)

BACKGROUND

Remote Monitoring (RMON) is a standard monitoring specification that enables various network monitors and console systems to exchange network-monitoring data. RMON provides network administrators with more freedom in selecting network-monitoring probes and consoles with features that meet their particular networking needs. This chapter provides a brief overview of the RMON specification, focusing on RMON groups.

The RMON specification defines a set of statistics and functions that can be exchanged between RMON-compliant console managers and network probes. As such, RMON provides network administrators with comprehensive network-fault diagnosis, planning, and performance-tuning information.

RMON was defined by the user community with the help of the Internet Engineering Task Force (IETF). It became a proposed standard in 1992 as RFC 1271 (for Ethernet). RMON then became a draft standard in 1995 as RFC 1757, effectively obsoleting RFC 1271.

Figure 51–1 illustrates an RMON probe capable of monitoring an Ethernet segment and transmitting statistical information back to an RMON-compliant console.

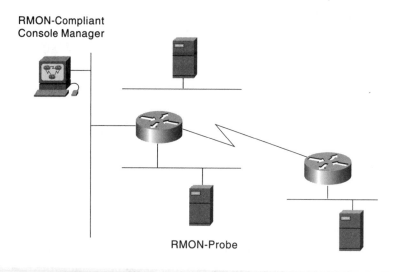

Figure 51–1

An RMON probe can send statistical information to an RMON console.

RMON GROUPS

RMON delivers information in nine RMON *groups* of monitoring elements, each providing specific sets of data to meet common network-monitoring requirements. Each group is optional so that vendors do not need to support all the groups within the Management Information Base (MIB). Some RMON groups require support of other RMON groups to function properly. Table 51-1 summarizes the nine monitoring groups specified in the RFC 1757 Ethernet RMON MIB.

RMON Group	Function	Elements
Statistics	Contains statistics measured by the probe for each monitored interface on this device.	Packets dropped, packets sent, bytes sent (octets), broadcast packets, multicast packets, CRC errors, runts, giants, fragments, jabbers, collisions, and counters for packets ranging from 64–128, 128–256, 256–512, 512–1024, and 1024–1518 bytes.
History	Records periodic statistical samples from a network and stores them for later retrieval.	Sample period, number of samples, item(s) sampled.
Alarm	Periodically takes statistical samples from variables in the probe and compares them with previously configured thresholds. If the monitored variable crosses a threshold, an event is generated.	Includes the alarm table and requires the implementation of the event group. Alarm type, interval, starting threshold, stop threshold.
Host	Contains statistics associated with each host discovered on the network.	Host address, packets, and bytes received and transmitted, as well as broadcast, multicast, and error packets.
HostTopN	Prepares tables that describe the hosts that top a list ordered by one of their statistics. The available statistics are samples of one of their base statistics over an interval specified by the management station. Thus, these statistics are rate-based.	Statistics, host(s), sample start and stop periods, rate base, duration.
Matrix	Stores statistics for conversations between sets of two addresses. As the device detects a new conversation, it creates a new entry in its table.	Source and destination address pairs and packets, bytes, and errors for each pair.

Continues

Table 51-1
RMON Monitoring Groups

RMON Group	Function	Elements
Filters	Enables packets to be matched by a filter equation. These matched packets form a data stream that might be captured or might generate events.	Bit-filter type (mask or not mask), filter expression (bit level), conditional expression (and, or, not) to other filters.
Packet Capture	Enables packets to be captured after they flow through a channel.	Size of buffer for captured packets, full status (alarm), number of captured packets.
Events	Controls the generation and notification of events from this device.	Event type, description, last time event sent.

Table 51-1
RMON Monitoring Groups

CHAPTER 52

Simple Network Management Protocol (SNMP)

BACKGROUND

The Simple Network Management Protocol is an application-layer protocol that facilitates the exchange of management information between network devices. It is part of the Transmission Control Protocol/Internet Protocol (TCP/IP) protocol suite. SNMP enables network administrators to manage network performance, find and solve network problems, and plan for network growth.

Two versions of SNMP exist: SNMP Version 1 (SNMPv1) and SNMP Version 2 (SNMPv2). Both versions have a number of features in common, but SNMPv2 offers enhancements, such as additional protocol operations. Standardization of yet another version of SNMP—SNMP Version 3 (SNMPv3)—is pending. This chapter provides descriptions of the SNMPv1 and SNMPv2 protocol operations. Figure 52–1 illustrates a basic network managed by SNMP.

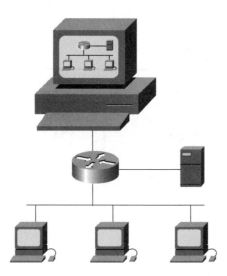

Figure 52–1
SNMP facilitates the exchange of network information between devices.

SNMP Basic Components

An SNMP managed network consists of three key components: *managed devices*, *agents*, and *network-management systems* (NMSs).

A managed device is a network node that contains an SNMP agent and resides on a managed network. Managed devices collect and store management information and make this information available to NMSs using SNMP. Managed devices, sometimes called network elements, can be routers and access servers, switches and bridges, hubs, computer hosts, or printers.

An agent is a network-management software module that resides in a managed device. An agent has local knowledge of management information and translates that information into a form compatible with SNMP.

An NMS executes applications that monitor and control managed devices. NMSs provide the bulk of the processing and memory resources required for network management. One or more NMSs must exist on any managed network.

Figure 52–2 illustrates the relationship between these three components.

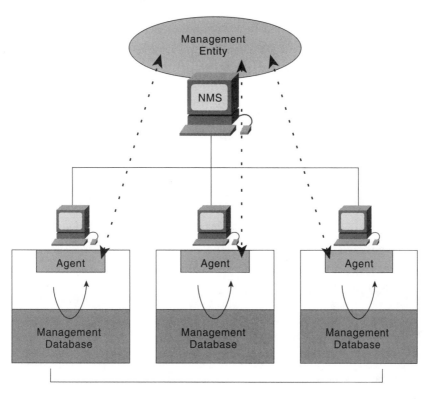

Figure 52–2
An SNMP managed network consists of managed devices, agents, and NMSs.

SNMP BASIC COMMANDS

Managed devices are monitored and controlled using four basic SNMP commands: *read*, *write*, *trap*, and *traversal operations*.

The read command is used by an NMS to monitor managed devices. The NMS examines different variables that are maintained by managed devices.

The write command is used by an NMS to control managed devices. The NMS changes the values of variables stored within managed devices.

The trap command is used by managed devices to asynchronously report events to the NMS. When certain types of events occur, a managed device sends a trap to the NMS.

Traversal operations are used by the NMS to determine which variables a managed device supports and to sequentially gather information in variable tables, such as a routing table.

SNMP MANAGEMENT INFORMATION BASE (MIB)

A *Management Information Base (MIB)* is a collection of information that is organized hierarchically. MIBs are accessed using a network-management protocol such as SNMP. They are comprised of managed objects and are identified by object identifiers.

A managed object (sometimes called a MIB object, an object, or a MIB) is one of any number of specific characteristics of a managed device. Managed objects are comprised of one or more object instances, which are essentially variables.

Two types of managed objects exist: *scalar* and *tabular*. Scalar objects define a single object instance. Tabular objects define multiple related object instances that are grouped together in MIB tables.

An example of a managed object is *atInput*, which is a scalar object that contains a single object instance, the integer value that indicates the total number of input AppleTalk packets on a router interface.

An object identifier (or object ID) uniquely identifies a managed object in the MIB hierarchy. The MIB hierarchy can be depicted as a tree with a nameless root, the levels of which are assigned by different organizations. Figure 52–3 illustrates the MIB tree.

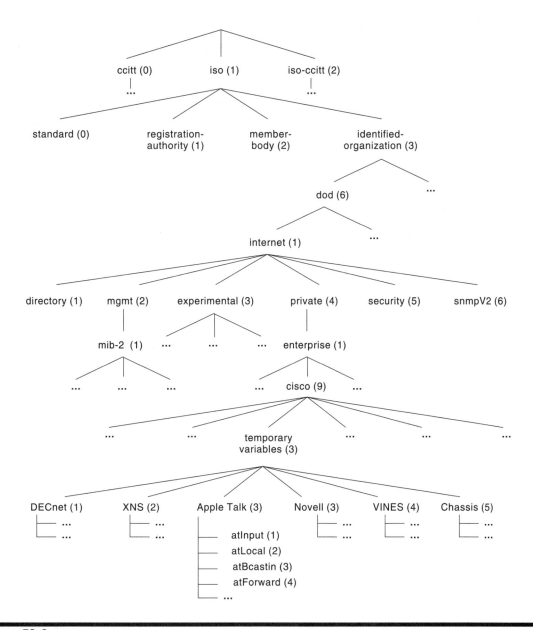

Figure 52–3

The MIB tree illustrates the various hierarchies assigned by different organizations.

The top-level MIB object IDs belong to different standards organizations, while lower-level object IDs are allocated by associated organizations.

Vendors can define private branches that include managed objects for their own products. MIBs that have not been standardized typically are positioned in the experimental branch.

The managed object *atInput* can be uniquely identified either by the object name—*iso.identified-organization.dod.internet.private.enterprise.cisco.temporary variables.AppleTalk.atInput*—or by the equivalent object descriptor: 1.3.6.1.4.1.9.3.3.1.

SNMP AND DATA REPRESENTATION

SNMP must account for and adjust to incompatibilities between managed devices. Different computers use different data-representation techniques, which can compromise the ability of SNMP to exchange information between managed devices. SNMP uses a subset of Abstract Syntax Notation One (ASN.1) to accommodate communication between diverse systems.

SNMP VERSION 1 (SNMPV1)

SNMP Version 1 (SNMPv1) is the initial implementation of the SNMP protocol. It is described in Request For Comments (RFC) 1157 and functions within the specifications of the Structure of Management Information (SMI). SNMPv1 operates over protocols such as User Datagram Protocol (UDP), Internet Protocol (IP), OSI Connectionless Network Service (CLNS), Apple-Talk Datagram-Delivery Protocol (DDP), and Novell Internet Packet Exchange (IPX). SNMPv1 is widely used and is the de facto network-management protocol in the Internet community.

SNMPv1 and Structure of Management Information (SMI)

The Structure of Management Information (SMI) defines the rules for describing management information, using Abstract Syntax Notation One

(ASN.1). The SNMPv1 SMI is defined in Request For Comments (RFC) 1155. The SMI makes three key specifications: ASN.1 data types, SMI-specific data types, and SNMP MIB tables.

SNMPv1 and ASN.1 Data Types

The SNMPv1 SMI specifies that all managed objects have a certain subset of Abstract Syntax Notation One (ASN.1) data types associated with them. Three ASN.1 data types are required: *name*, *syntax*, and *encoding*. The name serves as the object identifier (object ID). The syntax defines the data type of the object (for example, integer or string). The SMI uses a subset of the ASN.1 syntax definitions. The encoding data describes how information associated with a managed object is formatted as a series of data items for transmission over the network.

SNMPv1 and SMI-Specific Data Types

The SNMPv1 SMI specifies the use of a number of SMI-specific data types, which are divided into two categories: *simple data types* and *application-wide data types*.

Three simple data types are defined in the SNMPv1 SMI, all of which are unique values: *integers*, *octet strings*, and *object IDs*. The integer data type is a signed integer in the range of -2,147,483,648 to 2,147,483,647. Octet strings are ordered sequences of zero to 65,535 octets. Object IDs come from the set of all object identifiers allocated according to the rules specified in ASN.1.

Seven application-wide data types exist in the SNMPv1 SMI: *network addresses*, *counters*, *gauges*, *time ticks*, *opaques*, *integers*, and *unsigned integers*. Network addresses represent an address from a particular protocol family. SNMPv1 supports only 32-bit IP addresses. Counters are nonnegative integers that increase until they reach a maximum value and then return to zero. In SNMPv1, a 32-bit counter size is specified. Gauges are nonnegative integers that can increase or decrease but retain the maximum value reached. A time tick represents a hundredth of a second since some event. An opaque represents an arbitrary encoding that is used to pass arbitrary information strings that do not conform to the strict data typing used by the SMI. An integer represents signed integer-valued information. This data type redefines the integer data type, which has arbitrary precision in ASN.1 but bounded precision in the SMI. An unsigned integer represents unsigned integer-valued information and is useful when values are always nonnegative. This data type redefines the integer data type, which has arbitrary precision in ASN.1 but bounded precision in the SMI.

SNMP MIB Tables

The SNMPv1 SMI defines highly structured tables that are used to group the instances of a tabular object (that is, an object that contains multiple variables). Tables are composed of zero or more rows, which are indexed in a way that allows SNMP to retrieve or alter an entire row with a single Get, Get-Next, or Set command.

SNMPv1 Protocol Operations

SNMP is a simple request-response protocol. The network-management system issues a request, and managed devices return responses. This behavior is implemented by using one of four protocol operations: *Get*, *GetNext*, *Set*, and *Trap*. The Get operation is used by the NMS to retrieve the value of one or more object instances from an agent. If the agent responding to the Get operation cannot provide values for all the object instances in a list, it does not provide any values. The GetNext operation is used by the NMS to retrieve the value of the next object instance in a table or list within an agent. The Set operation is used by the NMS to set the values of object instances within an agent. The Trap operation is used by agents to asynchronously inform the NMS of a significant event.

SNMP VERSION 2 (SNMPV2)

SNMP Version 2 (SNMPv2) is an evolution of the initial version, SNMPv1. Originally, SNMPv2 was published as a set of proposed Internet standards in

1993; currently, it is a Draft Standard. As with SNMPv1, SNMPv2 functions within the specifications of the Structure of Management Information (SMI). In theory, SNMPv2 offers a number of improvements to SNMPv1, including additional protocol operations.

SNMPv2 and Structure of Management Information (SMI)

The Structure of Management Information (SMI) defines the rules for describing management information, using Abstract Syntax Notation One (ASN.1).

The SNMPv2 SMI is described in RFC 1902. It makes certain additions and enhancements to the SNMPv1 SMI-specific data types, such as including *bit strings*, *network addresses*, and *counters*. Bit strings are defined only in SNMPv2 and comprise zero or more named bits that specify a value. Network addresses represent an address from a particular protocol family. SNMPv1 supports only 32-bit IP addresses, but SNMPv2 can support other types of addresses as well. Counters are non-negative integers that increase until they reach a maximum value and then return to zero. In SNMPv1, a 32-bit counter size is specified. In SNMPv2, 32-bit and 64-bit counters are defined.

SMI Information Modules

The SNMPv2 SMI also specifies information modules, which specify a group of related definitions. Three types of SMI information modules exist: *MIB modules*, *compliance statements*, and *capability statements*. MIB modules contain definitions of interrelated managed objects. Compliance statements provide a systematic way to describe a group of managed objects that must be implemented for conformance to a standard. Capability statements are used to indicate the precise level of support that an agent claims with respect to a MIB group. An NMS can adjust its behavior toward agents according to the capabilities statements associated with each agent.

SNMPv2 Protocol Operations

The Get, GetNext, and Set operations used in SNMPv1 are exactly the same as those used in SNMPv2. SNMPv2, however, adds and enhances some protocol operations. The SNMPv2 Trap operation, for example, serves the same function as that used in SNMPv1. It, however, uses a different message format and is designed to replace the SNMPv1 Trap.

SNMPv2 also defines two new protocol operations: *GetBulk* and *Inform*. The GetBulk operation is used by the NMS to efficiently retrieve large blocks of data, such as multiple rows in a table. GetBulk fills a response message with as much of the requested data as will fit. The Inform operation allows one NMS to send trap information to another NMS and receive a response. In SNMPv2, if the agent responding to GetBulk operations cannot provide values for all the variables in a list, it provides partial results.

SNMP MANAGEMENT

SNMP is a distributed-management protocol. A system can operate exclusively as either an NMS or an agent, or it can perform the functions of both. When a system operates as both an NMS and an agent, another NMS might require that the system query managed devices and provide a summary of the information learned, or that it report locally stored management information.

SNMP SECURITY

SNMP lacks any authentication capabilities, which results in vulnerability to a variety of security threats. These include *masquerading, modification of information, message sequence and timing modifications*, and *disclosure*. Masquerading consists of an unauthorized entity attempting to perform management operations by assuming the identity of an authorized management entity. Modification of information involves an unauthorized entity attempting to alter a message generated by an authorized entity so that the message results in unauthorized accounting management or configuration management operations. Message sequence and timing modifications occur when an unauthorized entity reorders, delays, or copies and later replays a message generated by an authorized entity. Disclosure results when an unauthorized entity extracts values stored in managed objects, or learns of notifiable events by monitoring exchanges between managers and agents. Because SNMP does not implement authentication, many vendors do not implement Set operations, thereby reducing SNMP to a monitoring facility.

SNMP INTEROPERABILITY

As presently specified, SNMPv2 is incompatible with SNMPv1 in two key areas: message formats and protocol operations. SNMPv2 messages use different header and protocol data-unit (PDU) formats than SNMPv1 messages. SNMPv2 also uses two protocol operations that are not specified in SNMPv1. Furthermore, RFC 1908 defines two possible SNMPv1/v2 coexistence strategies: proxy agents and "bilingual" network-management systems.

Proxy Agents

An SNMPv2 agent can act as a proxy agent on behalf of SNMPv1 managed devices, as follows:

- An SNMPv2 NMS issues a command intended for an SNMPv1 agent.

- The NMS sends the SNMP message to the SNMPv2 proxy agent.

- The proxy agent forwards Get, GetNext, and Set messages to the SNMPv1 agent unchanged.

- GetBulk messages are converted by the proxy agent to GetNext messages and then are forwarded to the SNMPv1 agent.

- The proxy agent maps SNMPv1 trap messages to SNMPv2 trap messages and then forwards them to the NMS.

Bilingual Network-Management System

Bilingual SNMPv2 network-management systems support both SNMPv1 and SNMPv2. To support this dual-management environment, a management application in the bilingual NMS must contact an agent. The NMS then examines information stored in a local database to determine whether the agent supports SNMPv1 or SNMPv2. Based on the information in the database, the NMS communicates with the agent using the appropriate version of SNMP.

SNMP REFERENCE: SNMPv1 MESSAGE FORMATS

SNMPv1 messages contain two parts: a message header and a protocol data unit. Figure 52–4 illustrates the basic format of an SNMPv1 message.

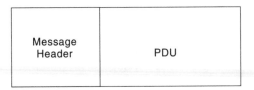

Figure 52–4
An SNVPv1 message consists of a header and a PDU.

SNMPv1 Message Header

SNMPv1 message headers contain two fields: *Version Number* and *Community Name*. The following descriptions summarize these fields:

- *Version Number*—Specifies the version of SNMP used.

- *Community Name*—Defines an access environment for a group of NMSs. NMSs within the community are said to exist within the same administrative domain. Community names serve as a weak form of authentication because devices that do not know the proper community name are precluded from SNMP operations.

SNMPv1 Protocol Data Unit (PDU)

SNMPv1 PDUs contain a specific command (Get, Set, and so on) and operands that indicate the object instances involved in the transaction. SNMPv1 PDU fields are variable in length, as prescribed by Abstract Syntax Notation One (ASN.1). Figure 52–5 illustrates the fields of the SNMPv1 Get, GetNext, Response, and Set PDUs transactions.

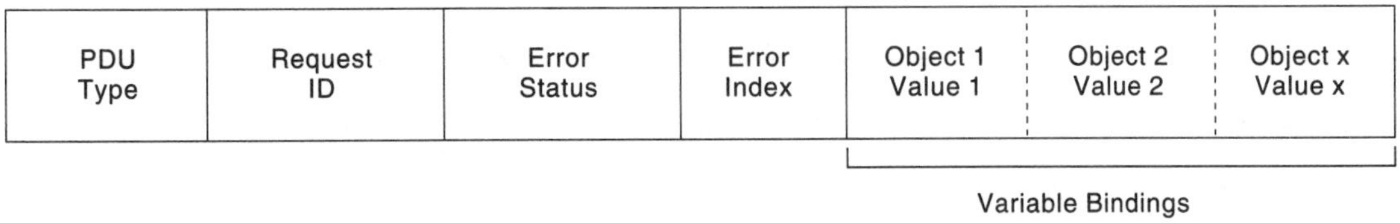

PDU Type	Request ID	Error Status	Error Index	Object 1 Value 1	Object 2 Value 2	Object x Value x

Variable Bindings

Figure 52–5
SNMPv1 Get, GetNext, Response, and Set PDUs contain the same fields.

The following descriptions summarize the fields illustrated in Figure 52–5:

- *PDU Type*—Specifies the type of PDU transmitted.

- *Request ID*—Associates SNMP requests with responses.

- *Error Status*—Indicates one of a number of errors and error types. Only the response operation sets this field. Other operations set this field to zero.

- *Error Index*—Associates an error with a particular object instance. Only the response operation sets this field. Other operations set this field to zero.

- *Variable Bindings*—Serves as the data field of the SNMPv1 PDU. Each variable binding associates a particular object instance with its current value (with the exception of Get and GetNext requests, for which the value is ignored).

Trap PDU Format

Figure 52–6 illustrates the fields of the SNMPv1 Trap PDU.

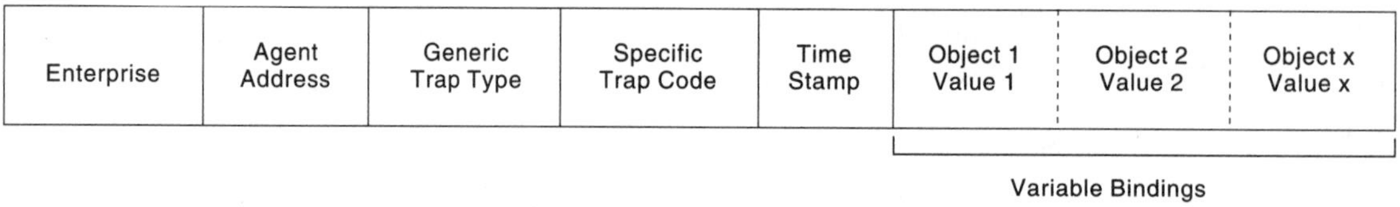

Enterprise	Agent Address	Generic Trap Type	Specific Trap Code	Time Stamp	Object 1 Value 1	Object 2 Value 2	Object x Value x

Variable Bindings

Figure 52–6

The SNMPv1 Trap PDU consists of eight fields.

The following descriptions summarize the fields illustrated in Figure 52–6:

- *Enterprise*—Identifies the type of managed object generating the trap.

- *Agent Address*—Provides the address of the managed object generating the trap.

- *Generic Trap Type*—Indicates one of a number of generic trap types.

- *Specific Trap Code*—Indicates one of a number of specific trap codes.

- *Time Stamp*—Provides the amount of time that has elapsed between the last network reinitialization and generation of the trap.

- *Variable Bindings*—The data field of the SNMPv1 Trap PDU. Each variable binding associates a particular object instance with its current value.

SNMP REFERENCE: SNMPv2 MESSAGE FORMAT

SNMPv2 messages consist of a header and a PDU. Figure 52–7 illustrates the basic format of an SNMPv2 message.

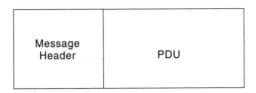

Figure 52–7
SNMPv2 messages also consist of a header and a PDU.

SNMPv2 Message Header

SNMPv2 message headers contain two fields: *Version Number* and *Community Name*. The following descriptions summarize these fields:

- *Version Number*—Specifies the version of SNMP that is being used.

- *Community Name*—Defines an access environment for a group of NMSs. NMSs within the community are said to exist within the same administrative domain. Community names serve as a weak form of authentication because devices that do not know the proper community name are precluded from SNMP operations.

SNMPv2 Protocol Data Unit (PDU)

SNMPv2 specifies two PDU formats, depending on the SNMP protocol operation. SNMPv2 PDU fields are variable in length, as prescribed by Abstract Syntax Notation One (ASN.1).

Figure 52–8 illustrates the fields of the SNMPv2 Get, GetNext, Inform, Response, Set, and Trap PDUs.

The following descriptions summarize the fields illustrated in Figure 52–8:

- *PDU Type*—Identifies the type of PDU transmitted (Get, GetNext, Inform, Response, Set, or Trap).

- *Request ID*—Associates SNMP requests with responses.

- *Error Status*—Indicates one of a number of errors and error types. Only the response operation sets this field. Other operations set this field to zero.

- *Error Index*—Associates an error with a particular object instance. Only the response operation sets this field. Other operations set this field to zero.

- *Variable Bindings*—Serves as the data field of the SNMPv2 PDU. Each variable binding associates a particular object instance with its current value (with the exception of Get and GetNext requests, for which the value is ignored).

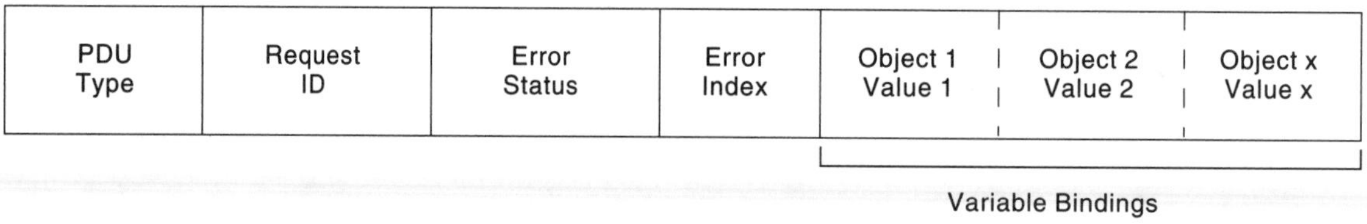

PDU Type	Request ID	Error Status	Error Index	Object 1 Value 1	Object 2 Value 2	Object x Value x

Variable Bindings

Figure 52–8
SNMPv2 Get, GetNext, Inform, Response, Set, and Trap PDUs contain the same fields.

GetBulk PDU Format

Figure 52–9 illustrates the fields of the SNMPv2 GetBulk PDU.

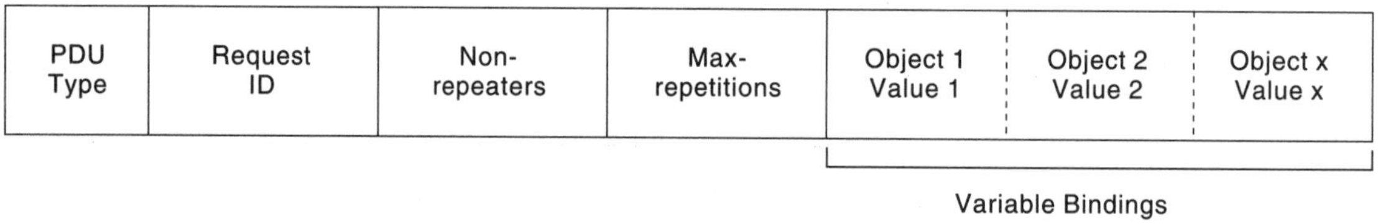

PDU Type	Request ID	Non-repeaters	Max-repetitions	Object 1 Value 1	Object 2 Value 2	Object x Value x

Variable Bindings

Figure 52–9
The SNMPv2 GetBulk PDU consists of seven fields.

The following descriptions summarize the fields illustrated in Figure 52–9:

- *PDU Type*—Identifies the PDU as a GetBulk operation.

- *Request ID*—Associates SNMP requests with responses.

- *Non-repeaters*—Specifies the number of object instances in the variable bindings field that should be retrieved no more than once from the beginning of the request. This field is used when some of the instances are scalar objects with only one variable.

- *Max Repetitions*—Defines the maximum number of times that other variables beyond those specified by the non-repeaters field should be retrieved.

- *Variable Bindings*—Serves as the data field of the SNMPv2 PDU. Each variable binding associates a particular object instance with its current value (with the exception of Get and GetNext requests, for which the value is ignored).

Internetworking Terms and Abbreviations

In the business world, computer networks are becoming too useful to do without. Using a Local-Talk network, Macintosh users in Marketing can share product bulletins, data sheets, and slide presentations. Digital minicomputer users in Accounting can access a common database of customer information using DECnet. In Engineering, Sun workstation users can share product specifications using TCP/IP over Ethernet. And in Manufacturing, IBM devices attached to a Token Ring network can process real-time data on material availability and fill orders sent in over serial links from remote offices.

This glossary attempts to gather and define the terms and abbreviations of internetworking. As with any growing technical field, some terms evolve several meanings. Where necessary, multiple definitions and abbreviation expansions are presented. Multiword terms are alphabetized as if there were no spaces; hyphenated terms, as if there were no hyphens.

Terms in this glossary are typically defined under their abbreviations. Each abbreviation expansion is listed separately, with a cross-reference to the abbreviation entry. In addition, many definitions contain cross-references to related terms.

We hope that this glossary adds to your understanding of internetworking technologies.

Numerics

10Base2   10-Mbps baseband Ethernet specification using 50-ohm thin coaxial cable. 10Base2, which is part of the IEEE 802.3 specification, has a distance limit of 185 meters per segment. *See also* Cheapernet, Ethernet, IEEE 802.3, and Thinnet.

10Base5   10-Mbps baseband Ethernet specification using standard (thick) 50-ohm baseband coaxial cable. 10Base5, which is part of the IEEE 802.3 baseband physical layer specification, has a distance limit of 500 meters per segment. *See also* Ethernet and IEEE 802.3.

10BaseF   10-Mbps baseband Ethernet specification that refers to the 10BaseFB, 10BaseFL, and 10BaseFP standards for Ethernet over fiber-optic cabling. *See also* 10BaseFB, 10BaseFL, 10BaseFP, and Ethernet.

10BaseFB   10-Mbps baseband Ethernet specification using fiber-optic cabling. 10BaseFB is part of the IEEE 10BaseF specification. It is not used to connect user stations, but instead provides a synchronous signaling backbone that allows additional segments and repeaters to be connected to the network. 10BaseFB segments can be up to 2,000 meters long. *See also* 10BaseF and Ethernet.

10BaseFL   10-Mbps baseband Ethernet specification using fiber-optic cabling. 10BaseFL is part of the IEEE 10BaseF specification and, although able to interoperate with FOIRL, is designed to replace the FOIRL specification. 10BaseFL segments can be up to 1,000 meters long if used with FOIRL, and up to 2,000 meters if 10BaseFL is used exclusively. *See also* 10BaseF, Ethernet, and FOIRL.

10BaseFP   10-Mbps fiber-passive baseband Ethernet specification using fiber-optic cabling. 10BaseFP is part of the IEEE 10BaseF specification. It organizes a number of computers into a star topology without the use of repeaters. 10BaseFP segments can be up to 500 meters long. *See also* 10BaseF and Ethernet.

10BaseT   10-Mbps baseband Ethernet specification using two pairs of twisted-pair cabling (Category 3, 4, or 5): one pair for transmitting data and the other for receiving data. 10BaseT, which is part of the IEEE 802.3 specification, has a distance limit of approximately 100 meters per segment. *See also* Ethernet and IEEE 802.3.

10Broad36   10-Mbps broadband Ethernet specification using broadband coaxial cable. 10Broad36, which is part of the IEEE 802.3 specification, has a distance limit of 3,600 meters per segment. *See also* Ethernet and IEEE 802.3.

100BaseFX   100-Mbps baseband Fast Ethernet specification using two strands of multimode fiber-optic cable per link. To guarantee proper signal timing, a 100BaseFX link cannot exceed 400 meters in length. Based on the IEEE 802.3 standard. *See also* 100BaseX, Fast Ethernet, and IEEE 802.3.

100BaseT   100-Mbps baseband Fast Ethernet specification using UTP wiring. Like the 10BaseT technology on which it is based, 100BaseT sends link pulses over the network segment when no traffic is present. However, these link pulses contain more information than do those used in 10BaseT. Based on the IEEE 802.3 standard. *See also* 10BaseT, Fast Ethernet, and IEEE 802.3.

100BaseT4   100-Mbps baseband Fast Ethernet specification using four pairs of Category 3, 4, or 5 UTP wiring. To guarantee proper signal timing, a 100BaseT4 segment cannot exceed 100 meters in length. Based on the IEEE 802.3 standard. *See also* Fast Ethernet and IEEE 802.3.

100BaseTX   100-Mbps baseband Fast Ethernet specification using two pairs of either UTP or STP wiring. The first pair of wires is used to receive data; the second is used to transmit. To guarantee proper signal timing, a 100BaseTX segment cannot exceed 100 meters in length. Based on the IEEE 802.3 standard. *See also* 100BaseX, Fast Ethernet, and IEEE 802.3.

100BaseX   100-Mbps baseband Fast Ethernet specification that refers to the 100BaseFX and 100BaseTX standards for Fast Ethernet over fiber-optic cabling. Based on the IEEE 802.3 standard. *See also* 100BaseFX, 100BaseTX, Fast Ethernet, and IEEE 802.3.

100VG-AnyLAN 100-Mbps Fast Ethernet and Token Ring media technology using four pairs of Category 3, 4, or 5 UTP cabling. This high-speed transport technology, developed by Hewlett-Packard, can be made to operate on existing 10BaseT Ethernet networks. Based on the IEEE 802.12 standard. *See also* IEEE 802.12.

24th channel signaling *See* A&B bit signaling.

370 block mux channel *See* block multiplexer channel.

4B/5B local fiber 4-byte/5-byte local fiber. FibreChannel physical media used for FDDI and ATM. Supports speeds of up to 100 Mbps over multimode fiber. *See also* TAXI 4B/5B.

4-byte/5-byte local fiber *See* 4B/5B local fiber.

8B/10B local fiber 8-byte/10-byte local fiber. Fiber channel physical media that supports speeds up to 149.76 Mbps over multimode fiber.

8-byte/10-byte local fiber *See* 8B/10B local fiber.

A

A&B bit signaling Procedure used in T1 transmission facilities in which each of the 24 T1 subchannels devotes one bit of every sixth frame to the carrying of supervisory signaling information. *Also called* 24th channel signaling.

AAL ATM adaptation layer. Service-dependent sublayer of the data link layer. The AAL accepts data from different applications and presents it to the ATM layer in the form of 48-byte ATM payload segments. AALs consist of two sublayers, CS and SAR. AALs differ on the basis of the source-destination timing used, whether they use CBR or VBR, and whether they are used for connection-oriented or connectionless mode data transfer. At present, the four types of AAL recommended by the ITU-T are AAL1, AAL2, AAL3/4, and AAL5. *See* AAL1, AAL2, AAL3/4, AAL5, CS, and SAR. *See also* ATM and ATM layer.

AAL1 ATM adaptation layer 1. One of four AALs recommended by the ITU-T. AAL1 is used for connection-oriented, delay-sensitive services requiring constant bit rates, such as uncompressed video and other isochronous traffic. *See also* AAL.

AAL2 ATM adaptation layer 2. One of four AALs recommended by the ITU-T. AAL2 is used for connection-oriented services that support a variable bit rate, such as some isochronous video and voice traffic. *See also* AAL.

AAL3/4 ATM adaptation layer 3/4. One of four AALs (merged from two initially distinct adaptation layers) recommended by the ITU-T. AAL3/4 supports both connectionless and connection-oriented links, but is primarily used for the transmission of SMDS packets over ATM networks. *See also* AAL.

AAL5 ATM adaptation layer 5. One of four AALs recommended by the ITU-T. AAL5 supports connection-oriented, VBR services, and is used predominantly for the transfer of classical IP over ATM and LANE traffic. AAL5 uses SEAL and is the least complex of the current AAL recommendations. It offers low bandwidth overhead and simpler processing requirements in exchange for reduced bandwidth capacity and error-recovery capability. *See also* AAL and SEAL.

AARP AppleTalk Address Resolution Protocol. Protocol in the AppleTalk protocol stack that maps a data-link address to a network address.

AARP probe packets Packets transmitted by AARP that determine whether a randomly selected node ID is being used by another node in a nonextended AppleTalk network. If the node ID is not being used, the sending node uses that node ID. If the node ID is being used, the sending node chooses a different ID and sends more AARP probe packets. *See also* AARP.

ABM Asynchronous Balanced Mode. An HDLC (and derivative protocol) communication mode supporting peer-oriented, point-to-point communications between two stations, where either station can initiate transmission.

ABR 1. available bit rate. QOS class defined by the ATM Forum for ATM networks. ABR is used for connections that do not require timing relationships between source and destination. ABR provides no guarantees in terms of cell loss or delay; it provides only best-effort service. Traffic sources adjust their transmission rates in response to information they receive describing the status of the network and its capability to successfully deliver data. *Compare with* CBR, UBR, and VBR.

2. area border router. Router located on the border of one or more OSPF areas that connects those areas to the backbone network. ABRs are considered members of both the OSPF backbone and the attached areas. They therefore maintain routing tables describing both the backbone topology and the topology of the other areas.

Abstract Syntax Notation One   *See* ASN.1.

access list   List kept by routers to control access to or from the router for a number of services (for example, to prevent packets with a certain IP address from leaving a particular interface on the router).

access method   1. Generally, the way in which network devices access the network medium.
2. Software within an SNA processor that controls the flow of information through a network.

access server   Communications processor that connects asynchronous devices to a LAN or WAN through network and terminal emulation software. Performs both synchronous and asynchronous routing of supported protocols. Sometimes called a network access server. *Compare with* communication server.

accounting management   One of five categories of network management defined by ISO for management of OSI networks. Accounting management subsystems are responsible for collecting network data relating to resource usage. *See also* configuration management, fault management, performance management, and security management.

ACF   Advanced Communications Function. A group of SNA products that provides distributed processing and resource sharing. *See also* ACF/NCP.

ACF/NCP   Advanced Communications Function/Network Control Program. The primary SNA NCP. ACF/NCP resides in the communications controller and interfaces with the SNA access method in the host processor to control network communications. *See also* ACF and NCP.

ACK   *See* acknowledgment.

acknowledgment   Notification sent from one network device to another to acknowledge that some event (for example, receipt of a message) has occurred. Sometimes abbreviated ACK. *Compare with* NAK.

ACR   allowed cell rate. Parameter defined by the ATM Forum for ATM traffic management. ACR varies between the MCR and the PCR, and is dynamically controlled using congestion control mechanisms. *See also* MCR and PCR.

ACSE   association control service element. An OSI convention used to establish, maintain, or terminate a connection between two applications.

active hub   A multiported device that amplifies LAN transmission signals.

active monitor   A device responsible for managing a Token Ring. A network node is selected to be the active monitor if it has the highest MAC address on the ring. The active monitor is responsible for management tasks such as ensuring that tokens are not lost or that frames do not circulate indefinitely. *See also* ring monitor and standby monitor.

adapter   *See* NIC (network interface card).

adaptive differential pulse code modulation   *See* ADPCM.

adaptive routing   *See* dynamic routing.

ADCCP   Advanced Data Communications Control Protocol. An ANSI standard bit-oriented data link control protocol.

address   A data structure or logical convention used to identify a unique entity, such as a particular process or network device.

addressed call mode A mode that permits control signals and commands to establish and terminate calls in V.25bis. *See also* V.25bis.

address mapping A technique that allows different protocols to interoperate by translating addresses from one format to another. For example, when routing IP over X.25, the IP addresses must be mapped to the X.25 addresses so that the IP packets can be transmitted by the X.25 network. *See also* address resolution.

address mask A bit combination used to describe which portion of an address refers to the network or subnet and which part refers to the host. Sometimes referred to simply as a mask. *See also* subnet mask.

address resolution Generally, a method for resolving differences between computer addressing schemes. Address resolution usually specifies a method for mapping network layer (Layer 3) addresses to data link layer (Layer 2) addresses. *See also* address mapping.

Address Resolution Protocol *See* ARP.

adjacency A relationship formed between selected neighboring routers and end nodes for the purpose of exchanging routing information. Adjacency is based on the use of a common media segment.

adjacent nodes 1. In SNA, nodes that are connected to a given node with no intervening nodes.
2. In DECnet and OSI, nodes that share a common network segment (in Ethernet, FDDI, or Token Ring networks).

administrative distance A rating of the trustworthiness of a routing information source. The higher the value, the lower the trustworthiness rating.

admission control *See* traffic policing.

ADPCM adaptive differential pulse code modulation. The process by which analog voice samples are encoded into high-quality digital signals.

ADSL Asymmetric Digital Subscriber Line. One of four DSL technologies. ADSL is designed to deliver more bandwidth downstream (from the central office to the customer site) than upstream. Downstream rates range from 1.5 to 9 Mbps, whereas upstream bandwidth ranges from 16 to 640 kbps. ADSL transmissions work at distances up to 18,000 feet (5,488 meters) over a single copper twisted pair.

ADSU ATM DSU. Terminal adapter used to access an ATM network via an HSSI-compatible device. *See also* DSU.

Advanced Communications Function *See* ACF.

Advanced Communications Function/Network Control Program *See* ACF/NCP.

Advanced Data Communications Control Protocol *See* ADCCP.

Advanced Peer-to-Peer Networking *See* APPN.

Advanced Program-to-Program Communication *See* APPC.

Advanced Research Projects Agency *See* ARPA.

Advanced Research Projects Agency Network *See* ARPANET.

advertising Router process in which routing or service updates are sent at specified intervals so that other routers on the network can maintain lists of usable routes.

AEP AppleTalk Echo Protocol. Used to test connectivity between two AppleTalk nodes. One node sends a packet to another node and receives a duplicate, or echo, of that packet.

AFI authority and format identifier. The portion of an NSAP-format ATM address that identifies the type and format of the IDI portion of an ATM address.

agent 1. Generally, software that processes queries and returns replies on behalf of an application.
2. In NMSs, a process that resides in all managed devices and reports the values of specified variables to management stations.

AIS alarm indication signal. In a T1 transmission, an all-ones signal transmitted in lieu of the normal signal to maintain transmission continuity and to indicate to the receiving terminal that there is a transmission fault that is located either at, or upstream from, the transmitting terminal. *See also* T1.

alarm   A message notifying an operator or administrator of a network problem. *See also* event and trap.

alarm indication signal   *See* AIS.

a-law   The ITU-T companding standard used in the conversion between analog and digital signals in PCM systems. A-law is used primarily in European telephone networks and is similar to the North American mu-law standard. *See also* companding and mu-law.

algorithm   A well-defined rule or process for arriving at a solution to a problem. In networking, algorithms are commonly used to determine the best route for traffic from a particular source to a particular destination.

alias   *See* entity.

alignment error   In IEEE 802.3 networks, an error that occurs when the total number of bits of a received frame is not divisible by eight. Alignment errors are usually caused by frame damage due to collisions.

allowed cell rate   *See* ACR.

all-rings explorer packet   *See* all-routes explorer packet.

all-routes explorer packet   An explorer packet that traverses an entire SRB network, following all possible paths to a specific destination. Sometimes called all-rings explorer packet. *See also* explorer packet, local explorer packet, and spanning explorer packet.

alternate mark inversion   *See* AMI.

AM   amplitude modulation. Modulation technique whereby information is conveyed through the amplitude of the carrier signal. *Compare with* FM and PAM. *See also* modulation.

American National Standards Institute   *See* ANSI.

American Standard Code for Information Interchange   *See* ASCII.

AMI   alternate mark inversion. Line-code type used on T1 and E1 circuits. In AMI, zeros are represented by 01 during each bit cell, and ones are represented by 11 or 00, alternately, during each bit cell. AMI requires that the sending device maintain ones density. Ones density is not maintained independent of the data stream. Sometimes called binary coded alternate mark inversion. *See also* ones density.

amplitude   The maximum value of an analog or a digital waveform.

amplitude modulation   *See* AM.

analog transmission   Signal transmission over wires or through the air in which information is conveyed through a variation of some combination of signal amplitude, frequency, and phase.

ANSI   American National Standards Institute. A voluntary organization comprising corporate, government, and other members that coordinates standards-related activities, approves U.S. national standards, and develops positions for the United States in international standards organizations. ANSI helps develop international and U.S. standards relating to, among other things, communications and networking. ANSI is a member of the IEC and the ISO. *See also* IEC and ISO.

ANSI X3T9.5   *See* X3T9.5.

APaRT   automated packet recognition/translation. A technology that allows a server to be attached to CDDI or FDDI without requiring the reconfiguration of applications or network protocols. APaRT recognizes specific data link layer encapsulation packet types and, when these packet types are transferred from one medium to another, translates them into the native format of the destination device.

API   application programming interface. A specification of function-call conventions that defines an interface to a service.

Apollo Domain   A proprietary network protocol suite developed by Apollo Computer for communication on proprietary Apollo networks.

APPC Advanced Program-to-Program Communication. IBM SNA system software that allows high-speed communication between programs on different computers in a distributed computing environment. APPC establishes and tears down connections between communicating programs, and consists of two interfaces: a programming interface and a data-exchange interface. The former replies to requests from programs requiring communication; the latter establishes sessions between programs. APPC runs on LU 6.2 devices. *See also* LU 6.2.

AppleTalk A series of communications protocols designed by Apple Computer. Two phases currently exist. Phase 1, the earlier version, supports a single physical network that can have only one network number and be in one zone. Phase 2, the more recent version, supports multiple logical networks on a single physical network and allows networks to be in more than one zone. *See also* zone.

AppleTalk Address Resolution Protocol *See* AARP.

AppleTalk Echo Protocol *See* AEP.

AppleTalk Remote Access *See* ARA.

AppleTalk Transaction Protocol *See* ATP.

AppleTalk Update-Based Routing Protocol *See* AURP.

AppleTalk zone *See* zone.

application layer Layer 7 of the OSI reference model. This layer provides services to application processes (such as electronic mail, file transfer, and terminal emulation) that are outside the OSI model. The application layer identifies and establishes the availability of intended communication partners (and the resources required to connect with them), synchronizes cooperating applications, and establishes agreement on procedures for error recovery and control of data integrity. Corresponds roughly with the transaction services layer in the SNA model. *See also* data link layer, network layer, physical layer, presentation layer, session layer, and transport layer.

application programming interface *See* API.

APPN Advanced Peer-to-Peer Networking. An enhancement to the original IBM SNA architecture. APPN handles session establishment between peer nodes, dynamic transparent route calculation, and traffic prioritization for APPC traffic. *Compare with* APPN+. *See also* APPC.

APPN+ A next-generation APPN that replaces the label-swapping routing algorithm with source routing. Also called high-performance routing. *See also* APPN.

ARA AppleTalk Remote Access. A protocol that provides Macintosh users direct access to information and resources at a remote AppleTalk site.

ARCnet Attached Resource Computer Network. A 2.5-Mbps token-bus LAN developed in the late 1970s and early 1980s by Datapoint Corporation.

area A logical set of network segments (either CLNS, DECnet, or OSPF based) and their attached devices. Areas are usually connected to other areas via routers, making up a single autonomous system. *See also* autonomous system.

area border router *See* ABR.

ARM asynchronous response mode. An HDLC communication mode involving one primary station and at least one secondary station, where either the primary or one of the secondary stations can initiate transmissions. *See also* primary station and secondary station.

ARP Address Resolution Protocol. An Internet protocol used to map an IP address to a MAC address. Defined in RFC 826. *Compare with* RARP. *See also* proxy ARP.

ARPA Advanced Research Projects Agency. A research and development organization that is part of the DoD. ARPA is responsible for numerous technological advances in communications and networking. ARPA evolved into DARPA, and then back into ARPA again (in 1994). *See also* DARPA.

ARPANET   Advanced Research Projects Agency Network. A landmark packet-switching network established in 1969. ARPANET was developed in the 1970s by BBN and funded by ARPA (and later DARPA). It eventually evolved into the Internet. The term ARPANET was officially retired in 1990. *See also* ARPA, BBN, DARPA, and Internet.

ARQ   automatic repeat request. A communication technique in which the receiving device detects errors and requests retransmissions.

AS   *See* autonomous system.

ASBR   autonomous system boundary router. An ABR located between an OSPF autonomous system and a non-OSPF network. ASBRs run both OSPF and another routing protocol, such as RIP. ASBRs must reside in a non-stub OSPF area. *See also* ABR, non-stub area, and OSPF.

ASCII   American Standard Code for Information Interchange. An 8-bit code for character representation (7 bits plus parity).

ASN.1   Abstract Syntax Notation One. An OSI language for describing data types independently of particular computer structures and representation techniques. Described by ISO International Standard 8824. *See also* BER (basic encoding rules).

association control service element   *See* ACSE.

associative memory   Memory that is accessed based on its contents, not on its memory address. Sometimes called content addressable memory (CAM).

AST   automatic spanning tree. A function that supports the automatic resolution of spanning trees in SRB networks, providing a single path for spanning explorer frames to traverse from a given node in the network to another. AST is based on the IEEE 802.1 standard. *See also* IEEE 802.1 and SRB.

ASTA   Advanced Software Technology and Algorithms. A component of the HPCC program intended to develop software and algorithms for implementation on high-performance computer and communications systems. *See also* HPCC.

Asynchronous Balanced Mode   *See* ABM.

asynchronous response mode   *See* ARM.

asynchronous time-division multiplexing   *See* ATDM.

Asynchronous Transfer Mode   *See* ATM.

asynchronous transmission   Digital signals that are transmitted without precise clocking. Such signals generally have different frequencies and phase relationships. Asynchronous transmissions usually encapsulate individual characters in control bits (called start and stop bits) that designate the beginning and end of each character. *Compare with* isochronous transmission, plesiochronous transmission, and synchronous transmission.

ATDM   asynchronous time-division multiplexing. A method of sending information that resembles normal TDM, except that time slots are allocated as needed rather than preassigned to specific transmitters. *Compare with* FDM, statistical multiplexing, and TDM.

ATM   Asynchronous Transfer Mode. An international standard for cell relay in which multiple service types (such as voice, video, or data) are conveyed in fixed-length (53-byte) cells. Fixed-length cells allow cell processing to occur in hardware, thereby reducing transit delays. ATM is designed to take advantage of high-speed transmission media such as E3, SONET, and T3.

ATM adaptation layer   *See* AAL.

ATM adaptation layer 1   *See* AAL1.

ATM adaptation layer 2   *See* AAL2.

ATM adaptation layer 3/4   *See* AAL3/4.

ATM adaptation layer 5   *See* AAL5.

ATM data service unit   *See* ADSU.

ATM Forum   An international organization jointly founded in 1991 by Cisco Systems, NET/ADAPTIVE, Northern Telecom, and Sprint that develops and promotes standards-based implementation agreements for ATM technology.

The ATM Forum expands on official standards developed by ANSI and ITU-T, and develops implementation agreements in advance of official standards.

ATM layer A service-independent sublayer of the data link layer in an ATM network. The ATM layer receives the 48-byte payload segments from the AAL and attaches a 5-byte header to each, producing standard 53-byte ATM cells. These cells are passed to the physical layer for transmission across the physical medium. *See also* AAL.

ATMM ATM management. A process that runs on an ATM switch that controls VCI translation and rate enforcement. *See also* ATM and VCI.

ATM management *See* ATMM.

ATM UNI *See* UNI.

ATM user-user connection A connection created by the ATM layer to provide communication between two or more ATM service users, such as ATMM processes. Such communication can be unidirectional, using one VCC, or bidirectional, using two VCCs. *See also* ATM layer, ATMM, and VCC.

ATP AppleTalk Transaction Protocol. A transport-level protocol that allows reliable request-response exchanges between two socket clients.

Attached Resource Computer Network *See* ARCnet.

attachment unit interface *See* AUI.

attenuation The loss of communication signal energy.

attribute Configuration data that defines the characteristics of database objects such as the chassis, cards, ports, or virtual circuits of a particular device. Attributes might be preset or user-configurable. On a LightStream 2020 ATM switch, attributes are set using the configuration program or CLI commands.

AUI attachment unit interface. An IEEE 802.3 interface between an MAU and a NIC (network interface card). Also called transceiver cable. *See also* IEEE 802.3, MAU, and NIC (network interface card).

AURP AppleTalk Update-Based Routing Protocol. A method of encapsulating AppleTalk traffic in the header of a foreign protocol, allowing the connection of two or more discontiguous AppleTalk internetworks through a foreign network (such as TCP/IP) to form an AppleTalk WAN. This connection is called an AURP tunnel. In addition to its encapsulation function, AURP maintains routing tables for the entire AppleTalk WAN by exchanging routing information between exterior routers. *See also* AURP tunnel and exterior router.

AURP tunnel A connection created in an AURP WAN that functions as a single, virtual data link between AppleTalk internetworks physically separated by a foreign network (a TCP/IP network, for example). *See also* AURP.

authority zone A section of the domain-name tree for which one name server is the authority. Associated with DNS. *See also* DNS.

Automated Packet Recognition/Translation *See* APaRT.

automatic call reconnect A feature permitting automatic call rerouting away from a failed trunk line.

automatic repeat request *See* ARQ.

automatic spanning tree *See* AST.

autonomous confederation A group of autonomous systems that rely on their own network reachability and routing information more than they rely on that received from other autonomous systems or confederations.

autonomous system A collection of networks under a common administration sharing a common routing strategy. Autonomous systems are subdivided by areas. An autonomous system must be assigned a unique 16-bit number by IANA. Sometimes abbreviated AS. *See also* area and IANA.

autonomous system boundary router *See* ASBR.

autoreconfiguration A process performed by nodes within the failure domain of a Token Ring network.

Nodes automatically perform diagnostics in an attempt to reconfigure the network around the failed areas.

available bit rate   *See* ABR.

average rate   The average rate, in kilobits per second (kbps), at which a given virtual circuit transmits.

B

B8ZS   binary 8-zero substitution. A line-code type, used on T1 and E1 circuits, in which a special code is substituted whenever eight consecutive zeros are sent through the link. This code is then interpreted at the remote end of the connection. This technique guarantees ones density independently of the data stream. Sometimes called bipolar 8-zero substitution. *Compare with* AMI. *See also* ones density.

backbone   The part of a network that acts as the primary path for traffic that is most often sourced from, and destined for, other networks.

back end   A node or software program that provides services to a front end. *See also* client, front end, and server.

backoff   The (usually random) retransmission delay enforced by contentious MAC protocols after a network node with data to transmit determines that the physical medium is already in use.

backplane   A physical connection between an interface processor or card and the data buses and power distribution buses inside a chassis.

back pressure   Propagation of network congestion information upstream through an internetwork.

backward explicit congestion notification   *See* BECN.

backward learning   An algorithmic process used for routing traffic that surmises information by assuming symmetrical network conditions. For example, if node A receives a packet from node B through intermediate node C, the backward-learning routing algorithm will assume that A can optimally reach B through C.

balanced configuration   In HDLC, a point-to-point network configuration with two combined stations.

balanced, unbalanced   *See* balun.

balun   balanced, unbalanced. A device used for matching impedance between a balanced and an unbalanced line, usually twisted-pair and coaxial cable.

bandwidth   The difference between the highest and lowest frequencies available for network signals. The term is also used to describe the rated throughput capacity of a given network medium or protocol.

bandwidth allocation   *See* bandwidth reservation.

bandwidth reservation   A process of assigning bandwidth to users and applications served by a network. It involves assigning priority to different flows of traffic based on how critical and delay sensitive they are. This makes the best use of available bandwidth, and if the network becomes congested, lower-priority traffic can be dropped. Sometimes called bandwidth allocation. *See also* call priority.

Banyan VINES   *See* VINES.

BARRNet   Bay Area Regional Research Network. A regional network serving the San Francisco Bay Area. The BARRNet backbone is composed of four University of California campuses (Berkeley, Davis, Santa Cruz, and San Francisco), Stanford University, Lawrence Livermore National Laboratory, and NASA Ames Research Center. BARRNet is now part of BBN Planet. *See also* BBN Planet.

baseband   A characteristic of a network technology in which only one carrier frequency is used. Ethernet is an example of a baseband network. Also called narrowband. *Compare with* broadband.

basic encoding rules   *See* BER.

Basic Rate Interface   *See* BRI.

Basic Research and Human Resources   *See* BRHR.

baud   Unit of signaling speed equal to the number of discrete signal elements transmitted per second. Baud is synonymous with bits per second (bps), if each signal element represents exactly 1 bit.

Bay Area Regional Research Network   *See* BARRNet.

BBN   Bolt, Beranek, and Newman, Inc. A high-technology company located in Massachusetts that developed and maintained the ARPANET (and later, the Internet) core gateway system. *See also* BBN Planet.

BBN Planet   A subsidiary company of BBN that operates a nationwide Internet access network composed in part by the former regional networks BARRNet, NEARNET, and SURAnet. *See also* BARRNet, BBN, NEARNET, and SURAnet.

Bc   Committed Burst. Negotiated tariff metric in Frame Relay internetworks. The maximum amount of data (in bits) that a Frame Relay internetwork is committed to accept and transmit at the CIR. *See also* Be and CIR.

B channel   bearer channel. In ISDN, a full-duplex, 64-kbps channel used to send user data. *Compare with* D channel, E channel, and H channel.

Be   Excess Burst. Negotiated tariff metric in Frame Relay internetworks. The number of bits that a Frame Relay internetwork attempts to transmit after Bc is accommodated. Be data is, in general, delivered with a lower probability than Bc data because Be data can be marked as DE by the network. *See also* Bc and DE.

beacon   A frame from a Token Ring or FDDI device indicating a serious problem with the ring, such as a broken cable. A beacon frame contains the address of the station assumed to be down.

bearer channel   *See* B channel.

Because It's Time Network   *See* BITNET.

BECN   backward explicit congestion notification. A bit set by a Frame Relay network in frames traveling in the opposite direction of frames encountering a congested path. DTE receiving frames with the BECN bit set can request that higher-level protocols take flow control action as appropriate. *Compare with* FECN.

Bell Communications Research   *See* Bellcore.

Bellcore   Bell Communications Research. An organization that performs research and development on behalf of the RBOCs.

Bellman-Ford routing algorithm   *See* distance vector routing algorithm.

Bell operating company   *See* BOC.

BER   1. bit error rate. The ratio of received bits that contain errors.
2. basic encoding rules. Rules for encoding data units described in the ISO ASN.1 standard. *See also* ASN.1.

Berkeley Standard Distribution   *See* BSD.

BERT   bit error rate tester. A device that determines the BER on a given communications channel. *See also* BER (bit error rate).

best-effort delivery   Delivery in a network system that does not use a sophisticated acknowledgment system to guarantee reliable delivery of information.

BGP   Border Gateway Protocol. An interdomain routing protocol that replaces EGP. BGP exchanges reachability information with other BGP systems. It is defined in RFC 1163. *See also* BGP4 and EGP.

BGP4   BGP Version 4. Version 4 of the predominant interdomain routing protocol used on the Internet. BGP4 supports CIDR and uses route aggregation mechanisms to reduce the size of routing tables. *See also* BGP and CIDR.

BIGA   Bus Interface Gate Array. A technology that allows the Catalyst 5000 to receive and transmit frames from its packet-switching memory to its MAC local buffer memory without the intervention of the host processor.

big-endian   A method of storing or transmitting data in which the most significant bit or byte is presented first. *Compare with* little-endian.

binary   A numbering system that uses ones and zeros (1 = on, 0 = off).

binary 8-zero substitution   *See* B8ZS.

binary coded alternate mark inversion   *See* AMI.

binary synchronous communication   *See* BSC.

biphase coding   A bipolar coding scheme originally developed for use in Ethernet. Clocking information is embedded into and recovered from the synchronous data stream without the need for separate clocking leads. The biphase signal contains no direct current energy.

bipolar   An electrical characteristic denoting a circuit with both negative and positive polarity. *Compare with* unipolar.

bipolar 8-zero substitution   *See* B8ZS.

BISDN   Broadband ISDN. ITU-T communication standards designed to handle high-bandwidth applications such as video. BISDN currently uses ATM technology over SONET-based transmission circuits to provide data rates from 155 to 622 Mbps and beyond. *Compare* with N-ISDN. *See also* BRI, ISDN, and PRI.

bisync   *See* BSC.

bit   A binary digit used in the binary numbering system. Can be 0 or 1.

bit error rate   *See* BER.

bit error rate tester   *See* BERT.

BITNET   "Because It's Time" Networking Services. Low-cost, low-speed academic network consisting primarily of IBM mainframes and 9600-bps leased lines. BITNET is now part of CREN. *See also* CREN.

BITNET III   A dial-up service providing connectivity for members of CREN. *See also* CREN.

bit-oriented protocol   A class of data link layer communication protocols that can transmit frames regardless of frame content. Compared with byte-oriented protocols, bit-oriented protocols provide full-duplex operation and are more efficient and reliable. *Compare with* byte-oriented protocol.

bit rate   The speed at which bits are transmitted, usually expressed in bits per second (bps).

bits per second   Abbreviated bps.

black hole   Routing term for an area of the internetwork where packets enter, but do not emerge, due to adverse conditions or poor system configuration within a portion of the network.

blocking   In a switching system, a condition in which no paths are available to complete a circuit. The term is also used to describe a situation in which one activity cannot begin until another has been completed.

block multiplexer channel   An IBM-style channel that implements the FIPS-60 channel, a U.S. channel standard. This channel is also referred to as OEMI channel and 370-block mux channel.

BNC connector   A standard connector used to connect IEEE 802.3 10Base2 coaxial cable to an MAU.

BNN   boundary network node. In SNA terminology, a subarea node that provides boundary function support for adjacent peripheral nodes. This support includes sequencing, pacing, and address translation. Also called boundary node.

BOC   Bell operating company. *See* RBOC.

Bolt, Beranek, and Newman, Inc.   *See* BBN.

BOOTP   A protocol used by a network node to determine the IP address of its Ethernet interfaces, in order to affect network booting.

boot programmable read-only memory   *See* boot PROM.

boot PROM   boot programmable read-only memory. A chip mounted on a printed circuit board used to provide executable boot instructions to a computer device.

border gateway   A router that communicates with routers in other autonomous systems.

Border Gateway Protocol   *See* BGP.

boundary function A capability of SNA subarea nodes to provide protocol support for attached peripheral nodes. Typically found in IBM 3745 devices.

boundary network node *See* BNN.

boundary node *See* BNN.

BPDU bridge protocol data unit. A Spanning-Tree Protocol hello packet that is sent out at configurable intervals to exchange information among bridges in the network. *See also* PDU.

bps bits per second.

BRHR Basic Research and Human Resources. A component of the HPCC program designed to support research, training, and education in computer science, computer engineering, and computational science. *See also* HPCC.

BRI Basic Rate Interface. An ISDN interface composed of two B channels and one D channel for circuit-switched communication of voice, video, and data. *Compare with* PRI. *See also* BISDN, ISDN, and N-ISDN.

bridge A device that connects and passes packets between two network segments that use the same communications protocol. Bridges operate at the data link layer (Layer 2) of the OSI reference model. In general, a bridge filters, forwards, or floods an incoming frame based on the MAC address of that frame. *See also* relay.

bridge forwarding A process that uses entries in a filtering database to determine whether frames with a given MAC destination address can be forwarded to a given port or ports. Described in the IEEE 802.1 standard. *See also* IEEE 802.1.

bridge number A number that identifies each bridge in an SRB LAN. Parallel bridges must have different bridge numbers.

bridge protocol data unit *See* BPDU.

bridge static filtering A process in which a bridge maintains a filtering database consisting of static entries. Each static entry equates a MAC destination address with a port that can receive frames with this MAC destination address and a set of ports on which the frames can be transmitted. Defined in the IEEE 802.1 standard. *See also* IEEE 802.1.

broadband A transmission system that multiplexes multiple independent signals onto one cable. In telecommunications terminology, any channel having a bandwidth greater than a voice-grade channel (4 kHz). In LAN terminology, a coaxial cable on which analog signaling is used. Also called wideband. *Compare with* baseband.

Broadband ISDN *See* BISDN.

broadcast Data packet that is sent to all nodes on a network. Broadcasts are identified by a broadcast address. *Compare with* multicast and unicast. *See also* broadcast address.

broadcast address A special address reserved for sending a message to all stations. Generally, a broadcast address is a MAC destination address of all ones. *Compare with* multicast address and unicast address. *See also* broadcast.

broadcast and unknown server *See* BUS.

broadcast domain The set of all devices that will receive broadcast frames originating from any device within the set. Broadcast domains are typically bounded by routers because routers do not forward broadcast frames.

broadcast search A propagation of a search request to all network nodes if the location of a resource is unknown to the requester. *See also* directed search.

broadcast storm An undesirable network event in which many broadcasts are sent simultaneously across all network segments. A broadcast storm uses substantial network bandwidth and, typically, causes network time-outs.

browser *See* WWW browser.

BSC binary synchronous communication. A character-oriented data link layer protocol for half-duplex applications. Often referred to simply as bisync.

BSD   Berkeley Standard Distribution. The term used to describe any of a variety of UNIX-type operating systems based on the UC Berkeley BSD operating system.

BT   burst tolerance. A parameter defined by the ATM Forum for ATM traffic management. For VBR connections, BT determines the size of the maximum burst of contiguous cells that can be transmitted. *See also* VBR.

buffer   A storage area used for handling data in transit. Buffers are used in internetworking to compensate for differences in processing speed between network devices. Bursts of data can be stored in buffers until they can be handled by slower processing devices. Sometimes referred to as a packet buffer.

burst tolerance   *See* BT.

BUS   broadcast and unknown server. A multicast server used in ELANs that is used to flood traffic addressed to an unknown destination and to forward multicast and broadcast traffic to the appropriate clients. *See also* ELAN.

bus   1. A common physical signal path composed of wires or other media across which signals can be sent from one part of a computer to another. Sometimes called highway. *See* bus topology.

bus and tag channel   An IBM channel developed in the 1960s that incorporates copper multiwire technology. Replaced by the ESCON channel. *See also* ESCON channel and parallel channel.

Bus Interface Gate Array   *See* BIGA.

bus topology   A linear LAN architecture in which transmissions from network stations propagate the length of the medium and are received by all other stations. *Compare with* ring topology, star topology, and tree topology.

bypass mode   An operating mode on FDDI and Token Ring networks in which an interface has been removed from the ring.

bypass relay   Allows a particular Token Ring interface to be shut down and thus effectively removed from the ring.

byte   A series of consecutive binary digits that are operated on as a unit (for example, an 8-bit byte).

byte-oriented protocol   A class of data-link communications protocols that use a specific character from the user character set to delimit frames. These protocols have largely been replaced by bit-oriented protocols. *Compare with* bit-oriented protocol.

byte reversal   A process of storing numeric data with the least-significant byte first. Used for integers and addresses on devices with Intel microprocessors.

C

cable   A transmission medium of copper wire or optical fiber wrapped in a protective cover.

cable range   A range of network numbers that is valid for use by nodes on an extended AppleTalk network. The cable range value can be a single network number or a contiguous sequence of several network numbers. Node addresses are assigned based on the cable range value.

cable television   *See* CATV.

caching   A form of replication in which information learned during a previous transaction is used to process later transactions.

California Education and Research Federation Network   *See* CERFnet.

call admission control   A traffic management mechanism used in ATM networks that determines whether the network can offer a path with sufficient bandwidth for a requested VCC.

call priority   A priority assigned to each origination port in circuit-switched systems. This priority defines the order in which calls are reconnected. Call priority also defines which calls can or cannot be placed during a bandwidth reservation. *See also* bandwidth reservation.

call setup time   The time required to establish a switched call between DTE devices.

CAM   content-addressable memory. *See* associative memory.

Canadian Standards Association *See* CSA.

carrier An electromagnetic wave or alternating current of a single frequency, suitable for modulation by another, data-bearing signal. *See also* modulation.

Carrier Detect *See* CD.

carrier sense multiple access collision detect *See* CSMA/CD.

Category 1 cabling One of five grades of UTP cabling described in the EIA/TIA-586 standard. Category 1 cabling is used for telephone communications and is not suitable for transmitting data. *Compare with* Category 2 cabling, Category 3 cabling, Category 4 cabling, and Category 5 cabling. *See also* EIA/TIA-586 and UTP.

Category 2 cabling One of five grades of UTP cabling described in the EIA/TIA-586 standard. Category 2 cabling is capable of transmitting data at speeds up to 4 Mbps. *Compare with* Category 1 cabling, Category 3 cabling, Category 4 cabling, and Category 5 cabling. *See also* EIA/TIA-586 and UTP.

Category 3 cabling One of five grades of UTP cabling described in the EIA/TIA-586 standard. Category 3 cabling is used in 10BaseT networks and can transmit data at speeds up to 10 Mbps. *Compare with* Category 1 cabling, Category 2 cabling, Category 4 cabling, and Category 5 cabling. *See also* EIA/TIA-586 and UTP.

Category 4 cabling One of five grades of UTP cabling described in the EIA/TIA-586 standard. Category 4 cabling is used in Token Ring networks and can transmit data at speeds up to 16 Mbps. *Compare with* Category 1 cabling, Category 2 cabling, Category 3 cabling, and Category 5 cabling. *See also* EIA/TIA-586 and UTP.

Category 5 cabling One of five grades of UTP cabling described in the EIA/TIA-586 standard. Category 5 cabling is used for running CDDI and can transmit data at speeds up to 100 Mbps. *Compare with* Category 1 cabling, Category 2 cabling, Category 3 cabling, and Category 4 cabling. *See also* EIA/TIA-586 and UTP.

catenet A network in which hosts are connected to diverse networks, which themselves are connected with routers. The Internet is a prominent example of a catenet.

CATV cable television. A communication system in which multiple channels of programming material are transmitted to homes using broadband coaxial cable. Formerly called Community Antenna Television.

CBDS Connectionless Broadband Data Service. A European high-speed, packet-switched, datagram-based WAN networking technology. Similar to SMDS. *See also* SMDS.

CBR constant bit rate. A QOS class defined by the ATM Forum for ATM networks. CBR is used for connections that depend on precise clocking to ensure undistorted delivery. *Compare with* ABR (available bit rate), UBR, and VBR.

CCITT Consultative Committee for International Telegraph and Telephone. An International organization responsible for the development of communications standards. Now called the ITU-T. *See* ITU-T.

CCS common channel signaling. A signaling system used in telephone networks that separates signaling information from user data. A specified channel is exclusively designated to carry signaling information for all other channels in the system. *See also* SS7.

CD Carrier Detect. A signal that indicates whether an interface is active. Also, a signal generated by a modem indicating that a call has been connected.

CDDI Copper Distributed Data Interface. An implementation of FDDI protocols over STP and UTP cabling. CDDI transmits over relatively short distances (about 100 meters), providing data rates of 100 Mbps using a dual-ring architecture to provide redundancy. Based on the ANSI Twisted-Pair Physical Medium Dependent (TPPMD) standard. *Compare with* FDDI.

CDPD Cellular Digital Packet Data. An open standard for two-way wireless data communication over high-frequency cellular telephone channels. Allows data transmissions between a remote cellular link and a NAP. Operates at 19.2 kbps.

CDVT cell delay variation tolerance. A parameter defined by the ATM Forum for ATM traffic management. In CBR transmissions, it determines the level of jitter that is tolerable for the data samples taken by the PCR. *See also* CBR and PCR.

cell The basic unit for ATM switching and multiplexing. Cells contain identifiers that specify the data stream to which they belong. Each cell consists of a 5-byte header and 48 bytes of payload. *See also* cell relay.

cell delay variation tolerance *See* CDVT.

cell loss priority *See* CLP.

cell relay A network technology based on the use of small, fixed-size packets, or cells. Because cells are fixed-length, they can be processed and switched in hardware at high speeds. Cell relay is the basis for many high-speed network protocols including ATM, IEEE 802.6, and SMDS. *See also* cell.

cells per second Abbreviated cps.

Cellular Digital Packet Data *See* CDPD.

cellular radio A technology that uses radio transmissions to access telephone-company networks. Service is provided in a particular area by a low-power transmitter.

central office *See* CO.

Centrex An AT&T PBX that provides direct inward dialing and automatic number identification of the calling PBX.

CEPT ConfÈrence EuropÈenne des Postes et des TÈlÈcommunications. An association of the 26 European PTTs that recommends communication specifications to the ITU-T.

CERFnet California Education and Research Federation Network. A TCP/IP network, based in Southern California, that connects hundreds of higher-education centers internationally while also providing Internet access to subscribers. CERFnet was founded in 1988 by the San Diego Supercomputer Center and General Atomics, and is funded by the NSF.

chaining SNA concept in which RUs are grouped together for the purpose of error recovery.

Challenge Handshake Authentication Protocol *See* CHAP.

channel 1. A communication path. Multiple channels can be multiplexed over a single cable in certain environments.
2. In IBM, the specific path between large computers (such as mainframes) and attached peripheral devices.

channel-attached Pertaining to attachment of devices directly by data channels (input/output channels) to a computer.

channelized E1 An access link operating at 2.048 Mbps that is subdivided into 30 B-channels and 1 D-channel. Supports DDR, Frame Relay, and X.25. *Compare with* channelized T1.

channelized T1 An access link operating at 1.544 Mbps that is subdivided into 24 channels (23 B-channels and 1 D-channel) of 64 kbps each. The individual channels or groups of channels connect to different destinations. Supports DDR, Frame Relay, and X.25. Also referred to as fractional T1. *Compare with* channelized E1.

channel service unit *See* CSU.

CHAP Challenge Handshake Authentication Protocol. A security feature supported on lines using PPP encapsulation that prevents unauthorized access. CHAP does not itself prevent unauthorized access; it merely identifies the remote end. The router or access server then determines whether that user is allowed access. *Compare with* PAP.

chat script A string of text that defines the login "conversation" that occurs between two systems. It consists of expect-send pairs that define the string the local system expects to receive from the remote system and what the local system should send as a reply.

Cheapernet An industry term used to refer to the IEEE 802.3 10Base2 standard or the cable specified in that standard. *Compare with* Thinnet. *See also* 10Base2, Ethernet, and IEEE 802.3.

checksum A method for checking the integrity of transmitted data. A checksum is an integer value computed from a sequence of octets taken through a series of arithmetic operations. The value is recomputed at the receiving end and compared for verification.

choke packet A packet sent to a transmitter to tell it that congestion exists and that it should reduce its sending rate.

CIA *See* classical IP over ATM.

CICNet A regional network that connects academic, research, nonprofit, and commercial organizations in the Midwestern United States. Founded in 1988, CICNet was a part of the NSFNET and was funded by the NSF until the NSFNET dissolved in 1995. *See also* NSFNET.

CICS Customer Information Control System. An IBM application subsystem that allows transactions entered at remote terminals to be processed concurrently by user applications.

CIDR classless interdomain routing. A technique supported by BGP4 and based on route aggregation. CIDR allows routers to group routes together in order to cut down on the quantity of routing information carried by the core routers. With CIDR, several IP networks appear to networks outside the group as a single, larger entity. *See also* BGP4.

CIR committed information rate. The rate at which a Frame Relay network agrees to transfer information under normal conditions, averaged over a minimum increment of time. CIR, measured in bits per second, is one of the key negotiated tariff metrics. *See also* Bc.

circuit A communications path between two or more points.

circuit group A grouping of associated serial lines that link two bridges. If one of the serial links in a circuit group is in the spanning tree for a network, any of the serial links in the circuit group can be used for load balancing. This load-balancing strategy avoids data ordering problems by assigning each destination address to a particular serial link.

circuit switching A switching system in which a dedicated physical circuit path must exist between sender and receiver for the duration of the "call." Used heavily in the telephone company network. Circuit switching can be contrasted with contention and token passing as a channel-access method, and with message switching and packet switching as a switching technique.

Class A station *See* DAS.

Class B station *See* SAS.

classical IP over ATM A specification for running IP over ATM in a manner that takes full advantage of the features of ATM. Defined in RFC 1577. Sometimes called CIA.

classless interdomain routing *See* CIDR.

class of service *See* COS.

CLAW Common Link Access for Workstations. A data link layer protocol used by channel-attached RISC System/6000 series systems and by IBM 3172 devices running TCP/IP off-load. CLAW improves efficiency of channel use and allows the CIP to provide the functionality of a 3172 in TCP/IP environments and support direct channel attachment. The output from TCP/IP mainframe processing is a series of IP datagrams that the router can switch without modifications.

Clear To Send *See* CTS.

client A node or software program (front-end device) that requests services from a server. *See also* back end, front end, and server.

client/server computing Computing (processing) network systems in which transaction responsibilities are divided into two parts: client (front end) and server (back end). Both terms (client and server) can be applied to software programs or actual computing devices. Also called distributed computing (processing). *Compare with* peer-to-peer computing. *See also* RPC.

CLNP   Connectionless Network Protocol. OSI network layer protocol that does not require a circuit to be established before data is transmitted. *See also* CLNS.

CLNS   Connectionless Network Service. An OSI network layer service that does not require a circuit to be established before data is transmitted. CLNS routes messages to their destinations independently of any other messages. *See also* CLNP.

CLP   cell loss priority. A field in the ATM cell header that determines the probability of a cell being dropped if the network becomes congested. Cells with CLP = 0 are insured traffic, which is unlikely to be dropped. Cells with CLP = 1 are best-effort traffic, which might be dropped in congested conditions in order to free up resources to handle insured traffic.

cluster controller   1. Generally, an intelligent device that provides the connections for a cluster of terminals to a data link.
2. In SNA, a programmable device that controls the input/output operations of attached devices. Typically, an IBM 3174 or 3274 device.

CMI   coded mark inversion. An ITU-T line coding technique specified for STS-3c transmissions. Also used in DS-1 systems. *See also* DS-1 and STS-3c.

CMIP   Common Management Information Protocol. An OSI network management protocol created and standardized by ISO for the monitoring and control of heterogeneous networks. *See also* CMIS.

CMIS   Common Management Information Services. An OSI network management service interface created and standardized by ISO for the monitoring and control of heterogeneous networks. *See also* CMIP.

CMNS   Connection-Mode Network Service. A service that extends local X.25 switching to a variety of media (Ethernet, FDDI, Token Ring). *See also* CONP.

CMT   connection management. A FDDI process that handles the transition of the ring through its various states (off, active, connect, and so on), as defined by the ANSI X3T9.5 specification.

CO   central office. A local telephone company office to which all local loops in a given area connect and in which circuit switching of subscriber lines occurs.

coaxial cable   Cable consisting of a hollow outer cylindrical conductor that surrounds a single inner wire conductor. Two types of coaxial cable are currently used in LANs: 50-ohm cable, which is used for digital signaling, and 75-ohm cable, which is used for analog signaling and high-speed digital signaling.

CODEC   coder-decoder. A device that typically uses PCM to transform analog signals into a digital bit stream and digital signals back into analog.

coded mark inversion   *See* CMI.

coder-decoder   *See* CODEC.

coding   Electrical techniques used to convey binary signals.

collapsed backbone   A nondistributed backbone in which all network segments are interconnected by way of an internetworking device. A collapsed backbone might be a virtual network segment existing in a device such as a hub, a router, or a switch.

collision   In Ethernet, the result of two nodes transmitting simultaneously. The frames from each device impact and are damaged when they meet on the physical media. *See also* collision domain.

collision detection   *See* CSMA/CD.

collision domain   In Ethernet, the network area within which frames that have collided are propagated. Repeaters and hubs propagate collisions; LAN switches, bridges, and routers do not. *See also* collision.

Committed Burst   *See* Bc.

committed information rate   *See* CIR.

common carrier A licensed, private utility company that supplies communication services to the public at regulated prices.

common channel signaling *See* CCS.

Common Link Access for Workstations *See* CLAW.

Common Management Information Protocol *See* CMIP.

Common Management Information Services *See* CMIS.

common part convergence sublayer *See* CPCS.

Common Programming Interface for Communications *See* CPI-C.

common transport semantic *See* CTS.

communication Transmission of information.

communication controller In SNA, a subarea node (such as an IBM 3745 device) that contains an NCP.

communication server A communications processor that connects asynchronous devices to a LAN or WAN through network and terminal emulation software. Performs only asynchronous routing of IP and IPX. *Compare with* access server.

communications line The physical link (such as wire or a telephone circuit) that connects one or more devices to one or more other devices.

community In SNMP, a logical group of managed devices and NMSs in the same administrative domain.

Community Antenna Television Now known as CATV. *See* CATV.

community string A text string that acts as a password and is used to authenticate messages sent between a management station and a router containing an SNMP agent. The community string is sent in every packet between the manager and the agent.

companding A contraction derived from the opposite processes of compression and expansion. Part of the PCM process whereby analog signal values are logically rounded to discrete scale-step values on a nonlinear scale. The decimal step number is then coded in its binary equivalent prior to transmission. The process is reversed at the receiving terminal, using the same nonlinear scale. *Compare with* compression and expansion. *See also* a-law and mu-law.

complete sequence number PDU *See* CSNP.

Compressed Serial Link Internet Protocol *See* CSLIP.

compression The running of a data set through an algorithm that reduces the space required to store or the bandwidth required to transmit the data set. Compare with companding and expansion.

Computer Science Network *See* CSNET.

concentrator *See* hub.

ConfÈrence EuropÈenne des Postes et des TÈlÈcommunications *See* CEPT.

configuration management One of five categories of network management defined by ISO for management of OSI networks. Configuration management subsystems are responsible for detecting and determining the state of a network. *See also* accounting management, fault management, performance management, and security management.

congestion Traffic in excess of network capacity.

connectionless Data transfer that occurs without the existence of a virtual circuit. Compare with connection-oriented. *See also* virtual circuit.

Connectionless Broadband Data Service *See* CBDS.

Connectionless Network Protocol *See* CLNP.

Connectionless Network Service *See* CLNS.

connection management *See* CMT.

Connection-Mode Network Service *See* CMNS.

connection-oriented Data transfer that requires the establishment of a virtual circuit. A Layer 4 protocol that creates with software a virtual circuit between devices to provide guaranteed transport of data. *See also* connectionless. *See also* virtual circuit.

Connection-Oriented Network Protocol *See* CONP.

CONP Connection-Oriented Network Protocol. An OSI protocol that provides connection-oriented operation to upper-layer protocols. *See also* CMNS.

console A DTE through which commands are entered into a host.

constant bit rate *See* CBR.

Consultative Committee for International Telegraph and Telephone *See* CCITT.

content-addressable memory *See* associative memory.

contention An access method in which network devices compete for permission to access the physical medium. *Compare with* circuit switching and token passing.

control point *See* CP.

convergence The speed and ability of a group of internetworking devices running a specific routing protocol to agree on the topology of an internetwork after a change in that topology.

convergence sublayer *See* CS.

conversation In SNA, an LU 6.2 session between two transaction programs.

Cooperation for Open Systems Interconnection Networking in Europe *See* COSINE.

Copper Distributed Data Interface *See* CDDI.

core gateway The primary routers in the Internet.

core router In a packet-switched star topology, a router that is part of the backbone and that serves as the single pipe through which all traffic from peripheral networks must pass on its way to other peripheral networks.

Corporation for Open Systems *See* COS.

Corporation for Research and Educational Networking *See* CREN.

COS 1. class of service. An indication of how an upper-layer protocol requires that a lower-layer protocol treat its messages. In SNA subarea routing, COS definitions are used by subarea nodes to determine the optimal route to establish a given session. A COS definition comprises a virtual route number and a transmission priority field. Also called TOS (type of service).
2. Corporation for Open Systems. An organization that promulgates the use of OSI protocols through conformance testing, certification, and related activities.

COSINE Cooperation for Open Systems Interconnection Networking in Europe. A European project financed by the European Community (EC) to build a communication network between scientific and industrial entities in Europe. The project ended in 1994.

cost An arbitrary value, typically based on hop count, media bandwidth, or other measures, that is assigned by a network administrator and used to compare various paths through an internetwork environment. Cost values are used by routing protocols to determine the most favorable path to a particular destination: The lower the cost, the better the path. Sometimes called path cost. *See also* routing metric.

count to infinity A problem that can occur in routing algorithms that are slow to converge, in which routers continuously increment the hop count to particular networks. Typically, some arbitrary hop-count limit is imposed to prevent this problem.

CP control point. In SNA networks, an element that identifies the APPN networking components of a PU 2.1 node, manages device resources, and can provide services to other devices. In APPN, CPs are able to communicate with logically adjacent CPs by way of CP-to-CP sessions. *See also* EN and NN.

CPCS common part convergence sublayer. One of the two sublayers of any AAL. The CPCS is service independent and is further divided into the CS and the SAR sublayers. The CPCS is responsible for preparing data for transport across the ATM network, including the creation of the 48-byte payload cells that are passed to the ATM layer. *See also* AAL, ATM layer, CS, SAR, and SSCS.

CPE customer premises equipment. Terminating equipment, such as terminals, telephones, and modems, supplied by the telephone company, installed at customer sites, and connected to the telephone company network.

CPI-C Common Programming Interface for Communications. A platform-independent API developed by IBM and used to provide portability in APPC applications. *See also* APPC.

cps cells per second.

CRC cyclic redundancy check. An error-checking technique in which the frame recipient calculates a remainder by dividing frame contents by a prime binary divisor and compares the calculated remainder to a value stored in the frame by the sending node.

CREN Corporation for Research and Educational Networking. The result of a merger of BITNET and CSNET. CREN is devoted to providing Internet connectivity to its members, which include the alumni, students, faculty, and other affiliates of participating educational and research institutions, via BITNET III. *See also* BITNET, BITNET III, and CSNET.

cross talk Interfering energy transferred from one circuit to another.

CS convergence sublayer. One of the two sublayers of the AAL CPCS, responsible for padding and error checking. PDUs passed from the SSCS are appended with an 8-byte trailer (for error checking and other control information) and padded, if necessary, so that the length of the resulting PDU is divisible by 48. These PDUs are then passed to the SAR sublayer of the CPCS for further processing. *See also* AAL, CPCS, SAR, and SSCS.

CSA Canadian Standards Association. An agency in Canada that certifies products that conform to Canadian national safety standards.

CSLIP Compressed Serial Link Internet Protocol. An extension of SLIP that, when appropriate, allows just header information to be sent across a SLIP connection, reducing overhead and increasing packet throughput on SLIP lines. *See also* SLIP.

CSMA/CD carrier sense multiple access collision detect. Media-access mechanism wherein devices ready to transmit data first check the channel for a carrier. If no carrier is sensed for a specific period of time, a device can transmit. If two devices transmit at once, a collision occurs and is detected by all colliding devices. This collision subsequently delays retransmissions from those devices for some random length of time. CSMA/CD access is used by Ethernet and IEEE 802.3.

CSNET Computer Science Network. A large internetwork consisting primarily of universities, research institutions, and commercial concerns. CSNET merged with BITNET to form CREN. *See also* BITNET and CREN.

CSNP complete sequence number PDU. A PDU sent by the designated router in an OSPF network to maintain database synchronization.

CSU channel service unit. A digital interface device that connects end-user equipment to the local digital telephone loop. Often referred to, together with DSU, as CSU/DSU. *See also* DSU.

CTS 1. Clear To Send. A circuit in the EIA/TIA-232 specification that is activated when DCE is ready to accept data from DTE.
2. common transport semantic. A cornerstone of the IBM strategy to reduce the number of protocols on networks. CTS provides a single API for developers of network software and enables applications to run over APPN, OSI, or TCP/IP.

Customer Information Control System *See* CICS.

customer premises equipment *See* CPE.

cut-through packet switching A packet switching approach that streams data through a switch so that the leading edge of a packet exits the switch at the output port before the packet finishes entering the input port. A device using cut-through packet switching reads, processes, and forwards packets as soon as the destination address is looked up and the outgoing port is determined. Also known as on-the-fly packet switching. *Compare with* store and forward packet switching.

cycles per second   *See* hertz.

cyclic redundancy check   *See* CRC.

D

D4 framing   *See* SF.

DAC   dual-attached concentrator. An FDDI or a CDDI concentrator capable of attaching to both rings of an FDDI or CDDI network. It can also be dual-homed from the master ports of other FDDI or CDDI concentrators.

DARPA   Defense Advanced Research Projects Agency. A U.S. government agency that funded research for and experimentation with the Internet. Evolved from ARPA, and then, in 1994, back to ARPA. *See also* ARPA.

DARPA Internet   An obsolete term referring to the Internet. *See* Internet.

DAS   dual attachment station. A device attached to both the primary and the secondary FDDI rings. Dual attachment provides redundancy for the FDDI ring; if the primary ring fails, the station can wrap the primary ring to the secondary ring, isolating the failure and retaining ring integrity. Also known as a Class A station. Compare with SAS.

database object   In general, a piece of information that is stored in a database. *See* DB connector.

data channel   *See* D channel.

data circuit-terminating equipment   *See* DCE.

data communications equipment   *See* DCE.

Data Country Code   *See* DCC.

Data Encryption Standard   *See* DES.

Data Exchange Interface   *See* DXI.

data flow control layer   Layer 5 of the SNA architectural model. This layer determines and manages interactions between session partners, particularly data flow. Corresponds to the session layer of the OSI model. *See also* data link control layer, path control layer, physical control layer, presentation services layer, transaction services layer, and transmission control layer.

datagram   A logical grouping of information sent as a network layer unit over a transmission medium without prior establishment of a virtual circuit. IP datagrams are the primary information units in the Internet. The terms frame, message, packet, and segment are also used to describe logical information groupings at various layers of the OSI reference model and in various technology circles.

Datagram Delivery Protocol   *See* DDP.

data-link connection identifier   *See* DLCI.

data link control layer   Layer 2 in the SNA architectural model. This layer is responsible for the transmission of data over a particular physical link. Corresponds roughly to the data link layer of the OSI model. *See also* data flow control layer, path control layer, physical control layer, presentation services layer, transaction services layer, and transmission control layer.

data link layer   Layer 2 of the OSI reference model. This layer provides reliable transit of data across a physical link. The data link layer is concerned with physical addressing, network topology, line discipline, error notification, ordered delivery of frames, and flow control. The IEEE has divided this layer into two sublayers: the MAC sublayer and the LLC sublayer. Sometimes simply called link layer. Roughly corresponds to the data link control layer of the SNA model. *See also* application layer, LLC, MAC, network layer, physical layer, presentation layer, session layer, and transport layer.

data-link switching   *See* DLSw.

Data Network Identification Code   *See* DNIC.

data set ready   *See* DSR.

data service unit *See* DSU.

data sink Network equipment that accepts data transmissions.

data stream All data transmitted through a communications line in a single read or write operation.

data terminal equipment *See* DTE.

data terminal ready *See* DTR.

dB decibels.

DB connector data bus connector. A type of connector used to connect serial and parallel cables to a data bus. DB connector names are of the format DB-*x*, where *x* represents the number of wires within the connector. Each line is connected to a pin on the connector, but in many cases, not all pins are assigned a function. DB connectors are defined by various EIA/TIA standards.

DCA Defense Communications Agency. A U.S. government organization responsible for DDN networks such as MILNET. Now called DISA. *See* DISA.

DCC Data Country Code. One of two ATM address formats developed by the ATM Forum for use by private networks. Adapted from the subnetwork model of addressing, in which the ATM layer is responsible for mapping network layer addresses to ATM addresses. *See also* ICD.

DCE data communications equipment (EIA expansion) or data circuit-terminating equipment (ITU-T expansion). The devices and connections of a communications network that comprise the network end of the user-to-network interface. The DCE provides a physical connection to the network, forwards traffic, and provides a clocking signal used to synchronize data transmission between DCE and DTE devices. Modems and interface cards are examples of DCE. Compare with DTE.

D channel 1. data channel. Full-duplex, 16-kbps (BRI) or 64-kbps (PRI) ISDN channel. *Compare with* B channel, E channel, and H channel.

2. In SNA, a device that connects a processor and main storage with peripherals.

DDM Distributed Data Management. Software in an IBM SNA environment that provides peer-to-peer communication and file sharing. One of three SNA transaction services. *See also* DIA and SNADS.

DDN Defense Data Network. A U.S. military network composed of an unclassified network (MILNET) and various secret and top-secret networks. DDN is operated and maintained by DISA. *See also* DISA and MILNET.

DDP Datagram Delivery Protocol. An Apple Computer network layer protocol that is responsible for the socket-to-socket delivery of datagrams over an AppleTalk internetwork.

DDR dial-on-demand routing. A technique whereby a Cisco router can automatically initiate and close a circuit-switched session as transmitting stations demand. The router spoofs keepalives so that end stations treat the session as active. DDR permits routing over ISDN or telephone lines using an external ISDN terminal adapter or modem.

DE discard eligible. *See* tagged traffic.

deadlock 1. Unresolved contention for the use of a resource.
2. In APPN, when two elements of a process each wait for action by or a response from the other before they resume the process.

decibels Abbreviated dB.

DECnet Group of communications products (including a protocol suite) developed and supported by Digital Equipment Corporation. DECnet/OSI (also called DECnet Phase V) is the most recent iteration and supports both OSI protocols and proprietary Digital protocols. Phase IV Prime supports inherent MAC addresses that allow DECnet nodes to coexist with systems running other protocols that have MAC address restrictions. *See also* DNA.

DECnet routing A proprietary routing scheme introduced by Digital Equipment Corporation in

DECnet Phase III. In DECnet Phase V, DECnet completed its transition to OSI routing protocols (ES-IS and IS-IS).

decryption The reverse application of an encryption algorithm to encrypted data, thereby restoring that data to its original, unencrypted state. *See also* encryption.

dedicated LAN A network segment allocated to a single device. Used in LAN switched network topologies.

dedicated line A communications line that is indefinitely reserved for transmissions, rather than switched as transmission is required. *See also* leased line.

de facto standard A standard that exists by nature of its widespread use. Compare with de jure standard. *See also* standard.

default route A routing table entry that is used to direct frames for which a next hop is not explicitly listed in the routing table.

Defense Advanced Research Projects Agency *See* DARPA.

Defense Communications Agency *See* DCA.

Defense Data Network *See* DDN.

Defense Information Systems Agency *See* DISA.

Defense Intelligence Agency *See* DIA.

de jure standard A standard that exists because of its approval by an official standards body. *Compare with* de facto standard. *See also* standard.

delay The time between the initiation of a transaction by a sender and the first response received by the sender. Also, the time required to move a packet from source to destination over a given path.

demand priority A media access method used in 100VG-AnyLAN that uses a hub that can handle multiple transmission requests and can process traffic according to priority, making it useful for servicing time-sensitive traffic such as multimedia and video. Demand priority eliminates the overhead of packet

collisions, collision recovery, and broadcast traffic typical in Ethernet networks. *See also* 100VG-AnyLAN.

demarc A demarcation point between carrier equipment and CPE.

demodulation The process of returning a modulated signal to its original form. Modems perform demodulation by returning an analog signal to its original (digital) form. *See also* modulation.

demultiplexing The separating of multiple input streams that have been multiplexed into a common physical signal back into multiple output streams. *See also* multiplexing.

dense mode PIM *See* PIM dense mode.

Department of Defense *See* DoD.

Department of Defense Intelligence Information System Network Security for Information Exchange *See* DNSIX.

Dependent LU *See* DLU.

Dependent LU Requester *See* DLUR.

Dependent LU Server *See* DLUS.

DES Data Encryption Standard. A standard cryptographic algorithm developed by the U.S. NBS.

designated bridge The bridge that incurs the lowest path cost when forwarding a frame from a segment to the route bridge.

designated router An OSPF router that generates LSAs for a multiaccess network and has other special responsibilities in running OSPF. Each multiaccess OSPF network that has at least two attached routers has a designated router that is elected by the OSPF Hello protocol. The designated router enables a reduction in the number of adjacencies required on a multiaccess network, which in turn reduces the amount of routing protocol traffic and the size of the topological database.

destination address The address of a network device that is receiving data. *See also* source address.

destination MAC   *See* DMAC.

destination service access point   *See* DSAP.

deterministic load distribution   A technique for distributing traffic between two bridges across a circuit group. Guarantees packet ordering between source-destination pairs and always forwards traffic for a source-destination pair on the same segment in a circuit group for a given circuit-group configuration.

Deutsche Industrie Norm   *See* DIN.

Deutsche Industrie Norm connector   *See* DIN connector.

device   *See* node.

DHCP   Dynamic Host Configuration Protocol. Provides a mechanism for allocating IP addresses dynamically so that addresses can be reused when hosts no longer need them.

DIA   Document Interchange Architecture. Defines the protocols and data formats needed for the transparent interchange of documents in an SNA network. One of three SNA transaction services. *See also* DDM and SNADS.

dial-on-demand routing   *See* DDR.

dial-up line   A communications circuit that is established by a switched-circuit connection using the telephone company network.

differential encoding   A digital encoding technique whereby a binary value is denoted by a signal change rather than a particular signal level.

differential Manchester encoding   A digital coding scheme where a mid-bit-time transition is used for clocking, and a transition at the beginning of each bit time denotes a zero. The coding scheme used by IEEE 802.5 and Token Ring networks.

Diffusing Update Algorithm   *See* DUAL.

Digital Network Architecture   *See* DNA.

digital signal level 0   *See* DS-0.

digital signal level 1   *See* DS-1.

digital signal level 3   *See* DS-3.

Dijkstra's algorithm   *See* SPF.

DIN   Deutsche Industrie Norm. A German national standards organization.

DIN connector   Deutsche Industrie Norm connector. A multipin connector used in some Macintosh and IBM PC-compatible computers, and on some network processor panels.

directed search   A search request sent to a specific node known to contain a resource. A directed search is used to determine the continued existence of the resource and to obtain routing information specific to the node. *See also* broadcast search.

direct memory access   *See* DMA.

directory services   Services that help network devices locate service providers.

DISA   Defense Information Systems Agency. A U.S. military organization responsible for implementing and operating military information systems, including the DDN. *See also* DDN.

discard eligible   *See* DE.

discovery architecture   APPN software that enables a machine configured as an APPN EN to automatically find primary and backup NNs when the machine is brought onto an APPN network.

discovery mode   A method by which an AppleTalk interface acquires information about an attached network from an operational node and then uses this information to configure itself. Also called dynamic configuration.

Distance Vector Multicast Routing Protocol   *See* DVMRP.

distance vector routing algorithm   A class of routing algorithms that iterate on the number of hops in a route to find a shortest-path spanning tree. Distance vector routing algorithms call for each router to send its entire routing table in each update, but only to its neighbors. Distance vector routing algorithms can be prone to routing loops, but are computationally simpler than link state routing algorithms. Also called Bellman-Ford routing algorithm. *See also* link state routing algorithm and SPF.

distortion delay A problem with a communication signal resulting from nonuniform transmission speeds of the components of a signal through a transmission medium. Also called group delay.

distributed computing (processing) *See* client/server computing.

Distributed Data Management *See* DDM.

Distributed Queue Dual Bus *See* DQDB.

DLCI data-link connection identifier. A value that specifies a PVC or SVC in a Frame Relay network. In the basic Frame Relay specification, DLCIs are locally significant (connected devices might use different values to specify the same connection). In the LMI extended specification, DLCIs are globally significant (DLCIs specify individual end devices). *See also* LMI.

DLSw data-link switching. An interoperability standard, described in RFC 1434, that provides a method for forwarding SNA and NetBIOS traffic over TCP/IP networks using data link layer switching and encapsulation. DLSw uses SSP instead of SRB, eliminating the major limitations of SRB, including hop-count limits, broadcast and unnecessary traffic, timeouts, lack of flow control, and lack of prioritization schemes. *See also* SRB and SSP.

DLU Dependent LU. An LU that depends on the SSCP to provide services for establishing sessions with other LUs. *See also* LU and SSCP.

DLUR Dependent LU Requester. The client half of the Dependent LU Requestor/Server enhancement to APPN. The DLUR component resides in APPN ENs and NNs that support adjacent DLUs by securing services from the DLUS. *See also* APPN, DLU, and DLUS.

DLUR node In APPN networks, an EN or NN that implements the DLUR component. *See also* DLUR.

DLUS Dependent LU Server. The server half of the Dependent LU Requestor/Server enhancement to APPN. The DLUS component provides SSCP services to DLUR nodes over an APPN network. *See also* APPN, DLU, and DLUR.

DLUS node In APPN networks, an NN that implements the DLUS component. *See also* DLUS.

DMA direct memory access. The transfer of data from a peripheral device, such as a hard disk drive, into memory without that data passing through the microprocessor. DMA transfers data into memory at high speeds with no processor overhead.

DMAC destination MAC. The MAC address specified in the Destination Address field of a packet. *Compare with* SMAC. *See also* MAC address.

DNA Digital Network Architecture. A network architecture developed by Digital Equipment Corporation. The products that embody DNA (including communications protocols) are collectively referred to as DECnet. *See also* DECnet.

DNIC Data Network Identification Code. Part of an X.121 address. DNICs are divided into two parts: The first specifies the country in which the addressed PSN (packet-switching node) is located and the second specifies the PSN itself. *See also* X.121.

DNS Domain Name System. A system used in the Internet for translating names of network nodes into addresses. *See also* authority zone.

DNSIX Department of Defense Intelligence Information System Network Security for Information Exchange. A collection of security requirements for networking defined by the U.S. Defense Intelligence Agency.

Document Interchange Architecture *See* DIA.

DoD Department of Defense. A U.S. government organization that is responsible for national defense. The DoD has frequently funded communication protocol development.

domain 1. In the Internet, a portion of the naming hierarchy tree that refers to general groupings of networks based on organization type or geography. 2. In SNA, an SSCP and the resources it controls. 3. In IS-IS, a logical set of networks.

Domain A networking system developed by Apollo Computer (now part of Hewlett-Packard) for use in its engineering workstations.

Domain Name System *See* DNS.

domain-specific part *See* DSP.

dot address The common notation for IP addresses in the form *n.n.n.n*, where each number *n* represents, in decimal, 1 byte of the 4-byte IP address. Also called dotted notation, dotted-decimal notation, or four-part dotted notation.

dotted notation *See* dot address.

downlink station *See* ground station.

downstream physical unit *See* DSPU.

DQDB Distributed Queue Dual Bus. A data link layer communication protocol, specified in the IEEE 802.6 standard, designed for use in MANs. DQDB, which permits multiple systems to interconnect using two unidirectional logical buses, is an open standard that is designed for compatibility with carrier transmission standards and is aligned with emerging standards for BISDN. SIP is based on DQDB. *See also* MAN.

DRAM dynamic random-access memory. RAM that stores information in capacitors that must be periodically refreshed. Delays can occur because DRAMs are inaccessible to the processor when refreshing their contents. However, DRAMs are less complex and have greater capacity than SRAMs. *See also* SRAM.

drop A point on a multipoint channel where a connection to a networked device is made.

drop cable Generally, a cable that connects a network device (such as a computer) to a physical medium. A type of AUI. *See also* AUI.

DS-0 digital signal level 0. A framing specification used in transmitting digital signals over a single channel at 64-kbps on a T1 facility. *Compare with* DS-1 and DS-3.

DS-1 digital signal level 1. A framing specification used in transmitting digital signals at 1.544 Mbps on a T1 facility (in the United States) or at 2.108 Mbps on an E1 facility (in Europe). *Compare with* DS-0 and DS-3.

DS-1 domestic trunk interface *See* DS-1/DTI.

DS-1/DTI DS-1 domestic trunk interface. An interface circuit used for DS-1 applications with 24 trunks.

DS-3 digital signal level 3. A framing specification used for transmitting digital signals at 44.736 Mbps on a T3 facility. *Compare with* DS-0 and DS-1. *See also* E3 and T3.

DSAP destination service access point. The SAP of the network node designated in the Destination field of a packet. *Compare with* SSAP. *See also* SAP (service access point).

DSP domain-specific part. The part of a CLNS address that contains an area identifier, a station identifier, and a selector byte.

DSPU downstream physical unit. In SNA, a PU that is located downstream from the host.

DSPU concentration *See* DSPU and PU.

DSR data set ready. An EIA/TIA-232 interface circuit that is activated when DCE is powered up and ready for use.

DSU data service unit. A device used in digital transmission that adapts the physical interface on a DTE device to a transmission facility such as T1 or E1. The DSU is also responsible for functions such as signal timing. Often referred to, together with CSU, as CSU/DSU. *See also* CSU.

DSX-1 A cross-connection point for DS-1 signals.

DTE data terminal equipment. A device at the user end of a user-network interface that serves as a data source, destination, or both. DTE connects to a data network through a DCE device (for example, a modem) and typically uses clocking signals generated by the DCE. DTE includes devices such as computers, protocol translators, and multiplexers. *Compare with* DCE.

DTMF   dual tone multifrequency. The use of two simultaneous voice-band tones for dialing (such as touch tone).

DTR   data terminal ready. An EIA/TIA-232 circuit that is activated to let the DCE know when the DTE is ready to send and receive data.

DUAL   Diffusing Update Algorithm. A convergence algorithm used in Enhanced IGRP that provides loop-free operation at every instant throughout a route computation. Allows routers involved in a topology change to synchronize at the same time, while not involving routers that are unaffected by the change. *See also* Enhanced IGRP.

dual-attached concentrator   *See* DAC.

dual attachment station   *See* DAS.

dual counter-rotating rings   A network topology in which two signal paths, whose directions are opposite one another, exist in a token-passing network. FDDI and CDDI are based on this concept.

dual-homed station   A device attached to multiple FDDI rings to provide redundancy.

dual homing   A network topology in which a device is connected to the network by way of two independent access points (points of attachment). One access point is the primary connection, and the other is a standby connection that is activated in the event of a failure of the primary connection.

Dual IS-IS   *See* Integrated IS-IS.

dual tone multifrequency   *See* DTMF.

DVMRP   Distance Vector Multicast Routing Protocol. An internetwork gateway protocol, largely based on RIP, that implements a typical dense mode IP multicast scheme. DVMRP uses IGMP to exchange routing datagrams with its neighbors. *See also* IGMP.

DXI   Data Exchange Interface. An ATM Forum specification, described in RFC 1483, that defines how a network device such as a bridge, router, or hub can effectively act as an FEP to an ATM network by interfacing with a special DSU that performs packet segmentation and reassembly.

dynamic address resolution   The use of an address resolution protocol to determine and store address information on demand.

dynamic configuration   *See* discovery mode.

dynamic random-access memory   *See* DRAM.

dynamic routing   Routing that adjusts automatically to network topology or traffic changes. Also called adaptive routing.

E

E1   A wide-area digital transmission scheme used predominantly in Europe that carries data at a rate of 2.048 Mbps. E1 lines can be leased for private use from common carriers. *Compare with* T1. *See also* DS-1.

E.164   An ITU-T recommendation for international telecommunication numbering, especially in ISDN, BISDN, and SMDS. An evolution of standard telephone numbers.

E3   A wide-area digital transmission scheme, used predominantly in Europe, that carries data at a rate of 34.368 Mbps. E3 lines can be leased for private use from common carriers. *Compare with* T3. *See also* DS-3.

early token release   A technique used in Token Ring networks that allows a station to release a new token onto the ring immediately after transmitting, instead of waiting for the first frame to return. This feature can increase the total bandwidth on the ring. *See also* Token Ring.

EARN   European Academic Research Network. A European network connecting universities and research institutes. EARN merged with RARE to form TERENA. *See also* RARE and TERENA.

EBCDIC extended binary coded decimal interchange code. Any of a number of coded character sets developed by IBM consisting of 8-bit coded characters. This character code is used by older IBM systems and telex machines. *Compare with* ASCII.

E channel echo channel. A 64-kbps ISDN circuit-switching control channel. The E channel was defined in the 1984 ITU-T ISDN specification, but was dropped in the 1988 specification. *Compare with* B channel, D channel, and H channel.

echo channel *See* E channel.

echoplex A mode in which keyboard characters are echoed on a terminal screen upon return of a signal from the other end of the line indicating that the characters were received correctly.

ECMA European Computer Manufacturers Association. A group of European computer vendors that have done substantial OSI standardization work.

EDI electronic data interchange. The electronic communication of operational data, such as orders and invoices, between organizations.

EDIFACT Electronic Data Interchange for Administration, Commerce, and Transport. A data exchange standard administered by the United Nations to be a multi-industry EDI standard.

EEPROM electrically erasable programmable read-only memory. EPROM that can be erased using electrical signals applied to specific pins. *See also* EPROM.

EGP Exterior Gateway Protocol. An Internet protocol for exchanging routing information between autonomous systems. Documented in RFC 904. Not to be confused with the general term exterior gateway protocol. EGP is an obsolete protocol that has been replaced by BGP. *See also* BGP.

EIA Electronic Industries Association. A group that specifies electrical transmission standards. The EIA and TIA have developed numerous well-known communications standards, including EIA/TIA-232 and EIA/TIA-449. *See also* TIA.

EIA-530 Refers to two electrical implementations of EIA/TIA-449: RS-422 (for balanced transmission) and RS-423 (for unbalanced transmission). *See also* RS-422, RS-423, and EIA/TIA-449.

EIA/TIA-232 A common physical layer interface standard, developed by EIA and TIA, that supports unbalanced circuits at signal speeds of up to 64 kbps. Closely resembles the V.24 specification. Formerly known as RS-232.

EIA/TIA-449 A popular physical layer interface developed by EIA and TIA. Essentially, a faster (up to 2 Mbps) version of EIA/TIA-232 capable of longer cable runs. Formerly called RS-449. *See also* EIA-530.

EIA/TIA-586 A standard that describes the characteristics and applications for various grades of UTP cabling. *See also* Category 1 cabling, Category 2 cabling, Category 3 cabling, Category 4 cabling, Category 5 cabling, and UTP.

EIGRP *See* Enhanced IGRP.

EISA Extended Industry-Standard Architecture. A 32-bit bus interface used in PCs, PC-based servers, and some UNIX workstations and servers. *See also* ISA.

ELAN emulated LAN. An ATM network in which an Ethernet or Token Ring LAN is emulated using a client/server model. ELANs are composed of an LEC, an LES, a BUS, and an LECS. Multiple ELANs can exist simultaneously on a single ATM network. ELANs are defined by the LANE specification. *See also* BUS, LANE, LEC, LECS, and LES.

electromagnetic interference *See* EMI.

electromagnetic pulse *See* EMP.

electrically erasable programmable read-only memory *See* EEPROM.

electronic data interchange *See* EDI.

Electronic Data Interchange for Administration, Commerce, and Transport *See* EDIFACT.

Electronic Industries Association *See* EIA.

electronic mail A widely used network application in which mail messages are transmitted electronically between end users over various types of networks using various network protocols. Often called e-mail.

Electronic Messaging Association *See* EMA.

electrostatic discharge *See* ESD.

EMA 1. Enterprise Management Architecture. A Digital Equipment Corporation network management architecture, based on the OSI network management model.
2. Electronic Messaging Association. A forum devoted to standards and policy work, education, and development of electronic messaging systems such as electronic mail, voice mail, and facsimile.

e-mail *See* electronic mail.

EMI electromagnetic interference. Interference by electromagnetic signals that can cause reduced data integrity and increased error rates on transmission channels.

EMIF ESCON Multiple Image Facility. A mainframe I/O software function that allows one ESCON channel to be shared among multiple logical partitions on the same mainframe. *See also* ESCON.

EMP electromagnetic pulse. Caused by lightning and other high-energy phenomena. Capable of coupling enough energy into unshielded conductors to destroy electronic devices. *See also* Tempest.

emulated LAN *See* ELAN.

emulation mode A function of an NCP that enables it to perform activities equivalent to those performed by a transmission control unit.

EN end node. An APPN end system that implements the PU 2.1, provides end-user services, and supports sessions between local and remote CPs. ENs are not capable of routing traffic and rely on an adjacent NN for APPN services. *Compare with* NN. *See also* CP.

encapsulation The wrapping of data in a particular protocol header. For example, Ethernet data is

wrapped in a specific Ethernet header before network transit. Also, when bridging dissimilar networks, the entire frame from one network is simply placed in the header used by the data link layer protocol of the other network. *See also* tunneling.

encapsulation bridging Bridging that carries Ethernet frames from one router to another across disparate media, such as serial and FDDI lines. *Compare with* translational bridging.

encoder A device that modifies information into the required transmission format.

encryption The application of a specific algorithm to data so as to alter the appearance of the data, making it incomprehensible to those who are not authorized to see the information. *See also* decryption.

end node *See* EN.

end of transmission *See* EOT.

endpoint A device at which a virtual circuit or virtual path begins or ends.

end system *See* ES.

End System-to-Intermediate System *See* ES-IS.

Energy Sciences Network *See* ESnet.

Enhanced IGRP Enhanced Interior Gateway Routing Protocol. An advanced version of IGRP developed by Cisco. Provides superior convergence properties and operating efficiency, and combines the advantages of link state protocols with those of distance vector protocols. *Compare with* IGRP. *See also* IGP, OSPF, and RIP.

Enhanced Interior Gateway Routing Protocol *See* Enhanced IGRP.

Enterprise Management Architecture *See* EMA.

enterprise network A large and diverse network connecting most major points in a company or other organization. Differs from a WAN in that it is privately owned and maintained.

Enterprise System Connection *See* ESCON.

Enterprise System Connection channel *See* ESCON channel.

entity Generally, an individual, manageable network device. Sometimes called an alias.

EOT end of transmission. Generally, a character that signifies the end of a logical group of characters or bits.

EPROM erasable programmable read-only memory. Nonvolatile memory chips that are programmed after they are manufactured and, if necessary, can be erased by some means and reprogrammed. *Compare with* EEPROM and PROM.

equalization A technique used to compensate for communications channel distortions.

erasable programmable read-only memory *See* EPROM.

error control A technique for detecting and correcting errors in data transmissions.

error-correcting code A code having sufficient intelligence and incorporating sufficient signaling information to enable the detection and correction of many errors at the receiver.

error-detecting code A code that can detect transmission errors through analysis of received data based on the adherence of the data to appropriate structural guidelines.

ES 1. end system. Generally, an end-user device on a network.
2. end system. A nonrouting host or node in an OSI network.

ESCON Enterprise System Connection. An IBM channel architecture that specifies a pair of fiber-optic cables, with either LEDs or lasers as transmitters and a signaling rate of 200 Mbps.

ESCON channel An IBM channel for attaching mainframes to peripherals such as storage devices, backup units, and network interfaces. This channel incorporates FibreChannel technology. The ESCON channel replaces the bus and tag channel. *Compare with* parallel channel. *See also* bus and tag channel.

ESCON Multiple Image Facility *See* EMIF.

ESD electrostatic discharge. A discharge of stored static electricity that can damage electronic equipment and impair electrical circuitry, resulting in complete or intermittent failures.

ESF Extended Superframe Format. A framing type used on T1 circuits that consists of 24 frames of 192 bits each, with the 193rd bit providing timing and other functions. ESF is an enhanced version of SF. *See also* SF.

ES-IS End System-to-Intermediate System. An OSI protocol that defines how end systems (hosts) announce themselves to intermediate systems (routers). *See also* IS-IS.

ESnet Energy Sciences Network. A data communications network managed and funded by the U.S. Department of Energy Office of Energy Research (DOE/OER). Interconnects the DOE to educational institutions and other research facilities.

Ethernet A baseband LAN specification invented by Xerox Corporation and developed jointly by Xerox, Intel, and Digital Equipment Corporation. Ethernet networks use CSMA/CD and run over a variety of cable types at 10 Mbps. Ethernet is similar to the IEEE 802.3 series of standards. *See also* 10Base2, 10Base5, 10BaseF, 10BaseT, 10Broad36, and IEEE 802.3.

EtherTalk AppleTalk protocols running on Ethernet.

ETSI European Telecommunication Standards Institute. An organization created by the European PTTs and the European Community (EC) to propose telecommunications standards for Europe.

EUnet European Internet. A European commercial Internet service provider. EUnet is designed to provide electronic mail, news, and other Internet services to European markets.

European Academic Research Network *See* EARN.

European Computer Manufacturers Association *See* ECMA.

European Telecommunication Standards Institute *See* ETSI.

European Internet *See* EUnet.

event A network message indicating operational irregularities in physical elements of a network or a response to the occurrence of a significant task, typically the completion of a request for information. *See also* alarm and trap.

Excess Burst *See* Be.

excess rate Traffic in excess of the insured rate for a given connection. Specifically, the excess rate equals the maximum rate minus the insured rate. Excess traffic is delivered only if network resources are available and can be discarded during periods of congestion. *Compare with* insured rate and maximum rate.

exchange identification *See* XID.

EXEC The interactive command processor of the Cisco IOS software.

expansion The process of running a compressed data set through an algorithm that restores the data set to its original size. *Compare with* companding and compression.

expedited delivery An option set by a specific protocol layer telling other protocol layers (or the same protocol layer in another network device) to handle specific data more rapidly.

explicit route In SNA, a route from a source subarea to a destination subarea, as specified by a list of subarea nodes and transmission groups that connect the two.

explorer frame A frame sent out by a networked device in a SRB environment to determine the optimal route to another networked device.

explorer packet A packet generated by an end station trying to find its way through a SRB network. Gathers a hop-by-hop description of a path through the network by being marked (updated) by each

bridge that it traverses, thereby creating a complete topological map. *See also* all-routes explorer packet, local explorer packet, and spanning explorer packet.

Extended Binary Coded Decimal Interchange Code *See* EBCDIC.

Extended Industry-Standard Architecture *See* EISA.

Extended Superframe Format *See* ESF.

exterior gateway protocol Any internetwork protocol used to exchange routing information between autonomous systems. Not to be confused with Exterior Gateway Protocol (EGP), which is a particular instance of an exterior gateway protocol.

Exterior Gateway Protocol *See* EGP.

exterior router A router connected to an AURP tunnel, responsible for the encapsulation and deencapsulation of AppleTalk packets in a foreign protocol header (for example, IP). *See also* AURP and AURP tunnel.

F

failure domain An area in which a failure has occurred in a Token Ring, defined by the information contained in a beacon. When a station detects a serious problem with the network (such as a cable break), it sends a beacon frame that includes the station reporting the failure, its NAUN, and everything in between. Beaconing in turn initiates a process called autoreconfiguration. *See also* autoreconfiguration, beacon, and NAUN.

fan-out unit A device that allows multiple devices on a network to communicate using a single network attachment.

Fast Ethernet Any of a number of 100-Mbps Ethernet specifications. Fast Ethernet offers a speed increase 10 times that of the 10BaseT Ethernet specification, while preserving qualities such as frame format, MAC mechanisms, and MTU. Such similarities allow the use of existing 10BaseT applications and network management tools on Fast Ethernet networks. Based on an extension to the IEEE 802.3 specification. *Compare with* Ethernet. *See also* 100BaseFX,

100BaseT, 100BaseT4, 100BaseTX, 100BaseX, and IEEE 802.3.

Fast Sequenced Transport *See* FST.

fast switching A Cisco feature whereby a route cache is used to expedite packet switching through a router. *Compare with* slow switching.

fault management One of five categories of network management defined by ISO for management of OSI networks. Fault management attempts to ensure that network faults are detected and controlled. *See also* accounting management, configuration management, performance management, and security management.

FCC Federal Communications Commission. A U.S. government agency that supervises, licenses, and controls electronic and electromagnetic transmission standards.

FCS frame check sequence. The extra characters added to a frame for error control purposes. Used in HDLC, Frame Relay, and other data link layer protocols.

FDDI Fiber Distributed Data Interface. A LAN standard, defined by ANSI X3T9.5, specifying a 100-Mbps token-passing network using fiber-optic cable, with transmission distances of up to 2 km. FDDI uses a dual-ring architecture to provide redundancy. *Compare with* CDDI and FDDI II.

FDDI II An ANSI standard that enhances FDDI. FDDI II provides isochronous transmission for connectionless data circuits and connection-oriented voice and video circuits. *Compare with* FDDI.

FDM frequency-division multiplexing. A technique whereby information from multiple channels can be allocated bandwidth on a single wire based on frequency. *Compare with* ATDM, statistical multiplexing, and TDM.

FECN forward explicit congestion notification. A bit set by a Frame Relay network to inform DTE receiving the frame that congestion was experienced in the path from source to destination. DTE-receiving frames with the FECN bit set can request that

higher-level protocols take flow-control action as appropriate. *Compare with* BECN.

Federal Communications Commission *See* FCC.

Federal Networking Council *See* FNC.

FEP front-end processor. A device or board that provides network interface capabilities for a networked device. In SNA, typically an IBM 3745 device.

Fiber Distributed Data Interface *See* FDDI.

fiber-optic cable A physical medium capable of conducting modulated light transmission. Compared with other transmission media, fiber-optic cable is more expensive, but is not susceptible to electromagnetic interference and is capable of higher data rates. Sometimes called optical fiber.

fiber-optic interrepeater link *See* FOIRL.

FID0 format indicator 0. One of several formats that an SNA TH can use. An FID0 TH is used for communication between an SNA node and a non-SNA node. *See also* TH.

FID1 format indicator 1. One of several formats that an SNA TH can use. An FID1 TH encapsulates messages between two subarea nodes that do not support virtual and explicit routes. *See also* TH.

FID2 format indicator 2. One of several formats that an SNA TH can use. An FID2 TH is used for transferring messages between a subarea node and a PU 2, using local addresses. *See also* TH.

FID3 format indicator 3. One of several formats that an SNA TH can use. An FID3 TH is used for transferring messages between a subarea node and a PU 1, using local addresses. *See also* TH.

FID4 format indicator 4. One of several formats that an SNA TH can use. An FID4 TH encapsulates messages between two subarea nodes that are capable of supporting virtual and explicit routes. *See also* TH.

file transfer A popular network application that allows files to be moved from one network device to another.

File Transfer, Access, and Management   *See* FTAM.

File Transfer Protocol   *See* FTP.

filter   Generally, a process or device that screens network traffic for certain characteristics, such as source address, destination address, or protocol, and determines whether to forward or discard that traffic based on the established criteria.

firewall   A router or access server, or several routers or access servers, designated as a buffer between any connected public networks and a private network. A firewall router uses access lists and other methods to ensure the security of the private network.

firmware   Software instructions set permanently or semipermanently in ROM.

flapping   A routing problem in which an advertised route between two nodes alternates (flaps) back and forth between two paths due to a network problem that causes intermittent interface failures.

Flash memory   A technology developed by Intel and licensed to other semiconductor companies. Flash memory is nonvolatile storage that can be electrically erased and reprogrammed. Allows software images to be stored, booted, and rewritten as necessary.

flash update   A routing update sent asynchronously in response to a change in the network topology. *Compare with* routing update.

flooding   A traffic-passing technique used by switches and bridges in which traffic received on an interface is sent out all of the interfaces of that device except the interface on which the information was originally received.

flow   A stream of data traveling between two endpoints across a network (for example, from one LAN station to another). Multiple flows can be transmitted on a single circuit.

flow control   A technique for ensuring that a transmitting entity, such as a modem, does not overwhelm a receiving entity with data. When the buffers on the receiving device are full, a message is sent to the sending device to suspend the transmission until the data in the buffers has been processed. In IBM networks, this technique is called pacing.

FM   frequency modulation. A modulation technique in which signals of different frequencies represent different data values. *Compare with* AM and PAM. *See also* modulation.

FNC   Federal Networking Council. A group responsible for assessing and coordinating U.S. federal agency networking policies and needs.

FOIRL   fiber-optic interrepeater link. A fiber-optic signaling methodology based on the IEEE 802.3 fiber-optic specification. FOIRL is a precursor of the 10BaseFL specification, which is designed to replace it. *See also* 10BaseFL.

format indicator 0   *See* FID0.

format indicator 1   *See* FID1.

format indicator 2   *See* FID2.

format indicator 3   *See* FID3.

format indicator 4   *See* FID4.

forward channel   A communications path carrying information from the call initiator to the called party.

forward delay interval   The amount of time an interface spends listening for topology change information after that interface has been activated for bridging and before forwarding actually begins.

forward explicit congestion notification   *See* FECN.

forwarding   The process of sending a frame toward its ultimate destination by way of an internetworking device.

Fourier transform   A technique used to evaluate the importance of various frequency cycles in a time series pattern.

four-part dotted notation   *See* dot address.

fractional T1   *See* channelized T1.

FRAD   Frame Relay access device. Any network device that provides a connection between a LAN and a Frame Relay WAN.

fragment A piece of a larger packet that has been broken down to smaller units.

fragmentation The process of breaking a packet into smaller units when transmitting over a network medium that cannot support a packet of the original size. *See also* reassembly.

frame A logical grouping of information sent as a data link layer unit over a transmission medium. Often refers to the header and trailer, used for synchronization and error control, that surround the user data contained in the unit. The terms datagram, message, packet, and segment are also used to describe logical information groupings at various layers of the OSI reference model and in various technology circles.

frame check sequence *See* FCS.

Frame Relay An industry-standard, switched data link layer protocol that handles multiple virtual circuits using HDLC encapsulation between connected devices. Frame Relay is more efficient than X.25, the protocol for which it is generally considered a replacement. *See also* X.25.

Frame Relay Access Device *See* FRAD.

Frame Relay bridging A bridging technique, described in RFC 1490, that uses the same spanning-tree algorithm as other bridging functions, but allows packets to be encapsulated for transmission across a Frame Relay network.

frame switch *See* LAN switch.

free-trade zone A part of an AppleTalk internetwork that is accessible by two other parts of the internetwork that are unable to directly access one another.

frequency The number of cycles, measured in hertz, of an alternating current signal per unit time.

frequency-division multiplexing *See* FDM.

frequency modulation *See* FM.

front end A node or software program that requests services of a back end. *See also* back end, client, and server.

front-end processor *See* FEP.

FST Fast Sequenced Transport. A connectionless, sequenced transport protocol that runs on top of IP. SRB traffic is encapsulated inside IP datagrams and is passed over an FST connection between two network devices (such as routers). Speeds up data delivery, reduces overhead, and improves the response time of SRB traffic.

FTAM File Transfer, Access, and Management. In OSI, an application layer protocol developed for network file exchange and management between diverse types of computers.

FTP File Transfer Protocol. An application protocol, part of the TCP/IP protocol stack, used for transferring files between network nodes. FTP is defined in RFC 959.

full duplex The capability for simultaneous data transmission between a sending station and a receiving station. *Compare with* half duplex and simplex.

full mesh A network in which devices are organized in a mesh topology, with each network node having either a physical circuit or a virtual circuit connecting it to every other network node. A full mesh provides a great deal of redundancy, but because it can be prohibitively expensive to implement, it is usually reserved for network backbones. *See also* mesh and partial mesh.

Fuzzball A Digital Equipment Corporation LSI-11 computer system running IP gateway software. The NSFNET used these systems as backbone packet switches.

G

G.703/G.704 An ITU-T electrical and mechanical specifications for connections between telephone company equipment and DTE using BNC connectors and operating at E1 data rates.

G.804 An ITU-T framing standard that defines the mapping of ATM cells into the physical medium.

gateway In the IP community, an older term referring to a routing device. Today, the term router is used to describe nodes that perform this function, and gateway refers to a special-purpose device that performs an application layer conversion of information from one protocol stack to another. *Compare with* router.

Gateway Discovery Protocol *See* GDP.

gateway host In SNA, a host node that contains a gateway SSCP.

gateway NCP An NCP that connects two or more SNA networks and performs address translation to allow cross-network session traffic.

Gateway-to-Gateway Protocol *See* GGP.

GB gigabyte.

GBps gigabytes per second.

Gb gigabit.

Gbps gigabits per second.

GDP Gateway Discovery Protocol. A Cisco protocol that allows hosts to dynamically detect the arrival of new routers as well as determine when a router goes down. Based on UDP. *See also* UDP.

generic routing encapsulation *See* GRE.

Get Nearest Server *See* GNS.

GGP Gateway-to-Gateway Protocol. A MILNET protocol specifying how core routers (gateways) should exchange reachability and routing information. GGP uses a distributed shortest-path algorithm.

GHz gigahertz.

gigabit Abbreviated Gb.

gigabits per second Abbreviated Gbps.

gigabyte Abbreviated GB.

gigabytes per second Abbreviated GBps.

gigahertz Abbreviated GHz.

GNS Get Nearest Server. A request packet sent by a client on an IPX network to locate the nearest active server of a particular type. An IPX network client issues a GNS request to solicit either a direct response from a connected server or a response from a router that tells it where on the internetwork the service can be located. GNS is part of the IPX SAP. *See also* IPX and SAP (Service Advertisement Protocol).

GOSIP Government OSI Profile. A U.S. government procurement specification for OSI protocols. Through GOSIP, the government has mandated that all federal agencies standardize on OSI and implement OSI-based systems as they become commercially available.

Government OSI Profile *See* GOSIP.

grade of service A measure of telephone service quality based on the probability that a call will encounter a busy signal during the busiest hours of the day.

graphical user interface *See* GUI.

GRE generic routing encapsulation. A tunneling protocol developed by Cisco that can encapsulate a wide variety of protocol packet types inside IP tunnels, creating a virtual point-to-point link to Cisco routers at remote points over an IP internetwork. By connecting multiprotocol subnetworks in a single-protocol backbone environment, IP tunneling using GRE allows network expansion across a single-protocol backbone environment.

ground station A collection of communications equipment designed to receive signals from (and usually transmit signals to) satellites. Also called a downlink station.

group address *See* multicast address.

group delay *See* distortion delay.

guard band An UNUSED frequency band between two communications channels that provides separation of the channels to prevent mutual interference.

GUI graphical user interface. A user environment that uses pictorial as well as textual representations of the input and output of applications and the hierarchical or other data structure in which information is stored. Use of conventions such as buttons, icons, and windows are typical, and many actions are performed using a pointing device (such as a mouse). Microsoft Windows and the Apple Macintosh are prominent examples of platforms utilizing a GUI.

H

half duplex The capability for data transmission in only one direction at a time between a sending station and a receiving station. *Compare with* full duplex and simplex.

handshake A sequence of messages exchanged between two or more network devices to ensure transmission synchronization.

hardware address *See* MAC address.

HBD3 A line code type used on E1 circuits.

H channel high-speed channel. A full-duplex ISDN primary rate channel operating at 384 kbps. *Compare with* B channel, D channel, and E channel.

HDLC High-Level Data Link Control. A bit-oriented synchronous data link layer protocol developed by ISO. Derived from SDLC, HDLC specifies a data encapsulation method on synchronous serial links using frame characters and checksums. *See also* SDLC.

headend The endpoint of a broadband network. All stations transmit toward the headend; the headend then transmits toward the destination stations.

header Control information placed before data when encapsulating that data for network transmission. *Compare with* trailer. *See also* PCI.

heartbeat *See* SQE.

HELLO An interior routing protocol used principally by NSFNET nodes. HELLO allows particular packet switches to discover minimal delay routes. Not to be confused with the Hello protocol.

hello packet A multicast packet that is used by routers for neighbor discovery and recovery. Hello packets

also indicate that a client is still operating and network ready.

Hello protocol A protocol used by OSPF systems for establishing and maintaining neighbor relationships. Not to be confused with HELLO.

helper address An address configured on an interface to which broadcasts received on that interface will be sent.

HEPnet High-Energy Physics Network. A research network that originated in the United States, but that has spread to most places involved in high-energy physics. Well-known sites include Argonne National Laboratory, Brookhaven National Laboratory, Lawrence Berkeley Laboratory, and the Stanford Linear Accelerator Center.

hertz A measure of frequency, abbreviated Hz. Synonymous with cycles per second.

heterogeneous network A network consisting of dissimilar devices that run dissimilar protocols and in many cases support dissimilar functions or applications.

hierarchical routing Routing based on a hierarchical addressing system. For example, IP routing algorithms use IP addresses, which contain network numbers, subnet numbers, and host numbers.

High-Energy Physics Network *See* HEPnet.

High-Level Data Link Control *See* HDLC.

High-Performance Computing and Communications *See* HPCC.

High-Performance Computing Systems *See* HPCS.

High-Performance Parallel Interface *See* HIPPI.

High-Performance Routing *See* HPR.

High-Speed Serial Interface *See* HSSI.

highway *See* bus.

HIPPI High-Performance Parallel Interface. A high-performance interface standard defined by

ANSI. HIPPI is typically used to connect supercomputers to peripherals and other devices.

holddown   A state into which a route is placed so that routers will neither advertise the route nor accept advertisements about the route for a specific length of time (the holddown period). Holddown is used to flush bad information about a route from all routers in the network. A route is typically placed in holddown when a link in that route fails.

homologation   Conformity of a product or specification to international standards, such as ITU-T, CSA, TUV, UL, or VCCI. Enables portability across company and international boundaries.

hop   The passage of a data packet between two network nodes (for example, between two routers). *See also* hop count.

hop count   A routing metric used to measure the distance between a source and a destination. RIP uses hop count as its sole metric. *See also* hop and RIP.

host   A computer system on a network. Similar to the term node except that host usually implies a computer system, whereas node generally applies to any networked system, including access servers and routers. *See also* node.

host address   *See* host number.

host node   An SNA subarea node that contains an SSCP.

host number   Part of an IP address that designates which node on the subnetwork is being addressed. Also called a host address.

Hot Standby Router Protocol   *See* HSRP.

HPCC   High-Performance Computing and Communications. A U.S. government funded program advocating advances in computing, communications, and related fields. The HPCC is designed to ensure U.S. leadership in these fields through education, research and development, industry collaboration, and implementation of high-performance technology. The five components

of the HPCC are ASTA, BRHR, HPCS, IITA, and NREN.

HPCS   High-Performance Computing Systems. A component of the HPCC program designed to ensure U.S. technological leadership in high-performance computing through research and development of computing systems and related software. *See also* HPCC.

HPR   High-Performance Routing. A second-generation routing algorithm for APPN. HPR provides a connectionless layer with nondisruptive routing of sessions around link failures, and a connection-oriented layer with end-to-end flow control, error control, and sequencing. Compare with ISR. *See also* APPN.

HSRP   Hot Standby Router Protocol. A protocol that provides high network availability and transparent network topology changes. HSRP creates a Hot Standby router group with a lead router that services all packets sent to the Hot Standby address. The lead router is monitored by other routers in the group, and if it fails, one of these standby routers inherits the lead position and the Hot Standby group address.

HSSI   High-Speed Serial Interface. A network standard for high-speed (up to 52 Mbps) serial connections over WAN links.

HTML   hypertext markup language. A simple hypertext document formatting language that uses tags to indicate how a given part of a document should be interpreted by a viewing application, such as a WWW browser. *See also* hypertext and WWW browser.

hub   1. Generally, a device that serves as the center of a star-topology network.
2. A hardware or software device that contains multiple independent but connected modules of network and internetwork equipment. Hubs can be active (where they repeat signals sent through them) or passive (where they do not repeat, but merely split, signals sent through them).
3. In Ethernet and IEEE 802.3, an Ethernet multiport repeater, sometimes referred to as a concentrator.

hybrid network An internetwork made up of more than one type of network technology, including LANs and WANs.

hypertext Electronically stored text that allows direct access to other texts by way of encoded links. Hypertext documents can be created using HTML, and often integrate images, sound, and other media that are commonly viewed using a WWW browser. *See also* HTML and WWW browser.

hypertext markup language *See* HTML.

Hz *See* hertz.

I

IAB Internet Architecture Board. A board of internetwork researchers who discuss issues pertinent to Internet architecture. Responsible for appointing a variety of Internet-related groups such as IANA, IESG, and IRSG. The IAB is appointed by the trustees of ISOC. *See also* IANA, IESG, IRSG, and ISOC.

IANA Internet Assigned Numbers Authority. An organization operated under the auspices of ISOC as a part of IAB. IANA delegates authority for IP address-space allocation and domain-name assignment to the NIC and other organizations. IANA also maintains a database of assigned protocol identifiers used in the TCP/IP stack, including autonomous system numbers. *See also* IAB, ISOC, and NIC.

ICD International Code Designator. One of two ATM address formats developed by the ATM Forum for use by private networks. Adapted from the subnetwork model of addressing in which the ATM layer is responsible for mapping network layer addresses to ATM addresses. *See also* DCC.

ICMP Internet Control Message Protocol. A network layer Internet protocol that reports errors and provides other information relevant to IP packet processing. Documented in RFC 792.

ICMP Router Discovery Protocol *See* IRDP.

IDI initial domain identifier. In OSI, the portion of the NSAP that specifies the domain.

IDN international data number. *See* X.121.

IDP initial domain part. The part of a CLNS address that contains an authority and format identifier and a domain identifier.

IDPR Interdomain Policy Routing. An interdomain routing protocol that dynamically exchanges policies between autonomous systems. IDPR encapsulates interautonomous system traffic and routes it according to the policies of each autonomous system along the path. IDPR is currently an IETF proposal. *See also* policy routing.

IDRP IS-IS Interdomain Routing Protocol. An OSI protocol that specifies how routers communicate with routers in different domains.

IEC International Electrotechnical Commission. An industry group that writes and distributes standards for electrical products and components.

IEEE Institute of Electrical and Electronics Engineers. A professional organization whose activities include the development of communications and network standards. IEEE LAN standards are the predominant LAN standards today.

IEEE 802.1 An IEEE specification which describes an algorithm that prevents bridging loops by creating a spanning tree. The algorithm was invented by Digital Equipment Corporation. The Digital algorithm and the IEEE 802.1 algorithm are not exactly the same, nor are they compatible. *See also* spanning tree, spanning-tree algorithm, and Spanning-Tree Protocol.

IEEE 802.12 An IEEE LAN standard that specifies the physical layer and the MAC sublayer of the data link layer. IEEE 802.12 uses the demand priority media-access scheme at 100 Mbps over a variety of physical media. *See also* 100VG-AnyLAN.

IEEE 802.2 An IEEE LAN protocol that specifies an implementation of the LLC sublayer of the data link layer. IEEE 802.2 handles errors, framing, flow control, and the network layer (Layer 3) service interface. Used in IEEE 802.3 and IEEE 802.5 LANs. *See also* IEEE 802.3 and IEEE 802.5.

IEEE 802.3   An IEEE LAN protocol that specifies an implementation of the physical layer and the MAC sublayer of the data link layer. IEEE 802.3 uses CSMA/CD access at a variety of speeds over a variety of physical media. Extensions to the IEEE 802.3 standard specify implementations for Fast Ethernet. Physical variations of the original IEEE 802.3 specification include 10Base2, 10Base5, 10BaseF, 10BaseT, and 10Broad36. Physical variations for Fast Ethernet include 100BaseT, 100BaseT4, and 100BaseX.

IEEE 802.4   An IEEE LAN protocol that specifies an implementation of the physical layer and the MAC sublayer of the data link layer. IEEE 802.4 uses token-passing access over a bus topology and is based on the token bus LAN architecture. *See also* token bus.

IEEE 802.5   An IEEE LAN protocol that specifies an implementation of the physical layer and MAC sublayer of the data link layer. IEEE 802.5 uses token passing access at 4 or 16 Mbps over STP cabling and is similar to IBM Token Ring. *See also* Token Ring.

IEEE 802.6   An IEEE MAN specification based on DQDB technology. IEEE 802.6 supports data rates of 1.5 to 155 Mbps. *See also* DQDB.

IESG   Internet Engineering Steering Group. An organization, appointed by the IAB, that manages the operation of the IETF. *See also* IAB and IETF.

IETF   Internet Engineering Task Force. A task force consisting of more than 80 working groups responsible for developing Internet standards. The IETF operates under the auspices of ISOC. *See also* ISOC.

IFIP   International Federation for Information Processing. A research organization that performs OSI prestandardization work. Among other accomplishments, IFIP formalized the original MHS model. *See also* MHS.

IGMP   Internet Group Management Protocol. A protocol used by IP hosts to report their multicast group memberships to an adjacent multicast router. *See also* multicast router.

IGP   Interior Gateway Protocol. An Internet protocol used to exchange routing information within an autonomous system. Examples of common Internet IGPs include IGRP, OSPF, and RIP. *See also* IGRP, OSPF, and RIP.

IGRP   Interior Gateway Routing Protocol. An IGP developed by Cisco to address the problems associated with routing in large, heterogeneous networks. *Compare with* Enhanced IGRP. *See also* IGP, OSPF, and RIP.

IIH   IS-IS Hello. A message sent by all IS-IS systems to maintain adjacencies. *See also* IS-IS.

IITA   Information Infrastructure Technology and Applications. A component of the HPCC program intended to ensure U.S. leadership in the development of advanced information technologies. *See also* HPCC.

ILMI   Interim Local Management Interface. A specification developed by the ATM Forum for incorporating network-management capabilities into the ATM UNI.

IMP   interface message processor. An old name for ARPANET packet switches. An IMP is now referred to as a PSN (packet-switching node). *See also* PSN (packet-switching node).

in-band signaling   A transmission within a frequency range normally used for information transmission. *Compare with* out-of-band signaling.

Industry-Standard Architecture   *See* ISA.

Information Infrastructure Technology and Applications   *See* IITA.

infrared   Electromagnetic waves whose frequency range is above that of microwaves, but below that of the visible spectrum. LAN systems based on this technology represent an emerging technology.

initial domain identifier   *See* IDI.

initial domain part   *See* IDP.

INOC Internet Network Operations Center. A BBN group that in the early days of the Internet monitored and controlled the Internet core gateways (routers). INOC no longer exists in this form.

input/output *See* I/O.

Institute of Electrical and Electronics Engineers *See* IEEE.

insured burst The largest burst of data above the insured rate that is temporarily allowed on a PVC and not tagged by the traffic policing function for dropping in the case of network congestion. The insured burst is specified in bytes or cells. *Compare with* maximum burst. *See also* insured rate.

insured rate The long-term data throughput, in bits or cells per second, that an ATM network commits to support under normal network conditions. The insured rate is 100 percent allocated; the entire amount is deducted from the total trunk bandwidth along the path of the circuit. *Compare with* excess rate and maximum rate. *See also* insured burst.

insured traffic Traffic within the insured rate specified for the PVC. This traffic should not be dropped by the network under normal network conditions. *See also* CLP and insured rate.

Integrated IS-IS A routing protocol based on the OSI routing protocol IS-IS, but with support for IP and other protocols. Integrated IS-IS implementations send only one set of routing updates, making it more efficient than two separate implementations. Formerly referred to as Dual IS-IS. *Compare with* IS-IS.

Integrated Services Digital Network *See* ISDN.

interarea routing Term used to describe routing between two or more logical areas. *Compare with* intra-area routing.

Interdomain Policy Routing *See* IDPR.

interface 1. A connection between two systems or devices.
2. In routing terminology, a network connection.

3. In telephony, a shared boundary defined by common physical interconnection characteristics, signal characteristics, and meanings of interchanged signals.
4. The boundary between adjacent layers of the OSI model.

interface message processor *See* IMP.

interference Unwanted communication channel noise.

Interim Local Management Interface *See* ILMI.

Interior Gateway Protocol *See* IGP.

Interior Gateway Routing Protocol *See* IGRP.

intermediate routing node *See* IRN.

Intermediate Session Routing *See* ISR.

intermediate system *See* IS.

Intermediate System-to-Intermediate System *See* IS-IS.

International Code Designator *See* ICD.

International Data Number *See* X.121.

International Electrotechnical Commission *See* IEC.

International Federation for Information Processing *See* IFIP.

International Organization for Standardization *See* ISO.

International Standards Organization An erroneous expansion of the acronym ISO. *See* ISO.

International Telecommunication Union Telecommunication Standardization Sector *See* ITU-T.

Internet A term that refers to the largest global internetwork, connecting tens of thousands of networks worldwide and having a "culture" that focuses on research and standardization based on real-life use. Many leading-edge network technologies come from the Internet community. The Internet evolved in part from ARPANET. At one time, called the DARPA Internet. Not to be confused with the general term internet. *See also* ARPANET.

internet Short for internetwork. Not to be confused with the Internet. *See* internetwork.

Internet Architecture Board *See* IAB.

Internet address *See* IP address.

Internet Assigned Numbers Authority *See* IANA.

Internet Control Message Protocol *See* ICMP.

Internet Engineering Steering Group *See* IESG.

Internet Engineering Task Force *See* IETF.

Internet Group Management Protocol *See* IGMP.

Internet Network Operations Center *See* INOC.

Internet Protocol *See* IP.

Internet protocol Any protocol that is part of the TCP/IP protocol stack. *See* TCP/IP.

Internet Research Steering Group *See* IRSG.

Internet Research Task Force *See* IRTF.

Internet Society *See* ISOC.

internetwork A collection of networks interconnected by routers and other devices that functions (generally) as a single network. Sometimes called an internet, which is not to be confused with the Internet.

internetworking The industry that has arisen around the problem of connecting networks together. The term can refer to products, procedures, and technologies.

Internetwork Packet Exchange *See* IPX.

interoperability The capability of computing equipment manufactured by different vendors to communicate with one another successfully over a network.

Inter-Switching System Interface *See* ISSI.

intra-area routing Routing within a logical area. *Compare with* interarea routing.

Inverse Address Resolution Protocol *See* Inverse ARP.

Inverse ARP Inverse Address Resolution Protocol. A method of building dynamic routes in a network. Allows an access server to discover the network address of a device associated with a virtual circuit.

I/O input/output.

IP Internet Protocol. A network layer protocol in the TCP/IP stack offering a connectionless internetwork service. IP provides features for addressing, type-of-service specification, fragmentation and reassembly, and security. Documented in RFC 791.

IP address A 32-bit address assigned to hosts using TCP/IP. An IP address belongs to one of five classes (A, B, C, D, or E) and is written as four octets separated with periods (dotted decimal format). Each address consists of a network number, an optional subnetwork number, and a host number. The network and subnetwork numbers together are used for routing, and the host number is used to address an individual host within the network or subnetwork. A subnet mask is used to extract network and subnetwork information from the IP address. Also called an Internet address. *See also* IP and subnet mask.

IP multicast A routing technique that allows IP traffic to be propagated from one source to a number of destinations or from many sources to many destinations. Rather than send one packet to each destination, one packet is sent to a multicast group identified by a single IP destination group address.

IP Security Option *See* IPSO.

IPSO IP Security Option. A U.S. government specification that defines an optional field in the IP packet header that defines hierarchical packet security levels on a per-interface basis.

IPX Internetwork Packet Exchange. A NetWare network layer (Layer 3) protocol used for transferring data from servers to workstations. IPX is similar to IP and XNS.

IPXWAN A protocol that negotiates end-to-end options for new links. When a link comes up, the first IPX packets sent across are IPXWAN packets negotiating the options for the link. When the IPXWAN options have been successfully determined, normal IPX transmission begins. Defined by RFC 1362.

IRDP ICMP Router Discovery Protocol. A protocol that enables a host to determine the address of a router that it can use as a default gateway. Similar to ES-IS, but used with IP. *See also* ES-IS.

IRN intermediate routing node. In SNA, a subarea node with intermediate routing capability.

IRSG Internet Research Steering Group. A group that is part of the IAB and oversees the activities of the IRTF. *See also* IAB and IRTF.

IRTF Internet Research Task Force. A community of network experts that consider Internet-related research topics. The IRTF is governed by the IRSG and is considered a subsidiary of the IAB. *See also* IAB and IRSG.

IS intermediate system. A routing node in an OSI network.

ISA Industry-Standard Architecture. A 16-bit bus used for Intel-based personal computers. *See also* EISA.

isarithmic flow control A flow control technique in which permits travel through the network. Possession of these permits grants the right to transmit. Isarithmic flow control is not commonly implemented.

ISDN Integrated Services Digital Network. A communication protocol, offered by telephone companies, that permits telephone networks to carry data, voice, and other source traffic. *See also* BISDN, BRI, N-ISDN, and PRI.

IS-IS Intermediate System-to-Intermediate System. An OSI link-state hierarchical routing protocol based on DECnet Phase V routing whereby ISs (routers) exchange routing information based on a single metric to determine network topology. *Compare with* Integrated IS-IS. *See also* ES-IS and OSPF.

IS-IS Hello *See* IIH.

IS-IS Interdomain Routing Protocol *See* IDRP.

ISO International Organization for Standardization. An international organization that is responsible for a wide range of standards, including those relevant to networking. ISO developed the OSI reference model, a popular networking reference model.

ISO 3309 HDLC procedures developed by ISO. ISO 3309:1979 specifies the HDLC frame structure for use in synchronous environments. ISO 3309:1984 specifies proposed modifications to allow the use of HDLC in asynchronous environments as well.

ISO 9000 A set of international quality-management standards defined by ISO. The standards, which are not specific to any country, industry, or product, allow companies to demonstrate that they have specific processes in place to maintain an efficient quality system.

ISOC Internet Society. An international nonprofit organization, founded in 1992, that coordinates the evolution and use of the Internet. In addition, ISOC delegates authority to other groups related to the Internet, such as the IAB. ISOC is headquartered in Reston, Virginia. *See also* IAB.

isochronous transmission An asynchronous transmission over a synchronous data link. Isochronous signals require a constant bit rate for reliable transport. *Compare with* asynchronous transmission, plesiochronous transmission, and synchronous transmission.

ISODE ISO development environment. A large set of libraries and utilities used to develop upper-layer OSI protocols and applications.

ISO development environment *See* ISODE.

ISP Internet service provider. A company that provides Internet access to other companies and individuals.

ISR Intermediate Session Routing. An initial routing algorithm used in APPN. ISR provides node-to-node connection-oriented routing. Network outages cause sessions to fail because ISR cannot provide nondisruptive rerouting around a failure. ISR has been replaced by HPR. *Compare with* HPR. *See also* APPN.

ISSI   Inter-Switching System Interface. A standard interface between SMDS switches.

ITU-T   International Telecommunication Union Telecommunication Standardization Sector. An international body that develops worldwide standards for telecommunications technologies. The ITU-T carries out the functions of the former CCITT. *See also* CCITT.

J

jabber   1. An error condition in which a network device continually transmits random, meaningless data onto the network.
2. In IEEE 802.3, a data packet whose length exceeds that prescribed in the standard.

JANET   Joint Academic Network. An X.25 WAN connecting university and research institutions in the United Kingdom.

Japan UNIX Network   *See* JUNET.

jitter   An analog communication line distortion caused by the variation of a signal from its reference timing positions. Jitter can cause data loss, particularly at high speeds.

John von Neumann Computer Network   *See* JvNCnet.

Joint Academic Network   *See* JANET.

jumper   An electrical switch consisting of a number of pins and a connector that can be attached to the pins in a variety of different ways. Different circuits are created by attaching the connector to different pins.

JUNET   Japan UNIX Network. A nationwide, noncommercial network in Japan, designed to promote communication between Japanese and other researchers.

JvNCnet   John von Neumann Computer Network. A regional network, owned and operated by Global Enterprise Services, Inc., composed of T1 and slower serial links, providing midlevel networking services to sites in the Northeastern United States.

K

Karn's algorithm   An algorithm that improves round-trip time estimations by helping transport layer protocols distinguish between good and bad round-trip time samples.

KB   kilobyte.

Kb   kilobit.

kbps   kilobits per second.

keepalive interval   The period of time between each keepalive message sent by a network device.

keepalive message   A message sent by one network device to inform another network device that the virtual circuit between the two is still active.

Kermit   A popular file-transfer and terminal-emulation program.

kilobit   Abbreviated Kb.

kilobits per second   Abbreviated kbps.

kilobyte   Abbreviated KB.

L

L2F Protocol   Layer 2 Forwarding Protocol. A protocol that supports the creation of secure virtual private dial-up networks over the Internet.

label swapping   A routing algorithm used by APPN in which each router that a message passes through on its way to its destination independently determines the best path to the next router.

LAN   local-area network. A high-speed, low-error data network covering a relatively small geographic area (up to a few thousand meters). LANs connect workstations, peripherals, terminals, and other devices in a single building or other geographically limited area. LAN standards specify cabling and signaling at the physical and data link layers of the OSI model. Ethernet, FDDI, and Token Ring are widely used LAN technologies. *Compare with* MAN and WAN.

LANE LAN emulation. A technology that allows an ATM network to function as a LAN backbone. The ATM network must provide multicast and broadcast support, address mapping (MAC-to-ATM), SVC management, and a usable packet format. LANE also defines Ethernet and Token Ring ELANs. *See also* ELAN.

LAN emulation *See* LANE.

LAN Emulation Client *See* LEC.

LAN Emulation Configuration Server *See* LECS.

LAN Emulation Server *See* LES.

LAN Manager Distributed NOS, developed by Microsoft, that supports a variety of protocols and platforms.

LAN Manager for UNIX *See* LM/X.

LAN Network Manager *See* LNM.

LAN Server A server-based NOS developed by IBM and derived from LNM. *See also* LNM.

LAN switch A high-speed switch that forwards packets between data-link segments. Most LAN switches forward traffic based on MAC addresses. This variety of LAN switch is sometimes called a frame switch. LAN switches are often categorized according to the method they use to forward traffic: cut-through packet switching or store-and-forward packet switching. Multilayer switches are an intelligent subset of LAN switches. *Compare with* multilayer switch. *See also* cut-through packet switching and store and forward packet switching.

LAPB Link Access Procedure, Balanced. A data link layer protocol in the X.25 protocol stack. LAPB is a bit-oriented protocol derived from HDLC. *See also* HDLC and X.25.

LAPD Link Access Procedure on the D channel. An ISDN data link layer protocol for the D channel. LAPD was derived from the LAPB protocol and is designed primarily to satisfy the signaling requirements of ISDN basic access. Defined by ITU-T Recommendations Q.920 and Q.921.

LAPM Link Access Procedure for Modems. An ARQ used by modems implementing the V.42 protocol for error correction. *See also* ARQ and V.42.

laser light amplification by stimulated emission of radiation. An analog transmission device in which a suitable active material is excited by an external stimulus to produce a narrow beam of coherent light that can be modulated into pulses to carry data. Networks based on laser technology are sometimes run over SONET.

LAT local-area transport. A network virtual terminal protocol developed by Digital Equipment Corporation.

LATA local access and transport area. A geographic telephone dialing area serviced by a single local telephone company. Calls within LATAs are called *local calls*. There are well over 100 LATAs in the United States.

latency 1. The delay between the time a device requests access to a network and the time it is granted permission to transmit.
2. The delay between the time a device receives a frame and the time the frame is forwarded out the destination port.

LCI logical channel identifier. *See* VCN.

LCN logical channel number. *See* VCN.

leaf internetwork In a star topology, an internetwork whose sole access to other internetworks in the star is through a core router.

learning bridge A bridge that performs MAC address learning to reduce traffic on the network. Learning bridges manage a database of MAC addresses and the interfaces associated with each address. *See also* MAC address learning.

leased line A transmission line reserved by a communications carrier for the private use of a customer. A leased line is a type of dedicated line. *See also* dedicated line.

LEC 1. LAN Emulation Client. An entity in an end system that performs data forwarding, address resolution, and other control functions for a single ES within a single ELAN. A LEC also provides a standard LAN service interface to any higher-layer entity that interfaces to the LEC. Each LEC is identified by a unique ATM address, and is associated with one or more MAC addresses reachable through that ATM address. *See also* ELAN and LES. 2. local exchange carrier. A local or regional telephone company that owns and operates a telephone network and the customer lines that connect to it.

LECS LAN Emulation Configuration Server. An entity that assigns individual LANE clients to particular ELANs by directing them to the LES that corresponds to the ELAN. There is logically one LECS per administrative domain, and this serves all ELANs within that domain. *See also* ELAN.

LED light emitting diode. A semiconductor device that emits light produced by converting electrical energy. Status lights on hardware devices are typically LEDs.

LEN node low-entry networking node. In SNA, a PU 2.1 that supports LU protocols, but whose CP cannot communicate with other nodes. Because there is no CP-to-CP session between a LEN node and its NN, the LEN node must have a statically defined image of the APPN network.

LES LAN Emulation Server. An entity that implements the control function for a particular ELAN. There is only one logical LES per ELAN, and it is identified by a unique ATM address. *See also* ELAN.

Level 1 router A device that routes traffic within a single DECnet or OSI area.

Level 2 router A device that routes traffic between DECnet or OSI areas. All Level 2 routers must form a contiguous network.

light amplification by stimulated emission of radiation *See* laser.

light emitting diode *See* LED.

limited resource link A resource defined by a device operator to remain active only when being used.

limited-route explorer packet *See* spanning explorer packet.

line 1. In SNA, a connection to the network. 2. *See* link.

line code type One of a number of coding schemes used on serial lines to maintain data integrity and reliability. The line code type used is determined by the carrier service provider. *See also* AMI and HBD3.

line conditioning The use of equipment on leased voice-grade channels to improve analog characteristics, thereby allowing higher transmission rates.

line driver An inexpensive amplifier and signal converter that conditions digital signals to ensure reliable transmissions over extended distances.

line of sight A characteristic of certain transmission systems, such as laser, microwave, and infrared systems, in which no obstructions in a direct path between transmitter and receiver can exist.

line printer daemon *See* LPD.

line turnaround The time required to change data transmission direction on a telephone line.

link A network communications channel consisting of a circuit or transmission path and all related equipment between a sender and a receiver. Most often used to refer to a WAN connection. Sometimes referred to as a line or a transmission link.

Link Access Procedure, Balanced *See* LAPB.

Link Access Procedure for Modems *See* LAPM.

Link Access Procedure on the D channel *See* LAPD.

link layer *See* data link layer.

link-layer address *See* MAC address.

link-state advertisement *See* LSA.

link-state packet *See* LSA.

link state routing algorithm   A routing algorithm in which each router broadcasts or multicasts information regarding the cost of reaching each of its neighbors to all nodes in the internetwork. Link state algorithms create a consistent view of the network and are therefore not prone to routing loops, but they achieve this at the cost of relatively greater computational difficulty and more widespread traffic (compared with distance vector routing algorithms). *Compare with* distance vector routing algorithm. *See also* Dijkstra's algorithm.

little-endian   A method of storing or transmitting data in which the least significant bit or byte is presented first. *Compare with* big-endian.

LLC   Logical Link Control. The higher of the two data link layer sublayers defined by the IEEE. The LLC sublayer handles error control, flow control, framing, and MAC-sublayer addressing. The most prevalent LLC protocol is IEEE 802.2, which includes both connectionless and connection-oriented variants. *See also* data link layer and MAC.

LLC2   Logical Link Control, type 2. A connection-oriented OSI LLC-sublayer protocol. *See also* LLC.

LMI   Local Management Interface. A set of enhancements to the basic Frame Relay specification. LMI includes support for a keepalive mechanism, which verifies that data is flowing; a multicast mechanism, which provides the network server with its local DLCI and the multicast DLCI; global addressing, which gives DLCIs global rather than local significance in Frame Relay networks; and a status mechanism, which provides an ongoing status report on the DLCIs known to the switch. Known as LMT in ANSI terminology.

LMT   *See* LMI.

LM/X   LAN Manager for UNIX. A monitor of LAN devices in UNIX environments.

LNM   LAN Network Manager. An SRB and Token Ring management package provided by IBM. It typically runs on a PC, and it monitors SRB and

Token Ring devices and can pass alerts up to NetView.

load balancing   In routing, the ability of a router to distribute traffic over all its network ports that are the same distance from the destination address. Good load-balancing algorithms use both line speed and reliability information. Load balancing increases the utilization of network segments, thus increasing effective network bandwidth.

local access and transport area   *See* LATA.

local acknowledgment   A method whereby an intermediate network node, such as a router, responds to acknowledgments for a remote end host. Use of local acknowledgments reduces network overhead and, therefore, the risk of time-outs. Also known as local termination.

local-area network   *See* LAN.

local-area transport   *See* LAT.

local bridge   A bridge that directly interconnects networks in the same geographic area.

local exchange carrier   *See* LEC.

local explorer packet   A packet generated by an end system in an SRB network to find a host connected to the local ring. If the local explorer packet fails to find a local host, the end system produces either a spanning explorer packet or an all-routes explorer packet. *See also* all-routes explorer packet, explorer packet, and spanning explorer packet.

local loop   A line from the premises of a telephone subscriber to the telephone company CO.

Local Management Interface   *See* LMI.

LocalTalk   An Apple proprietary baseband protocol that operates at the data link and physical layers of the OSI reference model. LocalTalk uses CSMA/CD media access scheme and supports transmissions at speeds of 230 kbps.

local termination   *See* local acknowledgment.

local traffic filtering   A process by which a bridge filters out (drops) frames whose source and destination MAC addresses are located on the same interface on the bridge, thus preventing unnecessary traffic from being forwarded across the bridge. Defined in the IEEE 802.1 standard. *See also* IEEE 802.1.

logical address   *See* network address.

logical channel   A nondedicated, packet-switched communications path between two or more network nodes. Packet switching allows many logical channels to exist simultaneously on a single physical channel.

logical channel identifier   *See* LCI.

logical channel number   *See* LCN.

Logical Link Control   *See* LLC.

Logical Link Control, type 2   *See* LLC2.

logical unit   *See* LU.

Logical Unit 6.2   *See* LU 6.2.

loop   A route in which packets never reach their destination, but simply cycle repeatedly through a constant series of network nodes.

loopback test   A test in which signals are sent and then directed back toward their source from some point along the communications path. Loopback tests are often used to test network interface usability.

lossy   A characteristic of a network that is prone to lose packets when it becomes highly loaded.

low-entry networking node   *See* LEN node.

LPD   line printer daemon. A protocol used to send print jobs between UNIX systems.

LSA   link-state advertisement. A broadcast packet used by link-state protocols that contains information about neighbors and path costs. LSAs are used by the receiving routers to maintain their routing tables. Sometimes called a link-state packet (LSP).

LSP   link-state packet. *See* LSA.

LU   logical unit. A primary component of SNA, an LU is an NAU that enables end users to communicate with each other and gain access to SNA network resources.

LU 6.2   Logical Unit 6.2. In SNA, an LU that provides peer-to-peer communication between programs in a distributed computing environment. APPC runs on LU 6.2 devices. *See also* APPC.

M

MAC   Media Access Control. The lower of the two sublayers of the data link layer defined by the IEEE. The MAC sublayer handles access to shared media, such as whether token passing or contention will be used. *See also* data link layer and LLC.

MAC address   A standardized data link layer address that is required for every port or device that connects to a LAN. Other devices in the network use these addresses to locate specific ports in the network and to create and update routing tables and data structures. MAC addresses are 6 bytes long and are controlled by the IEEE. Also known as a hardware address, a MAC-layer address, or a physical address. *Compare with* network address.

MAC address learning   A service that characterizes a learning bridge, in which the source MAC address of each received packet is stored so that future packets destined for that address can be forwarded only to the bridge interface on which that address is located. Packets destined for unrecognized addresses are forwarded out every bridge interface. This scheme helps minimize traffic on the attached LANs. MAC address learning is defined in the IEEE 802.1 standard. *See also* learning bridge and MAC address.

MacIP   A network layer protocol that encapsulates IP packets in DDS or transmission over AppleTalk. MacIP also provides proxy ARP services.

MAC-layer address   *See* MAC address.

Maintenance Operation Protocol   *See* MOP.

MAN   metropolitan-area network. A network that spans a metropolitan area. Generally, a MAN spans a larger geographic area than a LAN, but a smaller geographic area than a WAN. *Compare with* LAN and WAN.

managed object In network management, a network device that can be managed by a network management protocol.

Management Information Base *See* MIB.

management services SNA functions distributed among network components to manage and control an SNA network.

Manchester encoding A digital coding scheme, used by IEEE 802.3 and Ethernet, in which a mid-bit-time transition is used for clocking, and a 1 is denoted by a high level during the first half of the bit time.

Manufacturing Automation Protocol *See* MAP.

MAP Manufacturing Automation Protocol. A network architecture created by General Motors to satisfy the specific needs of the factory floor. MAP specifies a token-passing LAN similar to that of IEEE 802.4. *See also* IEEE 802.4.

mask *See* address mask and subnet mask.

MAU media attachment unit. A device used in Ethernet and IEEE 802.3 networks that provides the interface between the AUI port of a station and the common medium of the Ethernet. The MAU, which can be built into a station or can be a separate device, performs physical layer functions including the conversion of digital data from the Ethernet interface, collision detection, and injection of bits onto the network. Sometimes referred to as a media access unit, also abbreviated MAU, or as a transceiver. In Token Ring, a MAU is known as a multistation access unit and is usually abbreviated MSAU to avoid confusion. *See also* AUI and MSAU.

maximum burst The largest burst of data above the insured rate that is allowed temporarily on an ATM PVC but that is not dropped at the edge by the traffic policing function, even if it exceeds the maximum rate. This amount of traffic is allowed only temporarily; on average, the traffic source needs to be within the maximum rate. Specified in bytes or cells. *Compare with* insured burst. *See also* maximum rate.

maximum rate The maximum total data throughput allowed on a given virtual circuit, equal to the sum of the insured and uninsured traffic from the traffic source. The uninsured data might be dropped if the network becomes congested. The maximum rate, which cannot exceed the media rate, represents the highest data throughput the virtual circuit will ever deliver, measured in bits or cells per second. *Compare with* excess rate and insured rate. *See also* maximum burst.

maximum transmission unit *See* MTU.

MB megabyte.

Mb megabit.

MBONE multicast backbone. The multicast backbone of the Internet. MBONE is a virtual multicast network composed of multicast LANs and the point-to-point tunnels that interconnect them.

Mbps megabits per second.

MCA micro channel architecture. A bus interface commonly used in PCs and some UNIX workstations and servers.

MCI Multiport Communications Interface. A card on the AGS+ that provides two Ethernet interfaces and up to two synchronous serial interfaces. The MCI processes packets rapidly, without the interframe delays typical of other Ethernet interfaces.

MCR minimum cell rate. A parameter defined by the ATM Forum for ATM traffic management. MCR is defined only for ABR transmissions, and specifies the minimum value for the ACR. *See also* ABR (available bit rate), ACR, and PCR.

MD5 Message Digest 5. An algorithm used for message authentication in SNMP v.2. MD5 verifies the integrity of the communication, authenticates the origin, and checks for timeliness. *See also* SNMP2.

media Plural of medium. The various physical environments through which transmission signals pass. Common network media include twisted-pair, coaxial and fiber-optic cable, and the atmosphere (through which microwave, laser, and infrared transmission occurs). Sometimes called physical media.

Media Access Control   *See* MAC.

media access unit   *See* MAU.

media attachment unit   *See* MAU.

media interface connector   *See* MIC.

media rate   Maximum traffic throughput for a particular media type.

medium   *See* media.

megabit   Abbreviated Mb.

megabits per second   Abbreviated Mbps.

megabyte   Abbreviated MB.

mesh   A network topology in which devices are organized in a manageable, segmented manner with many, often redundant, interconnections strategically placed between network nodes. *See also* full mesh and partial mesh.

message   An application layer (Layer 7) logical grouping of information, often composed of a number of lower-layer logical groupings such as packets. The terms datagram, frame, packet, and segment are also used to describe logical information groupings at various layers of the OSI reference model and in various technology circles.

message handling system   *See* MHS.

Message Digest 5   *See* MD5.

Message Queuing Interface   *See* MQI.

message switching   A switching technique involving transmission of messages from node to node through a network. The message is stored at each node until such time as a forwarding path is available. *Compare with* circuit switching and packet switching.

message unit   A unit of data processed by any network layer.

metasignaling   A process running at the ATM layer that manages signaling types and virtual circuits.

metering   *See* traffic shaping.

metric   *See* routing metric.

metropolitan-area network   *See* MAN.

MHS   message handling system. ITU-T X.400 recommendations that provide message handling services for communications between distributed applications. NetWare MHS is a different (though similar) entity that also provides message-handling services. *See also* IFIP.

MIB   Management Information Base. A database of network management information that is used and maintained by a network management protocol such as SNMP or CMIP. The value of a MIB object can be changed or retrieved using SNMP or CMIP commands. MIB objects are organized in a tree structure that includes public (standard) and private (proprietary) branches.

MIC   media interface connector. An FDDI de facto standard connector.

micro channel architecture   *See* MCA.

microcode   The translation layer between machine instructions and the elementary operations of a computer. Microcode is stored in ROM and allows the addition of new machine instructions without requiring that they be designed into electronic circuits when new instructions are needed.

microsegmentation   The division of a network into smaller segments, usually with the intention of increasing aggregate bandwidth to network devices.

microwave   Electromagnetic waves in the range 1 to 30 GHz. Microwave-based networks are an evolving technology gaining favor due to high bandwidth and relatively low cost.

midsplit   A broadband cable system in which the available frequencies are split into two groups: one for transmission and one for reception.

Military Network   *See* MILNET.

millions of instructions per second *See* mips.

MILNET Military Network. An unclassified portion of the DDN. Operated and maintained by the DISA. *See also* DDN and DISA.

minimum cell rate *See* MCR.

mips millions of instructions per second. The number of instructions executed by a processor per second.

modem modulator-demodulator. A device that converts digital and analog signals. At the source, a modem converts digital signals to a form suitable for transmission over analog communication facilities. At the destination, the analog signals are returned to their digital form. Modems allow data to be transmitted over voice-grade telephone lines.

modem eliminator A device that allows connection of two DTE devices without modems.

modulation The process by which the characteristics of electrical signals are transformed to represent information. Types of modulation include AM, FM, and PAM. *See also* AM, FM, and PAM.

modulator-demodulator *See* modem.

monomode fiber *See* single-mode fiber.

MOP Maintenance Operation Protocol. A Digital Equipment Corporation protocol that provides a way to perform primitive maintenance operations on DECnet systems. For example, MOP can be used to download a system image to a diskless station.

Mosaic A public-domain WWW browser, developed at the National Center for Supercomputing Applications (NCSA). *See also* WWW browser.

MOSPF Multicast OSPF. An intradomain multicast routing protocol used in OSPF networks. Extensions are applied to the base OSPF unicast protocol to support IP multicast routing.

MQI Message Queuing Interface. An international standard API that provides functionality similar to that of the RPC interface. In contrast to RPC, MQI is implemented strictly at the application layer. *See also* RPC.

MSAU multistation access unit. A wiring concentrator to which all end stations in a Token Ring network connect. The MSAU provides an interface between these devices and the Token Ring interface. Sometimes abbreviated MAU.

MTU maximum transmission unit. The maximum packet size, in bytes, that a particular interface can handle.

mu-law A North American companding standard used in conversion between analog and digital signals in PCM systems. Similar to the European a-law. *See also* a-law and companding.

multiaccess network A network that allows multiple devices to connect and communicate simultaneously.

multicast Single packets copied by the network and sent to a specific subset of network addresses. These addresses are specified in the destination address field. *Compare with* broadcast and unicast.

multicast address A single address that refers to multiple network devices. Synonymous with group address. *Compare with* broadcast address and unicast address. *See also* multicast.

multicast backbone *See* MBONE.

multicast group A dynamically determined group of IP hosts identified by a single IP multicast address.

Multicast OSPF *See* MOSPF.

multicast router A router used to send IGMP query messages on their attached local networks. Host members of a multicast group respond to a query by sending IGMP reports noting the multicast groups to which they belong. The multicast router takes responsibility for forwarding multicast datagrams from one multicast group to all other networks that have members in the group. *See also* IGMP.

multicast server A server that establishes a one-to-many connection to each device in a VLAN, thus establishing a broadcast domain for each VLAN segment. The multicast server forwards incoming broadcasts only to the multicast address that maps to the broadcast address.

multidrop line A communications line that has multiple cable access points. Sometimes called a multipoint line.

multihomed host A host attached to multiple physical network segments in an OSI CLNS network.

multihoming An addressing scheme in IS-IS routing that supports assignment of multiple area addresses.

multilayer switch A switch that filters and forwards packets based on MAC addresses and network addresses. A subset of LAN switch. *Compare with* LAN switch.

multimode fiber An optical fiber supporting propagation of multiple frequencies of light. *See also* single-mode fiber.

multiple domain network An SNA network with multiple SSCPs. *See also* SSCP.

multiplexing A scheme that allows multiple logical signals to be transmitted simultaneously across a single physical channel. *Compare with* demultiplexing.

multipoint line *See* multidrop line.

Multiport Communications Interface *See* MCI.

multistation access unit *See* MSAU.

multivendor network A network that uses equipment from more than one vendor. Multivendor networks pose many more compatibility problems than single-vendor networks. *Compare with* single-vendor network.

N

Nagle's algorithm Two separate congestion control algorithms that can be used in TCP-based networks. One algorithm reduces the sending window; the other limits small datagrams.

NAK negative acknowledgment. A response sent from a receiving device to a sending device indicating that the information received contained errors. *Compare with* acknowledgment.

Name Binding Protocol *See* NBP.

name caching A method by which remotely discovered host names are stored by a router for use in future packet-forwarding decisions to allow quick access.

name resolution Generally, the process of associating a name with a network location.

name server A server connected to a network that resolves network names into network addresses.

NAP network access point. A location for interconnection of Internet service providers in the United States for the exchange of packets.

narrowband *See* baseband.

Narrowband ISDN *See* N-ISDN.

National Bureau of Standards *See* NBS.

National Institute of Standards and Technology *See* NIST.

National Research and Education Network *See* NREN.

National Science Foundation *See* NSF.

National Science Foundation Network *See* NSFNET.

NAU network addressable unit. An SNA term for an addressable entity. Examples include LUs, PUs, and SSCPs. NAUs generally provide upper-level network services. *Compare with* path control network.

NAUN nearest active upstream neighbor. In Token Ring or IEEE 802.5 networks, the closest upstream network device from any given device that is still active.

NBMA nonbroadcast multiaccess. A multiaccess network that either does not support broadcasting (such as X.25) or in which broadcasting is not feasible (for example, an SMDS broadcast group or an extended Ethernet that is too large). *See also* multiaccess network.

NBP Name Binding Protocol. An AppleTalk transport-level protocol that translates a character string name into an internetwork address.

NBS National Bureau of Standards. An organization that was part of the U.S. Department of Commerce. Now known as NIST. *See also* NIST.

NCP Network Control Program. In SNA, a program that routes and controls the flow of data between a communications controller (in which it resides) and other network resources.

NCP/Token Ring Interconnection *See* NTRI.

NDIS network driver interface specification. The specification for a generic, hardware- and protocol-independent device driver for NICs. Produced by Microsoft.

nearest active upstream neighbor *See* NAUN.

NEARNET A regional network in New England (United States) that links Boston University, Harvard University, and MIT. Now part of BBN Planet. *See also* BBN Planet.

negative acknowledgment *See* NAK.

neighboring routers In OSPF, two routers that have interfaces to a common network. On multiaccess networks, neighbors are dynamically discovered by the OSPF Hello protocol.

NET network entity title. Network addresses, defined by the ISO network architecture, and used in CLNS-based networks.

net Short for network.

NetBIOS Network Basic Input/Output System. An API used by applications on an IBM LAN to request services from lower-level network processes. These services might include session establishment and termination, and information transfer.

NetView An IBM network management architecture and related applications. NetView is a VTAM application used for managing mainframes in SNA networks. *See also* VTAM.

NetWare A popular distributed NOS developed by Novell. Provides transparent remote file access and numerous other distributed network services.

NetWare Link Services Protocol *See* NLSP.

NetWare Loadable Module *See* NLM.

network A collection of computers, printers, routers, switches, and other devices that are able to communicate with each other over some transmission medium.

network access point *See* NAP.

network access server *See* access server.

network address A network layer address referring to a logical, rather than a physical, network device. Also called a protocol address. *Compare with* MAC address.

network addressable unit *See* NAU.

network administrator A person responsible for the operation, maintenance, and management of a network. *See also* network operator.

network analyzer A hardware or software device that offers various network troubleshooting features, including protocol-specific packet decodes, specific preprogrammed troubleshooting tests, packet filtering, and packet transmission.

Network Basic Input/Output System *See* NetBIOS.

Network Control Program *See* NCP.

network driver interface specification *See* NDIS.

network entity title *See* NET.

Network File System *See* NFS.

Network Information Center *See* NIC.

Network Information Service *See* NIS.

network interface A boundary between a carrier network and a privately owned installation.

network interface card *See* NIC.

network layer Layer 3 of the OSI reference model. This layer provides connectivity and path selection between two end systems. The network layer is the layer at which routing occurs. Corresponds roughly with the path control layer of the SNA model. *See* *also* application layer, data link layer, physical layer, presentation layer, session layer, and transport layer.

network management   Systems or actions that help maintain, characterize, or troubleshoot a network.

network management system   *See* NMS.

network management vector transport   *See* NMVT.

Network-to-Network Interface   *See* NNI.

network node   *See* NN.

Network Node Interface   *See* NNI.

Network Node Server   An SNA NN that provides resource location and route selection services for ENs, LEN nodes, and LUs that are in its domain.

network number   Part of an IP address that specifies the network to which the host belongs.

network operating system   *See* NOS.

Network Operations Center   *See* NOC.

network operator   A person who routinely monitors and controls a network, performing tasks such as reviewing and responding to traps, monitoring throughput, configuring new circuits, and resolving problems. *See also* network administrator.

network service access point   *See* NSAP.

Next Hop Resolution Protocol   *See* NHRP.

NFS   Network File System. As commonly used, a distributed file system protocol suite developed by Sun Microsystems that allows remote file access across a network. In actuality, NFS is simply one protocol in the suite. NFS protocols include NFS, RPC, XDR (External Data Representation), and others. These protocols are part of a larger architecture that Sun refers to as ONC. *See also* ONC.

NHRP   Next Hop Resolution Protocol. A protocol used by routers to dynamically discover the MAC address of other routers and hosts connected to an NBMA network. These systems can then directly communicate without requiring traffic to use an

intermediate hop, increasing performance in ATM, Frame Relay, SMDS, and X.25 environments.

NIC   1. network interface card. A board that provides network communication capabilities to and from a computer system. Also called an adapter. *See also* AUI.
2. Network Information Center. An organization that serves the Internet community by supplying user assistance, documentation, training, and other services.

NIS   Network Information Service. A protocol developed by Sun Microsystems for the administration of networkwide databases. The service essentially uses two programs: one for finding a NIS server and one for accessing the NIS databases.

N-ISDN   Narrowband ISDN. A communications standards developed by the ITU-T for baseband networks. Based on 64-kbps B channels and 16- or 64-kbps D channels. *Compare with* BISDN. *See also* BRI, ISDN, and PRI.

NIST   National Institute of Standards and Technology. Formerly the NBS, a U.S. government organization that supports and catalogs a variety of standards. *See also* NBS.

NLM   NetWare Loadable Module. An individual program that can be loaded into memory and function as part of the NetWare NOS.

NLSP   NetWare Link Services Protocol. A link-state routing protocol based on IS-IS. *See also* IS-IS.

NMS   network management system. A system responsible for managing at least part of a network. An NMS is generally a reasonably powerful and well-equipped computer such as an engineering workstation. NMSs communicate with agents to help keep track of network statistics and resources.

NMVT   network management vector transport. An SNA message consisting of a series of vectors conveying network management[nd]specific information.

NN   network node. An SNA intermediate node that provides connectivity, directory services, route selection, intermediate session routing, data transport, and network management services to LEN nodes and ENs. The NN contains a CP that manages the resources of both the NN itself and those of the ENs and LEN nodes in its domain. NNs provide intermediate routing services by implementing the APPN PU 2.1 extensions. *Compare with* EN. *See also* CP.

NNI Network-to-Network Interface. An ATM Forum standard that defines the interface between two ATM switches that are both located in a private network or are both located in a public network. The interface between a public switch and a private one is defined by the UNI standard. Also, the standard interface between two Frame Relay switches meeting the same criteria. *Compare with* UNI.

NOC Network Operations Center. An organization responsible for maintaining a network.

node 1. An endpoint of a network connection or a junction common to two or more lines in a network. Nodes can be processors, controllers, or workstations. Nodes, which vary in routing and other functional capabilities, can be interconnected by links, and serve as control points in the network. Node is sometimes used generically to refer to any entity that can access a network and is frequently used interchangeably with device. *See also* host. 2. In SNA, the basic component of a network, and the point at which one or more functional units connect channels or data circuits.

noise Undesirable communications channel signals.

nonbroadcast multiaccess *See* NBMA.

nonreturn to zero *See* NRZ.

nonreturn to zero inverted *See* NRZI.

nonseed router In AppleTalk, a router that must first obtain and then verify its configuration with a seed router before it can begin operation. *See also* seed router.

non-stub area A resource-intensive OSPF area that carries a default route, static routes, intra-area

routes, interarea routes, and external routes. Non-stub areas are the only OSPF areas that can have virtual links configured across them and are the only areas that can contain an ASBR. *Compare with* stub area. *See also* ASBR and OSPF.

nonvolatile random-access memory *See* NVRAM.

normal response mode *See* NRM.

Northwest Net An NSF-funded regional network serving the Northwestern United States, Alaska, Montana, and North Dakota. Northwest Net connects all major universities in the region, as well as many leading industrial concerns.

NOS network operating system. Distributed file systems. Examples of NOSs include LAN Manager, NetWare, NFS, and VINES.

Novell IPX *See* IPX.

NREN National Research and Education Network. A component of the HPCC program designed to ensure U.S. technical leadership in computer communications through research and development efforts in state-of-the-art telecommunications and networking technologies. *See also* HPCC.

NRM normal response mode. An HDLC mode for use on links with one primary station and one or more secondary stations. In this mode, secondary stations can transmit only if they first receive a poll from the primary station.

NRZ nonreturn to zero. Signals that maintain constant voltage levels with no signal transitions (no return to a zero-voltage level) during a bit interval. *Compare with* NRZI.

NRZI nonreturn to zero inverted. Signals that maintain constant voltage levels with no signal transitions (no return to a zero-voltage level), but interpret the presence of data at the beginning of a bit interval as a signal transition and the absence of data as no transition. *Compare with* NRZ.

NSAP network service access point. Network addresses, as specified by ISO. An NSAP is the point at which OSI network service is made available to a transport layer (Layer 4) entity.

NSF National Science Foundation. A U.S. government agency that funds scientific research in the United States. The now-defunct NSFNET was funded by the NSF. *See also* NSFNET.

NSFNET National Science Foundation Network. A large network that was controlled by the NSF and provided networking services in support of education and research in the United States, from 1986 to 1995. NSFNET is no longer in service.

NTRI NCP/Token Ring Interconnection. A function used by ACF/NCP to support Token Ring[nd]attached SNA devices. NTRI also provides translation from Token Ring[nd]attached SNA devices (PUs) to switched (dial-up) devices.

null modem A small box or cable used to join computing devices directly, rather than over a network.

NVRAM nonvolatile RAM. RAM that retains its contents when a unit is powered off.

NYSERNet Network in New York (United States) with a T1 backbone connecting NSF, many universities, and several commercial concerns.

O

OAM cell operation, administration, and maintenance cell. An ATM Forum specification for cells used to monitor virtual circuits. OAM cells provide a virtual circuit[nd]level loopback in which a router responds to the cells, demonstrating that the circuit is up, and the router is operational.

OARnet Ohio Academic Resources Network. An Internet service provider that connects a number of U.S. sites, including the Ohio supercomputer center in Columbus, Ohio.

object instance An instance of an object type that has been bound to a value.

OC Optical Carrier. A series of physical protocols (OC-1, OC-2, OC-3, and so on), defined for SONET

optical signal transmissions. OC signal levels put STS frames onto multimode fiber-optic line at a variety of speeds. The base rate is 51.84 Mbps (OC-1); each signal level thereafter operates at a speed divisible by that number (thus, OC-3 runs at 155.52 Mbps). *See also* SONET, STS-1, and STS-3c.

ODA Open Document Architecture. An ISO standard that specifies how documents are represented and transmitted electronically. Formally called Office Document Architecture.

ODI Open Data-Link Interface. A Novell specification providing a standardized interface for NICs (network interface cards) that allows multiple protocols to use a single NIC. *See also* NIC (network interface card).

OEMI channel *See* block multiplexer channel.

Office Document Architecture *See* ODA.

Ohio Academic Resources Network *See* OARnet.

OIM OSI Internet Management. A group tasked with specifying ways in which OSI network management protocols can be used to manage TCP/IP networks.

ONC Open Network Computing. A distributed applications architecture designed by Sun Microsystems, currently controlled by a consortium led by Sun. The NFS protocols are part of ONC. *See also* NFS.

ones density A scheme that allows a CSU/DSU to recover the data clock reliably. The CSU/DSU derives the data clock from the data that passes through it. In order to recover the clock, the CSU/DSU hardware must receive at least one 1 bit value for every 8 bits of data that pass through it. Also called pulse density.

on-the-fly packet switching *See* cut-through packet switching.

open architecture An architecture with which third-party developers can legally develop products and for which public domain specifications exist.

open circuit A broken path along a transmission medium. Open circuits usually prevent network communication.

Open Data-Link Interface   *See* ODI.

Open Document Architecture   *See* ODA.

Open Network Computing   *See* ONC.

Open Shortest Path First   *See* OSPF.

Open System Interconnection   *See* OSI.

Open System Interconnection reference model   *See* OSI reference model.

operation, administration, and maintenance cell   *See* OAM cell.

Optical Carrier   *See* OC.

optical fiber   *See* fiber-optic cable.

Organizational Unique Identifier   *See* OUI.

OSI   Open System Interconnection. An international standardization program created by ISO and ITU-T to develop standards for data networking that facilitate multivendor equipment interoperability.

OSI Internet Management   *See* OIM.

OSINET   An international association designed to promote OSI in vendor architectures.

OSI reference model   Open System Interconnection reference model. A network architectural model developed by ISO and ITU-T. The model consists of seven layers, each of which specifies particular network functions such as addressing, flow control, error control, encapsulation, and reliable message transfer. The highest layer (the application layer) is closest to the user; the lowest layer (the physical layer) is closest to the media technology. The lower two layers are implemented in hardware and software, while the upper five layers are implemented only in software. The OSI reference model is used universally as a method for teaching and understanding network functionality. Similar in some respects to SNA. *See* application layer, data link layer, network layer, physical layer, presentation layer, session layer, and transport layer.

OSPF   Open Shortest Path First. A link-state, hierarchical IGP routing algorithm proposed as a

successor to RIP in the Internet community. OSPF features include least-cost routing, multipath routing, and load balancing. OSPF was derived from an early version of the IS-IS protocol. *See also* Enhanced IGRP, IGP, IGRP, IS-IS, and RIP.

OUI   Organizational Unique Identifier. The three octets assigned by the IEEE in a block of 48-bit LAN addresses.

outframe   The maximum number of outstanding frames allowed in an SNA PU 2 server at any time.

out-of-band signaling   Transmission using frequencies or channels outside the frequencies or channels normally used for information transfer. Out-of-band signaling is often used for error reporting in situations in which in-band signaling can be affected by whatever problems the network might be experiencing. *Compare with* in-band signaling.

P

pacing   *See* flow control.

packet   A logical grouping of information that includes a header containing control information and (usually) user data. Packets are most often used to refer to network layer units of data. The terms datagram, frame, message, and segment are also used to describe logical information groupings at various layers of the OSI reference model and in various technology circles. *See also* PDU.

packet assembler/disassembler   *See* PAD.

packet buffer   *See* buffer.

packet internet groper   *See* ping.

packet level protocol   *See* PLP.

packet switch   A WAN device that routes packets along the most efficient path and allows a communications channel to be shared by multiple connections. Sometimes referred to as a packet-switching node (PSN), and formerly called an IMP. *See also* IMP.

packet-switched data network   *See* PSN (packet-switching node).

packet-switched network *See* PSN (packet-switched network).

packet switching A networking method in which nodes share bandwidth with each other by sending packets. *Compare with* circuit switching and message switching. *See also* PSN (packet-switched network).

packet switch exchange *See* PSE.

packet-switching node *See* PSN (packet-switching node).

PAD packet assembler/disassembler. A device used to connect simple devices (such as character-mode terminals) that do not support the full functionality of a particular protocol to a network. PADs buffer data and assemble and disassemble packets sent to such end devices.

Palo Alto Research Center *See* PARC.

PAM pulse amplitude modulation. A modulation scheme in which the modulating wave is caused to modulate the amplitude of a pulse stream. *Compare with* AM and FM. *See also* modulation.

PAP Password Authentication Protocol. An authentication protocol that allows PPP peers to authenticate one another. The remote router attempting to connect to the local router is required to send an authentication request. Unlike CHAP, PAP passes the password and host name or username in the clear (unencrypted). PAP does not itself prevent unauthorized access, but merely identifies the remote end. The router or access server then determines whether that user is allowed access. PAP is supported only on PPP lines. *Compare with* CHAP.

parallel channel A channel that uses bus and tag cables as a transmission medium. *Compare with* ESCON channel. *See also* bus and tag channel.

parallelism Multiple paths existing between two points in a network. These paths may be of equal or unequal cost. Parallelism is often a network design goal; if one path fails, there is redundancy in the network to ensure that an alternate path to the same point exists.

parallel transmission A method of data transmission in which the bits of a data character are transmitted simultaneously over a number of channels. *Compare with* serial transmission.

PARC Palo Alto Research Center. A research and development center operated by XEROX. A number of widely used technologies were originally conceived at PARC, including the first personal computers and LANs.

PARC Universal Protocol *See* PUP.

parity check A process for checking the integrity of a character. A parity check involves appending a bit that makes the total number of binary 1 digits in a character or word (excluding the parity bit) either odd (for odd parity) or even (for even parity).

partial mesh A network in which devices are organized in a mesh topology, with some network nodes organized in a full mesh, but with others that are connected to only one or two other nodes in the network. A partial mesh does not provide the level of redundancy of a full mesh topology, but is less expensive to implement. Partial mesh topologies are generally used in the peripheral networks that connect to a fully meshed backbone. *See also* full mesh and mesh.

Password Authentication Protocol *See* PAP.

path control layer Layer 3 in the SNA architectural model. This layer performs sequencing services related to proper data reassembly. The path control layer is *also* responsible for routing. Corresponds roughly with the network layer of the OSI model. *See also* data flow control layer, data link control layer, physical control layer, presentation services layer, transaction services layer, and transmission control layer.

path control network An SNA concept that consists of lower-level components that control the routing and data flow through an SNA network and handle physical data transmission between SNA nodes. *Compare with* NAU.

path cost *See* cost.

path name   The full name of a UNIX, DOS, or LynxOS file or directory, including all directory and subdirectory names. Consecutive names in a path name are typically separated by a forward slash (/) or a backslash (\), as in /usr/app/base/config.

payload   The portion of a frame that contains upper-layer information (data).

PBX   private branch exchange. A digital or analog telephone switchboard located on the subscriber premises and used to connect private and public telephone networks.

PCI   protocol control information. Control information added to user data to comprise an OSI packet. The OSI equivalent of the term *header*. *See also* header.

PCM   pulse code modulation. The transmission of analog information in digital form through sampling and encoding the samples with a fixed number of bits.

PCR   peak cell rate. A parameter defined by the ATM Forum for ATM traffic management. In CBR transmissions, PCR determines how often data samples are sent. In ABR transmissions, PCR determines the maximum value of the ACR. *See also* ABR (available bit rate), ACR, and CBR.

PDN   public data network. A network operated either by a government (as in Europe) or by a private concern to provide computer communications to the public, usually for a fee. PDNs enable small organizations to create a WAN without all the equipment costs of long-distance circuits.

PDU   protocol data unit. An OSI term for packet. *See also* BPDU and packet.

peak cell rate   *See* PCR.

peak rate   The maximum rate, in kilobits per second, at which a virtual circuit can transmit.

peer-to-peer computing   Each network device runs both client and server portions of an application. Also, communication between implementations of the same OSI reference model layer in two different network devices. *Compare with* client/server computing.

performance management   One of five categories of network management defined by ISO for management of OSI networks. Performance management subsystems are responsible for analyzing and controlling network performance including network throughput and error rates. *See also* accounting management, configuration management, fault management, and security management.

peripheral node   In SNA, a node that uses local addresses and is therefore not affected by changes to network addresses. Peripheral nodes require boundary function assistance from an adjacent subarea node.

permanent virtual circuit   *See* PVC.

permanent virtual connection   *See* PVC.

permanent virtual path   *See* PVP.

permit processing   *See* traffic policing.

P/F   poll/final bit. A bit in bit-synchronous data link layer protocols that indicates the function of a frame. If the frame is a command, a 1 in this bit indicates a poll. If the frame is a response, a 1 in this bit indicates that the current frame is the last frame in the response.

PGP   Pretty Good Privacy. A public-key encryption application that allows secure file and message exchanges. There is some controversy over the development and use of this application, in part due to U.S. national security concerns.

phase   The location of a position on an alternating wave form.

phase shift   A situation in which the relative position in time between the clock and data signals of a transmission becomes unsynchronized. In systems using long cables at high transmission speeds, slight variances in cable construction, temperature, and other factors can cause a phase shift, resulting in high error rates.

PHY   physical sublayer. One of two sublayers of the FDDI physical layer. *See also* PMD.

physical address   *See* MAC address.

physical control layer   Layer 1 in the SNA architectural model. This layer is responsible for the physical specifications for the physical links between end systems. Corresponds to the physical layer of the OSI model. *See also* data flow control layer, data link control layer, path control layer, presentation services layer, transaction services layer, and transmission control layer.

physical layer   Layer 1 of the OSI reference model. The physical layer defines the electrical, mechanical, procedural, and functional specifications for activating, maintaining, and deactivating the physical link between end systems. Corresponds with the physical control layer in the SNA model. *See also* application layer, data link layer, network layer, presentation layer, session layer, and transport layer.

physical layer convergence procedure   *See* PLCP.

physical media   *See* media.

physical medium   *See* media.

physical medium dependent   *See* PMD.

physical sublayer   *See* PHY.

physical unit   *See* PU.

Physical Unit 2   *See* PU 2.

Physical Unit 2.1   *See* PU 2.1.

Physical Unit 4   *See* PU 4.

Physical Unit 5   *See* PU 5.

Physics Network   *See* PHYSNET.

PHYSNET   Physics Network. A group of many DECnet-based physics research networks, including HEPnet. *See also* HEPnet.

piggybacking   The process of carrying acknowledgments within a data packet to save network bandwidth.

PIM   Protocol Independent Multicast. A multicast routing architecture that allows the addition of IP multicast routing on existing IP networks. PIM is

unicast routing protocol independent and can be operated in two modes: dense mode and sparse mode. *See also* PIM dense mode and PIM sparse mode.

PIM dense mode   One of the two PIM operational modes. PIM dense mode is data driven and resembles typical multicast routing protocols. Packets are forwarded on all outgoing interfaces until pruning and truncation occurs. In dense mode, receivers are densely populated, and it is assumed that the downstream networks want to receive and will probably use the datagrams that are forwarded to them. The cost of using dense mode is its default flooding behavior. Sometimes called dense mode PIM or PIM DM. *Compare with* PIM sparse mode. *See also* PIM.

PIM DM   *See* PIM dense mode.

PIM SM   *See* PIM sparse mode.

PIM sparse mode   One of the two PIM operational modes. PIM sparse mode tries to constrain data distribution so that a minimal number of routers in the network receive it. Packets are sent only if they are explicitly requested at the RP (rendezvous point). In sparse mode, receivers are widely distributed, and the assumption is that downstream networks will not necessarily use the datagrams that are sent to them. The cost of using sparse mode is its reliance on the periodic refreshing of explicit join messages and its need for RPs. Sometimes called sparse mode PIM or PIM SM. *Compare with* PIM dense mode. *See also* PIM and RP (rendezvous point).

ping   packet internet groper. An ICMP echo message and its reply. Often used to test the reachability of a network device.

ping-ponging   The actions of a packet in a two-node routing loop.

PLCP   physical layer convergence procedure. A specification that maps ATM cells into physical media, such as T3 or E3, and defines certain management information.

plesiochronous transmission Digital signals that are sourced from different clocks of comparable accuracy and stability. *Compare with* asynchronous transmission, isochronous transmission, and synchronous transmission.

PLP packet level protocol. A network layer protocol in the X.25 protocol stack. Sometimes called X.25 Level 3 or X.25 Protocol. *See also* X.25.

PLU Primary LU. The LU that is initiating a session with another LU. *See also* LU.

PMD physical medium dependent. A sublayer of the FDDI physical layer that interfaces directly with the physical medium and performs the most basic bit transmission functions of the network. *See also* PHY.

PNNI Private Network-Network Interface. An ATM Forum specification that describes an ATM virtual circuit routing protocol, as well as a signaling protocol between ATM switches. Used to allow ATM switches within a private network to interconnect. Sometimes called Private Network Node Interface.

point of presence *See* POP.

Point-to-Point Protocol *See* PPP.

poison reverse updates Routing updates that explicitly indicate that a network or subnet is unreachable, rather than implying that a network is unreachable by not including it in updates. Poison reverse updates are sent to defeat large routing loops.

policy-based routing *See* policy routing.

policy routing A routing scheme that forwards packets to specific interfaces based on user-configured policies. Such policies might specify that traffic sent from a particular network should be forwarded out one interface, while all other traffic should be forwarded out another interface.

poll/final bit *See* P/F.

polling An access method in which a primary network device inquires, in an orderly fashion, whether secondaries have data to transmit. The inquiry occurs in the form of a message to each secondary that gives the secondary the right to transmit.

POP point of presence. A physical access point to a long-distance carrier interchange.

port 1. An interface on an internetworking device (such as a router).
2. In IP terminology, an upper-layer process that receives information from lower layers.
3. To rewrite software or microcode so that it will run on a different hardware platform or in a different software environment than that for which it was originally designed.

Post, Telephone, and Telegraph *See* PTT.

PPP Point-to-Point Protocol. A successor to SLIP that provides router-to-router and host-to-network connections over synchronous and asynchronous circuits. *See also* SLIP.

presentation layer Layer 6 of the OSI reference model. This layer ensures that information sent by the application layer of one system will be readable by the application layer of another. The presentation layer is also concerned with the data structures used by programs and therefore negotiates data transfer syntax for the application layer. Corresponds roughly with the presentation services layer of the SNA model. *See also* application layer, data link layer, network layer, physical layer, session layer, and transport layer.

presentation services layer Layer 6 of the SNA architectural model. This layer provides network resource management, session presentation services, and some application management. Corresponds roughly with the presentation layer of the OSI model. *See also* data flow control layer, data link control layer, path control layer, physical control layer, transaction services layer, and transmission control layer.

Pretty Good Privacy *See* PGP.

PRI Primary Rate Interface. ISDN interface to primary rate access. Primary rate access consists of a single 64-kbps D channel plus 23 (T1) or 30 (E1)

B channels for voice or data. *Compare with* BRI. *See also* BISDN, ISDN, and N-ISDN.

primary *See* primary station.

Primary LU *See* PLU.

Primary Rate Interface *See* PRI.

primary ring One of the two rings that make up an FDDI or CDDI ring. The primary ring is the default path for data transmissions. *Compare with* secondary ring.

primary station In bit-synchronous data link layer protocols such as HDLC and SDLC, a station that controls the transmission activity of secondary stations and performs other management functions, such as error control, through polling or other means. Primary stations send commands to secondary stations and receive responses. Also called, simply, a primary. *See also* secondary station.

print server A networked computer system that fields, manages, and executes (or sends for execution) print requests from other network devices.

priority queuing A routing feature in which frames in an interface output queue are prioritized based on various characteristics, such as packet size and interface type.

private branch exchange *See* PBX.

Private Network-Network Interface *See* PNNI.

Private Network Node Interface *See* PNNI.

process switching An operation that provides full route evaluation and per-packet load balancing across parallel WAN links. Involves the transmission of entire frames to the router CPU, where they are repackaged for delivery to or from a WAN interface, with the router making a route selection for each packet. Process switching is the most resource-intensive switching operation that the CPU can perform.

programmable read-only memory *See* PROM.

PROM programmable read-only memory. ROM that can be programmed using special equipment. A PROM can be programmed only once. *Compare with* EPROM.

propagation delay The time required for data to travel over a network, from its source to its ultimate destination.

protocol The formal description of a set of rules and conventions that govern how devices on a network exchange information.

protocol address *See* network address.

protocol control information *See* PCI.

protocol converter A device or software that enables equipment with different data formats to communicate by translating the data transmission code of one device to the data transmission code of another device.

protocol data unit *See* PDU.

Protocol Independent Multicast *See* PIM.

protocol stack A set of related communications protocols that operate together and, as a group, address communication at some or all of the seven layers of the OSI reference model. Not every protocol stack covers each layer of the model, and often a single protocol in the stack addresses a number of layers at once. TCP/IP is a typical protocol stack.

protocol translator A network device or software that converts one protocol into another, similar, protocol.

proxy An entity that, in the interest of efficiency, essentially stands in for another entity.

proxy Address Resolution Protocol *See* proxy ARP.

proxy ARP proxy Address Resolution Protocol. A variation of the ARP protocol in which an intermediate device (for example, a router) sends an ARP response on behalf of an end node to the requesting host. Proxy ARP can lessen bandwidth use on slow-speed WAN links. *See also* ARP.

proxy explorer   A technique that minimizes exploding explorer packet traffic propagating through an SRB network by creating an explorer packet reply cache, the entries of which are reused when subsequent explorer packets need to find the same host.

proxy polling   A technique that alleviates the load across an SDLC network by allowing routers to act as proxies for primary and secondary nodes, thus keeping polling traffic off the shared links. Proxy polling has been replaced by SDLC transport.

PSDN   packet-switched data network. *See* PSN (packet-switched network).

PSE   packet switch exchange. Essentially, a switch. The term PSE is generally used in reference to a switch in an X.25 PSN (packet-switching node). *See also* switch.

PSN   1. packet-switched network. A network that utilizes packet-switching technology for data transfer. Sometimes called a packet-switched data network (PSDN). *See* packet switching.
2. packet-switching node. A network node capable of performing packet switching functions. *See also* packet switching.

PSTN   Public Switched Telephone Network. The variety of telephone networks and services in place worldwide.

PTT   Post, Telephone, and Telegraph. A government agency that provides telephone services. PTTs exist in most areas outside North America and provide both local and long-distance telephone services.

PU   physical unit. An SNA component that manages and monitors the resources of a node, as requested by an SSCP. There is one PU per node.

PU 2   Physical Unit 2. An SNA peripheral node that can support only DLUs that require services from a VTAM host and that are only capable of performing the secondary LU role in SNA sessions.

PU 2.1   Physical Unit type 2.1. An SNA network node used for connecting peer nodes in a peer-oriented network. PU 2.1 sessions do not require that one

node reside on VTAM. APPN is based on PU 2.1 nodes, which can also be connected to a traditional hierarchical SNA network.

PU 4   Physical Unit 4. A component of an IBM FEP capable of full-duplex data transfer. Each such SNA device employs a separate data and control path into the transmit and receive buffers of the control program.

PU 5   Physical Unit 5. A component of an IBM mainframe or host computer that manages an SNA network. PU 5 nodes are involved in routing within the SNA path control layer.

public data network   *See* PDN.

Public Switched Telephone Network   *See* PSTN.

pulse amplitude modulation   *See* PAM.

pulse code modulation   *See* PCM.

pulse density   *See* ones density.

PUP   PARC Universal Protocol. A protocol similar to IP, developed at PARC.

PVC   permanent virtual circuit. A virtual circuit that is permanently established. PVCs save bandwidth associated with circuit establishment and tear down in situations where certain virtual circuits must exist all the time. Called a permanent virtual connection in ATM terminology. *Compare with* SVC.

PVP   permanent virtual path. A virtual path that consists of PVCs. *See also* PVC and virtual path.

Q

Q.920/Q.921   ITU-T specifications for the ISDN UNI data link layer. *See also* UNI.

Q.922A   An ITU-T specification for Frame Relay encapsulation.

Q.931   An ITU-T specification for signaling to establish, maintain, and clear ISDN connections. *See also* Q.93B.

Q.93B   An ITU-T specification signaling to establish, maintain, and clear BISDN network connections. An evolution of ITU-T recommendation Q.931. *See also* Q.931.

QLLC   Qualified Logical Link Control. A data link layer protocol defined by IBM that allows SNA data to be transported across X.25 networks.

QOS   quality of service. A measure of performance for a transmission system that reflects its transmission quality and service availability.

QOS parameters   quality of service parameters. The parameters that control the amount of traffic the source router in an ATM network sends over an SVC. If any switch along the path cannot accommodate the requested QOS parameters, the request is rejected, and a rejection message is forwarded to the originator of the request.

Qualified Logical Link Control   *See* QLLC.

quality of service   *See* QOS.

quartet signaling   A signaling technique used in 100VG-AnyLAN networks that allows data transmission at 100 Mbps over four pairs of UTP cabling at the same frequencies used in 10BaseT networks. *See also* 100VG-AnyLAN.

query   A message used to inquire about the value of some variable or set of variables.

queue   1. Generally, an ordered list of elements waiting to be processed.
2. In routing, a backlog of packets waiting to be forwarded over a router interface.

queuing delay   The amount of time that data must wait before it can be transmitted onto a statistically multiplexed physical circuit.

queuing theory   Scientific principles governing the formation or lack of formation of congestion on a network or at an interface.

R

RACE   Research on Advanced Communications in Europe. A project sponsored by the European Community (EC) for the development of broadband networking capabilities.

radio frequency   *See* RF.

radio frequency interference   *See* RFI.

RAM   random-access memory. Volatile memory that can be read and written by a microprocessor.

random-access memory   *See* RAM.

Rapid Transport Protocol   *See* RTP.

RARE   RÈseaux AssociÈs pour la Recherche EuropÈenne. Association of European universities and research centers designed to promote an advanced telecommunications infrastructure in the European scientific community. RARE merged with EARN to form TERENA. *See also* EARN and TERENA.

RARP   Reverse Address Resolution Protocol. A protocol in the TCP/IP stack that provides a method for finding IP addresses based on MAC addresses. Compare with ARP.

rate enforcement   *See* traffic policing.

rate queue   A value that is associated with one or more virtual circuits and that defines the speed at which an individual virtual circuit transmits data to the remote end. Each rate queue represents a portion of the overall bandwidth available on an ATM link. The combined bandwidth of all configured rate queues should not exceed the total bandwidth available.

RBHC   Regional Bell Holding Company. One of seven telephone companies created by the AT&T divestiture in 1984.

RBOC   Regional Bell Operating Company. A local or regional telephone company that owns and operates telephone lines and switches in one of seven U.S. regions. The RBOCs were created by the divestiture of AT&T. Also called Bell Operating Company (BOC).

rcp   remote copy. A protocol that allows users to copy files to and from a file system residing on a remote host or server on the network. The rcp protocol uses TCP to ensure the reliable delivery of data.

rcp server A router or another device that acts as a server for rcp. *See also* rcp.

read-only memory *See* ROM.

Ready To Send *See* RTS.

reassembly The putting back together of an IP datagram at the destination after it has been fragmented either at the source or at an intermediate node. *See also* fragmentation.

redirect The part of the ICMP and ES-IS protocols that allows a router to tell a host that using another router would be more effective.

redirector Software that intercepts requests for resources within a computer and analyzes them for remote access requirements. If remote access is required to satisfy the request, the redirector forms an RPC and sends the RPC to lower-layer protocol software for transmission through the network to the node that can satisfy the request.

redistribution Allowing routing information discovered through one routing protocol to be distributed in the update messages of another routing protocol. Sometimes called route redistribution.

redundancy 1. In internetworking, the duplication of devices, services, or connections so that, in the event of a failure, the redundant devices, services, or connections can perform the work of those that failed. *See also* redundant system.
2. In telephony, the portion of the total information contained in a message that can be eliminated without loss of essential information or meaning.

redundant system A computer, router, switch, or other computer system that contains two or more of each of the most important subsystems, such as two disk drives, two CPUs, or two power supplies.

Regional Bell Holding Company *See* RBHC.

Regional Bell Operating Company *See* RBOC.

registered jack connector *See* RJ connector.

relay OSI terminology for a device that connects two or more networks or network systems. A data link layer (Layer 2) relay is a bridge; a network layer (Layer 3) relay is a router. *See also* bridge and router.

reliability The ratio of expected to received keepalives from a link. If the ratio is high, the line is reliable. Used as a routing metric.

remote bridge A bridge that connects physically disparate network segments via WAN links.

remote copy *See* rcp.

remote job entry *See* RJE.

remote login *See* rlogin.

Remote Monitoring *See* RMON.

Remote Operations Service Element *See* ROSE.

remote-procedure call *See* RPC.

remote shell protocol *See* rsh.

remote source-route bridging *See* RSRB.

rendezvous point *See* RP.

repeater A device that regenerates and propagates electrical signals between two network segments. *See also* segment.

Request For Comments *See* RFC.

request/response unit *See* RU.

Research on Advanced Communications in Europe *See* RACE.

RÈseaux AssociÈs pour la Recherche EuropÈenne *See* RARE.

Reverse Address Resolution Protocol *See* RARP.

Reverse Path Multicasting *See* RPM.

RF radio frequency. A frequency that corresponds to radio transmissions. Cable TV and broadband networks use RF technology.

RFC Request For Comments. A document series used as the primary means for communicating information about the Internet. Some RFCs are designated by the IAB as Internet standards. Most RFCs document protocol specifications such as

Telnet and FTP, but some are humorous or historical. RFCs are available online from numerous sources.

RFI   radio frequency interference. A radio frequency that creates noise that interferes with information being transmitted across unshielded copper cabling.

RIF   Routing Information Field. A field in the IEEE 802.5 header that is used by a source-route bridge to determine through which Token Ring network segments a packet must transit. A RIF is made up of ring and bridge numbers as well as other information.

RII   Routing Information Identifier. A bit used by SRT bridges to distinguish between frames that should be transparently bridged and frames that should be passed to the SRB module for handling.

ring   A connection of two or more stations in a logically circular topology. Information is passed sequentially between active stations. Token Ring, FDDI, and CDDI are based on this topology.

ring latency   The time required for a signal to propagate once around a ring in a Token Ring or IEEE 802.5 network.

ring monitor   A centralized management tool for Token Ring networks based on the IEEE 802.5 specification. *See also* active monitor and standby monitor.

ring topology   A network topology that consists of a series of repeaters connected to one another by unidirectional transmission links to form a single closed loop. Each station on the network connects to the network at a repeater. Although logically a ring, ring topologies are most often organized in a closed-loop star. *Compare with* bus topology, star topology, and tree topology.

RIP   Routing Information Protocol. An IGP supplied with UNIX BSD systems. The most common IGP in the Internet. RIP uses hop count as a routing metric. *See also* Enhanced IGRP, hop count, IGP, IGRP, and OSPF.

RJ connector   registered jack connector. Standard connectors originally used to connect telephone lines.

RJ connectors are now used for telephone connections and for 10BaseT and other types of network connections. RJ-11, RJ-12, and RJ-45 are popular types of RJ connectors.

RJE   remote job entry. An application that is batch oriented, as opposed to interactive. In RJE environments, jobs are submitted to a computing facility, and output is received later.

rlogin   remote login. A terminal emulation program, similar to Telnet, offered in most UNIX implementations.

RMON   Remote Monitoring. An MIB agent specification described in RFC 1271 that defines functions for the remote monitoring of networked devices. The RMON specification provides numerous monitoring, problem detection, and reporting capabilities.

ROM   read-only memory. Nonvolatile memory that can be read, but not written, by the microprocessor.

root account   A privileged account on UNIX systems used exclusively by network or system administrators.

root bridge   A bridge that exchanges topology information with designated bridges in a spanning-tree implementation in order to notify all other bridges in the network when topology changes are required. This prevents loops and provides a measure of defense against link failure.

ROSE   Remote Operations Service Element. An OSI RPC mechanism used by various OSI network application protocols.

round-trip time   *See* RTT.

route   A path through an internetwork.

routed protocol   A protocol that can be routed by a router. A router must be able to interpret the logical internetwork as specified by that routed protocol. Examples of routed protocols include AppleTalk, DECnet, and IP.

route extension In SNA, a path from the destination subarea node, through peripheral equipment, to a NAU.

route map A method of controlling the redistribution of routes between routing domains.

route summarization The consolidation of advertised addresses in OSPF and IS-IS. In OSPF, this causes a single summary route to be advertised to other areas by an ABR (area border router).

router A network layer device that uses one or more metrics to determine the optimal path along which network traffic should be forwarded. Routers forward packets from one network to another based on network layer information. Occasionally called a gateway (although this definition of gateway is becoming increasingly outdated). *Compare with* gateway. *See also* relay.

route redistribution *See* redistribution.

routing The process of finding a path to a destination host. Routing is very complex in large networks because of the many potential intermediate destinations a packet might traverse before reaching its destination host.

routing domain A group of end systems and intermediate systems operating under the same set of administrative rules. Within each routing domain is one or more areas, each uniquely identified by an area address.

Routing Information Field *See* RIF.

Routing Information Identifier *See* RII.

Routing Information Protocol *See* RIP.

routing metric A method by which a routing algorithm determines that one route is better than another. This information is stored in routing tables. Metrics include bandwidth, communication cost, delay, hop count, load, MTU, path cost, and reliability. Sometimes referred to simply as a metric. *See also* cost.

routing protocol A protocol that accomplishes routing through the implementation of a specific routing algorithm. Examples of routing protocols are IGRP, OSPF, and RIP.

routing table A table stored in a router or some other internetworking device that keeps track of routes to particular network destinations and, in some cases, metrics associated with those routes.

Routing Table Maintenance Protocol *See* RTMP.

Routing Table Protocol *See* RTP.

routing update A message sent from a router to indicate network reachability and associated cost information. Routing updates are typically sent at regular intervals and after a change in network topology. *Compare with* flash update.

RP 1. rendezvous point. A router specified in PIM sparse mode implementations to track membership in multicast groups and to forward messages to known multicast group addresses. *See also* PIM sparse mode. 2. route processor. A processor module in the Cisco 7000 series routers that contains the CPU, system software, and most of the memory components that are used in the router. Sometimes called a supervisory processor.

RPC remote-procedure call. The technological foundation of client/server computing. RPCs are procedure calls that are built or specified by clients and executed on servers, with the results returned over the network to the clients. *See also* client/server computing.

RPM Reverse Path Multicasting. A multicasting technique in which a multicast datagram is forwarded out of all but the receiving interface if the receiving interface is one used to forward unicast datagrams to the source of the multicast datagram.

RS-232 A popular physical layer interface. Now known as EIA/TIA-232. *See* EIA/TIA-232.

RS-422 A balanced electrical implementation of EIA/TIA-449 for high-speed data transmission. Now referred to collectively with RS-423 as EIA-530. *See also* EIA-530 and RS-423.

RS-423 An unbalanced electrical implementation of EIA/TIA-449 for EIA/TIA-232 compatibility. Now referred to collectively with RS-422 as EIA-530. *See also* EIA-530 and RS-422.

RS-449 A popular physical layer interface. Now known as EIA/TIA-449. *See* EIA/TIA-449.

rsh remote shell protocol. A protocol that allows a user to execute commands on a remote system without having to log in to the system. For example, rsh can be used to remotely examine the status of a number of access servers without connecting to each communication server, executing the command, and then disconnecting from the communication server.

RSRB remote source-route bridging. An SRB over WAN links. *See also* SRB.

RSVP Resource Reservation Protocol. A protocol that supports the reservation of resources across an IP network. Applications running on IP end systems can use RSVP to indicate to other nodes the nature (bandwidth, jitter, maximum burst, and so forth) of the packet streams they want to receive. RSVP depends on IPv6. Also known as Resource Reservation Setup Protocol.

RTCP RTP Control Protocol. A protocol that monitors the QOS of an IPv6 RTP connection and conveys information about the on-going session.

RTMP Routing Table Maintenance Protocol. An Apple Computer proprietary routing protocol. RTMP was derived from RIP. *See also* RIP.

RTP 1. Routing Table Protocol. A VINES routing protocol based on RIP. Distributes network topology information and aids VINES servers in finding neighboring clients, servers, and routers. Uses delay as a routing metric. *See also* SRTP.
2. Rapid Transport Protocol. A protocol that provides pacing and error recovery for APPN data as it crosses the APPN network. With RTP, error recovery and flow control are done end-to-end rather

than at every node. RTP prevents congestion rather than reacts to it.

RTS   Ready To Send. An EIA/TIA-232 control signal that requests a data transmission on a communications line.   RTT round-trip time. The time required for a network communication to travel from the source to the destination and back. RTT includes the time required for the destination to process the message from the source and generate a reply. RTT is used by some routing algorithms to aid in calculating optimal routes.

RU request/response unit. The request and response messages exchanged between NAUs in an SNA network.

S

SAC single-attached concentrator. An FDDI or CDDI concentrator that connects to the network by being cascaded from the master port of another FDDI or CDDI concentrator.

sampling rate The rate at which samples of a particular waveform amplitude are taken.

SAP 1. service access point. A field defined by the IEEE 802.2 specification that is part of an address specification. Thus, the destination plus the DSAP define the recipient of a packet. The same applies to the SSAP. *See also* DSAP and SSAP.
2. Service Advertisement Protocol. An IPX protocol that provides a means of informing network clients, via routers and servers, of available network resources and services. *See also* IPX.

SAR segmentation and reassembly. One of the two sublayers of the AAL CPCS, responsible for dividing (at the source) and reassembling (at the destination) the PDUs passed from the CS. The SAR sublayer takes the PDUs processed by the CS and, after dividing them into 48-byte pieces of payload data, passes them to the ATM layer for further processing. *See also* AAL, ATM layer, CPCS, CS, and SSCS.

SAS single attachment station. A device attached only to the primary ring of an FDDI ring. Also known as a Class B station. *Compare with* DAS. *See also* FDDI.

satellite communication The use of orbiting satellites to relay data between multiple earth-based stations. Satellite communications offer high bandwidth and a cost that is not related to distance between earth stations, long propagation delays, or broadcast capability.

SBus A bus technology used in Sun SPARC-based workstations and servers. The SBus specification has been adopted by the IEEE as a new bus standard.

SCR sustainable cell rate. A parameter defined by the ATM Forum for ATM traffic management. For VBR connections, SCR determines the long-term average cell rate that can be transmitted. *See also* VBR.

SCTE serial clock transmit external. A timing signal that DTE echoes to DCE to maintain clocking. SCTE is designed to compensate for clock phase shift on long cables. When the DCE device uses SCTE instead of its internal clock to sample data from the DTE, it is better able to sample the data without error, even if there is a phase shift in the cable. *See also* phase shift.

SDH Synchronous Digital Hierarchy. A European standard that defines a set of rate and format standards that are transmitted using optical signals over fiber. SDH is similar to SONET, with a basic SDH rate of 155.52 Mbps, designated at STM-1. *See also* SONET and STM-1.

SDLC Synchronous Data Link Control. An SNA data link layer communications protocol. SDLC is a bit-oriented, full-duplex serial protocol that has spawned numerous similar protocols, including HDLC and LAPB. *See also* HDLC and LAPB.

SDLLC A feature that performs translation between SDLC and IEEE 802.2 type 2.

SDSU SMDS DSU. A DSU for access to SMDS via HSSIs and other serial interfaces.

SDU service data unit. A unit of information from an upper-layer protocol that defines a service request to a lower-layer protocol.

SEAL simple and efficient AAL. A scheme used by AAL5 in which the SAR sublayer segments CS PDUs

without adding additional fields. *See also* AAL, AAL5, CS, and SAR.

secondary *See* secondary station.

secondary ring One of the two rings that makes up an FDDI or CDDI ring. The secondary ring is usually reserved for use in the event of a failure of the primary ring. *Compare with* primary ring.

secondary station In bit-synchronous data link layer protocols such as HDLC, a station that responds to commands from a primary station. Sometimes referred to simply as a secondary. *See also* primary station.

security management One of five categories of network management defined by ISO for management of OSI networks. Security management subsystems are responsible for controlling access to network resources. *See also* accounting management, configuration management, fault management, and performance management.

seed router A router that responds to configuration queries from nonseed routers on its connected AppleTalk network, allowing those routers to confirm or modify their configurations accordingly. *See also* nonseed router.

segment 1. A section of a network that is bounded by bridges, routers, or switches.
2. In a LAN using a bus topology, a continuous electrical circuit that is often connected to other such segments with repeaters.
3. In the TCP specification, a single transport layer unit of information. The terms datagram, frame, message, and packet are also used to describe logical information groupings at various layers of the OSI reference model and in various technology circles.

segmentation and reassembly *See* SAR.

Sequenced Packet Exchange *See* SPX.

Sequenced Packet Protocol *See* \SPP.

Sequenced Routing Update Protocol *See* SRTP.

serial clock transmit external *See* SCTE.

Serial Line Internet Protocol *See* SLIP.

serial transmission A method of data transmission in which the bits of a data character are transmitted sequentially over a single channel. *Compare with* parallel transmission.

server A node or software program that provides services to clients. *See also* back end, client, and front end.

Server Message Block *See* SMB.

service access point *See* SAP.

Service Advertisement Protocol *See* SAP.

service data unit *See* SDU.

service point An interface between non-SNA devices and NetView that sends alerts from equipment unknown to the SNA environment.

service profile identifier *See* SPID.

service-specific convergence sublayer *See* SSCS.

session 1. A related set of communications transactions between two or more network devices. 2. In SNA, a logical connection enabling two NAUs to communicate.

session layer Layer 5 of the OSI reference model. This layer establishes, manages, and terminates sessions between applications and manages data exchange between presentation layer entities. Corresponds to the data flow control layer of the SNA model. *See also* application layer, data link layer, network layer, physical layer, presentation layer, and transport layer.

SF Super Frame. A common framing type used on T1 circuits. SF consists of 12 frames of 192 bits each, with the 193rd bit providing error checking and other functions. SF has been superseded by ESF, but is still widely used. Also called D4 framing. *See also* ESF.

SGMP Simple Gateway Monitoring Protocol. A network management protocol that was considered for Internet standardization and later evolved into SNMP. Documented in RFC 1028. *See also* SNMP.

shaping *See* traffic shaping.

shielded cable A cable that has a layer of shielded insulation to reduce EMI.

shielded twisted-pair *See* STP.

shortest path first algorithm *See* SPF.

shortest-path routing Routing that minimizes distance or path cost through application of an algorithm.

signaling The process of sending a transmission signal over a physical medium for purposes of communication.

signaling packet A packet generated by an ATM-connected device that wants to establish a connection with another such device. The signaling packet contains the ATM NSAP address of the desired ATM endpoint, as well as any QOS parameters required for the connection. If the endpoint can support the desired QOS, it responds with an accept message, and the connection is opened. *See also* QOS.

Signaling System number 7 *See* SS7.

signal quality error *See* SQE.

simple and efficient AAL *See* SEAL.

Simple Gateway Monitoring Protocol *See* SGMP.

Simple Mail Transfer Protocol *See* SMTP.

Simple Multicast Routing Protocol *See* SMRP.

Simple Network Management Protocol *See* SNMP.

simplex The capability for data transmission in only one direction between a sending station and a receiving station. *Compare with* full duplex and half duplex

single-attached concentrator *See* SAC.

single attachment station *See* SAS.

single-mode fiber Fiber-optic cabling with a narrow core that allows light to enter only at a single angle. Such cabling has higher bandwidth than multimode fiber, but requires a light source with a narrow spectral width (for example, a laser). Also called monomode fiber. *See also* multimode fiber.

single-route explorer packet *See* spanning explorer packet.

single-vendor network A network using equipment from only one vendor. Single-vendor networks rarely suffer compatibility problems. *See also* multivendor network.

SIP SMDS Interface Protocol. A protocol used in communications between CPE and SMDS network equipment. Allows the CPE to use SMDS service for high-speed WAN internetworking. Based on the IEEE 802.6 DQDB standard. *See also* DQDB.

sliding window flow control A method of flow control in which a receiver gives a transmitter permission to transmit data until a window is full. When the window is full, the transmitter must stop transmitting until the receiver advertises a larger window. TCP, other transport protocols, and several data link layer protocols use this method of flow control.

SLIP Serial Line Internet Protocol. A standard protocol for point-to-point serial connections using a variation of TCP/IP. A predecessor of PPP. *See also* CSLIP and PPP.

slotted ring A LAN architecture based on a ring topology in which the ring is divided into slots that circulate continuously. Slots can be either empty or full, and transmissions must start at the beginning of a slot.

slow switching Packet processing performed at process level speeds, without the use of a route cache. *Compare with* fast switching.

SMAC source MAC. A MAC address specified in the Source Address field of a packet. *Compare with* DMAC. *See also* MAC address.

SMB Server Message Block. A file-system protocol used in LAN Manager and similar NOSs to package data and exchange information with other systems.

SMDS Switched Multimegabit Data Service. A high-speed, packet-switched, datagram-based WAN networking technology offered by the telephone companies. *See also* CBDS.

SMDS Interface Protocol *See* SIP.

SMI Structure of Management Information. A document (RFC 1155) specifying rules used to define managed objects in the MIB. *See also* MIB.

smoothing *See* traffic shaping.

SMRP Simple Multicast Routing Protocol. A specialized multicast network protocol for routing multimedia data streams on enterprise networks. SMRP works in conjunction with multicast extensions to the AppleTalk protocol.

SMT Station Management. An ANSI FDDI specification that defines how ring stations are managed.

SMTP Simple Mail Transfer Protocol. An Internet protocol that provides electronic mail services.

SNA Systems Network Architecture. A large, complex, feature-rich network architecture developed in the 1970s by IBM. Similar in some respects to the OSI reference model, but with a number of differences. SNA is essentially composed of seven layers. *See* data flow control layer, data link control layer, path control layer, physical control layer, presentation services layer, transaction services layer, and transmission control layer.

SNA Distribution Services *See* SNADS.

SNA Network Interconnection *See* SNI.

SNADS SNA Distribution Services. Consists of a set of SNA transaction programs that interconnect and cooperate to provide asynchronous distribution of information between end users. One of three SNA transaction services. *See also* DDM and DIA.

SNAP Subnetwork Access Protocol. An Internet protocol that operates between a network entity in the subnetwork and a network entity in the end system. SNAP specifies a standard method of encapsulating IP datagrams and ARP messages on IEEE networks. The SNAP entity in the end system makes use of the services of the subnetwork and performs three key functions: data transfer, connection management, and QOS selection.

SNI   1. Subscriber Network Interface. An interface for SMDS-based networks that connects CPE and an SMDS switch. *See also* UNI.
2. SNA Network Interconnection. An IBM gateway connecting multiple SNA networks.

SNMP   Simple Network Management Protocol. A network management protocol used almost exclusively in TCP/IP networks. SNMP provides a means to monitor and control network devices, and to manage configurations, statistics collection, performance, and security. *See also* SGMP and SNMP2.

SNMP communities   Authentication scheme that enables an intelligent network device to validate SNMP requests from sources such as the NMS. *See also* SNMP.

SNMP2   SNMP Version 2. Version 2 of the popular network management protocol. SNMP2 supports centralized as well as distributed network management strategies, and includes improvements in the SMI, protocol operations, management architecture, and security. *See also* SNMP.

SNPA   subnetwork point of attachment. A data link layer address (such as an Ethernet address, an X.25 address, or a Frame Relay DLCI address). SNPA addresses are used to configure a CLNS route for an interface.

socket   A software structure operating as a communications endpoint within a network device.

SONET   Synchronous Optical Network. A high-speed (up to 2.5 Gbps) synchronous network specification developed by Bellcore and designed to run on optical fiber. STS-1 is the basic building block of SONET. Approved as an international standard in 1988. *See also* SDH, STS-1, and STS-3c.

source address   The address of a network device that is sending data. *See also* destination address.

source MAC   *See* SMAC.

source-route bridging   *See* SRB.

source-route translational bridging   *See* SR/TLB.

source-route transparent bridging   *See* SRT.

source service access point   *See* SSAP.

Southeastern Universities Research Association Network   *See* SURAnet.

span   A full-duplex digital transmission line between two digital facilities.

spanning explorer packet   A packet that follows a statically configured spanning tree when looking for paths in an SRB network. Also known as a limited-route explorer packet or a single-route explorer packet. *See also* all-routes explorer packet, explorer packet, and local explorer packet.

spanning tree   A loop-free subset of a network topology. *See also* spanning-tree algorithm and Spanning-Tree Protocol.

spanning-tree algorithm   An algorithm used by the Spanning-Tree Protocol to create a spanning tree. Sometimes abbreviated STA. *See also* spanning tree and Spanning-Tree Protocol.

Spanning-Tree Protocol   A bridge protocol that utilizes the spanning-tree algorithm, enabling a learning bridge to dynamically work around loops in a network topology by creating a spanning tree. Bridges exchange BPDU messages with other bridges to detect loops, and then remove the loops by shutting down selected bridge interfaces. Refers to both the IEEE 802.1 Spanning-Tree Protocol standard and the earlier Digital Equipment Corporation Spanning-Tree Protocol on which it is based. The IEEE version supports bridge domains and allows the bridge to construct a loop-free topology across an extended LAN. The IEEE version is generally preferred over the Digital version. Sometimes abbreviated STP. *See also* BPDU, learning bridge, MAC address learning, spanning tree, and spanning-tree algorithm.

sparse mode PIM   *See* PIM sparse mode.

speed matching   A feature that provides sufficient buffering capability in a destination device to allow a high-speed source to transmit data at its maximum rate, even if the destination device is a lower-speed device.

SPF   shortest path first. A routing algorithm that iterates on length of path to determine a shortest-path spanning tree. Commonly used in link-state routing algorithms. Sometimes called Dijkstra's algorithm. *See also* link state routing algorithm.

SPID   service profile identifier. A number that some service providers use to define the services to which an ISDN device subscribes. The ISDN device uses the SPID when accessing the switch that initializes the connection to a service provider.

split-horizon updates   A routing technique in which information about routes is prevented from exiting the router interface through which that information was received. Split-horizon updates are useful in preventing routing loops.

spoofing   A packet illegally claiming to be from an address from which it was not actually sent. Spoofing is designed to foil network security mechanisms such as filters and access lists.

spooler   An application that manages requests or jobs submitted to it for execution. Spoolers process the submitted requests in an orderly fashion from a queue. A print spooler is an example of a spooler.

\SPP   Sequenced Packet Protocol. A protocol that provides reliable, connection-based, flow-controlled packet transmission on behalf of client processes. Part of the XNS protocol suite.

SPX   Sequenced Packet Exchange. A reliable, connection-oriented protocol that supplements the datagram service provided by network layer (Layer 3) protocols. Novell derived this commonly used NetWare transport protocol from the SPP of the XNS protocol suite.

SQE   signal quality error. A transmission sent by a transceiver to the controller to let the controller know whether the collision circuitry is functional. Also called heartbeat.

SRAM   A type of RAM that retains its contents for as long as power is supplied. SRAM does not require constant refreshing, as does DRAM. *Compare with* DRAM.

SRB   source-route bridging. A method of bridging originated by IBM and popular in Token Ring networks. In an SRB network, the entire route to a destination is predetermined, in real time, prior to the sending of data to the destination. *Compare with* transparent bridging.

SRT   source-route transparent bridging. An IBM bridging scheme that merges the two most prevalent bridging strategies, SRB and transparent bridging. SRT employs both technologies in one device to satisfy the needs of all ENs. No translation between bridging protocols is necessary. *Compare with* SR/TLB.

SR/TLB   source-route translational bridging. A method of bridging in which source-route stations can communicate with transparent bridge stations with the help of an intermediate bridge that translates between the two bridge protocols. *Compare with* SRT.

SRTP   Sequenced Routing Update Protocol. A protocol that assists VINES servers in finding neighboring clients, servers, and routers. *See also* RTP (Routing Table Protocol).

SS7   Signaling System number 7. A standard CCS system used with BISDN and ISDN. Developed by Bellcore. *See also* CCS.

SSAP   source service access point. The SAP of the network node designated in the Source field of a packet. *Compare with* DSAP. *See also* SAP (service access point).

SSCP   system services control points. The focal points within an SNA network for managing network configuration, coordinating network operator and problem determination requests, and providing directory services and other session services for network end users.

SSCP-PU session　A session used by SNA to allow an SSCP to manage the resources of a node through the PU. SSCPs can send requests to and receive replies from individual nodes in order to control the network configuration.

SSCS　service-specific convergence sublayer. One of the two sublayers of any AAL. SSCS, which is service dependent, offers insured data transmission. The SSCS can be null as well, in classical IP over ATM or LAN emulation implementations. *See also* AAL, ATM layer, CPCS, CS, and SAR.

SSP　Switch-to-Switch Protocol. A protocol specified in the DLSw standard that routers use to establish DLSw connections, locate resources, forward data, and handle flow control and error recovery. *See also* DLSw.

STA　*See* spanning-tree algorithm.

stack　*See* protocol stack.

standard　A set of rules or procedures that are either widely used or officially specified. *See also* de facto standard and de jure standard.

standby monitor　A device placed in standby mode on a Token Ring network in case an active monitor fails. *See also* active monitor and ring monitor.

StarLAN　CSMA/CD LAN, based on IEEE 802.3, developed by AT&T.

star topology　A LAN topology in which endpoints on a network are connected to a common central switch by point-to-point links. A ring topology that is organized as a star implements a unidirectional closed-loop star, instead of point-to-point links. *Compare with* bus topology, ring topology, and tree topology.

start-stop transmission　*See* asynchronous transmission.

static route　A route that is explicitly configured and entered into the routing table. Static routes take precedence over routes chosen by dynamic routing protocols.

Station Management　*See* SMT.

statistical multiplexing　A technique whereby information from multiple logical channels can be transmitted across a single physical channel. Statistical multiplexing dynamically allocates bandwidth only to active input channels, making better use of available bandwidth and allowing more devices to be connected than with other multiplexing techniques. Also referred to as statistical time-division multiplexing or stat mux. *Compare with* ATDM, FDM, and TDM.

statistical time-division multiplexing　*See* statistical multiplexing.

stat mux　*See* statistical multiplexing.

STM-1　Synchronous Transport Module level 1. One of a number of SDH formats that specifies the frame structure for the 155.52-Mbps lines used to carry ATM cells. *See also* SDH.

store and forward packet switching　A packet-switching technique in which frames are completely processed before being forwarded out the appropriate port. This processing includes calculating the CRC and checking the destination address. In addition, frames must be temporarily stored until network resources (such as an unused link) are available to forward the message. *Compare with* cut-through packet switching.

STP　1. shielded twisted-pair. A two-pair wiring medium used in a variety of network implementations. STP cabling has a layer of shielded insulation to reduce EMI. *Compare with* UTP. *See also* twisted pair.
2. *See* Spanning-Tree Protocol.

Structure of Management Information　*See* SMI.

STS-1　Synchronous Transport Signal level 1. A basic building block signal of SONET, operating at

51.84 Mbps. Faster SONET rates are defined as STS-*n*, where *n* is a multiple of 51.84 Mbps. *See also* SONET.

STS-3c Synchronous Transport Signal level 3, concatenated. A SONET format that specifies the frame structure for the 155.52-Mbps lines used to carry ATM cells. *See also* SONET.

stub area An OSPF area that carries a default route, intra-area routes, and interarea routes, but does not carry external routes. Virtual links cannot be configured across a stub area, and they cannot contain an ASBR. *Compare with* non-stub area. *See also* ASBR and OSPF.

stub network A network that has only a single connection to a router.

subarea A portion of an SNA network that consists of a subarea node and any attached links and peripheral nodes.

subarea node An SNA communication controller or host that handles complete network addresses.

subchannel In broadband terminology, a frequency-based subdivision creating a separate communications channel.

subinterface One of a number of virtual interfaces on a single physical interface.

subnet *See* subnetwork.

subnet address A portion of an IP address that is specified as the subnetwork by the subnet mask. *See also* IP address, subnet mask, and subnetwork.

subnet mask A 32-bit address mask used in IP to indicate the bits of an IP address that are being used for the subnet address. Sometimes referred to simply as mask. *See also* address mask and IP address.

subnetwork 1. In IP networks, a network sharing a particular subnet address. Subnetworks are networks arbitrarily segmented by a network administrator in order to provide a multilevel, hierarchical routing structure while shielding the subnetwork from the addressing complexity of attached networks.

Sometimes called a subnet. *See also* IP address, subnet address, and subnet mask.
2. In OSI networks, a collection of ESs and ISs under the control of a single administrative domain and using a single network access protocol.

Subnetwork Access Protocol *See* SNAP.

subnetwork point of attachment *See* SNPA.

Subscriber Network Interface *See* SNI.

subvector A data segment of a vector in an SNA message. A subvector consists of a length field, a key that describes the subvector type, and subvector-specific data.

Super Frame *See* SF.

supervisory processor *See* RP (route processor).

SURAnet Southeastern Universities Research Association Network. A network connecting universities and other organizations in the Southeastern United States. SURAnet, originally funded by the NSF and a part of NSFNET, is now part of BBN Planet. *See also* BBN Planet, NSF, and NSFNET.

sustainable cell rate *See* SCR.

SVC switched virtual circuit. A virtual circuit that is dynamically established on demand and is torn down when transmission is complete. SVCs are used in situations where data transmission is sporadic. Called a switched virtual connection in ATM terminology. *Compare with* PVC.

switch 1. A network device that filters, forwards, and floods frames based on the destination address of each frame. The switch operates at the data link layer of the OSI model.
2. An electronic or mechanical device that allows a connection to be established as necessary and terminated when there is no longer a session to support.

switched LAN A LAN implemented with LAN switches. *See* LAN switch.

Switched Multimegabit Data Service *See* SMDS.

switched virtual circuit   *See* SVC.

switched virtual connection   *See* SVC.

Switch-to-Switch Protocol   *See* SSP.

synchronization   Establishment of common timing between sender and receiver.

Synchronous Data Link Control   *See* SDLC.

Synchronous Digital Hierarchy   *See* SDH.

Synchronous Optical Network   *See* SONET.

synchronous transmission   Digital signals that are transmitted with precise clocking. Such signals have the same frequency, with individual characters encapsulated in control bits (called start bits and stop bits) that designate the beginning and end of each character. *Compare with* asynchronous transmission, isochronous transmission, and plesiochronous transmission.

Synchronous Transport Module level 1   *See* STM-1.

Synchronous Transport Signal level 1   *See* STS-1.

Synchronous Transport Signal level 3, concatenated   *See* STS-3c.

sysgen   system generation. The process of defining network resources in a network.

system generation   *See* sysgen.

system services control points   *See* SSCP.

Systems Network Architecture   *See* SNA.

T

T1   A digital WAN carrier facility. T1 transmits DS-1[nd]formatted data at 1.544 Mbps through the telephone-switching network, using AMI or B8ZS coding. *Compare with* E1. *See also* AMI, B8ZS, and DS-1.

T3   A digital WAN carrier facility. T3 transmits DS-3[nd]formatted data at 44.736 Mbps through the telephone switching network. *Compare with* E3. *See also* DS-3.

TAC   Terminal Access Controller. An Internet host that accepts terminal connections from dial-up lines.

TACACS   Terminal Access Controller Access Control System. An authentication protocol, developed by the DDN community, that provides remote access authentication and related services, such as event logging. User passwords are administered in a central database rather than in individual routers, providing an easily scalable network security solution.

tag switching   A high-performance, packet-forwarding technology that integrates network layer (Layer 3) routing and data link layer (Layer 2) switching and provides scalable, high-speed switching in the network core. Tag switching is based on the concept of label swapping, in which packets or cells are assigned short, fixed-length labels that tell switching nodes how data should be forwarded.

tagged traffic   ATM cells that have their CLP bit set to 1. If the network is congested, tagged traffic can be dropped to ensure delivery of higher-priority traffic. Sometimes called DE (discard eligible) traffic. *See also* CLP.

TAXI 4B/5B   Transparent Asynchronous Transmitter/Receiver Interface 4-byte/5-byte. An encoding scheme used for FDDI LANs, as well as for ATM. Supports speeds of up to 100 Mbps over multimode fiber. TAXI is the chipset that generates 4B/5B encoding on multimode fiber. *See also* 4B/5B local fiber.

T-carrier   A TDM transmission method usually referring to a line or cable carrying a DS-1 signal.

TCP   Transmission Control Protocol. A connection-oriented transport layer protocol that provides reliable full-duplex data transmission. TCP is part of the TCP/IP protocol stack. *See also* TCP/IP.

TCP/IP   Transmission Control Protocol/Internet Protocol. A common name for the suite of protocols developed by the U.S. DoD in the 1970s to support the construction of worldwide internetworks. TCP and IP are the two best-known protocols in the suite. *See also* IP and TCP.

TCU   trunk coupling unit. In Token Ring networks, a physical device that enables a station to connect to the trunk cable.

TDM   time-division multiplexing. A technique in which information from multiple channels can be allocated bandwidth on a single wire based on preassigned time slots. Bandwidth is allocated to each channel, regardless of whether the station has data to transmit. *Compare with* ATDM, FDM, and statistical multiplexing.

TDR   time domain reflectometer. A device capable of sending signals through a network medium to check cable continuity and other attributes. TDRs are used to find physical layer network problems.

Technical Assistance Center   *See* TAC.

Technical Office Protocol   *See* TOP.

telco   Abbreviation for telephone company.

telecommunications   Communications (usually involving computer systems) over the telephone network.

Telecommunications Industry Association   *See* TIA.

telephony   The science of converting sound to electrical signals and transmitting it between widely removed points.

telex   A teletypewriter service that allows subscribers to send messages over PSTN.

Telnet   A standard terminal emulation protocol in the TCP/IP protocol stack. Telnet is used for remote terminal connection, enabling users to log in to remote systems and use resources as if they were connected to a local system. Telnet is defined in RFC 854.

Tempest   A U.S. military standard. Electronic products adhering to the Tempest specification are designed to withstand EMP. *See also* EMP.

TERENA   Trans-European Research and Education Networking Association. An organization that promotes information and telecommunications technologies development in Europe. Formed by the merging of EARN and RARE. *See also* EARN and RARE.

termid   SNA cluster controller identification. Termid is meaningful only for switched lines. Also called Xid.

terminal   A simple device at which data can be entered or retrieved from a network. Generally, a terminal has a monitor and a keyboard, but no processor or local disk drive.

Terminal Access Controller   *See* TAC.

Terminal Access Controller Access System   *See* TACACS.

terminal adapter   A device used to connect ISDN BRI connections to existing interfaces such as EIA/TIA-232. Essentially, an ISDN modem.

terminal emulation   A network application in which a computer runs software that makes it appear to a remote host as a directly attached terminal.

terminal server   A communications processor that connects asynchronous devices such as terminals, printers, hosts, and modems to any LAN or WAN that uses TCP/IP, X.25, or LAT protocols. Terminal servers provide the internetwork intelligence that is not available in the connected devices.

terminator   A device that provides electrical resistance at the end of a transmission line to absorb signals on the line, thereby keeping them from bouncing back and being received again by network stations.

Texas Higher Education Network   *See* THEnet.

TFTP   Trivial File Transfer Protocol. A simplified version of FTP that allows files to be transferred from one computer to another over a network.

TH   transmission header. An SNA header that is appended to the SNA basic information unit (BIU). The TH uses one of a number of available SNA header formats. *See also* FID0, FID1, FID2, FID3, and FID4.

THEnet   Texas Higher Education Network. A regional network comprising more than 60 academic and research institutions in the Texas area.

Thinnet   A thinner, less expensive version of the cable specified in the IEEE 802.3 10Base2 standard. *Compare with* Cheapernet. *See also* 10Base2, Ethernet, and IEEE 802.3.

throughput   The rate of information arriving at, and possibly passing through, a particular point in a network system.

TIA   Telecommunications Industry Association. An organization that develops standards relating to telecommunications technologies. Together, the TIA and the EIA have formalized standards, such as EIA/TIA-232, for the electrical characteristics of data transmission. *See also* EIA.

TIC   Token Ring interface coupler. A controller through which an FEP connects to a Token Ring.

time-division multiplexing   *See* TDM.

time domain reflectometer   *See* TDR.

Time Notify   *See* TNotify.

time-out   An event that occurs when one network device expects to hear from another network device within a specified period of time, but does not. The resulting time-out usually results in a retransmission of information or the dissolving of the session between the two devices.

Time To Live   *See* TTL.

TN3270   Terminal emulation software that allows a terminal to appear to an IBM host as a 3278 Model 2 terminal.

TNotify   Time Notify. Specifies how often SMT initiates neighbor notification broadcasts. *See also* SMT.

token   A frame that contains control information. Possession of the token allows a network device to transmit data onto the network. *See also* token passing.

token bus   A LAN architecture that uses token passing access over a bus topology. This LAN architecture is the basis for the IEEE 802.4 LAN specification. *See also* IEEE 802.4.

token passing   An access method by which network devices access the physical medium in an orderly fashion based on possession of a small frame called a token. *Compare with* circuit switching and contention. *See also* token.

Token Ring   A token-passing LAN developed and supported by IBM. Token Ring runs at 4 or 16 Mbps over a ring topology. Similar to IEEE 802.5. *See also* IEEE 802.5, ring topology, and token passing.

Token Ring interface coupler   *See* TIC.

TOP   Technical Office Protocol. An OSI-based architecture developed for office communications.

topology   The physical arrangement of network nodes and media within an enterprise networking structure.

TOS   type of service. *See* COS (class of service).

TP0   Transport Protocol Class 0. An OSI connectionless transport protocol for use over reliable subnetworks. Defined by ISO 8073.

TP4   Transport Protocol Class 4. An OSI connection-based transport protocol. Defined by ISO 8073.

traffic policing   A process used to measure the actual traffic flow across a given connection and compare it to the total admissible traffic flow for that connection. Traffic outside the agreed on flow can be tagged (where the CLP bit is set to 1) and can be discarded en route if congestion develops. Traffic policing is used in ATM, Frame Relay, and other types of networks. Also know as admission control, permit processing, rate enforcement, and UPC (usage parameter control). *See also* tagged traffic.

traffic shaping   The use of queues to limit surges that can congest a network. Data is buffered and then sent into the network in regulated amounts to ensure that the traffic will fit within the promised traffic envelope for the particular connection. Traffic shaping is used in ATM, Frame Relay, and other types of networks. Also known as metering, shaping, and smoothing.

trailer Control information appended to data when encapsulating the data for network transmission. *Compare with* header.

transaction A result-oriented unit of communication processing.

transaction services layer Layer 7 in the SNA architectural model. Represents user application functions, such as spreadsheets, word processing, or electronic mail, by which users interact with the network. Corresponds roughly with the application layer of the OSI reference model. *See also* data flow control layer, data link control layer, path control layer, physical control layer, presentation services layer, and transmission control layer.

transceiver *See* MAU.

transceiver cable *See* AUI.

Trans-European Research and Education Networking Association *See* TERENA.

transit bridging Bridging that uses encapsulation to send a frame between two similar networks over a dissimilar network.

translational bridging Bridging between networks with dissimilar MAC sublayer protocols. MAC information is translated into the format of the destination network at the bridge. *Compare with* encapsulation bridging.

transmission control layer Layer 4 in the SNA architectural model. This layer is responsible for establishing, maintaining, and terminating SNA sessions, sequencing data messages, and controlling session level flow. Corresponds to the transport layer of the OSI model. *See also* data flow control layer, data link control layer, path control layer, physical control layer, presentation services layer, and transaction services layer.

Transmission Control Protocol *See* TCP.

Transmission Control Protocol/Internet Protocol *See* TCP/IP.

transmission group In SNA routing, one or more parallel communications links treated as one communications facility.

transmission header *See* TH.

transmission link *See* link.

TRANSPAC A major packet data network run by France Telecom.

Transparent Asynchronous Transmitter/Receiver Interface 4-byte/5-byte *See* TAXI 4B/5B.

transparent bridging A bridging scheme often used in Ethernet and IEEE 802.3 networks in which bridges pass frames one hop at a time based on tables associating end nodes with bridge ports. Transparent bridging is so named because the presence of bridges is transparent to network end nodes. *Compare with* SRB.

transport layer Layer 4 of the OSI reference model. This layer is responsible for reliable network communication between end nodes. The transport layer provides mechanisms for the establishment, maintenance, and termination of virtual circuits, transport fault detection and recovery, and information flow control. Corresponds to the transmission control layer of the SNA model. *See also* application layer, data link layer, network layer, physical layer, presentation layer, and session layer.

Transport Protocol Class 0 *See* TP0.

Transport Protocol Class 4 *See* TP4.

trap A message sent by an SNMP agent to an NMS, console, or terminal to indicate the occurrence of a significant event, such as a specifically defined condition or a threshold that has been reached. *See also* alarm and event.

tree topology A LAN topology similar to a bus topology, except that tree networks can contain branches with multiple nodes. Transmissions from a station propagate the length of the medium and are received by all other stations. *Compare with* bus topology, ring topology, and star topology.

Trivial File Transfer Protocol   *See* TFTP.

trunk   A physical and logical connection between two ATM switches across which traffic in an ATM network travels. An ATM backbone is composed of a number of trunks.

trunk coupling unit   *See* TCU.

trunk up-down   *See* TUD.

TTL   Time To Live. A field in an IP header that indicates how long a packet is considered valid.

tunneling   An architecture that is designed to provide the services necessary to implement any standard point-to-point encapsulation scheme. *See also* encapsulation.

TUD   trunk up-down. A protocol used in ATM networks that monitors trunks and detects when one goes down or comes up. ATM switches send regular test messages from each trunk port to test trunk line quality. If a trunk misses a given number of these messages, TUD declares the trunk down. When a trunk comes back up, TUD recognizes that the trunk is up, declares the trunk up, and returns it to service. *See also* trunk.

TUV   A German test agency that certifies products to European safety standards.

twisted pair   A relatively low-speed transmission medium consisting of two insulated wires arranged in a regular spiral pattern. The wires can be shielded or unshielded. Twisted pair is common in telephony applications and is increasingly common in data networks. *See also* STP and UTP.

two-way simultaneous   *See* TWS.

TWS   two-way simultaneous. A mode that allows a router configured as a primary SDLC station to achieve better utilization of a full-duplex serial line. When TWS is enabled in a multidrop environment, the router can poll a secondary station and receive data from that station while it sends data to or receives data from a different secondary station on the same serial line.

TYMNET   *See* XStream.

Type 1 operation   IEEE 802.2 (LLC) connectionless operation.

Type 2 operation   IEEE 802.2 (LLC) connection-oriented operation.

type of service   *See* TOS.

U

UART   Universal Asynchronous Receiver/Transmitter. An integrated circuit, attached to the parallel bus of a computer, used for serial communications. The UART translates between serial and parallel signals, provides transmission clocking, and buffers data sent to or from the computer.

UB Net/One   Ungermann-Bass Net/One. A routing protocol, developed by UB Networks, that uses hello packets and a path-delay metric, with end nodes communicating using the XNS protocol. There are a number of differences between the manner in which Net/One uses the XNS protocol and the usage common among other XNS nodes.

UBR   unspecified bit rate. A QOS class defined by the ATM Forum for ATM networks. UBR allows any amount of data up to a specified maximum to be sent across the network, but there are no guarantees in terms of cell loss rate and delay. *Compare with* ABR (available bit rate), CBR, and VBR.

UDP   User Datagram Protocol. A connectionless transport layer protocol in the TCP/IP protocol stack. UDP is a simple protocol that exchanges datagrams without acknowledgments or guaranteed delivery, requiring that error processing and retransmission be handled by other protocols. UDP is defined in RFC 768.

UL   Underwriters Laboratories. An independent agency within the United States that tests product safety.

ULP   upper-layer protocol. A protocol that operates at a higher layer in the OSI reference model than other layers. ULP is sometimes used to refer to the next-highest protocol (relative to a particular protocol) in a protocol stack.

unbalanced configuration   HDLC configuration with one primary station and multiple secondary stations.

Underwriters Laboratories   *See* UL.

Ungermann-Bass Net/One   *See* UB Net/One.

UNI   User-Network Interface. An ATM Forum specification that defines an interoperability standard for the interface between ATM-based products (a router or an ATM switch) located in a private network and the ATM switches located within the public carrier networks. Also used to describe similar connections in Frame Relay networks. *See also* NNI, Q.920/Q.921, and SNI (Subscriber Network Interface).

unicast   A message sent to a single network destination. *Compare with* broadcast and multicast.

unicast address   An address that specifies a single network device. *Compare with* broadcast address and multicast address. *See also* unicast.

uninsured traffic   Traffic within the excess rate (the difference between the insured rate and maximum rate) for a VCC. This traffic can be dropped by the network if congestion occurs. *See also* CLP, insured rate, and maximum rate.

unipolar   One polarity (literally), the fundamental electrical characteristic of internal signals in digital communications equipment. *Compare with* bipolar.

unity gain   In broadband networks, the balance between signal loss and signal gain through amplifiers.

Universal Asynchronous Receiver/Transmitter   *See* UART.

Universal Resource Locator   *See* URL.

UNIX   An Operating system developed in 1969 at Bell Laboratories. UNIX has gone through several iterations since its inception. These include UNIX 4.3 BSD (Berkeley Standard Distribution), developed at the University of California at Berkeley, and UNIX System V, Release 4.0, developed by AT&T.

UNIX-to-UNIX Copy Program   *See* UUCP.

unnumbered frame   An HDLC frame used for a specific control or management purposes, including link startup and shutdown, and mode specification.

unshielded twisted-pair   *See* UTP.

unspecified bit rate   *See* UBR.

UPC   usage parameter control. *See* traffic policing.

upper-layer protocol   *See* ULP.

URL   Universal Resource Locator. A standardized addressing scheme for accessing hypertext documents and other services using a WWW browser. *See also* WWW browser.

usage parameter control   *See* traffic policing.

USENET   Initiated in 1979, one of the oldest and largest cooperative networks, with more than 10,000 hosts and a quarter million users. Its primary service is a distributed conferencing service called *news*.

User Datagram Protocol   *See* UDP.

User-Network Interface   *See* UNI.

UTP   unshielded twisted-pair. A four-pair wire medium used in a variety of networks. UTP does not require the fixed spacing between connections that is necessary with coaxial-type connections. There are five types of UTP cabling commonly used: Category 1 cabling, Category 2 cabling, Category 3 cabling, Category 4 cabling, and Category 5 cabling. *Compare with* STP. *See also* EIA/TIA-586 and twisted pair.

UUCP   UNIX-to-UNIX Copy Program. A protocol stack used for point-to-point communication between UNIX systems.

V

V.24   An ITU-T standard for a physical layer interface between DTE and DCE. V.24 is essentially the same as the EIA/TIA-232 standard. *See also* EIA/TIA-232.

V.25bis   An ITU-T specification describing procedures for call setup and teardown over the DTE-DCE interface in a PSDN.

V.32   An ITU-T standard serial line protocol for bidirectional data transmissions at speeds of 4.8 or 9.6 kbps. *See also* V.32bis.

V.32bis   An ITU-T standard that extends V.32 to speeds up to 14.4 kbps. *See also* V.32.

V.34   An ITU-T standard that specifies a serial line protocol. V.34 offers improvements to the V.32 standard, including higher transmission rates (28.8 kbps) and enhanced data compression. *Compare with* V.32.

V.35   An ITU-T standard describing a synchronous, physical layer protocol used for communications between a network access device and a packet network. V.35 is most commonly used in the United States and in Europe and is recommended for speeds up to 48 kbps.

V.42   An ITU-T standard protocol for error correction using LAPM. *See also* LAPM.

variable bit rate   *See* VBR.

variable-length subnet mask   *See* VLSM.

VBR   variable bit rate. A QOS class defined by the ATM Forum for ATM networks. VBR is subdivided into a real time (RT) class and a non-real time (NRT) class. VBR (RT) is used for connections in which there is a fixed timing relationship between samples. VBR (NRT) is used for connections in which there is no fixed timing relationship between samples, but that still need a guaranteed QOS. *Compare with* ABR (available bit rate), CBR, and UBR.

VC   *See* virtual circuit.

VCC   virtual channel connection. A logical circuit, made up of VCLs, that carries data between two endpoints in an ATM network. Sometimes called a virtual circuit connection. *See also* VCI, VCL, and VPI.

VCI   virtual channel identifier. A 16-bit field in the header of an ATM cell. The VCI, together with the VPI, is used to identify the next destination of a cell as it passes through a series of ATM switches on its way to its destination. ATM switches use the VPI/VCI fields to identify the next network VCL that a cell

needs to transit on its way to its final destination. The function of the VCI is similar to that of the DLCI in Frame Relay. *Compare with* DLCI. *See also* VCL and VPI.

VCL   virtual channel link. A connection between two ATM devices. A VCC is made up of one or more VCLs. *See also* VCC.

VCN   virtual circuit number. A 12-bit field in an X.25 PLP header that identifies an X.25 virtual circuit. Allows DCE to determine how to route a packet through the X.25 network. Sometimes called LCI (logical channel identifier) or LCN (logical channel number).

VDSL   Very-High-Data-Rate Digital Subscriber Line. One of four DSL technologies. VDSL delivers 13 to 52 Mbps downstream and 1.5 to 2.3 Mbps upstream over a single twisted copper pair. The operating range of VDSL is limited to 1,000 to 4,500 feet (304.8 to 1,372 meters).

vector   A data segment of an SNA message. A vector consists of a length field, a key that describes the vector type, and vector-specific data.

VINES   Virtual Integrated Network Service. A NOS developed and marketed by Banyan Systems.

virtual address   *See* network address.

virtual channel   *See* virtual circuit.

virtual channel connection   *See* VCC.

virtual channel identifier   *See* VCI.

virtual channel link   *See* VCL.

virtual circuit   A logical circuit created to ensure reliable communication between two network devices. A virtual circuit is defined by a VPI/VCI pair, and can be either permanent (a PVC) or switched (an SVC). Virtual circuits are used in Frame Relay and X.25. In ATM, a virtual circuit is called a virtual channel. Sometimes abbreviated VC. *See also* PVC, SVC, VCI, virtual route, and VPI.

virtual circuit connection   *See* VCC.

virtual circuit number *See* VCN.

Virtual Integrated Network Service *See* VINES.

virtualization The process of implementing a network based on virtual network segments. Devices are connected to virtual segments independent of their physical location and their physical connection to the network.

virtual LAN *See* VLAN.

virtual LAN internetwork *See* VLI.

virtual path A logical grouping of virtual circuits that connect two sites. *See also* virtual circuit.

virtual path connection *See* VPC.

virtual path identifier *See* VPI.

virtual path identifier/virtual channel identifier *See* VPI/VCI.

virtual path link *See* VPL.

virtual ring An entity in an SRB network that logically connects two or more physical rings either locally or remotely. The concept of virtual rings can be expanded across router boundaries.

virtual route In SNA, a logical connection between subarea nodes that is physically realized as a particular explicit route. SNA terminology for virtual circuit. *See also* virtual circuit.

virtual telecommunications access method *See* VTAM.

Virtual Terminal Protocol *See* VTP.

VLAN virtual LAN. A group of devices on a LAN that are configured (using management software) so that they can communicate as if they were attached to the same wire, when in fact they are located on a number of different LAN segments. Because VLANs are based on logical instead of physical connections, they are extremely flexible.

VLI virtual LAN internetwork. An internetwork composed of VLANs. *See* VLAN.

VLSM variable-length subnet mask. The ability to specify a different subnet mask for the same network number on different subnets. VLSM can help optimize available address space.

VPC virtual path connection. Grouping of VCCs that share one or more contiguous VPLs. *See also* VCC and VPL.

VPI virtual path identifier. An 8-bit field in the header of an ATM cell. The VPI, together with the VCI, is used to identify the next destination of a cell as it passes through a series of ATM switches on its way to its destination. ATM switches use the VPI/VCI fields to identify the next VCL that a cell needs to transit on its way to its final destination. The function of the VPI is similar to that of the DLCI in Frame Relay. *Compare with* DLCI. *See also* VCI and VCL.

VPI/VCI *See* VCI and VPI.

VPL virtual path link. Within a virtual path, a group of unidirectional VCLs with the same endpoints. Grouping VCLs into VPLs reduces the number of connections to be managed, thereby decreasing network control overhead and cost. A VPC is made up of one or more VPLs.

VPN virtual private network. A network that enables IP traffic to travel securely over a public TCP/IP network by encrypting all traffic from one network to another. A VPN uses tunneling to encrypt all information at the IP level.

VTAM virtual telecommunications access method. A set of programs that control communication between LUs. VTAM controls data transmission between channel-attached devices and performs routing functions.

VTP Virtual Terminal Protocol. An ISO application for establishing a virtual terminal connection across a network.

W

WAN wide-area network. A data communications network that serves users across a broad geographic area and often uses transmission devices provided by common carriers. Frame Relay, SMDS, and X.25 are examples of WANs. *Compare with* LAN and MAN.

watchdog packet   A packet used to ensure that a client is still connected to a NetWare server. If the server has not received a packet from a client for a certain period of time, it sends that client a series of watchdog packets. If the station fails to respond to a predefined number of watchdog packets, the server concludes that the station is no longer connected and clears the connection for that station.

watchdog spoofing   A subset of spoofing that refers specifically to a router acting for a NetWare client by sending watchdog packets to a NetWare server to keep the session between client and server active. *See also* spoofing.

watchdog timer   1. A hardware or software mechanism that is used to trigger an event or an escape from a process unless the timer is periodically reset. 2. In NetWare, a timer that indicates the maximum period of time a server will wait for a client to respond to a watchdog packet. If the timer expires, the server sends another watchdog packet (up to a set maximum). *See also* watchdog packet.

waveform coding   Electrical techniques used to convey binary signals.

wide-area network   *See* WAN.

wideband   *See* broadband.

wildcard mask   A 32-bit quantity used in conjunction with an IP address to determine which bits in an IP address should be ignored when comparing that address with another IP address. A wildcard mask is specified when setting up access lists.

wiring closet   A specially designed room used for wiring a data or voice network. Wiring closets serve as a central junction point for the wiring and wiring equipment that is used for interconnecting devices.

WISCNET   A TCP/IP network in Wisconsin connecting University of Wisconsin campuses and a number of private colleges. Links are 56 kbps and T1.

workgroup   A collection of workstations and servers on a LAN that are designed to communicate and exchange data with one another.

workgroup switching   A method of switching that provides high-speed (100-Mbps) transparent bridging between Ethernet networks and high-speed translational bridging between Ethernet and CDDI or FDDI.

World Wide Web   *See* WWW.

wrap   An action taken by an FDDI or CDDI network to recover in the event of a failure. The stations on each side of the failure reconfigure themselves, creating a single logical ring out of the primary and secondary rings.

WWW   World Wide Web. A large network of Internet servers providing hypertext and other services to terminals running client applications such as a WWW browser. *See also* WWW browser.

WWW browser   A GUI-based hypertext client application, such as Mosaic, used to access hypertext documents and other services located on innumerable remote servers throughout the WWW and Internet. *See also* hypertext, Internet, Mosaic, and WWW.

X

X.121   An ITU-T standard describing an addressing scheme used in X.25 networks. X.121 addresses are sometimes called IDNs.

X.21   An ITU-T standard for serial communications over synchronous digital lines. The X.21 protocol is used primarily in Europe and Japan.

X.21bis   An ITU-T standard that defines the physical layer protocol for communication between DCE and DTE in an X.25 network. Virtually equivalent to EIA/TIA-232. *See also* EIA/TIA-232 and X.25.

X.25   An ITU-T standard that defines how connections between DTE and DCE are maintained for remote terminal access and computer communications in PDNs. X.25 specifies LAPB, a data link layer protocol, and PLP, a network layer protocol. Frame

Relay has to some degree superseded X.25. *See also* Frame Relay, LAPB, and PLP.

X.25 Level 3 *See* PLP.

X.25 Protocol *See* PLP.

X.28 An ITU-T recommendation that defines the terminal-to-PAD interface in X.25 networks. *See also* PAD and X.25.

X.29 An ITU-T recommendation that defines the form for control information in the terminal-to-PAD interface used in X.25 networks. *See also* PAD and X.25.

X.3 An ITU-T recommendation that defines various PAD parameters used in X.25 networks. *See also* PAD and X.25.

X3T9.5 A number assigned to the ANSI Task Group of Accredited Standards Committee for their internal, working document describing FDDI.

X.400 An ITU-T recommendation specifying a standard for electronic mail transfer.

X.500 An ITU-T recommendation specifying a standard for distributed maintenance of files and directories.

X.75 An ITU-T specification that defines the signaling system between two PDNs. X.75 is essentially an NNI. *See also* NNI.

X Display Manager Control Protocol *See* XDMCP.

xDSL x digital subscriber line. A group term used to refer to ADSL, HDSL, SDSL, and VDSL. All are emerging digital technologies using the existing copper infrastructure provided by the telephone companies. xDSL is a high-speed alternative to ISDN.

Xerox Network Systems *See* XNS.

XID exchange identification. Request and response packets exchanged prior to a session between a router and a Token Ring host. If the parameters of the serial device contained in the XID packet do not match the configuration of the host, the session is dropped.

Xid *See* termid.

XDMCP X Display Manager Control Protocol. A protocol used to communicate between X terminals and workstations running UNIX.

XNS Xerox Network Systems. A protocol suite originally designed by PARC. Many PC networking companies, such as 3Com, Banyan, Novell, and UB Networks, used or currently use a variation of XNS as their primary transport protocol.

XRemote A protocol developed specifically to optimize support for X Window over a serial communications link.

XStream A major public PSN (packet-switched network) in the United States operated by MCI. Formerly called TYMNET.

X terminal A terminal that allows a user simultaneous access to several different applications and resources in a multivendor environment through implementation of X Window. *See also* X Window.

X Window A distributed, network-transparent, device-independent, multitasking windowing and graphics system originally developed by MIT for communication between X terminals and UNIX workstations. *See also* X terminal.

Z

zero code suppression A line coding scheme used for transmission clocking. Zero line suppression substitutes a one in the seventh bit of a string of eight consecutive zeros. *See also* ones density.

ZIP Zone Information Protocol. An AppleTalk session layer protocol that maps network numbers to zone names. *See also* ZIP storm and zone.

ZIP storm A broadcast storm that occurs when a router running AppleTalk propagates a route for which it currently has no corresponding zone name. The route is then forwarded by downstream routers, and a ZIP storm ensues. *See also* ZIP.

zone In AppleTalk, a logical group of network devices. *See also* ZIP.

Zone Information Protocol *See* ZIP.

Index